Get the eBook FREE!

(PDF, ePub, Kindle, and liveBook all included)

We believe that once you buy a book from us, you should be able to read it in any format we have available. To get electronic versions of this book at no additional cost to you, purchase and then register this book at the Manning website.

Go to https://www.manning.com/freebook and follow the instructions to complete your pBook registration.

That's it!
Thanks from Manning!

Optimization Algorithms

AI TECHNIQUES FOR DESIGN, PLANNING, AND CONTROL PROBLEMS

ALAA KHAMIS

MANNING
SHELTER ISLAND

For online information and ordering of this and other Manning books, please visit www.manning.com. The publisher offers discounts on this book when ordered in quantity.

For more information, please contact

  Special Sales Department
  Manning Publications Co.
  20 Baldwin Road
  PO Box 761
  Shelter Island, NY 11964
  Email: orders@manning.com

Manning Publications Co.
20 Baldwin Road
PO Box 761
Shelter Island, NY 11964

Development editor:	Doug Rudder
Technical editor:	Frances Buontempo
Review editor:	Adriana Sabo and Dunja Nikitović
Production editor:	Andy Marinkovich
Copyeditor:	Andy Carroll
Proofreader:	Melody Dolab
Technical proofreader:	Bin Hu
Typesetter:	Bojan Stojanović
Cover designer:	Marija Tudor

ISBN: 9781633438835
Printed in the United States of America

To my beautiful wife Nermein and my lovely children,
Renad and Kareem. You are the joy of my life.

brief contents

contents

  *Graph embedding   407 ▪ Attention mechanisms   415 ▪ Pointer
  networks   418*

11.4 Self-organizing maps   422

11.5 Machine learning for optimization problems   424

11.6 Solving function optimization using supervised machine
      learning   427

11.7 Solving TSP using supervised graph machine learning   432

11.8 Solving TSP using unsupervised machine learning   438

11.9 Finding a convex hull   441

12 ***Reinforcement learning   450***

12.1 Demystifying reinforcement learning   451

  *Markov decision process (MDP)   452 ▪ From MDP to
  reinforcement learning   453 ▪ Model-based versus model-free
  RL   458 ▪ Actor-critic methods   459 ▪ Proximal policy
  optimization   460 ▪ Multi-armed bandit (MAB)   464*

12.2 Optimization with reinforcement learning   470

12.3 Balancing CartPole using A2C and PPO   473

12.4 Autonomous coordination in mobile networks using
      PPO   481

12.5 Solving the truck selection problem using contextual
      bandits   485

12.6 Journey's end: A final reflection   490

      references   492
      index   497

The following bonus appendices are available in the ePub and
Kindle versions of this book, and you can read them online in
liveBook:

preface

Have you ever wondered how navigation apps like Google Maps and Apple Maps determine the fastest route from one place to another? Have you been curious about how ride-sharing companies like Uber, Lyft, or DiDi guide their drivers to the best spots to reduce your wait time and their travel distance, making things better for everyone? Or perhaps you've asked yourself how food delivery platforms like Uber Eats suggest food choices for you. Have you considered how last-mile delivery apps map out the fastest routes for parcel deliveries while minimizing empty return trips? Do you ever wonder how emergency responders are dispatched swiftly to incidents? Have you thought about the process behind selecting locations for electric vehicle charging stations? Or how to calculate the optimal price for a product, optimize investment portfolios, allocate resources, or schedule surgeries efficiently? This book dives into the world of artificial intelligence algorithms that tackle these real-world design, planning, and control problems. The book is written for practitioners interested in solving ill-structured search and optimization problems using modern derivative-free algorithms. This book will get you up to speed with the core concepts of search and optimization and endow you with the ability to deal with practical design, planning, and control problems.

This book has been written to take almost anyone with no prior knowledge of search and optimization, and with only an intermediate knowledge of Python and data structures, from never having solved search and optimization problems to being a well-rounded search and optimization practitioner able to select, implement, and adapt the right solver for the right problem. This book grew out of several courses related to search and optimization that I have taught at different universities and at industry training centers.

The book will take you you on a comprehensive journey through a diverse landscape of search and optimization algorithms. It begins with a deep dive into deterministic search algorithms that rigorously explore problem spaces for optimal solutions, utilizing both blind and informed strategies. The journey then progresses to trajectory-based algorithms, where you'll discover the effectiveness of simulated annealing and tabu search in overcoming local optima. As we advance, we'll delve into the domain of evolutionary computing algorithms, observing the prowess of genetic algorithms in tackling complex continuous and discrete optimization problems. This fascinating journey continues with an intriguing look at swarm intelligence algorithms, including particle swarm optimization, ant colony optimization, and the artificial bee colony algorithm. The final leg of our journey introduces machine learning-based methods, utilizing unsupervised, supervised, and reinforcement learning to address complex combinatorial optimization problems.

My 25 years working as an AI and robotics professor in academia and as a technical leader in industry have given me a wealth of experiences to share with you. Throughout this book, numerous examples and in-depth case studies are provided for both novices and experts. These examples and case studies are thoroughly explained and put into practice with cutting-edge Python libraries dedicated to search and optimization.

I hope that this book, which traverses the vast landscape of optimization algorithms, serves as a valuable guide and resource in your journey. Whether you are a novice or an expert, the insights you'll gain from this comprehensive exploration of various algorithms and their application to real-world problems can empower you to make impactful decisions and innovate in various domains. The field of optimization is continuously evolving, and with this book, you are equipped not just to keep pace with its advancements but also to contribute to shaping the future of this dynamic and critical discipline. Let the knowledge you gain here inspire you to tackle new challenges, forge new paths, and realize the immense potential that lies in optimization.

acknowledgments

The journey of writing a book is an endeavor that's never solitary, and demands the involvement and encouragement of many individuals.

I want to begin by expressing my deepest gratitude to my family, who stood by me with unwavering patience and encouragement throughout the lengthy process of writing this book. My beloved wife, Nermein, and my children, Renad and Kareem, have been my pillars of support. Your patience during the long hours I dedicated to this project and your constant encouragement were the driving force behind my determination to see it through. I am truly fortunate to have you in my life. Nermein, in particular, not only provided emotional support but also played a crucial role in editing the book's graphics. Your collective strength and support fueled my determination and made this book possible.

I am deeply grateful to Mike Stephens, the book's acquisitions editor, whose belief in this book's vision was a cornerstone in bringing it to life. The exceptional efforts of Doug Rudder and Patrick Barb, the developmental editors, have greatly enhanced the quality of this book.

My thanks also extend to Frances Buontempo, the book's technical editor, who worked diligently to provide feedback that greatly improved the technical quality of the book. Your insights were crucial in ensuring the accuracy and clarity of the content. And a big thank you as well to review editors Adriana Sabo and Dunja Nikitović and to all the reviewers who provided feedback—Alain Couniot, Anne Katrine Falk, Ayush Bihani, Chris Thomas, Christoffer Fink, Dirk Gomez, Dwipam Katariya, Janit Anjaria, Jeremy Chen, Jesús Antonino Juárez Guerrrero, Joseph Pachod, Kevin Cheung, Khai Win, Kim Gabrielsen,

Laud Bentil, Maxim Volgin, Mikael Dautrey, Nick Vazquez, Onofrei George, Pablo Roccatagliata, Rani Sharim, Richard Vaughan, Ruben Gonzalez-Rubio, Sergio Govoni, Simon Tschöke, Thomas Jeffries, Vidhya Vinay, and Wei Luo. Your suggestions helped make this book what it is.

Special thanks to Andy Carroll, the book's copy editor, for his thorough review and invaluable edits, and to Andy Marinkovich, the production editor, for his dedication in moving the book through production. Thanks also to technical proofreader, Bin Hu, for his valuable contributions. Grateful appreciation also to proofreader, Melody Dolab, and typesetter, Bojan Stojanović, for their contributions to the book's quality and presentation. And many thanks to the cover designer, Marija Tudor, for her stunning design.

I extend my gratitude to the entire team at Manning for their professional guidance and assistance at every stage of putting this book together. Your commitment to excellence has made this endeavor all the more rewarding.

I must also express my gratitude to my friends, colleagues, and students for their unwavering support throughout this journey. In particular, I want to thank Yinan Wang for his significant contributions to the first part of the book, Dr. Mostafa Hassan for his valuable input in the second part of the book, and my students Jonah Ruan, Peiqi Li, Ahmed Elgazwy, and Yilun Li for their contributions to some of the coding exercises.

To all those mentioned here, and to anyone else who contributed in any way, your involvement has been instrumental in bringing this book to fruition. Thank you for being a part of this remarkable journey.

about this book

Optimization Algorithms delves into the diverse world of optimization algorithms, offering an extensive exploration of deterministic graph search algorithms, trajectory-based algorithms, evolutionary computing algorithms, swarm intelligence algorithms, and machine learning-based methods. It is designed to cater to both novices and experts, featuring a wealth of examples and in-depth case studies that span a broad spectrum of design, planning, and control problems. These examples encompass a wide array of practical scenarios, including, but not limited to, routing problems, assembly line balancing, optimal pricing, composite laminate design, controller parameter tuning, political districting, product manufacturing planning, neural network training, facility allocation, doctor scheduling, supply/demand optimization, airline flight operations, electric motor control, and online advertising optimization. This book stands as a valuable resource for anyone looking to deepen their understanding and proficiency in the dynamic and ever-evolving field of optimization.

Who should read this book?

This book is tailored to meet the needs of a diverse range of readers, particularly working professionals who deal with optimization problems across various domains. It serves as an invaluable resource for practitioners seeking to deepen their understanding and skills in solving optimization problems. The content is also highly beneficial for continuing education and training centers, catering to general-interest readers and learners with a keen interest in optimization algorithms. Computer engineering/science and systems engineering students, along with researchers, will find this book a treasure trove of knowledge, enhancing their academic and practical understanding. Additionally, university professors can use this comprehensive guide in designing and enriching undergraduate and postgraduate courses on topics such as graph search, metaheuristic optimization, bio-inspired algorithms, cooperative and adaptive algorithms, and the application of machine learning in optimization. This book is a versatile and rich source of information, well-suited for anyone involved or interested in the dynamic field of optimization.

How this book is organized: A roadmap

The book is divided into five parts and 12 chapters with three appendices, 114 code listings, several projects, and more than 140 exercises and their solutions:

- This book will guide you through the realms of optimization algorithms, beginning with deterministic graph search algorithms in part 1, where foundational concepts and techniques are covered.
- Part 2 progresses into trajectory-based algorithms like simulated annealing and tabu search, applying them to diverse problems.
- In part 3, the focus shifts to evolutionary computing algorithms, delving into genetic algorithms and their applications.
- Part 4 explores swarm intelligence algorithms, including particle swarm optimization, ant colony optimization, and artificial bee colony algorithms, demonstrating their nature-inspired problem-solving capabilities.
- Part 5 converges on machine learning-based methods, bridging machine learning and optimization to address complex problems using techniques like self-organizing maps, graph machine learning, and reinforcement learning.

This book includes three appendices, serving as invaluable companions that offer practical insights and resources to enhance your understanding and proficiency in implementing optimization algorithms.

Appendix A guides you in setting up the Python environment and introduces various state-of-the-art Python libraries such as mathematical programming solvers, graph and mapping libraries, and machine learning libraries.

Appendix B provides a variety of relevant resources, including optimization test functions, combinatorial optimization benchmark datasets, geospatial datasets, and machine learning datasets.

Finally, Appendix C presents a comprehensive set of exercises and solutions organized chapter-wise. These exercises encompass various styles, including multiple-choice questions (MCQs), matching exercises, word search, cross-word puzzles, coding exercises, and problem-solving exercises. The purpose of these exercises is to actively reinforce and solidify your understanding of optimization concepts and algorithms explored throughout the book.

These bonus appendices are available in the ePub and Kindle versions of this book, and you can read them online in liveBook available here: https://www.manning.com/books/optimization-algorithms..

For readers looking to grasp the core concepts of search and optimization algorithms, I recommend starting with part 1, which lays the foundation. Afterward, you are free to explore the subsequent chapters in any order that aligns with your interests. Each chapter is crafted to stand on its own, providing flexibility in your learning journey.

A crucial aspect of this learning process is actively engaging with the included code listings. By experimenting with and tuning the algorithm parameters, you'll gain practical insights into, and a deeper understanding of, the subject matter. Additionally, I encourage you to attempt the exercises provided online in appendix C, as they are designed to reinforce your knowledge. If you encounter difficulties, the solutions are included, offering guidance to help you overcome any obstacles. This hands-on approach is essential for a thorough and rewarding learning experience.

About the code

This book is enriched with an extensive array of source code presented in numbered listings, numerous practical projects, and exercises (along with their solutions). It utilizes state-of-the-art Python libraries in the code listings to ensure a contemporary and effective learning experience. All of this code, which is implemented in the form of Python Jupyter notebooks—a web-based interactive computing platform—is readily available for download from the book's GitHub repository: https://github.com/Optimization-Algorithms-Book/Code-Listings. This setup not only facilitates an interactive and engaging learning process but also allows you to directly experiment with and modify the code. Note that the book is structured with the assumption that you have Python 3.6 or a newer version installed on your system.

You can also get executable snippets of code from the liveBook (online) version of this book at https://livebook.manning.com/book/optimization-algorithms. The complete code for the examples in the book is available for download from the Manning website at www.manning.com.

liveBook discussion forum

Purchase of *Optimization Algorithms* includes free access to liveBook, Manning's online reading platform. Using liveBook's exclusive discussion features, you can attach comments to the book globally or to specific sections or paragraphs. It's a snap to make notes for yourself, ask and answer technical questions, and receive help from the author and other users. To access the forum, go to https://livebook.manning.com/book/optimization-algorithms/discussion. You can also learn more about Manning's forums and the rules of conduct at https://livebook.manning.com/discussion.

Manning's commitment to our readers is to provide a venue where a meaningful dialogue between individual readers and between readers and the author can take place. It is not a commitment to any specific amount of participation on the part of the author, whose contribution to the forum remains voluntary (and unpaid). We suggest you try asking the author some challenging questions lest their interest stray! The forum and the archives of previous discussions will be accessible from the publisher's website for as long as the book is in print.

about the author

DR. ALAA KHAMIS works as AI & Smart Mobility Technical Leader at General Motors Canada. He is also a Lecturer at the University of Toronto, an Adjunct Professor at Ontario Tech University and Nile University, and an Affiliate Member of the Center of Pattern Analysis and Machine Intelligence (CPAMI) at the University of Waterloo. He worked as an Autonomous Vehicles Professor at Zewail City of Science and Technology, Head of AI at Sypron Solutions, Associate Professor and Head of Engineering Science Department at Suez University, Associate Professor and Director of Robotics and Autonomous Systems (RAS) research group at German University in Cairo (GUC), Research Assistant Professor at the University of Waterloo, Canada, Visiting Professor at Universidad Carlos III de Madrid, Spain, and Université de Sherbrooke, Canada, Visiting Researcher at the University of Reading, UK, and Distinguished Scholar at the University of Applied Sciences Ravensburg-Weingarten, Germany. His research interests include smart mobility, autonomous and connected vehicles, cognitive IoT, algorithmic robotics, intelligent data processing and analysis, machine learning, and combinatorial optimization. He has published five books and more than 200 scientific papers in refereed journals and international conferences. He has also filed 64 US patents, defensive publications, and trade secrets. For more information, please visit www.alaakhamis.org.

ABOUT THE TECHNICAL EDITOR

Frances Buontempo has many years of C++, Python, and machine learning experience. She has given talks on both and edits ACCU's *Overload* magazine. She has written two books: *Genetic Algorithms and Machine Learning for Programmers* (Pragmatic Bookshelf, 2019) and *Learn C++ by Example* (Manning, 2024). Frances has also often helped as a Manning editor, helping others be clearer, and she believes she can explain complicated things clearly.

about the cover illustration

The figure on the cover of *Optimization Algorithms* is "Insulaire de Oonalaska," or "Onalaska Islander," taken from a collection by Jacques Grasset de Saint-Sauveur, published in 1797. Each illustration is finely drawn and colored by hand.

In those days, it was easy to identify where people lived and what their trade or station in life was just by their dress. Manning celebrates the inventiveness and initiative of the computer business with book covers based on the rich diversity of regional culture centuries ago, brought back to life by pictures from collections such as this one.

Part 1

Deterministic search algorithms

Welcome to the first part of this book, where we'll embark on an exploration of deterministic graph search algorithms. This part consists of four chapters.

In chapter 1, you'll learn the fundamental concepts of search and optimization and understand their real-world significance. You'll discover how to define optimization problems, differentiate between well-structured and ill-structured problems, gain insight into the challenges of search algorithms, and understand the search dilemma.

Chapter 2 dives deeper into the classification of optimization problems. You'll learn how to categorize search and optimization algorithms based on different criteria. Additionally, you'll learn about heuristics, metaheuristics, and heuristic search strategies, with a sneak peek at nature-inspired algorithms.

In chapter 3, you'll explore graph search techniques, uncover graph traversal methods, and discover how to use blind search algorithms to find the shortest path between two nodes in a graph, all while solving practical routing problems.

In chapter 4, you'll delve into the concept of informed search. You'll learn how to solve the minimum spanning tree problem and find the shortest path using informed search algorithms, all while gaining practical problem-solving skills for real-world routing problems.

When you're finished with this part of the book, you'll have a solid grasp of the fundamentals of optimization, deterministic graph search algorithms, and practical problem-solving skills that are applicable to real-world scenarios, setting the stage for the diverse optimization algorithms explored in the following parts of this book.

Introduction to search and optimization

Optimization is deeply embedded in nature and in the systems and technologies we build. Nature is a remarkable testament to the ubiquity and prevalence of optimization. Take, for instance, the foraging behaviors of social insects like ants and honeybees. They have developed their own unique optimization methods, from navigating the shortest path to an existing food source to discovering new food sources in an unknown external environment. Honeybee colonies focus their foraging efforts on only the most profitable patches. They cooperatively build their honeycombs with hexagonal structures for efficient use of space (the maximum number of cells that can be built in a given area), material efficiency (using less beeswax), structural strength, and the optimal angle to prevent honey from spilling

3

out of the cells. Similarly, birds exhibit optimization behavior during their annual migrations. They undertake long voyages from their breeding grounds to their winter homes, and their migration routes have been optimized over generations to conserve energy. These routes account for factors such as prevailing wind patterns, food availability, and safety from predators. These examples underscore how nature intuitively applies optimization strategies for survival and growth, offering us lessons that can be translated into algorithmic problem-solving.

Optimization is also a regular aspect of our daily lives, often so seamlessly integrated that we barely notice its constant influence. As human beings, we strive to optimize our everyday lives. Consider the simple act of planning your day. We instinctively order or group tasks or errands in a way that minimizes travel time or maximizes our free time. We navigate the challenge of grocery shopping within a budget, trying to get the most value out of every dollar spent. We create workout routines aiming for the maximum fitness benefits within our limited time. Even at home, we optimize our energy usage to keep our utility bills in check.

Likewise, corporations maximize profits by increasing efficiency and eliminating waste. For example, logistics giants like FedEx, UPS, and Amazon spend millions of dollars each year researching new ways to trim the cost of delivering packages. Telecommunications agencies seek to determine the optimal placement of crucial infrastructure, like cellular towers, to service the maximum number of customers while investing in the minimum level of equipment. Similarly, transportation network companies like Uber, Lyft, and DiDi route drivers efficiently during passenger trips and direct drivers to ride-hailing hotspots during idle periods to minimize passenger wait time. As urbanization intensifies worldwide, local emergency services depend on efficient dispatching and routing platforms to select and route the appropriate vehicles, equipment, and personnel to respond to incidents across increasingly complex metropolitan road networks. Airlines need to solve several optimization problems, such as flight planning, fleet assignment, crew scheduling, aircraft routing, and aircraft maintenance planning. Healthcare systems also handle optimization problems such as hospital resource planning, emergency procedure management, patient admission scheduling, surgery scheduling, and pandemic containment. Industry 4.0, a major customer of optimization technology, deals with complex optimization problems such as smart scheduling and rescheduling, assembly line balancing, supply-chain optimization, and operational efficiency. Smart cities deal with large-scale optimization problems such as stationary asset optimal assignments, mobile asset deployment, energy optimization, water control, pollution reduction, waste management, and bushfire containment.

These examples show how ubiquitous and important optimization is as a way to maximize operational efficiency in different domains. In this book, we'll dive into the exciting world of optimization algorithms. We'll unravel how these algorithms can be used to tackle complex continuous and discrete problems in different domains.

1.1 *Why care about search and optimization?*

Search is the systematic examination of states, starting from an initial state and ending (hopefully) at the goal state. Optimization techniques are in reality search methods, where the goal is to find an optimal or a near-optimal state within the feasible search space. This feasible search space is a subset of the optimization problem space where all the problem's constraints are satisfied. It's hard to come up with a single industry that doesn't already use some form of search or optimization methods, software, or algorithms. It's highly likely that in your workplace or industry, you deal with optimization daily, though you may not be aware of it. While search and optimization are ubiquitous in almost all industries, using complicated algorithms to optimize processes may not always be practical. For example, consider a small pizzeria that offers food delivery to its local customers. Let's assume that the restaurant processes around ten deliveries on an average weeknight. While efficiency-improving strategies (such as avoiding left turns in right-driving countries or right turns in left-driving countries, avoiding major intersections, avoiding school zones during drop-off and pick-up times, avoiding bridges during lift times, and favoring downhill roads) may theoretically shorten delivery times and reduce costs, the scale of the problem is so tiny that implementing these kinds of changes may not lead to any noticeable effect.

In larger-scale problems, such as fleet assignment and dispatching, multicriteria stochastic vehicle routing, resource allocation, and crew scheduling, applying search and optimization techniques to a problem must be a qualified decision. Some firms or companies may not benefit from excessive process changes due to a lack of expertise or resources to implement those changes. There may also be concerns about a potential lack of follow-through from stakeholders. Implementing these changes could also cost more than the savings obtained through the optimization process. Later in this book, we will see how these costs can be accounted for when developing search and optimization algorithms.

This book will take most anyone from never having solved search and optimization problems to being a well-rounded search and optimization practitioner, able to select, implement, and adapt the right solver for the right problem. It doesn't assume any prior knowledge of search and optimization and only an intermediate knowledge of data structures and Python. For managers or professionals involved in high-level technological decisions at their workplace, these skills can be critical in understanding software-based approaches, their opportunities, and their limitations when discussing process improvement. In contrast, IT professionals will find these skills directly applicable when considering options for developing or selecting new software suites and technologies for in-house use. The following section describes the methodology we will follow throughout this book.

1.2   *Going from toy problems to the real world*

When discussing algorithms, many books and references present them as formal definitions and then apply them to so-called "toy problems." These trivial problems are helpful because they often deal with smaller datasets and search spaces while being solvable by hand iteration. This book follows a similar approach but takes it one step further by presenting real-world data implementations. Whenever possible, resources such as datasets and values are used to illustrate the direct applicability and practical drawbacks of the algorithms discussed. Initially, the scaled-down toy problems will help you appreciate the step-by-step operations involved in the various algorithms. Later, the Python implementations will teach you how to use multiple datasets and Python libraries to address the increased complexity and scope of real-world problems.

As illustrated in figure 1.1, the source of inspiration for each search or optimization algorithm is identified, and then the algorithm pseudocode, algorithm parameters, and heuristics/solution strategies used are presented. The algorithm's pros and cons and adaptation methods are then described. This book contains many examples that will allow you to carry out iterations by hand on a scaled-down version of the problem and fully understand how each algorithm works. It also includes many programming exercises in a special problem-solution-discussion format so you can see how a scaled-up version of the problem previously solved by hand can be solved using Python. Through programming, you can optimally tune the algorithm and study its performance and scalability.

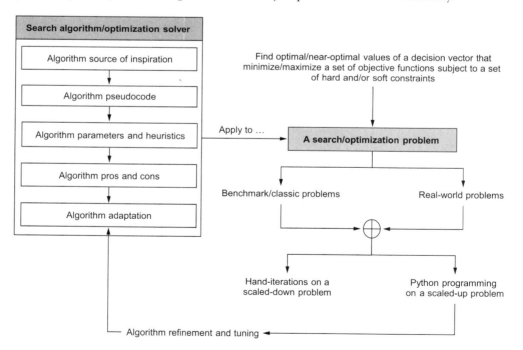

Figure 1.1   The book's methodology—each algorithm will be introduced following a pattern that goes from explanation to application.

Throughout this book, several classic and real-world optimization problems will be considered to show you how to use the search and optimization algorithms discussed in the book. Figure 1.2 shows examples of these optimization/search problems.

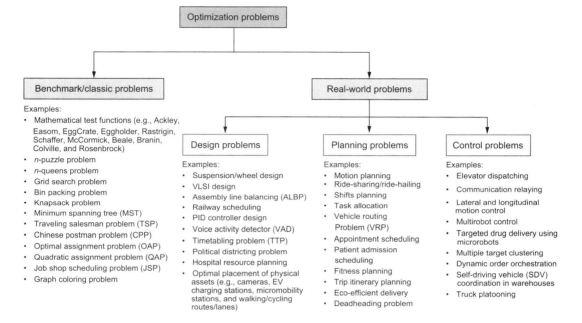

Figure 1.2   Examples of classic and real-world optimization problems

Real-world design problems, or strategic functions, can be used in situations when time is not as important as the quality of the solution and users are willing to wait (sometimes even a few days) to get optimal solutions. Planning problems, or tactical functions, need to be solved in a time span from a few seconds to a few minutes. Control problems, or operational functions, need to be solved repetitively and quickly, in a time span from a few milliseconds to a few seconds. To find a solution in such a short period of time, optimality is usually traded in for speed gains. In the next chapter, we'll discuss these problem types more thoroughly.

I highly recommend that you first perform the hand iterations for the examples following each algorithm and then try to recreate the Python implementations yourself. Feel free to play around with the parameters and problem scale in the code; one of the advantages of running optimization algorithms through software is the ability to tune for optimality.

1.3   Basic ingredients of optimization problems

Optimization refers to the practice of finding the "best" solutions to a given problem, where "best" usually means satisfactory or acceptable, possibly subject to a given set of constraints. The solutions can be classified into *feasible*, *optimal*, and *near-optimal* solutions:

- *Feasible solutions* are solutions that satisfy all the given constraints.
- *Optimal solutions* are both feasible and provide the best objective function value.
- *Near-optimal solutions* are feasible solutions that provide a superior objective function value but are not necessarily the best.

Assuming we have a minimization problem, where the goal is to find the values of a decision variable that minimize a certain objective function, a search space may combine multiple global minima, strong local minima, and weak local minima, as illustrated in figure 1.3:

- A *global optimum* (or a *global minimum* in the case of minimization problems) is the best of a set of candidate solutions (i.e., the lowest point of the entire feasible search space). Mathematically, if $f(x)$ is the objective function, a point x* is the global minimum if, for all x in the domain of f, $f(x^*) \leq f(x)$.
- A *strong local minimum* is a point where the function's value is less than (or equal to) the values of the function in a neighborhood around that point but is higher than the global minimum. Mathematically, a point x* is a strong local minimum if there is a neighborhood N of x^* such that $f(x^*) < f(x)$ for all x in N with $x \neq x^*$.
- A *weak local minimum* is a point where the function's value is less than or equal to the function's values at neighboring points, but there are sequences of points converging to this point for which the function's values strictly decrease. Mathematically, a point x^* is a weak local minimum if there is a neighborhood N of x^* such that $f(x^*) \leq f(x)$ for all x in N.

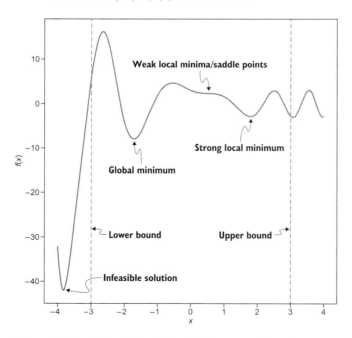

Figure 1.3 Feasible solutions fall within the constraints of the problem. A feasible search space may display a combination of global, strong local, and weak local minima.

These optimum seeking methods, also known as *optimization techniques,* are generally studied as a part of operations research (OR). OR, also referred to as *decision* or *management science,* is a field that originated at the beginning of World War II due to the urgent need to assign scarce resources in military operations. It is a branch of mathematics that applies advanced scientific analytical methods to decision-making and management problems to find the best or optimal solutions.

Optimization problems can generally be stated as follows. Find *X* which optimizes *f*, subject to a possible set of equality and inequality constraints:

$$g_i(X) = 0, i = 1, 2, \ldots, m$$
$$h_j(X) \leq 0, j = 1, 2, \ldots, p \qquad \text{1.1}$$

where

- $X = (x_1, x_2, \ldots, x_n)^T$ is the vector representing the decision variables
- $f(X) = (f_1(X), f_2(X), \ldots, f_M(X))$ is the vector of objectives to be optimized
- $g_i(X)$ is a set of equality constraints
- $h_j(X)$ is a set of inequality constraints

The following subsections describe three main components of optimization problems: decision variables, objective functions, and constraints.

1.3.1   *Decision variables*

Decision variables represent a set of unknowns or variables that affect the objective function's value. These are the variables that define the possible solutions to an optimization problem. If *X* represents the unknowns, also referred to as the independent variables, then *f(X)* quantifies the quality of the candidate solution or feasible solution.

For example, assume that an event organizer is planning a conference on search and optimization algorithms. The organizer plans to pay *a* for fixed costs (the venue rental, security, and guest speaking fees) and *b* for variable costs (pamphlets, lanyards, ID badges, and a catered lunch), which depend on the number of participants. Based on past conferences, the organizer predicts that demand for tickets will be as follows:

$$Q = 5000 - 20x \qquad \text{1.2}$$

where *x* is the ticket price and *Q* is the expected number of tickets to be sold. Thus, the company expects the following scenarios:

- If the company charges nothing ($x = 0$), they will give away 5,000 tickets for free.
- If the ticket price is $x = \$250$, the company will get no attendees, and the expected number of tickets will be 0.
- If the ticket price is $x < \$250$, the company will sell some number of tickets $0 \leq Q \leq 5,000$.

The profit $f(x)$ that the event organizer can expect to earn can be calculated as follows:

$$Profit = Revenue - Costs \qquad \text{1.3}$$

where *Revenue* = Qx and *Costs* = $a + Qb$. Altogether, the profit (or objective) function looks like this:

$$f(x) = Revenue - Costs = Qx - (a + Qb)$$
$$= -20x^2 + (5000 + 20b)x - 5000b - a \qquad \text{1.4}$$

In this problem, the predefined parameters include fixed costs, *a,* and variable costs, *b.* There is a single decision variable, *x,* which is the price of the ticket where $x_{LB} \le x \le x_{UB}$. The ticket price's lower bound x_{LB} and upper bound x_{UB} are considered boundary constraints. Solving this optimization problem focuses on finding the best value of *x* that maximizes the profit $f(x)$.

1.3.2   *Objective functions*

An objective function $f(x)$, also known as the criterion, merit function, utility function, cost function, stands for the quantity to be optimized. Without a loss of generality, optimization can be interpreted as the minimization of a value, since the maximization of a primal function $f(x)$ can be just the minimization of a dual problem generated after applying mathematical operations on $f(x)$. This means that if the primal function is a minimization problem, then the dual problem is a maximization problem (and vice versa). According to this duality aspect of optimization problems, a solution x^*, which is the minimum for the primal minimization problem, is also, at the same time, the maximum for the dual maximization problem, as illustrated in figure 1.4.

Moreover, simple mathematical operations like addition, subtraction, multiplication, and division do not change the value of the optimal point. For example, multiplying or dividing $f(x)$ by a positive constant or adding or subtracting a positive constant to or from $f(x)$ does not change the optimal value of the decision variable, as illustrated in figure 1.4.

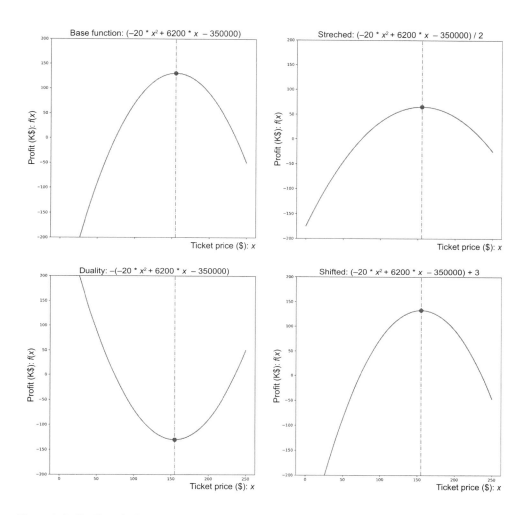

Figure 1.4 **Duality principle and mathematical operations on an optimization problem**

In the earlier ticket pricing problem, assume that $a = 50,000$, $b = 60$, $x_{LB} = 0$, and $x_{UB} = 250$. Using these values, we have a profit function: $f(x) = -20x^2 + 6,200x - 350,000$. Following a derivative-based approach, we can simply derive the function to find its maximum: $df/dx = -40x + 6,200 = 0$ or $40x = 6,200$. Thus, the optimal ticket price is \$155, which yields a net profit of \$130,500, as shown in figure 1.5.

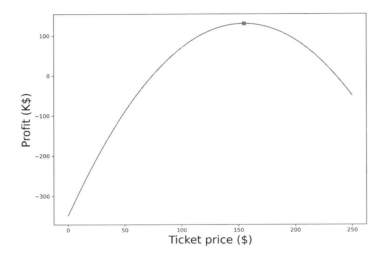

Figure 1.5   Ticket pricing problem—the optimal pricing that maximizes profit is \$155 per ticket.

In the ticket pricing problem, we have a single objective function to be optimized, which is the profit. In this case, the problem is called a *mono-objective optimization problem*. An optimization problem involving multiple objective functions is known as a *multi-objective optimization problem*. For example, assume that we want to design an electric vehicle (EV). This design problem's objective functions can be minimizing acceleration time and maximizing Environmental Protection Agency (EPA) driving range. The acceleration time is the time in seconds the EV takes to accelerate from 0 to 60 mph. The EPA driving range is the approximate number of miles that a vehicle can travel in combined city and highway driving (using a mix of 55% highway and 45% city driving) before needing to be recharged, according to the EPA's testing methodology. Decision variables can include the size of the wheels, the power of the electric motor, and the battery's capacity. A bigger battery is needed to extend the driving range of the EV, which adds extra weight, and therefore the acceleration time increases. In this example, the two objectives are in conflict, as we need to minimize acceleration time and maximize the EPA range, as shown in figure 1.6.

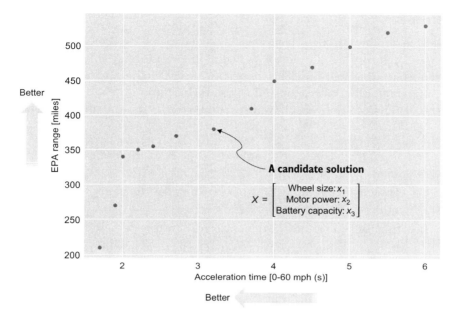

Figure 1.6   Electric vehicle design problem for maximizing EPA range and minimizing acceleration time

This multi-objective optimization problem can be handled using a preference-based multi-objective optimization procedure or by using a Pareto optimization approach. In the former approach, the duality principle is applied first to transform all the conflicting objectives for maximization (e.g., maximizing the EPA range and the inverse of the acceleration time) or for minimization (e.g., minimizing the acceleration time and the inverse of the EPA range). Then we combine these multiple objectives into an overall objective function by using a relative preference vector or a weighting scheme to scalarize the multiple objectives. For example, you may give more weight to EPA range over acceleration time. However, finding this preference vector or the weights is subjective, and sometimes it's not straightforward. The Pareto optimization approach relies on finding multiple trade-off optimal solutions and choosing one using higher-level information. This procedure tries to find the best trade-off by reducing the number of alternatives to an optimal set of nondominated solutions known as the Pareto frontier, which can be used to take strategic decisions in multi-objective space. Multi-objective optimization is discussed in chapter 8.

Constraint-satisfaction problems (CSPs) do not define an explicit objective function. Instead, the goal is to find a solution that satisfies a given set of constraints. The n-queen problem is an example of a CSP. In this problem, the aim is to put n queens on an n x n board with no two queens on the same row, column, or diagonal. The 4 x 4 queen CSP problem has two optimal solutions. Neither of these two optimal solutions is inherently or objectively better than the other. The only requirement of the problem is to satisfy the given constraints.

1.3.3   *Constraints*

Constrained optimization problems have a set of equality and/or inequality constraints $g_i(X)$, $l_j(X)$ that restrict the values assigned to the decision variables. In addition, most problems have a set of boundary constraints, which define the domain of values for each variable. Furthermore, constraints can be hard (must be satisfied) or soft (desirable to satisfy). Consider the following examples from a school timetabling problem:

- Not having multiple lectures in the same room at the same time is a *hard constraint*.
- Not having a teacher give multiple lectures at the same time is also a *hard constraint*.
- Guaranteeing a minimum of three teaching days for every teacher may be a *soft constraint*.
- Locating back-to-back lectures in nearby rooms may be a *soft constraint*.
- Avoiding scheduling very early or very late lectures may also be a *soft constraint*.

As another example of hard and soft constraints, navigation apps such as Google Maps, Apple Maps, Waze, or HERE WeGo may allow users to set preferences for routing:

- Avoiding ferries, toll roads, and highways would be *hard constraints*.
- Avoiding busy intersections, highways during rush hour, or school zones during drop-off and pick-up times might be *soft constraints*.

Soft constraints can be modeled by incorporating a reward/penalty function as part of the objective function. The function can reward solutions that satisfy the soft constraints and penalize those that do not.

As an example, assume that there are 10 parcels to be loaded in the cargo bike in figure 1.7.

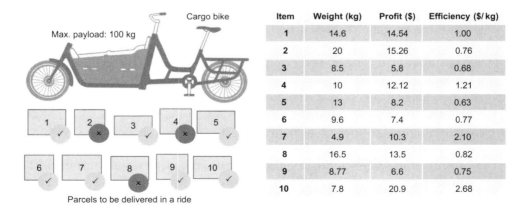

Item	Weight (kg)	Profit ($)	Efficiency ($/ kg)
1	14.6	14.54	1.00
2	20	15.26	0.76
3	8.5	5.8	0.68
4	10	12.12	1.21
5	13	8.2	0.63
6	9.6	7.4	0.77
7	4.9	10.3	2.10
8	16.5	13.5	0.82
9	8.77	6.6	0.75
10	7.8	20.9	2.68

Figure 1.7   The cargo bike loading problem is an example of a problem with a soft constraint. While the weight of the packages can exceed the bike's capacity, a penalty will be applied when the bike is overweight.

Each parcel has its own weight, profit, and efficiency value (profit per kg). The goal is to select the parcels to be loaded in such a way that the profit function f_1 is maximized and the weight function f_2 is minimized. This is a classic example of a combinatorial problem:

$$f_1 = \sum_{i=0}^{n} E_i$$

1.5

where n is the total number of packages and E_i is the efficiency of package i

$$f_2 = \left| \sum_{i=0}^{n} w_i - C \right|, \; 50 \text{ is added } iff \left[\sum_{i=0}^{n} w_i > C \right]$$

1.6

where w_i is the weight of package i and C is the maximum capacity of the bike. A penalty of 50 is added if and only if the total weight of the added parcels exceeds the maximum capacity.

Soft constraints can also be used to make the search algorithm more adaptive. For example, the severity of the penalty can be dynamically changed as the algorithm progresses, imposing less strict penalties at first to encourage exploration, but imposing more severe penalties near the end to generate a result largely bound by the constraint.

1.4 Well-structured problems vs. ill-structured problems

We can classify optimization problems based on their structure and the procedure that exists (or doesn't exist) for solving them. The following subsections introduce well-structured and ill-structured problems.

1.4.1 Well-structured problems

In "The Structure of Ill Structured Problems," Herbert Simon outlines six key characteristics of well-structured problems (WSPs) [1]. These include the presence of a clear criterion for testing proposed solutions, the existence of a problem space capable of representing the initial problem state and potential solutions, and the representation of attainable and considerable state changes within the problem space. Moreover, any knowledge acquired by the problem solver can be represented within these spaces, and if the problem involves interacting with the external world, the state changes reflect the laws governing the real world. Simon emphasizes that these conditions hold strongly, implying that the processes require feasible computation and that information necessary for problem-solving is effectively available without excessive search efforts.

Assume that we are planning a robotic pick-and-place task in an inspection system. In this scenario, the robot waits until receiving a signal from a presence sensor, which indicates the existence of a defective workpiece over the conveyor belt. The robot stops the conveyor belt, picks up the defective piece, and deposits it in a waste box. Then the robot reactivates the movement of the conveyor belt. After this operation, the robot returns to its initial position and the cycle repeats. As illustrated in figure 1.8, this problem has the following well-structured components:

- *Feasible states*—The position and speed of the robot arm and its orientation and status (open or closed and orientation) of its end-effector (gripper)
- *Operator (successor)*—Robot arm motion control command to move from one point to another following a certain singularity-free trajectory (positions or joint angles in space and motion speed) and end-effector control (orientation and open or closed)
- *Goal*—Pick and place a defective workpiece regardless of its orientation
- *Solution/path*—Optimal sequence through state space for the fastest pick-and-place operation
- *Stopping criteria*—Defective workpiece is picked from the conveyer belt and placed in the waste box, and the robot returns to its home position
- *Evaluation criteria*—Pick-and-place duration and/or the success rate of the pick-and-place process

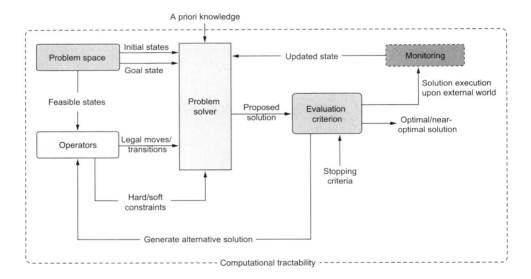

Figure 1.8   A WPS features a defined problem space, operators for allowable moves, clear evaluation criteria, and computational tractability.

As you can see, the work environment is highly structured, static, and fully observable. The problem can be mathematically modeled, and an optimal pick-and-place plan can be generated and executed with a high level of certainty. This pick-and-place problem can be considered a WSP.

1.4.2   Ill-structured problems

Ill-structured problems (ISPs) are complex discrete or continuous problems without algorithmic solutions or general problem solvers. ISPs are characterized by one or more of these characteristics:

- A problem space with different views of the problems, unclear goals, multimodality, and a dynamic nature
- A lack of exact mathematical models or a lack of well-proven algorithmic solutions
- Solutions that are contradictory, consequences that are difficult to predict, and risk that is difficult or impossible to calculate, resulting in a lack of clear evaluation criteria
- Considerable data imperfection in terms of uncertainty, partial observability, vagueness, incomplete information, ambiguity, or unpredictability that makes monitoring the execution of the solutions difficult and sometimes impossible
- Computational intractability

Assume that we need to find the optimal dispatching of four elevators to serve users between 10 floors, as illustrated in figure 1.9. This is a classic example of a problem too large to solve using traditional means.

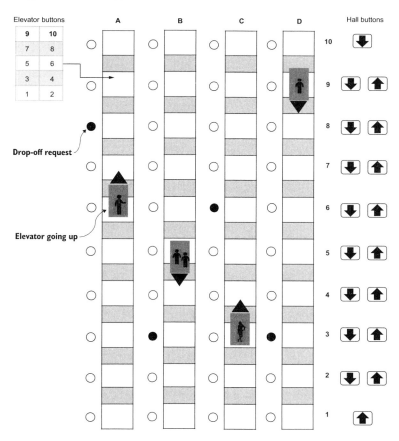

Figure 1.9 **Elevator dispatching problem—with four elevator cars and 10 floors, this problem has ~10^{21} possible states.**

The following objective functions can be considered in this optimal dispatching problem:

- Minimizing the average waiting time—how long the user waits before getting on an elevator
- Minimizing the average system time—how long the user waits before being dropped off at the destination floor
- Minimizing the percentage of users whose waiting time exceeds 60 seconds
- Ensuring fairness in serving all the users of the elevators

This optimal dispatching problem is an example of an ISP, as the problem space has a dynamic nature and partial observability; it is impossible to predict the user calls and destinations. Defining an optimum is almost impossible, as it can immediately change after a decision has been made based on the known situation (such as if a new request comes in for a move in the opposite direction). Moreover, the search space is huge due to the extremely high number of possible states, taking into consideration different elevator positions, elevator buttons, and hall call buttons:

- *Elevator position*—Each elevator can be on one of 10 floors. Therefore, for each elevator, there are 10 different possible states. Since there are four elevators, the number of combinations for elevator positions is 10^4.
- *Elevator buttons*—Each elevator has 10 buttons that can be either on (pressed) or off (not pressed). Therefore, for one elevator, there are 2^{10} different possible states. Since there are four elevators, the number of combinations for elevator buttons is 2^{40}.
- *Hall call buttons*—There are 18 hall call buttons (up and down buttons at each floor, except the first and the last floor) that can be either on or off. Therefore, the number of combinations for hall call buttons is 2^{18}.

Assuming that every combination of button presses is valid (i.e., ignoring the physical or logical limitations of an elevator system, such as not allowing both the up and down hall call buttons on the same floor to be pressed at the same time), the total number of states can be calculated as follows: number of possible states = 10^4 (elevator positions) * 2^{40} (elevator buttons) * 2^{18} (hall call buttons) = 2.88 x 10^{21} different states. The total number of states is more than the number of stars in the universe!

1.4.3   *WSP, but ISP in practice*

The traveling salesman problem (TSP) is an example of a problem that may be well-structured in principle, but in practice becomes ill-structured. This is because of the impractical amount of computational power required to solve the problem in real time.

Assume that a traveling salesman is assigned to make sales calls to a list of n cities. The salesman would like to visit all these cities in the minimum amount of time, as salespeople are generally paid by commission rather than hourly. Furthermore, the tour of the cities may be asymmetric; the time it takes to go from city A to city B may not be the same as the reverse due to infrastructure, traffic patterns, and one-way streets. For example, with 13 cities to visit, the problem may initially seem trivial. However, upon closer examination, the search space for this TSP results in $13! = 6,227,020,800$ different possible routes to be examined in the case of using naive algorithms! Fortunately, dynamic programming algorithms enable reduced complexity, as we will see in the next chapter.

This book largely focuses on ISPs, and on WSPs that are ISPs in practice, for a few reasons:

- WSPs tend to have well-known solving algorithms that often provide trivial, step-by-step procedures. As such, very efficient and well-known solutions often exist for these kinds of problems. Moreover, several WSPs can be solved using derivative-based generic solvers.

- The amount of computational power needed to solve WSPs is often negligible, or very manageable at worst. Especially with the continued improvement of consumer-grade computers, not to mention the vast resources available through cloud computing and distributed processing, we often do not have to settle for near-optimal WSP solutions resulting from computational bottlenecks.

- Most problems in the real world are ISPs, as the problem scope, state, and environment are dynamic and sometimes partially observable with certain degrees of uncertainties. Solutions or algorithms for ISPs, therefore, have much more applicability to real-world scenarios, and there is a greater incentive to find solutions to these problems.

Most of the algorithms explored in this book are derivative-free and stochastic; they use randomness in their parameters and decision processes. These algorithms are often well suited to solving ISPs, as the randomness of their initial states and operators allows the algorithms to escape local minima and find optimal or near-optimal solutions. In contrast, deterministic algorithms use well-defined and procedural paths to reach solutions and generally are not well suited for ISPs, as they either cannot work in unknown search spaces or are unable to return solutions in a reasonable amount of time. Moreover, most of the algorithms covered in this book are black-box solvers that deal with the optimization problem as a black box. This black box provides, for certain decision variable values, the corresponding values of the objective functions and constraint functions. Importantly, this approach eliminates the need to consider various properties of the objective and constraint functions, such as nonlinearity, differentiability, nonconvexity, monotonicity, discontinuities, or even stochastic noise.

1.5   *Search algorithms and the search dilemma*

The goal of any optimization method is to assign values to decision variables so that the objective function is optimized. To achieve this, optimization algorithms search the solution space for candidate solutions. Constraints are simply limitations on specific regions in the search space. Thus, all optimization techniques are, in reality, just search methods, where the goal is to find feasible solutions to satisfy constraints and maximize (or minimize) the objective functions. We'll define "search" as the systematic examination of feasible states, starting from the initial state, and ending (hopefully) at the goal state. However, while we explore the feasible search space, we may find a few reasonably good neighboring solutions, and the question is whether we should exploit this region or keep exploring, looking for better solutions in other regions of the feasible search space.

Exploration (or *diversification*) is the process of investigating new regions in the feasible search space with the hope of finding other promising solutions. On the other hand, *exploitation* (or *intensification*) is the process of directing the search agent to focus on an attractive region of the search space where good solutions have already been found.

This exploration–exploitation dilemma is one of the most important problems in search and optimization, and in life as well. We apply exploration–exploitation tactics in our lives. When we move to a new city, we start by exploring different stores and restaurants and then focus on shortlisted options around us. During a midlife crisis, some middle-aged individuals feel bored in their daily routine and lifestyle without satisfactory accomplishments, and they tend to take explorative actions. The US immigration system tries to avoid exploiting specific segments of applicants (e.g., family, skilled workers, refugees, and asylees) and enables more diversity through a computer-generated lottery. In social insects like honeybees, foraging for food sources is performed by two different worker groups, foragers and scouts (5–25% of the foragers). Forager bees focus on a specific food source while scouts are novelty seekers who keep scouting around for rich nectar. In search and optimization, the exploration–exploitation dilemma represents the trade-off between exploring new unvisited states or solutions in the search space and exploiting the elite solutions found in a certain neighborhood in the search space (figure 1.10).

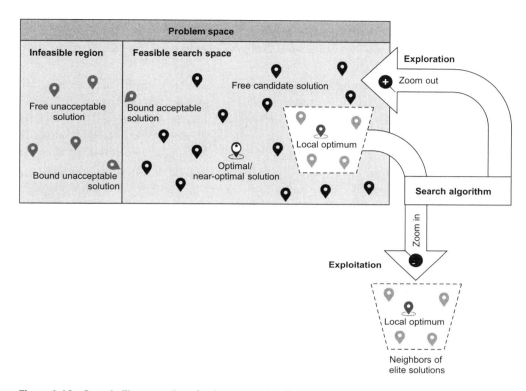

Figure 1.10 **Search dilemma—there is always a trade-off between branching out to new areas of the search space or focusing on an area with known good or elite solutions.**

Local search algorithms are exploitative algorithms that can be easily trapped in local optima if the search landscape is multimodal. On the other extreme, random search algorithms keep exploring the search space with a high chance of reaching global optima at the cost of an impractical search time. Generally speaking, explorative algorithms can find global optima at the cost of processing time, while exploitative algorithms risk getting stuck at local minima.

Summary

- Optimization is ubiquitous and pervasive in numerous areas of life, industry, and research.

- Decision variables, objective functions, and constraints are the main ingredients of optimization problems. Decision variables are the inputs that you have control over and that affect the objective function's value. An objective function is the function that needs to be optimized, either minimized or maximized. Constraints are the limitations or restrictions that the solution must satisfy.

- Optimization is a search process for finding the "best" solutions to a problem, providing the best objective function values, and possibly subject to a given set of hard (must be satisfied) and soft (desirable to satisfy) constraints.

- Ill-structured problems are complex discrete or continuous problems without exact mathematical models and/or algorithmic solutions or general problem solvers. They usually have dynamic and/or partially observable large search spaces that cannot be handled by classic optimization methods.

- In many real-life applications, quickly finding a near-optimal solution is better than spending a large amount of time searching for an optimal solution.

- Two key concepts you'll see frequently in future chapters are the exploration (or diversification) and exploitation (or intensification) search dilemmas. Achieving a trade-off between exploration and exploitation will allow the algorithm to find optimal or near-optimal solutions without getting trapped in local optima in an attractive region of the search space and without spending a large amount of time.

A deeper look at search and optimization

2

This chapter covers

- Classifying optimization problems based on different criteria
- Classifying search and optimization algorithms based on the way the search space is explored and how deterministic the algorithm is
- Introducing heuristics, metaheuristics, and heuristic search strategies
- A first look at nature-inspired search and optimization algorithms

Before we dive into the problems and algorithms that I hinted at in chapter 1, it will be useful to be clear about how we talk about these problems and algorithms. Classifying problems allows us to group similar problems together and potentially exploit existing solutions. For example, a traveling salesman problem involving geographic values (i.e., cities and roads) may be used as a model to find the minimum length of wires connecting pins in a very large-scale integration (VLSI) design. The same can be said for classifying the algorithms themselves, as grouping algorithms with similar properties can allow us to easily identify the right algorithm to solve a problem and meet expectations, such as the quality of the solution and the permissible search time.

Throughout this chapter, we'll discuss common classifications of optimization problems and algorithms. Heuristics and metaheuristics will also be introduced as general algorithmic frameworks or high-level strategies that guide the search process. Many of these strategies are inspired by nature, so we'll shed some light on nature-inspired algorithms. Let's start by discussing how we can classify optimization problems based on different criteria.

2.1 *Classifying optimization problems*

Optimization is everywhere! In everyday life, you'll face different kinds of optimization problems. For example, you may like to set the thermostat to a certain temperature to stay comfortable and at the same time save energy. You may select light fixtures and adjust the light levels to reduce energy costs. When you start driving your electric vehicle (EV), you may search for the fastest or most energy-efficient route to your destination. Before arriving at your destination, you may look for a parking spot that is affordable, provides the shortest walking distance to your destination, offers EV charging, and is preferably underground. These optimization problems have different levels of complexity that mainly depend on the type of problem. As mentioned in the previous chapter, the process of optimization involves selecting decision variables from a given feasible search space in such a way as to optimize (minimize or maximize) a given objective function or, in some cases, multiple objective functions.

Optimization problems are characterized by three main components: decision variables or design vectors, objective functions or criteria to be optimized, and a set of hard and soft constraints to be satisfied. The nature of these three components, the permissible time allowed for solving the problem, and the expected quality of the solutions lead to different types of optimization problems, as shown in figure 2.1.

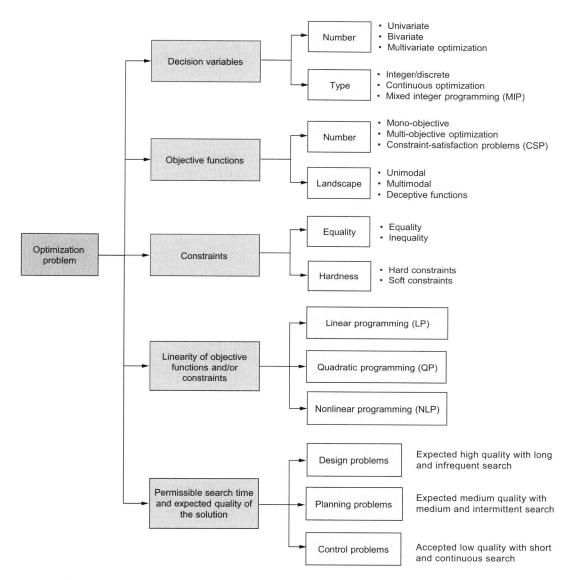

Figure 2.1   Optimization problem classification—an optimization problem can be broken down into its constituent parts, which form the basis for classifying such problems.

The following subsections explain these types in greater detail and provide examples of each type of optimization problem.

2.1.1 *Number and type of decision variables*

Based on the number of decision variables, optimization problems can be broadly grouped into univariate (single variable) or multivariate (multiple variable) problems. For example, vehicle speed, acceleration, and tire pressure are among the parameters that effect a vehicle's fuel economy, where fuel economy refers to how far a vehicle can travel on a specific amount of fuel. According to the US Department of Energy, controlling the speed and acceleration of a vehicle can improve its fuel economy by 15% to 30% at highway speeds and 10% to 40% in stop-and-go traffic. A study by the US National Highway Traffic Safety Administration (NHTSA) found that a 1% decrease in tire pressure correlated to a 0.3% reduction in fuel economy. If we are only looking for the optimal vehicle speed for maximum fuel economy, the problem is a univariate optimization problem. Finding the optimal speed and acceleration for maximum fuel economy is a bivariate optimization problem, whereas finding optimal speed, acceleration, and tire pressure is a multivariate problem.

Problem classification also varies according to the type of decision variables. A continuous problem involves continuous-valued variables, where $x_j \in R$. In contrast, if $x_j \in Z$, the problem is an integer or discrete optimization problem. A mixed-integer problem has both continuous-valued and integer-valued variables. For example, optimizing elevator speed and acceleration (continuous variables) and the sequence of picking up passengers (a discrete variable) is a mixed-integer problem. Problems where the solutions are sets, combinations, or permutations of integer-valued variables are referred to as combinatorial optimization problems.

Combination vs. permutation

Combinatorics is the branch of mathematics studying both the combination and permutation of a set of elements. The main difference between combination and permutation is the order. If the order of the elements doesn't matter, it is a combination, and if the order does matter, it is a permutation. Thus, permutations are ordered combinations. Depending on whether repetition of the elements is allowed or not, we can have different forms of combinations and permutations.

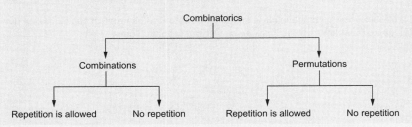

Combinations and permutations—permutations respect order and are thus ordered combinations. Both combinations and permutations have variants with and without repetition.

For example, assume we are designing a fitness plan that includes multiple fitness activities. Five types of exercises can be included in the fitness plan: jogging, swimming, biking, yoga, and aerobics. In a weekly plan, if we choose only three of these five exercises, and repetition is allowed, the number of possible combinations will be $(n + r - 1)! / r!(n - 1)! = (5 + 3 - 1)! / 3!(5 - 1)! = 7! / (3! \times 4!) = 35$. This means we can generate 35 different fitness plans by selecting three of the available five exercises and by allowing repetition.

However, if repetition is not allowed, the number of possible combinations will be $C(n,r) = n! / r!(n - r)! = 5! / (3! \times 2!) = 10$. This formula is often called "n choose r" (such as "5 choose 3"), and it's also known as the *binomial coefficient*. This means that we can generate only 10 plans if we don't want to repeat any of the exercises.

In both combination with and without repetition, the fitness plan doesn't include the order of performing the included exercises. If we respect specific order, the plan will take the form of a permutation. If repeating exercises is allowed, the number of possible permutations when selecting three of the five available exercises will be $n^r = 5^3 = 125$. However, if repetition is not allowed, the number of possible permutations will be $P(n,r) = n! / (n - r)! = 5! / (5 - 3)! = 60$.

Combinatorics can be implemented fairly easily in Python when coding from scratch, but there are excellent libraries available, such as SymPy, an open source Python library for symbolic mathematics. Its capabilities include, but are not limited to, statistics, physics, geometry, calculus, equation solving, combinatorics, discrete math, cryptography, and parsing. For example, the binomial coefficient can be calculated in SymPy using the following simple code:

```
from sympy import binomial
print(binomial(5,3))
```

See appendix A and the documentation for SymPy for more on implementing combinatorics in Python.

The traveling salesman problem (TSP) is a common example of a combinational problem whose solution is a permutation—a sequence of cities to be visited. In TSP, given n cities, a traveling salesman must visit all the cities and then return home, making a loop (a round trip). The salesman would like to travel in the most efficient way (such as the fastest, cheapest, or shortest route).

TSP can be subdivided into *symmetric TSP* (STSP) and *asymmetric TSP* (ATSP). In STSP, the distance between two cities is the same in both directions, forming an undirected graph. This symmetry halves the number of possible solutions. ATSP is a strict generalization of the symmetric version. In ATSP, paths may not exist in both directions, or the distances might be different, forming a directed graph. Traffic collisions, one-way streets, bridges, and airfares for cities with different departure and arrival fees are examples of how this symmetry could break down.

The search space in TSP is very large. For example, let's assume the salesman is to visit the 13 major cities in the Greater Toronto Area (GTA), as illustrated in figure 2.2. The naive solution's complexity is $O(n!)$. This means that there are $n! = 13! = 6,227,020,800$ possible tours in the case of ATSP. This is a huge search space in both STSP and ATSP. However, dynamic programming (DP) algorithms enable reduced complexity.

Figure 2.2   TSP in the Greater Toronto Area (GTA). The traveling salesman must visit all 13 cities and wishes to select the "best" path, whether that be based on distance, time, or some other criterion.

Dynamic programming is a method of solving optimization problems by breaking them down into smaller subproblems and solving each subproblem independently. For example, the complexity of the Bellman-Held-Karp algorithm [1] is $O(2^n \times n^2)$. There are other solvers and algorithms with different levels of computational complexity and approximation ratios such as the Concorde TSP solver, the 2-opt and 3-opt algorithms, branch and bound algorithms, the Christofides algorithm (or Christofides–Serdyukov algorithm), the Lin-Kernighan algorithm, metaheuristics-based algorithms, graph neural networks, and deep reinforcement learning methods. For example, the Christofides algorithm [2] is a polynomial-time approximation algorithm that produces a solution to TSP that is guaranteed to be no more than 50% longer than the optimal solution with a time complexity of $O(n^3)$. See appendix A for the solution of TSP using the Christofides algorithm implemented with the NetworkX package. We will discuss how to solve TSP using a number of these algorithms throughout this book.

A wide range of discrete optimization problems can be modeled as TSP. These problems include, but are not limited to, microchip manufacturing, permutation flow shop scheduling, arranging school bus routes for children in a school district, assigning routes for airplanes, transporting farming equipment, scheduling of service calls, meal delivery, and routing trucks for parcel delivery and pickup. For example, the capacitated vehicle routing problem (CVRP) is a generalization of TSP where one has to serve a set of customers using a fleet of vehicles based at a common depot. Each customer has a certain demand for goods that are initially located at the depot. The task is to design vehicle routes starting and ending at the depot such that all customer demands are fulfilled. Later in this book, we'll look at several examples of solving TSP and its variants using stochastic approaches.

Problem types

Decision problems are foundational in the study of algorithmic complexity. Generally speaking, a decision problem is a type of problem that requires determining whether a given input satisfies a certain property or condition. This problem can be answered with a simple "yes" or "no."

Decision problems are commonly classified based on their levels of complexity. These classes can also be applied to optimization problems, given that optimization problems can be converted into decision-making problems. For example, an optimization problem whose objective is to find an optimal or near-optimal solution within a feasible search space can be paraphrased as a decision-making problem that answers the question "Is there an optimal or a near-optimal solution within the feasible search space?" The answer will be "yes" or "no," or "true" or "false".

A generally accepted notion of an algorithm's efficiency is that its running time is polynomial. This means that the time or the computational cost to solve the problem can be described by a polynomial function of the size of the input for the algorithm. For example, in the context of TSP, the size of the input would typically be the number of cities that the salesperson needs to visit. Problems that can be solved in polynomial time are known as *tractable*. The following figure shows different types of problems and gives examples of commonly used benchmarks (toy problems) and real-life applications of each type.

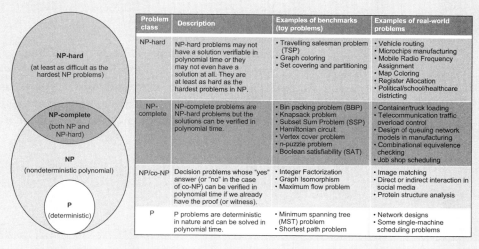

Problem class	Description	Examples of benchmarks (toy problems)	Examples of real-world problems
NP-hard	NP-hard problems may not have a solution verifiable in polynomial time or they may not even have a solution at all. They are at least as hard as the hardest problems in NP.	• Travelling salesman problem (TSP) • Graph coloring • Set covering and partitioning	• Vehicle routing • Microchips manufacturing • Mobile Radio Frequency Assignment • Map Coloring • Register Allocation • Political/school/healthcare districting
NP-complete	NP-complete problems are NP-hard problems but the solutions can be verified in polynomial time.	• Bin packing problem (BBP) • Knapsack problem • Subset Sum Problem (SSP) • Hamiltonian circuit • Vertex cover problem • n-puzzle problem • Boolean satisfiability (SAT)	• Container/truck loading • Telecommunication traffic overload control • Design of queuing network models in manufacturing • Combinational equivalence checking • Job shop scheduling
NP/co-NP	Decision problems whose "yes" answer (or "no" in the case of co-NP) can be verified in polynomial time if we already have the proof (or witness).	• Integer Factorization • Graph Isomorphism • Maximum flow problem	• Image matching • Direct or indirect interaction in social media • Protein structure analysis
P	P problems are deterministic in nature and can be solved in polynomial time.	• Minimum spanning tree (MST) problem • Shortest path problem	• Network designs • Some single-machine scheduling problems

Problem classes based on hardness and completeness. Problems can be categorized into NP-hard, NP-complete, NP, or P.

(continued)

For example, a complexity class P represents all decision problems that can be solved in polynomial time by deterministic algorithms (i.e., algorithms that do not guess at a solution). The NP or nondeterministic polynomial problems are those whose solutions are hard to find but easy to verify and are solved by a nondeterministic algorithm in polynomial time. NP-complete problems are those that are both NP-hard and verifiable in polynomial time. Finally, a problem is NP-hard if it is at least as hard as the hardest problem in NP-complete. NP-hard problems are usually solved by approximation or heuristic solvers, as it is hard to find efficient exact algorithms to solve such problems.

Clustering is a type of combinatorial problem whose solution takes the form of a combination where the order doesn't matter. In clustering, given n objects, we need to group them in k groups (clusters) such that all objects in a single group or cluster have a "natural" relation to one another, and objects not in the same group are somehow different. This means that the objects will be grouped based on some similarity or dissimilarity metric.

Stirling numbers can be used for counting partitions and permutations in combinatorial problems. Stirling numbers of the *first kind* count permutations according to their number of cycles, while Stirling numbers of the *second kind* represent the number of ways we can partition a set of objects into non-empty subsets. The following formula is for a Stirling number of the second kind (a *Stirling partition number*), and it gives the number of ways you can partition a set of n objects into k non-empty subsets in the context of our clustering problem:

$$S(n, k) = \begin{Bmatrix} n \\ k \end{Bmatrix} = \frac{1}{k!} \sum_{i=0}^{k} (-1)^i \begin{pmatrix} k \\ i \end{pmatrix} (k - i)^n$$

2.1

Let's consider smart cart clustering as an example. Shopping and luggage carts are commonly found in shopping malls and large airports. Shoppers or travelers pick up these carts at designated points and leave them in arbitrary places. It is a considerable task to re-collect them, and it is therefore beneficial if a "smarter" version of these carts could draw themselves together automatically to the nearest assembly points, as illustrated in figure 2.3.

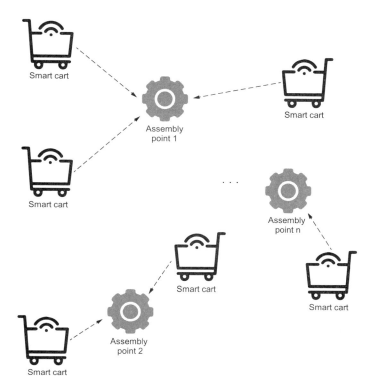

Figure 2.3   Smart cart clustering. Unused shopping or luggage carts congregate near designated assembly points to make collection and redistribution easier.

In practice, this problem is considered an NP-hard problem, as the search space can be very large based on the numbers of available carts and assembly points. To cluster these carts effectively, the centers of clustering (the *centroids*) must be found. The carts in each cluster will then be directed to the assembly point closest to the centroids.

For example, assume that 50 carts are to be clustered around four assembly points. This means that $n = 50$ and $k = 4$. Stirling numbers can be generated using the SymPy library. To do so, simply call the stirling function on two numbers, n and k:

```
from sympy.functions.combinatorial.numbers import stirling
print(stirling(50,4))
print(stirling(100,4))
```

The result is 5.3×10^{28}, and if *n* is increased to 100, the number becomes 6.7×10^{58}. Enumerating all possible partitions for large problems is not feasible.

2.1.2   *Landscape and number of objective functions*

An objective function's *landscape* represents the distribution of the function's values in the feasible search space. In this landscape, you'll find the optimal solution or the global minima in the lowest valley, assuming you are dealing with a minimization problem, or at the highest peak in the case of a maximization problem. According to the landscape of the objective function, if there is only one clear global optimal solution, the problem is *unimodal* (e.g., convex and concave functions). In a *multimodal* problem, more than one optimum exists. The objective function is called *deceptive* when the global minimum lies in a very narrow valley and there is also a strong local minimum with a wide basin of attraction, such that the value of this objective function is close to the value of an objective function at the global minimum [3]. Figure 2.4 is a 3D visualization of the landscapes of unimodal, multimodal, and deceptive functions generated using Python in the next listing. The complete listing is available in the GitHub repo for the book.

Listing 2.1   Examples of objective functions

```python
import numpy as np
import math
import matplotlib.pyplot as plt

def objective_unimodal(x, y):          # Unimodal function
    return x**2.0 + y**2.0

def objective_multimodal(x, y):        # Multimodal function
    return np.sin(x) * np.cos(y)

def objective_deceptive(x, y):         # Deceptive function
    return (1-(abs((np.sin(math.pi*(x-2))*np.sin(math.pi*(y-2)))/
    (math.pi*math.pi*(x-2)*(y-2))))**5)*(2+(x-7)**2+2*(y-7)**2)

fig = plt.figure(figsize = (25,25))
ax = fig.add_subplot(1,3,1, projection='3d')

x = np.arange(-3, 3, 0.01)
y = np.arange(-3, 3, 0.01)

X, Y = np.meshgrid(x, y)
Z = objective_unimodal(X, Y)
surf = ax.plot_surface(X, Y, Z, cmap=plt.cm.cividis)
ax.set_xlabel('x', fontsize=15)
ax.set_ylabel('y', fontsize=15)
ax.set_zlabel('Z', fontsize=15)
ax.set_title("Unimodal/Convex function", fontsize=18)
```

```
ax = fig.add_subplot(1,3,2, projection='3d')
Z = objective_multimodal(X, Y)
surf = ax.plot_surface(X, Y, Z, cmap=plt.cm.cividis)
ax.set_xlabel('x', fontsize=15)
ax.set_ylabel('y', fontsize=15)
ax.set_zlabel('Z', fontsize=15)
ax.set_title("Multimodal function", fontsize=18)

X, Y = np.meshgrid(x, y)
Z = objective_unimodal(X, Y)
ax = fig.add_subplot(1,3,3, projection='3d')
Z = objective_deceptive(X, Y)
surf = ax.plot_surface(X, Y, Z, cmap=plt.cm.cividis, antialiased=False)
ax.set_xlabel('x', fontsize=15)
ax.set_ylabel('y', fontsize=15)
ax.set_zlabel('Z', fontsize=15)
ax.set_title("Deceptive function", fontsize=18)

plt.show()
```

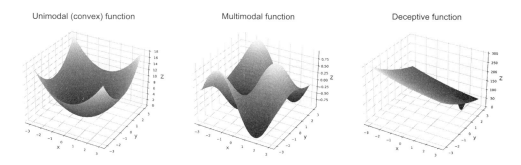

Figure 2.4   Unimodal, multimodal, and deceptive functions. Unimodal functions have one global optimum, whereas multimodal functions can have many. Deceptive functions contain false optima close to the value of an objective function at a global minimum, which can cause some algorithms to get stuck.

If the quantity to be optimized is expressed using only one objective function, the problem is referred to as a mono-objective or single-objective optimization problem (such as convex or concave functions). A multi-objective optimization problem specifies multiple objectives to be simultaneously optimized. Problems without an explicit objective function are called constraint-satisfaction problems (CSPs). The goal in this case is to find a solution that satisfies a given set of constraints.

The n-queen problem is an example of a CSP. In this problem, the aim is to put n queens on an $n \times n$ board with no two queens on the same row, column, or diagonal, as illustrated in figure 2.5. In this 4-queen problem, there are 5 conflicts in the first state ({Q1,Q2}, {Q1,Q3}, {Q2,Q3}, {Q2,Q4}, and {Q3,Q4}). After moving Q4, the number of conflicts reduces by 2, and after moving Q3, the number of conflicts is only 1, which is between Q1 and Q2.

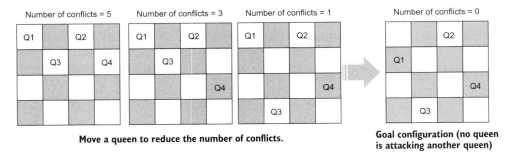

Move a queen to reduce the number of conflicts.

Goal configuration (no queen is attacking another queen)

Figure 2.5   The *n*-queen problem. This problem has no objective function, only a set of constraints that must be satisfied.

If we keep moving or placing the pieces, we can reach the goal state where the number of conflicts is 0, which means that no queen could attack any other queen horizontally, vertically, or diagonally. The next listing is a Python implementation of the 4-queen problem.

Listing 2.2   *n*-queen CSP

```python
from copy import deepcopy
import math
import matplotlib.pyplot as plt
import numpy as np

board_size = 4
board = np.full((board_size, board_size), False)    ◄──── Create an n x n board.

def can_attack(board, row, col):        Check for a queen on the
    if any(board[row]):                 same row.
        return True

    offset = col - row
    if any(np.diagonal(board, offset)):
        return True                                  Check for queens on the
    offset = (len(board) - 1 - col) - row            diagonals.
    if any(np.diagonal(np.fliplr(board), offset)):
        return True

    return False

board[0][0] = True
col = 1
states = [deepcopy(board)]
while col < board_size:
    row = 0
    while row < board_size:                          The piece can be placed
        if not can_attack(board, row, col):    ◄──── in this column.
            board[row][col] = True
            col += 1
            states.append(deepcopy(board))
```

```
        break
    row += 1
    if row == board_size:          ◄─────────────  The piece cannot be
        board = np.delete(board, 0, 1)              placed in this column.
        new_col = [[False]] * board_size
        board = np.append(board, new_col, 1)
        states.append(deepcopy(board))
        col -= 1
        continue
```

In the preceding listing, the `can_attack` function detects if a newly placed piece can attack a previously placed piece. A piece can attack another piece if it is in the same row, column, or diagonal. Figure 2.6 shows the solution obtained after six steps.

Figure 2.6 *n*-queen solution

The first piece is trivially placed in the first position. The second piece must be placed either in the third or fourth position, as the first two can be attacked. By placing it in the third position, however, the third piece cannot be placed. Thus, the first piece is removed (the board is "slid" one column over), and we try again. This continues until a solution is found.

The full code for this problem, including the code used to generate visualizations, can be found in the code file for listing 2.2, available in the book's GitHub repo. The solution algorithm is as follows:

1 Moving from top to bottom in a column, the algorithm attempts to place the piece while avoiding conflicts. For the first column, this will default to Q1 = 0.

2 Moving to the next column, if a piece cannot be placed at row 0, it will be placed at row 1, and so on.

3 When a piece has been placed, the algorithm moves to the next column.

4 If it is impossible to place a piece in a given column, the first column of the entire board is removed, and the current column is reattempted.

Constraint programming solvers available in Google OR-Tools can also be used to solve this $n \times n$ queen problem. The next listing shows the steps of the solution using OR-Tools.

Listing 2.3   Solving the n-queen problem using OR-Tools

```
import numpy as np
import matplotlib.pyplot as plt
import math
from ortools.sat.python import cp_model
```
Import a constraint programming solver that uses SAT (satisfiability) methods.

```
board_size = 4
```
Set the board size for the n x n queen problem.

```
model = cp_model.CpModel()
```
Define a solver.

```
queens = [model.NewIntVar(0, board_size - 1, 'x%i' % i)
➥for i in range(board_size)]
```
Define the variables. The array index represents the column, and the value is the row.

Define the constraint: all rows must be different.
```
model.AddAllDifferent(queens)

model.AddAllDifferent(queens[i] + i for i in range(board_size))
model.AddAllDifferent(queens[i] - i for i in range(board_size))
```

```
solver = cp_model.CpSolver()
solver.parameters.enumerate_all_solutions = True
solver.Solve(model)
```
Solve the model.

```
all_queens = range(board_size)
state=[]
for i in all_queens:
    for j in all_queens:
        if solver.Value(queens[j]) == i:
            # There is a queen in column j, row i.
            state.append(True)
        else:
            state.append(None)
```
Define the constraint: no two queens can be on the same diagonal.

```
states=np.array(state).reshape(-1, board_size)
fig = plt.figure(figsize=(5,5))
markers = [
    x.tolist().index(True) if True in x.tolist() else None
    for x in np.transpose(states)
]
res = np.add.outer(range(board_size), range(board_size)) % 2
plt.imshow(res, cmap="binary_r")
plt.xticks([])
plt.yticks([])
plt.plot(markers, marker="*", linestyle="None",
➥markersize=100/board_size, color="y")H
```
Visualize the solution.

Running this code produces the output in figure 2.7. More information about Google OR-Tools is available in appendix A.

Figure 2.7 The *n*-queen solution using OR-Tools

2.1.3 Constraints

Constrained problems have hard or soft constraints for equality, inequality, or both. Hard constraints must be satisfied, while soft constraints are nice to satisfy (but are not mandatory). If there are no constraints to be considered, aside from the boundary constraints, the problem is an unconstrained optimization problem.

Let's revisit the ticket pricing problem introduced in section 1.3.1. There is a wide range of derivative-based solvers in Python that can handle such kinds of differentiable mathematical optimization problems (see appendix A). The next listing shows how you can solve this simple ticket pricing problem using SciPy. SciPy is a library containing valuable tools for all things computation.

Listing 2.4 Optimal ticket pricing

```
import numpy as np
import scipy.optimize as opt
import matplotlib.pyplot as plt

def f(x):
    return -(-20*x**2+6200*x-350000)/1000

res=opt.minimize_scalar(f, method='bounded', bounds=[0, 250])

print("Optimal Ticket Price ($): %.2f" % res.x)
print("Profit f(x) in K$: %.2f" % -res.fun)
```

The objective function, required by minimize_scalar to be a minimization function

The bounded method is the constrained minimization procedure that finds the solution.

Running this code produces the following output:

```
Optimal Ticket Price ($): 155.00
Profit f(x) in K$: 130.50
```

This code finds the optimal ticket price in the range between $0 and $250 that maximizes the profit. As you may have noticed, the profit formula is converted into a minimization problem by adding a negative sign in the objective function to match with the `minimize` function in `scipy.optimize`. A minus sign is added in the `print` function to convert it back into profit.

What if we imposed an equality constraint on this problem? Let's assume that due to incredible international demand for our event, we are now considering using a different event planning company and opening up virtual attendance for our conference so that international guests can also participate. Interested participants can now choose between attending the event in person or joining via a live stream. All participants, whether in-person or virtual, will receive a physical welcome package, which is limited to 10,000 units. Thus, in order to ensure a "full" event, we must either sell 10,000 in-person tickets, 10,000 virtual tickets, or some combination thereof. The new event company is charging us a $1,000,000 flat rate for the event, so we want to sell as many tickets as possible (exactly 10,000). The following equation is associated with this problem:

Let x be the number of physical ticket sales, and let y be the number of virtual ticket sales. Additionally, let $f(x,y)$ be the function for profits generated from the event, where

$$f(x, y) = 155x + \left(0.001x^{\frac{3}{2}} + 70\right)y - 1000000 \qquad \text{2.2}$$

Essentially, we earn $155 profit on in-person attendance, and the profit for online attendance is $70, but it increases by some amount with the more physical attendance we have (let's say that as the event looks "more crowded," we can charge more for online attendees).

Suppose we add a constraint function, $x + y \le 10000$, which shows that the combined ticket sales cannot exceed 10,000. The problem is now a bivariate mono-objective constrained optimization problem. It is possible to convert this constrained optimization problem to an unconstrained optimization using the Lagrange multiplier, λ. We can use SymPy to implement Lagrange multipliers and solve for the optimal mix of virtual and physical ticket sales. The idea is to convert the constrained optimization problem defined by the objective function $f(x,y)$ with an equality constraint $g(x,y)$ into an unconstrained optimization problem using the Lagrangian function $L(x,y,\lambda) = f(x,y) + \lambda g(x,y)$. This function combines an objective function and constraints, enabling constrained optimization problems to be formulated as unconstrained problems through the use of Lagrange multipliers. To do so, we take the partial derivatives of the objective functions and the constraints, with respect to the decision variables x and y, to form the unconstrained optimization equations to be used by the SymPy solver, as illustrated in figure 2.8.

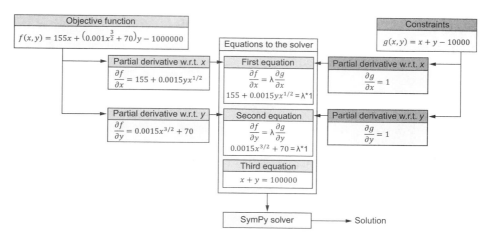

Figure 2.8 Steps for solving the ticket pricing problem using the Lagrange method

The next listing shows the Python implementation using SymPy.

Listing 2.5 Maximizing profits using Lagrange multipliers

```
import sympy as sym

x,y=sym.var('x, y', positive=True)          ◄——— Define the decision variables.

f=155*x+(0.001*x**sym.Rational(3,2)+70)*y-1000000   ◄——┐ Define the ticket pricing
                                                        │ objective function.
g=x+y-10000   ◄——— Define the equality constraint.

lamda=sym.symbols('lambda')   ◄——— Lagrange multiplier
Lagr=f-lamda*g   ◄——— Lagrangian function

eqs = [sym.diff(Lagr, x), sym.diff(Lagr, y), g]   ◄——— Equations to the solver

sol=sym.solve(eqs,[x,y,lamda], dict=True)   ◄——┐
                                               Solve these three equations
def getValueOf(k, L):                          in three variables
    for d in L:                                (x,y,lambda) using SymPy.
        if k in d:
            return d[k]

profit=[f.subs(p) for p in sol]

print("optimal number of physical ticket sales: x = %.0f" % getValueOf(x, sol))
print("optimal number of online ticket sales: y = %.0f" % getValueOf(y, sol))
print("Expected profil: f(x,y) = $%.4f" % profit[0])
```

By solving the preceding three equations, we get x and y values that correspond to the optimized quantities for virtual and physical ticket sales. With the code in listing 2.5, we can see that the best result is to sell 6,424 in-person tickets and 3,576 online tickets. This results in a maximum profit of $2,087,260.

2.1.4   *Linearity of objective functions and constraints*

If all the objective functions and associated constraint conditions are linear, the optimization problem is categorized as a *linear optimization problem* or *linear programming problem* (LPP or LP), where the goal is to find the optimal value of a linear function subject to linear constraints. Blending problems are a typical application of mixed integer linear programming (MILP), where a number of ingredients are to be blended or mixed to obtain a product with certain characteristics or properties. In the animal feed mix problem described in Paul Jensen's *Operations Research Models and Methods* [4], the optimum amounts of three ingredients in an animal feed mix need to be determined. The possible ingredients, their nutritive contents (in kilograms of nutrient per kilograms of ingredient), and the unit costs are shown in table 2.1.

Table 2.1   Animal feed mix problem

Ingredients	Nutritive content and price of ingredients			
	Calcium (kg/kg)	Protein (kg/kg)	Fiber (kg/kg)	Unit cost (cents/kg)
Corn	0.001	0.09	0.02	30.5
Limestone	0.38	0.0	0.0	10.0
Soybean meal	0.002	0.50	0.08	90.0

The mixture must meet the following restrictions:

- Calcium—At least 0.8% but not more than 1.2%
- Protein—At least 22%
- Fiber—At most 5%

The problem is to find the mixture that satisfies these constraints while minimizing cost. The decision variables are x_1, x_2, and x_3, which are proportions of limestone, corn, and soybean meal respectively.

The objective function $f = 30.5x_1 + 10x_2 + 90x_3$ needs to be minimized, subject to the following constraints:

- Calcium limits: $0.008 \leq 0.001x_1 + 0.38x_2 + 0.002x_3 \leq 0.012$
- Protein constraint: $0.09x_1 + 0.5x_3 \geq 0.22$
- Fiber constraint: $0.02x_1 + 0.08x_3 <= 0.05$
- Non-negativity restriction: x_1, x_2, $x_3 \geq 0$
- Conservation: $x_1 + x_2 + x_3 = 1$

In this problem, both the objective function and the constraints are linear, so it is an LPP. There are several Python libraries that can be used to solve mathematical optimization problems.

We'll try solving the animal feed mix problem using PuLP. PuLP is a Python linear programming library that allows users to define linear programming problems and solve them using optimization algorithms such as COIN-OR's linear and integer programming solvers. See appendix A for more information about PuLP and other mathematical programming solvers. The next listing shows the steps for solving the animal feed mix problem using PuLP.

Listing 2.6 Solving a linear programming problem using PuLP

```
from pulp import *

model = LpProblem("Animal_Feed_Mix_Problem", LpMinimize)
```
Create a linear programming model.

```
x1 = LpVariable('Corn', lowBound = 0, upBound = 1, cat='Continous')
x2 = LpVariable('Limestone', lowBound = 0, upBound = 1, cat='Continous')
x3 = LpVariable('Soybean meal', lowBound = 0, upBound = 1, cat='Continous')
```
Define three variables that represent the percentages of corn, limestone, and soybean meal in the mixture.

```
model += 30.5*x1 + 10.0*x2 + 90*x3, 'Cost'
```
Define the total cost as the objective function to be minimized.

```
model +=0.008 <= 0.001*x1 + 0.38*x2 + 0.002*x3 <= 0.012, 'Calcium limits'
model += 0.09*x1 + 0.5*x3 >=0.22, 'Minimum protein'
model += 0.02*x1 + 0.08*x3 <=0.05, 'Maximum fiber'
model += x1+x2+x3 == 1, 'Conservation'
```
Add the constraints.

```
model.solve()
```
Solve the problem using PuLP's choice of solver.

```
for v in model.variables():
    print(v.name, '=', round(v.varValue,2)*100, '%')

print('Total cost of the mixture per kg = ',
      round(value(model.objective)/100, 2), '$')
```
Print the results (the optimal percentages of the ingredients and the cost of the mixture per kg).

As you can see in this listing, we start by importing PuLP and creating a model as a linear programming problem. We then define LP variables with the associated parameters, such as name, lower bound, and upper bound for each variable's range and the type of variable (e.g., integer, binary, or continuous). A solver is then used to solve the problem. PuLP supports several solvers, such as GLPK, GUROBI, CPLEX, and MOSEK. The default solver in PuLP is Cbc (COIN-OR branch and cut). Running this code gives the following output:

```
Corn = 65.0%
Limestone = 3.0%
Soybean_meal = 32.0%
Total cost of the mixture per kg = 0.4916$
```

If one of the objective functions, or at least one of the constraints, is nonlinear, the problem is considered a nonlinear optimization problem or nonlinear programming problem (NLP), and it's harder to solve than a linear problem. A special case of NLP, when the objective function is quadratic, is called quadratic programming (QP). For example, the plant layout problem (PLP) or facility location problem (FLP) is a quadratic assignment problem (QAP) that aims at assigning different facilities (departments) *F* to different locations *L* in order to minimize a given function cost, such as the total material handling cost, as shown in figure 2.9.

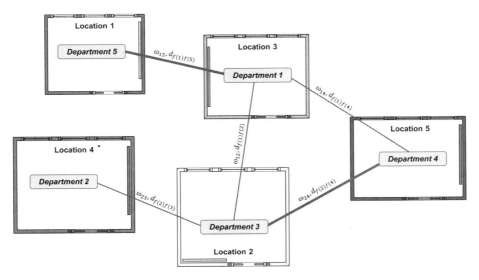

Figure 2.9   Plant layout problem—what is the optimal location for each department that minimizes the overall material handling costs?

Assume that ω_{ij} is the frequency of interaction or the flow of products between these facilities and $d_{f(i)f(j)}$ is the distance between facilities *i* and *j*. The material handling cost (MHC) is

$$\text{MHC}_{ij} = \text{flow} \times \text{distance} = \omega_{ij} \times d_{f(i)f(j)} \qquad \textbf{2.3}$$

and the total material handling cost (TMHC) is the summation of all the material handling costs inside the material handling cost matrix. In matrix notation, the problem can be formulated as

$$\text{Find } X \text{ which minimizes } trace(W X D X^T)$$

where *X* represents the assignment vector, *W* is the flow matrix, and *D* is the distance matrix. Trace is the sum of elements on the main diagonal (from the upper left to the lower right) of the resultant material handling cost matrix.

In a more general case, NLP includes nonlinear objective functions, or at least nonlinear constraints, of any form. For example, imagine you're designing a landmine detection and disposal unmanned ground vehicle (UGV) [5]. In outdoor applications like humanitarian demining, UGVs should be able to navigate through rough terrain. Sandy soils, rocky terrain with obstacles, steep inclines, ditches, and culverts can be difficult for vehicles to negotiate. The locomotion systems of such vehicles need to carefully designed to guarantee motion fluidity.

Assume that you are in charge of finding optimal values for wheel parameters (e.g., diameter, width, and loading) that will

- Minimize the wheel sinkage, which is the maximum amount the wheel sinks in the soil that it is moving on
- Minimize motion resistance, which is the overall resistance faced by the UGV unit due to the different components of resistance (compaction, gravitational, etc.)
- Minimize drive torque, which is the driving torque required from the actuating motors for each wheel
- Minimize drive power, which is the driving power required from the actuating motors for each wheel
- Maximize the slope negotiability, which represents the maximum slope that can be climbed by the UGV unit considering its weight and the soil parameters.

Due to availability in the market or manufacturing concerns and costs, the wheel diameter should be in the range of 4 to 8.2 inches, wheel width should be in the range of 3 to 5 inches, and wheel loading should be in the range of 22 to 24 pounds per wheel. This wheel design problem (figure 2.10) can be stated as follows:

Find X which optimizes f, subject to a possible set of boundary constraints, where X is a vector that is composed of a number of decision variables such as

- x_1 = wheel diameter, $x_1 \in [4, 8.2]$
- x_2 = wheel width, $x_2 \in [3, 5]$
- x_3 = wheel loading, $x_3 \in [22, 24]$

We can also consider the objective functions $f = \{f_1, f_2, ...\}$. For example, the function for wheel sinkage might look like this:

$$f_1 = \left(\frac{3x_3}{(3 - n)(k_c + x_2 k_\phi \sqrt{x_1})} \right)^{\frac{2}{2n+1}} \qquad \textbf{2.4}$$

where n is the exponent of sinkage, k_c is the cohesive modulus of soil deformation, and k_φ is the frictional modulus of soil deformation. This problem is considered to be nonlinear because the objective function is nonlinear.

Figure 2.10   The MineProbe wheel design problem [5]

The catenary problem discussed in Veselić's "Finite catenary and the method of Lagrange" article [6] is another example of a nonlinear optimization problem. A catenary is a flexible hanging object composed of multiple parts, such as a chain or telephone cable (figure 2.11). In this problem, we are provided with n homogenous beams, with lengths $d_1, d_2, \ldots d_n > 0$ and masses $m_1, m_2, \ldots m_n > 0$, which are connected by $n + 1$ joints $G_0, G_2, \ldots G_{n+1}$. The location of each joint is represented by the Cartesian coordinates (x_i, y_i, z_i). The ends of the catenary are G_0 and G_{n+1}, which both have the same y and z values (they are at the same height and in line with each other).

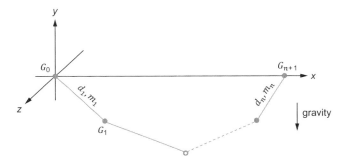

Figure 2.11   Finite catenary problem—the catenary (or chain) is suspended from two points, G_0 and G_{n+1}.

Assuming that the beam lengths and masses are predefined parameters, our goal is to look for stable equilibrium positions in the field of gravity—those positions where the potential energy is minimized. The potential energy to be minimized is defined as follows:

$$E = \sum_{i=1}^{n+1} m_i \gamma \frac{y_i + y_{i-1}}{2}, \gamma > 0$$

2.5

subject to the following constraints:

$$g_i = (x_i - x_{i-1})^2 + (y_i - y_{i-1})^2 + (z_i - z_{i-1})^2 - d_i^2 = 0, i = 0, 2, \ldots, n \quad \textbf{2.6}$$

where γ is the gravitational constant. The nonlinearity of the constraints makes this problem nonlinear, despite having a linear objective function.

2.1.5   *Expected quality and permissible time for the solution*

Optimization problems can also be categorized according to the expected quality of the solutions and the time allowed to find the solutions. Figure 2.12 shows three main types of problems: design problems (strategic functions), planning problems (tactical functions), and control problems (operational functions).

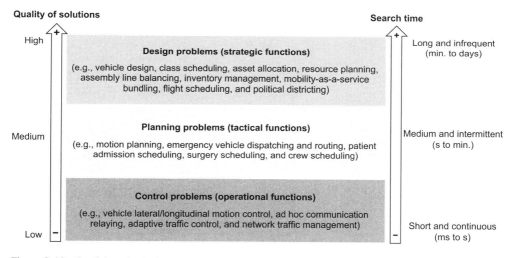

Figure 2.12   Qualities of solutions vs. search time. Some types of problems require fast computations but do not require incredibly accurate results, while others (such as design problems) allow more processing time in return for higher accuracy.

In *design problems*, time is not as important as the quality of the solution, and users are willing to wait (sometimes even a few days) to get an optimal, or near-optimal, result. These problems can be solved offline, and the optimization process is usually carried out only once in a long time. Examples of design problems include vehicle design, class scheduling, asset allocation, resource planning, assembly line balancing, inventory management, flight scheduling, and political districting.

Let's discuss political districting as a design problem in more detail. Districting is the problem of grouping small geographic areas, called *basic units*, into larger geographic clusters, called *districts*, in such a way that the latter are acceptable according to relevant planning criteria [7]. Typical examples of basic units are customers, streets, or zip code areas. The planning criteria may include the following:

- Balance or equity in terms of demographic background, equitable size, balanced workload, equal sales potential, or the number of customers
- Contiguity to enable traveling between the basic units of the district without having to leave the district
- Compactness to allow for round- or square-shaped undistorted districts without holes
- Respect of boundaries, such as administrative boundaries, railroads, rivers, or mountains
- Socio-economic heterogeneity, to allow for better representation of residents with different incomes, ethnicities, concerns, or views

Political districting, school districting, districting for health services, districting for EV charging stations, districting for micro-mobility stations (e.g., for e-bikes and e-scooters), and districting for sales or delivery are all examples of districting problems.

Political districting is a problem that has plagued societies since the advent of representative democracy in the Roman Republic. In a representative democracy, officials are nominated and elected to represent the interests of the people who elected them. In order to have a greater say when deciding on matters that concern the entire state, the party system came about, which defines political platforms that nominees use to differentiate themselves from their competitors. Manipulating the shapes of electoral districts to determine the outcome of elections is called *gerrymandering* (named after the early nineteenth century Massachusetts governor Elbridge Gerry who redrew the map of the Senate's districts in 1810 in order to weaken the opposing federalist party). Figure 2.13 shows how manipulating the shapes of the districts can sway the vote in favor of a decision that otherwise wouldn't have won.

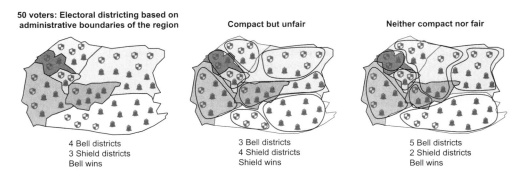

Figure 2.13   Example of gerrymandering. The two major political parties, Shield and Bell, try to gain an advantage by manipulating the district boundaries to suppress undesired interests and promote their own.

An effective and transparent political districting strategy is needed to avoid gerrymandering and generate a solution that preserves the integrity of individual subdistricts and divides the population into almost equal voting populations in a reproducible way.

In many countries, electoral districts are reviewed from time to time to reflect changes and movements in the country's population. For example, the Constitution of Canada requires that federal electoral districts be reviewed after each 10-year census.

Political districting is defined as aggregating n subregions of a territory into m electoral districts subject to constraints such as

- The districts should have near-equal voting population.
- The socioeconomic homogeneity inside each district, as well as the integrity of different communities, should be maximized.
- The districts have to be compact, and the subregions of each district have to be contiguous.
- Subregions should be considered as indivisible political units, and their boundaries should be respected.

The problem can be formulated as an optimization problem in which a function that quantifies the preceding factors is maximized. Here is an example of this function:

$$F(x) = \alpha_{\text{pop}} f_{\text{pop}}(x) + \alpha_{\text{comp}} f_{\text{comp}}(x) + \alpha_{\text{soc}} f_{\text{soc}}(x) + \alpha_{\text{sim}} f_{\text{sim}}(x) \qquad \textbf{2.7}$$

where x is a solution to the problem or the electoral districts, α_i are user-specified multipliers $0 \leq \alpha_i \leq 1$, and f_{pop}, f_{comp}, f_{soc}, f_{int}, and f_{sim} are functions that quantify the population equality, compactness of districts, socioeconomic homogeneity, integrity of different communities, and similarity to existing districts respectively. In the upcoming chapters, I will show you how we can use offline optimization algorithms to handle optimal multicriteria assignment design problems.

Planning problems need to be solved faster than design problems, in a time span from a few seconds to a few minutes. To find a solution in such a short time, optimality is usually traded for speed. Examples of planning problems include vehicle motion planning, emergency vehicle dispatching and routing, patient admission scheduling, surgery scheduling, and crew scheduling. Let's consider the ride-sharing problem as an example of a planning problem.

Ride-sharing involves a fleet of pay-per-use vehicles and a set of passengers with predefined pick-up and drop-off points (figure 2.14). The dispatch service needs to assign a set of passengers in a specific order to each driver to achieve a set of objectives. This ride-sharing problem is a multi-objective constrained optimization problem. A non-comprehensive list of optimization goals for ride-sharing includes

- Minimizing the total travel distance or time of drivers' trips
- Minimizing the total travel time of passengers' trips
- Maximizing the number of matched (served) requests
- Minimizing the cost of the drivers' trips
- Minimizing the cost of the passengers' trips

- Maximizing the drivers' earnings
- Minimizing passengers' waiting time
- Minimizing the total number of drivers required

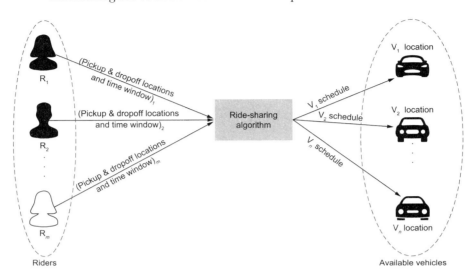

Figure 2.14   **Ride-sharing problem—this planning problem needs to be solved in a shorter amount of time, as delays could mean lost trips and a bad user experience.**

For the ride-sharing problem, both the search time and the quality of the solutions are important. On many popular ride-sharing platforms, dozens if not hundreds of users may simultaneously be searching for rides at the same place in a given district. Overly costly and time-consuming solutions would lead to higher operating costs (i.e., employing more drivers than necessary or calling in drivers from other districts) as well as the potential for lost business (bad user experiences may dissuade passengers from using the platform a second time) and high driver turnover.

In practice, the assignment of drivers to passengers goes well beyond the distance between passenger and driver—it may also include factors such as driver reliability, passenger rating, vehicle type, and pickup and destination location types. For example, a customer going to the airport may request a larger vehicle to accommodate luggage. In the upcoming chapters, we will discuss how to solve planning problems using different search and optimization algorithms.

Control problems require very fast solutions in real time. In most cases, this means a time span from a millisecond to a few seconds. Vehicle lateral or longitudinal motion control, surgical robot motion control, disruptions management, and ad hoc communication relaying are examples of control problems. Online optimization algorithms are required to handle these kinds of problems. Optimization tasks in both planning and control problems are often carried out repetitively—new orders will, for instance, continuously arrive in a production facility and need to be scheduled to machines in a way that minimizes the waiting time for all jobs.

Imagine a real-world situation where a swarm of unmanned aerial vehicles (UAVs) or micro aerial vehicles (MAVs) is deployed to search for victims trapped on untraversable terrain after a natural disaster, like an earthquake, avalanche, tsunami, tornado, wildfire, etc. The mission consists of two phases: a search phase and a relay phase. During the search phase, the MAVs will conduct a search according to the deployment algorithm. When a target is found, the swarm of MAVs will self-organize to utilize their range-limited communication capabilities and set up an ad hoc communication relay network between the victim and the base station, as illustrated in figure 2.15.

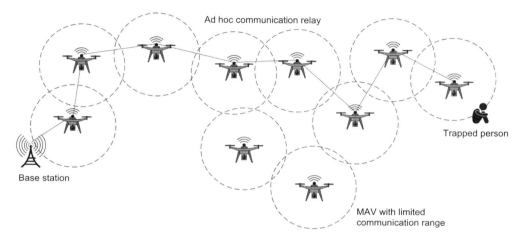

Figure 2.15 Communication relaying problem—a swarm of MAVs must form an ad hoc communication relay between a base station and a trapped victim. The movement of the MAVs is a control problem that must be solved repeatedly, multiple times per second. In this case, speed is more important than accuracy, as minor errors can be immediately corrected during the next cycle.

During the search phase, MAVs can be deployed to maximize the area covered. After they detect a victim, the MAVs can be repositioned to maximize the victim's visibility. The ad hoc communication relay network is then established to maximize the radio coverage in the swarm and find the shortest path between the MAV that detected the victim and the base station, given the following assumptions:

- MAVs are capable of situational awareness by combining data from three noise-prone sensors: a magnetic compass for direction, a speedometer for speed, and an altimeter for altitude.
- MAVs are capable of communicating via a standard protocol such as IEEE 802.11b with a limited range of 100 m.
- MAVs are capable of relaying ground signals as well as controlling signals sent among MAVs.
- MAVs have enough onboard power to sustain 30 minutes of continuous flight, at which point they must return to the base to recharge. However, the amount of flight time varies depending on the amount of signaling completed during flight.

- MAVs are capable of quickly accelerating to a constant flight speed of 10 m/s.
- MAVs are not capable of hovering and have a minimum turn radius of approximately 10 m.

For control problems such as MAV repositioning, search time is of paramount importance. As the MAVs cannot hover and thus must remain in constant motion, delayed decisions may lead to unexpected situations, such as mid-air collisions or a loss of signal. As instructions are sent (or repeated) every few milliseconds, each MAV must be able to decide its next move within that span of time. A MAV must account not only for its current position, target position, and velocity, but must also consider obstacles, communications signal strength, wind, and other environmental effects. Minor errors are acceptable, as they can be corrected in subsequent searches. In the upcoming chapters, we will discuss how to solve control problems like this.

This book will largely focus on complex, ill-structured problems that cannot be handled by traditional mathematical optimization or derivative-based solvers. We'll look at examples of design, planning and control problems in various domains. Next, let's take a look at how search and optimization algorithms are classified.

2.2   *Classifying search and optimization algorithms*

When we search, we try to examine different states to find a path from the start (initial) state to the goal state. Often, an optimization algorithm searches for an optimum solution by iteratively transforming a current state or a candidate solution into a new, hopefully better, solution. Search algorithms can be classified based on the way the search space is explored:

- *Local search* uses only local information about the search space surrounding the current solution to produce new solutions. Since only local information is used, local search algorithms (also known as local optimizers) locate local optima (which may or may not be global optima).
- *Global search* uses more information about the search space to locate global optima.

In other words, global search algorithms explore the entire search space, while local search algorithms only exploit neighborhoods.

Yet another classification distinguishes between deterministic and stochastic algorithms, as illustrated in figure 2.16:

- *Deterministic algorithms* follow a rigorous procedure in their path, and both the values of their design variables and their functions are repeatable. From the same starting point, they will follow the same path, whether you run the program today or tomorrow. Examples include, but are not limited to, graphical methods, gradient and Hessian-based methods, penalty methods, gradient projection methods, and graph search methods. Graph search methods can be further subdivided into blind search methods (e.g., depth-first, breadth-first, or Dijkstra) and informed search methods (e.g., hill climbing, beam search, best-first, A*, or contraction hierarchies). Deterministic methods are covered in part 1 of this book.

- *Stochastic algorithms* explicitly use randomness in their parameters or decision-making process or both. For example, genetic algorithms use some random or pseudo-random numbers, resulting in individual paths that are not exactly repeatable. With stochastic algorithms, the time taken to obtain an optimal solution cannot be accurately foretold. Solutions do not always get better, and stochastic algorithms sometimes miss the opportunity to find optimal solutions. This behavior can be advantageous, however, because it can prevent them from becoming trapped in local optima. Examples of stochastic algorithms include tabu search, simulated annealing, genetic algorithms, differential evolution algorithms, particle swarm optimization, ant colony optimization, artificial bee colony, firefly algorithm, etc. Most statistical machine learning algorithms are stochastic because they make use of randomness during the learning stage and they make predictions during the inference stage with a certain level of uncertainty. Moreover, some machine learning models are, like people, unpredictable. Models trained using human behavior-based data as independent variables are more likely to be unpredictable than those trained using independent variables that strictly follow physical laws. For example, the human intent recognition model is less predictable than a model that predicts the stress-strain curve of a material. Due to the uncertainty associated with machine learning predictions, machine learning–based algorithms used to solve optimization problems can be considered stochastic methods. Stochastic algorithms are covered in parts 2 to 5 of this book.

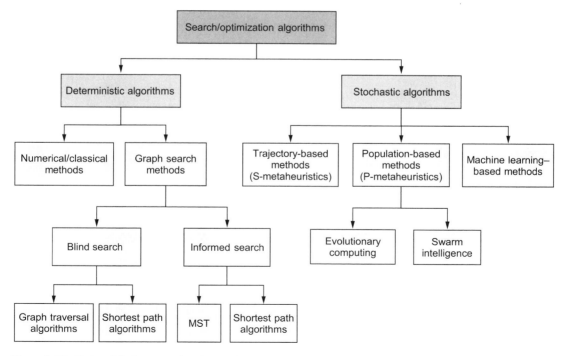

Figure 2.16 **Deterministic vs. stochastic algorithms. Deterministic algorithms follow a set procedure, and the results are repeatable, while stochastic searches have elements of randomness built into the algorithms.**

Treasure-hunting mission

The search for an optimal solution in a given search space can be likened to a treasure-hunting mission. Imagine you and a group of friends decided to visit an island looking for pirate treasure.

All the areas on the island (except the active volcano area) correspond to the feasible search space of the optimization problem. The treasure corresponds to the optimal solution in this feasible space. You and your friends are the "search agents" launched to search for the solution, each following different search approaches. If you don't have any information that can guide you while searching, you are following a blind (uninformed) search approach, which is usually inefficient and time-consuming. If you know that the pirates used to hide the treasure in elevated spots, you could then directly climb up the steepest cliff and try to reach the highest peak. This scenario corresponds to the classic hill-climbing technique (informed search). Uninformed and informed search algorithms are presented in the next two chapters. You could also follow a trial-and-error approach, looking for hints and repeatedly moving from one place to another plausible place until you find the treasure. This corresponds to trajectory-based search, which we'll discuss in part 2 of the book.

If you do not want to take the risk of getting nothing and decide to share information with your friends instead of treasure-hunting alone, you will be following a population-based search approach. While working in a team, you may notice that some treasure hunters show better performance than others. In this case, only better-performing hunters can be kept, and new ones can be recruited to replace the lesser-performing hunters. This is akin to evolutionary algorithms, such as genetic algorithms, where the fittest hunters survive. Genetic algorithms are covered in part 3 of the book. Alternatively, you and other friends can try to emulate the success of the outperforming hunters in each area of the treasure island without getting rid of any team members and without recruiting new ones. This scenario uses the so-called swarm intelligence and corresponds to population-based optimization algorithms such as particle swarm optimization, ant colony optimization, and artificial bee colony algorithm. These algorithms will be discussed in part 4 of the book.

You alone, or with the help of your friends, can build a mental model based on historical data of previous and similar treasure-hunting missions, or you can train a reward predictor based on trial-and-error interaction with the treasure island (search space), taking the strength of the metal detector signal as a reward indicator. After a few iterations, you will learn to maximize the reward from the predictor and improve your behavior until you fulfill the desired goal and find the treasure. This corresponds to a machine learning–based approach, which we'll discuss in part 5 of this book.

2.3   *Heuristics and metaheuristics*

Heuristics (also known as *mental shortcuts* or *rules of thumb*) are solution strategies, seeking methods, or rules that can facilitate finding acceptable (optimal or near-optimal) solutions to a complex problem in a practical time. Despite the fact that heuristics can seek near-optimal solutions at a reasonable computational cost, they cannot guarantee either feasibility or degree of optimality.

"Eureka! Eureka!"

The word *heuristic* comes from the Greek word *heuriskein*, which means "to find or discover." The past tense of this verb, *eureka*, was used by the Greek mathematician, physicist, engineer, astronomer, and inventor Archimedes. Archimedes was contracted to detect fraud in the manufacture of a golden crown, and he accepted the challenge. During a subsequent visit to the public baths, he had a revelation. As his body submerged in the water, he observed that the more he sank, the more water was displaced, offering an exact measure of his volume. Realizing the principle at play, he deduced that a crown containing silver, being less dense than pure gold, would need to have greater volume to match the weight of a pure gold crown. Consequently, it would displace more water. Recognizing the solution, Archimedes leaped out of the bath and hurried home, exclaiming "Eureka! Eureka!" which translates to "I've found it! I've found it!"

The term metaheuristic is a combination of two Greek words: *meta*, which means "beyond, on a higher level," and *heuristics*. It's a term coined by Fred Glover, inventor of the tabu search (discussed in chapter 6) to refer to high-level strategies used to guide and modify other heuristics to enhance their performance. The goal of metaheuristics is to efficiently explore the search space in order to find optimal or near-optimal solutions. Metaheuristics may incorporate mechanisms to achieve a trade-off between exploration (diversification) and exploitation (intensification) of the search space to avoid getting trapped in confined areas of the search space while also finding optimal or near-optimal solutions in a reasonable amount of time. Finding this balance of exploration and exploitation is crucial in heuristics, as discussed in section 1.5. Metaheuristic algorithms are often global optimizers that can be applied to different linear and nonlinear optimization problems with relatively few modifications for specific problems. These algorithms are often robust and can handle different problem sizes, problem instances, and random variables.

Let's assume that we have 6 objects with different sizes (2, 4, 3, 6, 5, and 1) and we need to pack them into a minimum number of bins. Each bin has a limited size of 7, so the total size of the objects in the bin should be 7 or less. If we have n objects, there are $n!$ possible ways of packing the objects. The minimum number of bins we need is the *lower bound*. To calculate this lower bound, we need to find the total number of object sizes ($2 + 4 + 3 + 6 + 5 + 1 = 21$). The lower bound is $21 / 7 = 3$ bins. This means that we need at least 3 bins to pack these objects. Figure 2.17 illustrates two heuristics that can be used to solve this bin packing problem.

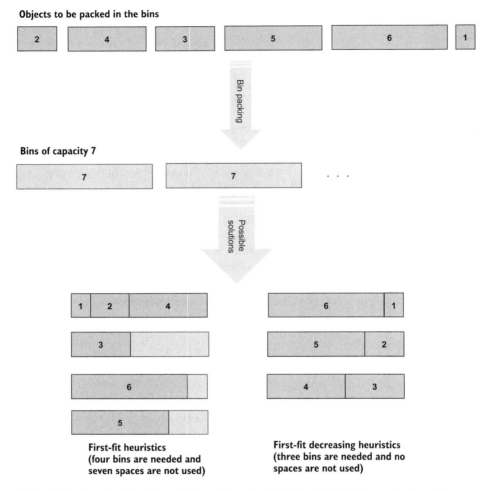

Figure 2.17   Handling the bin packing problem using first-fit and first-fit decreasing heuristics

First-fit heuristics pack the objects following their order without taking into consideration their sizes. This results in the need for four bins that are not fully utilized, as there are seven spaces left in three of these bins. If we apply the first-fit decreasing heuristic, we will order the objects based on their sizes and pack them following this order. This heuristic allows us to pack all the objects in three fully utilized bins, which is the lower bound.

In the previous example, all the objects have the same height. However, in a more generalized version, let's consider objects with different widths and heights, as illustrated in figure 2.18. Applying heuristics such as smallest-first can allow us to load the container much faster. Some heuristics do not guarantee optimality; for example, the largest-first heuristic gives a suboptimal solution, as one object is left out. This can be considered an infeasible solution if we need to load all the objects into the container, or it will be a suboptimal solution if the objective is to load as many objects as possible.

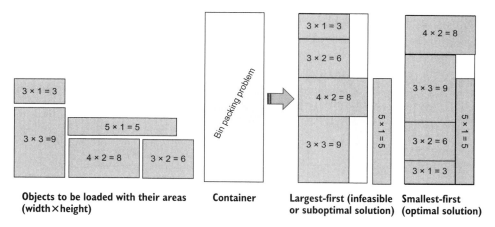

Figure 2.18   Bin packing problem. Using heuristics allows us to solve the problem much faster than with a brute-force approach. However, some heuristic functions may result in infeasible or suboptimal solutions, and they do not guarantee optimality.

To solve this problem in Python, let's first define the objects, the containers, and what it means to place an object inside a container. For the sake of simplicity, the following listing avoids custom classes and uses numpy arrays instead.

Listing 2.7   Bin packing problem

```
import numpy
import matplotlib.pyplot as plt
from matplotlib import cm
from matplotlib.colors import rgb2hex

width = 4
height = 8
container = numpy.full((height,width), 0)

objects = [[3,1],[3,3],[5,1],[4,2],[3,2]]

def fit(container, object, obj_index, rotate=True):
    obj_w = object[0]
    obj_h = object[1]
    for i in range(height - obj_h + 1): C
        for j in range(width - obj_w + 1):
            placement = container[i : i + obj_h, j : j + obj_w]
            if placement.sum() == 0:
                container[i : i + obj_h, j : j + obj_w] = obj_index
                return True
        return fit(container, object[::-1], obj_index, rotate=False)
```

> **Define the dimensions of the container, and initialize the numpy array to 0s.**

> **Represent objects to be placed as [width, height].**

> **The fit function places objects into the container, either through direct placement, shifting, or rotation.**

The fit function attempts to write a value to a 2D slice of the container, provided there are no values in that slice already (the sum is 0). If that fails, it shifts along the container from top to bottom, from left to right, and tries again. As a last resort, it tries the same thing but with the object rotated by 90 degrees.

The first heuristic prioritizes fitting by object area in descending order:

```
def largest_first(container, objects):
    excluded = []
    assigned = []
    objects.sort(key=lambda obj: obj[0] * obj[1], reverse=True)
    for obj in objects:
        if not fit(container, obj, objects.index(obj) + 1):
            excluded.append(objects.index(obj) + 1)
        else:
            assigned.append(objects.index(obj) + 1)
    if excluded: print(f"Items excluded: {len(excluded)}")
    visualize(numpy.flip(container, axis=0), assigned)
```

Sort elements by area in descending order.

Some objects may not fit; we can keep track of them using a list.

Visualize the filled container.

The output of this code is shown in figure 2.19. The code for visualizing this result is included in the full code files for listing 2.7, available in the book's GitHub repo.

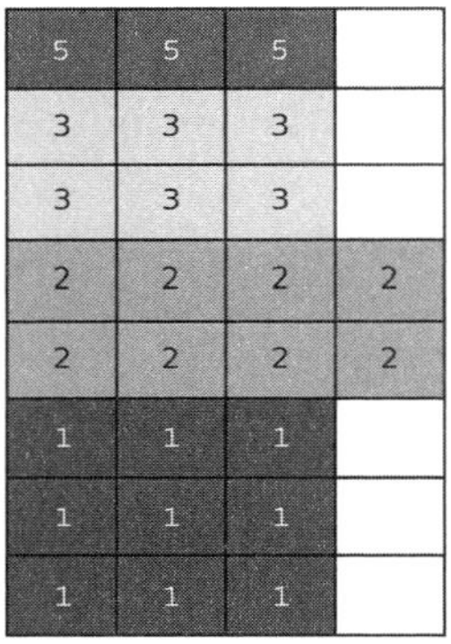

Figure 2.19   Bin packing using the largest-first heuristic—one object has been excluded, as it does not fit in the remaining space.

The second heuristic sorts first by width and then by total area, in ascending order:

```
def smallest_width_first(container, objects):
    excluded = []
    assigned = []
    objects.sort(key=lambda obj: (obj[0], obj[0] * obj[1]))
    for obj in objects:
        if not fit(container, obj, objects.index(obj) + 1):
            excluded.append(objects.index(obj) + 1)
        else:
            assigned.append(objects.index(obj) + 1)
    if excluded: print(f"Items excluded: {len(excluded)}")
    visualize(numpy.flip(container, axis=0), assigned)
```

Sort by width as primary key, and then by area in ascending order.

Visualize the solution.

The `smallest_width_first` heuristic manages to successfully fit all the objects into the container, as shown in figure 2.20.

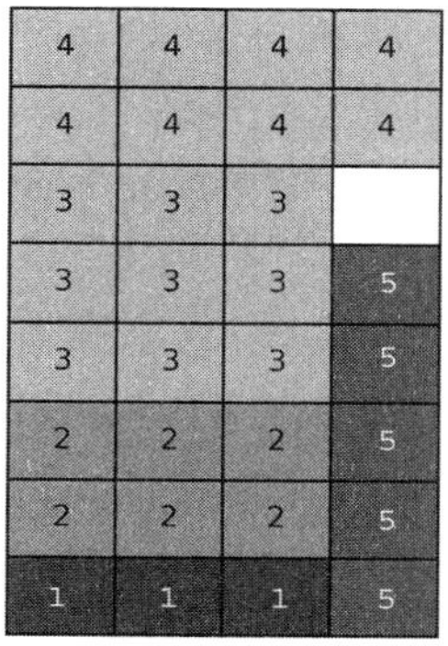

Figure 2.20   **Bin packing problem using the smallest-first heuristic—all five objects have been successfully placed in the container.**

Different heuristic search strategies can be used to generate candidate solutions. These strategies include, but are not limited to, search by repeated solution construction (e.g., graph search and ant colony optimization), search by repeated solution modification (e.g., tabu search, simulated annealing, genetic algorithm, and particle swarm optimization), and search by repeated solution recombination (e.g., genetic algorithm and differential evolution).

Let's reconsider the cargo bike loading problem discussed in section 1.3.3. We can order the items to be delivered based on their efficiency (profit per kg), as shown in table 2.2.

Table 2.2   **Packages ranked by efficiency. The efficiency of a package is defined as the profit per kilogram.**

Item	Weight (kg)	Profit ($)	Efficiency ($/kg)
10	7.8	20.9	2.68
7	4.9	10.3	2.10
4	10	12.12	1.21
1	14.6	14.54	1
8	16.5	13.5	0.82
6	9.6	7.4	0.77
2	20	15.26	0.76
9	8.77	6.6	0.75
3	8.5	5.8	0.68
5	13	8.2	0.63

Using a search strategy based on the *repeated solution construction* heuristic, we can start by applying a greedy principle and pick items based on their efficiency until we reach the maximum payload of the cargo bike (100 kg) as a hard constraint. The steps for this are shown in table 2.3.

Table 2.3   Repeated solution construction—packages are added to the bike until the maximum capacity is reached.

Step	Item	Add?	Total weight (kg)	Total profit ($)
1	10	Yes	7.8	20.9
2	7	Yes	12.7	31.2
3	4	Yes	22.7	43.32
4	1	Yes	37.3	57.86
5	8	Yes	53.8	71.36
6	6	Yes	63.4	78.76
7	2	Yes	83.4	94.02
8	9	Yes	92.17	100.62
9	3	No	(100.67)	-
10	5	No	(113.67)	-

We obtain the following subset of items: 10, 7, 4, 1, 8, 6, 2, and 9. This can also be written as $(1,1,0,1,0,1,1,1,1,1)$, which when read from left to right shows that we include items 1, 2, 4, 6, 7, 8, 9, and 10 (and exclude items 3 and 5). This results in a total profit of \$100.62 and a weight of 92.17 kg. We can generate more solutions by repeating the process of adding objects, starting with an empty container.

Instead of creating one or more solutions completely from scratch, we could also think about ways of modifying an existing feasible solution—this is a *repeated solution modification-based* heuristic search strategy. Consider the previous solution generated for the cargo-bike problem: $(1,1,0,1,0,1,1,1,1,1)$. We know that this feasible solution is not optimal, but how can we improve it? We could do so by removing item 9 from the cargo bike and adding item 5. This process of removing and adding results in a new solution, $(1,1,0,1,1,1,1,1,0,1)$, with a total profit of \$102.22 and a weight of 96.4 kg.

Another approach is to combine existing solutions to generate new solutions to progress in the search space—this is *repeated solution recombination*. Suppose the following two solutions are given:

- $S_1 = (1,1,1,1,1,0,0,1,0,1)$ with a weight of 75.8 kg and a profit of \$75.78
- $S_2 = (0,1,0,1,1,0,1,1,1,1)$ with a weight of 80.97 kg and a profit of \$86.88

As illustrated in figure 2.21, we can take the configuration of the first two items of S_1 and the last eight items of S_2 to get a new solution. This means that we include items 1, 2, 4, 5, 7, 8, 9, and 10 in the new solution and exclude items 3 and 6. This yields a new solution: $S_3 = (1,1,0,1,1,0,1,1,1,1)$ with a weight of 95.57 kg and a higher profit of \$101.42.

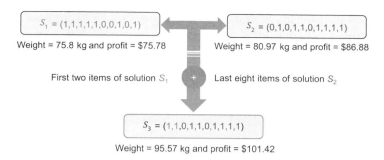

Figure 2.21   Repeated solution recombination—taking the first two elements of S₁ and adding the last eight elements of S₂ yields a new, better solution.

2.4   *Nature-inspired algorithms*

Nature is the ultimate source of inspiration. Problems in nature are usually ill-structured, dynamic, partially observable, nonlinear, multimodal, and multi-objective with hard and soft constraints and with no or limited access to global information. Nature-inspired algorithms are computational models that mimic or reverse engineer the intelligent behaviors observed in nature. Examples include molecular dynamics, cooperative foraging, division of labor, self-replication, immunity, biological evolution, learning, flocking, schooling, and self-organization, just to name just a few.

Molecular dynamics (the science of simulating the motions of a system of particles) and thermal annealing inspired scientists to create an optimization algorithm called *simulated annealing*, which we'll discuss in chapter 5. Evolutionary computing algorithms such as genetic algorithm (GA), genetic programming (GP), evolutionary programming (EP), evolutionary strategies (ES), differential evolution (DE), cultural algorithms (CA), and co-evolution (CoE) are inspired by evolutionary biology (the study of the evolutionary processes) and biological evolution. Part 3 of this book will cover a number of evolutionary computing algorithms.

Ethology (the study of animal behavior) is the main source of inspiration for swarm intelligence algorithms such as particle swarm optimization (PSO), ant colony optimization (ACO), artificial bee colony (ABC), firefly algorithm (FA), bat algorithm (BA), social spider optimization (SSO), butterfly optimization algorithm (BOA), dragonfly algorithm (DA), krill herd (KH), shuffled frog leaping algorithm (SFLA), fish school search (FSS), dolphin partner optimization (DPO), dolphin swarm optimization algorithm (DSOA), cat swarm optimization (CSO), monkey search algorithm (MSA), lion optimization algorithm (LOA), cuckoo search (CS), cuckoo optimization algorithm (COA), wolf search algorithm (WSA), and grey wolf optimizer (GWO). Swarm intelligence-based optimization algorithms are covered in part 4 of this book.

Neural networks (NNs) are computational models inspired by the structure and functioning of biological neural networks. How NNs can be used to solve search and optimization problems is described in part 5 of this book. Tabu search (explained in chapter 6) is based on evolving memory (adaptive memory and responsive exploration), which is studied in behavioral psychology (the science of behavior and mind). Reinforcement learning is a branch of machine learning that draws inspiration from several sources such as psychology, neuroscience, and control theory, and it can be used to solve search and optimization problems, as described in the last chapter of the book.

Other nature-inspired search and optimization algorithms include, but are not limited to, bacterial foraging optimization algorithm (BFO), bacterial swarming algorithm (BSA), biogeography-based optimization (BBO), invasive weed optimization (IWO), flower pollination algorithm (FPA), forest optimization algorithm (FOA), water flow-like algorithm (WFA), water cycle algorithm (WCA), brainstorm optimization algorithm (BSO), stochastic diffusion search (SDS), alliance algorithm (AA), black hole algorithm (BH), black hole mechanics optimization (BHMO), adaptive black hole algorithm (BHA), improved black hole algorithm (IBH), levy flight black hole (LBH), multiple population levy black hole (MLBH), spiral galaxy-based search algorithm (GbSA), galaxy-based search algorithm (GSA), big-bang big-crunch (BBBC), ray optimization (RO), quantum annealing (QA), quantum-inspired genetic algorithm (QGA), quantum-inspired evolutionary algorithm (QEA), quantum swarm evolutionary algorithm (QSE), and quantum-inspired particle swarm optimization (QPSO). For a comprehensive list of metaheuristic algorithms, see S.M. Almufti's "Historical survey on metaheuristics algorithms" [8].

In the five parts of this book, we'll explore five primary categories of search and optimization algorithms: graph search algorithms, trajectory-based optimization, evolutionary computing, swarm intelligence algorithms, and machine learning methods. The following algorithms are covered within these categories:

- Graph search methods (blind or uninformed search and informed search algorithms)
- Simulated annealing (SA)
- Tab search (TS)
- Genetic algorithm (GA)
- Particle swarm optimization (PSO)
- Ant colony optimization (ACO)
- Artificial bee colony (ABC)
- Graph convolutional network (GCN)
- Graph Attention Network (GAT)
- Self-organizing map (SOM)
- Actor-Critic (A2C) architecture
- Proximal policy optimization (PPO)
- Multi-armed bandit (MAB)
- Contextual multi-armed bandit (CMAB)

Throughout this book, we'll look at several real-world problems and see how these algorithms can be applied.

Summary

- Search and optimization problems can be classified based on the number of decision variables (univariate and multivariate problems), the types of decision variables (continuous, discrete, or mixed-integer), the number of objective functions (mono-objective, multi-objective, or constraint-satisfaction problems), the landscape of the objective function (unimodal, multimodal, or deceptive), the number of constraints (unconstrained and constrained problems), and the linearity of the objective functions and constraints (linear problems and nonlinear problems).

- Based on the expected quality of the solutions and the search time permitted to find the solutions, optimization problems can also be categorized as design problems (strategic functions), planning problems (tactical functions), or control problems (operational functions).

- Search and optimization algorithms can be classified based on the way the search space is explored (local versus global search), on their optimization speeds (online versus offline optimization), and the determinism of the algorithm (deterministic versus stochastic).

- Heuristics (also known as *mental shortcuts* or *rules of thumb*) facilitate finding acceptable (optimal or near-optimal) solutions to complex problems in a reasonably practical time.

- Metaheuristics are high-level strategies used to guide and modify other heuristics to enhance their performance.

- Nature-inspired algorithms are computational models that mimic or reverse engineer the intelligent behaviors observed in nature to solve complex ill-structured problems.

Blind search algorithms

You were introduced to deterministic and stochastic algorithms in chapter 2. In this chapter, we will focus on deterministic algorithms, specifically blind search algorithms, and their applications in exploring tree or graph structures and finding the shortest path between nodes. Using these algorithms, you can explore a maze from an initial state to a goal state, solve n-puzzle problems, figure out the distance between you and any other person on a social media graph, search a family tree to determine the exact relationship between any two related people, or find the shortest path between any origin (e.g., your home) and any destination. Blind search algorithms are important, as they are often more efficient and practical to use when dealing with simple, well-defined problems.

3.1   Introduction to graphs

A *graph* is a nonlinear data structure composed of entities known as *vertices* (or nodes) and the relationships between them, known as *edges* (or *arcs* or *links*). This data structure does not follow a sequential pattern, making it *nonlinear*, unlike arrays, stacks, or queues, which are linear structures.

A graph can be represented mathematically by G, where $G = (V, E)$. V represents the set of nodes or vertices, and E represents the set of edges or links. Various attributes can also be added as components to the edge tuple, such as edge length, capacity, or any other unique properties (e.g., road material). Graphs can be classified as undirected, directed, multigraph, acyclic, and hypergraphs.

An *undirected graph* is one where a set of nodes are connected using bidirectional edges. This means that the order of two connected nodes is not essential.

NetworkX is a commonly used Python library for creating, manipulating, and studying the structure, dynamics, and functions of graphs and complex networks (see appendix A for more information about graph libraries). The following listing shows how you can use NetworkX to create an undirected graph.

Listing 3.1   Creating an undirected graph using NetworkX

```
import networkx as nx
import matplotlib.pyplot as plt

graph = nx.Graph()

nodes = list(range(5))          ◀──── Generate a list of nodes from 0 to 4.
graph.add_nodes_from(nodes)

edges = [(0,1),(1,2), (1,3), (2,3),(3,4)]   ◀──── Define a list of edges.
graph.add_edges_from(edges)

nx.draw_networkx(graph, font_color="white")
```

The output of this code is shown in figure 3.1. The actual layout you get might be different, but the connections among the vertices will be the same as shown here.

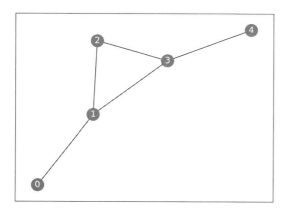

Figure 3.1   An undirected graph

A *directed graph* is a graph in which a set of nodes are connected using directional edges. Directed graphs have many applications, such as representing flow constraints (e.g., one-way streets), relations (e.g., causal relationships), and dependencies (e.g., tasks that depend on the completion of other tasks). The following listing shows how to use NetworkX to create a directed graph.

> **Listing 3.2   Creating a directed graph using NetworkX**

```
import networkx as nx
import matplotlib.pyplot as plt
                              ┌─ DiGraph allows for
graph = nx.DiGraph() ◄────────┘  directed edges.
nodes = list(range(5))
edges = [(0,1),(1,2), (1,3), (2,3),(3,4)]
graph.add_edges_from(edges)
graph.add_nodes_from(nodes)
nx.draw_networkx(graph, font_color="white")
```

The code output is shown in figure 3.2. Note the arrows indicating the edge directions.

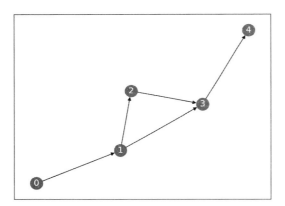

Figure 3.2   A directed graph

A *multigraph* is a graph in which multiple edges may connect the same pair of vertices. These edges are called *parallel edges*. Multigraphs can be used to represent complex relationships between nodes, such as multiple parallel roads between two locations in traffic routing, multiple capacities and demands in resource allocation problems, and multiple relationships between individuals in social networks, to name just a few. Unfortunately, NetworkX is not particularly good at visualizing multigraphs with parallel edges. This listing shows how you can use NetworkX in conjunction with the Matplotlib library to create a multigraph.

Listing 3.3 Creating a multigraph using NetworkX

```
import networkx as nx
import matplotlib.pyplot as plt

graph = nx.MultiGraph()
nodes = list(range(5))
edges = [(0,1),(0,1),(4,3),(1,2), (1,3), (2,3),(3,4),(0,1)]
graph.add_nodes_from(nodes)
graph.add_edges_from(edges)

pos = nx.kamada_kawai_layout(graph)    ◄── Node positions are generated using
ax = plt.gca()                              the Kamada-Kawai path-length cost
                                            function.

for e in graph.edges:
    ax.annotate("",xy=pos[e[0]], xycoords='data', xytext=pos[e[1]],
    ➥textcoords='data', arrowprops=dict(arrowstyle="-",
    ➥connectionstyle=f"arc3, rad={0.3*e[2]}"),zorder=1)

nx.draw_networkx_nodes(graph, pos)      #C
nx.draw_networkx_labels(graph,pos, font_color='w')       #C

plt.show()
```

Draw each edge one at a time, modifying the curvature of the edge based on its index (i.e., the second edge between nodes 0 and 1).

Draw nodes and node labels.

It is worth noting that kamada_kawai_layout attempts to position nodes on the space so that the geometric (Euclidean) distance between them is as close as possible to the graph-theoretic (path) distance between them. Figure 3.3 shows an example of a multigraph generated by this code.

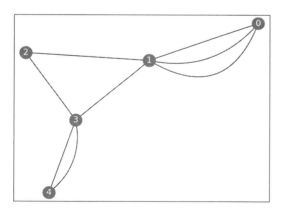

Figure 3.3 Example of a multigraph. Notice the three parallel edges connecting nodes 0 and 1, as well as the two edges connecting nodes 3 and 4.

As the name implies, an *acyclic graph* is a graph without cycles. A *tree*, as a specialized case of a graph, is a connected graph with no cycles or self-loops. In graph theory, a connected graph is a type of graph in which there is a path between every pair of vertices. A *cycle*, also called a *self-loop* or a *circuit*, is an edge in a graph that connects a vertex (or node) to itself. In task scheduling, acyclic graphs can be used to represent the relationships between tasks where each node represents a task and each directed edge represents a precedence constraint. This constraint means that the task represented by the end node cannot start until the task represented by the start node is completed. We'll discuss the assembly line balancing problem in chapter 6 as an example of scheduling problems.

The following listing shows how you can use NetworkX to create and verify an acyclic graph. An example of an acyclic graph is shown in figure 3.4

Listing 3.4   **Creating an acyclic graph using NetworkX**

```
import networkx as nx
import matplotlib.pyplot as plt

graph = nx.DiGraph()
nodes = list(range(5))
edges = [(0,1), (0,2),(4,1),(1,2),(2,3)]
graph.add_nodes_from(nodes)
graph.add_edges_from(edges)

nx.draw_networkx(graph, nx.kamada_kawai_layout(graph), with_labels=True,
➥ font_color='w')
plt.show()
                                                    Check if the graph is
nx.is_directed_acyclic_graph(graph) ◀───           acyclic.
```

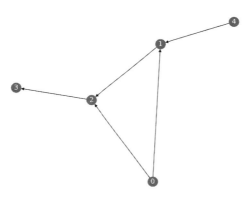

Figure 3.4   An acyclic graph—no path cycles back to any starting node.

A *hypergraph* is a generalization of a graph in which the generalized edges (called *hyperedges*) can join any number of nodes. Hypergraphs are used to represent complex networks because they can capture higher-order many-to-many relationships. They're used in domains such as social media, information systems, computational geometry, computational pathology, and neuroscience. For example, a group of people working on a project can be represented by a hypergraph. Each person is represented by a node, and the project is represented by a hyperedge. The hyperedge connects all the people working on the project, regardless of how many people are involved. The hyperedge can also contain other attributes, such as the project's name, the start and end dates, the budget, etc.

The following listing shows how you can use HyperNetX (HNX) to create a hypergraph. HNX is a Python library that enables us to model the entities and relationships found in complex networks as hypergraphs. Figure 3.5 shows an example of a hypergraph.

Listing 3.5 Creating a hypergraph using HyperNetX

```
import hypernetx as hnx

data = {
    0: ("A","B","G"),
    1: ("A","C","D","E","F"),
    2: ("B","F"),
    3: ("A","B","D","E","F","G")
}
H = hnx.Hypergraph(data)
hnx.draw(H)
```

The data for the hypergraph comes as key-value pairs of hyperedge name/hyperedge node groups.

Create a hypergraph for the provided data.

Visualize the hypergraph.

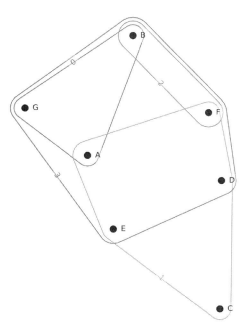

Figure 3.5 An example of a hypergraph. Hyperedges can connect more than two nodes, such as hyperedge 0, which links nodes A, B, and G.

Graphs can also be weighted or unweighted. In a *weighted graph*, a weight, or value, is assigned to each edge. For example, in the case of road networks, the edges could have weights that represent the cost of traversing the road. This weight could represent distance, time, or any other metric. In telecommunications networks, the weight might represent the cost of utilizing that edge or the strength of the connections between the communication devices.

Listing 3.6 shows how you could create and visualize a weighted graph between telecommunication devices. The weights in this example represent the speed of connections between the devices in Mbps. Running this code generated the weighted graph in figure 3.6.

Listing 3.6 Creating a weighted graph using NetworkX

```python
import networkx as nx
import matplotlib.pyplot as plt

G = nx.Graph()   ◀──────────────┤ Create an empty weighted graph.

G.add_node("Device1", pos=(0,0))
G.add_node("Device2", pos=(0,2))       Add nodes to the graph
G.add_node("Device3", pos=(2,0))       (representing devices).
G.add_node("Device4", pos=(2,2))

G.add_weighted_edges_from([("Device1", "Device2", 45.69),     Add weighted edges to
                           ("Device1", "Device3", 56.34),     the graph (representing
                           ("Device2", "Device4", 18.5)])  ◀─ connections).

pos = nx.get_node_attributes(G, 'pos')  ◀─          Get node position attributes
nx.draw_networkx(G, pos, with_labels=True)          from the graph.
nx.draw_networkx_edge_labels(G, pos,
➥edge_labels={(u, v): d['weight'] for       Draw the graph.
➥u, v, d in G.edges(data=True)})
plt.show()
```

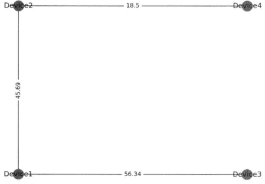

Figure 3.6   Example of a weighted graph

Graphs are everywhere. Search engines like Google see the internet as a giant graph where each web page is a node, and two pages are joined by an edge if there is a link from one page to the other. A social media platform like Facebook treats each user profile as a node on a social graph, and two nodes are said to be connected if they are each other's friends or have social ties. The concept of "following" a user, such as on a platform like X (previously Twitter), can be represented by a directional edge, where user *A* can follow user *B*, but the reverse is not necessarily true. Table 3.1 shows the meanings of nodes and edges on different social media platforms.

Table 3.1 Examples of graphs in the context of social media

Social media platform	Nodes	Edges	Type of edge
Facebook	Users, groups, posts, and events	Friendship, group membership, messages, creation of posts, and reactions on posts	Undirected: a like, or react, or comment Directed: a friend request
X (previously Twitter)	Users, groups, unregistered persons, and posts	Following, group membership, messages, creation of posts, and reactions on posts	Undirected: a mention or a retweet Directed: the following relationship (when you follow a person, they do not automatically follow you back)
LinkedIn	Users, groups, unregistered persons, posts, skills, and jobs	Connections, group membership, posting, reactions on posts, messages, endorsements, invitations, recommending jobs	Undirected: an endorsement or recommendation Directed: a connection
Instagram	Users, comments, containers for publishing posts, hashtags, media (e.g., photo, video, story, or album), and pages (Facebook page)	Relationships between users such as following, liking, and commenting	Undirected: a like or a comment Directed: a follow relationship
TikTok	Users, videos, hashtags, locations, and keywords	Relationships between users such as following, liking, and commenting	Undirected: a like or comment Directed: a follow relationship

In a road network graph, the nodes represent landmarks such as intersections and points of interest (POI), and the edges represent the roads. In such a graph, most of the edges are directed, meaning that they have specific directions, and they may have additional information such as length, speed limit, capacity, etc. Each edge is a two-endpoint connection between two nodes, where the direction of the edge represents the direction of traffic flow. A *route* is a sequence of edges connecting the origin node to the destination node.

OSMnx is a Python library developed to simplify the retrieving and manipulating of data from OpenStreetMap (OSM; openstreetmap.org). OSM is a crowdsourced geographic database of the world (see appendix B for more information about how to fetch data from open geospatial data sources). OSMnx lets you download filtered data from OSM and returns the network as a NetworkX graph data structure. It can also convert a text descriptor of a place into a NetworkX graph (see appendix A for more information about graph and mapping libraries). The following listing uses the University of Toronto as an example.

Listing 3.7   University of Toronto example

```
import osmnx as ox
import matplotlib.pyplot as plt

place_name = "University of Toronto"

graph = ox.graph_from_address(place_name)
ox.plot_graph(graph,figsize=(10,10))
```

A graph_from_address can also take city names and mailing addresses as input.

Figure 3.7 shows an OSM map of the area around the St. George campus of the University of Toronto. The graph shows the edges and nodes of the road network surrounding the campus in downtown Toronto.

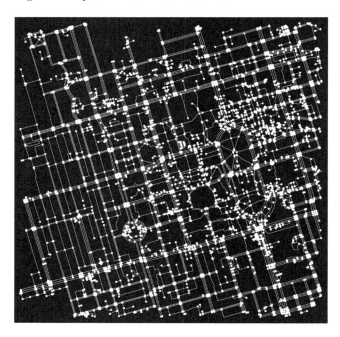

Figure 3.7   St. George campus, University of Toronto

While the map may look visually interesting, it lacks the context of surrounding geographic features. Let's use the folium library (see appendix A) to create a base layer map with street names, neighborhood names, and even building footprints.

```
graph = ox.graph_from_address(place_name)
ox.folium.plot_graph_folium(graph)
```

Figure 3.8 shows the road network surrounding the St. George campus.

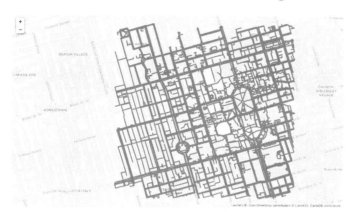

Figure 3.8   Road network around St. George campus, University of Toronto

Suppose you want to get from one location to another on this campus. For example, imagine you're starting at the King Edward VII equestrian statue near Queen's Park in Toronto, and you need to cross the campus to attend a lecture at the Bahen Centre for Information Technology. Later in this chapter, you will see how you can calculate the shortest path between these two points.

For now, let's just plot these two locations on the map using the folium library. Figure 3.9 shows the folium map and markers.

Listing 3.8   Plotting with folium

```
import folium

center=(43.662643, -79.395689)
source_point = (43.664527, -79.392442)
destination_point = (43.659659, -79.397669)

m = folium.Map(location=center, zoom_start=15)
folium.Marker(location=source_point,icon=folium.
➥Icon(color='red',icon='camera', prefix='fa')).add_to(m) #E
folium.Marker(location=center,icon=folium.Icon(color='blue',
➥icon='graduation-cap', prefix='fa')).add_to(m) #E
folium.Marker(location=destination_point,icon=folium.Icon(color='green',
➥icon='university', prefix='fa')).add_to(m) #E
```

The GPS coordinates (latitude and longitude) of the University of Toronto

The GPS coordinates of the equestrian statue as a source point

The GPS coordinates of the Bahen Centre for Information Technology as the destination

Create a map centered around a specified point.

Add markers with icons.

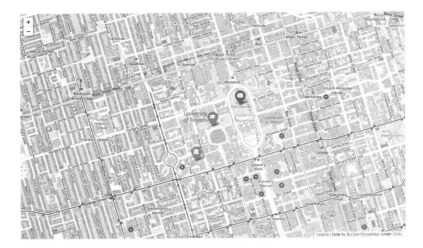

Figure 3.9   Visualizing points of interest using folium markers

The output of the code is interactive and allows for features such as zooming, panning, and even layer filtering (when enabled). Appendix A provides more details about map visualization libraries in Python.

3.2   *Graph search*

As I mentioned in chapter 2, search algorithms can be broadly classified into deterministic and stochastic algorithms. In *deterministic search*, the search algorithm follows a rigorous procedure, and its path and the values of both the design variables and the functions are repeatable. The algorithm will follow the same path for the same starting point whenever you run the program, whether it's today or ten years in the future. In *stochastic search*, on the other hand, the algorithm always has some randomness, and the solution is not exactly repeatable. Each time you run the algorithm, you may get slightly different results.

Based on the availability of information about the search space or domain knowledge (e.g., the distance from the current state to the goal), deterministic search algorithms can be broadly classified into *blind* (or *uninformed*) search and *informed* search, as illustrated in figure 3.10. Some of these algorithms, such as Kruskal's minimum spanning tree (MST) algorithm, will be covered in the next chapter. This chapter focuses on blind search algorithms. Blind search is a search approach where no information about the search space is needed.

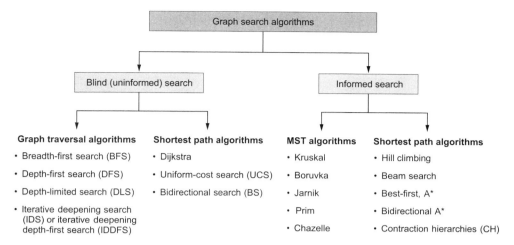

Figure 3.10   Graph search methods

A blind search may conclude upon discovering the first solution, depending on the algorithm's termination criteria. However, the search space may contain numerous valid but non-optimal solutions, so a blind search may return a solution that meets all the requirements but does so in a non-optimal way. An optimal solution can be found by running a blind search following an exhaustive search or brute-force strategy to find all the feasible solutions, which can then be compared to select the best one. This is similar to applying the British Museum algorithm, which finds a solution by checking all possibilities one by one. Given the fact that blind search treats every node in the graph or tree equally, this search approach is often referred to as a *uniform search.*

Examples of blind search algorithms include, but are not limited to, the following:

- *Breadth-first search* (BFS) is a graph traversal algorithm that builds the search tree by levels.

- *Depth-first search* (DFS) is a graph traversal algorithm that first explores nodes going through one adjacent to the root, then the next adjacent, until it finds a solution or it reaches a dead end.

- *Depth-limited search* (DLS) is a DFS with a predetermined depth limit.

- *Iterative deepening search* (IDS), or *iterative deepening depth-first search* (IDDFS), combines DFS's space efficiency and BFS's fast search by incrementing the depth limit until the goal is reached.

- *Dijkstra's algorithm* solves the single-source shortest-path problem for a weighted graph with non-negative edge costs.

- *Uniform-cost* search (UCS) is a variant of Dijkstra's algorithm that uses the lowest cumulative cost to find a path from the source to the destination. It is equivalent to the BFS algorithm if the path cost of all edges is the same.
- *Bidirectional* search (BS) is a combination of forward and backward search. It searches forward from the start and backward from the goal simultaneously.

The following sections discuss graph traversal algorithms and shortest path algorithms, focusing on BFS, DFS, Dijkstra's algorithm, UCS, and BS as examples of blind search approaches.

3.3   Graph traversal algorithms

Graph traversal is the process of exploring the structure of a tree or a graph by visiting the nodes following a specific, well-defined rule. This category of graph search algorithms only seeks to find a path between two nodes without optimizing for the length of the final route.

3.3.1   Breadth-first search

Breadth-first search (BFS) is an algorithm where the traversal starts at a specified node (the source or starting node) and follows the graph layerwise, thus exploring all of the current node's neighboring nodes (those directly connected to the current node). Then, if a result has not been found, the algorithm searches the next-level neighbor nodes. This algorithm finds a solution if one exists, assuming that a finite number of successors, or branches, always follow any node. Algorithm 3.1 shows the BFS steps.

Algorithm 3.1   Breadth-first search (BFS)

```
Inputs: Source node, Destination node
Output: Route from source to destination

Initialize queue ← a FIFO initialized with source node
Initialize explored ← empty
Initialize found ← False

While queue is not empty and found is False do
    Set node ← queue.dequeue()
    Add node to explored
    For child in node.expand() do
        If child is not in explored and child is not in queue then
            If child is destination then
                Update route ← child route()
                Update found ← True
            Add child to queue
Return route
```

BFS uses the queue as a data structure to maintain the states to be explored. A queue is a first in, first out (FIFO) data structure, where the node that has been sitting on the queue for the longest time is the next node to be expanded. BFS dequeues a state off the queue and then enqueues its successors back on the queue.

Let's consider the 8-puzzle problem (sometimes called the *sliding-block problem* or *tile-puzzle problem*). The puzzle consists of an area divided into a 3 × 3 grid. The tiles are numbered 1 through 8, except for an empty (or blank) tile. The blank tile can be moved by swapping its position with any tile directly adjacent (up, down, left, right). The puzzle's goal is to place the tiles so that they are arranged in order. Variations of the puzzle allow the empty tile to end up either at the first or last position. This problem is an example of a well-structured problem (WSP) with the following well-defined components:

- States—Location of the blank and location of the eight tiles
- Operator (successor)—Blank moves left, right, up, and down
- Goal—Match the state given by the goal state
- Solution/path—Sequence through state space
- Stopping criteria—An ordered puzzle (reaching the Goal state)
- Evaluation criteria—Number of steps or path cost (the path length)

Figure 3.11 illustrates the BFS steps for solving the 8-puzzle problem and the search tree traversal order. In this figure, the state represents the physical configuration of the 8-puzzle problem, and each node in the search tree is a data structure that includes information about its parent, children, depth, and the cost of the path from the initial state to this node. Level 1 nodes are generated from left to right by moving the blank title left, up, and right respectively. Moving forward, level 2 nodes are generated by expanding the previously generated nodes in level 1, avoiding the previously explored nodes. We keep repeating this procedure to traverse all the possible nodes or until we hit the goal (the shaded grid). The number of steps to reach the goal will depend mainly on the initial state of the 8-puzzle board. The highlighted numbers show the order of traverse. As you can see, BFS progresses horizontally before it proceeds vertically.

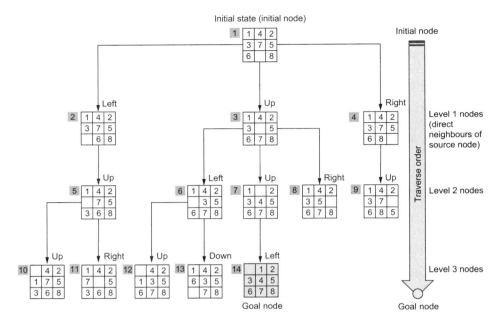

Figure 3.11   Using BFS to solve the 8-puzzle problem

Listing 3.9 utilizes a generic BFS algorithm developed for this book, which can be found in the Optimization Algorithm Tools (optalgotools) Python package (see appendix A for installation instructions). The algorithm takes starting and goal states as inputs and returns a `solution` object. This `solution` object contains the actual result and some performance metrics, such as processing time, maximum space used, and the number of solution states explored. The `State` class and `visualize` function are defined in the complete listing available in the book's GitHub repo. The `State` class helps manage some data structures and utility functions, and it will allow us to reuse this problem's structure later with different algorithms.

Listing 3.9   Solving the 8-puzzle problem using BFS

```
#!pip install optalgotools
from optalgotools.algorithms.graph_search import BFS    ◄───┐ The BFS algorithm is
                                                              imported from a library
init_state = [[1,4,2], [3,7,5], [6,0,8]]                      called optalgotools.

goal_state = [[0,1,2], [3,4,5], [6,7,8]]

                                                    ┌─ See the State class in the
init_state = State(init_state)   ◄──────────────────┘  complete listing.
goal_state = State(goal_state)


if not init_state.is_solvable():   ◄────────────────┐ Some boards are not solvable.
    print("This puzzle is not solvable.")
```

```
else:

    solution = BFS(init_state, goal_state)
    print(f"Process time: {solution.time} s")
    print(f"Space required: {solution.space} bytes")
    print(f"Explored states: {solution.explored}")
    visualize(solution.result)  ◄─────────────────
```

See the visualize function in the complete listing.

This is an example solution, given the preceding inputs:

```
Process time: 0.015625 s
Space required: 624 bytes
Explored states: 7
```

Figure 3.12 shows the state changes following the BFS algorithm.

Initial state		
1	4	2
3	7	5
6		8

State 1		
1	4	2
3		5
6	7	8

State 2		
1		2
3	4	5
6	7	8

Goal state		
	1	2
3	4	5
6	7	8

Figure 3.12 **The step-by-step BFS solution using Python. BFS searches for a solution but does not consider optimality.**

To really understand how BFS works, let's look at the steps involved in a simple path-planning problem. This problem finds a collision-free path for a mobile robot or autonomous vehicle from a start position to a given destination amidst a collection of obstacles.

1 Add the source node to the queue (figure 3.13).

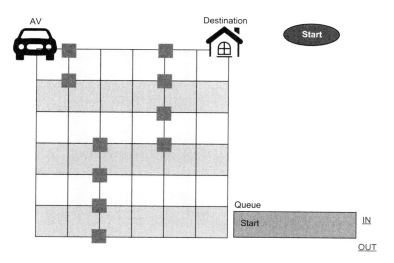

Figure 3.13 **Solving the path-planning problem using BFS—step 1**

2 The robot can only move to the south (S) node, as the east (E) and southeast (SE) nodes are obstructed (figure 3.14).

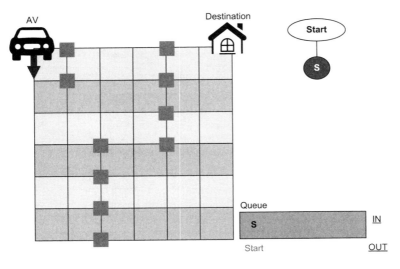

Figure 3.14   Solving the path-planning problem using BFS—step 2

3 Take S out (FIFO), and explore its neighboring nodes, S and SE, with E being an obstructed node (figure 3.15).

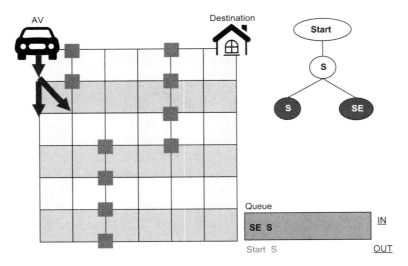

Figure 3.15   Solving the path-planning problem using BFS—step 3

4 Take S out (FIFO), and explore its neighboring nodes, S and SE (figure 3.16).

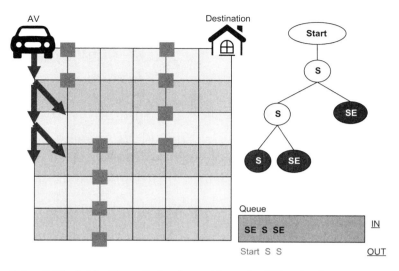

Figure 3.16 Solving the path-planning problem using BFS—step 4

5   Take SE out (FIFO), and explore its neighboring nodes, E and NE (figure 3.17).

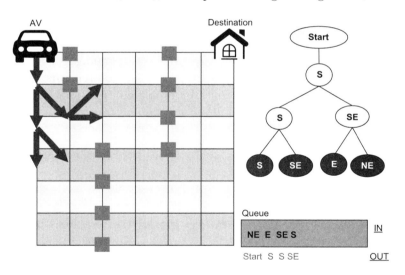

Figure 3.17 Solving the path-planning problem using BFS—step 5

6   The FIFO queue continues until the destination node is found (figure 3.18). For simplicity, assuming that the robot wants to reach node E shown in figure 3.18, we can trace back up the tree to find the path from the source node to the goal, which will be Start-S-SE-E.

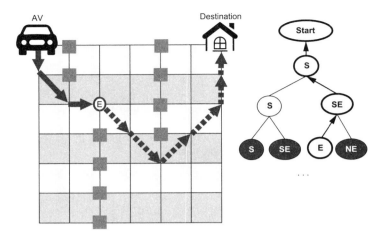

Figure 3.18   Solving the path-planning problem using BFS—final routes for an intermediate goal node E and the final destination

In BFS, every node generated must remain in memory. The number of nodes generated is at most $O(b^d)$, where b represents the maximum branching factor for each node (i.e., the number of children the node has) and d is the depth one must expand to reach the goal. In the previous example, with E as a goal node (b=2, d=3), the total number of traversed nodes is 2^3=8, including the start node.

Aside from the algorithm's ability to solve the problem at hand, algorithm efficiency is evaluated based on run time (time complexity), memory requirements, and the number of primitive operations required to solve the problem in the worst case. Examples of these primitive operations include, but are not limited to, expression evaluation, variable value assignment, array indexing, and method or function calls.

Big *O* notation

Big *O* notation describes the performance or complexity of an algorithm, usually under the worst-case scenario. Big *O* notation helps us answer the question, "Will the algorithm scale?"

To obtain the big *O* notation for a function f(x), if f(x) is a sum of several terms, the one with the largest growth rate is kept, and all others are omitted. Moreover, if f(x) is a product of several factors, any constants (terms in the product that do not depend on x) are omitted.

As an example, let's look at the ticket pricing problem presented in chapter 1: $f(x) = -20x^2 + 6200x - 350000$. Assume that x is a vector with size n that represents n different ticket prices. This function is the sum of three terms, of which the one with the highest growth rate is the one with the largest exponent as a function of x, namely $-20x^2$. We can now apply the second rule: $-20x^2$ is a product of -20 and x^2, in which the first factor does not depend on x. Dropping this factor results in the simplified form x^2. Thus, we say that $f(x)$ is a big *O* of n^2, where n is the size of the decision variable x. Mathematically we can write $f(x) \in O(n^2)$ (pronounced "order n squared" or "*O* of n squared"), which represents a quadratic complexity (i.e., the growth rate is proportional to the square of the size of the ticket price vector).

Table 3.2 shows examples of algorithm complexities, and figure 3.19 shows examples of big O notations.

Table 3.2 Algorithm complexity

Notation	Name	Effectiveness	Description	Examples
$O(1)$	Constant	Excellent	Running time does not depend on the input size. As the input size grows, the number of operations is not affected.	Variable declaration Accessing an array element Retrieving information from a hash-table lookup Inserting and removing from a queue Pushing and popping on a stack
$O(\log n)$	Logarithmic	High	As the input size grows, the number of operations grows very slowly. Whenever n doubles or triples, etc., the running time increases by a constant.	Binary search
$O(n^c)$, $0 < c < 1$	Fractional power or sublinear	High	As the input size grows, the number of operations is replicated in multiplication.	Testing graph connectedness Approximating the number of connected components in a graph Approximating the weight of the minimum spanning tree (MST)
$O(n)$	Linear	Medium	As the input size grows, the number of operations increases linearly. Whenever n doubles, the running time doubles.	Printing out an array's elements Simple search Kadane's algorithm
$O(n \log n) = O(\log n!)$	Linearithmic, loglinear, or quasilinear	Medium	As the input size grows, the number of operations increases slightly faster than linear.	Merge sort Heapsort Timsort
$O(n^c)$, $c > 1$	Polynomial or algebraic	Low	As the input size grows, the number of operations increases as the exponent increases.	Minimum spanning tree (MST) Matrix determinant
$O(n^2)$	Quadratic	Low	Whenever n doubles, the running time increases four-fold. The quadratic function is practical for use only on small problems.	Selection sort Bubble sort Insertion sort

Table 3.2   Algorithm complexity (*continued*)

Notation	Name	Effectiveness	Description	Examples
$O(n^3)$	Cubic	Low	Whenever *n* doubles, the running time increases eightfold. The cubic function is practical for use only on small problems.	Matrix multiplication
$O(c^n)$, $c > 1$	Exponential	Very low	As the input size grows, the number of operations increases exponentially. It is slow and usually not appropriate for practical use.	Power set Tower of Hanoi Password cracking Brute force search
$O(n!)$	Factorial	Extremely low	Extremely slow, as all possible permutations of the input data need to be checked. The factorial algorithm is even worse than the exponential function.	Traveling salesman problem Permutations of a string

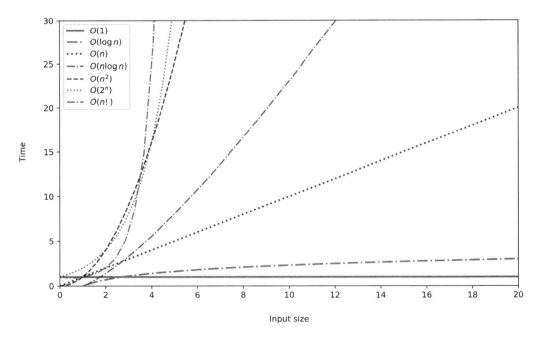

Figure 3.19   Examples of big *O* notations

Assume a computer with a processor speed of one million operations per second is used to handle a problem of size *n* = 20,000. Table 3.3 shows the running time according to the big *O* notation of the algorithm used to solve this problem.

Table 3.3 Algorithm complexity and the running time

Big *O*	Running time
$O(1)$	10^{-6} seconds
$O(\log n)$	14×10^{-6} seconds
$O(n)$	0.02 seconds
$O(n \log n) = O(\log n!)$	0.028 seconds
$O(n^2)$	6.66 minutes
$O(n^3)$	92.6 days
$O(c^n), c = 2$	$1262.137 \times 10^{6015}$ years
$O(n!)$	$5768.665 \times 10^{77331}$ years (this is many orders of magnitude larger than the age of the universe, which is around 13.7 billion years)

For a huge workspace where the goal is deep, the number of nodes could expand exponentially and demand a large memory requirement. In terms of time complexity, for a graph G = (V, E), BFS has a running time of $O(|V| + |E|)$, since each vertex is enqueued at most once and each edge is checked either once (for a directed graph) or at most twice (for an undirected graph). The time and space complexity of BFS is also defined in terms of a branching factor *b* and the depth of the shallowest goal *d*. Time complexity is $O(b^d)$, and space complexity is also $O(b^d)$.

Let's consider a graph with a constant branching factor *b* = 5, nodes of size 1 KB, and a limit of 1,000 nodes scanned per second. The total number of nodes *N* is given by the following equation:

$$N = \frac{b(d + 1) - 1}{b - 1}$$

3.1

Table 3.4 shows the time and memory requirements to traverse this graph using BFS.

Table 3.4 BFS time and space complexity

Depth *d*	Nodes *N*	Time	Memory
2	31	31 ms	31 KB
4	781	0.781 second	0.78 MB
6	19,531	5.43 hours	19.5 MB
8	488,281	56.5 days	488 MB
10	12,207,031	3.87 years	12.2 GB
12	305,175,781	96.77 years	305 GB
14	7,629,394,531	2,419.26 years	7.63 TB

Next, we'll take a look at the counterpart to the BFS algorithm, which searches deep into a graph first, rather than breadth-wise.

3.3.2   *Depth-first search*

Depth-first search (DFS) is a recursive algorithm that uses the idea of backtracking. It involves exhaustive searches of all the nodes by first going as deep as possible into the graph. Then, when it reaches the last layer with no result (i.e., when a dead end is reached), it backtracks up a layer and continues the search. In DFS, the deepest nodes are expanded first, and nodes of equal depth are ordered arbitrarily. Algorithm 3.2 shows the DFS steps.

Algorithm 3.2   Depth-first search (DFS)

```
Inputs: Source node, Destination node
Output: Route from source to destination

Initialize Stack ← a LIFO initialized with sourcenode
Initialize Explored ← empty
Initialize Found ← False

While stack is not empty and found is False do
    Set node ← stack.pop()
    Add node to explored
    For child in node.expand() do
        If child is not in explored and child is not in stack then
            If child is destination then
                Update route ← child.route()
                Update found ← True
            Add child to stack
Return route
```

As you may have noticed, the only difference between DFS and BFS is in how the data structure works. Rather than working down layer by layer (FIFO), DFS drills down to the bottommost layer and moves its way back to the starting node, using a last in, first out (LIFO) data structure known as a *stack*. The stack contains the list of discovered nodes. The most recently discovered node is pushed onto the top of the LIFO stack. Subsequently, the next node to be expanded is popped from the top of the stack, and all of its successors are then added to the stack.

Figure 3.20 shows the DFS solution for the 8-puzzle problem we looked at before, based on moving the blank tile. As you can see, when the algorithm reaches a dead end or terminal node (such as node 7), it goes back to the last decision point (node 3) and proceeds with another alternative (node 8 and so on). In this example, a depth bound of 5 is placed to constrain the node expansion. This depth bound makes nodes 6, 7, 10, 11, 13, 14, 16, 17, 22, 23, 26, and 27 terminal nodes in the search tree (i.e., they have no successors).

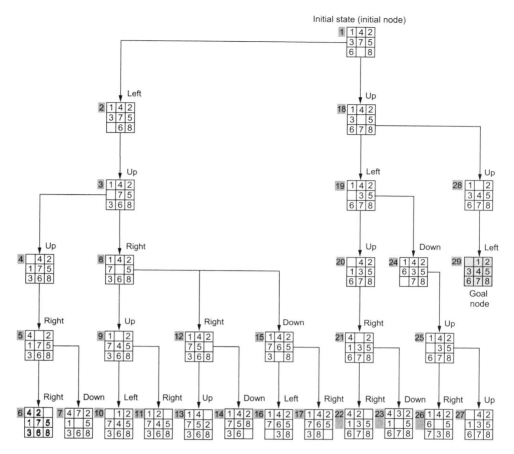

Figure 3.20   Using DFS to solve the 8-puzzle problem

As you can see in listing 3.10, we only need to change the algorithm in the code to use DFS. I've also omitted the solution visualization, the reason for which you'll see shortly. The `State` class is defined in the complete listing available in the book's GitHub repo.

Listing 3.10   Solving the 8-puzzle problem using DFS

```
from optalgotools.algorithms.graph_search import DFS

init_state = [[1,4,2],[3,7,5],[6,0,8]]
goal_state = [[0,1,2],[3,4,5],[6,7,8]]

init_state = State(init_state)
goal_state = State(goal_state)
```

```
if not init_state.is_solvable():          Some puzzles
    print("This puzzle is not solvable.")  are not solvable.
else:                                      The inputs for DFS are
    solution = DFS(init_state, goal_state)  the same as for BFS.
    print(f"Process time: {solution.time} s")
    print(f"Space required: {solution.space} bytes")
    print(f"Explored states: {solution.explored}")
    print(f"Number of steps: {len(solution.result)}")
```

Here's the output of this code run with the preceding inputs:

```
Process time: 0.5247 s
Space required: 624 bytes
Explored states: 29
Number of steps: 30
```

As you can see, DFS is not great when dealing with very deep graphs, where the solution may be located closer to the top. You can also see why I opted not to visualize the final solution: there are a lot more steps in the solution than we had in BFS! Because the solution to this problem is closer to the root node, the solution generated by DFS is a lot more convoluted (30 steps) than with BFS.

Revisiting the path-planning problem, DFS can be used to generate an obstacle-free path from the start location to the destination as follows:

1 Add the source node to the stack (figure 3.21).

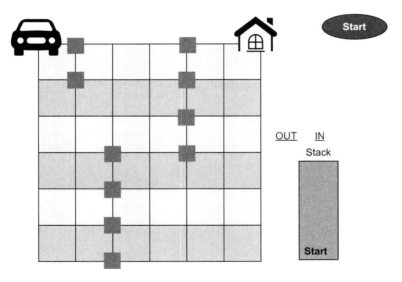

Figure 3.21   Solving the path-planning problem using DFS—step 1

2 Explore the S node, as the E and SE nodes are obstructed (figure 3.22).

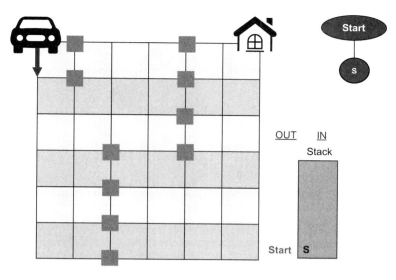

Figure 3.22   Solving the path-planning problem using DFS—step 2

3 Take S out (LIFO), and explore its neighboring nodes, S and SE, as E is an obstructed node (figure 3.23).

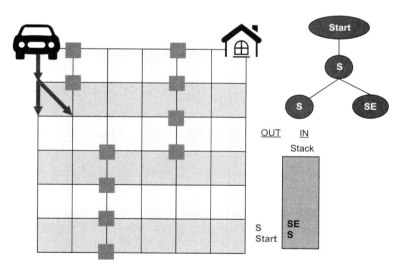

Figure 3.23   Solving the path-planning problem using DFS—step 3

4 Take SE out (LIFO), and explore its neighboring nodes, SW, S, E, and NE (figure 3.24).

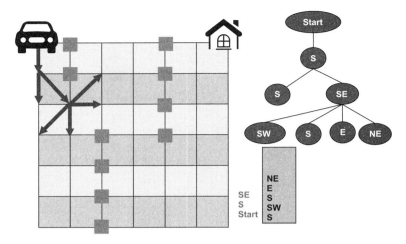

Figure 3.24   Solving the path-planning problem using DFS—step 4

5   The next node to be expanded would be NE, and its successors would be added to the stack. The LIFO stack continues until the goal node is found. Once the goal is found, you can then trace back through the tree to obtain the path for the vehicle to follow (figure 3.25).

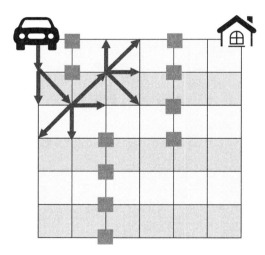

Figure 3.25   Solving the path-planning problem using DFS—step 5

DFS usually requires considerably less memory than BFS. This is mainly because DFS does not always expand every single node at each depth. However, DFS could continue down an unbounded branch forever in the case of a search tree with infinite depth, even if the goal is not located on that branch.

One way to handle this problem is to use *constrained depth-first search*, where the search stops after reaching a certain depth. Time complexity of DFS is $O(b^d)$ where b is the branching factor and d is the maximum depth of the search tree. This is terrible if d is much larger than b, but if solutions are found deep in the tree, it may be much faster than BFS. The space complexity of DFS is $O(bd)$, which is linear space! This space complexity represents the maximum number of nodes to be stored in memory.

Table 3.5 summarizes the differences between BFS and DFS.

Table 3.5 BFS versus DFS

	Breadth-first search (BFS)	Depth-first search (DFS)
Space complexity	More expensive	Less expensive. Requires only $O(d)$ space, irrespective of the number of children per node.
Time complexity	More time efficient. A vertex at a lower level (closer to the root) is visited first before visiting a vertex that is at a higher level (far away from the root).	Less time efficient
When it is preferred	• If the tree is very deep • If the branching factor is not excessive • If the solution appears at a relatively shallow level (i.e., the solution is near the starting point in the tree) • Example: Search the British royal family tree for someone who died a long time ago, as they would be closer to the top of the tree (e.g., King George VI).	• If the graph or tree is very wide with too many adjacent nodes • If no path is excessively deep • If solutions occur deeply in the tree (i.e., the target is far from the source) • Example: Search the British royal family tree for someone who is still alive, as they would be near the bottom of the tree (e.g., Prince William).

In applications where the weights of the edges in a graph are all equal (e.g., all length 1), the BFS and DFS algorithms outperform shortest path algorithms like Dijkstra's in terms of time. Shortest path algorithms will be explained in the next section.

3.4   *Shortest path algorithms*

Suppose that you were looking for the quickest way to go from your home to work. Graph traversal algorithms like BFS and DFS may eventually get you to your destination, but they certainly do not optimize for the distance traveled. We'll discuss Dijkstra's algorithm, uniform-cost search (UCS), and bidirectional Dijkstra's search as examples of blind search algorithms that try to find the shortest path between a source node and a destination node.

3.4.1   *Dijkstra's search*

Dijkstra's algorithm is a graph search algorithm that solves the single-source shortest path problem for a fully connected graph with non-negative edge path costs, producing a shortest-path tree. Dijkstra's algorithm was published in 1959, and it's named after Dutch computer scientist Edsger Dijkstra. This algorithm is the base of several other graph search algorithms that are commonly used to solve routing problems in popular navigation apps, as illustrated in figure 3.26. The algorithm follows dynamic programming approaches where the problem is recursively divided into simple subproblems. Dijkstra's algorithm is uninformed, meaning it does not need to know the target node beforehand and doesn't use heuristic information.

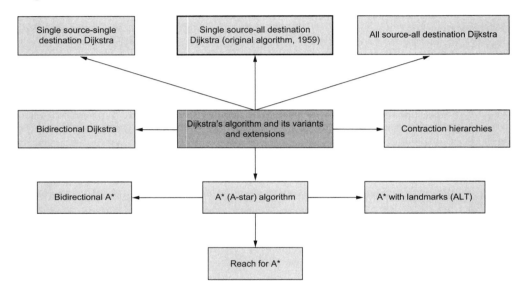

Figure 3.26   Dijkstra's algorithm and examples of its variants and extensions

Algorithm 3.3 shows the steps of the original version of Dijkstra's algorithm for finding the shortest path between a known single source node to all other nodes in the graph or tree.

Algorithm 3.3   Dijkstra's algorithm

```
Inputs: A graph with weighted edges and a source node
Output: Shortest path from the source to all other nodes in the graph

Initialize shortest_dist ← empty
Initialize unrelaxed_nodes ← empty
Initialize seen ← empty
```

```
For node in graph
    Set shortest_dist[node] = Infinity
    Add node to unrelaxed_nodes
    Set shortest_dist[source] ← 0

While unrelaxed_nodes is not empty do
    Set node ← unrelaxed_nodes.pop()
    Add node to seen
    For child in node.expand() do
        If child in seen then skip
        Update distance ← shortest_dist[node] + length of edge to child
        If distance < shortest_dist[child] then
            Update shortest_dist[child] ← distance
            Update child.parent ← node
Return shortest_dist
```

Dijkstra's algorithm and its variants presented in the code for this book are all modified to require a target node. This improves the processing time when working with large graphs (e.g., road networks).

Let's look at how Dijkstra's algorithm finds the shortest path between any two nodes in a graph. The priority queue is used to pop the element of the queue with the highest priority according to some ordering function (in this case, the shortest distance between the node and the source node).

0 Initial list, no predecessors: priority queue = {} (figure 3.27).

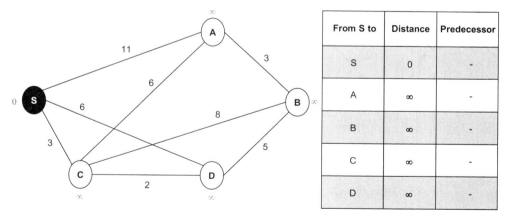

Figure 3.27 **Finding the shortest path using Dijkstra's algorithm—step 0**

1 The closest node to the source node is S, so add it to the priority queue. Update the cumulative distances (i.e., distances from the source node *S* to get to the node) and predecessors for A, C, and D. Priority queue = {S} (figure 3.28).

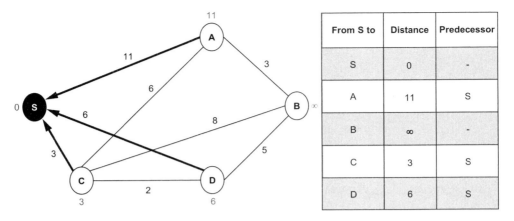

Figure 3.28   Finding the shortest path using Dijkstra's algorithm—step 1

   2 The next closest node is C, so add it to the priority queue. Update the distances and predecessors for A and D. Priority queue = {S, C} (figure 3.29).

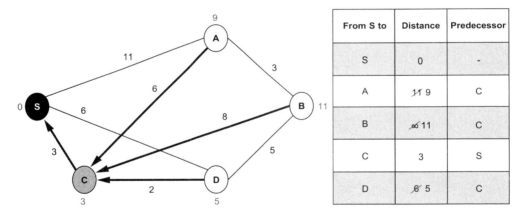

Figure 3.29   Finding the shortest path using Dijkstra's algorithm—step 2

   3 The next closest node is D, so add it to the priority queue. Update the distances and predecessor for B. Priority queue = {S, C, D} (figure 3.30).

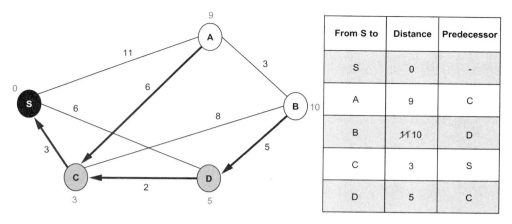

Figure 3.30   Finding the shortest path using Dijkstra's algorithm—step 3

4   The next closest node to the source node is A, so add it to the priority queue. Priority queue = {S, C, D, A} (figure 3.31).

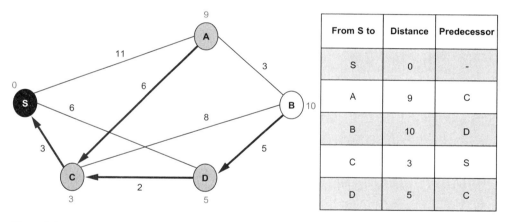

Figure 3.31   Finding the shortest path using Dijkstra's algorithm—step 4

5   The next step is to add the remaining node B to complete the search (figure 3.32). Priority queue = {S, C, D, A, B}. All nodes are now added.

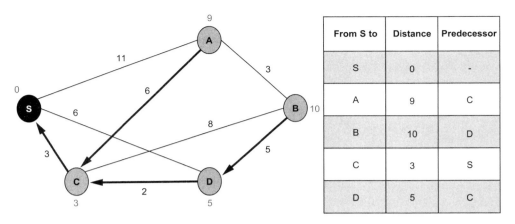

Figure 3.32   Finding the shortest path using Dijkstra's algorithm—step 5

From S to	Distance	Predecessor
S	0	-
A	9	C
B	10	D
C	3	S
D	5	C

Once the search is complete, you can choose your goal node and find the shortest path from the table. For example, if the goal node is A, the shortest path between S and A is S-C-A with length 9. Likewise, if the goal node is B, the shortest path between S and B is S-C-D-B with a distance of 10.

Note that we can't use Dijkstra's search on our 8-puzzle problem as Dijkstra's search requires knowledge of the entire problem space beforehand. While the problem has a finite number of possible states (exactly $9!/2$), the scale of that solution space makes the Dijkstra's search not very feasible.

3.4.2   *Uniform-cost search (UCS)*

The uniform-cost search (UCS) algorithm is a blind search algorithm that uses the lowest cumulative cost to find a path from the origin to the destination. Essentially, the algorithm organizes nodes to be explored either by their cost (with the lowest cost as the highest priority) for minimization problems, or by their utility (with the highest utility as the highest priority) in the case of maximization problems.

As nodes are popped from the queue, we add the node's children to the queue. If a child already exists in the priority queue, the priorities of both copies of the child are compared, and the lowest cost (the highest priority) in a minimization problem is accepted. This ensures that the path to each child is the shortest one available. We also maintain a visited list so we can avoid revisiting nodes that have already been popped from the queue. UCS behaves like BFS when all the edge costs in the graph are equal or identical. In this case, UCS will expand nodes in the same order as BFS—level by level or breadth-first. Algorithm 3.4 shows the steps of the UCS algorithm.

Algorithm 3.4   Uniform-cost search (UCS)

```
Inputs: A graph with edges, a source node, a destination node
Output: Shortest path from source to destination in the graph
```

```
Initialize priority_queue ← source
Initialize found ← False
Initialize seen ← source

While priority_queue is not empty and found is False do
    Set node ← priority_queue.pop()
    Update seen ← node
    Update node_cost ← cumulative distance from source
    If node is destination then
        Update route ← node.route()
        Update found ← True
    For child in node.expand() do
        If child in priority_queue then
            If child.priority < priority_queue[child].priority then
                Set priority_queue[child].priority = child.priority
        Else
            Update priority_queue ← child
        Update priority_queue[child].priority ← node_cost
Return route
```

UCS is a variant of Dijkstra's algorithm that is useful for large graphs because it is less time-consuming and has fewer space requirements. Whereas Dijkstra's adds all nodes to the queue at the start with an infinite cost, UCS fills the priority queue gradually. For example, consider the problem of finding the shortest path between every node pair in a graph. As a graph's size and complexity grows, it quickly becomes apparent that UCS is more efficient, as it does not require knowing the entire graph beforehand. Table 3.6 shows the difference in processing time between Dijkstra's and UCS on graphs of different sizes. These numbers were collected using the code in Comparison. ipynb, available in the book's GitHub repo, on an Intel Core i9-9900K at 3.60 GHz without multiprocessing or multithreading.

Table 3.6   UCS versus Dijkstra's

Graph size = |V| + |E|	Dijkstra time	Uniform-Cost Search (UCS) time
108	0.25 s	0.14 s
628	84.61 s	58.23 s
1,514	2,082.97 s	1,360.98 s

Note that running UCS on our 8-puzzle problem requires a distance property for each state (this defaults to 1), and it generates decent results overall (around 6.2 KB of space used and 789 states explored). It is important to note that because the edge lengths are all equal, UCS cannot prioritize new nodes to explore. Thus, the solution loses the advantage of shortest path algorithms, namely, the ability to optimize for a more compact solution. In the next chapter, you'll see ways of calculating artificial distances between these states, ultimately generating solutions quickly and minimizing the number of steps required.

3.4.3   *Bidirectional Dijkstra's search*

Bidirectional search simultaneously applies forward search and backward search. As illustrated in figure 3.33, it runs a search forward from the initial source state S→G and backward from the final goal state G→S until they meet.

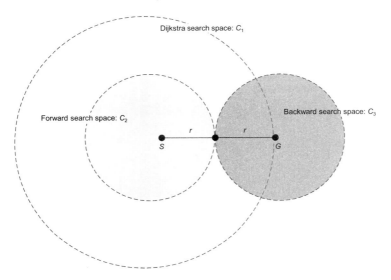

Figure 3.33   Bidirectional Dijkstra

As shown in figure 3.33, the Dijkstra's search space is $C_1 = 4\pi r^2$, and the bidirectional Dijkstra's search space is represented by $C_2 + C_3 = 2\pi r^2$. This means that we reduce the search space by about a factor of two. The following algorithm shows the steps of the bidirectional Dijkstra's algorithm.

Algorithm 3.5   Bidirectional Dijkstra's

```
Inputs: A graph, a source node, a destination node
Output: Shortest path from source to destination in the graph

Initialize frontier_f ← initialized with source
Initialize frontier_b ← initialized with destination
Initialize explored_f ← empty
Initialize explored_b ← empty
Initialize found ← False
Initialize collide ← False
Initialize altr_expand ← False

While frontier_f is not empty and frontier_b is not empty and not collide and
not found do
    If altr_expand then
        Set node ← frontier_f.pop()
        Add node to explored_f
```

```
        For child in node.expand() do
            If child in explored_f then continue
            If child is destination then
                Update route ← child.route()
                Update found ← True
            If child in explored_b then
                Update route ← child.route() + reverse(overlapped.route())
                Update collide ← True
            Add child to frontier_f
        Update altr_expand ← not altr_expand
    Else
        Update node ← frontier_b.pop()
        Add node to explored_b
        For child in node.expand() do
            If child in explored_b then continue
            If child is origin then
                Update route ← child.route()
                Update found ← True
            If child in explored_f then
                Update route ← reverse(child.route()) + overlapped.route()
                Update collide ← True
            Add child to frontier_b
        Update altr_expand ← not altr_expand
Return route
```

This approach is more efficient because of the time complexities involved. For example, a BFS search with a constant branching factor b and depth d would have an overall $O(b^d)$ space complexity. However, by running two BFS searches in opposite directions with only half the depth $(d/2)$, the space complexity becomes $O(b^{d/2} + b^{d/2})$ or simply $O(b^{d/2})$, which is significantly lower.

Figure 3.34 shows the difference between the Dijkstra's and bidirectional Dijkstra's algorithms in exploring 50,841 nodes in the City of Toronto.

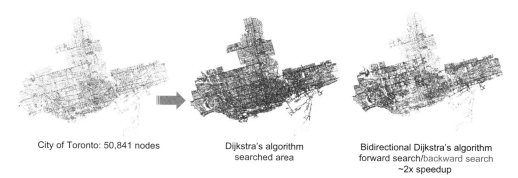

City of Toronto: 50,841 nodes   Dijkstra's algorithm searched area   Bidirectional Dijkstra's algorithm forward search/backward search ~2x speedup

Figure 3.34   Dijkstra's vs. bidirectional Dijkstra's—forward exploration from the left and backward exploration from the right

3.5   *Applying blind search to the routing problem*

Puzzle games and simple grid routing problems are nice for understanding how an algorithm works. However, it's time we look at some real-world examples and outcomes of using these algorithms. For example, imagine that you are visiting the King Edward VII equestrian statue at Queen's Park in Toronto when you suddenly remember you have a meeting at the Bahen Centre for Information Technology at the University of Toronto. I initially presented this problem when we first discussed road network graphs at the beginning of this chapter. There are a couple of assumptions we'll make when considering this problem:

- You aren't able to open a navigation app or call a friend for help, as your phone is out of battery power.
- You know your destination is somewhere in Toronto, but you have no clue where it is with reference to your starting location. (In later chapters, you'll learn how knowing your destination's direction can help generate near-optimal solutions in a very short amount of time.)
- Once you start using a rule for routing to your destination, you'll stick to that rule.

Let's look at how we might be able to simulate our pathfinding skills using BFS, DFS, Dijkstra's, UCS, and bidirectional Dijkstra's. The code for this example is located in the book's GitHub repo (Comparison.ipynb). Figures 3.35 to 3.37 show the routes generated by these blind search algorithms.

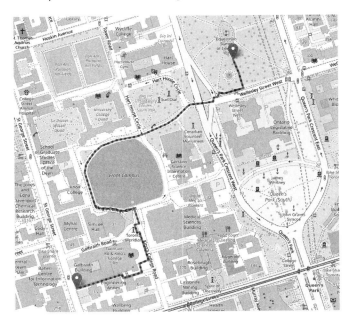

Figure 3.35   Shortest path generated using BFS. BFS searches each layer first before moving to the next. This works best for graphs that are not very broad and that have a solution near the root node.

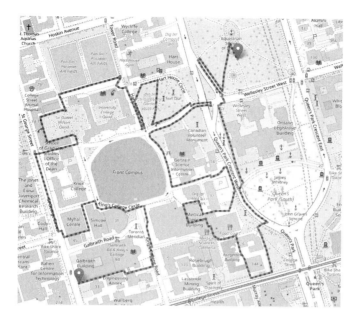

Figure 3.36   Shortest path generated using DFS. DFS searches as deep in the graph as possible before backtracking. This works best when the graph is not very deep and solutions are located further away from the root node.

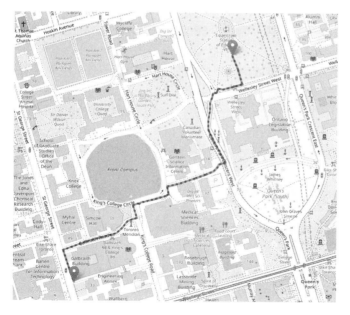

Figure 3.37   Shortest path generated using Dijkstra's, UCS, and bidirectional Dijkstra's. All three of these algorithms will produce the same solution (the optimal routing) but will handle memory use and node exploration differently.

It is worth noting that the `dijkstra_path` function in NetworkX uses Dijkstra's method to compute the shortest weighted path between two nodes in a graph. Our optalgotools package also provides an implementation for different graph search algorithms such as BFS, DFS, Dijkstra's, UCS, and bidirectional Dijkstra's. The implementation of Dijkstra's algorithm in optalgotools has been modified to work with our OSM data because graphs generated from maps will naturally have self-loops and parallel edges. Parallel edges may result in a route that is not the shortest available, as the route length depends heavily on which parallel edge was chosen when a particular path was generated. In figure 3.38, the shortest path from 0 to 2 may be returned as having a length of 7 if the top edge connecting 0 and 1 is chosen when calculating that path, versus a length of 3 when selecting the bottom edge.

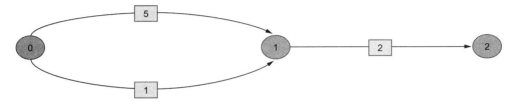

Figure 3.38   Parallel edges may be problematic because finding the shortest path depends on which parallel edge is selected during graph exploration.

Self-loops also cause trouble for the original Dijkstra's algorithm. If a graph contains a self-loop, the shortest path to a node might come from itself. At that point, we would be unable to generate a route (figure 3.39).

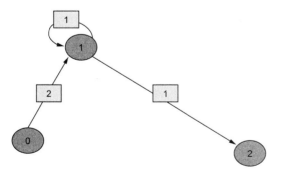

Figure 3.39   Self-loops may disrupt the chain of parent-child nodes, which prevents us from retracing the route after a solution has been found.

These two problems are generally easy but nontrivial to avoid. For parallel edges, we select the edge with the lowest weight (shortest length) and discard any other parallel edge. With self-loops, we can ignore the loop entirely, as negative-weight loops do not exist in most routing problems (a road cannot have a negative length), and positive-weight loops cannot be part of the shortest path. Additionally, the version of Dijkstra's algorithm used in this book terminates upon finding the target node, as opposed to the traditional implementation, which ends only when the shortest path from the root node to all other nodes is found.

Table 3.7 compares BFS, DFS, Dijkstra's, and UCS with regards to path length, process time, space required, and the number of explored nodes. As you can see from these results, Dijkstra's, UCS, and the bidirectional Dijkstra's algorithms produce optimal results, with varying degrees of time and space cost. While both BFS and DFS find feasible solutions in the shortest time, the solutions delivered are not optimal and, in the case of DFS, are not even plausible. On the other hand, DFS requires knowing the entire graph beforehand, which is costly and sometimes not very practical. Much of selecting an appropriate search algorithm for a specific problem involves determining the ideal balance between processing time and space requirements. In later chapters, we'll look at algorithms that produce near-optimal solutions and that are often used when optimal solutions are either impossible or impractical to find. Note that all these solutions are feasible; they all produce a valid (if sometimes convoluted) path from point A to point B.

Table 3.7 Comparing BFS, DFS, Dijkstra's, and UCS, where b is the branching factor, m is the maximum depth of the search tree, d is the shallowest graph depth, E is the number of edges, and V is the number of vertices.

Algorithm	Cost (meters)	Process time (s)	Space (bytes)	Explored nodes	Worst-case time	Worst-case space	Optimality
BFS	955.962	0.015625	1,152	278	$O(b^d)$	$O(b^d)$	No
DFS	3347.482	0.015625	1,152	153	$O(b^m)$	$O(bm)$	No
Dijkstra's	806.892	0.0625	3,752	393	$O(|E| + |V| \log |V|)$	$O(|V|)$	Yes
UCS		0.03125	592	393	$O((b + |E|) * d)$	$O(b^d)$	Yes
Bidirectional Dijkstra's		0.046875	3,752	282	$O(b^{d/2})$	$O(b^{d/2})$	Yes

In the next chapter, we will look at how search can be optimized if we utilize domain-specific knowledge instead of searching blindly. We'll dive right into informed search methods and see how we can use these algorithms to solve minimum spanning tree and shortest path problems.

Summary

- Conventional graph search algorithms (blind and informed search algorithms) are deterministic search algorithms that explore a graph either for general discovery or for explicit search.

- A graph is a nonlinear data structure consisting of vertices and edges.

- Blind (uninformed) search is a search approach where no information about the search space is used.

- Breadth-first search (BFS) is a graph traversal algorithm that examines all the nodes in a search tree on one level before considering any of the nodes on the next level.

- Depth-first search (DFS) is a graph traversal algorithm that starts at the root or an initial node or vertex, follows one branch as far as possible, and then backtracks to explore other branches until a solution is found or all paths are exhausted.

- Depth-limited search (DLS) is a constrained version of DFS with a predetermined depth limit, preventing it from exploring paths beyond a certain depth.

- Iterative deepening search (IDS), or iterative deepening depth-first search (IDDFS), combines DFS's space efficiency and BFS's fast search by incrementing the depth limit until the goal is reached.

- Dijkstra's algorithm solves the single-source shortest path problem for a weighted graph with non-negative edge costs.

- Uniform-cost search (UCS) is a variant of Dijkstra's algorithm that uses the lowest cumulative cost to find a path from the source to the destination. It is equivalent to the BFS algorithm if the path costs of all edges are the same.

- Bidirectional search (BS) is a combination of forward and backward search. It searches forward from the start and backward from the goal simultaneously.

- Selecting a search algorithm involves determining the target balance between time complexity, space complexity, and prior knowledge of the search space, among other factors.

Informed search algorithms

In the previous chapter, we covered blind search algorithms, which are algorithms in which no information about the search space is needed. In this chapter, we'll look at how search can be further optimized if we utilize some information about the search space during the search.

As problems and search spaces become larger and more complex, the complexity of the algorithms themselves increases. I'll start by introducing informed search algorithms, and then we'll discuss minimum spanning tree algorithms and shortest path search algorithms. A routing problem will be presented as a real-life application to show how you can use these algorithms.

4.1   *Introducing informed search*

As we discussed in the previous chapter, *blind search algorithms* work with no information about the search space, other than the information needed to distinguish the goal state from the others. Like the colloquial expression, "I'll know it when I see it," blind search follows a set framework of rules (e.g., breadth-first, depth-first, or Dijkstra's algorithm) to systematically navigate the search space. *Informed search algorithms* differ from blind search algorithms in the sense that the algorithm uses knowledge acquired during the search to guide the search itself. This knowledge can take the form of distance to target or incurred costs.

For example, in the 8-puzzle problem, we might use the number of misplaced tiles as a heuristic to determine how far any given state is from the goal state. In this way, we can determine at any given iteration of the algorithm how well it is performing and modify the search method based on current conditions. The definition of "good performance" depends on the heuristic algorithm being used.

Informed search algorithms can be broadly classified into those that solve for minimum spanning tree (MST) problems and those that compute the shortest path between two specific nodes or states, as outlined in figure 4.1.

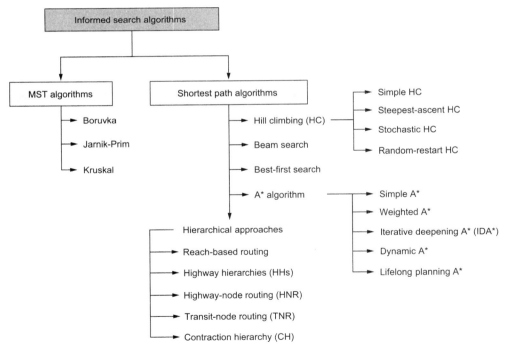

Figure 4.1   Examples of informed search algorithms. Each algorithm has multiple variants based on improvements, specific use cases, and specialized domains.

Several algorithms have been proposed to solve MST problems:

- *Borůvka's algorithm* finds an MST in a graph for which all edge weights are distinct. It also finds a minimum spanning forest, in the case of a graph that is not connected. It starts with each node as its own tree, identifies the cheapest edge leaving each tree, and then merges the trees joined by these edges. No edge presorting is needed or maintained in a priority queue.

- *Jarník-Prim's algorithm* starts from the root vertex and finds the lowest-weight edge from an MST vertex to a non-MST vertex and adds it to MST at each step.

- *Kruskal's algorithm* sorts edges by increasing weight and starts from the least-weighted edge to form a small MST component and then grows them into one large MST. I will describe this algorithm in more detail in the next section.

Hill climbing (HC), beam search, the A* algorithm, and contraction hierarchies (CH) are examples of informed search algorithms that can be used to find the shortest path between two nodes:

- *Hill climbing* is a local search algorithm that continuously moves in the direction of optimizing the objective function, increasing in the case of maximization problems, or decreasing in the case of minimization problems.

- *Beam search* explores a graph or tree by expanding the most promising node within a limited predefined set.

- *The A* algorithm* combines both the cost accrued up to a node and heuristic information, such as the straight-line distance between this node and the destination node, to select new nodes for expansion.

- *Hierarchical approaches*, such as reach-based routing, highway hierarchies (HHs), highway-node routing (HNR), transit-node routing (TNR), and contraction hierarchy (CH), are hierarchical approaches that take into consideration node importance and try to prune the search space by admissible heuristics.

The next section introduces the concept of an MST and presents an algorithm that can generate an MST for any given graph.

4.2 Minimum spanning tree algorithms

Imagine that you are the infrastructure manager for a small, remote rural town. Unlike most towns, there isn't really a main street or downtown area, so most points of interest are scattered. Additionally, budget cuts in previous years have left the roads either damaged or non-existent. The damaged roads are all buried under mud and are essentially impassable. You've been given a small budget to fix or build roads to improve the situation, but the money isn't enough to repair all the existing roads or to build new ones. Figure 4.2 shows a map of the town, as well as the locations of the existing damaged roads.

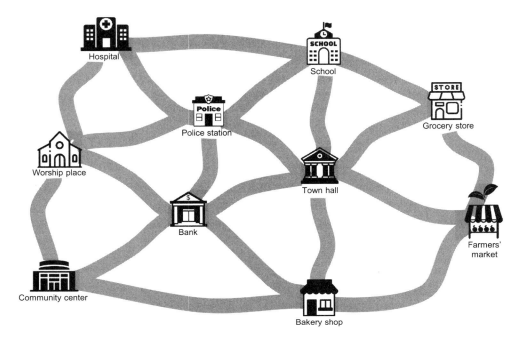

Figure 4.2   The muddy city problem. The roads in this town are badly damaged, but there isn't enough money to repair them all.

There are several ways to approach this problem, ranging from the not feasible (repair all the damaged roads and live with the consequences of a bankrupt town) to the overly conservative (only fix a few roads, or none at all, and ignore all the complaining towns-people). This problem is typically known as the muddy city problem, where various nodes in a graph must be connected while minimizing the edge weights. These weights can present the cost of fixing or paving the road, which may vary depending on the road's condition, length, and topology.

The mathematical way of solving the muddy city problem involves the idea of a minimum spanning tree (MST). A spanning tree, in general, is a cycle-free or loop-free subgraph of an undirected graph that connects all the vertices of the graph with the minimum number of edges. In figure 4.3, the left tree shows a graph *G* with nodes from A to F, while the middle and right trees show spanning trees of *G*. Notice that generic spanning trees do not require the edges to be weighted (i.e., to have a length, speed, time, or cost associated with them).

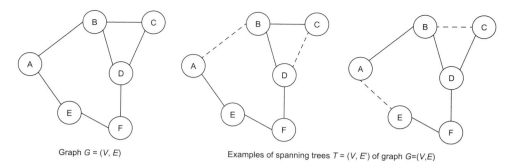

Graph G = (V, E)   Examples of spanning trees *T* = (*V*, *E*') of graph *G*=(*V*,*E*)

Figure 4.3 Examples of spanning trees. The middle and right trees reach every node of graph G with no loops or cycles.

An MST or minimum-weight spanning tree of an edge-weighted graph is a spanning tree whose weight (the sum of the weights of its edges) is no larger than the weight of any other spanning tree.

If $G=(V, E)$ is a graph, then any subgraph of G is a spanning tree if both of the following conditions are met:

- The subgraph contains all vertices V of G.
- The subgraph is connected with no circuits and no self-loops.

For a given spanning tree T for a graph G, the weight w of the spanning tree is the sum of the weights of all the edges in T. If the weight of T is the lowest of the weights of all the possible spanning trees of G, then we can call this an MST.

The previously described muddy city problem will be solved as an MST. Kruskal, Borůvka, Jarník-Prim, and Chazelle are all examples of algorithms that can be used to find an MST. Algorithm 4.1 shows the pseudocode for Kruskal's algorithm.

Algorithm 4.1   Kruskal's algorithm

```
Input: Graph G = (V, E) with each edge e ∈ E having a weight w(e)
Output: A minimum spanning tree T

Create a new graph T:= Ø with the same vertices as G, but with no edges.
Define a list S containing all the edges in the graph G
Sort the edges list S in ascending order of their weights.
For each edge e in the sorted list:
   If adding edge e to T does not form a cycle:
      Add this edge to T.
   Else:
      Skip this edge and move to the next edge in the list.
Continue this process until all the edges are processed.
Return T as the minimum spanning tree of graph G.
```

To better understand these steps, let's apply Kruskal's algorithm to solve the muddy city problem. Figure 4.4 shows the original graph. The numbers near the edges represent edge weights, and no edges have been added to the MST yet. The following steps will generate the MST by hand iteration.

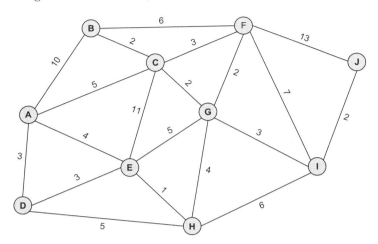

Figure 4.4   Solving the muddy city problem using Kruskal's algorithm—original graph

   1 The shortest edge is E-H with a length of 1, so it is highlighted and added to the MST (figure 4.5).

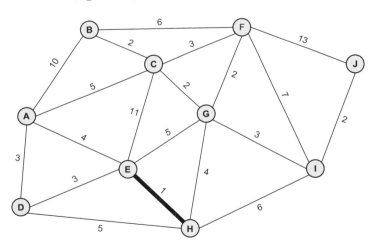

Figure 4.5   Solving the muddy city problem using Kruskal's algorithm—step 1

   2 B-C, C-G, G-F, and I-J are now the shortest edges with lengths of 2. B-C is chosen arbitrarily and is highlighted, followed by C-G, G-F, and I-J, as they don't form a cycle (figure 4.6).

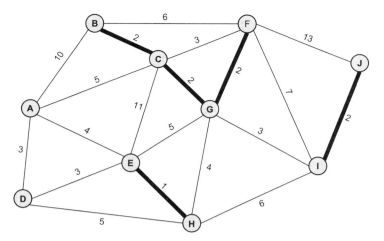

Figure 4.6 Solving the muddy city problem using Kruskal's algorithm—step 2

3 C-F, F-J, G-I, A-D, and D-E are now the shortest edges with lengths of 3. C-F cannot be chosen, as it forms a cycle. A-D is chosen arbitrarily and is highlighted, followed by D-E and G-I. F-J cannot be chosen, as it forms a cycle (figure 4.7).

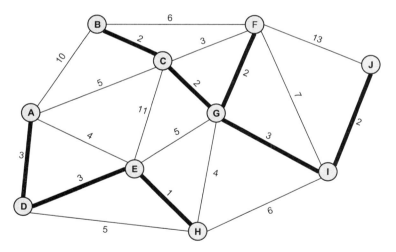

Figure 4.7 Solving the muddy city problem using Kruskal's algorithm—step 3

4 The next-shortest edges are A-E and G-H with lengths 4. A-E cannot be chosen because it forms a cycle, so the process finishes with the edge G-H. The minimum spanning tree has been found (figure 4.8).

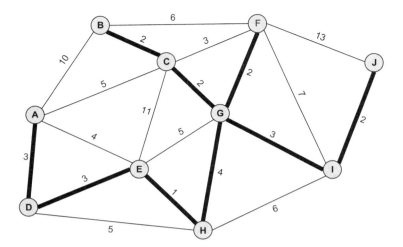

Figure 4.8   Solving the muddy city problem using Kruskal's algorithm—step 4

Figure 4.9 shows the final solution with all nodes in the graph connected.

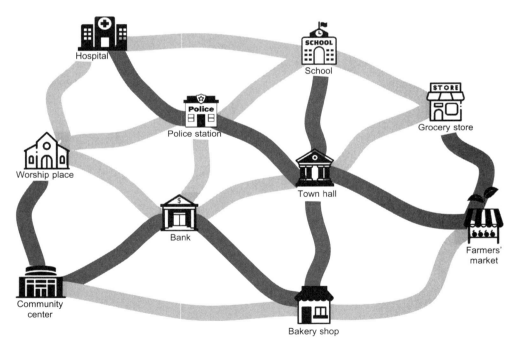

Figure 4.9   Solving the muddy city problem using Kruskal's algorithm. The algorithm adds edges to the final tree by ascending weight order, ignoring edges that will form a cycle.

This algorithm can be implemented easily in Python by using NetworkX's `find_cycle()` and `is_connected()` methods, which determine if an edge is a viable candidate for the MST, as well as the overall algorithm's termination condition, respectively. For the purposes of visual presentation, I've also used `spring_layout()` for the positions of the nodes and edges of the graph. The `spring_layout()` method uses a random number generator internally to generate these positions, and we can pass a seed (which allows a deterministic generation of so-called "pseudo-random" numbers) to guarantee a specific layout on each execution. Try modifying the seed parameter, and see what happens.

Listing 4.1   Solving the muddy city problem using Kruskal's algorithm

```python
import matplotlib.pyplot as plt
import networkx as nx

G = nx.Graph()
G.add_nodes_from(["A", "B", "C", "D", "E", "F", "G", "H", "I", "J"])

edges = [
    ("A", "B", {"weight": 10}),
    ("A", "C", {"weight": 5}),
    ("A", "D", {"weight": 3}),
    ("A", "E", {"weight": 4}),
    ("B", "C", {"weight": 2}),
    ("B", "F", {"weight": 6}),
    ("C", "E", {"weight": 11}),
    ("C", "F", {"weight": 3}),
    ("C", "G", {"weight": 2}),
    ("D", "E", {"weight": 3}),
    ("D", "H", {"weight": 5}),
    ("E", "G", {"weight": 5}),
    ("E", "H", {"weight": 1}),
    ("F", "G", {"weight": 2}),
    ("F", "I", {"weight": 7}),
    ("F", "J", {"weight": 13}),
    ("G", "H", {"weight": 4}),
    ("G", "I", {"weight": 3}),
    ("H", "I", {"weight": 6}),
    ("I", "J", {"weight": 2}),
]

G.add_edges_from(edges)
pos = nx.spring_layout(G, seed=74)

def Kruskal(G, attr = "weight"):
    edges = sorted(G.edges(data=True), key=lambda t: t[2].get(attr, 1))
    mst = nx.Graph()
    mst.add_nodes_from(G)
    for e in edges:
        mst.add_edges_from([e])
```

Create an undirected graph and populate it with nodes and edges.

Using a seed with the spring_layout method guarantees the same placement of nodes every time.

Sort edges by weight in ascending order.

```
try:
    nx.find_cycle(mst)
    mst.remove_edge(e[0], e[1])
except:
    if nx.is_connected(mst):
        break
    continue
return mst
```

find_cycle raises an error if no cycles exist in the graph. We can try/catch this error to determine if adding a new edge creates a cycle.

The set of edges in mst is a spanning tree if the graph formed by those edges is connected.

As a continuation of listing 4.1, the following code snippet is used to generate an MST using Kruskal and to visualize the MST:

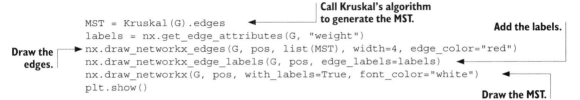

Call Kruskal's algorithm to generate the MST.

Add the labels.

Draw the edges.

```
MST = Kruskal(G).edges
labels = nx.get_edge_attributes(G, "weight")
nx.draw_networkx_edges(G, pos, list(MST), width=4, edge_color="red")
nx.draw_networkx_edge_labels(G, pos, edge_labels=labels)
nx.draw_networkx(G, pos, with_labels=True, font_color="white")
plt.show()
```

Draw the MST.

As you can see in figure 4.10, our Python implementation of the muddy city problem produces the exact same results that we achieved using hand iteration. Node G, which is the town hall, becomes a sort of central hub for the town's transportation infrastructure, and the total cost of road construction is minimized. It's worth noting, however, that while MST minimizes the total cost of connecting all nodes, it doesn't usually produce the most "convenient" solution. Should someone wish to travel from the place of worship to the hospital, for example, the shortest achievable distance would be 7 (passing through the police station), while our road network requires a total distance of 15.

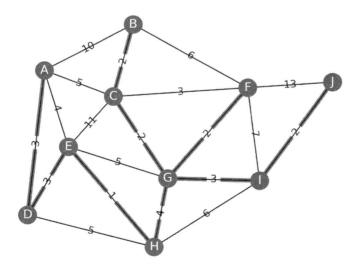

Figure 4.10   The muddy city problem solved using Kruskal's algorithm. The highlighted edges are part of the MST.

Let's apply this algorithm and this code to find the MST for all nodes in a search space surrounding the University of Toronto. Imagine that we have been tasked with installing new communications cables across the city, and we want to minimize the length of cable we use.

Listing 4.2   University of Toronto MST

```
import networkx as nx
import osmnx
import matplotlib.pyplot as plt
from optalgotools.algorithms.graph_search import Kruskal

reference = (43.661667, -79.395)
G = osmnx.graph_from_point(
    reference, dist=1000, clean_periphery=True, simplify=True, network_
type="drive"
)
fig, ax = osmnx.plot_graph(G)

undir_G = G.to_undirected()
sorted_edges = sorted(undir_G.edges(data=True), key=lambda t:
 t[2].get("length",1))

mst = Kruskal(G, sorted_edges=True, edges= sorted_edges,
 graph_type=nx.MultiDiGraph)

highlight_edges = ['b' if e in mst.edges else 'r' for e in G.edges]
edge_alphas = [1 if e in mst.edges else 0.25 for e in G.edges]
osmnx.plot_graph(
    G,
    edge_linewidth=2,
    edge_color=highlight_edges,
    edge_alpha=edge_alphas
)
plt.show()
```

Use the drive network to only focus on drivable roads. This prevents the code from building an MST with a combination of roads and sidewalks.

Get an undirected copy of the graph, and sort the road network edges by edge length.

Visualize the MST by highlighting the included edges.

Call the Kruskal algorithm from optalgotools, using a presorted list and specifying the graph type.

Figure 4.11 shows the resulting MST generated by Kruskal's algorithm. The road network graph in the figure may seem like one big connected component, but it isn't. There are one-way streets that seem to connect adjacent nodes on the graph, but in reality, they are not connected (you can go from A to B but not the reverse). We overcome this by converting the directed graph into an undirected graph using the to_undirected function in NetworkX.

The version of Kruskal's algorithm used in the listing is the same as was used for the muddy city problem. We're importing it from optalgotools to reduce the amount of code needed.

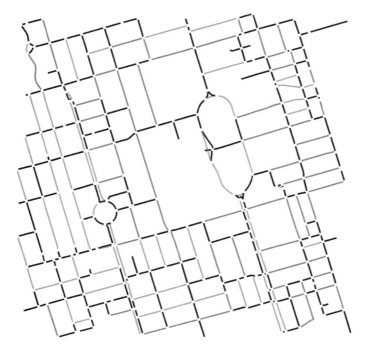

Figure 4.11   The MST generated by Kruskal's algorithm. All the edges included in the MST are highlighted. There are no cycles in the MST, and the total weight of the tree is minimized.

MSTs have a wide variety of applications in the real world, including network design, image segmentation, clustering, and facility location problems. MSTs are especially useful when dealing with problems concerning budgeting, such as planning networks, as they allow all nodes to be connected with a minimum total cost. As previously mentioned, informed search algorithms can be used to find MSTs as described in this section and with shortest path algorithms, which are discussed in the next section.

4.3   *Shortest path algorithms*

Informed search algorithms can be used to find the shortest path between two nodes by using knowledge about the problem (domain-specific knowledge) to prune the search. This knowledge, in the form of a heuristic function, gives an estimate of the distance to the goal. Examples of informed search algorithms include hill climbing, beam search, best-first, A*, and contraction hierarchies. The following subsections discuss these algorithms in detail.

4.3.1   Hill climbing algorithm

Assume that you are trying to climb to the top of a mountain in a dense fog. There is only one path up and down the mountain, but you aren't sure exactly where the peak is. Thus, you are only able to judge your progress by looking one step behind you and seeing if you've gone uphill or downhill since your last step. How can you know when you've reached the summit? A good guess would be when you're no longer going uphill!

Starting with a known (non-optimized) solution to a function or with an initial state, the hill climbing algorithm checks the neighbors of that solution and chooses the neighbor that is more optimized. This process is repeated until no better solution can be found, at which point the algorithm terminates.

The hill climbing algorithm is a local greedy search algorithm that tries to improve the efficiency of depth-first by incorporating domain-specific knowledge or heuristic information, so it can be considered as an informed depth-first algorithm. The hill climbing algorithm's pseudocode applied to graph search is shown in the algorithm 4.2 assuming minimization problem.

Algorithm 4.2   The hill climbing algorithm

```
Inputs: Source node, Destination node
Output: Route from source to destination

Initialize current ← random route from source to destination
Initialize neighbours ← children of current

While min(neighbours) > current do
    Set current ← min(neighbours)
    Update neighbours ← children of current
Return current as the route from source to destination
```

The algorithm sorts the successors of a node (according to their heuristic values) before adding them to the list to be expanded. This algorithm demands very little in the way of memory and computational overhead, as it simply remembers the current successors as the current path it is working on. It's a non-exhaustive technique; it does not examine the entire tree, so its performance will be reasonably fast. However, while this algorithm works relatively well with convex problems, functions with multiple local maxima will often result in an answer that is not the global maximum. It also performs poorly when there are plateaus (a local set of solutions that are all similarly optimized).

As shown in figure 4.12, depending on the initial state, the hill climbing algorithm may get stuck in local optima. Once it reaches the top of a hill, the algorithm will stop, since any new successor will be down the hill. This is analogous to climbing the mountain in the fog, reaching a smaller peak, and thinking that you've reached the main summit.

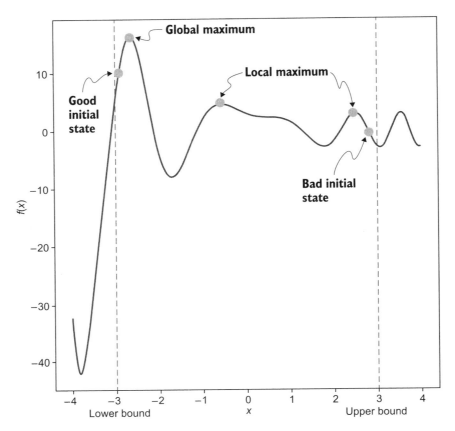

Figure 4.12   Depending on the initial state, the hill climbing algorithm may get stuck in local optima. Once it reaches a peak, the algorithm will stop, since any new successor will be down the hill.

Simple hill climbing, steepest-ascent hill climbing, stochastic hill climbing, and random-restart hill climbing are all variants of the hill climbing algorithm, as shown in figure 4.13.

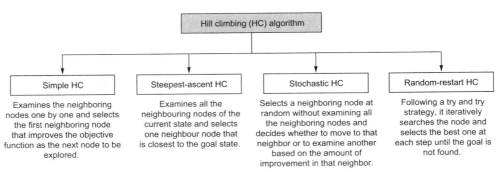

Figure 4.13   Variants of the hill climbing algorithm

Simple hill climbing examines the neighboring nodes one by one and selects the first neighboring node that optimizes the objective function as the next node to be explored. *Steepest-ascent or steepest-descent hill climbing* is a variation on the simple hill-climbing algorithm that first examines all the neighboring nodes of the current state and selects one neighbor node that is closest to the goal state. *Stochastic hill climbing* is a randomized version of a hill climbing algorithm that selects a neighboring node at random without examining all the neighboring nodes. This algorithm decides whether to move to that neighbor or to examine another based on the amount of improvement in that neighbor. Random-restart hill climbing or first-choice hill climbing follows a try-and-try strategy and iteratively searches the nodes and selects the best one at each step until the goal is found. If it gets stuck in a local maximum, it restarts the process from a new random initial state. Compared to the other hill climbing variants, this algorithm is better able to reach the destination if there are plateaus, local optima, and ridges.

Gradient descent algorithm

The *gradient descent algorithm* is widely used in machine learning to train models and make predictions. Gradient descent and hill climbing are two fundamentally different algorithms and cannot be confused with each other. Instead of climbing up a hill, gradient descent can be seen as hiking down to the bottom of a valley. Gradient descent is an iterative algorithm that looks at the slope of the local neighbors and moves in the direction with the steepest slope or the direction of negative gradient to optimize a continuous differentiable function. Alternatively, in the case of a maximization problem, *gradient ascent* moves in the direction with a positive gradient to optimize the objective function.

The gradient descent algorithm usually converges to a global minimum if the function is convex (i.e., if any local minimum is also a global minimum) and the learning rate is properly chosen. The hill climbing algorithm is a heuristic greedy algorithm that can easily get stuck in local optima. It is used mainly for discrete optimization problems, such as the traveling salesman, as it doesn't require the objective function to be differentiable.

Assume we have the simple graph shown in figure 4.14. The source node is S and the destination node is G.

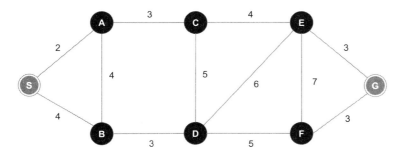

Figure 4.14   An 8 points of interest (POIs) road network in the form of a graph

This graph can be converted into a tree by finding a spanning tree that includes all the vertices of the original graph and that is connected and acyclic, as shown in figure 4.15.

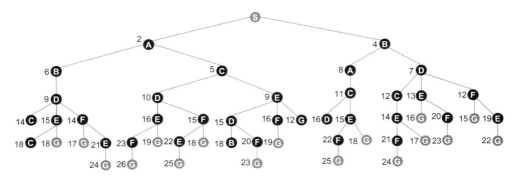

Figure 4.15   An 8 points of interest (POIs) road network in the form of a tree

As you can see, there are multiple ways to go from S to G, each with different costs. Following the hill climbing algorithm, the shortest path between S and G will be S→A→C→E→G, as illustrated in figure 4.16.

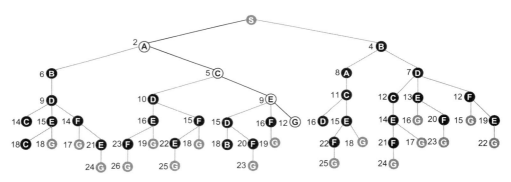

Figure 4.16   Shortest path between S and G using the hill climbing algorithm

Let's now use the 8-puzzle problem to illustrate the hill climbing approach. Figure 4.17 shows how the hill climbing search progresses, using the number of misplaced tiles, excluding the blank tile, as heuristic information $h(n)$. For example, in step 2, tiles 1, 4, 6, and 7 are wrongly placed, so $h = 4$. In step 3, tiles 1, and 4 are misplaced, so $h = 2$.

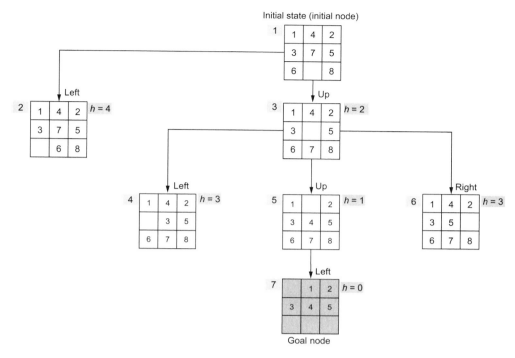

Figure 4.17   Using the hill climbing algorithm to solve the 8-puzzle problem. At each iteration, the algorithm explores neighboring states, looking for the minimum heuristic value.

Listing 4.3 shows a simple implementation of hill climbing in Python. The code selects nodes to explore by minimizing the heuristic value of the next node. A more complex version, involving generating shortest paths, will be presented at the end of this chapter.

Listing 4.3   Solving the 8-puzzle problem using hill climbing

```
import matplotlib.pyplot as plt

def Hill_Climbing(origin, destination, cost_fn):
    costs = [cost_fn(origin)]
    current = origin
    route = [current]
    neighbours = current.expand()
    shortest = min(neighbours, key=lambda s: cost_fn(s))
```

The neighbor nodes of the current state can be generated using expand().

The "closest" neighbor is the one with the lowest cost function (i.e., the fewest misplaced tiles).

```
        costs.append(cost_fn(shortest))
        route.append(shortest)

        while cost_fn(shortest) < cost_fn(current):
            current = shortest
            neighbours = current.expand()
            shortest = min(neighbours, key=lambda s: cost_fn(s))
            costs.append(cost_fn(shortest))
            route.append(shortest)
            if shortest == destination:        ◀─────    Terminate the algorithm
                break                                     if the goal state has been
                                                          reached.
        return route, costs
                                                    Calculate and return the
def misplaced_tiles(state: State):                  number of misplaced tiles that
    flat = state.flatten()                          are not in their goal positions.
    goal = range(len(flat))
    return sum([0 if goal[i] == flat[i] else 1 for i in range(len(flat))])
```

NOTE   The State class and visualize function are defined in the complete listing, available in the book's GitHub repo.

The following code snippet defines the initial and goal states of the puzzle and uses hill climbing to solve the puzzle:

```
init_state = [[1,4,2],
              [3,7,5],
              [6,0,8]]

goal_state = [[0,1,2],
              [3,4,5],
              [6,7,8]]

init_state = State(init_state)
goal_state = State(goal_state)
                                            Check if there is
if not init_state.is_solvable():    ◀────   even a solution.
    print("This puzzle is not solvable.")
else:                                                            Solve the puzzle
    solution, costs = Hill_Climbing(init_state, goal_state,      using hill climbing.
      ➥ misplaced_tiles)    ◀─────────────────────────────
    plt.xticks(range(len(costs)))
    plt.ylabel("Misplaced tiles")               Plot the search progress,
    plt.title("Hill climbing: 8 Puzzle")        and visualize the solution.
    plt.plot(costs)
    visualize(solution)
```

The output is shown in figure 4.18.

Initial state | State 1 | State 2 | Goal state

1	4	2
3	7	5
6		8

1	4	2
3		5
6	7	8

1		2
3	4	5
6	7	8

	1	2
3	4	5
6	7	8

Figure 4.18   States of the hill climbing solution for the 8-puzzle problem. Each subsequent state is selected by minimizing its cost compared to its neighbors. As the 8-puzzle problem has not only a well-defined but also an achievable goal state, the algorithm's termination condition (the goal being reached) coincides with the "peak" of the hill (which in this case is a valley, as it is a minimization problem).

As the 8-puzzle problem uses a heuristic as a cost, it essentially becomes a minimization problem. This implementation differs from the standard hill climbing in that, as a solution can always be found, and the graph is fully connected (you can transition from any state to another state through some combination of tile movements), the algorithm is guaranteed to find the optimal solution eventually. More complex problems will often generate solutions that are near-optimal.

4.3.2   *Beam search algorithm*

The *beam search algorithm* tries to minimize the memory requirements of the breadth-first algorithm, so it can be seen as an informed breadth-first algorithm. While hill climbing maintains a single best state throughout the run, beam search keeps w states in memory, where w is the beam width. At each iteration, it generates the neighbors for each of the states and puts them into a pool with the states from the original beam. It then selects the best w states from the pool at each level to become the new beam, and the rest of the states are discarded. This process then repeats. The algorithm expands only the first w promising nodes at each level.

This is a non-exhaustive search, but it is also a hazardous process, because a goal state might be missed. As this is a local search algorithm, it is also susceptible to getting stuck at a local optima. A beam search with w equal to the number of nodes in each level is the same as a BFS. Because there is the risk that a state that could lead to the optimal solution might be discarded, beam searches are incomplete (they may not terminate with the solution).

Algorithm 4.3 shows the pseudocode for the beam search algorithm applied to a graph search.

Algorithm 4.3   The beam search algorithm

```
Inputs: A source node, a destination node, and beam width w
Output: A route from source to destination

Initialize Seen ← nil
Initialize beam ← random w routes from source to destination
```

```
Add beam to seen
Initialize pool ← children of routes in the beam with consideration of seen +
beam
Initialize last_beam ← nil
While beam is not last_beam do
    Update last_beam ← beam
    Update beam ← the best w routes from pool
    If last_beam == beam then break
    Add beam to seen
    Update pool ← children of routes in the beam + beam

Return optimal route in beam
```

In section 2.3.1, you saw that BFS has an exponential complexity of $O(b^d)$, where b represents the maximum branching factor for each node and d is the depth one must expand to reach the goal. In the case of beam search, we only explore $w \times b$ nodes at any depth, saving many unneeded nodes compared to BFS. However, finding the best states or routes requires sorting, which is time-consuming if $w \times b$ is a huge number. A beam threshold can be used to handle this problem, where the best node is selected based on the heuristic function $h(n)$ within a certain threshold, and all the nodes outside this are pruned away.

Revisiting the simple routing problem with 8 points of interest (figure 4.14) and following the beam search algorithm with $w = 2$, the shortest path between S and G will be S-A-C-E-G, as illustrated in figure 4.19.

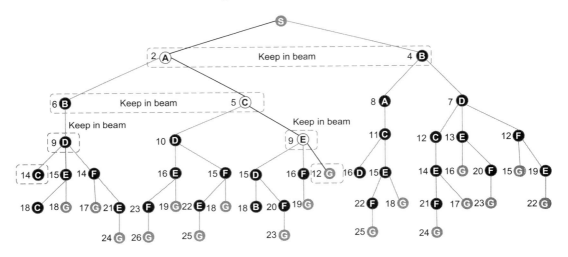

Figure 4.19   The shortest path between S and G using a beam search algorithm. With a beam width $w = 2$, two states are kept in the beam at each iteration. After generating the neighbors of each element in the beam, only the best w beams are kept.

The following listing shows a basic implementation of beam search used for a simple routing problem. See the full code in the GitHub repo to see how the graph is initialized, as well as how the visualization is generated (it is quite similar to that of listing 4.1).

Listing 4.4 Simple routing with beam search

```python
import matplotlib.pyplot as plt
import networkx as nx
import heapq
from optalgotools.structures import Node
from optalgotools.routing import cost

G = nx.Graph()
G.add_nodes_from(["A", "B", "C", "D", "E", "F", "G", "S"])
edges = [
    ("A", "B", {"weight": 4}),
    ("A", "C", {"weight": 3}),
    ("A", "S", {"weight": 2}),
    ("B", "D", {"weight": 3}),
    ("B", "S", {"weight": 4}),
    ("C", "E", {"weight": 4}),
    ("C", "D", {"weight": 5}),
    ("D", "E", {"weight": 6}),
    ("D", "F", {"weight": 5}),
    ("E", "F", {"weight": 7}),
    ("E", "G", {"weight": 3}),
    ("F", "G", {"weight": 3}),
]
G.add_edges_from(edges)
G=G.to_directed()

def Beam_Search(G, origin, destination, cost_fn, w=2, expand_kwargs=[],
    cost_kwargs=[]):
    seen = set()
    seen.add(origin)
    last_beam = None
    pool = set(origin.expand(**expand_kwargs))
    beam = []
    while beam != last_beam:
        last_beam = beam
        beam = heapq.nsmallest(
            w, pool, key=lambda node: cost_fn(G, node.path(),
            **cost_kwargs))
        current = beam.pop(0)
        seen.add(current)
        pool.remove(current)
        children = set(current.expand(**expand_kwargs))
        for child in children:
            if child in seen: next
            else:    #D
                if child == destination:
                    return child.path()
                beam.append(child)
        pool.update(beam)
    return None
```

Create a directed graph.

Get the neighbors of the node using the origin class's expand() method, passing any necessary arguments.

Prune the pool down to only the best k paths, passing any necessary arguments to the cost function.

Child routes are generated for each route by adding one extra node to the route. For each of these new routes, they are rejected (already explored), added to the beam (and then to the pool), or accepted (because they reach the destination).

None is returned if a path cannot be found.

This function can be called with the following example parameters:

```
result = Beam_Search(
    G,
    Node(G, "S"),
    Node(G, "G"),
    cost,
    expand_kwargs={"attr_name": "weight"},
    cost_kwargs={"attr_name": "weight"},
)
```

Visualizing the output of this algorithm produces the graph in figure 4.20, where the highlighted line represents the solution path from S to G.

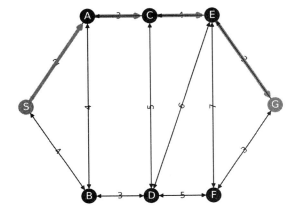

Figure 4.20   **Solution using a beam width of w = 2. The highlighted line represents the solution path.**

As you will see in a later section, when applying beam search to a real-life routing problem, generating the children in a beam search can become very complicated and time consuming.

4.3.3   *A* search algorithm*

The *A** (pronounced A-star) algorithm is an informed search algorithm widely used in pathfinding and graph traversal. This algorithm is a special case of the best-first algorithm. Best-first search is a kind of mixed depth- and breadth-first search that expands the most desirable unexpanded node based on either the cost to reach the node or an estimate or heuristic value of the cost to reach the goal from that node. The A* algorithm takes into account both the cost to reach the node and the estimated cost to reach the goal in order to find the optimal solution.

The pseudocode for A* is shown in algorithm 4.4.

Algorithm 4.4   A* algorithm

```
Inputs: Source node, Destination node
Output: Route from source to destination

Initialize A* heuristic ← sum of straight-line distance to source and
destination
Initialize PQ ← min heap according to A* heuristic
```

```
Initialize frontier ← a PQ initialized with source
Initialize explored ← empty
Initialize found ← False

While frontier is not empty and found is False do
    Set node ← frontier.pop()
    Add node to explored
    For child in node.expand() do
        If child is not in explored and child is not in frontier then
            If child is destination then
                Update route ← child.route()
                Update found ← True
            Add child to frontier

Return route
```

A* search tries to reduce the total number of states explored by incorporating both the actual cost and a heuristic estimate of the cost to get to the goal from a given state. The driving force behind A* is the selection of a new vertex (or node) to explore based on the lowest value. The value of the evaluation function $f(n)$ is computed using the following formula:

$$f(n) = g(n) + h(n)$$

4.1

In equation 4.1, $g(n)$ is the actual cost of the partial path already traveled from the source node S to node n. The heuristic information $h(n)$ can be the straight-line distance between node n and destination node G, or some other function. When $h(n) = 0$ for all nodes, A* will behave like a uniform-cost search (UCS), which was explained in section 3.4.2, so the node with the lowest cost will be expanded regardless of the estimated cost to reach the goal.

In *weighted A**, a constant weight is added to the heuristic function as follows:

$$f(n) = g(n) + w \times h(n)$$

4.2

To increase the importance of $h(n)$, w should be greater than 1. A dynamic weight $w(n)$ can be also used. The choice of the heuristic information is critical to the search results. The heuristic information $h(n)$ is admissible if and only if $h(n)$ is less than the actual cost to reach the goal state from n for every node n. This means that admissible heuristics never overestimate the cost to reach the goal and can lead to optimal solutions only when the heuristic function is close to the true remaining distance.

The A* heuristic algorithm operates by choosing the next vertex for exploration in a *greedy* manner, prioritizing nodes based on the value of the heuristic function. As the sum of the distance to the origin and destination is minimized when n lies on a straight line from S to G, this heuristic prioritizes nodes that are closer to the straight-line distance from origin to destination.

To better understand the A* procedure, let's consider the simple problem of finding the shortest path between a source node S and a goal node G in an 8 points of interest

(POIs) road network. This is the same POI graph from figure 4.14 but with heuristic values added for each node. An example of heuristic information is the straight-line distance to the goal as shown above each vertex in figure 4.21.

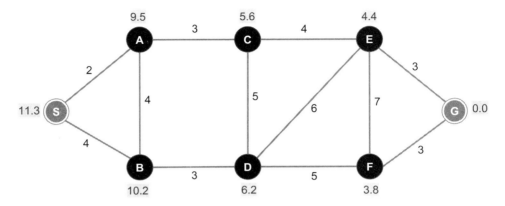

Figure 4.21　An 8 POIs road network in the form of a graph with heuristic information (straight-line distance to the goal) shown above each vertex

Figure 4.22 shows the steps for using A* to find the shortest path from S to G.

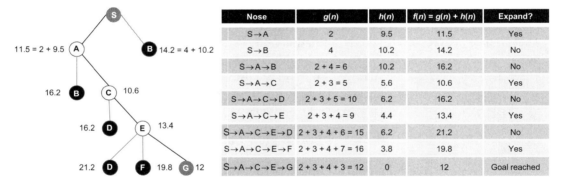

Nose	g(n)	h(n)	f(n) = g(n) + h(n)	Expand?
S→A	2	9.5	11.5	Yes
S→B	4	10.2	14.2	No
S→A→B	2 + 4 = 6	10.2	16.2	No
S→A→C	2 + 3 = 5	5.6	10.6	Yes
S→A→C→D	2 + 3 + 5 = 10	6.2	16.2	No
S→A→C→E	2 + 3 + 4 = 9	4.4	13.4	Yes
S→A→C→E→D	2 + 3 + 4 + 6 = 15	6.2	21.2	No
S→A→C→E→F	2 + 3 + 4 + 7 = 16	3.8	19.8	Yes
S→A→C→E→G	2 + 3 + 4 + 3 = 12	0	12	Goal reached

Figure 4.22　The A* steps to find the shortest path between the source node S and goal node G in an 8 POIs road network. The sum of the already incurred costs and the distance to the goal is used as the heuristic value to determine whether to expand a certain node.

This algorithm may look complex since it seems to need to store incomplete paths and their lengths at various places. However, using a recursive best-first search implementation can solve this problem in an elegant way without the need for explicit path storing. The quality of the lower-bound goal distance from each node greatly influences the timing complexity of the algorithm. The closer the given lower bound is to the true distance, the shorter the execution time.

We can apply the A* algorithm to the simple routing problem as follows (see the book's GitHub repo for the full code, containing graph initialization and visualization).

Listing 4.5 Simple routing using A* search

```
import matplotlib.pyplot as plt
from optalgotools.structures import Node
from optalgotools.routing import cost
import networkx as nx
import heapq

def A_Star(
    G, origin, destination, heuristic_fn, cost_fn, cost_kwargs=[],
    ➥ expand_kwargs=[]
):
    toDestination = heuristic_fn(G, origin, destination)
    toOrigin = {}
    route = []
    frontier = list()
    frontier.append(origin)
    toOrigin[origin] = 0
    explored = set()
    found = False
    while frontier and not found:
        node = min(frontier, key=lambda node: toOrigin[node] +
        ➥ toDestination[node])
        frontier.remove(node)
        explored.add(node)
        for child in node.expand(**expand_kwargs):
            if child not in explored and child not in frontier:
                if child == destination:
                    route = child.path()
                    found = True
                    continue
                frontier.append(child)
                toOrigin[child] = cost_fn(G, child.path(), **cost_kwargs)
    return route
```

Choose a node based on its heuristic value.

Expand the node's children, adding them to the frontier or terminating if the destination is found.

Add the toOrigin value for each node on the fly.

The implementation of A* in listing 4.5 doesn't use a "real" A* heuristic algorithm for two reasons:

- The straight line or haversine distance from any node to the destination cannot be readily determined, as we only have edge weights and no real spatial data (coordinates) to situate each node. To get around this, I created a function called `dummy_astar_heuristic` that returns static, arbitrarily generated distances for the purposes of this example.

- The distance from the origin to any node (straight line or otherwise) cannot be determined ahead of time for the same reasons as in the previous point. Thus, we use the traveled distance (i.e., the cost from the origin to the node as far as has been explored), and we update that value as the algorithm discovers new nodes. Later in this chapter, we will see how working with geographic data (such as road networks) allows us to capture this information beforehand.

A_Star can be called as follows, with some example parameters:

```
result = A_Star(
    G,
    Node(G, "S"),
    Node(G, "G"),
    dummy_astar_heuristic,
    cost,
    expand_kwargs={"attr_name": "weight"},
    cost_kwargs={"attr_name": "weight"},)
```

This gives us the same result as with beam search and hill climbing: a path of S-A-C-E-G.

Haversine distance

The haversine formula is used to calculate the geographic distance between two points on earth, given their longitudes and latitudes, based on a mean spherical earth radius. This distance is also known as the great-circle distance and is calculated using the following formula:

$$d = R \times C \text{ and } C = 2 \times \text{atan2}\left(\sqrt{a}, \sqrt{1 - a}\right) \qquad \text{4.3}$$

In the preceding equation, $a = \sin^2(\Delta lat/2) + \cos(lat1) \times \cos(lat2) \times \sin^2(\Delta lon/2)$, R is the earth radius (6,371 km or 3,691 miles), and d is the final distance between the two points. The following figure shows the haversine distance between Los Angeles, USA (34.0522° N, 118.2437° W) and Madrid, Spain (40.4168° N, 3.7038° W).

Haversine distance between Los Angeles and Madrid

The following Python code can be used to calculate the haversine distance:

```
!pip install haversine
from haversine import haversine
```
Install the Haversine package, and import the haversine function.

```
LA = (34.052235, -118.243683)
```
Set coordinates of two points in (latitude, longitude) format.

```
Madrid = (40.416775, -3.703790)  ◄──────  Set coordinates of two points in
                                           (latitude, longitude) format.

                                           Calculate the distance
distance = haversine(LA, Madrid)  ◄──────  in kilometers.
print(distance)
```

The implementation of the A* heuristic in optalgotools defaults to calculating distances as if the earth were flat. For local searches, this yields the best results. If the size of the search area is larger, it is better to calculate distance by passing `optalgotools.utilities.haversine_distance` into the `measuring_dist` parameter, which considers the curvature of the earth.

4.3.4 *Hierarchical approaches*

When facing routing problems at larger scales, such as those involving entire countries or graphs with millions of nodes, it is simply implausible to use basic approaches like Dijkstra's. In the previous chapter, you saw that bidirectional Dijkstra's gives a two times speedup compared to Dijkstra's algorithm. However, much faster routing algorithms are needed for interactive applications like navigation apps. One way to achieve this is to precompute certain routes and cache them on servers so that response times to user queries are reasonable. Another method involves pruning the search space. Hierarchical search algorithms prune the search space by generating admissible heuristics that abstract the search space.

> **NOTE** For more details about the general approaches of hierarchical methods, see Leighton, Wheeler, and Holte, "Faster optimal and suboptimal hierarchical search" [1].

Highway hierarchies involve the assignment of hierarchy "levels" to each road in a road network graph. This distinguishes the type of road segment (e.g., residential roads, national roads, highways). This is further supplemented by relevant data such as the maximum designated driving speed as well as the number of turns in the road. After the heuristics are generated for the graph, the data is passed through a modified search function (bidirectional Dijkstra's, A*, etc.) that considers the distance to the destination and the potential expansion node type. Highway hierarchy algorithms will generally consider highways as viable expansion nodes when they are further away from the target and will start to include national roads, and finally residential streets, as they near the destination. During the trip, less important roads merge with more important roads (e.g., residential roads merge with national roads, and national roads merge with highways). This allows us to avoid exploring millions of nodes.

Take, for example, a long-distance driving trip from New York to Miami. In the beginning, you will need to navigate local roads toward a highway or interstate. In the middle section of the trip, you will drive exclusively on the interstate or highway. Nearing your destination, you will leave the interstate and once again take local roads. While this approach makes sense, there are some disadvantages. First, the algorithm overlooks what kind of roads humans prefer to drive on. While a highway might make sense for a given route, the user may prefer to take local roads (such as when driving to a friend's house who lives nearby). Second, highway hierarchies do not consider factors such as traffic, which fluctuates often and adds significant cost to an "optimal" route. You can learn more about highway hierarchies in Sanders and Schultes' article "Highway hierarchies hasten exact shortest path queries" [2].

The contraction hierarchies (CH) algorithm is another hierarchical approach. It is a speed-up technique that improves the performance of shortest-path computations by pruning the search space based on the concept of node contraction. For example, for an 80 mile single-source single-destination shortest path search query, the bidirectional Dijkstra's algorithm explores 220,000 nodes, unidirectional A* explores 50,000 nodes, and bidirectional A* improves on those by exploring about 25,000 nodes. Contraction hierarchies solve the same problem by exploring only about 600 nodes. This makes CH much faster than Dijkstra's, bidirectional Dijkstra's, and A*.

NOTE Contraction hierarchies were introduced in Geisberger et al.'s 2008 "Contraction hierarchies: Faster and simpler hierarchical routing in road networks" article [3]. The 80 mile single-source single-destination shortest path search query is discussed on the *GraphHopper* blog (http://mng.bz/n142).

The CH algorithm encompasses two main phases:

1 The *preprocessing phase* is where nodes and edges are categorized based on some notion of importance. Important nodes can be major cities, major intersections, bridges connecting the two sides of a city, or points of interest that shortest paths go through. Each node is contracted based on the level of importance from least important to most important. During the contraction process, a set of shortcut edges is added to the graph to preserve shortest paths.

2 The *query phase* is where a bidirectional Dijkstra's search (or any other search) is run on the preprocessed graph, considering only increasingly important edges. This results in selectively ignoring less important nodes, and overall improving querying speed.

It's worth noting that the CH algorithm is mainly a preprocessing algorithm, which means that it is used before querying the shortest path. This preprocessing phase takes some time, but once it's done, the query phase is very fast. The algorithm can handle large graphs and can be used for various types of graphs, not only road networks. Let's dive into both phases in further detail.

THE CH PREPROCESSING PHASE

The preprocessing phase takes as input the original graph, and it returns an augmented graph and node order to be used during the query phase.

Assume a weighted directed graph $G = (V,E)$. The nodes of this graph are ordered based on node importance. In the case of road networks, node importance can be based on road type: residential roads, national roads, and motorways or highways. The basic intuition here is that closer to the source or target, we usually consider residential roads; far away from the source or target, national roads are considered; and even further away from the source or the target, it makes sense to consider highways. Some other heuristics that affect the node importance include the maximum speed, toll rates, the number of turns, etc.

Once the node order is determined, the vertex set or nodes are ordered by importance: $V = \{1,2,3\ldots,n\}$. Nodes are contracted or removed in this order using the following procedure:

```
for each pair (u,v)and (v,w)of edges:
    if <u,v,w> is a unique shortest path then
        add shortcut(u,w) with weight ω(<u,v,w>)or ω(<u,w>)+ω(<v,w>)
```

As illustrated in figure 4.23, node v can be contracted from graph G. If necessary, a shortcut or edge with a cost of 5 should be added to ensure that the shortest distance between u and w is preserved or remains the same, even after v has been contracted. Contracting a node v means replacing the shortest paths going through v with shortcuts. The new graph is called an *overlay graph* or an *augmented graph* (i.e., a graph with an augmented set of edges). This graph contains the same set of vertices as the initial graph and all the edges, plus all the added edges (shortcuts) used to preserve shortest distances in the original graph.

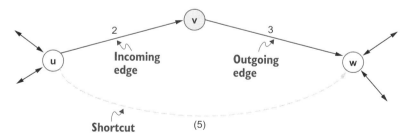

Figure 4.23   Node contraction operation—the number in brackets denotes the cost of the added shortcut.

When contracting node v, no shortcut is needed if there is a path P between u and w with $w(P) <= w(<u,v,w>)$. This path is called a *witness path*, as shown in figure 4.24.

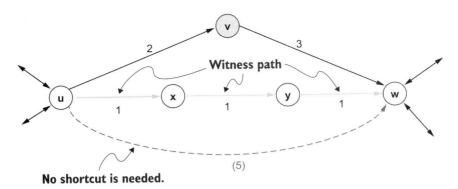

No shortcut is needed.

Figure 4.24   Witness path—there is another path from *u* to *w* that is shorter, so no shortcut is needed when contracting *v*.

During the CH preprocessing phase, since the nodes are ordered based on importance, a node can be iteratively contracted, and an additional shortcut arc can be
added to preserve short distances and to form an augmented graph. We end up with a
contraction hierarchy, with one overlay graph for each individual node. This preprocessing is done offline, and the augmented graph is used later during the query phase.

Let's consider a simple graph with four nodes. Figure 4.25 shows the steps of the contraction process. We will contract each node following the order of importance from
the least to the most important node (i.e., following the importance or hierarchy level
from 1 to n). This process will form shortcuts, which will allow us to search the graph
much faster, as we can ignore nodes that have been pruned. The initial graph is shown
in figure 4.25a:

1   By contracting the least important node, node 1, nothing happens, as the short-
    est path between the neighboring nodes 2 and 4 does not pass by node 1 (figure
    4.25b).

2   Moving forward and contracting the next most important node, node 2, we
    have now changed the shortest path for 1→3, 1→4, and 3→4. We can encode
    these shortest paths by creating new edges (shortcuts). The numbers in brackets
    denote the costs of the added shortcuts (figure 4.25c).

3   Contracting node 3 does not cause any change, as there is a shorter path between
    nodes 2 and 4 that does not pass by node 3 (figure 4.25d).

4   We do not need to contract node 4, as it is the last node in the graph (figure
    4.25e).

The generated overlay graph after the contraction process is shown in figure 4.25f.
The nodes are ordered based on importance.

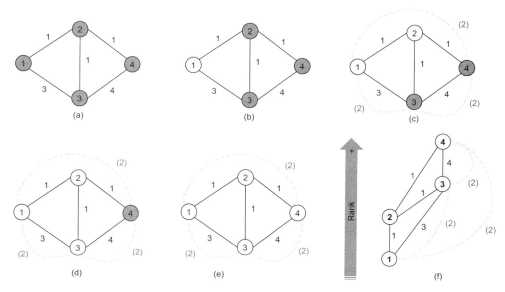

Figure 4.25 An example of the CH preprocessing phase

The order of contraction does not affect the success of CH, but it will affect the prepro-cessing and query time. Some contraction ordering systems minimize the number of shortcuts added in the augmented graph and thus the overall running time.

To begin, we need to use some notion of importance and keep all the nodes in a priority queue by decreasing importance. Edge difference, lazy updates, the number of contracted neighbors, and shortcut cover (all explained shortly) are examples of importance criteria. The *importance* of each node in the graph is its *priority*. This metric guides the order in which nodes are contracted. This *priority* term is dynamic and is continuously updated as nodes are contracted. The typical importance criteria include

- *Lazy updates*—The priority of the node on top of the priority queue (i.e., the node with the smallest priority) is updated before it is removed. If this node is still on top after the update, it will be contracted. Otherwise, the new topmost node will be processed in the same way.
- *Edge difference* (ED)—The ED of a node is the number of edges that need to be added versus the number of edges to be removed. We want to minimize the num-ber of edges added to the augmented graph. For a node v in a graph, assume that
  - ○ in(v) is the incoming degree (i.e., the number of edges coming into a node)
  - ○ out(v) is the outgoing degree (i.e., the number of outgoing edges emanating from a node)

- $\deg(v)$ is the total degree of the node, which is the sum of its in and out degrees so $\deg(v) = \operatorname{in}(v) + \operatorname{out}(v)$
- $\operatorname{add}(v)$ is the number of added shortcuts
- $\operatorname{ED}(v)$ is the edge difference after contracting node v, and it's given by $\operatorname{ED}(v) = \operatorname{add}(v) - \deg(v)$

The next two figures show how the edge difference is calculated and used to choose between contracting an edge node like A (figure 4.26) and a hub node like E (figure 4.27)

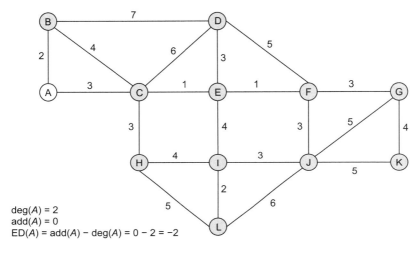

Figure 4.26   Edge difference in the case of edge node A

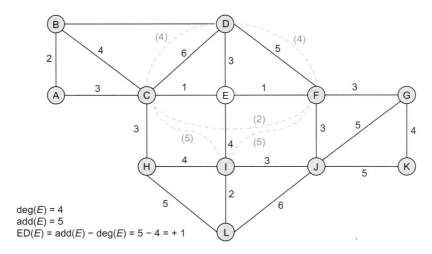

Figure 4.27   Edge difference in case of a hub node. The numbers in brackets denote the cost of the added shortcuts.

- *Number of contracted neighbors*—This reflects how nodes are spread across the map. It is better to avoid contracting all nodes in a small region of the graph and to ensure uniformity during the contraction process. We first contract the node with the smallest number of contracted neighbors.

- *Shortcut cover*—This method approximates how unavoidable the node is (e.g., a bridge connecting two parts of a city across a river). It represents the number of neighbors of a node, and thus how many shortcuts we'll need to create to or from them after contracting the node, because they're unavoidable nodes. Nodes with a smaller number of shortcut covers are contracted first.

The priority of a node estimates the attractiveness of contracting the node and can be a weighted linear combination of the previously described importance criteria, such as edge difference, number of contracted neighbors, and shortcut cover. The least important node is extracted in each iteration. The contraction process may affect the importance of a node, so we need to recompute this node importance. The newly updated importance is then compared with the node on the top of the priority queue (with the lowest importance) to decide whether or not this node needs to be contracted. The node with the smallest updated importance is always contracted.

THE CH QUERY PHASE

During the CH query phase, we apply bidirectional Dijkstra's to find the shortest path between the source and the target, as follows (figure 4.28):

- Dijkstra's algorithm from the source only considers edges u,v where level(u) > level(v), so you only want to relax nodes with a higher level than the node you have relaxed at that iteration. This is called the *upward graph*. In the context of Dijkstra's algorithm, *relaxing* a node refers to the process of updating the estimated distance or cost to reach that node from a source node by considering shorter paths through neighboring nodes. This helps refine the estimate of the shortest path to the node from the source.

- Dijkstra's algorithm from the target only considers edges u,v where level(u) < level(v), so you only want to relax nodes with a lower level than the node you have relaxed at that iteration. This is called the *downward graph*.

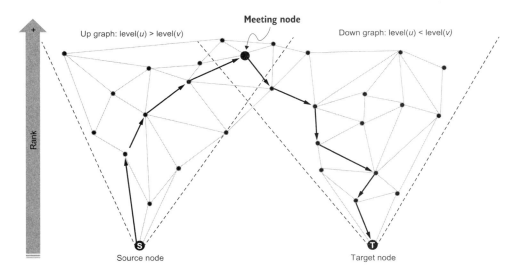

Figure 4.28 CH query phase

A CH EXAMPLE

Consider the following network with an arbitrary node ordering (figure 4.29). The numbers in the circles are the order in which the nodes will be contracted. The numbers on the edges represent the costs.

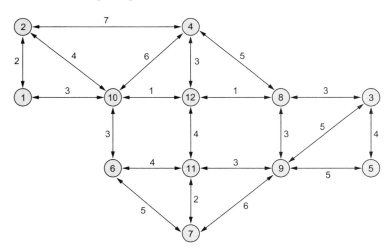

Figure 4.29 A CH example

Let's run the CH algorithm on this graph to get the shortest path between two nodes in this road network. The following steps show how to apply the CH algorithm:

1   *Contracting node 1*—There's no need to add a shortcut, as we do not lose a shortest path (figure 4.30).

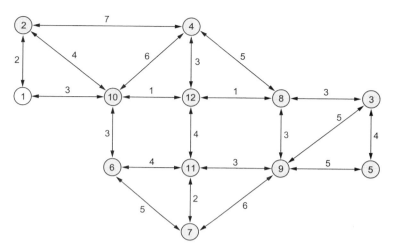

Figure 4.30   Graph contraction using an arbitrary node ranking—contracting node 1

2   *Contracting node 2*—There's no need to add a shortcut, as we do not lose a shortest path (figure 4.31).

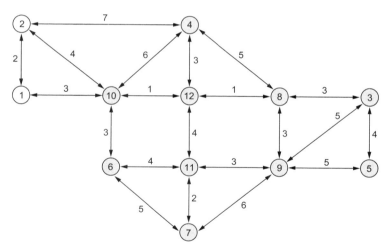

Figure 4.31   Graph contraction using an arbitrary node ranking—contracting node 2

3   *Contracting node 3*—A shortcut needs to be added to preserve the shortest path between 8 and 5, as there is no witness path. The cost of the added arc is 7 (figure 4.32).

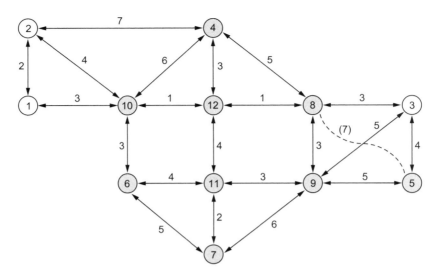

Figure 4.32   Graph contraction using an arbitrary node ranking—contracting node 3

4   *Contracting node 4*—No shortcuts need to be added (figure 4.33).

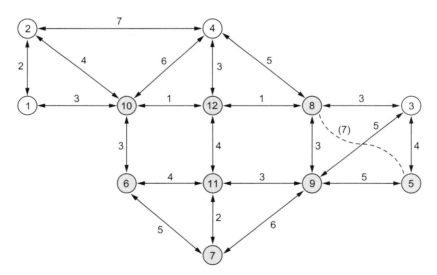

Figure 4.33   Graph contraction using an arbitrary node ranking—contracting node 4

5   *Contracting node 5*—No shortcuts need to be added (figure 4.34).

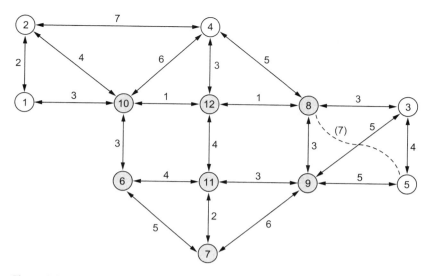

Figure 4.34   Graph contraction using an arbitrary node ranking—contracting node 5

6 *Contracting node 6*—No shortcuts need to be added, as there is a witness path between 7 and 10, which is 7-11-12-10 (figure 4.35).

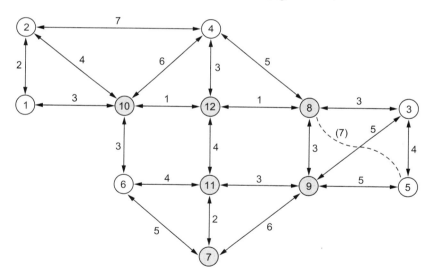

Figure 4.35   Graph contraction using an arbitrary node ranking—contracting node 6

7 *Contracting node 7*—No shortcuts need to be added (figure 4.36).

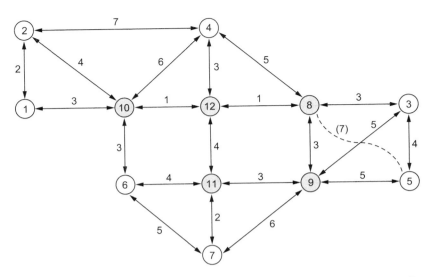

Figure 4.36   Graph contraction using an arbitrary node ranking—contracting node 7

8   *Contracting node 8*—A shortcut needs to be added to preserve the shortest path between 9 and 12 (figure 4.37).

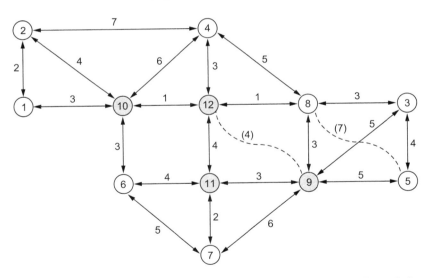

Figure 4.37   Graph contraction using an arbitrary node ranking—contracting node 8

9   *Contracting node 9*—No shortcuts need to be added (figure 4.38).

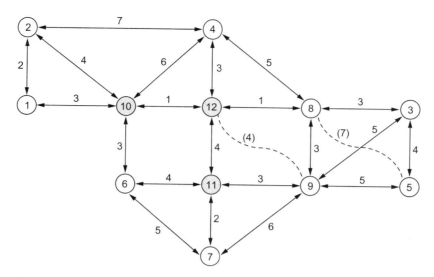

Figure 4.38   Graph contraction using an arbitrary node ranking—contracting node 9

10 *Contracting node 10*—No shortcuts need to be added (figure 4.39).

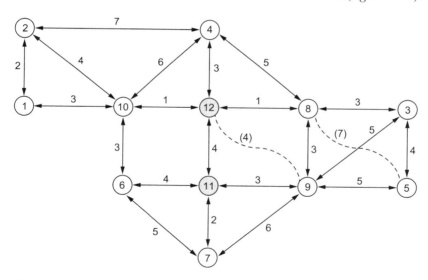

Figure 4.39   Graph contraction using an arbitrary node ranking—contracting node 10

11 *Contracting node 11*—No shortcuts need to be added (figure 4.40).

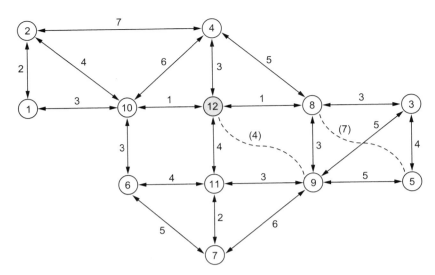

Figure 4.40   Graph contraction using an arbitrary node ranking—contracting node 11

12 *Contracting node 12*—No shortcuts need to be added (figure 4.41).

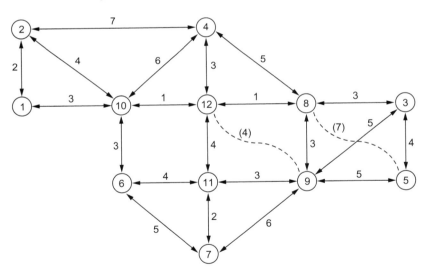

Figure 4.41   Graph contraction using an arbitrary node ranking—contracting node 12

The contracted graph can now be queried using a bidirectional Dijkstra's search. In the following figures, the numbers in brackets denote the cost of the added shortcut.

The upward graph in figure 4.42 shows the forward Dijkstra's search from the source to the target. The solid lines represent the visited edges, and the bold solid lines represent the shortest path between the source node and the meeting node.

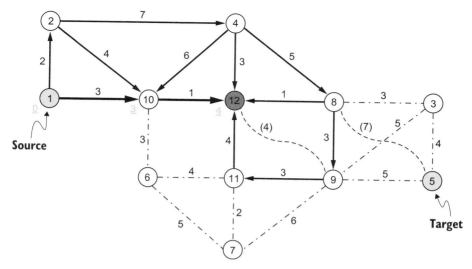

Figure 4.42   Solving a road network problem using the CH algorithm—upward graph

The downward graph in figure 4.43 shows the backward Dijkstra's search from the target to the source. The solid lines represent the visited edges, and the bold solid lines represent the shortest path between the target node and the meeting node.

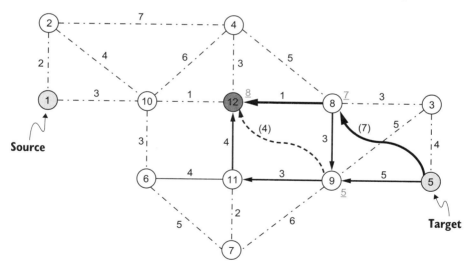

Figure 4.43   Solving a road network problem using the CH algorithm—downward graph

The minimum is at node 12 $(4 + 8 = 12)$, so node 12 is the meeting point (figure 4.44).

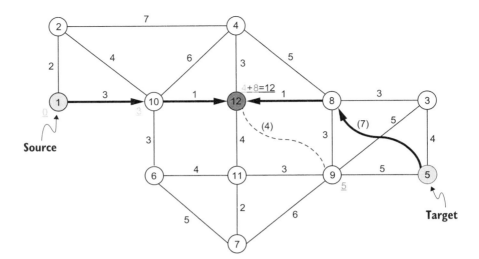

Figure 4.44   Solving a road network problem using the CH algorithm—meeting point

The shortest path will be 1-10-12-8-5. However, this path contains a shortcut (5-8). The actual arc (8-3-5) needs to be unpacked according to the shortcut pointer (node 3) stored during the contraction process. The actual shortest path is 1-10-12-8-3-4 with a cost of 12 (figure 4.45).

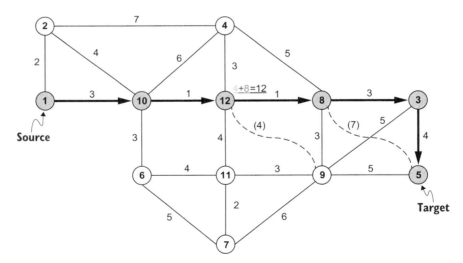

Figure 4.45   Solving a road network problem using the CH algorithm—shortest path

Listing 4.6 shows the implementation in Python. Note that the code for graph initialization has been omitted here, as it is similar to previous examples, but it can be viewed in the full listing in the book's GitHub repo. Likewise, the code for graph visualization is also in the full listing.

Listing 4.6   Contraction hierarchy with predetermined node order

```
import networkx as nx

shortcuts = {}
shortest_paths = dict(nx.all_pairs_dijkstra_path_length(G,
➥ weight="weight"))
current_G = G.copy()
for node in G.nodes:
    current_G.remove_node(node)
    current_shortest_paths = dict(
        nx.all_pairs_dijkstra_path_length(current_G, weight="weight")
    )
    for u in current_shortest_paths:
        if u == node:
            continue
        SP_contracted = current_shortest_paths[u]
        SP_original = shortest_paths[u]
        for v in SP_contracted:
            if u == v or node == v:
                continue
            if (
                SP_contracted[v] != SP_original[v]
                and G.has_edge(node, u)
                and G.has_edge(node, v)
            ):
                G.add_edge(u, v, weight=SP_original[v],contracted=True)
                shortcuts[(u,v)] = node
```

Copy the main graph so that the nodes are only removed from the copy, not the main graph.

Contract the node by removing it from the copied graph.

Recalculate the shortest path matrix, now with the node contracted.

Add a shortcut edge to replace the changed shortest path, and keep track of it so we can uncontract it when querying later.

You will notice that the preceding code creates two shortcut edges for each contraction, one from *u* to *v*, and one in reverse from *v* to *u*. As we are using an undirected graph, this duplication has no effect, since the edge (*u*, *v*) is the same as the edge (*v*, *u*).

Querying the generated graph requires a simple modified bidirectional Dijkstra's search, where neighbor nodes are disqualified for expansion if they are lower in the hierarchy than the current node. For the purposes of this book, we will use `networkx .algorithms.shortest_paths.weighted.bidirectional_dijkstra`, with a slight change (only nodes of higher hierarchy than the current node can be explored). As a continuation of listing 4.6, the following code snippet shows the querying process. The full code for the modified algorithm can be found in listing 4.6 in the book's GitHub repo:

Run bidirectional Dijkstra's using NetworkX.

```
sln = bidirectional_dijkstra(G, 1, 5, hierarchy, weight="weight")

uncontracted_route = [sln.result[0]]
for u, v in zip(sln.result[:-1], sln.result[1:]): ]]
    if (u, v) in shortcuts: ]]
        uncontracted_route.append(shortcuts[(u, v)])
    uncontracted_route.append(v)
```

Unpack any edges that are marked as contracted, and generate the unpacked route.

The preceding code will generate an unpacked route that can be visualized as in figure 4.46.

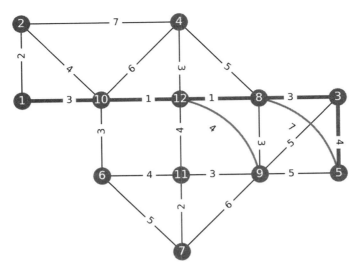

Figure 4.46   The solution path after unpacking the contracted edges. The original route returned by bidirectional Dijkstra's passes through the contracted edge (8,5), which is then unpacked into (8,3) and (3,5).

Contraction hierarchies expend a great deal of processing time on the preprocessing phase, but a correctly pruned graph (i.e., where the node contraction order is good) allows for much faster queries. While the small reduction in search space is negligible on a graph with 21 nodes, some graphs can be pruned up to 40%, resulting in significant cost and time savings when querying. In the example from listing 4.6, the search from node 1 to node 5 explores 11 nodes, as compared to the original 16 nodes in a normal bidirectional Dijkstra's. That's almost a 33% reduction!

4.4   *Applying informed search to a routing problem*

Let's look again at the University of Toronto routing problem introduced in section 3.5. We need to find the shortest path from the King Edward VII Equestrian statue at Queen's Park to the Bahen Centre for Information Technology. The search space is represented by a road network in which the intersections and points of interest (including the origin and destination) are nodes, and edges are used to represent road segments with weight (e.g., distance, travel time, fuel consumption, number of turns, etc.). Let's look at how we can find the shortest path using the informed search algorithms discussed in this chapter.

4.4.1   *Hill climbing for routing*

Listing 4.7 uses two functions from `optalgotools.routing` that generate random and child routes. While the actual HC algorithm is deterministic, the randomized initial route means that different results can be achieved over different runs. To counter this, we'll use a higher *n* value, which allows a broader diversity of children routes, so an optimal (or near optimal) solution will more likely be achieved.

Listing 4.7   U of T routing using the hill climbing algorithm

```
def Hill_Climbing(G, origin, destination, n=20):
    time_start = process_time()
    costs = []

    current = randomized_search(G, origin.osmid, destination.osmid)
    costs.append(cost(G, current))

    neighbours = list(islice(get_child(G, current), n))
    space_required = getsizeof(neighbours)
    shortest = min(neighbours, key=lambda route: cost(G, route))

    while cost(G, shortest) < cost(G, current):
        current = shortest
        neighbours = list(islice(get_child(G, current), n))
        shortest = min(neighbours, key=lambda route: cost(G, route))
        costs.append(cost(G, current))

    route = current
    time_end = process_time()
    return Solution(route, time_end - time_start, space_required, costs)
```

Track time and costs for comparison.

Generate an initial route randomly.

Get k neighbors (children).

While the implementation in listing 4.7 is deterministic, the initial route is still randomized. That means it is possible to get different results across runs. Hill climbing will return some decent results, as there are few local optimal points in the route function. However, larger search spaces will naturally have more local maxima and plateaus, and the HC algorithm will get stuck quickly.

Figure 4.47 shows a final solution of 806.892 m, which happens to be the same as the result generated by Dijkstra's algorithm in chapter 3 (an optimal solution).

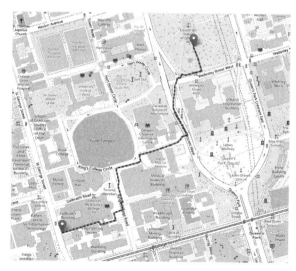

Figure 4.47   Shortest path solution generated using hill climbing. The solution shown here uses an *n* value of 100, which increases the total processing time but returns better and more consistent results.

4.4.2　*Beam search for routing*

A beam search for routing will follow much the same format as the HC search, with the exception that a "beam" of solutions is kept for comparison at each iteration. The full code for listing 4.8, with the graph initialization and visualization, is in the book's GitHub repo.

Listing 4.8　U of T routing using the beam search algorithm

```python
def get_beam(G, beam, n=20):
    new_beam = []
    for route in beam:
        neighbours = list(islice(get_child(G, route), n))   ◀── Generate child
        new_beam.extend(neighbours)                              routes for each
    return new_beam                                              route in the beam.

def Beam_Search(G, origin, destination, k=10, n=20):
    start_time = process_time()
    seen = set()
    costs = []
    beam = [randomized_search(G, origin.osmid, destination.osmid) for _ in
    ➥ range(k)]

    for route in beam:          ◀──────────────────────────┐
        seen.add(tuple(route))                              │

    pool = []
    children = get_beam(G, beam, n)                         The seen routes must be
    costs.append([cost(G, r) for r in beam])               converted to a tuple so
    for r in children:                                     they are hashable and
        if tuple(r) in seen:                               can be stored in a set.
            continue
        else:
            pool.append(r)
            seen.add(tuple(r))
    pool += beam                        Keep the k best routes at
    space_required = getsizeof(pool)    each iteration until
    last_beam = None                    generating new beams no
    while beam != last_beam:        ◀──┘ longer finds better solutions.
        last_beam = beam
        beam = heapq.nsmallest(k, pool, key=lambda r: cost(G, r))

        for route in beam:
            seen.add(tuple(route))

        pool = []
        children = get_beam(G, beam, n)
        costs.append([cost(G, r) for r in beam])
        for r in children:
            if tuple(r) in seen:
                continue
            else:
                pool.append(r)
                seen.add(tuple(r))
```

Initialize empty sets to keep track of visited nodes and path costs.

```
        pool += beam
        space_required = (
            getsizeof(pool) if getsizeof(pool) > space_required else
          ➥ space_required
        )
    route = min(beam, key=lambda r: cost(G, r))  ◄─┐ The final route is the best
    end_time = process_time()                       └─ route in the last beam.
    return Solution(

                                                    Return the final route, its cost,
                                                    processing time, and space required.
        route, end_time - start_time, space_required, np.rot90(costs))  ◄─────┘
```

Beam searches for routing are particularly costly, as they require multiple child routes to be generated for each beam. Like HC, generating more children results in a broader penetration of the search space, and thus is more likely to return a solution that is closer to or reaches the optimal solution. Figure 4.48 shows a final solution generated by beam search.

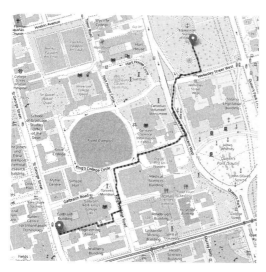

Figure 4.48 **Shortest path using a beam search algorithm. This solution was generated using *k* = 10 and *n* = 20, which means that 20 routes were generated for each route in the beam, and the top 10 routes were kept for each new beam. Lower *k* and *n* values will improve processing time but reduce the likelihood of generating a near-optimal or optimal solution.**

4.4.3 A* for routing

The next listing shows how we can use A* search to find the shortest route between two points of interest.

Listing 4.9 U of T routing using A*

```
import osmnx
from optalgotools.routing import (cost, draw_route, astar_heuristic)
from optalgotools.structures import Node
from optalgotools.algorithms.graph_search import A_Star
from optalgotools.utilities import haversine_distance

reference = (43.661667, -79.395)  ◄─── Set up King's College Cir, Toronto, ON as a reference.

G = osmnx.graph_from_point(reference, dist=300, clean_periphery=True,
```

```
 ➥  simplify=True)  ◀────┛ Create a graph.
                                          Set up the King Edward VII
 origin = (43.664527, -79.392442) ◀────  equestrian statue as the origin.
 destination = (43.659659, -79.397669) ◀────  Set up the Bahen Centre for Information
                                               Technology at U of T as the destination.

 origin_id = osmnx.distance.nearest_nodes(G, origin[1], origin[0])
 destination_id = osmnx.distance.nearest_nodes(G, destination[1],
 ➥  destination[0])
```

Get the osmid of the nearest nodes to the points.

```
 origin = Node(graph=G, osmid=origin_id)
 destination = Node(graph=G, osmid=destination_id)
```

Convert the source and destination nodes to Node.

```
 solution = A_Star(G, origin, destination, astar_heuristic,
 ➥  heuristic_kwargs={"measuring_dist": haversine_distance})
 route = solution.result
 print(f"Cost: {cost(G,route)} m")
 print(f"Process time: {solution.time} s")
 print(f"Space required: {solution.space} bytes")
 print(f"Explored nodes: {solution.explored}")
 draw_route(G,route)
```

Find the shortest path using A*.

Print the cost, processing time, space required, and explored nodes, and draw the final route.

The optimality of the A* search depends on the heuristic used. In this case, the solution returned is not optimal, but the incredibly high processing speed achieved is more important for most applications. Figure 4.49 shows a final solution generated by A* search.

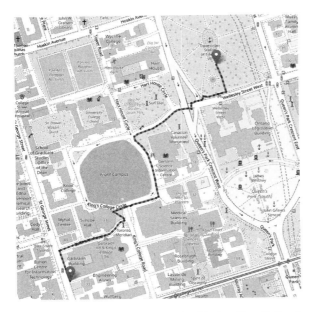

Figure 4.49   Shortest path using the A* algorithm. Better heuristic functions that closely approach the actual costs from any node to the goal will return better results.

4.4.4   Contraction hierarchies for routing

In order to run CH on the road network graph, we first need to rank the nodes by importance and then contract the graph. For this example, we are selecting edge difference (ED) as our measure of node importance.

Listing 4.10   U of T routing using CH

```
def edge_differences(G, sp):
    ed = {}
    degrees = dict(G.degree)
    for node in G.nodes:
        req_edges = 0
        neighbours = list(G.neighbors(node))

        if len(neighbours)==0: ed[node] = - degrees[node]

        for u, v in G.in_edges(node):
            for v, w in G.out_edges(node):
                if u == w: continue
                if v in sp[u][w]:
                    req_edges += 1
        ed[node] = req_edges - degrees[node]

    return dict(sorted(ed.items(), key=lambda x: x, reverse=True))
```

Some nodes are essentially dead ends, where they have no outbound edges. These nodes have an ED equal to their degree.

We can ignore two-way edges—an inbound edge and an outbound edge that originate and terminate at the same node.

The edge difference is the difference between edges that need to be added to the graph and the degree of the node.

Contracting the graph is as simple as adding an edge for every shortest path that gets altered by the contraction. The full code for graph contraction can be found in the book's GitHub repo. Contracted edges are marked with an attribute called *midpoint*, which stores the ID of the node that was contracted. Following a modified bidirectional Dijkstra's similar to that used in listing 4.6, the final route can be easily unpacked using the following snippet of code:

```
def unpack(G, u,v):
    u = int(u)
    v = int(v)
    if "midpoint" in G[u][v][0]:
        midpoint = G[u][v][0]["midpoint"]
        return unpack(G,u,midpoint) + unpack(G,midpoint, v)
    return [u]

route = []
for u,v in zip(solution.result[:-1], solution.result[1:]):
    route.extend(unpack(G,u,v))
route += [solution.result[-1]]
print(route)
```

For every midpoint unpacked, recursively unpack the resulting two edges, as some contracted edges may contain other contracted edges.

Unpack every node pair in the contracted route.

The GitHub repo also contains the full Python implementation of CH for routing. The route generated is identical to that shown by a normal bidirectional Dijkstra's algorithm (such as in chapter 3). If you will recall, running the normal bidirectional Dijkstra's in chapter 3 yielded a result where 282 nodes were explored during the search. For our CH result, only 164 nodes were explored, which means more than a 40% reduction of search space! Thus, while the optimality of the algorithm remains unchanged, contraction hierarchies allow for much bigger spaces to be searched in a reasonable amount of time.

Table 4.1 compares the search algorithms discussed in this chapter when applied to the U of T routing problem. A similar table can be found in chapter 3 for blind search algorithms.

Table 4.1   Comparing informed search algorithms in terms of time and space complexities, where *b* is the branching factor, *w* is the beam width, *d* is the shallowest graph depth, *E* is the number of edges, and *V* is the number of vertices

Algorithm	Cost (meters)	Time (s)	Space (bytes)	Explored	Time complexity	Space complexity
Hill climbing	806.892	21.546	976	400 nodes	$O(\infty)$	$O(b)$
Beam search	825.929	44.797	1,664	800 nodes	$O(wd)$	$O(wb)$
A* search	846.92	0.063	8,408	80 nodes	$O(b^d)$	$O(b^d)$
CH with bidirectional Dijkstra's	806.892	0.0469	72	164 nodes	$O(E + V \log V)$	$O(b^d/2)$

NOTE   The time listed for CH with bidirectional Dijkstra's is only for querying. Remember that the preprocessing step is usually quite costly. In this case, contracting the road network of 404 nodes took around 24.03125 seconds.

While hill climbing and beam search produced respectable results, they were too costly in terms of time to be useful for larger graphs. A* gives the fastest results but a non-optimal heuristic function, and it required excessive space for the heuristic values, so it has its own disadvantages. CH with bidirectional Dijkstra's is the only algorithm in table 4.1 that guarantees optimality, but the costly preprocessing step may not be suitable for all applications.

When comparing search algorithms, it is important to be aware of the constraints for any given problem and to select an algorithm based on those constraints. For example, certain implementations of hill climbing may result in rapid exit conditions. If the goal is to maximize the number of problems solved (and if local maxima are an acceptable result), HC algorithms result in quick solutions that have some degree of optimality. On the other hand, preprocessing-heavy algorithms like CH offer incredibly low space costs (even more so when implemented with a bidirectional search), as well as rapid searches for guaranteed optimal solutions (if using Dijkstra's algorithm). For high-volume usage implementations where preprocessing is not a concern (e.g., Uber), contraction hierarchies are a viable choice. In fact, the osrm package used in this book is primarily based on an implementation of contraction hierarchies.

Pandana, a Python library for network analysis, uses CH to calculate shortest paths and fast travel accessibility metrics. In Pandana, the backend code for CH is in C++ but can be accessed using Python. Pyrosm is another Python library for reading and parsing OpenStreetMap data. It is similar to OSMnx but faster, and it works with Pandana.

The next listing is a snippet of code that calculates the shortest distances to an amenity of interest in a selected city using the CH algorithm implemented in Pandana. The complete code is available in the book's GitHub repo.

Listing 4.11 Using CH to calculate the shortest distances to amenities

```
from pyrosm import OSM, get_data
import numpy as np
import matplotlib.pyplot as plt

osm = OSM(get_data("Toronto"))
nodes, edges = osm.get_network(network_type="driving", nodes=True)
hospitals = osm.get_pois({"amenity": ["hospital"]})

G = osm.to_graph(nodes, edges, graph_type='pandana')

hospitals['geometry'] = hospitals.centroid #E
hospitals = hospitals.dropna(subset=['lon', 'lat'])

G.precompute(1000)

G.set_pois(category='hospitals', maxdist=1000, maxitems=10,
    x_col=hospitals.lon, y_col=hospitals.lat)

nearest_five = G.nearest_pois(1000, "hospitals", num_pois=5)
```

- Get data for the city, region, or country of interest.
- Get nodes and edges from the road network with a "driving" type.
- Get points of interest for a certain amenity in the city.
- Create a network graph.
- Precompute distances up to 1,000 meters.
- Ensure all hospitals are represented as points.
- Attach hospitals to the Pandana graph.
- For each node, find the distances to the five closest hospitals up to 1,000 meters away.

In this example, OpenStreetMap is used to get data on the city of Toronto, and a subset is created to contain data on the city's hospitals. A Pandana object is then created, and the range queries are precomputed, given a horizon distance (e.g., 1,000 meters) to represent the reachable nodes within this distance. For each node in the network, we can find distances to the five closest hospitals up to 1,000 meters away using the fast CH algorithm implemented in Pandana.

In the next part of the book, we'll look at trajectory-based algorithms starting with the simulated annealing algorithm and then the tabu search algorithm. These algorithms improve local search and are less susceptible to getting stuck in local optima than the previously discussed greedy algorithms, which only accept improving moves.

Summary

- Informed search algorithms use domain-specific knowledge or heuristic information to streamline the search process while striving for optimal solutions or accepting near-optimal ones if necessary.
- Informed search algorithms can be used to solve minimum spanning tree (MST) problems and to find the shortest path between two nodes in a graph.

- The Borůvka algorithm, Jarník-Prim algorithm, and Kruskal algorithm are informed search algorithms for solving MST problems. An MST is a tree that contains the least weight among all the other spanning trees of a connected weighted graph. Kruskal's algorithm is a greedy algorithm that computes the MST for an undirected connected weighted graph by repeatedly adding the next shortest edge that doesn't produce a cycle.

- Hill climbing (HC), beam search, best-first search, the A* algorithm, and contraction hierarchies (CH) are examples of informed search algorithms that can be used to find the shortest path between two nodes.

- The HC algorithm is a local greedy search algorithm that tries to improve on the efficiency of depth-first by incorporating domain-specific knowledge or heuristic information.

- Beam search expands the most promising node within a limited predefined set defined by the beam width.

- Best-first search is a greedy algorithm that always expands the node that is closest to the goal node based on heuristic information only.

- The A* algorithm is a special case of a best-first algorithm that incorporates both the actual cost and a heuristic estimate of the cost to get to the goal from a given state.

- CH is a speed-up technique for improving the performance of pathfinding. During the preprocessing phase, each node is contracted in order of importance (from least important to most important), and shortcuts are added to preserve the shortest paths. Then the bidirectional Dijkstra's algorithm is applied to the resultant augmented graph to compute the shortest path between the source node and the target node.

Part 2

Trajectory-based algorithms

Now that part 1 has armed you with a solid foundation in optimization, we'll continue our journey into the realm of optimization algorithms, focusing on trajectory-based algorithms. This part of the book, consisting of two chapters, will take your optimization knowledge to the next level.

In chapter 5, you'll learn about trajectory-based optimization algorithms and, specifically, the simulated annealing algorithm—you'll discover how simulated annealing can be applied to solve continuous and discrete optimization problems. You'll explore function optimization as an example of continuous optimization, tackle puzzle games like Sudoku as instances of constraint satisfaction problems, delve into permutation problems such as the traveling salesman problem, and even apply simulated annealing to real-world problems, like optimizing delivery routes for semi-trucks.

Chapter 6 will introduce you to tabu search as another trajectory-based optimization algorithm. You'll learn the fundamentals of local search and how tabu search builds upon this foundation. This chapter will take you through solving constraint satisfaction problems, continuous optimization problems, routing problems, and balancing assembly lines in manufacturing.

By the end of this part, you'll have a deep understanding of trajectory-based optimization algorithms and the diverse problem domains they can effectively address. These chapters will equip you with valuable tools to tackle complex optimization problems across a wide range of applications.

Simulated annealing 5

In this chapter, we'll look at simulated annealing as a trajectory-based metaheuristic optimization technique. We'll discuss different elements of this algorithm and its adaptation aspects. A number of case studies will be presented to show the ability of this metaheuristic algorithm to solve continuous and discrete optimization problems.

5.1   *Introducing trajectory-based optimization*

Imagine yourself on a hiking trip looking for the lowest valley in a rugged landscape that has many valleys and hills. You don't have access to global information or a map that shows the location of the lowest valley. You start your hiking journey by randomly choosing a direction. You keep moving step by step until you get stuck in a local valley surrounded by hills. You are not highly satisfied with the location, as you believe that there is a lower valley in the area that may be behind the hills. Your curiosity drives you to move up one of the hills to find the lowest valley.

This is exactly what simulated annealing (SA) does. The basic idea of the SA algorithm is to use a stochastic search that follows a trial-and-error approach, accepting changes that improve the objective function and also keeping some changes that are not ideal. In a minimization problem, for example, any better moves or changes that decrease the value of the objective function will be accepted. However, some moves that increase the objective function will also be accepted with a certain probability. SA is a trajectory-based metaheuristic algorithm that can be used to find the global optimum solution for complex optimization problems.

Generally speaking, *metaheuristic algorithms* can be classified into *trajectory-based* and *population-based* algorithms, as shown in figure 5.1.

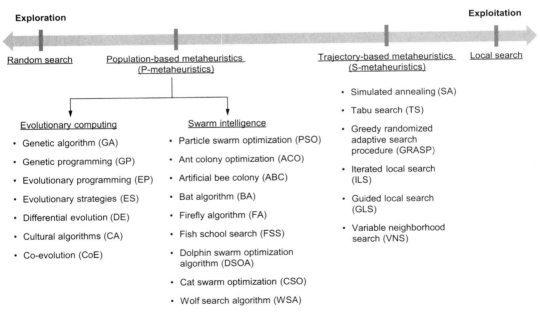

Figure 5.1   Exploration and exploitation of optimization algorithms

Trajectory-based metaheuristic algorithms or *S-metaheuristics*, such as SA or tabu search, use a single search agent that moves through the search space in a piecewise style. A better move or solution is always accepted, while a not-so-good move can be accepted with a certain probability. The steps, or moves, trace a trajectory in the search space, with a nonzero probability that this trajectory can reach the global optimum.

In contrast, *population-based algorithms* or *P-metaheuristics*, such as genetic algorithms, particle swarm optimization, and ant colony optimization, use multiple agents to search for an optimal or near-optimal global solution.

Due to the large diversity of initial populations, population-based algorithms are naturally more exploration-based, whereas single or trajectory-based algorithms are more exploitation-based. The following section explains the SA algorithm in more detail.

5.2   The simulated annealing algorithm

Whether you need to solve a complex nonlinear nondifferential function optimization problem, a puzzle game like Sudoku, an academic course scheduling problem, a travelling salesman problem (TSP), a network design problem, a task allocation problem, a circuit partitioning and placement problem, a production planning and scheduling problem, or even a tennis tournament planning problem, SA can be used as a generic solver for these different continuous and discrete optimization problems.

Let's first look at the details of this solver before we use it to solve different problems. We'll start by shedding some light on the physical annealing process, which was the inspiration for SA.

5.2.1   Physical annealing

Annealing, as a heat treatment process, has been used for centuries across various industries, including metallurgy, glassmaking, and ceramics. For example, in the context of making glass bottles, annealing removes the stresses and strains in the glass resulting from shaping. This is an important step, and if it's not done, the glass may shatter due to the buildup of tension caused by uneven cooling. After the bottles have cooled to room temperature, they are inspected and finally packaged.

Annealing alters a material, causing changes in its properties, such as strength and hardness. This process heats the material to above the recrystallization temperature, maintains a suitable temperature, and then cools the material. As the temperature reduces, the mobility of molecules reduces, with the tendency that molecules will align themselves in a crystalline structure (figure 5.2).

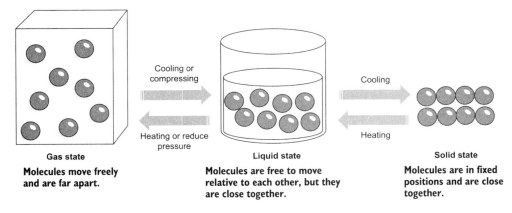

Figure 5.2   **The effect of temperature on the mobility of the molecules**

The aligned structure is the minimum energy state for the system. To ensure that this alignment is obtained, cooling must occur at a sufficiently slow rate. If the substance is cooled too rapidly, a noncrystalline state with irregular three-dimensional patterns may be reached, as illustrated in figure 5.3. Quartz, sodium chloride, diamond, and sugar are examples of crystalline solids that have a regular order for the arrangement of constituent particles, atoms, ions, or molecules. Glass, rubber, pitch, and many plastics are examples of noncrystalline amorphous solids. As you may know, quartz crystals are harder than glass thanks to their symmetrical molecular structure.

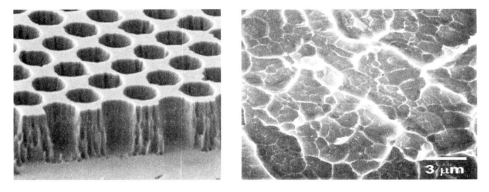

Figure 5.3   **Physical annealing. Left: a metal with a crystalline structure. Right: an amorphous metal with a disordered atomic-scale structure.**

NOTE   The annealing process involves the careful control of the temperature and cooling rate, often called the annealing or cooling schedule. The annealing time should be long enough for the material to undergo the required transformation. If the difference in the temperature rate of change between the outside and inside of a material is too big, this may cause defects and cracks.

The fact that the aligned structure represents the minimum energy state for the system inspired scientists to think about mimicking this process to solve optimization problems. *Simulated* annealing is a computational model that mimics the physical annealing process. In the context of mathematical optimization, the minimum of an objective function represents the minimum energy of the system. SA is an algorithmic implementation of the cooling process, used to find the optimum of an objective function. Table 5.1 outlines the analogy between SA and the physical annealing process.

Table 5.1 **The physical annealing and simulated annealing analogy**

Physical annealing	Simulated annealing
State of a material	Solution of an optimization problem
The energy of a state	The cost of a solution
Temperature	Control parameter (temperature)
High temperature makes molecules move freely	High temperature favors search space exploration
Low temperature restricts molecules' motion	Low temperature leads to exploiting the search space
Gradual cooling helps to reduce stress and increase homogeneity and structural stability.	Gradual cooling helps to avoid getting stuck in suboptimal local minima and to find the globally optimal or near-optimal solution.

In 1953, the first computational model that replicated the physical process of annealing was introduced. This model was presented as a universal method for computing the properties of substances that can be considered collections of individual molecules interacting with each other. S. Kirkpatrick et al. were trailblazers in utilizing SA for optimization, as described in their paper "Optimization by Simulated Annealing" [1]. The following subsection explains the steps involved in the SA algorithm.

5.2.2 *SA pseudocode*

SA employs a Markov chain-based random search approach, which not only accepts new solutions that decrease the objective function (assuming a minimization problem) but can also accept probabilistic solutions that increase objective function values.

Markov chain

The Markov property, named after Russian mathematician Andrey Markov (1856–1922), is a memoryless random process. This means that the next state depends only on the current state and not on the sequence of events that preceded it. A Markov chain (MC) is a stochastic or probabilistic model that describes a sequence of possible moves in which the probability of each move depends only on the state attained in the previous move. This means that the transition from one state to another depends only on the current fully observable state and a transition probability.

(continued)

Following this memoryless random process, the transition between the current known state A, for example, to a next neighboring state B is governed by a transition probability as illustrated in the following figure. Markov chains are used in different domains such as stochastic optimization, economy, speech recognition, weather prediction, and control systems. It's also worth mentioning that Google's PageRank algorithm uses a Markov chain to model the behavior of users navigating the web. SymPy provides a Python implementation for a finite discrete time-homogeneous Markov chain through the class `sympy.stats.DiscreteMarkovChain`.

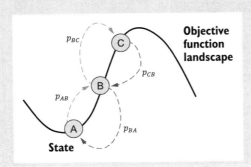

Markov chain—p_{AB}, p_{BA}, p_{BC}, and p_{CB} are transition probabilities between the states A, B, and C.

As illustrated in figure 5.4, a new neighboring solution or state x_k is always accepted if it's an improving solution (i.e., $f(x_k) < f(x_i)$). An improving solution is a solution that gives a lower value for the objective function if we're dealing with a minimization problem or gives a higher value in the case of a maximization problem. In the case of non-improving solutions, such as x_j, the solution can still be probabilistically accepted as a way to avoid the risk of getting trapped in a local minimum. This contrasts with a greedy algorithm's tendency to accept only improving solutions, making greedy algorithms more susceptible to getting stuck in local minima.

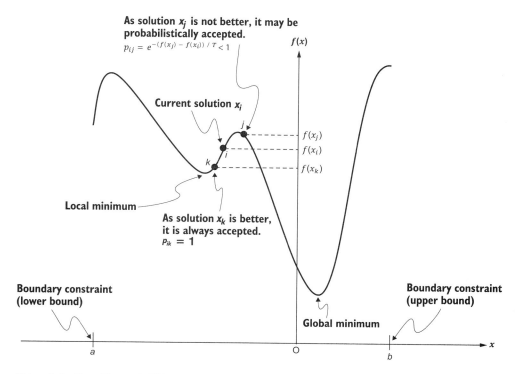

Figure 5.4 Transition probability, assuming a minimization problem. As solution x_k is an improving move, it is always accepted, and as solution x_j is non-improving, it may be probabilistically accepted based on the transition probability.

Temperature T appears in the transition probability and controls the exploration and exploitation in the search space. At high temperatures, non-improving moves will have a good chance of being accepted, but as the temperature decreases, the probability of accepting worse moves decreases. We'll discuss this in more detail in the following subsections.

The steps in SA can be summarized in the following pseudocode.

Algorithm 5.1   The SA algorithm

```
Objective function f(x), x = (x_1, . . . , x_p)^T
Initialize initial temperature T_o, initial guess x_o, iteration counter n=0
and iteration per temperature counter k=0
Set final temperature T_f, kmax maximum number of iterations per temperature
and max number of iterations N
```

```
Define cooling schedule
Begin
While T > T_f and n < N do
     While k<k_{max}
             Move randomly to a new location/state x_n + 1
             Calculate ∆f = f_{n+1}(x_{n+1}) - f_n(x_n)
             If the new solution if better then
                Accept the new solution
             Else
                Generate a random number r
                Accept if exp(-∆f/T)>r
             k=k+1
     End
     Update T according to the cooling schedule
     n = n + 1
End
Return the final solution
```

SA has the advantages of ease of use and the ability to provide optimal or near-optimal solutions for a wide range of continuous and discrete problems. The main drawbacks of this algorithm are the need to tune many parameters and the occasional slow convergence of the algorithm to the optimal or near-optimal solutions.

Aside from this original SA algorithm—classical simulated annealing (CSA)—various variants have been proposed to improve the algorithm's performance. For example, fast simulated annealing (FSA) is a semi-local search and consists of occasional long jumps. Dual annealing is a stochastic global optimization algorithm that is useful for dealing with complex nonlinear optimization problems. It is based on the combined classical simulated annealing and fast simulated annealing algorithms. The generalized simulated annealing (GSA) algorithm uses a distorted Cauchy-Lorentz visiting distribution [2].

Quantum annealing (QA)

In quantum mechanics, a quantum particle is treated as an electromagnetic wave that can penetrate with a certain probability through a potential barrier. Due to the wave nature of matter on the quantum level, there is indeed some probability that a quantum particle can traverse such a barrier if the barrier is thin enough. This phenomenon is known as quantum tunneling. The quantum tunneling effect is a phenomenon whereby wave functions or particles can penetrate through a supposedly impassable barrier even if the total energy of the particle is less than the barrier height.

As illustrated in the following figure, SA uses a thermal jump to push the search particle out of the local valley to avoid getting trapped in local minima. QA, on the other hand, searches an energy landscape to find an optimal or near-optimal solution by applying quantum effects. Instead of just walking through the landscape of the function, quantum annealing can tunnel through. This allows the algorithm to escape from local minima using quantum tunneling (tunnel effect) instead of the thermal jumps used in SA.

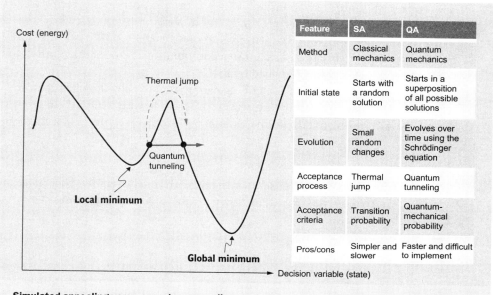

Simulated annealing versus quantum annealing

In QA, a number of candidate states are initialized with equal weights. Quantum-mechanical probability is used to change adiabatically and gradually the amplitudes of all states in parallel. For more information and an example of quantum annealers, see the D-Wave implementation: https://docs.dwavesys.com/docs/latest/c_gs_2.html.

The following subsections explain the different components of the SA algorithm, starting with the transition probability that allows SA to accept or reject non-improving moves.

5.2.3   *Acceptance probability*

Unlike hill climbing (see section 4.3.1), SA probabilistically allows downward steps, controlled by the current temperature and how bad the move is. In SA, better moves are always accepted. As shown in figure 5.4, non-improving moves can be probabilistically accepted based on the Boltzmann-Gibbs distribution.

In thermodynamics, a state at a temperature t has a probability of an increase in the energy magnitude ΔE given by the Boltzmann-Gibbs distribution as in equation 5.1:

$$p(\Delta E) = e^{-\frac{\Delta E}{k \times t}}$$

5.1

where k is the Boltzmann constant, which is the proportionality factor that relates the average relative kinetic energy of particles in a gas with the thermodynamic temperature of the gas, and which has the value of $1.380,649 \times 10^{-23}$ m² kg s⁻² K⁻¹. However, there's no need to use this constant in a computational model that mimics the physical annealing process, so it's replaced by 1.

Moreover, the change in the energy can be replaced by the change in the objective function as a way to quantify the search progress toward the optimal or near-optimal state. So ΔE can be linked with the change of the objective function using equation 5.2:

$$\Delta E = \gamma \Delta f \qquad\qquad \textbf{5.2}$$

where γ is a real constant. For simplicity, and without altering the core meaning, we can use $k = 1$ and $\gamma = 1$. Thus, the transition probability p simply becomes

$$p(\Delta f, T) = e^{-\frac{\Delta f}{T}} \qquad\qquad \textbf{5.3}$$

where T is the temperature of the system. To determine whether or not we accept a change, we usually use a random number r in the interval [0,1] as a threshold. Thus, if $p > r$, or $p = e^{(-\Delta f/T)} > r$, the move is accepted. Otherwise, the move is rejected.

If P_{ij} is the probability of moving from point x_i to x_j, then P_{ij} is calculated using

$$P_{ij} = e^{-\Delta f/T} > r \qquad\qquad \textbf{5.4}$$

The probability P_{ij} is called transition or acceptance probability. Accepting non-improving moves probabilistically makes the algorithm able to avoid getting trapped in some local minima. If the acceptance probability is set to 0, SA behaves similarly to hill climbing, as it will only accept solutions that are better than the current one. Conversely, if the acceptance probability is set to 1, SA becomes more exploratory, as it will always accept worse solutions, making it more akin to a random search.

The probability of accepting a worse state is a function of both the temperature of the system and the change in the cost function. As the temperature decreases, the probability of accepting worse moves decreases. Temperature can be seen as a parameter to balance the exploration and the exploitation in the search space. At high temperatures, the acceptance probability is high, which means that the algorithm accepts most of the moves to explore the parameter space. On the other hand, when the temperature is low, the acceptance probability is low, meaning that the algorithm restricts exploration. As shown in figure 5.5, if $T = 0$, no non-improving moves are accepted. In this case, SA is converted into hill climbing. As can be seen, the cooling process has an important effect on the search progress. The next section will present the different components of the cooling schedules used in SA.

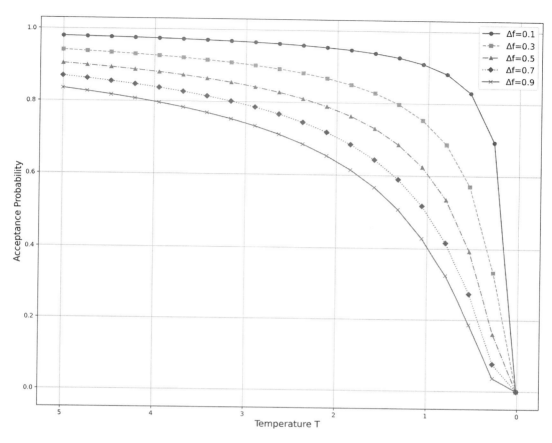

Figure 5.5 **Change of acceptance probability with the temperature and the change in the objective function.** The objective function change is the difference in the objective function's value between the current solution and a candidate solution. In minimization problems, a positive objective function change indicates that the candidate solution is worse than the current solution. The acceptance probability gets lower as the objective function change increases. At high temperatures, SA tends to explore more by accepting non-improving moves. As the temperature gets lower, the algorithm restricts exploration, favoring exploitation.

Given that the Boltzmann-based acceptance probability takes significant computational time (~1/3 of the SA computations), lookup tables or non-exponential probability formulas can be used instead. A lookup table can be generated by performing the exponential calculations offline only once for a range of values for changes in f and T. Other non-exponential probability formulas, such as $p(\Delta f) = 1 - \Delta f / T$, can be used as an acceptance probability. This formula should be normalized to make sure that the maximum value is 1 and the minimum value is 0.

In a computational model like SA, there is no need to strictly mimic the thermo-dynamic models that govern the physical annealing process. Figure 5.6 shows the difference between exponential and non-exponential acceptance probability functions. The code is available in the book's GitHub repo. The difference between exponential and non-exponential acceptance probability functions is small for small changes in the objective function—you can experiment with this using the provided code.

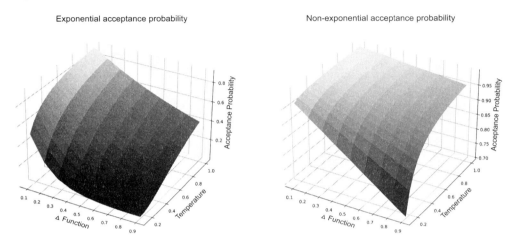

Figure 5.6   Exponential versus non-exponential acceptance probability

As temperature is part of the acceptance probability, it plays an important role in controlling the behavior of SA. The following subsection looks at how we can control the temperature to achieve a trade-off between exploration and exploitation.

5.2.4   *The annealing process*

The annealing process in SA involves the careful control of temperature and the cooling rate, often called the *annealing schedule*. This process involves defining the following parameters:

- Starting temperature
- Temperature decrement following a cooling schedule
- Number of iterations at each temperature
- Final temperature

This is shown in figure 5.7.

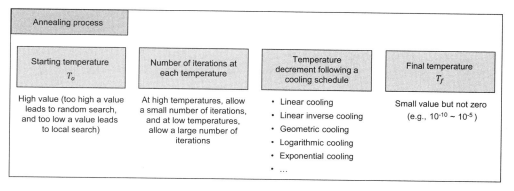

Figure 5.7   Annealing process parameters

The following subsections provide in-depth information about each of these parameters.

INITIAL TEMPERATURE

The choice of the right initial temperature is crucially important. As shown in equation 5.4, for a given change Δf

- If T is too high ($T \to \infty$), then $p \to 1$, which means almost all the changes will be accepted and the algorithm will behave like a random search algorithm.
- If T is too low ($T \to 0$), then any $\Delta f > 0$ (worse solution assuming a minimization problem) will rarely be accepted as $p \to 0$, and thus the diversity of the solution is limited, but any improvement (i.e., any $\Delta f < 0$ in the case of a minimization problem) will almost always be accepted. In this case, SA behaves like a local search and may easily become trapped in local minima.

To find a suitable starting temperature, we can use any available information about the objective function. If we know the maximum change $\max(\Delta f)$ of the objective function, we can use this to estimate an initial temperature T_0 for a given acceptance probability p_0 using equation 5.5:

$$T_o \approx -\frac{\max(\Delta f)}{\ln(p_o)}$$

5.5

If the potential maximum alteration of the objective function is unknown, we can use the following heuristic approach:

1. Initiate evaluations at a very high temperature to allow for nearly all changes to be accepted.

2 Reduce the temperature quickly until roughly 50% to 60% of the inferior moves are accepted.

3 Use this temperature as the new initial temperature T_o for proper and relatively slow cooling processing.

TEMPERATURE DECREMENT

The cooling schedule is the rate at which the temperature is systematically decreased as the algorithm proceeds. This schedule is among the tunable parameters of SA. The following cooling schedules are commonly used:

- *Linear cooling schedule*—The temperature is decremented linearly using equation 5.6:

$$T = T_o - \beta_i \qquad \textbf{5.6}$$

where T_o is the initial temperature, i is the pseudo time for iterations, and β is the cooling rate, which should be chosen in such a way that $T \to 0$ when $i \to i_f$ (or the maximum number N of iterations). This usually gives

$$\beta = \frac{T_o - T_f}{i_f} \qquad \textbf{5.7}$$

This cooling schedule is simple and easy to implement, but may not be the best choice for all types of problems. Moreover, it requires prior knowledge or assumptions about the maximum number of iterations.

- *Linear-inverse cooling schedule*—In linear-inverse cooling, the temperature decreases quickly at high temperatures and more gradually at low temperatures, as per equation 5.8. In this equation, a is the cooling factor and should be between 0 and 1:

$$T(i) = \frac{T_o}{1 + \alpha_i} \qquad \textbf{5.8}$$

- *Geometric cooling schedule*—A geometric cooling schedule essentially decreases the temperature by a cooling factor $0 < a < 1$ following equation 5.9:

$$T(i) = T_o \alpha^i \qquad \textbf{5.9}$$

The cooling process should be slow enough to allow the system to stabilize easily. In practice, $a = 0.7 \sim 0.95$ is commonly used. The higher the value of a, the longer it will take to reach the final (low) temperature. The main advantage of the geometric method is that $T \to 0$ when $i \to \infty$, and thus there is no need to specify the maximum number of iterations. Moreover, the geometric annealing schedule provides more gradual cooling, as shown in figure 5.8.

- *Logarithmic cooling schedule*—In this cooling schedule, the temperature is decreased logarithmically according to equation 5.10:

$$T(i) = \frac{T_o}{1 + \alpha \log(1 + i)}$$

5.10

where $\alpha > 1$. Theoretically, this cooling process asymptotically converges toward the global minimum. However, it requires prohibitive computing time.

- *Exponential cooling schedule*—In this cooling schedule, the temperature is decreased exponentially according to equation 5.11:

$$T(i) = T_o e^{-\alpha i^{\frac{1}{n}}}$$

5.11

where α is the cooling factor and n is the dimensionality of the model space. In this cooling process, the temperature is decreased very quickly during the first iterations, but the speed of the exponential decay is slowed down later and can be controlled using the cooling factor.

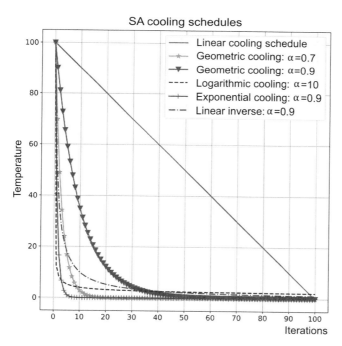

Figure 5.8 Different SA cooling schedules

As you can see, these cooling schedules are all monotonically decreasing functions that don't explicitly take into consideration how the search is progressing. In section 5.2.5, we'll look at a nonmonotonic adaptive cooling schedule.

ITERATIONS AT EACH TEMPERATURE

Before applying the cooling schedule (i.e., decreasing the temperature), it is important to allow a sufficient number of iterations at each temperature level to stabilize the system at that temperature. Typically, this is achieved by using a constant value. For example, the number of iterations at each temperature might be exponential to the problem size (e.g., the number of cities in TSP as a discrete problem or the dimensionality of a mathematical function in the case of continuous problems). However, this value can be altered dynamically.

One way to accomplish this is by limiting the number of iterations during the exploration phase of the search at the beginning, when the temperature is high. For example, when the temperature is high, we could perform a small number of iterations at each temperature and then implement the cooling process. As the search continues and the temperature decreases, we can shift toward exploitation by conducting a larger number of iterations at lower temperatures.

FINAL TEMPERATURE

It is usual to let the temperature decrease until it reaches zero. However, this can make the algorithm run a lot longer, especially when certain cooling schedules, such as geometric cooling, are used. In reality, it is not necessary to let the temperature reach zero if the chances of accepting a non-improving move at the current temperature are almost the same as if the temperature were zero. Therefore, the stopping criteria can be either of the following:

- A suitably low temperature ($T_f = 10^{-10} \sim 10^{-5}$)
- When the system reaches a "frozen" or minimum energy state (assuming a minimization problem), where neither better nor worse moves are accepted

5.2.5   *Adaptation in SA*

Several parameters in SA can be used to make the algorithm more adaptive to the search's progress. The initial temperature, the cooling schedule, and the number of iterations per temperature are the most critical of these parameters. Other components include the cost function, the method of generating neighborhood solutions, and the acceptance probability.

As illustrated in figure 5.9, the initial temperature can be used to control the exploration and exploitation behavior of SA. A high temperature leads to a high level of exploration, and a low temperature results in exploitative behavior (i.e., restricting the search around neighbors).

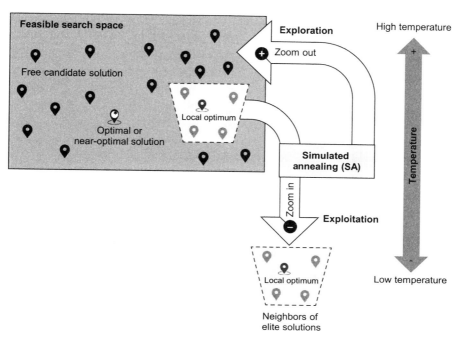

Figure 5.9   Effect of temperature in SA. High temperatures result in more exploration, whereas a low temperature restricts the exploration and leads to more exploitation in the search space.

You can think about it in terms of the movement of molecules. Assume that the molecule is the search agent. At high temperatures, the molecule moves freely in the search space, exploring different solutions. At low temperatures, the movement of the molecule becomes limited, so the exploration is restricted, and the search agent focuses on a specific part of the search space. With high temperatures at the beginning of the search, SA oscillates due to the exploration behavior that makes the algorithm accept non-improving moves with high probability. As the search progresses and the temperature gets lower, the algorithm starts to stabilize due to the exploitation behavior that makes the algorithm accept fewer non-improving moves and instead focus on the elite improving solutions.

It is always recommended that you start with a high temperature and gradually decrease it as the search progresses. However, the right initial temperature is problem-dependent. You can try different values and see which leads to better solutions. Some researchers suggest doing this adaptively, using other search methods or metaheuristics, such as a genetic algorithm.

Cooling schedules can also be used to make the algorithm more adaptive. Different cooling schedules can be used in different phases of the search, taking into consideration that most useful work is done in the middle of the schedule. Reheating can also be tried if no progress is observed. Cooling may take place every time a move (or a specific number of moves) is accepted. A nonmonotonic adaptive cooling schedule can be tried, where an adaptive factor is used, based on the difference between the current solution objective and the best objective achieved by the algorithm up to that moment, according to the following formula:

$$T = \left(\frac{1 + (f_i - f^*)}{f_i} \right) T(i)$$

5.12

where T is the system temperature at each state transition, $T(i)$ is the current temperature, f_i is the value of the objective function at iteration i, and f is the best value of the objective function obtained so far.

Another adaptation parameter is the number of iterations per temperature. This number can be adaptively changed by allowing a small number of iterations at high temperatures and allowing a large number of iterations at low temperatures to fully explore the local optimum.

The adaptation ability of the SA algorithm can be also influenced by the objective function and the representation of problem constraints utilized. As a general rule, it is advisable to steer clear of cost functions that yield the same result for multiple states (e.g., the number of edges incorporated in a TSP route). This type of function does not guide the search because it may not change in the objective function from one state to another.

For example, imagine two feasible routes with the same number of edges (i.e., $\Delta f = 0$). Counting on the number of edges as a cost function wouldn't be a good idea. However, many problems have constraints that can be represented in the cost function using reward or penalty terms. One way to make the algorithm more adaptive is to dynamically change the weighting of the reward and penalty terms. In the initial phase, the constraints can be relaxed more than in the advanced phases of the search.

There have been numerous efforts to make the selection and control of SA parameters totally adaptive. One example of such an effort was proposed by Ingber in "Adaptive simulated annealing (ASA): Lessons learned" [3]. ASA automatically adjusts the algorithm parameters that control the temperature schedule, requiring the user to only specify the cooling rate. The method uses a linear random combination of previously accepted steps and parameters to estimate new steps and parameters.

An ASA algorithm with greedy search (ASA-GS) is proposed by Geng et al. to solve the TSP [4]. ASA-GS is based on the classical SA algorithm and utilizes a greedy search technique to speed up the convergence rate. ASA utilizes dynamic adjustments in parameters like the temperature cooling coefficient, greedy search iterations, compulsive accept instances, and probability of accepting a new solution. These adaptive parameter controls aim to enhance the trade-off between quality and time efficiency.

SA finds extensive application across various domains. Its utility extends to solving diverse optimization problems encompassing nonlinear function optimization, TSP, academic course scheduling, network design, task allocation, circuit partitioning and placement, robot motion planning, and vehicle routing, as well as resource allocation and scheduling. The following sections show how you can use SA to solve continuous and discrete optimization problems in different domains.

5.3 *Function optimization*

As an example of continuous optimization problems, let's consider the following simple function optimization problem: find x which minimizes $f(x) = (x - 6)^2$, subject to the constraint $0 \leq x \leq 31$.

We can start with an initial random solution from the range of x. Different neighboring solutions can be generated by adding a random floating value chosen from a Gaussian or normal distribution with a given mean and standard deviation. The random.gauss() function in Python can be used as follows:

```
import random
mu, sigma = 0, 1 # mean and standard deviation
print(random.gauss(mu, sigma))
```

Assume that the initial temperature $T_0 = 5$, the number of iterations per temperature is 2, and the geometric cooling factor $\alpha = 0.85$. Let's carry out a few hand iterations to show how SA can solve this problem:

- *Initialization*—An initial solution is randomly generated, and its cost is evaluated as follows: $x = 2$ and $f(2) = 16$.
- *Iteration 1*—A new solution $x = 2.25$ is generated by adding a random value from a Gaussian distribution using the following code:

  ```
  import numpy as np
  x=x+np.random.normal(mu, sigma, 1)
  ```

  $f(2.25) = 14.06$ is an improving solution and so is accepted.
- *Iteration 2*—A new solution is generated by adding a random value to the last accepted solution from the previous iteration. The new solution $x = 2.25 - 1.07 = 1.18$, $f(1.18) = 23.23$ is a non-improving solution, so the acceptance probability must be calculated: $p = e^{-\Delta f / T} = e^{-(23.23 - 14.06)/5} = 0.1597$. We generate a random number r between $(0,1)$, and let's say it was $r = 0.37$. As $p \not> r$, we reject this solution.
- *Iteration 3*—We update the temperature because we have used the initial temperature $T_0 = 5$ for two iterations so far. Following geometric cooling, the new temperature is $T_1 = T_0 \alpha^i = 5*0.85^1 = 4.25$. We'll use this value for two iterations starting with this iteration. We'll now generate a new solution based on the last accepted solution by adding a random value from a Gaussian distribution. The new solution is $x = 2.25 + 1.57 = 3.82$ with $f(3.82) = 4.75$. This is an improving solution, so it's accepted, and the search continues.

SciPy provides Python implementations for SA algorithms and other algorithms to handle mathematical optimization problems. `scipy.optimize.anneal` is deprecated in SciPy, and a `dual_annealing()` function is available instead. The following listing shows the Bohachevsky function (which has the formula $f(x_1, x_2) = x_1^2 + 2x_2^2 - 0.3\cos(3\pi x_1) - 0.4\cos(3\pi x_2) + 0.7$) solution using the SciPy dual annealing algorithm. The complete listing is available in the book's GitHub repo.

Listing 5.1   Function optimization using `scipy.optimize.dual_annealing`

```
#!pip install scipy
import numpy as np
from scipy.optimize import dual_annealing

def objective_function(solution):
    return solution[0]**2 +2*(solution[1]**2) - 0.3*np.cos(3*np.
pi*solution[0]) -
 0.4*np.cos(4*np.pi*solution[1]) + 0.7

bounds = np.asarray([[-100, 100], [-100, 100]])

res_dual = dual_annealing(objective_function, bounds=bounds, maxiter = 100)

print('Dual Annealing Solution: f(%s) = %.5f' % (res_dual['x'], res_
dual['fun']))
```

Define the objective function or functions (e.g., Bohachevsky function).

Define the boundary constraints of the decision variables.

Perform the dual annealing search.

Print the dual annealing solution.

MEALPY is another Python library that provides implementations of different nature-inspired metaheuristic algorithms (see appendix A for more details). As a continuation, the following code shows the Bohachevsky function solution using MEALPY SA (the complete version of listing 5.1 is available in the book's GitHub repo):

```
#!pip install mealpy
from numpy import exp, arange
import matplotlib.pyplot as plt
from pylab import meshgrid,cm,imshow,contour,clabel,colorbar,axis,title,show
from mealpy.physics_based.SA import OriginalSA

problem = {"fit_func": objective_function,"lb": [bounds[0][0], bounds[1][0]],
"ub":
 [bounds[0][1], bounds[1][1]], "minmax": "min", "obj_weights": [1, 1]}

epoch = 100
pop_size = 10
max_sub_iter = 2
t0 = 1000
t1 = 1
move_count = 5
mutation_rate = 0.1
mutation_step_size = 0.1
mutation_step_size_damp = 0.99
```

Define the problem.

Define the MEALPY algorithm parameters to perform an SA search using MEALPY.

```
model = OriginalSA(epoch, pop_size, max_sub_iter, t0, t1, move_count,
mutation_rate,
   ↪ mutation_step_size, mutation_step_size_damp)
```
◀── | **Define a MEALPY SA solver.**

```
mealpy_solution, mealpy_value = model.solve(problem)

print('MEALPY SA Solution: f(%s) = %.5f' % (mealpy_solution, mealpy_value)) ◀──
```

| **Solve the problem using a defined solver.**   **Print the MEALPY SA solution.** |

Figure 5.10 shows the Bohachevsky function's solution. The performance of the algorithm depends mainly on its parameter tuning and stopping criteria. MEALPY runs a parallel version of SA and exposes many parameters to be tuned.

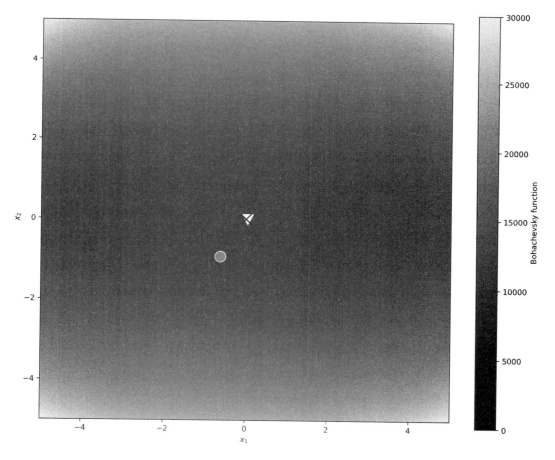

Figure 5.10   Solution of a continuous function optimization problem using SA. The cross in the center is the optimal solution. The triangle is the solution obtained by MEALPY SA. The dot is the SciPy dual annealing solution.

NOTE Appendix A shows how to use SA in other Python packages to solve mathematical optimization problems.

Let's implement an SA algorithm from scratch so we can gain more control and better handle different types of continuous and discrete optimization problems. In our implementation in the optalgotools package, we decouple the problem definition from the solver so we can use the solvers to handle different problems.

Let's apply our implementation to find the global minimum of the aforementioned simple function optimization problem and of more complex function optimization problems as well. There are several complex mathematical functions in multidimensional space, such as Rosenbrock's function, the Ackley function, the Rastrigin function, the Schaffer function, the Schwefel function, the Langermann function, the Levy function, the Bukin function, the Eggholder function, the cross-in-tray function, the drop wave function, and the Griewank function. Examples of function optimization test problems and datasets can be found in appendix B.

Listing 5.2 shows how SA can be used to solve the following mathematical functions:

- *A simple quadratic equation*—This is what we used in the hand iterations.
- *The Bohachevsky function (global minimum 0)*—This is a 2D unimodal function with a bowl shape. This function is known to be continuous, convex, separable, differentiable, nonmultimodal, nonrandom, and nonparametric, so derivate-based solvers can efficiently handle it. Note that a function whose variables can be separated is known as a *separable function*. Nonrandom functions contain no random variables. Nonparametric functions assume that the data distribution cannot be defined in terms of a finite set of parameters.
- *The Bukin function*—This function has many local minima, all of which lie on a ridge, and one global minimum $f(x_0) = 0$ at $x_0 = f(-10,1)$. This function is continuous, convex, nonseparable, nondifferentiable, multimodal, nonrandom, and nonparametric. This requires a derivative-free solver (also known as a black-box solver) such as SA.
- *The Gramacy & Lee function*—This is a 1D function with multiple local minima and local and global trends. This function is continuous, nonconvex, separable, differentiable, nonmultimodal, nonrandom, and nonparametric.
- *The Griewank 1D, 2D, and 3D functions*—These have many widespread local minima. These functions are continuous, nonconvex, separable, differentiable, multimodal, nonrandom, and nonparametric.

In our implementation, these are the SA parameters:

- A maximum number of iterations: `max_iter=1000`
- Maximum iterations per temperature: `max_iter_per_temp=100`
- An initial temperature: `initial_temp=1000`
- A final temperature: `final_temp=0.0001`

- A cooling schedule: `cooling_schedule='geometric'` (available options: `'linear'`, `'geometric'`, `'logarithmic'`, `'exponential'`, `'linear_inverse'`)
- A cooling factor: `cooling_alpha=0.9`
- A debug option: `debug=1` (`debug=1` prints the initial and final solution; `debug=2` provides hand-iteration tracing)

Feel free to change these settings and observe their effect on the performance of the algorithm.

Listing 5.2   Continuous function optimization using SA

```python
import random
import math
import numpy as np
from optalgotools.algorithms import SimulatedAnnealing
from optalgotools.problems import ProblemBase, ContinuousFunctionBase

def simple_example(x):
    return (x-6)**2

simple_example_bounds = np.asarray([[0, 31]])
simple_example_obj = ContinuousFunctionBase(simple_example, simple_example_
➥ simple_example_bounds)
sa = SimulatedAnnealing(max_iter=1000, max_iter_per_temp=100,
➥ initial_ temp=1000, final_temp=0.0001, cooling_schedule='geometric',
➥ cooling_alpha=0.9, debug=1)
sa.run(simple_example_obj)

def Bohachevsky(x_1, x_2):
    return x_1**2 +2*(x_2**2)-0.3*np.cos(3*np.pi*x_1)-0.4*np.cos(4*np.
pi*x_2)+0.7

Bohachevsky_bounds = np.asarray([[-100, 100], [-100, 100]])
Bohachevsky_obj = ContinuousFunctionBase(Bohachevsky, Bohachevsky_bounds, 5)
sa.run(Bohachevsky_obj)

def bukin(x_1, x_2):
    return 100*math.sqrt(abs(x_2-0.01*x_1**2)) + 0.01 * abs(x_1 + 10)

bukin_bounds = np.asarray([[-15, -5], [-3, 3]])
bukin_obj = ContinuousFunctionBase(bukin, bukin_bounds, 5)
sa.run(bukin_obj)

def gramacy_and_lee(x):
    return math.sin(10*pi*x)/(2*x) + (x-1)**4

gramacy_and_lee_bounds = np.asarray([[0.5, 2.5]])
gramacy_and_lee_obj = ContinuousFunctionBase(gramacy_and_lee, gramacy_and_
➥ lee_bounds, .1)
sa.run(gramacy_and_lee_obj)
```

Annotations in left margin:
- **Quadratic function SA-based solution** (brace spanning the simple_example block)
- **Bohachevsky SA-based solution** (brace spanning the Bohachevsky block)
- **Bukin SA-based solution** (brace spanning the bukin block)
- **Gramacy & Lee SA-based solution** (brace spanning the gramacy_and_lee block)

```
def griewank(*x):
    x = np.asarray(x)
    return np.sum(x**2/4000) - np.prod(np.cos(x/np.sqrt(np.asarray(range(1,
    ➥ len(x)+1)))))) + 1

griewank_bounds = np.asarray([[-600, 600]])
griewank_1d=ContinuousFunctionBase(griewank, griewank_bounds, 10)
sa.run(griewank_1d)
```

```
griewank_bounds_2d = np.asarray([[-600, 600]]*2)
griewank_2d=ContinuousFunctionBase(griewank, griewank_bounds_2d,
➥ (griewank_bounds_2d[:, 1] - griewank_bounds_2d[:, 0])/10)
sa.run(griewank_2d)
```

```
griewank_bounds_3d = np.asarray([[-600, 600]]*3)
griewank_3d=ContinuousFunctionBase(griewank, griewank_bounds_3d,
➥ (griewank_bounds_3d[:, 1] - griewank_bounds_3d[:, 0])/10)
sa.run(griewank_3d)
```

This is an example of the output for the Bukin function:

```
Simulated annealing is initialized:
current value = 60.73784664253138, current temp=1000
Simulated Annealing is done:
curr iter: 154, curr best value: 0.6093437608551259, curr
temp:9.97938882337113e-05, curr best: sol: [-14.63282848    2.14122839]
global minimum: x = -14.6328, 2.1412, f(x) = 0.6093
```

As can be seen, SA is able to handle different multidimensional, nonlinear function optimization problems. This stochastic global optimization algorithm is able to adapt to the landscape of the objective function and avoid getting trapped in local minima. However, in the case of multidimensional functions such as Griewank 2D and 3D, SA takes time to converge. The following sections show how SA can handle discrete problems such as Sudoku and TSP.

5.4   *Solving Sudoku*

Sudoku, also known as Su Doku, is one of the most popular number puzzles of all time. This game is adapted from a mathematical concept called a *Latin square*. The first version of the Sudoku puzzle was created by a retired architect named Howard Garns and appeared in the late 1970s as a puzzle in *Dell Pencil Puzzles and Word Games*. The game subsequently showed up in Japan in 1984 under the name "Sudoku," which is abbreviated from the Japanese "Sūji wa dokushin ni kagiru," which means the numbers (or digits) must remain single. Nowadays, Sudoku games are popular around the globe and are published in game websites, puzzle booklets, and newspapers.

The Sudoku game can be seen as a constraint-satisfaction problem (CSP) that is solved by correctly filling a 9×9 grid with digits so that each column, each row, and each of the nine 3×3 subgrids (aka "boxes," "blocks," or "regions") contain all of the digits from 1 to 9. Any row or column or 3×3 subgrid shouldn't contain more than one of the same number from 1 to 9.

Aside from entertainment, Sudoku is used in real-life applications such as developmental psychology and steganography. For example, several studies have showed that solving Sudoku or crosswords or other brain games may help in keeping your brain 10 years younger and can slow down the progression of conditions such as Alzheimer's. Sudoku can also be used as a tool to improve problem-solving skills, critical thinking, and attention. Finally, steganography is the technique of hiding images, messages, files, or other secret data within something that isn't a secret. In secret data delivery applications, digital images can be used to conceal secret data. The Sudoku puzzle is then used to modify selected pixel pairs in the cover image, based on a specially designed reference matrix, to insert secret digits.

Latin square

Latin squares were devised in the 10th century by Arabic numerologists who dealt with the mystical power of numbers. Islamic amulets, known as wafq majazi, from the 13th century have been found, and they were sketched in the margins of a 16th century Arabic medical text. The name "Latin" was inspired by the famous Swiss mathematician Leonhard Euler (1707–1783) who used Latin letters as symbols in the squares.

A *Latin square* is an *n* × *n* array filled with *n* different numbers, symbols, or colors arranged in such a way that no orthogonal (row or column) contains the same number, symbol, or color twice. An example of a 4 × 4 Latin square is shown here:

1	2	3	4
2	1	4	3
3	4	1	2
4	3	2	1

Latin squares are different from *magic squares*. A magic square is a square array of positive integers 1, 2, ..., n^2 arranged such that the sum of the *n* numbers in any horizontal, vertical, or main diagonal line is always the same number. Sudoku is based on Latin squares. In fact, any solution to a Sudoku puzzle is a Latin square. KenKen and KenDoku are other number puzzles based on an enhanced version of Latin squares and require some degree of arithmetic skills.

Generally speaking, the search space of Sudoku is huge. There are 6.671×10^{21} possible solvable Sudoku grids that yield a unique result [5]. According to Encyclopedia Britannica, if each human on earth solves one Sudoku puzzle every second, they wouldn't get through all of them until about the year 30,992. However, taking out symmetries, such as rotations, reflections, permuting columns and rows, and swapping digits, the number of essentially different Sudoku grids is reduced to 5,472,730,538 $\approx 5.473 \times 10^9$ [6]. The generalized $n \times n$ Sudoku problem is an NP-complete problem. However, some instances, such as standard 9×9 Sudoku, are not NP-complete. Constant-time algorithms exist to solve some instances of 9×9 Sudoku, in $O(1)$ time, as each and every 9×9 Sudoku can be listed, enumerated, and indexed in a finite dictionary or a lookup table used to find a solution. However, these algorithms cannot handle arbitrary generalized $n \times n$ Sudoku problems.

Backtracking, dancing links, and Crook's pencil-and-paper are common algorithms for solving Sudoku, especially if the size of the problem is small. *Backtracking* is mainly a classical depth-first search that tests a whole branch until that branch violates the rules or returns a solution.

Dancing links (DLX), invented by Donald Knuth in 2000, uses algorithm X to solve Sudoku puzzles, handled as exact cover problems. In the exact cover problem, given a binary matrix (i.e., a matrix composed only of 0 and 1), it is necessary to find a set of rows containing exactly one 1 in each column. Algorithm X, a recursive search algorithm, is applied to solve the exact cover problem using the backtracking method.

In *Crook's pencil-and-paper algorithm*, all possible numbers in each cell are listed. This list of numbers is called marking-up of the cell. We then try to find out if there is a row, column, or block with only one possible value throughout the row, column, or block. Once found, we fill in this cell with this number and update the markups in any affected row, column, or box. The next step is to find preemptive sets. As described in Crook's paper, a preemptive set is composed of numbers from the set $[1,2,\ldots,9]$ and is a set of size m, $2 \le m \le 9$, whose numbers are potential occupants of m cells exclusively, where exclusively means that no other numbers in the set $[1,2,\ldots,9]$, other than the members of the preemptive set, are potential occupants of those m cells. The last step is to eliminate possible numbers outside preemptive sets.

Backtracking

Backtracking algorithms are commonly used to solve search and optimization problems by recursion. The backtracking algorithm builds a feasible solution or a set of feasible solutions incrementally. Given a 9×9 Sudoku board, the algorithm visits all the empty cells following depth-first traversal order, filling the digits incrementally, and it backtracks when a number is not found to be valid. The following figure illustrates the backtracking algorithm steps for a 9×9 Sudoku puzzle.

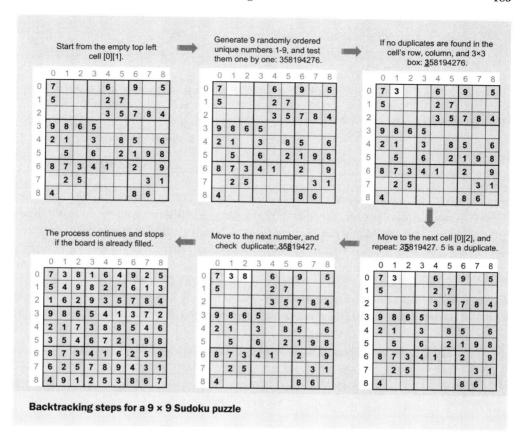

Backtracking steps for a 9 × 9 Sudoku puzzle

The next listing shows how a 9 × 9 Sudoku is solved using the SA algorithm.

Listing 5.3   Solving Sudoku using SA

```
from optalgotools.algorithms import SimulatedAnnealing     ◄──┐ Import the SA solver.
from optalgotools.problems import Sudoku  ◄─────┐
                                                 │ Import a Sudoku problem.
sa = SimulatedAnnealing(max_iter=100000, max_iter_per_temp=1000,
➥ initial_temp=500, final_temp=0.001, cooling_schedule='geometric',
➥ cooling_alpha=0.9, debug=1)  ◄───────┐
                                         │ Create a SA solver with the selected parameters.

Sudoku_hard = [
    [9, 0, 0, 1, 0, 0, 0, 5, 4],
    [0, 0, 0, 0, 8, 0, 0, 0, 0],
    [0, 0, 5, 0, 0, 9, 0, 0, 3],
```

```
    [0, 9, 0, 0, 3, 5, 0, 4, 1],
    [0, 0, 0, 0, 1, 0, 0, 0, 0],
    [4, 1, 0, 2, 6, 0, 0, 8, 0],
    [7, 0, 0, 3, 0, 0, 1, 0, 0],
    [0, 0, 0, 0, 4, 0, 0, 0, 0],
    [3, 5, 0, 0, 0, 1, 0, 0, 6],
]
sudoku_prob = Sudoku(Sudoku_hard)
sudoku_prob.print()

sudoku_prob.solve_backtrack()
sa.run(sudoku_prob, 0)
```

Create a hard 9 × 9 Sudoku (available variants include trivial, easy, medium, hard, and evil).

Solve the Sudoku using the backtracking algorithm.

Solve the Sudoku using SA.

You can try different variants of Sudoku by changing the puzzle configuration. In easy Sudoku problems, cells contain more prefilled numbers than medium or hard ones. Evil Sudoku is the highest level of puzzle difficulty. Table 5.2 compares the time it takes for SA, backtracking, and the Python Linear Programming (PuLP) library to solve different instances of 9 × 9 Sudoku puzzles. PuLP provides linear and mixed programming solvers. The default solver used in PuLP is Cbc (COIN-OR branch and cut), which is an open source solver for mixed integer linear programming problems. More information about PuLP is available in appendix A.

Table 5.2   SA versus backtracking versus PuLP in solving a 9 × 9 Sudoku puzzle

Time to find the solution(s)	Trivial	Easy	Medium	Hard	Evil
Backtracking	0.01	0.01	0.11	0.69	1.58
PuLP	0.69	0.12	0.11	0.13	0.12
Classical SA	0.10	0.07	0.01	3:17	Suboptimal in 3:16

As you can see, classical SA does not outperform the backtracking approach and is much slower in the case of hard and evil instances of Sudoku problems. PuLP is efficiently able to handle different variants of Sudoku in a consistent time, compared to backtracking and SA.

In the case of evil Sudoku, SA converges to a suboptimal solution despite trying different parameter settings. Given that this is a constraint-satisfaction problem, the notion of suboptimality is not valid, as a suboptimal solution is an invalid solution. This means that SA doesn't manage to solve the evil instance of Sudoku. Being a well-structured problem, 9 × 9 Sudoku with different levels of difficulty can be easily solved using a backtracking algorithm. Generally speaking, if the problem is well-structured with a well-known algorithm solution, metaheuristics approaches don't usually outperform these classical and more deterministic approaches.

5.5   *Solving TSP*

As described in section 2.1.1, the traveling salesman problem (TSP) is used as a platform for the study of general methods that can be applied to a wide range of discrete optimization problems. Consider solving the instance of TSP shown in figure 5.11 using SA. In this TSP, a traveling salesman must visit five cities and return home, making a loop (a round trip).

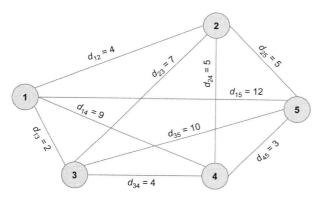

Figure 5.11   TSP for five cities—there are 5!/2 = 60 possible tours, assuming symmetric TSP. The weights on the edges of the graph represent the travel distances between the cities.

Assume the following values: initial temperature = 500, final temperature = 50, a linear decrement rate of 50, and one iteration at each temperature. A TSP solution takes the form of a permutation as follows: Solution = [1, 3, 4, 2, 5]. The objective function is the total distance of the route. Swapping is a suitable operator that can be used to generate neighboring solutions:

- *Iteration 0*—The initial solution is Solution = [1, 3, 4, 2, 5], cost = 2 + 4 + 5 + 5 + 12 = 28, as shown in figure 5.12.

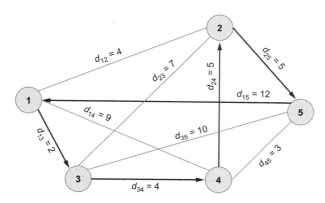

Figure 5.12   SA iteration 0 of a 5-city TSP

- *Iteration 1*—To generate a candidate solution, select two random cities (e.g., 2 and 3), and swap them. This results in a new solution [1, 2, 4, 3, 5] with a cost of 35 (figure 5.13).

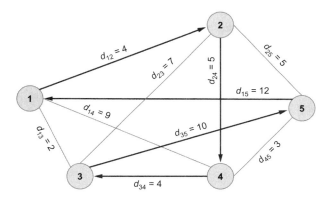

Figure 5.13   SA iteration 1 of a 5-city TSP

Since the new solution has a longer tour length, it will be conditionally accepted, according to a probability of $p = e^{-\Delta f/T} = e^{-(35-28)/T} = e^{-7/T}$ (at higher temperatures, there's a higher probability of acceptance). We pick a random value r within 0 and 1. If $P > r$, we accept this solution. Otherwise, we reject this solution. Assuming the new solution was not accepted, we generate a different one, starting from the initial solution:

- *Iteration 2*—A solution is generated by swapping cities 2 and 5 in the initial solution. The tour length of the candidate solution is 18 (figure 5.14).

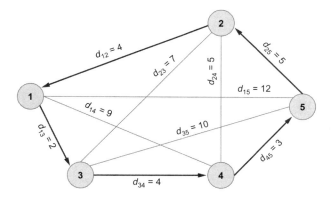

Figure 5.14   SA iteration 2 of a 5-city TSP

Since this solution has a shorter tour length, it will be accepted, and the search continues until the termination criteria are met. The following listing shows an SA solution for this simple TSP problem.

Listing 5.4   Solving TSP using SA

```
from optalgotools.algorithms import SimulatedAnnealing
from optalgotools.problems import TSP

dists = [ [0] * 5 for _ in range(5)]
dists[0][1] = dists[1][0] = 4
dists[0][2] = dists[2][0] = 2
dists[0][3] = dists[3][0] = 9
dists[0][4] = dists[4][0] = 12
dists[1][2] = dists[2][1] = 7
dists[1][3] = dists[3][1] = 5
dists[1][4] = dists[4][1] = 5
dists[2][3] = dists[3][2] = 4
dists[2][4] = dists[4][2] = 10
dists[3][4] = dists[4][3] = 3

tsp_sample = TSP(dists, 'random_swap')  ◄──────

sa = SimulatedAnnealing(max_iter=10000, max_iter_per_temp=1, initial_
temp=500,
➥ final_temp=50, cooling_schedule='linear_inverse', cooling_alpha=0.9,
debug=2)  ◄──────
sa.run(tsp_sample)  ◄──────
```

Create an instance of a TSP problem.

Run the SA solver, and show the results in each iteration.

Create an instance of the SA solver.

Let's now consider some benchmark instances of TSP, such as Berlin52 from TSPLIB (http://comopt.ifi.uni-heidelberg.de/software/TSPLIB95/). This dataset contains 52 locations in the city of Berlin. The shortest route obtained for the Berlin52 dataset is 7,542. The next listing shows how we can solve this TSP instance using our SA implementation.

Listing 5.5   Solving the Berlin52 TSP using SA

```
from optalgotools.problems import TSP
from optalgotools.algorithms import SimulatedAnnealing
import matplotlib.pyplot as plt

berlin52_tsp_url = 'https://raw.githubusercontent.com/coin-or/jorlib/
b3a41ce773e9b3b5b73c149d4c06097ea1511680/jorlib-core/src/test/resources/
tspLib/tsp/berlin52.tsp'  ◄──────
                            │ Permanent URL for the Berlin52 dataset
berlin52_tsp = TSP(load_tsp_url=berlin52_tsp_url, gen_method='mutate',
➥ rand_len=True, init_method='random')  ◄──────
                                          │ Create a TSP object for Berlin52.
sa = SimulatedAnnealing(max_iter=1200, max_iter_per_temp=500, initial_
temp=150,
➥ final_temp=0.01, cooling_schedule='linear', debug=1)  ◄──────
                                                          │ Create an SA model.
sa.run(berlin52_tsp, repetition=1)
print(sa.val_allbest)

berlin52_tsp.plot(sa.s_best)  ◄──────
```

Run SA, and evaluate the best solution distance.

Plot the route.

Here is an example of the output:

```
sol: [0, 48, 34, 35, 33, 43, 45, 36, 37, 47, 23, 4, 14, 5, 3, 24, 11, 50, 10,
51, 13, 12, 26, 27, 25, 46, 28, 15, 49, 19, 22, 29, 1, 6, 41, 20, 30, 17, 16,
2, 44, 18, 40, 7, 8, 9, 32, 42, 39, 38, 31, 21, 0]
8106.88
```

Figure 5.15 shows the route generated by SA for Belin52 TSP.

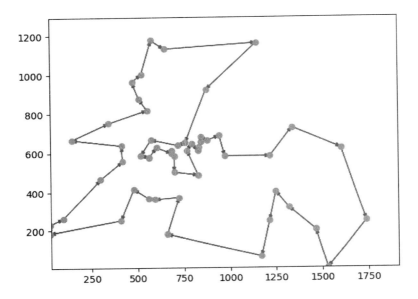

Figure 5.15   Solution of Belin52 using SA

As you can see, the near-optimal solution found by SA is 8,106.88. This value is a bit higher than the best-known solution for the Berlin52 TSP, which is 7,542. Parameter tuning and algorithm adaptation can help improve the results. For example, Geng et al.'s "Solving the traveling salesman problem based on an adaptive simulated annealing algorithm with greedy search" paper discusses using three kinds of mutations (vertex insert mutation, block insert mutation, and block reverse mutation) with different probabilities during the search to improve the accuracy of SA in solving TSP problems. Moreover, parameters such as the cooling coefficient of the temperature, the times of greedy search used to speed up the convergence rate, the times of compulsive accept, and the probability of accepting a new solution, can be adapted according to the size of the TSP instances. An implementation of this adaptive algorithm is available from this GitHub repo: https://github.com/ildoonet/simulated-annealing-for-tsp.

The effect of the algorithm's parameters can be studied, such as the initial temperature, the cooling schedule, the number of iterations per temperature, and the final temperature. For example, SA was applied for the Berlin52 TSP instance with the following settings:

- Maximum number of iterations = 1200
- Number of iterations per each temperature T = 500
- $T_{initial}$ = 150
- T_{final} = 0.01
- Linear cooling

Our implementation supports the following methods for mutating a new solution from an old one:

- `random_swap`—Swap two cities in the path. This can be done multiple times for the same solution by using `num_swaps`. Also, the swap can be done in a smaller window of the whole path using `swap_wind = [1 - n]`. For example, suppose the route is [A, B, C, D, F]. Swapping two random cities, like B and F, will result in a new route [A, F, C, D, B].

- `reverse`—Reverse the order of a subset of the cities with either a random length, using `rand_len`, or using `rev_len`, which has a default of 2. For example, starting with the solution [A, B, C, D, F], if we apply `reverse` with length 3, we can get a new solution [A, D, C, B, F].

- `insert`—Pick a random city, remove it from the path, and reinsert it before a different random city. For example, starting from the solution [A, B, C, D, F], we could pick city B and insert it before city F so we get a new solution [A, C, D, B, F].

- `mutate`—Randomly pick a number of consecutive cities from the current solution, and shuffle them. For example, starting from the solution [A, B, C, D, F], we may pick C, D, F and shuffle them so we get a new solution [A, B, F, C, D].

The implementation also supports two methods of initializing the path:

- `random`—This means the path is generated completely randomly.
- `greedy`—This tries to select a possibly suboptimal initial path by selecting the pairwise shortest distances between cities. This will not lead to the shortest path, but it may be better than the random initialization.

It is worth noting that the results of the SA algorithm may not be exactly repeatable. Due to the randomness included in the algorithm, each time you run the algorithm, you may get slightly different results. To avoid this, the `run` function included in the `SimulatedAnnealing` class contains a `repetition` argument that allows you to report the best solution generated out of multiple runs, as follows:

```
run(self, problem_obj=None, stoping_val=None, init=None, repetition=1)
```

You can set repetition to be 10, so the algorithm reports the best solution generated out of 10 runs.

5.6   *Solving a delivery semi-truck routing problem*

Let's consider a more real-life example of TSP. Assume that Walmart Supercenters are points of interest (POIs) to be visited by a delivery semi-truck. The vehicle will start from Walmart Supercenter number 3001, located at 270 Kingston Rd. E in Ajax, Ontario. It is required to find the shortest possible route the truck can follow to visit each POI only once and get back to the home location. There are 18 Walmart Supercenters in the selected part of the Greater Toronto Area (GTA), as shown in figure 5.16. This results in 18! possible routes to visit these stores located in Durham Region, York Region, and Toronto, Ontario.

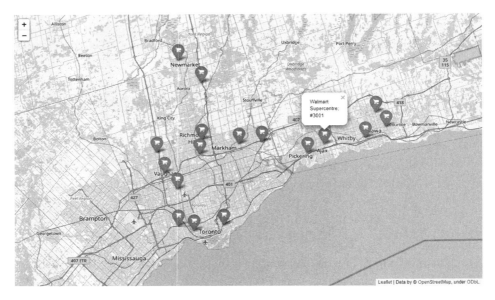

Figure 5.16   Selected Walmart Supercenters in the Greater Toronto Area (GTA)

The GPS coordinates (longitude and latitude) of each POI and the addresses are available on the POI Factory website (www.poi-factory.com/node/25560) and are included in the Walmart_United States&Canada.csv file that can be downloaded for free (for noncommercial use) after registration. Google Places API, Here Places API, and Safe-Graph on ArcGIS Marketplace can also be used to get data about points of interest such as hospitals, restaurants, retail stores, and grocery stores. Appendix B provides more details about open data sources.

The OSMnx library is used in this example to create a NetworkX graph that represents the supercenter locations. Pyrosm can also be used instead of OSMnx. The shortest distances between these locations are computed using the NetworkX built-in function `shortest_path`, which uses Dijkstra's algorithm as a default method (see section 3.4.1). Supercenter locations are rendered on OpenStreetMap based on their GPS coordinates using the folium library. Appendix A provides more details about these libraries.

In our implementation, the problem solver is decoupled from the problem object. We start by creating a TSP object for this discrete problem. We then create an SA object to solve the TSP problem. An initial solution is generated using the `mutate` method. As shown in figure 5.17, this initial solution is far from optimal. The total length of the initial route is 593.88 km, and this route is not convenient or easy to follow in practice.

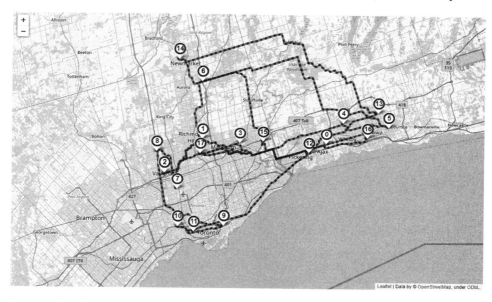

Figure 5.17   Initial solution for the Walmart delivery semi-truck route with a total distance of 593.88 km

Let's run SA with the following parameters:

- Maximum number of iterations = 10000
- Maximum interaction per temperature = 100
- Initial temperature = 85
- Final temperature = 0.0001
- Linear cooling schedule

Other cooling schedules could also be used. For example, geometric cooling can generate consistent, superior-quality, and timely solutions compared to other schemes. However, this is one of the algorithm parameters that can be tuned, as it sometimes depends on the nature of the problem. Figure 5.18 shows the shortest route with a total distance of 227.17 km.

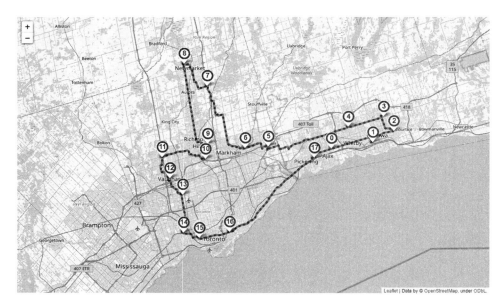

Figure 5.18   SA solution for the Walmart delivery semi-truck route with a total distance of 227.17 km

The next listing is a snippet of the code used to generate the shortest route for the delivery semi-truck using SA. The complete code is available in the book's GitHub repo.

Listing 5.6   Generating a Walmart delivery semi-truck route using SA

```
from optalgotools.algorithms import SimulatedAnnealing
from optalgotools.problems import TSP
import numpy as np
import pandas as pd
import osmnx as ox
import networkx as nx
import folium
import folium.plugins
```
Load a list of all Walmart locations in Ontario.

```
wal_df = pd.read_csv("https://raw.githubusercontent.com/Optimization-
Algorithms-
➥Book/Code-Listings/main/Appendix%20B/data/TSP/Walmart_ON.csv")
```

```
cities_list = [city for city, region in cityToRegion.items() if city in
➥wal_df.city.unique() and region in ['Durham Region', 'York Region',
'Toronto']]
```
Select cities that are in Durham Region, York Region, or Toronto.

```
gta_part = wal_df[wal_df.store_number.str.startswith('Walmart Supercentre') &
➥ wal_df.city.isin(cities_list)].reset_index(drop=True)
wal_gta_count = gta_part.shape[0]
```
Select Walmart stores that are in the preceding list and are Supercenters.

```
gta_part_loc = gta_part[['latitude', 'longitude']]

G = ox.graph_from_point(tuple(gta_part_loc.mean().to_list()), dist=42000,
➥ dist_type='network', network_type='drive', clean_periphery=True,
simplify=True,
➥ retain_all=True, truncate_by_edge=True)

gta_part['osmid'], gta_part['osmid_dist_m'] = zip(*gta_part.apply(lambda row:
➥ox.nearest_nodes(G, row.longitude, row.latitude, return_dist=True), axis =
1))

gta_part_dists = np.zeros([wal_gta_count, wal_gta_count])
gta_part_pathes = [[[] for i in range(wal_gta_count)] for j in range(wal_gta_
count)]
for i in range(wal_gta_count):
    for j in range(wal_gta_count):
        if i==j:
            continue
        gta_part_pathes[i][j] = nx.shortest_path(G=G, source=gta_part.
osmid[i],
➥ target=gta_part.osmid[j], weight='length', method='dijkstra')
        gta_part_dists[i][j] = nx.shortest_path_length(G=G,
➥source=gta_part.osmid[i], target=gta_part.osmid[j], weight='length',
➥ method='dijkstra')/1000

gta_part_tsp = TSP(dists=gta_part_dists, gen_method='mutate')

sa = SimulatedAnnealing(max_iter=1000, max_iter_per_temp=100, initial_
temp=85,
➥ final_temp=0.0001, cooling_schedule='linear')
sa.init_annealing(gta_part_tsp)
sa.run(gta_part_tsp)
```

Get the lat. and long. locations of the preceding set of Walmarts, and create a graph of roads that connects them and that is within 42 km.

Calculate the distances between the Walmart locations using the graph.

Create a TSP object for the problem.

Create an SA object to help solve the TSP problem.

Get an initial random solution, and check its length.

Run SA, and evaluate the best solution distance.

As you can see, we separated the solver class from the problem object in optalgotools. The solver is imported from `algorithms`, and the problem is an instance of the TSP problem in the `problems` class. This implementation allows you to change the problem instances and tune the parameters of the algorithm to reach an optimal or near-optimal solution. You may consider trying the adaptation aspects of SA explained in section 5.2.5 to figure out their effect on the algorithm's performance in terms of the length of the obtained route and the run time (CPU time and wall-clock time).

A metaheuristic algorithm like SA seeks optimal or near-optimal solutions at a reasonable computational cost, but it cannot guarantee either their feasibility or degree of optimality. With proper parameter tuning, the algorithm can provide acceptable solutions without further postprocessing. In the next chapter, we will discuss tabu search as another trajectory-based optimization algorithm.

Summary

- Metaheuristic algorithms can be broadly classified into trajectory-based algorithms and population-based algorithms. A trajectory-based metaheuristic algorithm, or S-metaheuristic, uses a single search agent that moves through the design or search space in a piecewise style. Population-based algorithms, or P-metaheuristics, use multiple agents to search for an optimal or near-optimal global solution. Simulated annealing is a trajectory-based metaheuristic algorithm.

- Simulated annealing mimics the annealing process in material processing, where a metal cools and freezes into a crystalline state with the minimum energy and larger crystal size so as to reduce the defects in metallic structures. The annealing process involves the careful control of temperature and cooling rate, often called the annealing schedule.

- Simulated annealing runs a series of moves under different thermodynamic conditions and always accepts improving moves and can probabilistically accept non-improving moves.

- The acceptance probability is proportional to the temperature. A high temperature increases the chance of accepting non-improving moves to favor exploration of the search space at the beginning of the search. As the search progresses, the temperature is decremented to restrict exploration and favor exploitation.

- As the temperature goes to zero, SA acts greedily like hill climbing, and as the temperature goes to infinity, SA behaves like a random walk. The temperature should decrease gradually to achieve the best trade-off between exploration and exploitation.

- Simulated annealing is a stochastic search algorithm and a derivative-free solver that can be used when derivative information is unavailable, unreliable, or prohibitively expensive. SA seeks optimal or near-optimal solutions at a reasonable computational cost but it cannot guarantee either the feasibility or degree of optimality.

- Adaptive simulated annealing can dynamically change its parameters with the search progress to control the exploration and exploitation behavior.

- Simulated annealing is an easy-to-implement probabilistic approximation algorithm that can be used to solve continuous and discrete problems in different domains.

Tabu search

6

This chapter covers

- Understanding local search
- Understanding how tabu search extends local search
- Solving constraint-satisfaction problems
- Solving continuous problems
- Solving routing problems
- Solving assembly line balancing problems

In the previous chapter, you were introduced to trajectory-based metaheuristics, and you learned about simulated annealing (SA) as an example of these metaheuristic algorithms. The actual first use of a metaheuristic is probably Fred Glover's *tabu search* (TS) in 1986, although his seminal article on tabu search was published later, in 1997 [1]. The word "tabu" (also spelled "taboo") originated from the Polynesian languages of the South Pacific. It is a term used to describe something that is prohibited, forbidden, or considered socially unacceptable within a particular culture or society. Tabu search is called "tabu" because it uses a memory structure to keep track of solutions that have been recently explored so it can avoid returning to them, especially in the early stage of the search, in order to avoid getting stuck in local optima.

TS is a powerful trajectory-based optimization technique that has been successfully applied to solve different optimization problems in different areas, such as scheduling, design, allocation, routing, production, inventory and investment, telecommunications, logic and artificial intelligence, technology, graph optimization, and general combinatorial optimization. TS can be considered a combination of local search and memory structures.

This chapter presents tabu search as a trajectory-based metaheuristic optimization technique, discusses its pros and cons, and looks at its applications in different domains. To illustrate how this algorithm can be used to solve optimization problems, a variety of case studies and exercises will be presented. Let's start by closely exploring local search.

6.1   *Local search*

Imagine yourself enjoying a vacation at a resort that features multiple restaurants, each offering a diverse selection of dishes to satisfy your every craving. During the initial day of your stay, you might choose a restaurant randomly or select the nearest one to your room if you are exhausted from your journey. You may continue dining at that particular restaurant or explore other options within the resort. In this case, you are applying local search by limiting your options to those found within the resort, without considering the possibility of ordering food online or leaving the resort to dine elsewhere.

Local search (LS) is a search technique that iteratively explores a subset of a search space in the neighborhood of the current solution or state in order to improve this solution with local changes. The type of local changes that may be applied to a solution is defined by a *neighborhood structure*. For a finite set of candidate solutions S, a neighborhood structure represents a set of neighboring solutions $N(s) \subseteq S$ that can be generated by making a small change to the current solution $s \in S$. The horizon of $N(s)$ as a neighborhood of s varies from exploring all the possible neighbors of the current solutions (random search) to only considering one neighbor (local search). The former can be computationally demanding, while the latter has a very limited horizon or search space and is highly vulnerable to getting trapped in a local minimum.

As shown in algorithm 6.1, a local search algorithm starts from an initial feasible solution and iteratively moves to a neighboring solution as long as the new neighboring solution is better than the old one.

Algorithm 6.1   Local search

```
Input: an initial feasible solution
Output: optimal solution
Begin
    While termination criteria not met do
        Generate a neighboring solution by applying a series of local
modifications (or moves)
        if the new solution is better then
            Replace the old one
```

Typically, every feasible solution has more than one neighboring solution. The name "local search" implies that the algorithm searches for a new solution in the neighborhood of the current one. For example, hill climbing can be considered a local search technique where a new neighboring solution that is locally maximizing the criterion or objective function is considered in each iteration. The hill climbing algorithm is a greedy algorithm, as it accepts only improving solutions. This sometimes makes it converge to local optima, which are usually average solutions unless the search is extremely lucky. The solution quality and the computation time are usually dependent on the chosen local moves.

Local search algorithms have been successfully applied to solve many hard combinatorial optimization problems in reasonable time. Application domains include areas such as operations research, management science, engineering, and bioinformatics. The performance of LS-based approaches can be further enhanced by introducing mechanisms for escaping from local minima in the search space. These mechanisms include, but are not limited to, simulated annealing, random noise, mixed random walk, and tabu search. Tabu search was originally proposed to allow LS to overcome the difficulty of local optima and prevent cycling by allowing non-improving moves and memorizing the recent history of the search.

Let's now discuss the various components of TS.

6.2 Tabu search algorithm

Going back to our resort example, even if you enjoyed your first meal at a particular restaurant within the resort, you may opt to dine at a different one on the following day to explore other options and to avoid becoming trapped in a local optimum. Suppose you promise yourself not to dine at the same restaurant for several days so you can explore the other dining options at the resort. Once you have sampled various restaurants, you might opt to return to one of the restaurants you previously visited and dine there for the remainder of your stay. You apply tabu search by memorizing your impressions of each meal at each restaurant you try, and you can search for alternatives, taking into consideration your previously memorized favorites. This allows you to enhance your local search by using memory to explore the search space more flexibly and responsively beyond local optimality.

This example demonstrates that tabu search incorporates adaptive memory and responsive exploration. *Adaptive memory* involves remembering information that is relevant or useful during the search process, such as recent moves made by the algorithm and the promising solutions found. *Responsive exploration* is a problem-solving approach that adapts and adjusts the behavior of the solver based on new information and the search history to find superior solutions faster.

Tabu search

"Tabu search is based on the premise that problem solving, in order to qualify as intelligent, must incorporate adaptive memory and responsive exploration. The adaptive memory feature of TS allows the implementation of procedures that are capable of searching the solution space economically and effectively. Since local choices are guided by information collected during the search, TS contrasts with memoryless designs that heavily rely on semi-random processes that implement a form of sampling. The emphasis on responsive exploration in tabu search, whether in a deterministic or probabilistic implementation, derives from the supposition that a bad strategic choice can often yield more information than a good random choice." (From Glover, Laguna, and Marti, "Principles of tabu search" [2].)

Tabu search is an iterative neighborhood search algorithm where the neighborhood changes dynamically. This algorithm was originally proposed to allow local search to overcome local optima. TS enhances local search by actively avoiding points in the search space already visited. By avoiding already visited points, loops in search trajectories are avoided and local optima can be escaped. Tabu search employs memory through a tabu list, which prohibits revisiting recently explored neighborhoods. This is done to avoid getting stuck in local optima. This combination can substantially increase the efficiency of solving some problems. The main feature of TS is the use of an explicit memory, which has two purposes: to avoid revisiting previously explored solutions and to explore unvisited regions of the solution space. The TS process starts with an initial randomized solution and then finds neighboring solutions. The best solution is then chosen and added to a tabu list. In subsequent iterations, tabu-active items are excluded as potential candidates unless enough time has elapsed and they can be reconsidered. This method helps prevent TS from getting stuck in local optima. Furthermore, to mitigate the effect of a tabu list excluding some good solutions, an aspiration criterion $A(s)$ can be employed, which allows previously tabu moves to be reconsidered if they result in a better solution than the current best-known solution.

Algorithm 6.2 shows how tabu search combines local search and memory structures.

Algorithm 6.2   Tabu search

```
Input: an initial feasible solution
Output: optimal solution
Begin
    While termination criteria not met do
        Choose the best: s'∈N(s) ← N(s)-T(s)+A(s)
        Memorize s' if it improves the best known solution
        s←s'
        Update Tab list T(S) and Aspiration criterion A(s)
```

As the algorithm shows, tabu search starts by using an initial feasible solution s and explores the search space iteratively to generate an optimal or near-optimal solution. At each iteration, and while the termination criteria are not met, the algorithm creates a candidate list of moves that lead to new solutions from the current solution within the neighborhood $N(s)$. If the new solution s' is an improving solution that is not listed as tabu-active $T(s)$ or is an admissible solution considering the aspiration criteria $A(s)$, the obtained solution is designated as the new current solution. Admissibility is then revised by updating the tabu restrictions and aspiration criteria.

Figure 6.1 summarizes the steps of TS in a flowchart. We start by obtaining a solution from initialization or from an intermediate or long-term memory component. We then create a candidate list of moves by applying an operator on the current solution, such as swapping, deleting and inserting, etc., depending on the nature of the problem at hand. These candidate neighboring solutions are evaluated, and the best admissible candidate is chosen. We keep updating the admissibility conditions, tabu restrictions, and aspiration criteria if the stopping criteria are not satisfied.

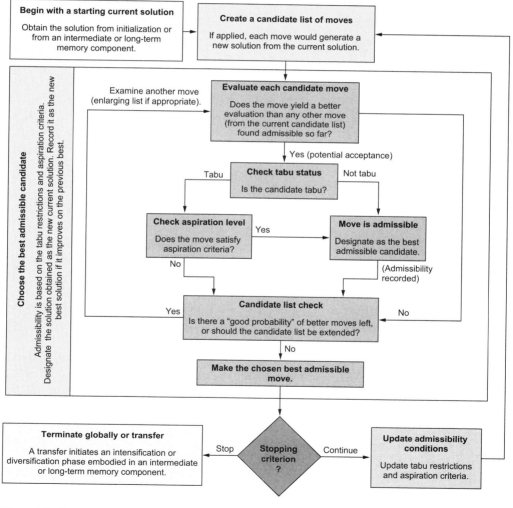

Figure 6.1   Tabu search steps (based on F. Glover's "Tabu search and adaptive memory programming—advances, applications and challenges" [1])

The following criteria may be used to terminate TS:

- The neighborhood is empty, meaning that all possible neighboring solutions have already been explored.
- The number of iterations performed since the last improvement exceeds a specified limit.
- There is external evidence that an optimal or a near-optimal solution has been reached.

To gain a better understanding of the TS algorithm, let's consider a simplified version of a symmetric traveling salesman problem (TSP) with only four cities, as illustrated in figure 6.2.

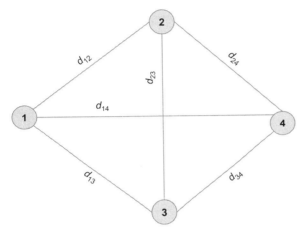

Figure 6.2   A 4-city TSP. The weights on the edges of the graph represent the travel distances between the cities.

A feasible solution can be represented as a sequence of cities or nodes where each city is visited exactly once. Assuming that the home city is city 1, an initial feasible solution can be selected randomly or using a greedy approach. A possible greedy approach is to choose the unvisited node closest to the current node and to continue this process until all nodes have been visited, resulting in a complete feasible tour that covers all nodes. This initial solution can be represented using permutation, such as {1,2,4,3}.

To generate a neighboring solution, we can apply a swapping operator. The neighborhood represents a set of neighboring solutions that can be generated by a pairwise exchange of any two cities in the solution. For this 4-city TSP, and fixing node 1 as the starting node or home city, the number of neighbors is the number of combinations without repetition $C(n,k)$ or n-choose-k:

$$C(n, k) = \frac{n!}{k!(n - k)!} = \frac{3!}{2!(3 - 2)!} = 3 \text{ neighbors}$$

Given the initial solution is {1,2,4,3}, the following three feasible neighboring solutions can be generated by applying the swapping operator:

- {1,2,3,4} by swapping 3 and 4
- {1,3,4,2} by swapping 2 and 3
- {1,4,2,3} by swapping 2 and 4

At each iteration, the neighboring solution with the best objective value (minimum total distance) is selected.

6.2.1 Memory structure

Local search strategies are often memoryless ones that keep no record of their past moves or solutions. The main feature of TS is the use of an explicit memory. *Explicit memory* refers to a mechanism that remembers the moves that have been previously visited during the search process. A simple TS usually implements the following two forms of adaptive memory mechanisms:

- *A recency-based or short-term memory*—This is a mechanism that keeps track of recently visited moves during the search process. It plays a role in preventing the algorithm from revisiting moves that have been explored recently.
- *A frequency-based or long-term memory*—This is a mechanism that tracks the historical frequency of specific moves throughout the entire search process and penalizes moves that have been visited frequently without success or that have proven to be less promising.

Memory types

According to the Atkinson–Shiffrin model (also known as the multi-store model or modal model), human memory has three components: sensory memory, working memory (sometimes called short-term memory), and long-term memory, as shown in the following figure.

Sensory memory is a very brief memory that automatically results from our perceptions and generally disappears after the original stimulus has ceased. Each of our five senses has a different memory store. For example, visual info is stored in iconic memory, while auditory info is stored in echoic memory.

The amount of information stored in short-term memory depends on the attention paid to the elements of sensory memory. Working memory is a more recent extension of the concept of short-term memory. This memory allows you to store and use the temporary information required to execute specific tasks. Rehearsal and repetition can help in increasing the duration of short-term memory. For example, imagine yourself as a customer-service associate in a fast food or beverage drive-thru, taking orders from customers and ensuring those orders are fulfilled. The order information provided by the customers is stored in your short-term or working memory, and once the order is fulfilled, this information is not kept in your memory.

(continued)

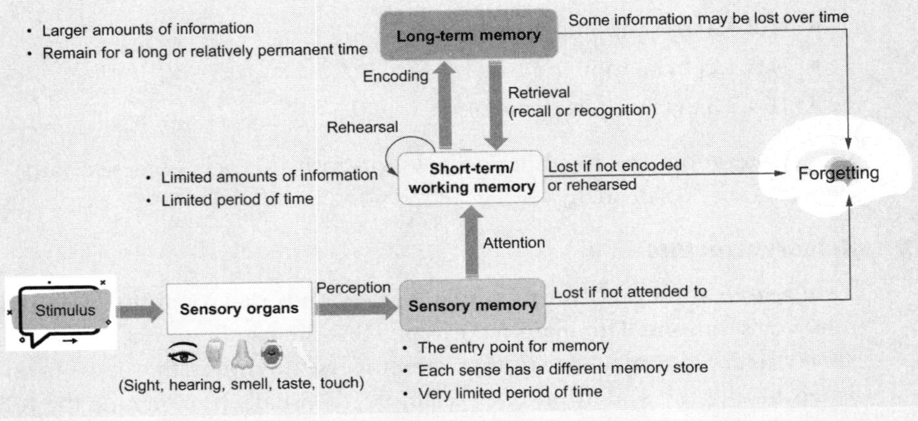

Memory types

Long-term memory holds your lifelong memories and a vast amount of information, such as your birthday, your address, work skills you've learned, etc. Some important information captured by working memory can be encoded and stored in long-term memory. The purpose of encoding is to assign a meaning to the information being memorized. For example, you might encode the word "omelet" as "egg, beaten, fried." If you could not recall the word "omelet" spontaneously, you can still retrieve it by invoking one of the indexes that you used to encode it, such as "egg." This is similar to encoding information using a lookup table for quick information retrieval.

Figure 6.3 shows a knapsack problem as an example. In this problem, each item has a *utility* and a *weight*, and we want to maximize the utility of the contents of the knapsack without exceeding the maximum weight. The problem is constrained by the capacity of the knapsack. Neighboring solutions can be generated by swapping items in and out of the knapsack.

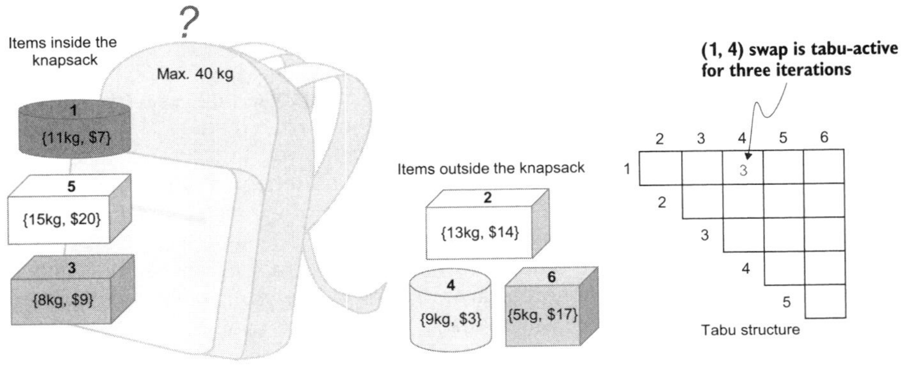

Figure 6.3 A knapsack problem

As illustrated in figure 6.3, a new candidate solution can be generated by swapping items 1 and 4. In this case, this swap will be tabu-active for the next three iterations, as shown in the tabu structure in the figure. *Tabu-active* moves are currently on the tabu list and cannot be selected for exploration in the current iteration. We could also generate neighboring solutions by adding or removing different items. If a neighborhood structure considers "add" and "remove" as separate moves, it might be a good idea to keep separate tabu lists for each type of move. Frequency-based memory keeps track of the frequency of the different swaps performed during a specified time interval. The idea is to penalize swaps that have been visited frequently.

The use of recency and frequency memory in TS serves primarily to prevent the searching process from cycling, which involves endlessly repeating the same sequence of moves or revisiting identical sets of solutions. Moreover, these two memory mechanisms play a role in achieving a trade-off between exploration and exploitation, as illustrated in figure 6.4.

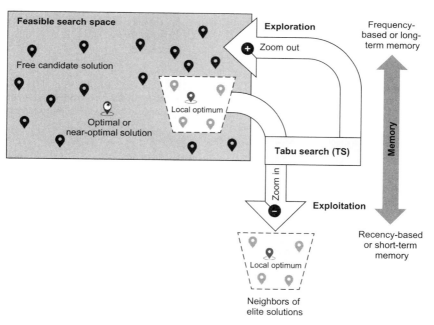

Figure 6.4   TS short-term memory and long-term memory and the search dilemma

The recency-based memory restricts the search to within a set of potentially prosperous or elite solutions to intensify the search while avoiding repetition or reversal of previously visited solutions. Frequency-based memory emphasizes the frequency of different moves to guide the algorithm toward new regions in the search space that might have not been explored. By discouraging the repetition of recent moves, recency-based memory contributes to exploration to a certain extent, but the primary reinforcement for exploration comes from frequency-based memory. The interplay between these memory mechanisms maintains a balance, allowing the algorithm to efficiently navigate the feasible search space.

For the 4-city TSP, a tabu structure can be used to represent both forms of memory, as shown in figure 6.5. In recency-based memory, the tabu structure stores the number of iterations for which a given swap is prohibited.

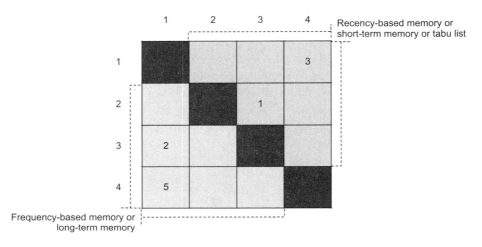

Figure 6.5   Tabu structure for the 4-city TSP. The numbers in recency-based memory represent the number of iterations remaining for tabu-active moves; the numbers in long-term memory represent the frequency count of using the move.

This recency-based memory mechanism is implemented using a tabu list as a data structure to keep track of the forbidden or tabu-active moves, preventing the algorithm from revisiting them for a specified number of iterations, called the *tabu tenure*. At each iteration, the tenure of each move already in the tabu list is decreased by 1, and those moves with zero tenure are dropped from the tabu list. The tabu tenure T can be chosen using different methods:

- *Static*—Choose T to be a constant, which may depend on the problem size, such as using guidelines like $\sqrt{N}$ or $N/10$ iterations where N is the problem size. It has been shown that a static tabu tenure cannot always prevent cycling [3].
- *Dynamic*—Choose T to vary randomly between a specific range T_{min} and T_{max} following the search progress. The threshold T_{min} and T_{max} can vary based on how the solution is improving during a certain number of iterations.

In the previous 4-city TSP example (figure 6.2), let's assume the tabu tenure is set as 3 iterations. If a solution is generated based on swap (1,4), this swap will be tabu-active for three iterations, meaning that it cannot be performed for the next three iterations.

Frequency-based memory, shown in the lower-left corner of figure 6.5, contains values that correspond to the frequency count of the swap. Whenever a swap occurs between two cities, the frequency counters of the respective swap values in the frequency table will increase by 1. When searching for the optimal solution, the values in the frequency counter are taken into account as a penalty for solutions which have been visited frequently. A penalized value directly proportional to the frequency count can be added to the cost or the fitness function of the solution.

6.2.2 Aspiration criteria

Avoiding tabu-active moves is necessary, but some of these moves may possess significant potential. In such instances, the tabu restrictions may hinder promising solutions, even in the absence of cycling risks. This problem is known as *stagnation*. In tabu search, stagnation can occur when the algorithm keeps rejecting candidate moves because they are tabu-active, and all tabu-inactive moves have already been explored or are non-improving moves. This can result in the algorithm revisiting the same solutions repeatedly without making any significant progress toward better solutions.

Aspiration criteria can mitigate this stagnation by allowing the algorithm to consider moves that are tabu-active but that lead to better solutions than the current best solution. By temporarily lifting tabu conditions for certain attributes of the solution, the algorithm can explore new regions of the search space and potentially discover better solutions. A commonly used aspiration criterion in almost all tabu search implementations is to allow the tabu activation rule to be overridden if the move yields a solution better than the best obtained so far (the incumbent solution) and when few iterations are left before this tabu-active move will get out of the tabu list.

6.2.3 Adaptation in TS

TS is applicable in both discrete and continuous solution spaces. For some complex problems, such as scheduling, quadratic assignment, and vehicle routing, tabu search obtains solutions that often surpass the best solutions previously found by other approaches. However, to achieve the best results, many parameters need to be carefully tuned, and the number of iterations required may also be large.

As is the case for all metaheuristics algorithms, a global optimum may not be found, depending on the parameter settings. TS parameters include the initial solution generation method (random, greedy, heuristic, etc.), tabu tenure, neighborhood structure, aspiration criteria, stopping criteria, and penalized value of the frequency count. These parameters can be pretuned or autotuned to improve the performance of TS. Parameter tuning refers to finding suitable values for the different algorithm parameters before the algorithm is run, but adaptation can also be done on the fly while the algorithm is running, following deterministic, adaptive, or self-adaptive approaches to balance exploration and exploitation:

- *Deterministic tuning* is when the control parameter is changed according to some deterministic update rule without taking into account any information from the search algorithm.

- *Adaptive tuning* is when the update rule takes information from the search algorithm and changes the control parameter accordingly.
- *Self-adaptive tuning* is when the update rule itself is adapted.

One of the most important parameters of TS is the tabu tenure. Figure 6.6 illustrates the effect of tabu tenure on the performance of TS. A tabu tenure that is too short may result in frequent cycling, where the algorithm performs the same moves or revisits the same solutions in a repetitive manner. This hinders the exploration of diverse areas in the solution space and may prevent the discovery of optimal or near-optimal solutions. Moreover, tabu tenures that are too short may lift restrictions on moves quickly, potentially causing the algorithm to overlook promising solutions that were temporarily deemed unfavorable. In contrast, a tabu tenure that is excessively long may lead to stagnation, where certain moves remain prohibited for an extended period. This can prevent the algorithm from exploring new regions of the solution space, potentially hindering the discovery of better solutions. Moreover, long tabu tenures increase the memory footprint of the algorithm, potentially leading to inefficiency and increased computational demands. This can be particularly problematic for large-scale problems.

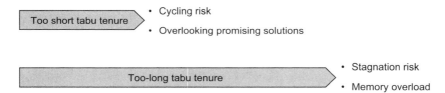

Figure 6.6   Effect of tabu tenure

One of the adaptive approaches incorporated into TS is to allow the length of the short-term memory (the tabu tenure) to vary dynamically and intensify the search when indicators identify promising regions or to promote diversification if the improvements seem to be minimal or a local optimum is detected. For example, you can set a lower bound L_{min} and an upper bound L_{max} for the tabu tenure. You can then decrement the tabu tenure by 1 if the solution has improved over the last iteration so the search will focus in a region of potential improvement. If the solution has deteriorated over the last iteration, you can increment the tabu tenure by 1 to guide the search away from an apparently bad region, as illustrated in figure 6.7. The values of L_{min} and L_{max} can be randomly changed every specific number of iterations.

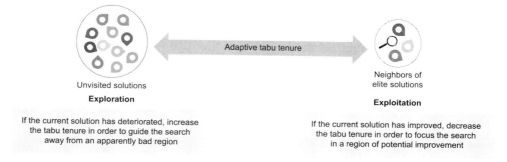

Figure 6.7   Dynamically controlling the tabu tenure

Reactive TS prevents the cycle occurrence by automatically learning the optimal tabu tenure [4]. In this approach, two possible reaction mechanisms are considered. An *immediate reaction mechanism* increases the tabu tenure to discourage additional repetitions. After a number of R immediate reactions, the geometric increase is sufficient to break any limit cycle. A second mechanism, called an *escape mechanism*, counts the number of moves that are repeated many times (more than *REP* times). When this number is greater than a predefined threshold *REP*, a diversifying escape movement is enforced. Other algorithm parameters, such as applying frequency-based memory or aspiration criterion, can be also considered when creating an adaptive version of tabu search.

Now that you have a good understanding of the various components of tabu search, let's explore how this algorithm can be used to solve a variety of optimization problems.

6.3   Solving constraint satisfaction problems

The *n*-queens problem is a classic puzzle that involves placing n chess queens on an $n \times n$ chessboard in such a way that no two queens threaten each other. In other words, no two queens should share the same row, column, or diagonal. This is a constraint-satisfaction problem (CSP) that does not define an explicit objective function. Let's suppose we are attempting to solve a 7-queens problem using tabu search. In this problem, the number of collisions in the initial random configuration shown in figure 6.8a is 4: {Q1 – Q2}, {Q2 – Q6}, {Q4 – Q5}, and {Q6 – Q7}.

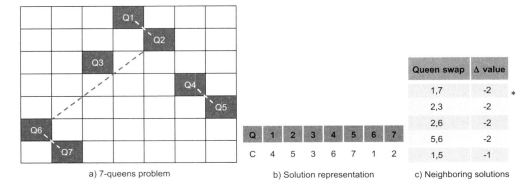

Figure 6.8   TS initialization for a 7-queens problem. At the left, the dotted lines show the 4 collisions between the queens. In the middle, C represents the column where a queen Q is placed. At the right, * denotes the swap that gives the best neighboring solution.

The initial solution in figure 6.8a can be represented as the ordering shown in figure 6.8b. A number of candidate neighboring solutions can be generated by swapping as shown in figure 6.8c. Swaps (Q1,Q7), (Q2,Q3), (Q2,Q6), and (Q5,Q6) give the same value, so let's assume that (Q1,Q7) is arbitrarily selected as a move that gives a new solution, which is shown in figure 6.9. In the initial iteration, Q1 was placed in column 4, and Q7 was placed in column 2. Swapping Q1 and Q7 means placing Q1 in column 2 and Q7 in column 4.

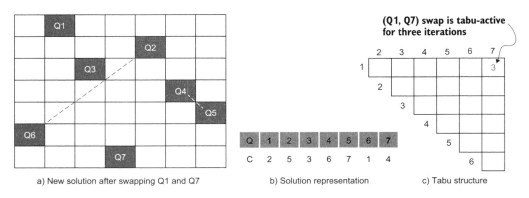

Figure 6.9   A 7-queens problem—TS iteration 1

The number of collisions is now reduced to 2, which are {Q2-Q6} and {Q4-Q5}. The tabu structure is updated as shown in figure 6.9c, forbidding the recently performed swap (Q1,Q7) for three iterations, assuming that the tabu tenure is 3.

In the next iteration, other neighboring solutions can be generated by swapping Q2 and Q4, as illustrated in figure 6.10. Swap (Q2,Q4) gives a new candidate solution, as it reduces the collisions by 1. The associated number of collisions for this solution is 1. The tabu structure is updated, and the search continues.

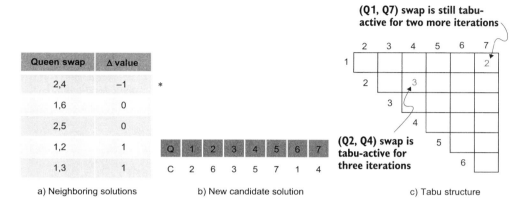

Figure 6.10   A 7-queens problem—TS iteration 2

In the next iteration (figure 6.11), swap (Q1,Q3) is selected as a move that gives a new solution.

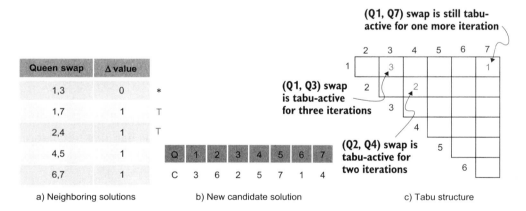

Figure 6.11   A 7-queens problem—TS iteration 3

In the new iteration (figure 6.12), swap (Q5,Q7) is selected. The *T* in figure 6.12a denotes the tabu-active moves.

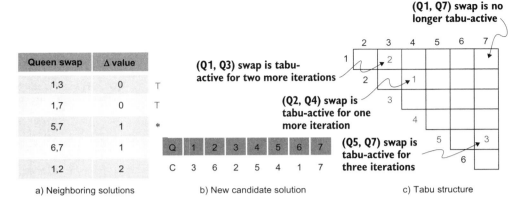

Figure 6.12   A 7-queens problem—TS iteration 4

In the next iteration, the (Q4,Q7) swap is selected (figure 6.13).

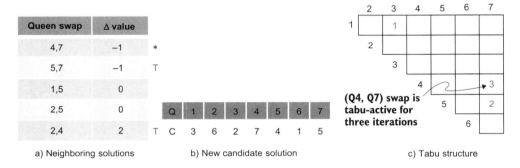

Figure 6.13   A 7-queens problem—TS iteration 5

In the next iteration, as the improving swaps are tabu-active, we can apply aspiration criteria to select swap (Q1,Q3) because there is only one iteration left before this swap is out of the tabu list (figure 6.14).

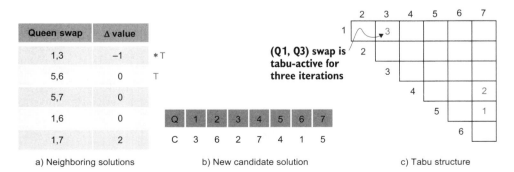

Figure 6.14   A 7-queens problem—TS iteration 6

Based on this solution, the board configuration will be as shown in figure 6.15. This is one of various possible solutions.

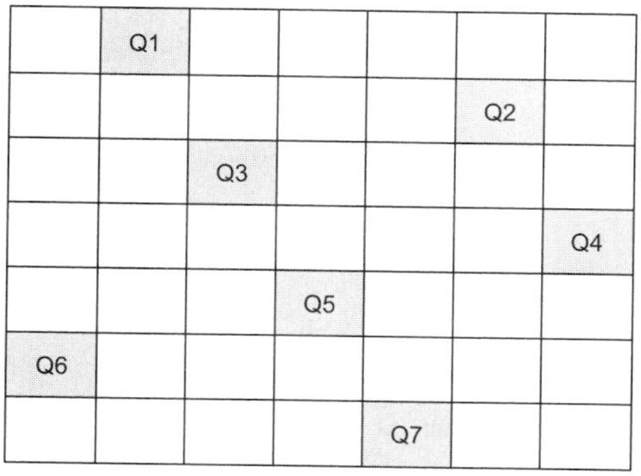

Figure 6.15 **A 7-queens solution generated by hand-iteration**

Let's explore how we can use Python to solve this problem using tabu search. To begin, we'll import the following Python libraries for random number generation and multi-dimensional arrays and plotting. Then we'll define a function to generate a random configuration for a *n*-queens board, based on a predefined board size.

Listing 6.1 Solving the 7-queens problem

```python
import random
import numpy as np
import matplotlib.pyplot as plt
def get_initial_state(board_size):
    queens = list(range(board_size))
    random.shuffle(queens)
    return queens
```

Assuming that the board size is 7, calling this function returns a random board configuration such as [0, 4, 1, 5, 6, 2, 3]. This means that Q1, Q2, Q3, Q4, Q5, Q6, and Q7 are placed in columns 1, 5, 2, 6, 7, 3, and 4 respectively.

We can then define a function to compute the number of queens that are attacking each other on the board. This function is defined as follows:

```python
def num_attacking_queens(queens):
    board_size = len(queens)
    num_attacks = 0
    for i in range(board_size):
        for j in range(i + 1, board_size):
            if queens[i]==queens[j] or abs(queens[i] - queens[j]) == j - i:
                num_attacks += 1
    return num_attacks
```

Next, we can create a function to determine the best possible move that decreases the number of attacks on the board, while ensuring that the move is not currently on the tabu list (i.e., not tabu-active). This function is defined as follows:

```python
def get_best_move(queens, tabu_list):
    board_size = len(queens)
    best_move = None
    best_num_attacks = board_size * (board_size - 1) // 2
    for i in range(board_size):
        for j in range(board_size):
            if queens[i] != j:
                new_queens = queens.copy()
                new_queens[i] = j
                if str(new_queens) not in tabu_list:
                    num_attacks = num_attacking_queens(new_queens)
                    if num_attacks < best_num_attacks:
                        best_move = (i, j)
                        best_num_attacks = num_attacks
    return best_move
```

As you may have noticed, the best number of attacks is initialized as the maximum number of attacks, which is $n * (n - 1) / 2$. In a 7-queens problem, this number is $7 * 6 / 2 = 21$.

We also need to implement a function that updates the tabu list based on a predefined tabu tenure. Here is the definition of this function:

```python
def update_tabu_list(tabu_list, tabu_tenure, move):
    tabu_list.append(str(move))
    if len(tabu_list) > tabu_tenure:
        tabu_list.pop(0)
```

The following function executes the steps of the tabu search, taking input parameters such as the maximum number of iterations, the tabu tenure, and the maximum number of moves without improvement before concluding that the solution is stuck, and the initial solution:

```python
def tabu_search(num_iterations, tabu_tenure, max_non_improvement, queens):
    num_non_improvement = 0
    best_queens = queens
    best_num_attacks = num_attacking_queens(queens)
    tabu_list = []

    for i in range(num_iterations):
        move = get_best_move(queens, tabu_list)
        if move is not None:
            queens[move[0]] = move[1]
            update_tabu_list(tabu_list, tabu_tennure, move)
            num_attacks = num_attacking_queens(queens)
            if num_attacks < best_num_attacks:
                best_queens = queens
                best_num_attacks = num_attacks
                num_non_improvement = 0
        else:
```

```
        num_non_improvement += 1
        if num_non_improvement >= max_non_improvement:
            break

    return best_queens, num_attacks
```

For a board size of 7, the maximum number of iterations is 2,000, the tabu tenure is 10, and the maximum number of moves without improvement before considering the solution to be stuck is 50. Calling the tabu search gives the solution [5, 1, 4, 0, 3, 6, 2], which is shown in figure 6.16.

Figure 6.16 A 7-queens solution generated by Python code

The full code for this implementation can be found in listing 6.1 in the book's GitHub repository. The number of iterations is used in the code as a stopping criterion. As an exercise, you can modify the code to add a stopping criterion that terminates the search once a solution with zero attacks has been found.

The *n*-queens problem is a discrete problem, as it involves finding a feasible configuration of chess queens on a discrete chessboard. In the following section, we'll explore how tabu search can be applied to continuous problems in the form of function optimization.

6.4 *Solving continuous problems*

As an illustration of continuous problems, let's begin with function optimization. The Himmelblau function $(f(x,y) = (x^2 + y - 11)^2 + (x + y^2 - 7)^2)$, named after David Mautner Himmelblau (1924–2011), is a multimodal function that is often used as a test problem for optimization algorithms. It is a nonconvex function with four identical local minima at (3.0, 2.0), (−2.805118, 3.131312), (−3.779310, −3.283186), and (3.584428, −1.848126), as shown in figure 6.17.

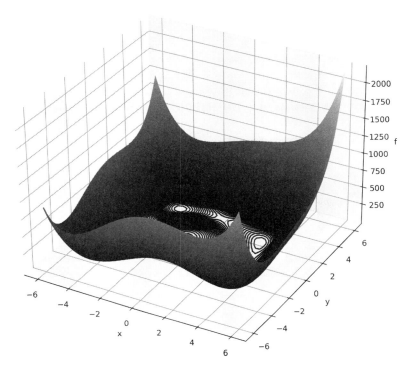

Figure 6.17   Himmelblau's function has four identical local minima at (3.0, 2.0), (−2.805118, 3.131312), (−3.779310, −3.283186), and (3.584428, −1.848126).

A generic Python implementation of tabu search is available as part of our optalgo-tools package. In this implementation, a hash table or dictionary as an indexed data structure is used to implement the tabu structure. A hashmap is a set of key–value pairs with no duplicate keys. It can be used to quickly retrieve data no matter how much data there is, as it has a big $O(1)$ for add, get, and delete functions.

The generic TS solver takes the following arguments:

- Maximum number of iterations (default `max_iter=1000`)
- Tabu tenure (default `tabu_tenure=1000`)
- Neighborhood size (default `neighbor_size=10`)
- Aspiration criteria (default `use_aspiration=True`)
- Remaining number of iterations to get out of tabu (default `aspiration_limit=None`)
- Incorporating frequency-based memory (default `use_longterm=False`)

The next listing shows how we can solve the minimization problem of Himmelblau's function using the generic tabu search solver implemented in optalgotools.

Listing 6.2   Solving Himmelblau's function using tabu search

Import the generic tabu search solver from optalgotools.   **Import the continuous problem base.**

```
import numpy as np
from optalgotools.algorithms import TabuSearch
from optalgotools.problems import ProblemBase, ContinuousFunctionBase
```

Define the objective function.   **Define the bounds.**

```
def Himmelblau(x,y):
      return (((x**2+y-11)**2) + (((x+y**2-7)**2)))

Himmelblau_bounds = np.asarray([[-6, 6], [-6, 6]])
```

Create a continuous function object.

```
Himmelblau_obj = ContinuousFunctionBase(Himmelblau, Himmelblau_bounds)

ts = TabuSearch(max_iter=100, tabu_tenure=5, neighbor_size=50, use_
aspiration=True,
➥    aspiration_limit=2, use_longterm=False, debug=1)
ts.run(Himmelblau_obj)
```

Define the TS solver.
Add debug = 1 to print the initial and final solution.
Run the solver.

Running this code gives a potential solution for Himmelblau's function:

```
Tabu search is initialized:
current value = 148.322
Tabu search is done:
curr iter: 100, curr best value: 0.005569730862620958, curr best: sol:
[3.00736837 1.98045825], found at iter: 21
```

Proper tuning of the various algorithm parameters allows you to find an optimal or near-optimal solution. Several other optimization test functions are available in appendix B. You may consider trying different functions by modifying listing 6.2.

Next, let's examine how tabu search can address the traveling salesman problem.

6.5   Solving TSP and routing problems

Let's look at using tabu search, implemented in Google OR-Tools, to solve the Berlin52 instance of TSP. This dataset contains 52 locations in the city of Berlin (http:// comopt.ifi.uni-heidelberg.de/software/TSPLIB95/STSP.html). The objective of the problem is to find the shortest possible tour that visits each location exactly once and then return to the starting location. The shortest route obtained for the Berlin52 dataset is 7,542, as explained in the previous chapter.

We'll start by importing the TSP problem class, the OR-Tools constraint programming solver, and the protocol buffer module that defines various enumerations (enums) used in the routing library of OR-Tools. We'll then create a tsp object from our generic tsp class implemented in optalgotools. We'll extract points of interest, nodes, or cities and calculate pairwise distances. The pairwise distances will be converted into integers as required by OR-Tools. Then we'll store the problem data in the form of a dictionary. In this dictionary, distance_matrix will represent the pairwise distances between the points of interest in the dataset.

Listing 6.3   Solving Belin52 TSP using OR-Tools tabu search

Import the TSP problem class from optalgotools.

Import the protocol buffer module.

Import the Python wrapper for the C++ constraint programming solver in OR-Tools.

```
import numpy as np
from optalgotools.problems import TSP
from ortools.constraint_solver import pywrapcp
from ortools.constraint_solver import routing_enums_pb2
import matplotlib.pyplot as plt

berlin52_tsp_url = 'https://raw.githubusercontent.com/coin-or/jorlib/
b3a41ce773e9b3b5b73c149d4c06097ea1511680/jorlib-core/src/test/resources/
tspLib/tsp/berlin52.tsp'
```
Get berlin52 from a permalink.

```
berlin52_tsp = TSP(load_tsp_url=berlin52_tsp_url, gen_method='mutate',
    init_method='random')
```
Create a different tsp object from the problem class.

```
cities = berlin52_tsp.cities
tsp_dist=berlin52_tsp.eval_distances_from_cities(cities)
tsp_dist_int=list(np.array(tsp_dist).astype(int))
```
Define the problem parameters.

We need to create a routing model by defining `data`, an index manager (`manager`), and a routing model (`routing`). The pairwise distances between any two nodes will be returned by the `distance_callback` function, which also converts from the routing variable `Index` to the distance matrix `NodeIndex`. The cost of the edge joining any two points of interest in the dataset is computed using an arc cost evaluator that tells the solver how to calculate the cost of travel between any two locations.

The data model is where the distance matrix, number of vehicles, and home city or initial depot are defined:

```
def create_data_model():
    data = {}
    data['distance_matrix'] = tsp_dist_int
    data['num_vehicles'] = 1
    data['depot'] = 0
    return data
```

The following function returns the pair-wise distance between any two nodes:

```
def distance_callback(from_index, to_index):
    from_node = manager.IndexToNode(from_index)
    to_node = manager.IndexToNode(to_index)
    return data['distance_matrix'][from_node][to_node]
```

The obtained route and its cost, or length, can be printed using the following function:

```
def print_solution(manager, routing, solution):
    print('Objective: {} meters'.format(solution.ObjectiveValue()))
    index = routing.Start(0)
    plan_output = 'Route for vehicle 0:\n'
    route_distance = 0
```

```
while not routing.IsEnd(index):
    plan_output += ' {} ->'.format(manager.IndexToNode(index))
    previous_index = index
    index = solution.Value(routing.NextVar(index))
    route_distance += routing.GetArcCostForVehicle(previous_index, index, 0)
plan_output += ' {}\n'.format(manager.IndexToNode(index))
plan_output += 'Route distance: {}meters\n'.format(route_distance)
```

Let's now look at how we can actually solve the TSP using the tabu search implemented in OR-Tools. We'll start by using the preceding functions to create a data model, which generates the data necessary for the TSP, such as the distance matrix between the cities, the number of vehicles, and the home city or the initial depot.

Next, we'll define a manager to manage the indices of the routing problem. For this, we'll use the `RoutingIndexManager` class from the `pywrapcp` module in the OR-Tools. This module provides a Python wrapper for the CP-SAT solver, a constraint programming solver developed by Google.

Then we'll create the `RoutingModel` object by using the `RoutingIndexManager` object. This `RoutingModel` object is used to define the constraints and objectives of the capacitated vehicle routing problem (CVRP), which is considered a generalization of TSP. The `RegisterTransitCallback()` method will register a callback function that calculates the distance between two cities. This callback function is defined in the `distance_callback` function.

The `SetArcCostEvaluatorOfAllVehicles()` method will set the arc cost evaluator of all the vehicles to the transit callback index, which calculates the distance between two nodes. In our case, we have a single traveling salesman or a single vehicle (so `num_vehicles=1`), but this code can also handle multiple TSP (mTSP) or multiple vehicles as well.

The `DefaultRoutingSearchParameters()` method will create an object of the `RoutingSearchParameters` class, which specifies the search parameters for solving the routing problem. In this case, the local search metaheuristic is set to tabu search, and the time limit is set to 30 seconds. Other available methods include GREEDY_DESCENT, SIMULATED_ANNEALING, and GENERIC_TABU_SEARCH. The main difference between TABU_SEARCH and GENERIC_TABU_SEARCH is in the way they handle the tabu list. TABU_SEARCH maintains a tabu list for each variable and applies tabu constraints to the current assignment. GENERIC_TABU_SEARCH, on the other hand, maintains a single tabu list for the entire search and applies tabu constraints to the moves made by the search.

The `SolveWithParameters()` method solves the routing problem with the specified search parameters. If a solution is found, it calls the `print_solution()` function to print the solution:

```
data = create_data_model()    ◄────────| Create the model.
manager = pywrapcp.RoutingIndexManager(len(data['distance_matrix']),
                                       data['num_vehicles'], data['depot'])
```

```
routing = pywrapcp.RoutingModel(manager)

transit_callback_index = routing.RegisterTransitCallback(distance_callback)

routing.SetArcCostEvaluatorOfAllVehicles(transit_callback_index)

search_parameters = pywrapcp.DefaultRoutingSearchParameters()
search_parameters.local_search_metaheuristic = (
       routing_enums_pb2.LocalSearchMetaheuristic.TABU_SEARCH)
search_parameters.time_limit.seconds = 30
search_parameters.log_search = True

solution = routing.SolveWithParameters(search_parameters)
if solution:
    print_solution(manager, routing, solution)
```

Set TABU_SEARCH as the solver.

Find the solution.

The following get_routes() function can then be called to extract the routes for each vehicle from the solution. This function iterates through each vehicle, starting with the start node, and adds the nodes visited by the vehicle until it reaches the end node. It then returns a list of routes for each vehicle:

```
def get_routes(solution, routing, manager):
  routes = []
  for route_nbr in range(routing.vehicles()):
    index = routing.Start(route_nbr)
    route = [manager.IndexToNode(index)]
    while not routing.IsEnd(index):
      index = solution.Value(routing.NextVar(index))
      route.append(manager.IndexToNode(index))
    routes.append(route)
  return routes

routes = get_routes(solution, routing, manager)

for i, route in enumerate(routes):
  print('Route', i, route)
berlin52_tsp.plot(route)
```

Print the route.

Visualize the route.

Running this code produces the following results and the route shown in figure 6.18:

```
Objective: 7884 meters
Route for vehicle 0:
 0 -> 21 -> 31 -> 44 -> 18 -> 40 -> 7 -> 8 -> 9 -> 42 -> 32 -> 50 -> 11 -> 10
-> 51 -> 13 -> 12 -> 26 -> 27 -> 25 -> 46 -> 28 -> 29 -> 1 -> 6 -> 41 -> 20
-> 16 -> 2 -> 17 -> 30 -> 22 -> 19 -> 49 -> 15 -> 43 -> 45 -> 24 -> 3 -> 5 ->
14 -> 4 -> 23 -> 47 -> 37 -> 36 -> 39 -> 38 -> 33 -> 34 -> 35 -> 48 -> 0
```

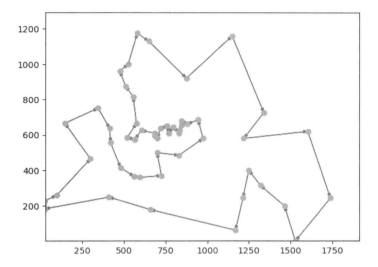

Figure 6.18   A TSP solution using the tabu search in OR-Tools. The graph shows the x and y locations of the points of interest included in the dataset in km.

The preceding implementation applies a simple aspiration criterion, where a solution is accepted if it is better than any other solution encountered so far. OR-Tools is very efficient in solving this problem (the obtained route length is 7,884, while the optimal solution is 7,542). However, the implemented tabu search is mainly used to solve routing problems.

As a continuation of listing 6.3, the following code snippet shows a generic tabu search solver in optalgotools that can be used to solve the same problem:

Create a TSP object for the problem.   **Create a TS object to help in solving the TSP problem.**

```
from optalgotools.algorithms import TabuSearch

ts = TabuSearch(max_iter=100, tabu_tenure=5, neighbor_size=10000,
     use_aspiration=True, aspiration_limit=2, use_longterm=False, debug=1)

ts.init_ts(berlin52_tsp,'random')
ts.val_cur
```
Get an initial random solution, and check its length.

```
ts.run(berlin52_tsp, repetition=1)
```
Run TS, and evaluate the best solution distance.

```
print(ts.s_best)
print(ts.val_best)
```
Print the best route.
Print the route length.

```
berlin52_tsp.plot(ts.s_best)
```
Visualize the best route.

Running this code produces the following results:

```
sol: [0, 21, 17, 2, 16, 20, 41, 6, 1, 29, 28, 15, 45, 47, 23, 36, 33, 43, 49,
19, 22, 30, 44, 18, 40, 7, 8, 9, 42, 32, 50, 10, 51, 13, 12, 46, 25, 26, 27,
11, 24, 3, 5, 14, 4, 37, 39, 38, 35, 34, 48, 31, 0], found at iter: 51
7982.79
```

As you can see, the obtained route length using our tabu search solver is 7,982.79, while the tabu search implemented in OR-Tools provides 7,884, and the optimal solution is 7,542. The tabu search algorithm implemented in optalgotools is also slower than the optimized tabu search implemented in Google's OR-Tools.

Let's revisit the delivery semi-truck routing problem discussed in section 5.6. In this problem, we need to find the optimal route for a delivery semi-truck to visit 18 Walmart Supercenters in a selected part of the Greater Toronto Area (GTA) starting from Walmart Supercenter number 3001, located at 270 Kingston Rd. E in Ajax, Ontario. The next listing shows how we can use the generic tabu search solver to handle this problem. A complete listing is available in the book's GitHub repo.

Listing 6.4   Solving the delivery semi-truck problem using tabu search

Get an initial random solution, and check its length.

Create a TS object to help solve the TSP problem.

Create a TSP object for the problem.

```
from optalgotools.algorithms import TabuSearch
from optalgotools.problems import TSP

gta_part_tsp = TSP(dists=gta_part_dists, gen_method='mutate')

ts = TabuSearch(max_iter=1000, tabu_tenure=5, neighbor_size=100,
    use_aspiration=True, aspiration_limit=2, use_longterm=False, debug=1)

ts.init_ts(gta_part_tsp,'random')

draw_map_path(G, ts.s_cur, gta_part_loc, gta_part_pathes)

ts.run(gta_part_tsp, repetition=5)

print(ts.s_allbest)
print(ts.val_allbest)

draw_map_path(G, ts.s_allbest, gta_part_loc, gta_part_pathes)
```

Draw the path of the random initial solution.

Run tabu search five times, and return the best solution.

Print the best solution.

Print the best route length.

Visualize the obtained route.

The generated route for the delivery semi-truck problem is shown in figure 6.19.

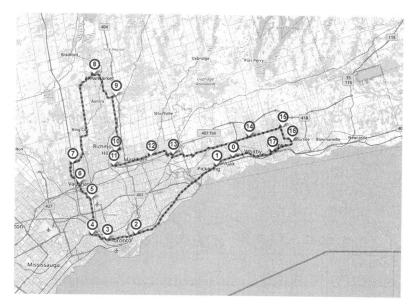

Figure 6.19   The TS solution for the Walmart delivery semi-truck route with a total distance of 223.53 km

Tabu search generates a slightly shorter route (223.53 km) than simulated annealing (227.17 km). Compared to the tabu search algorithm implemented in OR-Tools, the tabu search algorithm in optalgotools gives you more freedom to tune more parameters and to handle different types of discrete and continuous problems.

In the next section, we will delve into another notable challenge that the manufacturing sector faces.

6.6   *Assembly line balancing problem*

Henry Ford designed and installed an assembly line for car mass production in 1913. This development of assembly line manufacturing enabled mass production during the second industrial revolution and beyond. An *assembly line* is a flow-oriented production system where the productive units performing the operations, referred to as *workstations* or simply *stations*, are aligned sequentially. The work pieces visit the stations successively as they are moved along the line, usually by some kind of transportation system, such as a conveyor belt. At each workstation, new parts are added or new assemblies take place, resulting in a finished product at the end.

For example, figure 6.20 shows an example of a bike assembly line with five workstations. Beginning at the initial workstation WS-1, workers focus on assembling the frame, laying the foundation for subsequent tasks. Moving along the line, WS-2 takes charge of installing the forks and handlebars, while WS-3 attaches the wheels. Following this, at WS-4, workers undertake the intricate assembly of crankset, chain, derailleurs, gears, and pedals. Finally, at WS-5, the seat is securely affixed and other accessories are added, completing the assembly process. Three lamps are used to indicate the status of operation of each workstation: emergency, finish, and work in progress (WIP).

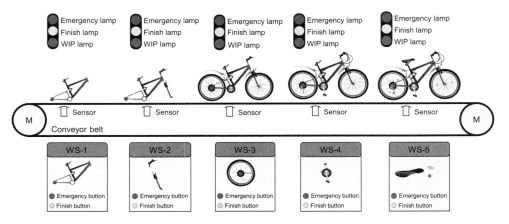

Figure 6.20   Assembly line balancing problem

It is crucial to optimize the design of an assembly line before implementing it, as assembly lines are designed to ensure high production efficiency, and reconfiguring them can result in significant investment costs. The assembly line balancing problem (ALBP) addresses the assignment of tasks (work elements) to workstations in order to minimize the amount of idle time of the line, while satisfying specific constraints. ALBP generally comprises all tasks and decisions related to equipping and aligning the productive units for a given production process before the actual assembly process can start. This encompasses setting the system capacity, which includes cycle time, number of stations, and station equipment, as well as assigning work content to productive units, which includes task assignment and determining the sequence of operations. This *balancing* of assembly lines is a difficult combinatorial optimization problem arising frequently in manufacturing.

Assembly line balancing problems can be categorized into two main groups: simple assembly line balancing problems (SALBPs) and generalized assembly line balancing problems (GALBPs). An SALBP involves the production of a single product in a serial line on one-sided workstations, while a GALBP considers different assembly line objectives, such as mixed model assembly lines, parallel lines, U-shaped lines, and two-sided lines.

In SALBP, we have a number of tasks that need to be completed by a number of workstations. Each task i has a time requirement t_i, and we are given a maximum number of workstations. Each workstation has a cycle time C, which refers to the time allocated for each station in the assembly line to complete its assigned tasks and pass the product to the next station. The goal is to minimize the number of workstations needed.

To capture more realistic conditions for ALBPs in industry, the time and space assembly line balancing problem (TSALBP) incorporates additional space constraints. A TSALBP involves assigning a set of n tasks with temporal and spatial attributes and a precedence graph. Each task must be assigned to only one station, provided that

- All precedence constraints are met
- The workload time for each station does not exceed the cycle time
- The required space for each station does not exceed the global available space

Different variations on TSALBP with different levels of complexity are shown in table 6.1.

Table 6.1   TSALBP variations: F (feasibility problem), OP (mono-objective optimization problem), MOP (multi-objective optimization problem)

Problem	# of stations	Cycle time	Space or layout of the stations	Type
TSALBP-F	Given	Given	Given	F
TSALBP-1	Minimize	Given	Given	OP
TSALBP-2	Given	Minimize	Given	OP
TSALBP-3	Given	Given	Minimize	OP
TSALBP-1/2	Minimize	Minimize	Given	MOP
TSALBP-1/3	Minimize	Given	Minimize	MOP
TSALBP-2/3	Given	Minimize	Minimize	MOP
TSALBP-1/2/3	Minimize	Minimize	Minimize	MOP

In the bike assembly line illustrated in figure 6.20, installing the forks and handlebar depends on the availability of an assembled frame. Similarly, attaching the wheels depends on the frame and forks assembly being completed. This dependency is defined by a precedence diagram, which shows the relationships between tasks, indicating which tasks must be completed before others can begin. For example, task 2 should be performed before starting tasks 3 and 4, as per the precedence diagram depicted in figure 6.21. In ALBPs, the sequence of the tasks should not violate the specified precedence due to the dependency relations between them.

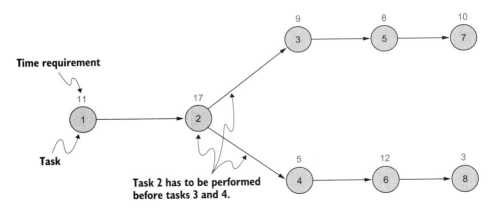

Figure 6.21   A precedence diagram

Simple assembly line balancing problems can be classified into two types: type 1 (SALBP-1) and type 2 (SALBP-2). Under type 1 (SALBP-1), the objective is to minimize the number of stations for a given cycle time. Conversely, under type 2 (SALBP-2), the goal is to minimize the cycle time for a given number of stations. Let's consider a type 1 (SALBP-1) problem that consists of minimizing the number of stations NS given fixed values of the cycle time CT and of the available area per station A. TSALBP-1 is equivalent to SALBP-1 if $A \to \infty$. We'll use smoothing index (SI) as a quantitative measure to evaluate the uniformity of workload distribution among the workstations. Each neighboring solution will be quantitatively evaluated using this SI. The SI aims to get the optimal task assignment for each station to minimize the idle time between stations, taking into account that the constraints imposed on the station's workload cannot exceed the cycle time.

SI is calculated as in equation 6.1:

$$SI = \sqrt{\frac{\sum_{i=1}^{NS} (WL_{max} - WL_i)^2}{NS}}$$

6.1

where

- WL_i is the workload of workstation i
- WL_{max} is the maximum workload
- NS is the number of stations

Tasks are assigned to the stations such that the workload doesn't exceed the cycle time and without violating their precedence. Assume that the cycle time CT is 4 minutes and the number of tasks n is 6, with the precedence diagram given in figure 6.22.

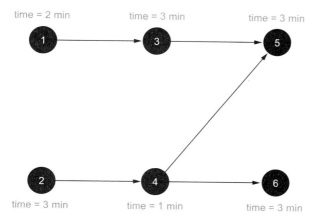

Figure 6.22   Precedence diagram example for six tasks

Let's perform hand iterations to understand how TS can be used to solve this problem, considering a tabu tenure of 3. A random initial solution is generated, as shown in figure 6.23, and its SI is evaluated using equation 6.1. The tabu structure or neighborhood can be defined as any other solution that is obtained by a pair-wise exchange of any two tasks in the solution. In our case, we have six tasks (i.e., $n = 6$) and a pairwise exchange (i.e., $k = 2$). So the maximum number of neighbors is the number of combinations without repetition $C(n,k)$, or n-choose-k, or $n!\ /\ k!\,(n - k)! = 6!\ /\ 2!4! = 15$ neighbors. The solution is presented as a permutation of tasks. For example, the initial solution [1 2 3 4 5 6] reflects the order of execution of the six tasks, taking into consideration the precedence constraint.

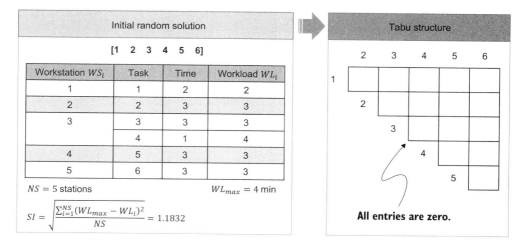

Figure 6.23   TS initialization for SALBP

Figure 6.24 shows the first iteration of TS for solving the SALBP. To generate a neighboring solution, we have to check the precedence diagram (figure 6.22). For example, for task 5 to start, both predecessor tasks 3 and 4 must have finished. Following this precedence diagram, when task 4 finishes, then both tasks 5 and 6 can start.

Let's use the swap method to find a neighboring solution. For this iteration, the neighboring feasible solutions are (1-2), (2-3), (3-4), and (5-6). As the three swaps lead to the same SI, we can arbitrarily pick one, such as (1-2), that results in a new order of task execution (i.e., a new candidate solution). This solution is [2 1 3 4 5 6]. The (1-2) swap should be added to the tabu structure for three iterations, assuming that the tabu tenure is 3.

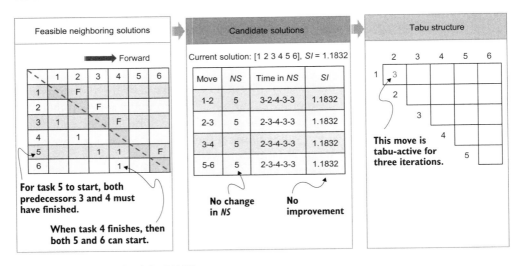

Figure 6.24   TS iteration 1 for SALBP

Moving forward, figure 6.25 shows the second iteration of tabu search. For this iteration, the neighboring feasible solutions are (2-1), (2-3), (3-4), and (5-6). Note that the move (2-1) is tabu-active. The (3-4) swap is selected because it has the smallest SI. The new solution is [2 1 4 3 5 6] with SI = 0, calculated with equation 6.1.

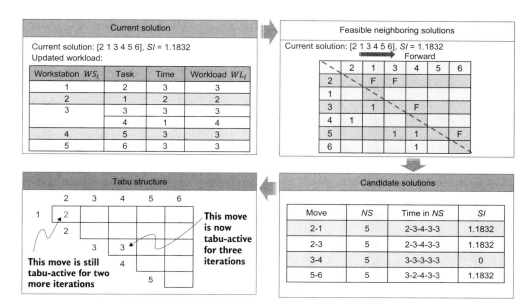

Figure 6.25   TS iteration 2 for SALBP

The tabu list is updated before we start the next iteration, as shown in the figure. The next listing shows a snippet of the tabu search implementation for solving SALBP. A complete listing is available in the book's GitHub repo.

Listing 6.5   Solving SALBP using tabu search

```
import pandas as pd
import numpy as np
import random as rd
import math
import matplotlib.pyplot as plt

tasks = pd.DataFrame(columns=['Task', 'Duration'])
tasks= pd.read_csv("https://raw.githubusercontent.com/Optimization-Algorithms
    -Book/Code-Listings/main/Appendix%20B/data/ALBP/ALB_TS_DATA.txt", sep
=",")
Prec= pd.read_csv("https://raw.githubusercontent.com/Optimization-Algorithms
    -Book/Code-Listings/main/Appendix%20B/data/ALBP/ALB_TS_PRECEDENCE.txt",
    sep =",")
Prec.columns=['TASK', 'IMMEDIATE_PRECEDESSOR']
```

Read data from appendix B directly.

```
Cycle_time = 4
```
Define the cycle time.

```
tenure = 3
max_itr=100
```

Get an initial solution.

Ensure the feasibility of the solution, considering the task precedence constraint.

```
solution = Initial_Solution(len(tasks))
soln_init = Make_Solution_Feasible(solution, Prec)
```

```
sol_best, SI_best=tabu_search(max_itr, soln_init, SI_init, tenure, WS, tasks,
    Prec_Matrix, Cycle_time)
```
Run the tabu search.

```
Smoothing_index(sol_best, WS, tasks, Cycle_time, True)
```
Calculate the SI of the best solution.

```
plt = Make_Solution_to_plot(sol_best, WS, tasks, Cycle_time)
plt.show()
```
Visualize the solution.

Running this code produces the following output:

```
The Smoothing Index value for ['T3', 'T5', 'T6', 'T1', 'T4', 'T2'] solution
sequence is: 0.0
The number of workstations for ['T3', 'T5', 'T6', 'T1', 'T4', 'T2'] solution
sequence is: 5
The workloads of workstation for ['T3', 'T5', 'T6', 'T1', 'T4', 'T2']
solution sequence are: [3. 3. 3. 3. 3.]
```

Figure 6.26 shows the initial and the final solution found by tabu search with a fair load balance between the workstations.

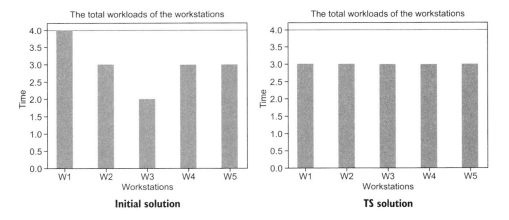

Figure 6.26   SALBP initial and final solutions

Let's now use the generic tabu search solver that's implemented as part of our optalgotools package. There are several benchmark datasets for ALBPs. These datasets are available in appendix B of the book's GitHub repo, and you can access them directly by using the URL to the raw content of the file, which can be obtained by using the "Raw" view in GitHub. Precedence graphs are provided in files with an .IN2 extension.

The next listing shows how to use the generic solver to solve the MANSOOR benchmark SALBP (best *NS* for a given *CT* = 48 is 4). The solution shows both the minimum number of workstations and the SI.

> **Listing 6.6   Assembly line balancing problem benchmarking**

Import the tabu search solver from optalgotools.

```
from optalgotools.algorithms import TabuSearch  ◄
from optalgotools.problems import ALBP  ◄
```

Import the ALBP class from the generic problem class.

```
data_url="https://raw.githubusercontent.com/Optimization-Algorithms-Book/
Code-Listings/main/Appendix%20B/data/ALBP/SALBP-data-sets/precedence%20
graphs/"  ◄
```
Define the URL of the datasets.

```
albp_instance= ALBP(data_url, "MANSOOR.IN2", 48.0)  ◄
```
Create an ALBP instance.

```
ts = TabuSearch(max_iter=20, tabu_tenure=4, neighbor_size=5, use_
aspiration=True,
⮱ aspiration_limit=None, use_longterm=False)  ◄
ts.init_ts(albp_instance)
ts.run(albp_instance, repetition=5)  ◄
```
Create an instance of the tabu search solver.

Solve the problem using tabu search.

```
SI = albp_instance.Smoothing_index(list(ts.s_best), ts.val_best,
⮱ albp_instance.tasks, True)  ◄
print(SI)
```
Print the results.

Calculate the SI of the solution.

Running this code gives the following results:

```
The Smoothing Index value for ['T1', 'T2', 'T4', 'T5', 'T6', 'T7', 'T9',
'T8', 'T10', 'T3', 'T11'] solution sequence is: 12.296340919151518
The number of workstations for ['T1', 'T2', 'T4', 'T5', 'T6', 'T7', 'T9',
'T8', 'T10', 'T3', 'T11'] solution sequence is: 5
The workloads of workstation for ['T1', 'T2', 'T4', 'T5', 'T6', 'T7', 'T9',
'T8', 'T10', 'T3', 'T11'] solution sequence are: [42. 44. 20. 45. 34.]
```

The complete listing in the book's GitHub repo shows several different datasets, including the following:

- MITCHELL (best NS for a given CT = 26 is 5)
- SAWYER30 (best NS for a given CT = 26 is 10)
- HAHN (best NS for a given CT = 2338 is 7)
- GUNTHER (best NS for a given CT = 44 is 12)
- BUXEY (best NS for a given CT = 47 is 7)
- LUTZ2 (best NS for a given CT = 11 is 49)
- BARTHOL2 (best NS for a given CT = 104 is 41)
- JACKSON (best NS for a given CT = 9 is 6)
- TONGE70 (best NS for a given CT = 293 is 13)

That concludes the second part of this book. We'll now shift our focus to evolutionary computation algorithms like genetic algorithms. These algorithms feature inherent parallelism and the capability to adapt their search for optimal solutions dynamically.

Summary

- Local search iteratively explores a subset of the search space in the neighborhood of the current solution or state in order to improve the solution by making local changes.
- Tabu search extends local search by combining it with adaptive memory structures. It guides a local search procedure to explore the solution space beyond any local optimality.
- Adaptive memory structures are used to remember recent algorithm moves and capture promising solutions.
- A tabu list is a data structure that keeps track of tabu-active moves.
- Tabu tenure refers to the specified number of iterations for which certain moves or solutions are marked as tabu-active.
- A too-short tabu tenure can result in cycling and the neglect of promising solutions, while a too-long tabu tenure may lead to stagnation and memory overload.
- As a way to avoid search stagnation, aspiration criteria allow tabu-active moves to be accepted by relaxing or temporarily lifting the tabu condition.
- A crucial aspect of adaptive tabu search involves striking a balance between exploiting search and exploration.

Part 3

Evolutionary computing algorithms

As we continue our journey into the world of optimization algorithms, this part will introduce you to the fascinating realm of genetic algorithms, a prime example of population-based metaheuristic algorithms. Within the two chapters of this part, you'll delve into the heart of evolutionary computation and unlock the potential of genetic algorithms as versatile tools for solving a wide range of optimization problems.

In chapter 7, you'll learn about population-based optimization algorithms and, more specifically, genetic algorithms. You'll discover the inner workings of evolutionary computation and gain a comprehensive understanding of the various components that make up genetic algorithms. We'll take a hands-on approach by implementing genetic algorithms in Python, allowing you to apply this powerful technique to practical problem-solving.

Chapter 8 will take you further into the world of genetic algorithms, exploring variants that enhance their adaptability to different problem types. You'll delve into Gray-coded genetic algorithms, explore real-valued genetic algorithms and their genetic operators, and understand permutation-based genetic algorithms and their applications. Additionally, you'll discover the concept of multi-objective optimization and learn how to fine-tune genetic algorithms to strike a balance between exploration and exploitation. Through practical examples, you'll see how genetic algorithms can efficiently solve both continuous and discrete optimization problems.

Genetic algorithms

7

This chapter covers

- Introducing population-based optimization algorithms
- Understanding evolutionary computation
- Understanding the different components of genetic algorithms
- Implementing genetic algorithms in Python

Suppose you're on a treasure-hunting mission and you don't want the risk of searching alone and returning empty-handed. You might decide to collaborate with a group of friends and share information. This approach follows a population-based search strategy, where multiple agents are involved in the search process.

During this collaborative effort, you may notice that some hunters perform better than others. In this case, you may choose to retain only the best-performing hunters and replace the less competent ones with new recruits. This process resembles the workings of evolutionary algorithms such as genetic algorithms, where the fittest individuals survive and pass on their traits to the next generation.

In this chapter, the binary-coded genetic algorithm is presented and discussed as an evolutionary computing algorithm. We'll look at different elements of this algorithm and at the implementation details. Other variants of genetic algorithms, such as the gray-coded genetic algorithm, real-valued genetic algorithm, and permutation-based genetic algorithm will be discussed in the next chapter.

7.1   *Population-based metaheuristic algorithms*

Population-based metaheuristic algorithms (P-metaheuristics), such as genetic algorithms, particle swarm optimization, and ant colony optimization, utilize multiple agents to search for an optimal or near-optimal global solution. As these algorithms begin with a diverse set of initial populations, they are naturally more exploration-based, allowing for the possibility of finding better solutions that might be missed by trajectory-based (S-metaheuristic) algorithms, which are more exploitation-based.

Population-based metaheuristic algorithms can be classified into two main categories based on their source of inspiration: *evolutionary computation algorithms* and *swarm intelligence algorithms*, as shown in figure 7.1.

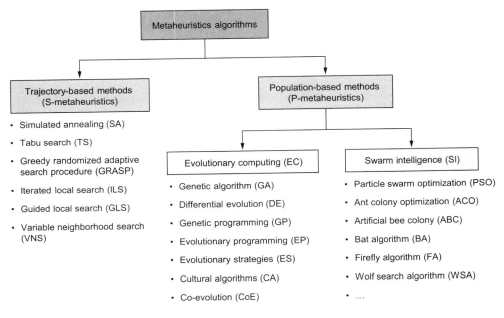

Figure 7.1   Metaheuristic algorithms

Evolutionary computation (EC) algorithms, as the name suggests, are inspired by the process of biological evolution. These algorithms use a population of potential solutions, which undergo genetic operations, such as mutation and crossover, to create new offspring that may have better fitness values. The process of selection determines which individuals in the population are selected to reproduce and create the next generation. Genetic algorithm (GA), differential evolution (DE), genetic programming (GP), evolutionary programming (EP), evolutionary strategies (ES), cultural algorithms (CA), and co-evolution (CoE) are examples of evolutionary computation algorithms.

Swarm intelligence (SI) algorithms, on the other hand, are inspired by the collective behavior of social organisms such as ants, bees, and birds, and they'll be discussed in part 4 of this book. These algorithms use a population of agents that interact with each other to find a solution. They use a variety of mechanisms, such as communication, cooperation, and self-organization, to optimize the search process. Examples of swarm intelligence algorithms include particle swarm optimization (PSO), ant colony optimization (ACO), artificial bee colony (ABC), the firefly algorithm (FA), the bat algorithm (BA), and the wolf search algorithm (WSA).

Both evolutionary computation and swarm intelligence algorithms are population-based algorithms that begin their search for the optimal or near-optimal solution from an initial population of candidate solutions. The quality and diversity of the initial population significantly influences the performance and efficiency of the algorithm. A well-constructed initial population provides a good starting point for the search process and can help the algorithm quickly converge toward a promising region of the search space. In contrast, a poorly constructed initial population may result in a premature convergence to a suboptimal solution, may get the algorithm stuck in a suboptimal region, or may take longer to converge toward a solution. To ensure a good balance between exploration and exploitation, the initial population should be diverse and cover a wide range of potential solutions.

A comparison between different initialization strategies for population-based metaheuristics is provided in El-Ghazali Talbi's *Metaheuristics: From Design to Implementation* [1], based on three key aspects: diversity, computational cost, and the quality of initial solutions. Initial solutions can be generated using a pseudo-random process or a quasi-random search. Initial solutions can also be generated sequentially (sequential diversification) or concurrently (parallel diversification) to achieve very high diversity. Heuristics involve using local search or greedy methods to generate initial solutions.

As shown in table 7.1, a pseudo-random strategy provides moderate diversity, low computational cost, and low-quality initial solutions. A quasi-random strategy exhibits higher diversity with comparable computational cost and low-quality initial solutions. Sequential diversification and parallel diversification both stand out with very high diversity, but the former incurs moderate computational cost, while the latter has low computational cost; both methods result in low-quality initial solutions. In contrast, the use of heuristics, such as local search or a greedy heuristic, yields high-quality initial solutions but with low diversity and high computational cost.

Table 7.1 Initialization strategies for population-based metaheuristics

Initialization strategy	Diversity	Computational cost	Quality of initial solution
Pseudo-random	Moderate	Low	Low
Quasi-random	High	Low	Low
Sequential diversification	Very high	Moderate	Low
Parallel diversification	Very high	Low	Low
Heuristics (e.g., local search or greedy heuristic)	Low	High	High

It is often beneficial to use a randomized approach to generate the initial population, where the candidates are samples from different regions of the search space to maximize the chances of finding the optimal solution. The next listing shows how we can sample initial solutions using Python. Let's start by generating 200 pseudo-random numbers.

Listing 7.1   Generating initial populations in Python

```
import math
import numpy as np
import matplotlib.pyplot as plt

np.random.seed(6345245)

N=200
P_random_pseudo=np.random.rand(N,N)
```

Set a seed for the random number generator.

Number of samples

Pseudo-random sampling

NOTE Random numbers are inherently unpredictable, pseudo-random numbers are deterministic but appear random, and quasi-random numbers are deterministic with evenly distributed patterns.

The generalized Halton number generator in the ghalton library can be used to generate quasi-random numbers. This method is based on the Halton sequence, which uses coprime numbers as its bases. You can use the generalized Halton number generator as follows:

```
!pip install ghalton
import ghalton

sequencer = ghalton.GeneralizedHalton(7,23)
P_random_quasi = np.array(sequencer.get(N))
```

The Box-Muller transform is used to generate pairs of independent, standard, normally distributed random numbers from pairs of uniformly distributed random numbers. Box-Muller is a 2D Gaussian sampling method that can be used as follows:

```
u1 = np.random.uniform(size=(N))
u2 = np.random.uniform(size=(N))

P_BM_x = np.sqrt(-2*np.log(u1))*np.cos(2*math.pi*u2)
P_BM_y = np.sqrt(-2*np.log(u1))*np.sin(2*math.pi*u2)
```

Generate uniformly distributed values between 0 and 1.

Calculate x and y values using Box-Muller.

One of the drawbacks of the Box-Muller transform is its tendency to cluster values around the mean due to its dependency on uniform distribution. Additionally, calculating the square root can be costly.

Central limit theorem (CLT) sampling is another sampling method where the distribution of the sample means approximates a normal distribution as the sample size gets larger, regardless of the population's distribution. The following code snippet shows how to implement this method:

```
import random

P_CLT_x=[2.0 * math.sqrt(N) * (sum(random.randint(0,1) for x in range(N)) /
N - 0.5)
➟ for x in range(N)]
P_CLT_y=[2.0 * math.sqrt(N) * (sum(random.randint(0,1) for x in range(N)) /
N - 0.5)
➟ for x in range(N)]
```

The Sobol low-discrepancy sequence (LDS) is a quasi-random sampling method available in the sobol_seq package. This method generates a sequence of points that are evenly spaced and distributed throughout the sample space, such that the gaps between adjacent points are as small as possible. It can be used as follows:

```
!pip install sobol_seq
import sobol_seq
P_sobel=sobol_seq.i4_sobol_generate(2,N)
```

Latin hypercube sampling is a parallel diversification method where the search space is decomposed into 25 blocks, and a solution is generated pseudo-randomly in each block. An example of using the Latin hybercube sampling method in the pyDOE (Design of Experiments) Python package is shown here:

```
!pip install pyDOE
from pyDOE import *
P_LHS=lhs(2, samples=N, criterion='center')
```

Let's visualize all of these sampling methods so we can get a good sense of the differences between them:

```
f, (ax1, ax2) = plt.subplots(ncols=2, figsize=(18,8))
f, (ax3,ax4) = plt.subplots(ncols=2, figsize=(18,8))
f, (ax5, ax6) = plt.subplots(ncols=2, figsize=(18,8))
ax1.scatter(P_random_pseudo[:,0], P_random_pseudo[:,1], color="gray")
ax2.scatter(P_random_quasi[:100], P_random_quasi[100:], color="red")
ax3.scatter(P_BM_x, P_BM_y, color="green")
ax4.scatter(P_CLT_x, P_CLT_y, color="cyan")
ax5.scatter(P_sobel[:,0], P_sobel[:,1], color="magenta")
ax6.plot(P_LHS[:,0], P_LHS[:,1], "o")

ax1.set_title("Pseudo-random")
ax2.set_title("Quasi-random")
ax3.set_title("Box-Muller")
ax4.set_title("Central Limit Theorem")
ax5.set_title("Sobol")
ax6.set_title("Latin Hypercube")
plt.show()
```

Running this code generates the plots shown in figure 7.2. In this figure, candidate solutions have been sampled from a feasible search space using various sampling methods, with each point representing a different solution. The level of diversity achieved by each sampling method can be evaluated by observing the gaps between the points and their dispersion.

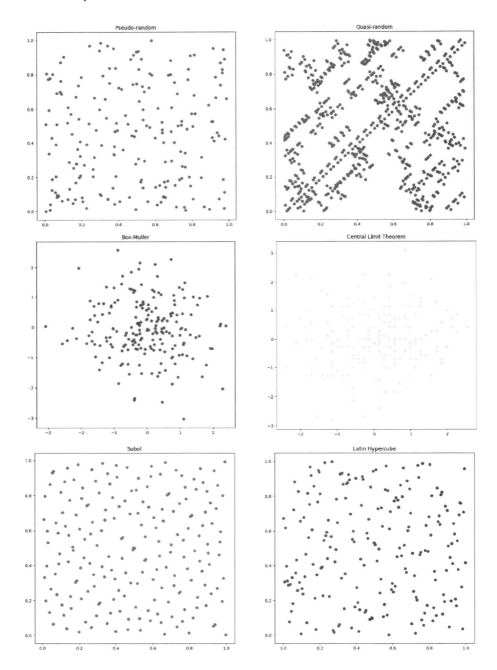

Figure 7.2   Sampling methods for generating an initial population

As mentioned in appendix A (see liveBook), there are several Python packages for evolutionary computation. In this chapter, we will focus on using pymoo: multi-objective optimization in Python. Pymoo provides different sampling methods for creating an initial population or an initial search point. Examples include random sampling and Latin hypercube sampling. As a continuation of listing 7.1, the following code snippet shows random sampling in pymoo:

```
!pip install -U pymoo
from pymoo.core.problem import Problem
from pymoo.operators.sampling.rnd import FloatRandomSampling
from pymoo.util import plotting

problem = Problem(n_var=2, xl=0, xu=1)
sampling = FloatRandomSampling()

X = sampling(problem, 200).get("X")
plotting.plot(X, no_fill=True)
```

Import an instance of the problem class.

Import the random sampling method.

Import the visualization method.

Create a problem with two variables, and specify the lower and upper bounds.

Create an instance of the random sampler.

Generate 200 random solutions/individuals.

Visualize the generated individuals.

The following code generates and visualizes 200 initial solutions using Latin hypercube sampling:

```
from pymoo.operators.sampling.lhs import LHS

sampling = LHS()

X = sampling(problem, 200).get("X")
plotting.plot(X, no_fill=True)
```

Import the Latin hypercube sampling module.

If the solutions take the form of permutations, random permutations can be generated as follows:

```
per1=np.random.permutation(10)
print(per1)

per2 = np.array([5, 4, 9, 0, 1, 2, 6, 8, 7, 3])
np.random.shuffle(per2)
print(per2)

pop_init = np.arange(50).reshape((10,5))
np.random.permutation(pop_init)

from itertools import combinations
size=5
ones=2

for pos in map(set, combinations(range(size), ones)):
    print([int(i in pos) for i in range(size)], sep='\n')
```

Randomly permute a sequence, or return a permuted range.

Randomly shuffle a sequence.

Population of the initial solution as real-value permutations

Population of the initial solution as binary permutations with the number of bits in the binary string and the number of ones in each binary string

You can also generate a random route between two points using the following code:

```
import osmnx as ox
import random
from collections import deque
from optalgotools.structures import Node
```

```
G = ox.graph_from_place("University of Toronto")
fig, ax = ox.plot_graph(G)

def randomized_search(G, source, destination):
    origin = Node(graph = G, osmid = source)
    destination = Node(graph = G, osmid = destination)

    route = []
    frontier = deque([origin])
    explored = set()
    while frontier:
        node = random.choice(frontier)
        frontier.remove(node)
        explored.add(node.osmid)

        for child in node.expand():
            if child not in explored and child not in frontier:
                if child == destination:
                    route = child.path()
                    return route
                frontier.append(child)

    raise Exception("destination and source are not on same component")

random_route = randomized_search(G, 24959528, 1480794706)

fig, ax = ox.plot_graph_route(G, random_route)
```

This is a typical graph search with a shuffled frontier.

This is the randomization part.

Generate random routes between two nodes.

Visualize the random routes.

The preceding code modifies a typical graph search algorithm by scrambling the frontier nodes. This means that candidates for expansion are "random," which means different routes are yielded when it's called repeatedly. Some generated random routes are shown in figure 7.3.

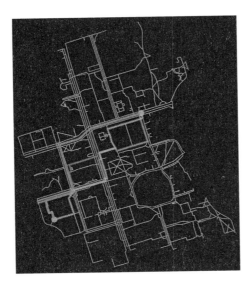

**Figure 7.3
Generating random
initial routes**

In the next section, I'll introduce evolutionary computation as population-based metaheuristics.

7.2 Introducing evolutionary computation

Evolution can be considered an optimization process in the sense that it involves the gradual improvement of the characteristics of living organisms over time, resulting in adaptation to dynamically changing and competitive environments and an enhanced ability to survive in these environments. In this section, I'll provide an overview of the fundamental concepts of biological evolution. Understanding these principles is important for gaining insight into evolutionary computation.

7.2.1 A brief recap of biology fundamentals

The *nucleus* is the central part of any living cell that contains the genetic information. This genetic information is stored in the *chromosomes*, each of which is built of deoxyribonucleic acid (DNA), which carries the genetic information used in the growth, development, functioning, and reproduction of all living organisms. Humans have a total of 23 pairs of chromosomes, or 46 chromosomes in total, in each of their cells. Each chromosome is made up of many different sections called *genes*, which are responsible for coding specific properties of an individual. The variant form of a gene that determines these properties, found at a specific location on a chromosome, is called an *allele*. Every gene has a unique position on the chromosome called a *locus*. The entire combination of genes is called a *genotype*, and it's the genotype that provides the genetic blueprint for an organism, determining the potential for an individual's traits and characteristics. The term *phenotype* refers to the observable physical, behavioral, and physiological characteristics of an organism, which result from the interaction between its genotype and the environment.

To illustrate the concept of genes and their role in determining the characteristics of a living organism, let's consider an example where a DNA molecule consists of four genes that are responsible for different traits: appetite, movement, feet, and skin type. The appetite gene may have different values that reflect the diet of the organism, such as herbivore (H), carnivore (C), or insectivore (I). The movement gene may determine the organism's mode of movement, such as climbing (CL), flying (FL), running (R), or swimming (SW). The feet gene may determine the type of feet or limbs that the organism has, such as claws (CLW), flippers (FLP), hooves (HV), or wings (WNG). Finally, the skin gene may determine the skin covering of the organism, such as fur (F), scales (S), or feathers (FTH), as illustrated in figure 7.4.

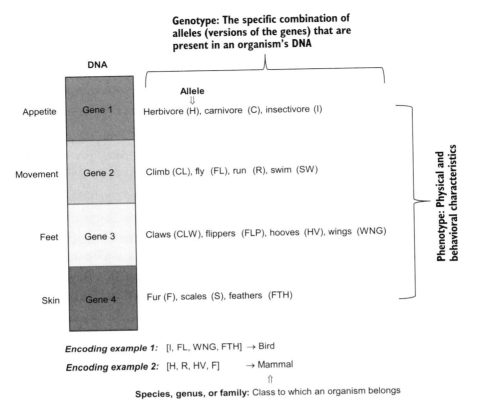

Figure 7.4   Genotype, phenotype, and taxonomic classification

In this example, the *genotype* refers to the specific genetic makeup of an organism, which is determined by the specific combination of alleles that an individual inherits from its parents. The specific values of these genes will determine the *phenotype*, or observable characteristics, of the organism. For example, an organism with an insectivore appetite gene, a flying movement gene, a wings feet gene, and a feather skin gene would likely be a bird. On the other hand, an organism with an herbivorous appetite gene, a running movement gene, a hooves feet gene, and a fur skin gene would likely be a mammal, such as a white-tailed deer.

The class to which an organism belongs, such as the species, genus, or family, is determined by its taxonomic classification based on shared characteristics with other organisms.

7.2.2   *The theory of evolution*

The theory of evolution explains how species of living organisms have changed over time and diversified into the forms we see today. This theory, developed by Charles Darwin, offers an explanation of biological diversity and its underlying mechanisms.

According to the theory, *natural selection* is a major mechanism that drives evolution. Over the course of numerous generations, adaptations arise from the cumulative effects of successive, minor, stochastic alterations in traits, and natural selection favors those variants that are best suited to their environment. This phenomenon is known as survival of the fittest: selected individuals reproduce, passing their properties to their offspring. Other individuals die without mating, and their properties are thus discarded. Over time, natural selection plays a significant role in shaping the characteristics and adaptations of populations, promoting the transmission of advantageous traits and eliminating less beneficial ones.

The theory of evolution

The theory of evolution by natural selection can be summarized as follows:

- In a world with limited resources and stable populations, each individual competes with others for survival.
- Those individuals with the "best" characteristics (traits) are more likely to survive and to reproduce, and those characteristics will be passed on to their offspring.
- These desirable characteristics are inherited by subsequent generations, and (over time) become dominant among the population.
- During production of a child organism, random events cause random changes to the child organism's characteristics.
- If these new characteristics are a benefit to the organism, the chances of survival for that organism are increased.

Evolutionary computation techniques mimic biological evolution and process a sequence of operations, such as creating an initial population (a collection of chromosomes), evaluating the population, and then evolving the population through multiple generations.

7.2.3 Evolutionary computation

Computational intelligence (CI) is a subfield of artificial intelligence (AI) that emphasizes the design, application, and development of algorithms that can learn and adapt to solve complex problems. It focuses on soft computing methods such as fuzzy logic, neural networks, evolutionary computation, and swarm intelligence. *Evolutionary computation* (EC), as a branch of CI, employs various computational methods inspired by biological evolution. These methods have computational mechanisms of natural selection, survival of the fittest, and reproduction as the core elements of their computational systems.

Generally speaking, EC algorithms consist of the following main components:

- *Population of individuals*—This is a set of candidate solutions that are initially generated randomly or by some heuristic methods and are then improved over time. The population size is usually large in order to explore a wide range of possible solutions to the problem. However, the optimal population size depends on various factors, such as the complexity of the problem, the number of variables in the problem, the required accuracy of the solution, and the computational resources available. In practice, the optimal population size is often determined through experimentation, with the performance of the algorithm being evaluated for different population sizes and the best performing size being selected.

- *Fitness function*—This function evaluates the quality of candidate solutions. It determines how well each solution solves the given problem by assigning a fitness value to each individual in the population. The higher the fitness value, the better the solution.

- *Parent selection method*—This method is used to select the most promising individuals from the population in order to create new offspring for the next generation.

- *Genetic operators*—These operators include *crossover* and *mutation*, and they are used to create new offspring from selected parents. The crossover operator exchanges genetic material between two selected individuals to create new offspring with a combination of traits from both parents. The mutation operator introduces random changes to the offspring's genetic makeup to add diversity to the population and prevent stagnation.

- *Survival methods*—These methods determine which individuals in a population will survive to the next generation.

Together, these five components form the basis of EC algorithms, which can effectively solve various optimization problems. As illustrated in figure 7.5, there are several EC paradigms.

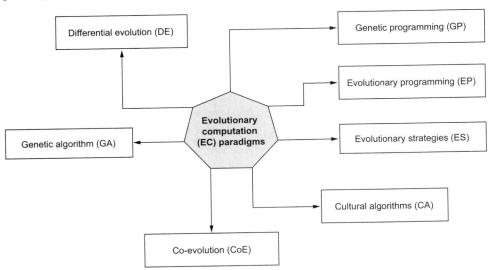

Figure 7.5 EC paradigms

These paradigms mainly vary in their approaches to representing individuals, parents, survival selection methods, and genetic operators:

- *Genetic algorithm (GA)*—This search algorithm mimics natural evolution, where each individual is a candidate solution encoded as a binary, real-valued, or permutation vector. We will discuss genetic algorithms in detail in this part of the book.

- *Differential evolution (DE)*—This algorithm uses real-valued vectors as individuals and generates new solutions by adding weighted differences between pairs of existing solutions. It is similar to GA, differing in the reproduction mechanism used.

- *Genetic programming (GP)*—This is a special case of GA, where each individual is a computer program encoded as a variable-length tree. This tree structure is used to represent functions and operators, such as `if-else` statements and mathematical operations.

- *Evolutionary programming (EP)*—This is similar to GP, but it focuses on evolving behavioral traits rather than program structure. It is an open framework where any representation and mutation operation can be applied, but there is no recombination.

- *Evolutionary strategies (ES)*—This algorithm uses real-valued vectors as individuals and adapts mutation and recombination parameters during evolution. Plus-selection, comma-selection, greedy selection, and distance-based selection are used as selection methods.

- *Cultural algorithm (CA)*—This approach incorporates social learning from a shared belief space into the traditional population-based evolution process. CA models the evolution of a population's culture and how it influences the genetic and phenotypic evolution of individuals.

- *Co-evolution (CoE)*—This is based on the reciprocal evolutionary change that occurs between interacting populations, where each represents a given species, together optimizing coupled objectives.

EC is a powerful approach to optimization that has several advantages, as well as a few drawbacks. The advantages include the following:

- EC algorithms do not make any presumptions about the problem space, making them applicable to a wide range of problems.

- They are widely applicable across different domains and can be used to solve continuous and discrete problems in various fields.

- The solutions produced by EC algorithms are more interpretable than those of neural networks or other black-box optimization techniques. This is mainly because EC algorithms use a more transparent process of selection, mutation, and recombination that can be tracked and understood step by step, whereas neural networks are often considered "black boxes" due to their complex, layered structures and nonlinear operations.

- EC algorithms provide multiple alternative solutions, which can be useful in cases where there is no single best solution.

- EC algorithms exhibit inherent parallelism, making them well-suited for simple parallel implementations on modern hardware.

The disadvantages of EC include the following:

- EC algorithms can be computationally expensive, meaning that they may be slow to converge or require a significant amount of computational resources to run.

- While EC algorithms, like many metaheuristic algorithms, cannot guarantee finding an optimal solution, they often converge to a near-optimal solution within a finite time frame.

- EC algorithms often require parameter tuning to achieve good performance, which can be time-consuming and challenging.

This chapter primarily focuses on genetic algorithms. The following section will look at the various components of genetic algorithms.

7.3   *Genetic algorithm building blocks*

Genetic algorithms are the most widely used form of EC. They are adaptive heuristic search algorithms that are designed to simulate processes in natural systems necessary for evolution, as proposed by Charles Darwin in his theory of evolution. These algorithms represent an intelligent exploitation of a random search within a defined search space.

The first genetic algorithm, named simple genetic algorithm (SGA) and also known as the classical or canonical GA, was developed by John Holland in 1975. Through his research, Holland provided insights into the design of artificial systems that are robust, adaptive, and capable of evolving to meet new challenges. By studying the processes of natural systems, he sought to create algorithms and computational models that could solve complex problems much like natural systems can. Holland defined GA as a computer program that evolves in ways that resemble natural selection and that can solve complex problems that even their creators do not fully understand. GA is based on the principles of evolution via natural selection, employing a population of individuals that undergo selection in the presence of variation-inducing operators such as mutation and crossover (recombination). A fitness function is used to evaluate individuals, and their reproductive success varies with their fitness. Figure 7.6 shows an analogy between GA and natural evolution.

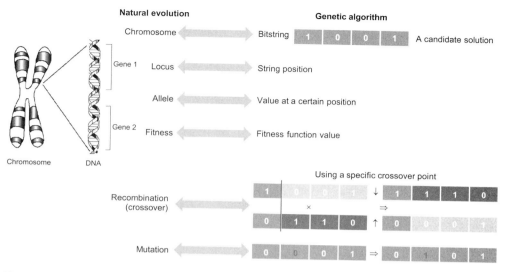

Figure 7.6   GA versus natural evolution

GA starts by initializing a population of individuals or candidate solutions. The fitness of all the individuals in the population is evaluated based on a defined fitness function, and then a new population is created by performing crossover and mutation, which generate children or new solutions. In constrained optimization problems, a feasibility check and repair should be applied after the offspring are produced.

The population keeps evolving until certain stopping criteria are met, as illustrated in figure 7.7. These termination criteria could be

- A specified number of generations or fitness evaluations (100 or 150 generations)
- An adequate solution that reaches a minimum threshold
- When there is no improvement in the best individual for a specified number of generations
- When memory or time constraints are reached
- Any combination of the preceding points

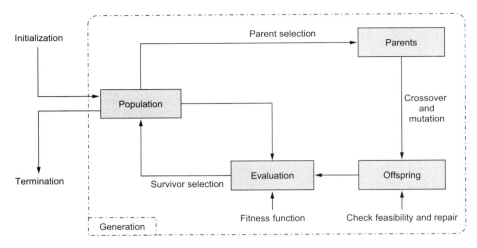

Figure 7.7   GA steps

Algorithm 7.1 summarizes the main steps of genetic algorithms.

Algorithm 7.1   Genetic algorithm

```
Initialization: Randomly generate an initial population M(0)

Evaluate all individuals: Compute and save the fitness f(m) for each
individual in the current population M(t)

While termination criteria are not met
    Select parents: Define selection probabilities p(m)for each individual p
in M(t)
    Apply crossover: Generate M(t+1) by probabilistically selecting
individuals from M(t) to produce offspring via genetic operators
    Apply mutation: Introduce random changes to individuals
    Evaluate: evaluate the fitness of the new individuals
    Select survivors: select individuals to form the next generation
```

The concept of GA is straightforward and easy to understand, as it emulates the process of natural evolution. It is a modular algorithm that can operate in parallel and can be easily distributed. GA is versatile and can handle multi-objective optimization problems effectively. It is particularly effective in noisy environments. GA is widely employed for tackling complex continuous and discrete optimization problems, and it excels in scenarios featuring numerous combinatorial parameters and nonlinear interdependencies among variables. Notably, as of the publication of this book in 2024, a search for "genetic algorithm" as a composite keyword returns approximately 100,000 results on Google Patent Search, while Google Scholar presents a staggering 1,940,000 results. This volume reflects the substantial interest in and diverse applications of genetic algorithms across academic and industrial domains.

7.3.1   *Fitness function*

As mentioned earlier, GA mimics nature's survival-of-the-fittest principle in a search process. Therefore, genetic algorithms are naturally suitable for solving maximization problems. However, various mathematical transformations can be used to convert minimization problems into maximization problems, such as these:

- *Negation transformation*—The simplest transformation is to negate the objective function. For example, maximizing a fitness function $f(x) = -O(x)$ is the same as minimizing the original objective function $O(x)$.
- *Reciprocal transformation*—Another way to convert a minimization problem into a maximization problem is to take the reciprocal of the objective function. This works only if the objective function is always non-negative. Equation 7.1 shows an example:

$$f(x) = \frac{1}{1 + O(x)}$$

7.1

- *Other mathematical transformations*—Equation 7.2 shows another transformation that converts an objective function in a minimization problem $O(x)$ into a fitness function in a maximization problem $f(x)$. In this equation, O_i is the objective function value of individual i, N is the population size, and V is a large value to ensure non-negative fitness values. The value of V can be the maximum value of the second term of the equation, so that the fitness value corresponding to the maximum value of the objective function is zero:

$$f(x) = V - \frac{O_i(x) \times N}{\sum_{i=1}^{N} O_i(x)}$$

7.2

According to the duality principal introduced in section 1.3.2, these transformations do not alter the location of the minima but convert a minimization problem to an equivalent maximization problem.

7.3.2   *Representation schemes*

An *encoding* is a data structure for representing candidate solutions, and a good encoding is probably the most important factor for the performance of GA. In GA, the parameters of a candidate solution (the genes) are concatenated to form a string (a chromosome). Binary encoding, real-value encoding, and permutation encoding can be used to encode the solution. Binary encoding is used in binary-coded GA (BGA) where the solution is represented as a binary string, as illustrated in figure 7.8.

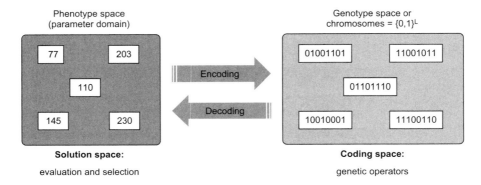

Figure 7.8 Binary encoding

Let's look again at the ticket pricing example introduced in section 1.3.1, where an event organizer is planning a conference and wants to determine the optimal ticket price to maximize the profit. The expected profit is given by the following equation:

$$\text{Profit} f(x) = -20x^2 + 6,200x - 350,000 \qquad \textbf{7.3}$$

where x is the ticket price. The binary genetic algorithm (BGA) can be used to find the optimal ticket price to maximize the profit, subject to the boundary constraint $75.0 \leq x \leq 235.0$, which will make sure that profit is positive. BGA features a simple binary encoding. The boundary constraint on the preceding function requires us to use an 8-bit binary encoding, as explained in the following sidebar. Hence, the chromosomes are represented by bit strings of length 8.

Calculating the minimum number of bits for a solution

To calculate the number of bits required to represent a range between the lower bound (*LB*) and upper bound (*UB*) with a desired precision p, follow these steps:

1. Calculate the range size: $R = (UB - LB)$.
2. Divide the range size by the desired precision: R / P.
3. Round up to the nearest whole number: *number_of_steps* = ceil(R / P), where ceil is the ceiling function that rounds up to the nearest integer.
4. Calculate the number of bits: *number_of_bits* = ceil($\log_2$(*number_of_steps*)), where $\log_2$ is the logarithm to the base 2.

Let's calculate the number of bits we'll need for the ticket pricing problem: $75.0 \leq x \leq 235.0$, assuming a precision of 0.1:

1. Calculate the range size: (235.0 – 75.0) = 160
2. Divide the range size by the desired precision: 160 / 0.1 = 1600
3. Round up to the nearest whole number: 1600. Now you have 1600 steps (values) to represent the numbers from 75.0 to 235.0 with a precision of 0.1.

4 To find the minimum number of bits required, you can use the formula *number_of_bits* = ceil(log$_2$(*number_of_steps*)):

number_of_bits = ceil(log$_2$(1600)) ≈ ceil(10.64) = 11

So you'll need 11 bits to represent the numbers from 75.0 to 235.0 with a precision of 0.1. If you want to consider integer values only (i.e., a precision of 1), you would need ceil(logs(160)) = ceil(7.32) = 8 bits.

As mentioned previously, GA starts with an initial population of candidate solutions. Population size has to be carefully selected, as very big population size usually does not improve performance of GA. Some research also shows that the best population size depends on the size of encoded string (chromosomes). It means that if you have chromosomes with 32 bits, the population should be higher than for chromosomes with 16 bits.

In the ticket pricing problem, assume that we start with a population of size 5. Table 7.2 shows examples of random solutions that can be generated to form the initial population.

Table 7.2 Initial population

Candidate solutions x	Values of x in the solution space	Candidate solutions in the binary coding space	Objective function $f(x)$
x_1	77	01001101	8,820
x_2	203	11001011	84,420
x_3	110	01101110	90,000
x_4	145	10010001	128,500
x_5	230	11100110	18,000

Once we have an initial population, we can proceed to select the parents that will be subjected to genetic operators (crossover and mutation). We'll look at the selection operators next.

7.3.3 *Selection operators*

There are different methods (operators) for parent selection, and they have different levels of selective pressure. *Selective pressure* refers to the probability of the best individual being selected compared to the average probability of selection for all individuals. When using an operator with a high selective pressure in a genetic algorithm, the diversity within the population decreases at a faster rate than it would using operators with a lower selective pressure. This may sound good, but it can result in the population converging prematurely towards suboptimal solutions, thus limiting the exploration abilities of the population and eliminating individuals that do not fit the specific criteria determined by the selective pressure. This can lead to a lack of diversity in the population, which reduces the chances of finding better solutions.

It is important to balance selective pressure with the exploration capabilities of the population to avoid premature convergence and to encourage the discovery of a diverse range of optimal solutions. Figure 7.9 illustrates some selection methods.

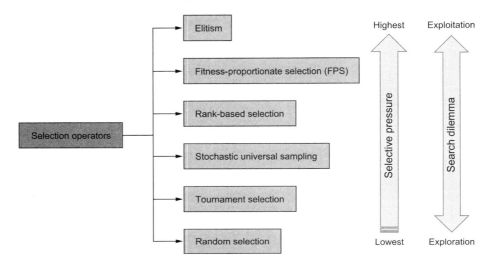

Figure 7.9   **Selection methods with their selective pressure**

ELITISM

Elitism in genetic algorithms involves selecting the fittest individuals for crossover and mutation and preserving the top-performing individuals of the current population to propagate into the next generation. The greater the number of individuals that are preserved, the lower the diversity of the succeeding population. This selection method has the highest selective pressure, as illustrated in figure 7.9.

In the ticket pricing example, the best solutions (x_4 and x_3) will be selected parents to generate offspring, as shown in table 7.3.

Table 7.3   **Solution ranking**

Candidate solutions x	Values of x in the solution space	Candidate solutions in the binary coding space	Objective function f(x)	Ranking
x_1	77	01001101	8,820	5
x_2	203	11001011	84,420	3
x_3	**110**	**01101110**	**90,000**	**2 (second-best individual)**
x_4	**145**	**10010001**	**128,500**	**1 (best individual)**
x_5	230	11100110	18,000	4

FITNESS-PROPORTIONATE SELECTION

Fitness-proportionate selection (FPS) is a selection method that favors the selection of the fittest individuals in a population. This method creates a probability distribution where the probability of an individual being selected is directly proportional to its fitness value. Individuals are chosen from this distribution by sampling it randomly. The individual fitness assignment relative to the whole population can be calculated as follows:

$$F(x_i) = \frac{f(x_i)}{\sum_{i=1}^{N} f(x_i)}$$

7.4

where *f* is the solution represented by an individual chromosome and *N* is the population size. Roulette wheel selection is an example of an FPS operator.

In our ticket pricing example, the roulette wheel can be constructed by implementing the following steps:

1 Calculate the total fitness for the population: F = 8,820 + 84,420 + 90,000 + 128,500 + 18,000 = 329,740.

2 Calculate the selection probability p_k for each chromosome x_k where $p_k = f(x_k) / F$. Table 7.4 shows the calculated selection probabilities.

Table 7.4   Selection probabilities

Candidate solutions *x*	Values of *x* in the solution space	Candidate solutions in the binary coding space	Objective function *f(x)*	Selection probability p_k
x_1	77	01001101	8,820	0.03
x_2	203	11001011	84,420	0.26
x_3	110	01101110	90,000	0.27
x_4	145	10010001	128,500	0.39
x_5	230	11100110	18,000	0.05

3 Calculate the cumulative probability q_k for each chromosome x_k where $q_k = \mathrm{sum}(p_j)$, $j = \{1, k\}$. Table 7.5 shows the calculated cumulative probabilities.

Table 7.5   Cumulative probabilities

Candidate solutions *x*	Values of *x* in the solution space	Candidate solutions in the binary coding space	Objective function *f(x)*	Selection probability p_k	Cumulative probability q_k
x_1	77	01001101	8,820	0.03	0.03
x_2	203	11001011	84,420	0.26	0.28
x_3	110	01101110	90,000	0.27	0.56
x_4	145	10010001	128,500	0.39	0.95
x_5	230	11100110	18,000	0.05	1.00

4   Generate a random number r from the range $[0,1]$.

5   If $q_1 >= r$, then select the first chromosome x_1; otherwise, select the kth chromosome x_k $(2 \le k \le N)$ such that $q_{k-1} < r \le q_k$. If we assume that the randomly generated number $r = 0.25$, then x_2 with $q_2 = 0.28$ is selected because $q_2 > 0.25$, and if $r = 0.58$, $x4$ will be selected because $q_4 > 0.58$. Figure 7.10 illustrates the roulette wheel for the ticket pricing example.

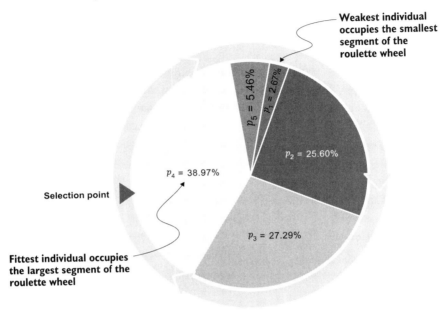

Figure 7.10   Roulette wheel for the ticket pricing example

As you can see, the fittest individual occupies the largest segment of the roulette wheel, and the weakest individual occupies the smallest segment of the wheel. Due to the direct correlation between fitness and selection in proportional selection, there is a potential for dominant individuals to disproportionately contribute to the next generation's offspring, leading to a reduction in the diversity of the population. This implies that proportional selection results in a high selective pressure.

RANK-BASED SELECTION

One way to address the limitations of FPS in genetic algorithms is to use relative fitness instead of absolute fitness to determine selection probabilities—individuals are selected based on their fitness relative to the fitness of other individuals in the population. This approach ensures that the selection process is not dominated by the best individual in the population.

Linear ranking and nonlinear ranking can be used. In *linear ranking*, the rank-based probability of an individual i being selected is calculated using the following equation:

$$p(i) = (2 - SP) + (SP - 1)\frac{r(i) - 1}{(N - 1)}$$

7.5

where N is the size of the population, SP is the selection pressure $(1.0 < SP \leq 2.0)$, and $r(i)$ is the rank associated with individual i (a higher rank is better). In the ticket pricing example, where $N = 5$, and assuming that $SP = 1.5$, the rank-based selection probability of each individual in the population is shown in table 7.6.

Table 7.6   Rank-based selection probabilities

Candidate solutions x	Values of x in the solution space	Candidate solutions in the binary coding space	Objective function f(x)	Rank r_i	FPS cumulative probability q_k	Rank-based selection probability
x_1	77	01001101	8,820	1	0.03	0.50
x_2	203	11001011	84,420	3	0.28	0.75
x_3	110	01101110	90,000	4	0.56	0.88
x_4	145	10010001	128,500	5	0.95	1.00
x_5	230	11100110	18,000	2	1.00	0.63

As you can see, rank-based selection reduces the bias of FPS by assigning greater probabilities of selection to less-fit individuals.

Nonlinear ranking permits higher selective pressures than linear ranking does. The selection probability is calculated using the following equation:

$$p(i) = \frac{N \cdot X^{i-1}}{\sum_{i=1}^{N} X^{i-1}}$$

7.6

where X is computed as the root of the polynomial $(SP - N) \cdot X^{N-1} + SP \cdot X^{N-2} + \ldots + SP \cdot X + SP = 0$. This nonlinear ranking allows values of selective pressure in the interval $[1, N - 2]$.

STOCHASTIC UNIVERSAL SAMPLING

Stochastic universal sampling (SUS) is another approach to mitigating the potential bias in the roulette-wheel selection approach. This method involves placing an outer roulette wheel around the pie with m evenly spaced pointers. With SUS, a single spin of the roulette wheel is used to simultaneously select all m individuals for reproduction. Figure 7.11 shows SUS for the ticket pricing problem using four selection points.

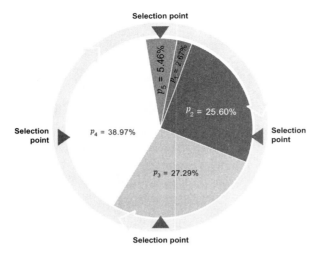

Figure 7.11   Stochastic universal sampling (SUS) strategy

TOURNAMENT SELECTION

Tournament selection involves randomly selecting a group of k individuals from the current population, where k is the size of the tournament group. Once the group is formed, a tournament is held among its members to identify the best-performing individual based on their fitness values. The individual with the highest fitness score is the winner and advances to the next stage of the genetic algorithm. Figure 7.12 shows the tournament selection process.

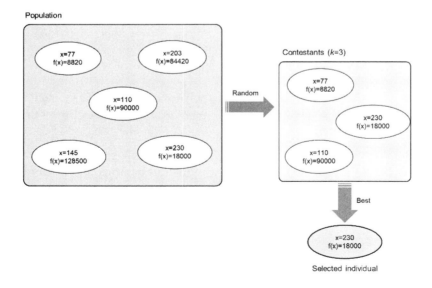

Figure 7.12   Tournament selection

To select *m* individuals for reproduction, the tournament procedure is carried out *m* times. In each iteration, a new tournament group is randomly chosen from the population, and the individuals in the group compete against each other until the best-performing individual is identified. The winners from each tournament are then selected for reproduction, which involves applying genetic operators such as crossover and mutation to create new offspring.

RANDOM SELECTION

Random selection is the simplest selection operator, where each individual has the same selection probability of $1/N$ (where N is the population size). No fitness information is used, which means that the best and the worst individuals have exactly the same probability of being selected. Random selection has the lowest selective pressure among the selection operators, as all individuals within the population have the same chance of being selected.

OTHER SELECTION METHODS

Other selection methods include, but are not limited to, Boltzmann Selection, (μ, λ)-and $(\mu + \lambda)$-selection, and hall of fame. The random selection and tournament selection methods are implemented as part of the `pymoo.operators.selection` class in pymoo.

After we select the parents, we need to produce offspring by applying reproduction operators.

7.3.4   *Reproduction operators*

Genetic algorithms employ two primary genetic operators, namely crossover and mutation, to generate offspring. Let's look at these two reproduction operators in detail.

CROSSOVER

Crossover is inspired by the biological process of recombination, where a portion of the genetic information is exchanged between two chromosomes. This exchange of genetic material results in the production of offspring, so two parents can thus give rise to two offspring. In order to ensure that the best individuals are able to contribute their genetic material, superior individuals are typically given more opportunities to reproduce through crossover. This mechanism promotes the effective combination of schemata, which are subsolutions located on different chromosomes. 1-point crossover, *n*-point crossover, and uniform crossover are commonly used crossover methods.

In *1-point crossover*, we start by choosing a random point on the two parents and splitting parents at this crossover point. Two children are then created by exchanging tails, as illustrated in figure 7.13. This crossover operation produces two new children (candidate solutions), which in the figure are 01010001 and 01001101 (or 81 and 77 in decimal, respectively) as potential ticket prices. These solutions result in total profits of $20,980 and $8,820 respectively, based on equation 7.3.

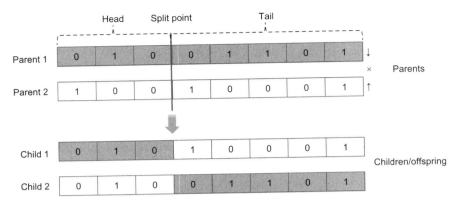

Figure 7.13   1-point crossover

In *n-point crossover*, which is a generalization of 1-point crossover, we choose n random crossover points and split along those points. The children are generated by gluing parts together and alternating between parents, as illustrated in figure 7.14. Following the 2-point crossover illustrated in figure 7.14, two candidate solutions are generated, which are 141 and 81 with fitness values of $126,580 and $20,980 respectively.

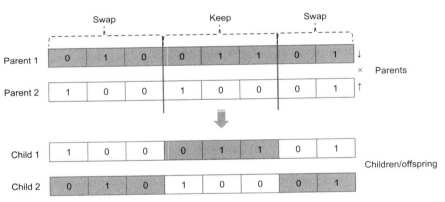

Figure 7.14   *n*-point crossover

In *uniform crossover*, random bit positions from two parents are swapped to create two offspring. One parent is assigned the label "heads" and the other "tails." For the first child, a coin is flipped for each gene to determine whether it should come from the "heads" or "tails" parent. The second child is created by taking the inverse of each gene in the first child, as shown in figure 7.15. In this example, applying uniform crossover results in 217 and 5 with fitness values of $53,620 and $–319,500. As you can see, 5 is not a feasible solution because it is not within the boundary constraints of {75.0,235.0}. This solution is rejected.

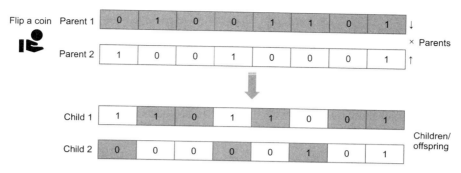

Figure 7.15   **Uniform crossover**

In pymoo, the repair operator can be used make sure the algorithm only searches in the feasible space. It is applied after the offspring have been produced.

MUTATION

Mutation is a process that introduces new genetic material into an individual, which helps to increase the diversity of the population. This diversity is important because it allows the population to explore a wider range of possible solutions to the problem at hand. Mutation is often used in combination with crossover to ensure that the full range of alleles is accessible for each gene. In the case of mutation, selection mechanisms could focus on "weak" individuals in the hope that mutation will introduce better traits to those individuals, increasing their chances of survival.

In binary genetic algorithms, mutation is performed by altering each gene independently with a probability p_m. For each gene, we generate a random number r between 0 and 1. If $p_m > r$, we alter the gene. Figure 7.16 illustrates mutating one of the individuals of the ticket pricing problem.

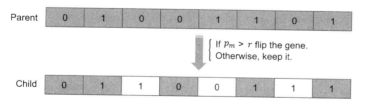

Figure 7.16   **Mutation**

NEW POPULATION

After applying crossover and mutation, we will have new offspring that represent new candidate solutions. To start a new generation, we need to create a new population by selecting individuals from the old population and from the newly generated offspring. The size of the new population will remain the same as the old population.

Generational GA and steady-state GA are two models used in genetic algorithms. As shown in figure 7.17, in *generational GA* models, the whole population is replaced by its offspring to start a "next generation." In *steady-state GA*, the number of generated offspring is less than the population size. Old individuals may be replaced by new ones. The process of selecting individuals for the new population is known as *survivor selection*. We'll look at survivor selection methods next.

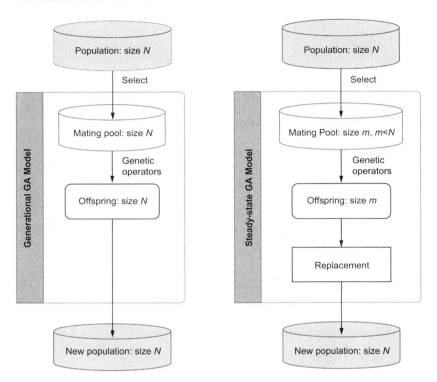

Figure 7.17   GA generational and steady-state models

7.3.5   *Survivor selection*

Random selection, age-based selection, fitness-proportionate selection, and tournament selection are examples of survivor selection methods that can preserve the best individuals while also introducing diversity to a population by making use of the newly generated offspring:

- In *random selection*, the new population is formed by random selection of N individuals.
- With *age-based selection* (or first in, first out), the oldest individuals will be deleted.

- *Fitness-proportionate selection* (FPS) takes into consideration the fitness of each individual—we can delete or replace individuals based on the inverse of fitness, always keeping the best individuals or deleting the worst individuals. For example, *elitist selection* involves simply selecting the best individuals from both the old population and the new offspring to create the new population. This method ensures that the best solutions are preserved from generation to generation.

- Tournament selection involves selecting individuals from both the old population and the new offspring at random and then selecting the best individuals from each group to create the new population. This method can be more effective at preserving diversity in the population.

In the ticket pricing example, if we apply elitist selection, the new population will be formed by the selected solutions shown in table 7.7.

Table 7.7   Elitist selection

Source	Candidate solutions x in the solution space	Candidate solutions in the binary coding space	Objective function f(x)	Ranking	Selected
Old individuals	77	01001101	8,820	7	No
	203	11001011	84,420	3	Yes
	110	01101110	90,000	2	Yes
	145	10010001	128,500	1	Yes
	230	11100110	18,000	6	No
New individuals generated by 1-point crossover	81	01010001	20,980	5	Yes
	77	01001101	8,820	7	No
New individuals generated by mutating individual 77	103	01100111	76,420	4	Yes

You may have noticed that 1-point crossover generated a solution that already exists in the initial population. This phenomenon is not necessarily a problem, as it is an expected outcome when applying genetic operators in a search process. Crossover and mutation can result in both explorative and exploitative behaviors. For example, in 1-point or *n*-point crossover and based on the random split point position, a new solution can be the same as or close to the parents or can generate more diverse offspring.

7.4   *Implementing genetic algorithms in Python*

A genetic algorithm is an easy algorithm to implement. Let's see how we can solve the ticket pricing problem using GA in Python.

We'll start by importing the necessary packages and defining the problem.

> **Listing 7.2   Solving the ticket pricing problem using binary GA**

```python
import numpy as np
import random
from tqdm.notebook import tqdm
from copy import copy
import matplotlib.pyplot as plt

def profit(x):
    return -20*x*x+6200*x-350000
```

Because we're solving this problem using a binary GA, we need to generate an initial random population. As a continuation of listing 7.2, the following `init_pop` function takes two arguments as input—pop_size, which represents the population size, and chromosome_length, which represents the length of each chromosome:

```python
def init_pop(pop_size, chromosome_length):
    ints = [random.randint(75,235) for i in range(pop_size)]
    strs = [bin(n)[2:].zfill(chromosome_length) for n in ints]
    bins = [[int(x) for x in n] for n in strs]
    return bins
```

Generate a list of random integers.

Convert the integers to binary strings.

Convert the binary strings to lists of binary digits.

Return the final list of binary chromosomes.

The `init_pop` function starts by generating a list of random integers from 75 to 235 (inclusive) with a length equal to `pop_size`. This list will later be converted to binary representations. The integers in the `ints` list are then converted to binary strings using the `bin()` function, which returns a binary string representation of a given number with the prefix `0b`. To remove this prefix, we use slicing with `[2:]`. Then we use the `zfill()` method to pad the binary string with leading zeros to ensure it has the same length as `chromosome_length`. The binary strings in the `strs` list are converted to lists of binary digits (0 or 1). This is done using a nested list comprehension that iterates through each character in the binary strings and converts it to an integer. The function finally returns a list of binary chromosomes, where each chromosome is a list of binary digits.

For a given population, we can calculate the fitness of each element in the population using the following `fitness_score` function. This fitness function essentially determines how "good" a particular offspring is. It converts each unit in the population to a binary number (the genotype), evaluates the function to optimize profit, and then returns the "best" offspring. The function mainly takes a population as input and returns a tuple containing two lists, one of the sorted fitness values and another of the sorted population:

```python
def fitness_score(population):
    fitness_values = []
    num = []
    for i in range(len(population)):
```

Convert binary to decimal.

```
num.append(int("".join(str(x) for x in population[i]), base=2))
fitness_values.append(profit(num[i]))
tuples = zip(*sorted(zip(fitness_values, population),reverse=True))
fitness_values, population = [list(t) for t in tuples]
return fitness_values, population
```

Evaluate the fitness of each chromosome and append the fitness value to the fitness_values list.

Create tuples of fitness values and their corresponding chromosomes, and then sort them in descending order based on fitness values.

Return the sorted fitness values and population.

Unzip the sorted tuples back into separate lists for fitness values and the population.

Let's now select two parents using the random selection method implemented in the following `select_parent` function. This function takes two arguments as input: `population`, which is a list of individuals in the population, and `num_parents`, which represents the number of parents to select. It returns a list of selected parents:

```
def select_parent(population, num_parents):
    parents=random.sample(population, num_parents)
    return parents
```

Randomly select a specified number of unique parents from the given population.

Return the list of selected parents.

The `select_parent` function implements a simple random sampling selection method, which gives each individual in the population an equal chance of being selected as a parent. Other selection methods, such as FPS or roulette wheel selection, can also be used to give higher chances to individuals with better fitness values.

The following `roulette_wheel_selection` function shows the steps of roulette wheel selection. The function takes two arguments as input—`population`, which is a list of individuals in the population, and `num_parents`, which represents the number of parents to select:

```
def roulette_wheel_selection(population, num_parents):
    fitness_values, population = fitness_score(population)
    total_fitness = sum(fitness_values)
    probabilities = [fitness / total_fitness for fitness in fitness_values]

    selected_parents = []
    for i in range(num_parents):
        r = random.random()

        cumulative_probability = 0
        for j in range(len(population)):
            cumulative_probability += probabilities[j]
            if cumulative_probability > r:
                selected_parents.append(population[j])
                break

    return selected_parents
```

Calculate total fitness.

Calculate selection probabilities for each individual.

Select only two parents.

Generate a random number r between 0 and 1.

Find the individual whose cumulative probability includes r.

After selecting the parents, it's time to apply genetic operators to produce the offspring. The following `crossover` function implements 1-point crossover. The function takes two arguments as input: `parents`, which is a list of two parent chromosomes, and `crossover_prob`, which represents the probability of crossover occurring between the parents. It returns a list of parents and offspring. The first offspring is generated by taking the first part (up to and including the crossover point) of the first parent and the second part (from the crossover point + 1 to the end of the chromosome) of the second parent. Similarly, the second offspring is generated by taking the first part (up to and including the crossover point) of the second parent and the second part (from the crossover point + 1 to the end of the chromosome) of the first parent:

Choose a random crossover point within the range of chromosome indices.

Apply crossover if, and only if, crossover probability is greater than a randomly generated number.

```
def crossover(parents, crossover_prob):
    chromosome_length = len(parents[0])
    if crossover_prob > random.random():
        cross_point = random.randint(0,chromosome_length)
        parents+=tuple([(parents[0][0:cross_point+1] +parents[1][cross_
point+1])])
        parents+=tuple([(parents[1][0:cross_point+1] +parents[0][cross_
point+1])])
    return parents
```

Create the first offspring.
Create the second offspring.

Return the original parents and the new offspring generated by the crossover operation.

Let's now apply the mutation process. The following `mutation` function performs mutation operations on a given population of chromosomes. It takes two arguments as input: `population`, which is a list of binary chromosomes, and `mutation_prob`, which represents the probability of mutation occurring at each gene in the chromosomes. It returns the mutated population:

Iterate through each chromosome in the population.

Iterate through each gene in the chromosome, except the last one.

```
def mutation(population, mutation_prob) :
    chromosome_length = len(population[0])
    for i in range(len(population)):
        for j in range(chromosome_length-1):
            if mutation_prob > random.random():
                if population[i][j]==1:
                    population[i][j]=0
                else:
                    population[i][j]=1
    return population
```

Apply mutation if, and only if, the mutation probability is greater than a randomly generated number.

Flip the value of the gene.

Return the mutated population.

Let's now put everything together and define the binary genetic algorithm (BGA) function. This function takes the following arguments as input:

- `population`—The initial population of binary chromosomes
- `num_gen`—The number of generations the algorithm will run for
- `num_parents`—The number of parents to select for crossover
- `crossover_prob`—The probability of crossover occurring between parents
- `mutation_prob`—The probability of mutation occurring at each gene
- `use_tqdm` (optional, default=`False`)—A Boolean flag to enable or disable a progress bar using the tqdm library

This is the BGA function:

```
def BGA(population, num_gen, num_parents, crossover_prob, mutation_prob, use_
tqdm =
False):
    states = []
    best_solution = []
    best_score = 0
    if use_tqdm: pbar = tqdm(total=num_gen)
    for _ in range(num_gen):
```

Initialization

Run the genetic algorithm for num_gen generations using a for loop.

Calculate the fitness scores and sort the population based on the fitness values by calling the fitness_ score function.

Update the best solution and best score.

Parent selection using the select_parent random method. You can replace this method with roulette_wheel_ selection(population, num_parents).

Perform mutation.

Perform crossover on the selected parents.

Return the best solution.

```
if use_tqdm: pbar.update()
scores, population = fitness_score(population)
current_best_score = scores[0]
current_best_solution = population[0]
states.append(current_best_score)
if current_best_score > best_score:
    best_score = current_best_score
    best_solution = int("".join(str(x) for x in
    ➥ copy(current_best_solution)), base=2)
parents = select_parent(population, num_parents)
parents = crossover(parents, crossover_prob)
population = mutation(population,mutation_prob)
return best_solution, best_score, states
```

This function returns the best solution, the best score, and the list of best scores at each generation.

Now we can solve the ticket pricing problem, starting with generating an initial population with the following parameters:

```
num_gen = 1000
pop_size = 5
crossover_prob = 0.7
mutation_prob = 0.3
num_parents = 2

chromosome_length = 8
best_score = -100000

population = init_pop(pop_size, chromosome_length)
print("Initial population: \n", population)
```

Running this code produced the following initial population:

```
Initial population: [[1, 1, 1, 0, 1, 0, 0, 0], [1, 0, 0, 0, 0, 1, 1, 0], [1,
1, 0, 1, 1, 1, 0, 1], [1, 1, 0, 0, 0, 0, 1, 1], [1, 0, 1, 0, 0, 0, 0, 0]]
```

We can now run the binary GA solver to get the solutions, as follows:

```
best_solution, best_score, states = BGA(population, num_gen, num_parents,
➥ crossover_prob, mutation_prob, use_tqdm=True)
```

Running this code produces the same solution obtained by the SciPy optimizer (see listing 2.4):

```
Optimal ticket price ($): 155
Profit ($): 130500
```

Rather than writing your own genetic algorithm code from scratch, you can take advantage of existing Python packages that offer GA implementations. Numerous open source Python libraries can help streamline the development process and save time. These libraries often include genetic operators, selection methods, and other features that make it easier to adapt a genetic algorithm to different optimization problems. Examples of these libraries include, but are not limited to, the following:

- *Pymoo* (Multi-objective Optimization in Python; https://pymoo.org/algorithms/moo/nsga2.html)—A Python library for multi-objective optimization using evolutionary algorithms and other metaheuristic techniques. Pymoo offers a variety of algorithms such as GA, differential evolution, evolutionary strategy, non-dominated sorting genetic algorithm (NSGA-II), NSGA-III, and particle swarm optimization (PSO).

- *DEAP* (Distributed Evolutionary Algorithms in Python; https://deap.readthedocs.io/en/master/—A Python library for implementing genetic algorithms in Python. It provides tools for defining, training, and evaluating genetic algorithm models, as well as for visualizing the optimization process. DEAP provides a variety of built-in genetic operators, including mutation, crossover, and selection, as well as support for custom operators tailored to specific optimization problems.

- *PyGAD* (Python Genetic Algorithm; https://pygad.readthedocs.io/en/latest/)—A Python library for implementing genetic algorithms and differential evolution (DE) algorithms. PyGAD is suitable for both single-objective and multi-objective optimization tasks and can be used in a wide range of applications, including machine learning, and other problem domains.

- *jMetalPy* (https://github.com/jMetal/jMetalPy)—A Python library designed for developing and experimenting with metaheuristic algorithms for solving multi-objective optimization problems. It provides support for a variety of metaheuristic algorithms, including popular evolutionary algorithms like non-dominated sorting genetic algorithm (NSGA-II), NSGA-III, strength Pareto evolutionary algorithm (SPEA2), and multi-objective evolutionary algorithm based on decomposition (MOEA/D), as well as other optimization techniques such as simulated annealing and particle swarm optimization.

- *PyGMO* (Python Parallel Global Multi-objective Optimizer; https://esa.github.io/pygmo/)—A scientific library providing a large number of optimization problems and algorithms such as NSGA-II, SPEA2, non-dominated sorting particle swarm optimization (NS-PSO), and parameter adaptive differential evolution (PaDE). It uses the generalized island-model paradigm for the coarse grained parallelization of optimization algorithms and, therefore, allows users to develop asynchronous and distributed algorithms.

- *Inspyred* (Bio-inspired Algorithms in Python; https://pythonhosted.org/inspyred/)—A library for creating and working with bio-inspired computational intelligence algorithms. It supports a variety of bio-inspired optimization algorithms, such as GA, evolution strategy, simulated annealing, differential evolution algorithm, estimation of distribution algorithm, Pareto archived evolution strategy (PAES), nondominated sorting genetic algorithm (NSGA-II), particle swarm optimization (PSO), and ant colony optimization (ACO).

- *Platypus* (https://platypus.readthedocs.io/en/latest/)—A framework for evolutionary computing in Python with a focus on multi-objective evolutionary algorithms (MOEAs). It provides tools for analyzing and visualizing algorithm performance and solution sets.

- *MEALPY* (https://mealpy.readthedocs.io/en/latest/index.html)—A Python library that provides implementations for population-based meta-heuristic algorithms such as evolutionary computing algorithms, swarm inspired computing, physics inspired computing, human inspired computing, and biology inspired computing.

- *Mlrose* (Machine Learning, Randomized Optimization and Search; https://mlrose.readthedocs.io/en/stable/index.html)—An open source Python library that provides an implementation of standard GA to find the optimum for a given optimization problem.

- *Pyevolve* (https://pyevolve.sourceforge.net/)—An open source Python library designed for working with genetic algorithms and other EC techniques

- *EasyGA* (https://github.com/danielwilczak101/EasyGA)—A Python package designed to provide an easy-to-use GA. It's worth noting that EasyGA and Pyevolve are simple libraries with less functionality and predefined problems than other libraries such as DEAP and Pymoo.

Listing A.3, available in the book's GitHub repo, shows how to use some of these libraries.

In this book, we will focus on utilizing the pymoo library, as it is a comprehensive framework that offers several optimization algorithms, visualization tools, and decision-making capabilities. This library is particularly well-suited for multi-objective optimization, which we'll explore in more detail in the next chapter. Pymoo's extensive features make it an excellent choice for implementing and analyzing genetic algorithms in various problem domains. Table 7.8 summarizes a comparative study of selected evolutionary computing frameworks, including pymoo [2].

Table 7.8 Comparing selected evolutionary computing frameworks in Python

Library	License	Pure Python	Visualization	Focus on multi-objective	Decision making
jMetalPy	MIT	Yes	Yes	Yes	No
PyGMO	GPL-3.0	No (C++ with Python wrappers)	No	Yes	No
Platypus	GPL-3.0	Yes	No	Yes	No
DEAP	LGPL-3.0	Yes	No	No	No
inspyred	MIT	Yes	No	No	No
pymoo	Apache 2.0	Yes	Yes	Yes	Yes

The following listing shows the steps for solving the ticket pricing problem using GA implemented in pymoo. We'll start by importing various classes and functions from the pymoo library.

Listing 7.3   Solving the ticket pricing problem using GA in pymoo

```
from pymoo.algorithms.soo.nonconvex.ga import GA
from pymoo.operators.crossover.pntx import PointCrossover,
➥ SinglePointCrossover,
➥ TwoPointCrossover
from pymoo.operators.mutation.pm import PolynomialMutation
from pymoo.operators.repair.rounding import RoundingRepair
from pymoo.operators.sampling.rnd import FloatRandomSampling
from pymoo.core.problem import Problem
from pymoo.optimize import minimize
```

The GA class represents a single-objective genetic algorithm in the pymoo library. The PointCrossover, SinglePointCrossover, and TwoPointCrossover classes represent different crossover operators for combining the genetic material of parent chromosomes to create offspring. The PolynomialMutation class represents a mutation operator that introduces small, random changes in the chromosomes' genes. The RoundingRepair class represents a repair operator that rounds the variable values of the chromosomes, ensuring that they stay within a specific range or meet certain constraints. The FloatRandomSampling class represents a random sampling operator that generates an initial population of chromosomes with random float values. The Problem class is used to define optimization problems by specifying objectives, constraints, and variable bounds. Finally, the minimize function is used to perform the optimization process. It is worth noting that pymoo can only handle minimization problems, so if you need to use it with a maximization problem, you'll have to convert the problem into a minimization problem, as discussed in section 7.3.1.

After importing the necessary classes and functions from the pymoo library, we can define the TicketPrice problem by subclassing the Problem class from the pymoo library as follows:

```
class TicketPrice(Problem):
    def __init__(self):                    ← Define the constructor for the TicketPrice class.
        super().__init__(n_var=1,
                        n_obj=1,
                        n_constr=0,
                        xl=75.0,
                        xu=235.0, vtype=float)   ← Call the constructor of the parent Problem class.

    def _evaluate(self, x, out, *args, **kwargs):   ← Define the evaluation function for the TicketPrice class.
        out["F"]= 20*x*x-6200*x+350000
```
Evaluate the value of the objective function using the given formula.

As can be seen, the constructor of the parent Problem class contains the following components with customized values applied to the ticket pricing problem:

- n_var=1—The number of decision variables in the problem, which is set to 1, indicating a single decision variable for the ticket price.
- n_obj=1—The number of objectives in the problem, which is set to 1, indicating a single-objective optimization problem.

- n_constr=0—The number of constraints in the problem, which is set to 0, indicating that there are no constraints in this optimization problem.
- xl=75.0—The lower bound for the decision variable, which is set to 75.0.
- xu=235.0—The upper bound for the decision variable, which is set to 235.0.
- vtype=float—The variable type for the decision variables, which is set to float. Other types include int and bool.

Now we can apply GA to solve the problem as follows:

```
problem = TicketPrice()          Create an instance of the
algorithm = GA(                  TicketPrice problem.
    pop_size=100,
    sampling=FloatRandomSampling(),
    crossover=PointCrossover(prob=0.8, n_points=2),
    mutation = PolynomialMutation(prob=0.3, repair=RoundingRepair()),
    eliminate_duplicates=True
)          Instantiate a GA object.                              Run the solver.
res = minimize(problem, algorithm, ('n_gen', 100), seed=1, verbose=True)

print(f"Optimal ticket price ($): {res.X}")    Print the optimal ticket price.
print(f"Profit ($): {-res.F}")
                                      Print the profit. Negate the objective
GA parameters include the following:  value when printing the result.
```

- pop_size=100—Set the population size to 100 individuals.
- sampling=FloatRandomSampling()—Use the FloatRandomSampling class to generate an initial population of chromosomes with random float values.
- crossover=PointCrossover(prob=0.8, n_points=2)—Use the PointCrossover class as the crossover operator with a probability of 0.8 and two crossover points.
- mutation=PolynomialMutation(prob=0.3, repair=RoundingRepair())—Use the PolynomialMutation class as the mutation operator with a probability of 0.3, and apply the RoundingRepair class to repair mutated solutions if needed. The repair makes sure every solution that is evaluated is, in fact, feasible.
- eliminate_duplicates=True—Set the flag to eliminate duplicate individuals in the population.
- res = minimize(...)—Call the minimize function from pymoo to run the optimization process.

Running listing 7.3 produces the following output:

```
Optimal ticket price ($): [155]
Profit ($): [130500.]
```

So far, we've only scratched the surface of genetic algorithms. We'll dive into the details, study different variants of genetic algorithms, and address more practical use cases in the next chapter.

Summary

- Metaheuristic algorithms that are population-based, often referred to as P-metaheuristics, employ multiple agents to find an optimal or near-optimal global solution. These algorithms can be divided into two main categories, depending on their source of inspiration: evolutionary computation (EC) algorithms and swarm intelligence (SI) algorithms.

- EC algorithms draw inspiration from the process of biological evolution. Examples of EC algorithms include the genetic algorithm (GA), differential evolution (DE), genetic programming (GP), evolutionary programming (EP), evolutionary strategies (ES), cultural algorithms (CA), and co-evolution (CoE).

- The genetic algorithm is the most widely used form of EC. It is an adaptive heuristic search method designed to mimic the natural system's processes required for evolution, as outlined in Charles Darwin's theory of evolution.

- Pseudo-random strategies, quasi-random strategies, sequential diversification, parallel diversification, and heuristics represent various initialization strategies for P-metaheuristics like genetic algorithms. Each strategy offers distinct levels of diversity, computational cost, and initial solution quality.

- In genetic algorithms, the crossover and mutation operators play essential roles in searching the solution space and maintaining diversity within the population. The primary purpose of these operators is to handle the search dilemma by balancing exploration (searching new areas of the solution space) and exploitation (refining the existing solutions).

- A high crossover rate and a low mutation rate are recommended to balance exploration and exploitation. The high crossover rate facilitates the sharing of good traits between individuals, while the low mutation rate introduces small, random changes to maintain diversity and prevent premature convergence. This combination allows the algorithm to efficiently search the solution space and find high-quality solutions.

- In the generational model of genetic algorithms, the entire population is replaced, whereas in the steady-state model of genetic algorithms, a small fraction of the population is replaced. The steady-state model has lower computation costs than the generational model in genetic algorithms, but the generational model improves diversity preservation compared to the steady-state models.

- A wide range of open source Python libraries exist for working with genetic algorithms. One such library, pymoo (Multi-objective Optimization in Python), includes popular algorithms such as genetic algorithms, differential evolution, evolutionary strategies, the non-dominated sorting genetic algorithm (NSGA-II), NSGA-III, and particle swarm optimization (PSO).

Genetic algorithm variants

This chapter covers

- Introducing the Gray-coded genetic algorithm
- Understanding real-valued GA and its genetic operators
- Understanding permutation-based GA and its genetic operators
- Understanding multi-objective optimization
- Adapting genetic algorithms to strike a balance between exploration and exploitation
- Solving continuous and discrete problems using GA

This chapter continues with the topic of chapter 7: we will look at various forms of genetic algorithms (GAs) and delve deeper into their real-world applications. We'll also look at a number of case studies and exercises, such as the traveling salesman problem (TSP), proportional integral derivative (PID) controller design, political districting, the cargo bike loading problem, manufacturing planning, facility allocation, and the opencast mining problem in this chapter and its supplementary exercises included in the online appendix C.

8.1   *Gray-coded GA*

The Hamming cliff effect refers to the fact that small changes in a chromosome can result in large changes in a solution's fitness, which can lead to a sharp drop-off in the fitness landscape and cause the algorithm to converge prematurely. In binary genetic algorithms, the crossover and mutation operations can significantly affect the solution due to this Hamming cliff effect, especially when the bits that are to be changed are among the most significant bits in the binary string. To mitigate the Hamming cliff effect, Gray-coded GA uses a Gray-code encoding scheme for the chromosomes.

The reflected binary code, commonly referred to as *Gray code* after its inventor Frank Gray, is a unique binary numbering system characterized by adjacent numerical values differing by only one bit, as shown in table 8.1. In this numeral system, each value has a unique representation that is close to the representations of its neighboring values, which helps minimize the effect of crossover and mutation operations on the solution. This coding ensures a smooth transition between values and minimizes the risk of errors during conversions or when used in various applications, such as rotary encoders and digital-to-analog converters. Table 8.1 shows the decimal numbers 1 to 15 and their corresponding binary and Gray equivalents.

Table 8.1   Decimal, binary, and Gray coding

Decimal number	Binary code	Gray code
0	0000	0000
1	0001	0001
2	0010	0011
3	0011	0010
4	0100	0110
5	0101	0111
6	0110	0101
7	0111	0100
8	1000	1100
9	1001	1101
10	1010	1111
11	1011	1110
12	1100	1010
13	1101	1011
14	1110	1001
15	1111	1000

Exclusive OR (XOR) gates are used to convert 4-bit binary numbers to Gray codes, as illustrated in figure 8.1 for the ticket pricing example discussed in the previous chapter. These XOR gates result in 1 only if the inputs are different and 0 if the inputs are the same.

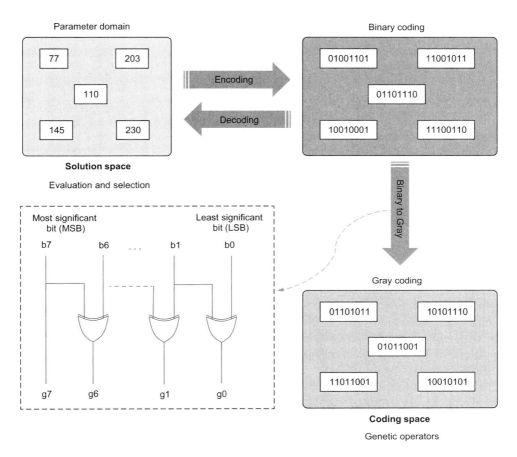

Figure 8.1   Gray coding and binary-to-Gray conversion

In Gray code, two successive values differ by only one bit. This property reduces the Hamming distance between adjacent numbers, leading to a smoother search space or smoother genotype-to-phenotype mapping.

Hamming cliff problem

One of the drawbacks of encoding variables as binary strings is the presence of Hamming cliffs. In binary-coded GAs, a small change in the encoded value (e.g., flipping a single bit) can lead to a significant change in the decoded value, especially if the flipped bit is located toward the most significant bit position. This abrupt change between two adjacent numbers in the search space is referred to as a Hamming cliff. This problem negatively affects binary-coded GAs by disrupting the search space's smoothness, causing poor convergence and leading to inefficient exploration and exploitation. To address the Hamming cliff problem, alternative representations like Gray code or real-valued encoding can be used, as they offer better locality and smoother search spaces, minimizing the disruptive effects of small changes on decoded values.

(continued)
For example, assume that we have a decision variable in the range [0, 15], as shown in the following figure. In binary-coded GA, we would use 4-bit binary representation to encode the candidate solutions. Let's assume we have two adjacent solutions in the search space: 7 and 8, or 0111 and 1000 in binary representation. The Hamming distance is the number of bit-wise differences, so the Hamming distance between 1000 and 0111 is 4. These two solutions (7 and 8) are neighbors in the search space, but when you look at their binary representations, you can see that they differ in all 4 bits. Flipping the most significant bit causes a significant change in the decoded value. In the case of Gray code, the Hamming distance between the Gray code representation 0100 (7 in decimal) and 1100 (8 in decimal) is only 1. This means that these Gray code representations for the two adjacent solutions differ by only 1 bit, providing a smoother search space and potentially improving the performance of the GA.

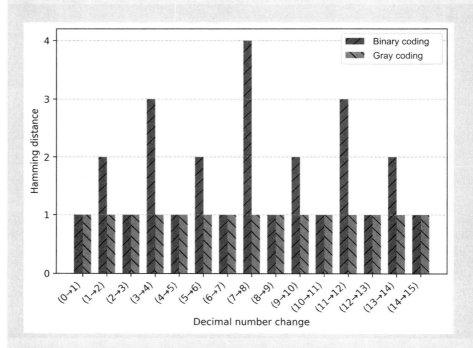

Hamming distances for decimal number change from 0 to 15 for binary and Gray coding

Gray code representations provide better locality, meaning that small changes in the encoded value result in small changes in the decoded value. This property can improve the convergence of the GA by reducing the likelihood of disruptive changes during crossover and mutation operations. However, it is worth noting that the performance improvements offered by Gray coding are problem-dependent, and this representation method is not commonly used compared to binary-coded GA.

8.2 Real-valued GA

Real-valued GA is a variation on the standard GA that uses real numbers for encoding chromosomes instead of binary or Gray code representations. Many optimization problems involve continuous variables or real-valued parameters, such as curve fitting, function optimization with real-valued inputs, proportional integral derivative (PID) controller parameter tuning, or optimizing the weights of a neural network. To handle these continuous problems, it's recommended that we use real-value GA directly for the following reasons:

- *Precision*—Real-valued GAs can achieve a higher level of precision in the search space than binary GAs. Binary encoding requires the discretization of the search space into a finite number of possible solutions, which can limit the accuracy of the search. Real-valued encoding, on the other hand, allows for a continuous search space, which can provide a more precise search.

- *Efficiency*—Real-valued GAs can require fewer bits to encode a solution compared to binary GAs. For example, assume that the decision variable to be represented has a lower bound (LB) of 0 and an upper bound (UB) of 10, and we need to represent the solution with a precision (P) of 0.0001. As explained in the previous chapter, the number of bits required to represent a range between LB and UB with a desired precision P is $number\_of\_bits = \mathrm{ceil}(\log2((UB - LB)/P)) = \mathrm{ceil}(\log2(\mathrm{ceil}(10/0.0001))) = \mathrm{ceil}(\log2(100000)) = 17$ bits. A real-valued encoding can use floating-point numbers with a smaller number of bits to represent a wider range of values than a binary encoding. This can result in a more efficient use of the available memory and computation resources.

- *Smoothness*—Real-valued GAs can maintain the continuity and smoothness of the search space, which can be important in some applications. In contrast, binary GAs can suffer from the Hamming cliff effect, as discussed in the previous section.

- *Adaptability*—Real-valued GAs can adapt more easily to changes in the search space or the fitness landscape. For example, if the fitness landscape changes abruptly, real-valued GAs can adjust the step size or mutation rate to explore the new landscape more effectively. Binary GAs, on the other hand, can require a more extensive redesign of the encoding or operator parameters to adapt to changes in the search space.

In the following subsections, we'll look at the crossover and mutation methods used in real-valued GA.

8.2.1 Crossover methods

Some popular crossover methods for real-valued GAs are single arithmetic crossover, simple arithmetic crossover, and whole arithmetic crossover.

SINGLE ARITHMETIC CROSSOVER

The *single arithmetic crossover method* involves picking a gene (k) at random and generating a random weight α, which lies in the range $[0, 1]$. Genes with indices i before and after the crossover point ($i < k$ or $i > k$) will inherit the genes from the corresponding parent chromosome. For genes at the crossover point ($i = k$), we create the offspring genes by taking a weighted average of the corresponding genes in the parent chromosomes:

$$Child_1 Gene_i = \alpha \times Parent_1 Gene_i + (1 - \alpha) \times Parent_2 Gene_i$$
$$Child_2 Gene_i = \alpha \times Parent_2 Gene_i + (1 - \alpha) \times Parent_1 Gene_i$$

Figure 8.2 illustrates the single arithmetic crossover in real-valued GA.

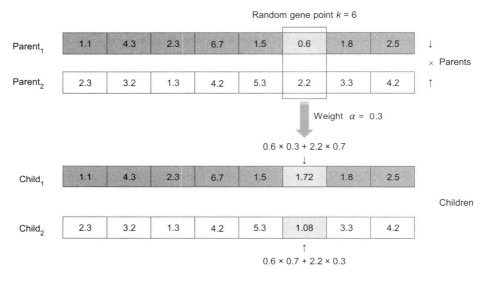

Figure 8.2   Single arithmetic crossover in real-valued GA

SIMPLE ARITHMETIC CROSSOVER

Simple arithmetic crossover is similar to single arithmetic crossover. Before a randomly picked crossover point ($i < k$), the genes are inherited from the corresponding parent chromosome. After the crossover point ($i >= k$), we create the offspring genes by taking a weighted average of the corresponding genes in the parent chromosomes. Figure 8.3 illustrates the simple arithmetic crossover in real-valued GA.

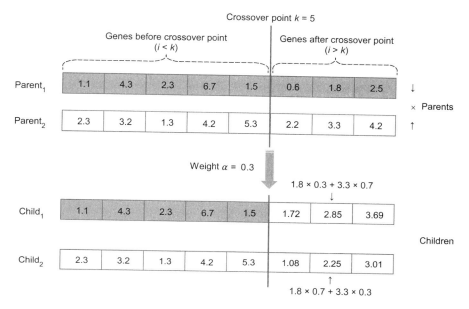

Figure 8.3   Simple arithmetic crossover in real-valued GA

WHOLE ARITHMETIC CROSSOVER

In the *whole arithmetic crossover* method, we take a weighted average of the entire parent chromosomes to create the offspring. Figure 8.4 illustrates this method in real-valued GA.

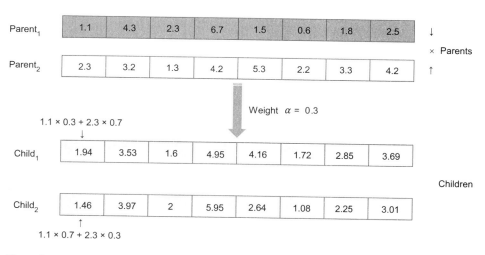

Figure 8.4   Whole arithmetic crossover in real-valued GA

SIMULATED BINARY CROSSOVER

Simulated binary crossover (SBX) [1] is another crossover method in real-valued GA. In SBX, real values can be represented by a binary notation, and then the point crossovers can be performed. SBX is designed to generate offspring close to the parent chromosomes by creating a probability distribution function, thus maintaining a balance between exploration and exploitation in the search space. SBX is implemented in pymoo.

8.2.2 *Mutation methods*

The simplest way to mutate a continuous variable is to introduce small, random perturbations to the genes of an individual to maintain diversity in the population and help the search process escape from local optima. There are several common mutation methods used in real-valued GAs:

- *Gaussian mutation*—Gaussian mutation adds a random value to the gene, where the random value is sampled from a Gaussian distribution with 0 mean and a specified standard deviation σ. The standard deviation controls the magnitude of the mutation (aka the *mutation step*).

- *Cauchy mutation*—Similar to Gaussian mutation, Cauchy mutation adds a random value to the gene, but the random value is sampled from a *Cauchy distribution* (aka a *Lorentz distribution* or *Cauchy–Lorentz distribution*) instead of a Gaussian distribution. The Cauchy distribution has heavier tails than the Gaussian distribution, leading to a higher probability of larger mutations.

- *Boundary mutation*—In boundary mutation, the mutated gene is randomly drawn from the uniform distribution within the variable's range, defined by the lower bound (*LB*) and upper bound (*UB*). This method is analogous to the bit-flipping mutation in a binary-coded GA, and it helps explore the boundaries of the search space. It may be useful when optimal solutions are located near the variable limits.

- *Polynomial mutation*—Polynomial mutation is a method that generates offspring close to the parent by creating a probability distribution function [2]. A distribution index (η) controls the shape of the probability distribution function, with higher values resulting in offspring closer to their parents (exploitation) and lower values leading to offspring more spread out in the search space (exploration).

To illustrate these genetic operators, let's consider a curve-fitting example. Assume we have the data points shown in table 8.2 and that we want to fit a third-order polynomial to these data points using real-valued GA.

Table 8.2   Curve-fitting problem data

x	0	1.25	2.5	3.75	5
y	1	5.22	23.5	79.28	196

The third-order polynomial takes the form $y = ax^3 + bx^2 + cx + d$. A real-valued GA can be used to find the four coefficients of the polynomial: a, b, c, and d. This problem is treated as a minimization problem where the objective is to minimize the mean squared error (MSE) that measures how close a fitted polynomial is to given data points. MSE is calculated using the following formula:

$$MSE = \frac{1}{n} \sum_{i=1}^{n} (y_i - y'_i)^2$$

8.1

where n is the number of data points, y is the y-coordinate value of each data point, and y' is the desired value that sits on the line we created.

In real-valued GA, a candidate solution is represented by a vector of parameters a, b, c, and d that can be represented by real values. Let's start with the following initial random solution: $Parent_1 = [1\ 2\ 3\ 4]$. We calculate its fitness by substituting these values in the function $(y = x^3 + 2x^2 + 3x + 4)$, calculating y' for each corresponding x and calculating the MSE as in table 8.3.

Table 8.3 MSE calculation for parent 1

x	0	1.25	2.5	3.75	5
y	1	5.22	23.5	79.28	196
y'	4	12.83	39.63	96.11	194
Square of error	9	57.88	260	283.23	4
MSE	122.83				

Let's generate another random solution: $Parent_2 = [2\ 2\ 2\ 2]$, which gives the formula $2x^3 + 2x^2 + 2x + 2$ and the MSE in table 8.4.

Table 8.4 MSE calculation for parent 2

x	0	1.25	2.5	3.75	5
y	1	5.22	23.5	79.28	196
y'	2	11.53	50.75	143.09	312
Square of error	1	39.83	742.56	4,072.2	13,456
MSE	3,662.32				

Applying whole arithmetic crossover on the two parents $P_1 = [1\ 2\ 3\ 4]$ and $P_2 = [2\ 2\ 2\ 2]$ with weight $\alpha = 0.2$ results in the following offspring:

$$Child_1 = \alpha P_1 + (1 - \alpha)P_2$$
$$= [0.2\ 0.4\ 0.6\ 0.8] + [1.6\ 1.6\ 1.6\ 1.6]$$
$$= [1.8\ 2\ 2.2\ 2.4], MSE = 2434.07$$

$$Child_2 = \alpha P_2 + (1 - \alpha)P_1$$
$$= [0.4\ 0.4\ 0.4\ 0.4] + [0.8\ 1.6\ 2.4\ 3.2]$$
$$= [1.2\ 2\ 2.8\ 3.6], MSE = 310.37$$

Let's assume $Child_1$ is subject to Gaussian mutation. This mutation process results in another child as follows: $Child_3 = Child_1 + N(0, \sigma)$, where $N(0, \sigma)$ is a random number from a normal distribution with a mean of 0 and a standard deviation of σ. Assuming that $\sigma = 1.2$, a random value of 0.43 is generated by `numpy.random.normal(0, 1.2)`, so $Child_3 = [1.8\ 2\ 2.2\ 2.4] + 0.43 = [2.23\ 2.43\ 2.63\ 2.83]$.

Listing 8.1 shows how to perform this curve-fitting using real-valued GA implemented in pymoo. We'll start by generating a dataset driven by a third-order polynomial, to be used later as a ground truth. Feel free to replace this synthetically generated data with any experimental data you may have.

Listing 8.1   Curve fitting using real-valued GA

```
import numpy as np

def third_order_polynomial(x, a, b, c, d):
    return a * x**3 + b * x**2 + c * x + d

a, b, c, d = 2, -3, 4, 1

x = np.linspace(0, 5, 5)

y = third_order_polynomial(x, a, b, c, d)

data_samples = np.column_stack((x, y))
```

Define coefficients for the third-order polynomial.

Generate five values as in the hand-iteration example.

Calculate y values using the third-order polynomial function.

Combine x and y values into an array of data samples.

As a continuation of listing 8.1, we can define a problem for curve fitting by subclassing pymoo's `Problem` class, ensuring we pass the parameters to the superclass and provide an _evaluate function. The `CurveFittingProblem` class has an initializer method that sets the number of decision variables to 4, the number of objectives to 1, the number of constraints to 0, the lower bound of the decision variables to −10.0, and the upper bound of the decision variables to 10.0. The `vtype` parameter specifies the data type of the decision variables, which is set to `float`. This initializer method creates an instance of the problem to be solved using the genetic algorithm. The _evaluate method takes as input a set of candidate solutions (x) and an output dictionary (out) and returns the fitness of each candidate solution in the F field of the out dictionary:

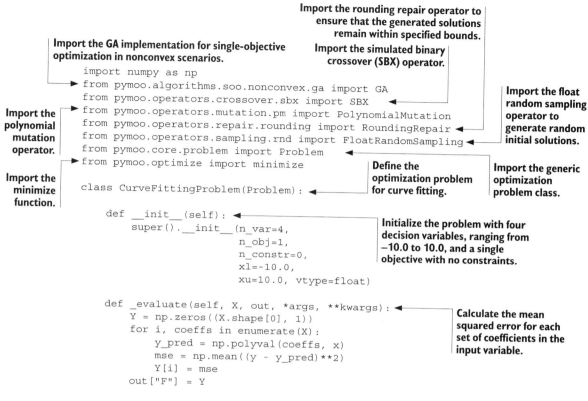

Import the GA implementation for single-objective optimization in nonconvex scenarios.

Import the rounding repair operator to ensure that the generated solutions remain within specified bounds.

Import the simulated binary crossover (SBX) operator.

Import the polynomial mutation operator.

Import the float random sampling operator to generate random initial solutions.

Import the minimize function.

Define the optimization problem for curve fitting.

Import the generic optimization problem class.

Initialize the problem with four decision variables, ranging from −10.0 to 10.0, and a single objective with no constraints.

Calculate the mean squared error for each set of coefficients in the input variable.

```python
import numpy as np
from pymoo.algorithms.soo.nonconvex.ga import GA
from pymoo.operators.crossover.sbx import SBX
from pymoo.operators.mutation.pm import PolynomialMutation
from pymoo.operators.repair.rounding import RoundingRepair
from pymoo.operators.sampling.rnd import FloatRandomSampling
from pymoo.core.problem import Problem
from pymoo.optimize import minimize

class CurveFittingProblem(Problem):

    def __init__(self):
        super().__init__(n_var=4,
                         n_obj=1,
                         n_constr=0,
                         xl=-10.0,
                         xu=10.0, vtype=float)

    def _evaluate(self, X, out, *args, **kwargs):
        Y = np.zeros((X.shape[0], 1))
        for i, coeffs in enumerate(X):
            y_pred = np.polyval(coeffs, x)
            mse = np.mean((y - y_pred)**2)
            Y[i] = mse
        out["F"] = Y
```

Now we can instantiate the `CurveFittingProblem` class to create an instance of the problem to be solved. We can then define the genetic algorithm to be used for the optimization. The GA class is used to define the algorithm, and the `pop_size` parameter sets the population size to 50. The `sampling` parameter uses the `FloatRandomSampling` operator to generate the initial population of candidate solutions randomly. The `crossover` parameter uses the `SBX` operator with a crossover probability of 0.8. The `mutation` parameter uses the `PolynomialMutation` operator with a mutation probability of 0.3 and a rounding repair operator to ensure that the decision variables remain within the specified bounds. The `eliminate_duplicates` parameter is set to `True` to remove duplicate candidate solutions from the population.

Next, we can run the genetic algorithm to solve the curve fitting problem using the `minimize` function. This function takes three arguments: the instance of the problem to be solved (`problem`), the instance of the algorithm to be used (`algorithm`), and a tuple specifying the stopping criterion for the algorithm (`'n_gen'`, `100`), which specifies that the algorithm should run for 100 generations. The `seed` parameter is set to 1 to ensure the reproducibility of the results. The `verbose` parameter is set to `True` to display the progress of the algorithm during the optimization:

```
problem = CurveFittingProblem()
```
Initialize an instance of the CurveFittingProblem class.

```
algorithm = GA(
    pop_size=50,
    sampling=FloatRandomSampling(),
    crossover= SBX(prob=0.8),
    mutation = PolynomialMutation(prob=0.3, repair=RoundingRepair()),
    eliminate_duplicates=True
)
```
Create a GA solver.

Perform the optimization for 100 generations.

```
res = minimize(problem, algorithm, ('n_gen', 100), seed=1, verbose=True)
```

You can print the four coefficients obtained by GA as follows:

```
best_coeffs = res.X
print("Coefficients of the best-fit third-order polynomial:")
print("a =", best_coeffs[0])
print("b =", best_coeffs[1])
print("c =", best_coeffs[2])
print("d =", best_coeffs[3])
```

This results in the following output:

```
Coefficients of the best-fit third-order polynomial:
a = 2, b = -3, c = 4, d = 1
```

As you can see, the estimated values of the four coefficients are same as the coefficients of the ground truth polynomial (a, b, c, d = 2, –3, 4, 1). You can experiment with the code by changing the polynomial coefficients, using your own data, and using different crossover and mutation methods.

Next, we'll look at permutation-based GA.

8.3 *Permutation-based GA*

Permutation-based GAs are designed to solve optimization problems where the solutions are permutations of a set of elements. Examples of such problems include the traveling salesman problem (TSP), vehicle routing problem, sports tournament scheduling, and job scheduling problem. In these problems, the solutions are represented as optimal orders or permutations of a set of elements or events.

There are typically two main types of problems where the goal is to determine the optimal order of events:

- *Resource or time-constrained problems*—In these problems, the events rely on limited resources or time, making the order of events crucial for optimal solutions. One example of this type of problem is ride-sharing scheduling, where the goal is to efficiently allocate resources like vehicles and drivers to serve the maximum number of passengers in the shortest possible time.

■ *Adjacency-based problems*—In these problems, the proximity or adjacency of elements plays a significant role in finding the best solution. An example of such a problem is the traveling salesman problem (TSP), where the aim is to visit a set of cities while minimizing the total travel distance, taking into account the distances between adjacent cities in the tour.

These problems are often formulated as permutation problems. In a permutation representation, if there are n variables, the solution is a list of n distinct integers, each occurring exactly once. This representation ensures that the order or adjacency of the elements in the solution is explicitly encoded, which is essential for finding the optimal sequence of events in these types of problems. For example, let's consider the following TSP for 8 cities. A candidate solution for this TSP is represented by a permutation such as [1, 2, 3, 4, 5, 6, 7, 8]. In permutation-based GA, specialized crossover and mutation operators are employed to preserve the constraints of the permutation problem, such as maintaining a valid sequence of cities in the TSP, where each city appears only once.

The following subsections describe commonly used crossover and mutation methods in permutation-based GAs. The choice of crossover and mutation methods in GAs depends on the problem being solved, the type of solutions being sought, and the objectives of the optimization problem. By carefully selecting and designing these operators, GAs can effectively explore and exploit the search space to find high-quality solutions.

8.3.1 Crossover methods

Several crossover methods are commonly used in permutation-based GAs, such as partially mapped crossover (PMX), edge crossover (EC), order 1 crossover (OX1), and cycle crossover (CX).

PARTIALLY MAPPED CROSSOVER

The *partially mapped crossover* (PMX) method creates offspring by combining the genetic information from two parent chromosomes while preserving the feasibility of the resulting offspring with the procedure shown in algorithm 8.1.

Algorithm 8.1 Partially mapped crossover (PMX)

```
Input: two parents P1 and P2
Output: two children C1 and C2
1. Initialize: Choose two random crossover points and copy the segment
between these two points from parent P1 to child C1 and from the second
parent P2 to the second child C2.
2. For each element in the copied segment of C1:
3.    Find the corresponding element in P2's segment.
4.    If the corresponding element is not already in C1:
5.        Replace the element in C1 at the same position as in P2 with the
          corresponding element from P2.
```

6. Fill the remaining positions in the offspring with the elements from the
other parent, ensuring that no duplicates are introduced.
7. Repeat steps 2-6 for the second offspring, using P1's segment as the
reference.
8. Return C1 and C2.

Figure 8.5 illustrates these steps for an 8-city TSP. In step 1, two random crossover points are chosen, and the cities between these two points are copied from parent P1 to child C1 and from the second parent P2 to the second child C2. Then we follow steps 2 to 5 for the cities that were not included in step 1. For the first city in C1, which is 3, we need to find the corresponding city in the P2 segment, which is 7. City 7 is not already included in C1, so we need to place city 7 in the place where city 3 appears in P2, which is the last position on the right, as shown by the solid black arrow in figure 8.5.

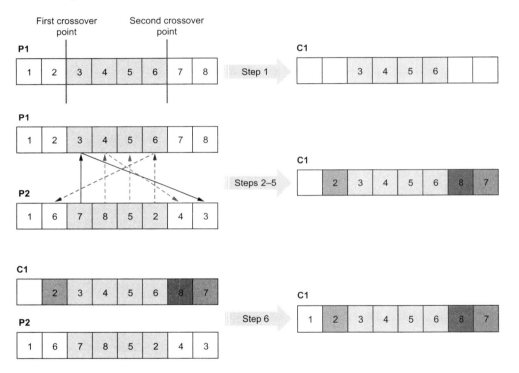

Figure 8.5 Partially mapped crossover (PMX)

The following listing shows code that performs a partially mapped crossover on two parents to generate two offspring.

Listing 8.2   Partially mapped crossover (PMX)

```
import random

def partially_mapped_crossover(parent1, parent2):

    n = len(parent1)

    point1, point2 = sorted(random.sample(range(n), 2))   ← Select two random
                                                             crossover points.
    child1 = [None] * n
    child2 = [None] * n
    child1[point1:point2+1] = parent1[point1:point2+1]
    child2[point1:point2+1] = parent2[point1:point2+1]

    for i in range(n):
        if child1[i] is None:
            value = parent2[i]                         ┐ Map the remaining elements
            while value in child1:                     │ from the other parent.
                value = parent2[parent1.index(value)]  ┘
            child1[i] = value

        if child2[i] is None:
            value = parent1[i]
            while value in child2:
                value = parent1[parent2.index(value)]
            child2[i] = value
                                         ┐ Return the generated
    return child1, child2   ←────────────┘ offspring.
```

Copy the segment between crossover points from a parent to a child.

Running this code will produce output like that shown in figure 8.6, depending on the generated random sample.

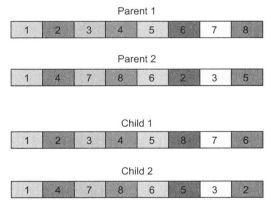

Figure 8.6   PMX results

The complete version of listing 8.2 is available in the book's GitHub repository.

EDGE CROSSOVER

The *edge crossover* (EC) method preserves the connectivity and adjacency information between elements from the parent chromosomes. In order to achieve this, an *edge table* (or *adjacency list*) is constructed. For example, in the 8-cities TSP, the edge table for two parents P1 = [1, 2, 3, 4, 5, 6, 7, 8] and P2 = [1, 6, 7, 8, 5, 2, 4, 3] is created by counting the adjacent elements in both parents, as in table 8.5. The "+" signs in the table denote a common edge between the two parents.

Table 8.5   An edge table (or adjacency list)

City	1	2	3	4	5	6	7	8
Edges	2,8,6,3	1,3,5,4	2,4+,1	3+,5,2	4,6,8,2	5,7+,1	6+,8+	7+,1,5

Algorithm 8.2 shows the steps involved in edge crossover.

Algorithm 8.2   Edge crossover (EC)

```
Input: two parent P1 and P2
Output: offspring C
1. Construct an edge table.
2. Start by selecting an arbitrary element from one of the parents as the
starting point for the offspring.
3. For the current element in the offspring, compare its edges.
4. If an edge is common in both parents, choose that as the next element in
the offspring.
5. If there is no common edge or the common edge is already in the offspring,
choose the next element from the parent with the shortest edge list.
6. Repeat until the offspring is complete.
7. Return C
```

Figure 8.7 illustrates these steps for the 8-cities TSP. This figure illustrates how to construct the edge table or adjacency list of each city. The process of counting the edges is shown in this figure. For example, cities 3 and 5 are adjacent cities or edges to city 4 in the first parent. In the second parent, cities 2 and 3 are edges for city 4. This means that city 3 is a common edge.

Creating a child starts by selecting city 1 randomly or as a home city. In the second row of the table, we list the adjacent cities of city 1, which are 2, 8, 6 and 3. Note that cities loop around, meaning city 1 is adjacent to city 8 in the first parent, and city 1 is adjacent to city 3 in the second parent. Discarding the already visited city 1, these cities have the following adjacent cities {3,5,4} for city 2, {7,5} for city 8, {5,7} for city 6, and {2,4} for city 3. We discard city 2, as it has three adjacent cities, and we select city 3 arbitrarily from 8, 6, and 3, as they have the same number of edges. We keep adding cities to the child following algorithm 8.2 until all the cities are added.

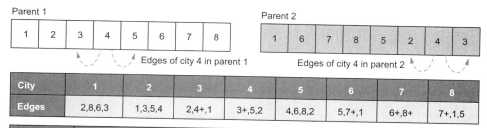

City	1	2	3	4	5	6	7	8
Edges	2,8,6,3	1,3,5,4	2,4+,1	3+,5,2	4,6,8,2	5,7+,1	6+,8+	7+,1,5

Choices	Element selected	Reason	Partial results - offspring
All	1	Random choice/home city	[1]
2,8,6,3	3	Arbitrarily chosen from 8, 6, and 3 as they have shortest lists	[1 3]
2,4+,1	4	Common edge	[1 3 4]
3+,5,2	2	Shortest list	[1 3 4 2]
1,3,5,4	5	Only item in the list	[1 3 4 2 5]
4,6,8,2	6	Arbitrarily chosen (both 6 and 8 have the same items)	[1 3 4 2 5 6]
5,7+,1	7	Only item and common edge	[1 3 4 2 5 6 7]
6+,8+	8	Last element	[1 3 4 2 5 6 7 8]

Figure 8.7 Edge crossover

The complete version of listing 8.2 is available in the book's GitHub repository. It shows the Python implementation of edge crossover with a TSP example.

ORDER 1 CROSSOVER

Order 1 crossover (OX1) creates offspring by combining the genetic information from two parent chromosomes while preserving the relative order of the elements in the resulting solutions. Algorithm 8.3 shows the steps involved in order 1 crossover.

Algorithm 8.3   Order 1 crossover (OX1)

```
Input: two parents P1 and P2
Output: offspring C1 and C2
1. Choose two random crossover points within the chromosomes and copy the
segment between the crossover points from P1 to C1 and from P2 to C2.
2. Starting from the second crossover point, go through the remaining
elements in P2.
3. If an element is not already present in C1, append it to the end in the
same order as it appears in P2.
4. Wrap around P2 and continue appending the elements until C1 is complete.
Repeat steps 2-4 for C2, using P1 as the reference.
5. Return C1 and C2
```

Figure 8.8 illustrates these steps for the 8-cities TSP. Starting from the second crossover point, cities 4 and 3 cannot be added, as they are already included in C1. The next element in P2 is city 1, so it is added to C1 after the second crossover point, followed by city 7, as city 6 is already included. City 8 is added next, followed by city 2, as city 5 is already included in C1.

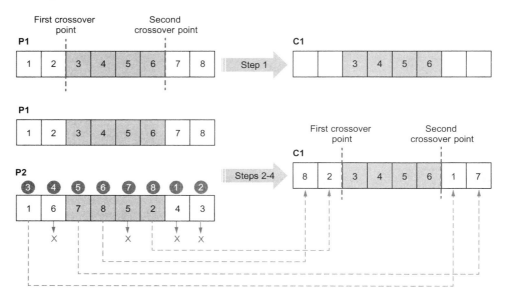

Figure 8.8   Order 1 crossover (OX1)—The numbers in circles show the sequence in which elements are added from parent 2 to child 1.

The complete version of listing 8.2 is available in the book's GitHub repository, and it shows the Python implementation of OX1 with the TSP example.

CYCLE CROSSOVER

Cycle crossover (CX) operates by dividing the elements into cycles, where a *cycle* is a subset of elements that consistently appear together in pairs when the two parent chromosomes are aligned. Given two parents, a cycle is formed by selecting an element from the first parent, finding its corresponding position in the second parent, and then repeating this process with the element at that position until returning to the starting element. The CX operator effectively combines the genetic information from both parents while preserving the order and adjacency relationships among the elements in the resulting offspring and maintaining the feasibility and diversity of the offspring solutions. Algorithm 8.4 shows the steps of this crossover method.

Algorithm 8.4   Cycle crossover (CX)

```
Input: two parents P1 and P2
Output: offspring C1 and C2
```

1. Identify cycles between the two parents. A cycle of elements from a parent P1 is created following these steps:
    a) Begin with the starting element of P1.
    b) Look at the element at the corresponding position in P2.
    c) Move to the position with the same element in P1.
    d) Include this element in the cycle.
    e) Iterate through steps b to d until you reach the starting element of P1.
2. Create offspring by placing the elements of the identified cycles, preserving their positions from the corresponding parents.
3. Fill in the remaining positions in C1 with elements from P2 and the remaining positions of C2 with elements from P1 that were not included in the identified cycles. Maintain the order of the elements as they appear in the parents.
4. Return C1 and C2.

Figure 8.9 illustrates these steps for the 10-cities TSP.

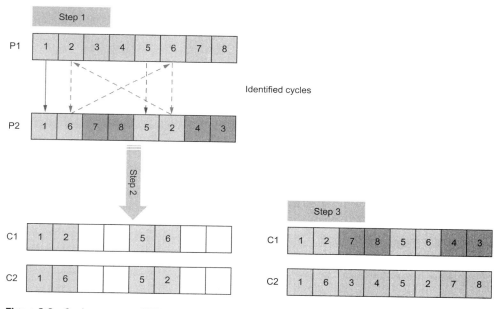

Figure 8.9   Cycle crossover (CX)

A Python implementation of CX with a TSP example is included in the complete version of listing 8.2, available in the book's GitHub repository. It's important to note that the performance of crossover operators is often problem-dependent and may also be influenced by the specific parameter settings of the genetic algorithm, such as population size, mutation rate, and selection pressure. Therefore, it is recommended that you experiment with different crossover operators and fine-tune the genetic algorithm's parameters to suit the problem being addressed.

8.3.2   *Mutation methods*

Insert, swap, inversion, and scramble are commonly used mutation methods in permutation-based GA. These methods are designed to introduce small perturbations to the solution while still preserving its feasibility:

- *Insert mutation*—Pick two gene values at random, and move the second to follow the first, shifting the rest along to accommodate them. This method primarily maintains the order and adjacency information of the genes.
- *Swap mutation*—Pick two genes at random, and swap their positions. This method mainly retains adjacency information while causing some disruption to the original order.
- *Inversion mutation*—Randomly select two genes, and invert the substring between them. This method largely maintains adjacency information but is disruptive to the order information.
- *Scramble mutation*—Randomly select two gene values, and rearrange the genes between the chosen positions non-contiguously, applying a random order.

Figure 8.10 illustrates these methods on the first parent as a selected individual in the 8-cities TSP.

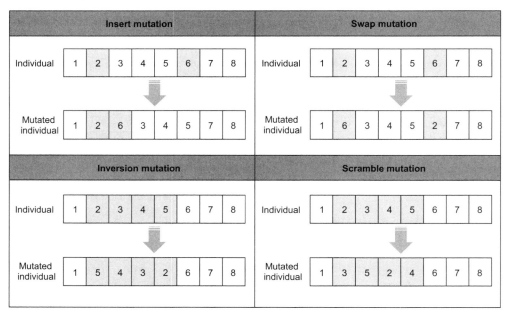

Figure 8.10   Mutation methods in permutation-based GA

As a continuation of listing 8.2, the following code snippet shows how you can implement inversion mutation in Python:

```
def inversion_mutation(individual, mutation_rate):
    n = len(individual)
    mutated_individual = individual.copy()

    if random.random() < mutation_rate:
        i, j = sorted(random.sample(range(n), 2))
        mutated_individual[i:j+1] = reversed(mutated_individual[i:j+1])

    return mutated_individual
```

Running this code will produce output like that in figure 8.11.

Figure 8.11 Inversion mutation result

The complete version of listing 8.2, available in the book's GitHub repository, includes implementations of different crossover and mutation methods commonly used in permutation-based genetic algorithms.

8.4 *Multi-objective optimization*

As mentioned earlier in section 1.3.2, optimization problems with multiple objective functions are known as multi-objective optimization problems (MOPs). These problems can be handled using a preference-based multi-objective optimization procedure or by using a Pareto optimization approach. In the former approach, the multiple objectives are combined into a single or overall objective function by using a relative preference vector or a weighting scheme to scalarize the multiple objectives. However, finding this preference vector or weight is subjective and sometimes is not straightforward.

Pareto optimization, named after Italian economist and sociologist Vilfredo Pareto (1848–1923), relies on finding multiple trade-off optimal solutions and choosing one using higher-level information. This procedure tries to find the best trade-off by reducing the number of alternatives to an optimal set of nondominated solutions known as the Pareto front (or Pareto frontier), which can be used to make strategic decisions in multi-objective space. A solution is Pareto optimal if there is no other solution that improves one objective without worsening another objective, in the case of conflicting objective functions. Thus, the optimal solution for MOPs is not a single solution, as for mono-objective or single optimization problems (SOPs), but a set of solutions defined as *Pareto optimal solutions*. These Pareto optimal solutions are also known as acceptable, efficient, nondominated, or non-inferior solutions. *Nondominated solutions* in Pareto optimization represent the best compromises that are not outperformed by any other solution across multiple conflicting objectives.

In chapter 1, we looked at an electric vehicles example: acceleration time and driving range are conflicting objective functions, as we need to minimize the acceleration time and maximize the driving range of the vehicle. There is no universal best vehicle that achieves both, as shown in figure 8.12, which is based on real data retrieved from the *Inside EVs* website (https://insideevs.com/). For example, the Lucid Air Dream Edition has the highest driving range but not the lowest acceleration time. The dotted line shows the Pareto front—the vehicles that achieve the best trade-off between the acceleration time and the driving range.

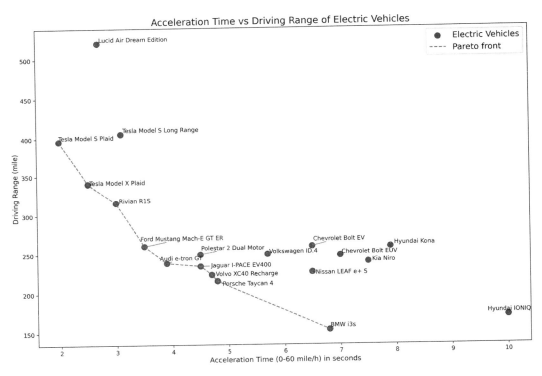

Figure 8.12   Acceleration time vs. driving range of 19 electric vehicles, as per September 2021

Multi-objective optimization algorithms

There are several algorithms for solving multi-objective optimization problems. The non-dominated sorting genetic algorithm (NSGA-II) is one of the most commonly used. Other algorithms include, but are not limited to, the strength Pareto evolutionary algorithm 2 (SPEA2), the Pareto-archived evolution strategy (PAES), the niched-Pareto genetic algorithm (NPGA), multi-objective selection based on dominated hypervolume (SMS-EMOA), and multi-objective evolutionary algorithm based on decomposition (MOEA/D).

These algorithms have their own strengths and weaknesses, and your choice of algorithm will depend on the specific problem being solved and your preferences. NSGA-II has several advantages, such as diversity maintenance, non-dominated sorting, and fast convergence. For more details about multi-objective optimization, see Deb's "Multi-objective optimization using evolutionary algorithms" [3] and Zitzler's "Evolutionary algorithms for multiobjective optimization" [4].

Let's solve a MOP using NSGA-II in an example. Assume that a manufacturer produces two products, P1 and P2, involving two different machines, M1 and M2. Each machine can only produce one product at a time, and each product has a different production time and cost on each machine:

- P1 requires 2 hours on M1 and 3 hours on M2, with production costs of $100 and $150 respectively.

- P2 requires 4 hours on M1 and 1 hour on M2, with production costs of $200 and $50 respectively.

In each shift, the two machines, M1 and M2, have the capacity of producing 100 units of P1 and 500 units of P2. The manufacturer wants to produce at least 80 units of P1 and 300 units of P2 while minimizing production costs and minimizing the difference in production times between the two machines.

We'll let x_1 and x_2 be the number of units of P1 produced on M1 and M2, respectively, and y_1 and y_2 be the number of units of P2 produced on M1 and M2, respectively. The problem can be formulated as follows:

$$\text{Minimize} f_1(x_1, x_2, y_1, y_2) = 100x_1 + 150x_2 + 200y_1 + 50y_2$$
$$\text{Minimize} f_2(x_1, x_2, y_1, y_2) = |(2x_1 + 4y_1) - (3x_2 + y_2)|$$

Subject to:

$$x_1 + x_2 \geq 80$$
$$y_1 + y_2 \geq 300$$
$$x_1, x_2, y_1, y_2 \geq 0$$

The first objective function (f_1) represents the total production costs, and the second objective function (f_2) represents the difference in production times between the two machines. Listing 8.3 shows the code for finding the optimal number of units to be produced in a shift using NSGA-II.

We'll start by inheriting from `ElementwiseProblem`, which allows us to define the optimization problem in an element-wise manner. n_var specifies the number of variables (4 in this case), n_obj defines the number of objectives (2), and n_ieq_constr indicates the number of inequality constraints (2). The xl and xu parameters define the lower and upper bounds for each variable respectively. The _evaluate method takes an input x (a solution candidate) and computes the objective values f1 and f2, as well as the inequality constraints g1 and g2. The third constraint is boundary constraint represented by the lower and upper bounds of the decision variables.

Listing 8.3   Solving a manufacturing problem using NSGA-II

```
import numpy as np
import matplotlib.pyplot as plt
from pymoo.core.problem import ElementwiseProblem          Import an instance
                                                           of the problem class.
class ManufacturingProblem(ElementwiseProblem):

    def __init__(self):
        super().__init__(n_var=4,                          Define the number
                         n_obj=2,                          of variables, objective
                         n_ieq_constr=2,                   functions, constraints,
                         xl=np.array([0,0,0,0]),           and lower and upper
                         xu=np.array([100,100,500,500]))   bounds.

    def _evaluate(self, x, out, *args, **kwargs):
        f1 = 100*x[0] + 150*x[1] + 200*x[2] + 50*x[3]
        f2 = np.abs((2*x[0] + 4*x[2]) - (3*x[1] + x[3]))
                                           Difference in production times
                                           between the two machines as
        g1 = -x[0] - x[1] + 80            a second-objective function
        g2 = -x[2] - x[3] + 300

Define the          out["F"] = [f1, f2]                Total production costs as a
constraints.        out["G"] = [g1, g2]                    first-objective function


problem = ManufacturingProblem()
```

We can now set up an instance of the NSGA-II algorithm as the solver:

Import simulated binary crossover   Import the NSGA-II class.   Import polynomial
(SBX) as a crossover operator.   mutation (PM) as a
                                                                           mutation operator.

```
from pymoo.algorithms.moo.nsga2 import NSGA2
from pymoo.operators.crossover.sbx import SBX
from pymoo.operators.mutation.pm import PM
from pymoo.operators.sampling.rnd import FloatRandomSampling
```
                                           Import the FloatRandomSampling
                                           method to generate random
                                           floating-point values for each
                                           variable within a specified range.

```
algorithm = NSGA2(
    pop_size=40,
    n_offsprings=10,
    sampling=FloatRandomSampling(),
    crossover=SBX(prob=0.9, eta=15),
    mutation=PM(eta=20),              Set up an instance
    eliminate_duplicates=True        of NSGA-II.
)
```

The solver has a population size (pop_size) of 40 individuals, generates 10 offspring using FloatRandomSampling, employs SBX crossover with a probability of 0.9, and fine-tunes the exponential distribution with an eta parameter of 15. PM mutation is used with an eta parameter of 20. This eta parameter controls the spread of the mutation distribution. eliminate_duplicates is set to True so that duplicate candidate solutions will be removed from the population at each generation.

We define the termination criterion by specifying the number of generations as follows:

```
from pymoo.termination import get_termination
termination = get_termination("n_gen", 40)
```

We can now run the solver to minimize both objective functions simultaneously:

```
from pymoo.optimize import minimize

res = minimize(problem,
               algorithm,
               termination,
               seed=1,
               save_history=True,
               verbose=True)
X = res.X
F = res.F
```

Finally, we print the best 10 solutions as follows:

```
print("Solutions found: ")
print("Number of units of product P1 produced on machines M1 and M2\n and
➥ Number of units of product P2 produced on machines M1 and M2 are:\n",
➥ np.asarray(X, dtype = 'int'))
np.set_printoptions(suppress=True, precision=3)
print("The total production costs and \n difference in production times
➥ between the two machines are:\n",F)
```

This code will produce output representing the best 10 non-dominated solutions obtained by NSGA-II and will look like this:

```
Solutions found:
Number of units of product P1 produced on machines M1 and M2
and Number of units of product P2 produced on machines M1 and M2 are:
[[ 90   18   39 300]
 [ 91   19   39 297]
 [ 91   16   12 300]
 [ 90   12   30 310]
 [ 90   14   21 300]
 [ 90   14   47 328]
 [ 34   48    1 305]
 [ 87   13    3 299]
 [ 91   11    7 297]
```

```
[ 30  51   0 300]]
The total production costs and
difference in production times between the two machines are:
[[34757.953    16.105]
[34935.538    13.813]
[29235.912   114.763]
[32498.687    43.463]
[30481.316    79.233]
[37228.051     0.652]
[26307.998   378.004]
[26388.316   150.968]
[27199.394   118.385]
[25980.561   392.176]]
```

As there is no universal best solution for these two objective functions, multi-criteria decision-making can be applied to select the best trade-off—the Pareto optimal. In pymoo, the decision-making procedure starts by defining boundary points called *ideal* and *nadir* points:

- *The ideal point*—This refers to the best possible values for each objective function that can be achieved in the entire feasible region of the problem. This point represents the scenario where all the objective functions are minimized simultaneously.
- *The nadir point*—This is the point where each objective function is maximized while satisfying all the constraints of the problem. It is the opposite of the ideal point and represents the worst possible values for each objective function in the entire feasible region of the problem.

These points are used in multi-objective optimization problems to normalize the objective functions and convert them to a common scale, allowing for a fair comparison of different solutions. The two points are calculated as follows:

```
approx_ideal = F.min(axis=0)
approx_nadir = F.max(axis=0)
nF = (F - approx_ideal) / (approx_nadir - approx_ideal)
```

We then define weights, which are required by the decomposition functions, based on the level of importance of each objective function from the developer's perspective:

```
weights = np.array([0.2, 0.8])  ◀────────  Weights for f1 and f2 respectively
```

A decomposition method is defined using the augmented scalarization function (ASF), discussed in Wierzbicki's "The use of reference objectives in multiobjective optimization" [5]:

```
from pymoo.decomposition.asf import ASF
decomp = ASF()
```

To find the best solutions, we choose the minimum ASF values calculated from all the solutions and use the inverse of the weights as required by ASF:

```
i = decomp.do(nF, 1/weights).argmin()

print("Best regarding ASF: Point \ni = %s\nF = %s" % (i, F[i]))

plt.figure(figsize=(7, 5))
plt.scatter(F[:, 0], F[:, 1], s=30, facecolors='none', edgecolors='blue')
plt.scatter(F[i, 0], F[i, 1], marker="x", color="red", s=200)
plt.title("Objective Space")
plt.xlabel("Total production costs")
plt.ylabel("Difference in production times")
plt.show()
```

The output is shown in figure 8.13.

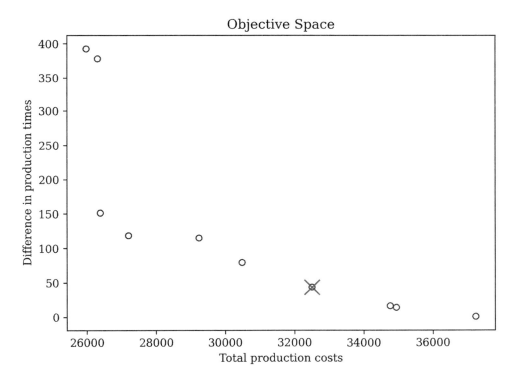

Figure 8.13   Manufacturing problem solution—the point marked with the X represents the selected Pareto optimal or best trade-off.

Running the code produces the following output:

```
The best solution found:
Number of units of product P1 produced on machines M1 and M2 are 90 and 12
respectively
Number of units of product P2 produced on machines M1 and M2 are 30 and 310
respectively
The total production costs are 32498.69
The difference in production times between the two machines is 43
```

The complete version of listing 8.3 is available in the book's GitHub repository. It includes another method using pseudo-weights to choose a solution from a solution set in the context of multi-objective optimization.

8.5   *Adaptive GA*

Adaptation methods help genetic algorithms strike a balance between exploration and exploitation, using different parameters such as initialization population size, crossover operators, and mutation operators. These parameters can be deterministically or dynamically adapted based on the search progress, allowing the algorithm to converge on high-quality solutions for complex optimization problems.

For example, population size can be adaptive. A larger population size promotes diversity and exploration, while a smaller size allows for faster convergence. The population size can be increased if the algorithm is struggling to find better solutions or decreased if the population has become too diverse.

Mutation operator parameters can be used to adapt the genetic algorithm and balance its exploration and exploitation aspects. For example, in the case of Gaussian mutation, we can adaptively set the value of the standard deviation σ of the Gaussian distribution during the run. The standard deviation of the Gaussian distribution can be changed following a deterministic approach, an adaptive approach, or a self-adaptive approach. If you're using a deterministic approach, the value of σ can be calculated in each generation using this formula: $\sigma(i) = 1 - 0.9 * i / N$ where i is the generation number, ranging from 0 to N (the maximum generation number). In this case, the value of σ is 1 at the beginning of the optimization process and gradually reduces to 0.1 toward the end to move the search algorithm's behavior from exploration to exploitation.

The adaptive approach incorporates feedback from the search process to adjust the variance and improve the search performance. Rechenberg's *1/5 success rule* is a well-known method that adjusts the step size of the search by monitoring the success rate of the search. This rule involves increasing the variance if a certain percentage of the previous mutations were successful in finding better solutions (i.e., if there was more than one successful mutation out of five tries), favoring exploration in order to avoid getting trapped in local optima. Otherwise, if there was a lower success rate, the variance should be decreased to favor exploitation. This allows the search to fine-tune its parameters based on its progress, leading to better performance and faster convergence to optimal solutions.

Figure 8.14 shows the steps of applying Rechenberg's 1/5 success rule. This update rule is applied in every generation, and a constant $0.82 <= c <= 1$ is used to update the standard deviation of the Gaussian distribution. As you can see, the higher the standard deviation, the higher the value of x, and the higher the deviation from the current solution (more exploration), and vice versa.

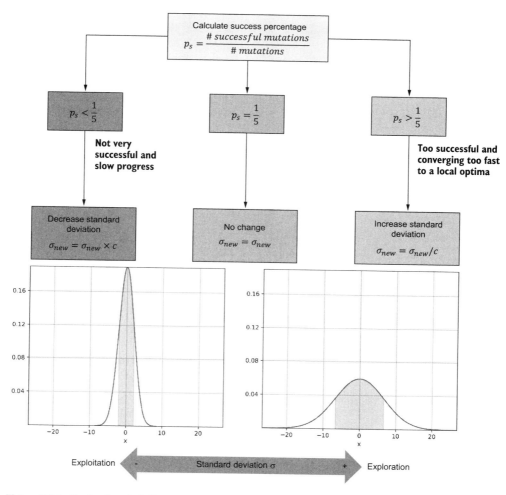

Figure 8.14 Rechenberg's 1/5 success rule. Following this rule, the Gaussian distribution's standard deviation is updated by a constant. The higher the standard deviation, the higher the value of x (i.e., larger step size), the higher the deviation from the current solution (more exploration), and vice versa.

The self-adaptive approach incorporates the mutation step size into each individual—a technique originally employed in evolution strategies (ES). In this method, the value of σ (the standard deviation or the mutation step size) evolves alongside the individual, resulting in distinct mutation step sizes for each individual in the population. The following equations are used in this self-adaptive approach:

$$\sigma' = \sigma e^{N(0, \tau_0)}$$

8.2

$$x_i' = x_i + N(0, \sigma')$$ **8.3**

where τ_o is the learning rate.

Now that you have a solid understanding of the various components of GAs, we can apply this powerful optimization technique to real-world problems. In the following sections, we will use GAs to solve three distinct problems: the traveling salesman problem, tuning the parameters of a PID controller, and the political districting problem.

8.6   *Solving the traveling salesman problem*

Let's consider the following traveling salesman problem (TSP) for 20 major cities in the USA, starting from New York City, as illustrated in figure 8.15.

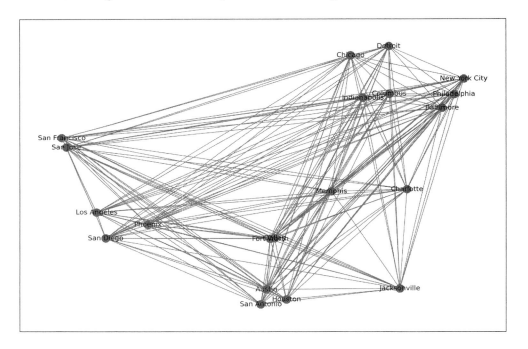

Figure 8.15   The 20 major US cities TSP

In listing 8.4, we start by importing the libraries we'll use and defining the TSP. First, we define the city names and their latitudes and longitudes. We then use those coordinates to create a haversine distance matrix and then convert the data dictionary into a dataframe.

Listing 8.4   Solving TSP using GA

```
import numpy as np
import pandas as pd
import networkx as nx
```

```
from collections import defaultdict
from haversine import haversine
import matplotlib.pyplot as plt
from pymoo.core.problem import ElementwiseProblem
from pymoo.core.repair import Repair
from pymoo.algorithms.soo.nonconvex.ga import GA
from pymoo.optimize import minimize
from pymoo.operators.sampling.rnd import PermutationRandomSampling
from pymoo.operators.crossover.ox import OrderCrossover
from pymoo.operators.mutation.inversion import InversionMutation
from pymoo.termination.default import DefaultSingleObjectiveTermination
from pymoo.optimize import minimize

cities = {
    'New York City': (40.72, -74.00),
    'Philadelphia': (39.95, -75.17),
    'Baltimore': (39.28, -76.62),
    'Charlotte': (35.23, -80.85),
    'Memphis': (35.12, -89.97),
    'Jacksonville': (30.32, -81.70),
    'Houston': (29.77, -95.38),
    'Austin': (30.27, -97.77),
    'San Antonio': (29.53, -98.47),
    'Fort Worth': (32.75, -97.33),
    'Dallas': (32.78, -96.80),
    'San Diego': (32.78, -117.15),
    'Los Angeles': (34.05, -118.25),
    'San Jose': (37.30, -121.87),
    'San Francisco': (37.78, -122.42),
    'Indianapolis': (39.78, -86.15),
    'Phoenix': (33.45, -112.07),
    'Columbus': (39.98, -82.98),
    'Chicago': (41.88, -87.63),
    'Detroit': (42.33, -83.05)
}
```

Define city names, latitudes, and longitudes for 20 major US cities.

```
distance_matrix = defaultdict(dict)
for ka, va in cities.items():
    for kb, vb in cities.items():
        distance_matrix[ka][kb] = 0.0 if kb == ka else
haversine((va[0], va[1]),
    (vb[0], vb[1]))
```

Create a haversine distance matrix based on latitude-longitude coordinates.

```
distances = pd.DataFrame(distance_matrix)
city_names=list(distances.columns)
distances=distances.values
```

Convert the distance dictionary into a dataframe.

```
G=nx.Graph()
for ka, va in cities.items():
    for kb, vb in cities.items():
        G.add_weighted_edges_from({(ka,kb, distance_matrix[ka][kb])})
        G.remove_edges_from(nx.selfloop_edges(G))
```

Create a networkx graph.

We can then create `TravelingSalesman` as a subclass of the `ElementwiseProblem` class available in pymoo. This class defines the number of cities and the intercity distances as problem parameters, and it evaluates the total path length as an objective function to be minimized:

```
class TravelingSalesman(ElementwiseProblem):

    def __init__(self, cities, distances, **kwargs):
        self.cities = cities
        n_cities = len(cities)
        self.distances = distances

        super().__init__(
            n_var=n_cities,
            n_obj=1,
            xl=0,
            xu=n_cities,
            vtype=int,
            **kwargs
        )

    def _evaluate(self, x, out, *args, **kwargs):
        f = 0
        for i in range(len(x) - 1):
            f += distances[x[i], x[i + 1]]
        f += distances[x[-1], x[0]]
        out["F"] = f
```

The following function is a subclass of the `Repair` class, and it provides a method to repair solutions for the TSP, ensuring that each solution starts with the city indexed as 0 (New York City, in this example). The repair operator in pymoo is used to make sure the algorithm is only searching the feasible space. It is applied after the offspring have been reproduced:

```
class StartFromZeroRepair(Repair):

    def _do(self, problem, X, **kwargs):
        I = np.where(X == 0)[1]

        for k in range(len(X)):
            i = I[k]
            X[k] = np.concatenate([X[k, i:], X[k, :i]])

        return X
```

It's time now to define a GA solver and apply it to solve the problem.

```
problem = TravelingSalesman(cities,distance_matrix)    ◄─── Create a TSP instance
                                                            for the given cities and
                                                            intercity distances.
algorithm = GA(
    pop_size=20,
    sampling=PermutationRandomSampling(),
    mutation=InversionMutation(),
    crossover=OrderCrossover(),
```

```
        repair=StartFromZeroRepair(),
        eliminate_duplicates=True
)
```
Define the GA solver.

```
termination = DefaultSingleObjectiveTermination(period=300, n_max_gen=np.inf)
```
Terminate (and disable the max generations) if the algorithm did not improve in the last 300 generations.

```
res = minimize(
    problem,
    algorithm,
    termination,
    seed=1,
    verbose=False
)
```
Find the shortest path.

We can print the found route and its length as follows:

```
Order = res.X
Route = [city_names[i] for i in Order]
arrow_route = ' → '.join(Route)
print("Route:", arrow_route)
print("Route length:", np.round(res.F[0], 3))
print("Function Evaluations:", res.algorithm.evaluator.n_eval)
```

This results in the following output:

```
Route: New York City → Detroit → Columbus → Indianapolis → Chicago → San
Francisco → San Jose → Los Angeles → San Diego → Phoenix → San Antonio →
Austin → Houston → Fort Worth → Dallas → Memphis → Jacksonville → Charlotte →
Baltimore → Philadelphia
Route length: 10934.796
Function Evaluations: 6020
```

The following code is used to visualize the obtained route using NetworkX:

```
fig, ax = plt.subplots(figsize=(15,10))
```
Create an independent shallow copy of the problem graph and attributes.

```
H = G.copy()
```
Reverse latitude and longitude for correct visualization.

```
reversed_dict = {key: value[::-1] for key, value in cities.items()}
```

```
keys_list = list(cities.keys())
```
Create a list of keys in the original dictionary.

```
included_cities = {keys_list[index]: cities[keys_list[index]] for index in
    list(res.X)}
included_cities_keys=list(included_cities.keys())
```
Create a new dictionary with the keys in the desired order.

```
edge_list =list(nx.utils.pairwise(included_cities_keys))
```
Create an edge list.

```
nx.draw_networkx_edges(H, pos=reversed_dict, edge_color="gray", width=0.5)
```

```
ax=nx.draw_networkx(
    H,
    pos=reversed_dict,
    with_labels=True,
    edgelist=edge_list,
    edge_color="red",
```
Draw the closest edges on each node only.

```
    node_size=200,
    width=3,
)
plt.show()
```
**Draw and show
the route.**

Figure 8.16 shows the obtained route for this traveling salesman problem.

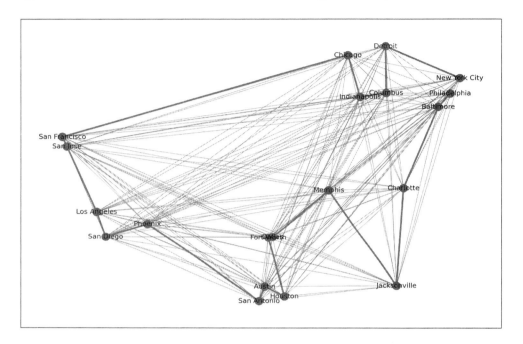

Figure 8.16   The 20 major US cities TSP solution

You can experiment with the full code in the book's GitHub repository by changing the problem data and the genetic algorithm parameters, such as population size, sampling, crossover, and mutation methods.

8.7   *PID tuning problem*

Have you ever wondered how your room stays at a comfortable temperature? Have you ever thought about how the heating or cooling system knows when to turn on and off automatically to maintain the temperature set on the thermostat? This is where control systems come into the picture. Control systems are like behind-the-scenes wizards that ensure things work smoothly and efficiently. They are sets of rules and mechanisms that guide devices or processes to achieve specific goals.

One type of control system is a *closed-loop system*. Picture this: you've set your room's thermostat to a cozy 22°C (72°F), and the heating or cooling system kicks in to reach that temperature. But what happens if it becomes too chilly or too warm? That's when the closed-loop system starts to take action. It's continually tracking the room's current temperature, comparing it to the desired temperature, and making the necessary heating or cooling tweaks.

The proportional integral derivative (PID) controller is the most commonly used algorithm in control systems engineering. This controller is designed to compensate for any error between the measured state (e.g., the current room temperature) and the desired state (e.g., the desired temperature value). Let's consider room temperature control using a PID controller as an example.

As shown in figure 8.17, the controller takes the error signal $e(t)$ (the difference between the desired state and the feedback signal) and produces the appropriate control signal $u(t)$ to turn on or off the heater in order to minimize the difference between the current room temperature and the desired value. The control signal is calculated using equation 8.4:

$$u(t) = K_p e(t) + K_i \int_o^t e(t)dt + K_d \frac{d}{dt} e(t)$$

8.4

As shown in this equation, the *proportional term* $K_p e(t)$ tends to produce a control signal that is proportional to the error and aims to rectify it. The *integral term* (the second term on the right side of the equation) tends to produce a control signal that is proportional to the magnitude of the error and its duration, or the area under the error curve. The *derivative term* (the third term on the right side of the equation) tends to produce a control signal that is proportional to the rate of error change, thus providing an anticipatory control signal.

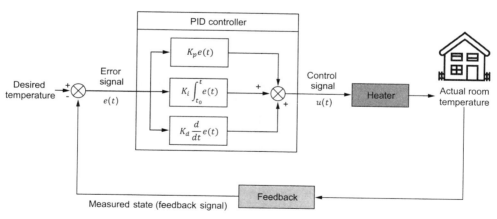

Figure 8.17 **PID-based closed-loop control system—the PID controller takes the error signal and produces a control signal to reduce the error to zero.**

Utilizing a PID controller allows the system (e.g., an air conditioner or heater) to follow the specified input and attain a desired or optimal steady-state error, rise time, settling time, and overshoot:

- *Rise time*—The rise time is the time required for the response to rise from 10% to 90% of its final value.
- *Peak overshoot*—The peak overshoot (aka maximum overshoot) is the deviation of the response at peak time from the final value of the response.
- *Settling time*—The settling time is the time required for the response to reach the steady state and stay within the specified tolerance bands (e.g., 2–5% of the final value) after the transient response has settled.
- *Steady-state error*—The steady-state error is the difference between the desired value and the actual value of the system output when the system has reached a stable condition.

As shown in figure 8.18, the heater is turned on (i.e., energized) when the current room temperature is lower than the set point or the desired value. The heater is turned off (i.e., de-energized) when the temperature is above the set point.

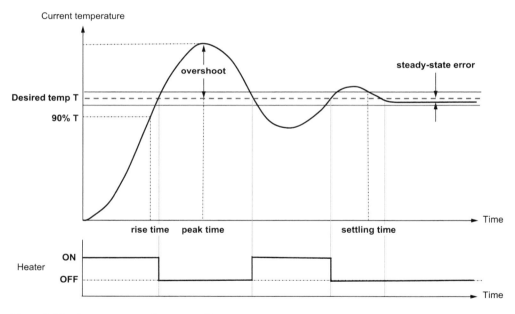

Figure 8.18   Step response of a system. The heater is turned on or off according to the difference between the actual temperature and the desired value.

Table 8.6 shows the effect of PID controller parameters on the time response of the system. Note that these correlations may not be exactly accurate, because K_p, K_i, and K_d are dependent on each other. In fact, changing one of these variables can change the effect of the other two. For this reason, the table should only be used as a reference when you are determining the values for K_p, K_i, and K_d.

Table 8.6 Effects of adding PID controller parameters on the system's response

Parameter	Rise time	Overshoot	Settling time	Steady-state error
K_p	Decreases	Increases	Small change	Decreases
K_i	Decreases	Increases	Increases	Decreases significantly
K_d	Small change	Decreases	Decreases	Small change

Finding the optimal values of the PID controller parameters for an optimal controller response is a multivariate optimization problem commonly referred to as the *PID tuning problem*. The following four performance metrics are commonly used to evaluate the quality of a control system such as a PID controller:

- *ITAE (integral time absolute error)*—This metric penalizes errors that persist over time, making it suitable for systems where transient response and settling time are important. It is calculated using this formula: ITAE $= \int (t|e(t)|) \ dt$, where t is the time, $e(t)$ is the error at time t defined as $e(t) = r(t) - y(t)$, $r(t)$ is the reference signal (desired output) at time t (for step response $r(t) = 1$), and $y(t)$ is the actual output of the system at time t.

- *ITSE (integral time square error)*—Like ITAE, this metric also penalizes errors that last for a long time but places more emphasis on larger errors due to the squared term. It is calculated using this formula: ITSE $= \int (te(t)^2) \ dt$.

- *IAE (integral absolute error)*—This metric measures the overall magnitude of the error without considering the duration of the error. This is a simple and widely used performance metric, and it's calculated using this formula: IAE $= \int |e(t)| \ dt$.

- *ISE (integral squared error)*—This metric emphasizes larger errors due to the squared term, making it useful for systems where minimizing large errors is a priority. It is calculated using this formula: ISE $= \int e(t)^2 \ dt$. It penalizes errors more heavily if they occur later in the evolution of the response. It also penalizes an error E for time dt more heavily than E/α for time αdt, where $\alpha > 1$. This expected response may have a slow rise time but with a more oscillatory behavior.

- *Combined criteria*—This metric combines overshoot, rise time, settling time, and steady-state error [6]. It is calculated using this formula: $W = (1 - e^{-\beta})(M_p + error_{ss}) + e^{-\beta}(t_s - t_r)$, where M_p is the overshoot, $error_{ss}$ is the steady-state error, t_s is the settling time, t_r is the rise time, and β is a balancing factor in the range of 0.8 to 1.5. You can set β to be larger than 0.7 to reduce the overshoot and steady-state error. On the other hand, you can set β to be smaller than 0.7 to reduce the rise time and settling time.

Each of these metrics quantifies the error between the desired output and the actual output of the system in different ways, emphasizing different aspects of the control system's performance. Note that performance metrics are not strictly confined to the aforementioned metrics. Engineers have the flexibility to devise custom performance metrics tailored to the specific goals and characteristics of the control system under consideration.

Figure 8.19 shows a closed-loop control system where a transfer function is used to describe the relationship between the input and output of the system in a Laplace domain. This domain is a generalization of a frequency domain, providing a more comprehensive representation that includes transient behavior and initial conditions. Assume that T_{sp} is the set point or the desired output and G represents the transfer functions indicated in the block diagram.

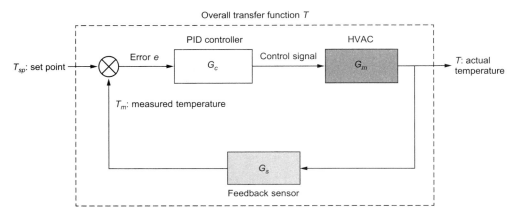

Figure 8.19   Closed-loop control system

All variables are a function of s, which is the output variable from a Laplace transform. The transfer function of a PID controller is given by this equation:

$$G_c(s) = \left(K_p + \frac{K_i}{s} + K_d s \right) = \frac{K_d s^2 + K_p s + K_i}{s} \qquad \textbf{8.5}$$

where K_p is the proportional gain, K_i is the integral gain, and K_d is the derivative gain. Assume that the transfer function of the HVAC system is given by this equation:

$$G_m(s) = \frac{1}{s^2 + 10s + 20} \qquad \textbf{8.6}$$

Assuming that $G_s = 1$ (unity feedback) and using block diagram reduction, we can find the overall transfer function $T(s)$ of the closed loop system:

$$T(s) = \frac{K_d s^2 K_p s + K_i}{s^3 + (K_d + 10) s^2 + (K_p + 20) s + K_i} \qquad \textbf{8.7}$$

Let's now look at how we can find the optimal values for the PID parameters with Python. In the next listing, we start by importing the libraries we'll use and defining the overall transfer function of the control system.

Listing 8.5   Solving the PID tuning problem using GA

```python
import numpy as np
import control          ← Import the control module.
import math
import matplotlib.pyplot as plt
from pymoo.algorithms.soo.nonconvex.ga import GA
from pymoo.operators.crossover.pntx import PointCrossover
from pymoo.operators.mutation.pm import PolynomialMutation
from pymoo.operators.repair.rounding import RoundingRepair
from pymoo.operators.sampling.rnd import FloatRandomSampling
from pymoo.core.problem import Problem
from pymoo.optimize import minimize          Take PID parameters as input.

def transfer_function(Kp,Ki,Kd):          ←
    num = np.array([Kd,Kp,Ki])          ←          Define the numerator of the
                                                   transfer function.
    den = np.array([1,(Kd+10),(Kp+20),Ki])          ←
                                                   Define the denominator of
    T = control.tf(num, den)          ←          the transfer function.
    t, y = control.step_response(T)          ←          Get time response output
    return T, t, y                                  using a step function as a
#A Import the control module.                       system input.
```

Create a transfer function. → `T = control.tf(num, den)`

Next, we can define the objective functions or performance criteria:

```python
def objective_function(t, error, Kp,Ki,Kd, criterion):

    if criterion == 1:
        ITAE = np.trapz(t, t*error)          ←          ITAE (integral time absolute error)
        objfnc= ITAE
    elif criterion == 2:
        ITSE = np.trapz(t, t*error**2)          ←          ITSE (integral time square error)
        objfnc= ITSE
    elif criterion == 3:
        IAE =  np.trapz(t, error)          ←          IAE (integral absolute error)
        objfnc= IAE
    elif criterion == 4:
        ISE = np.trapz(t, error**2)          ←          ISE (integral squared error)
        objfnc= ISE
    elif criterion == 5:
        T, _, _ =transfer_function(Kp,Ki,Kd)
        info = control.step_info(T)
        beta = 1
        Mp = info['Overshoot']
        tr = info['RiseTime']
        ts = info['SettlingTime']                                  W (combined criteria)
        ess = abs(1-info['SteadyStateValue'])
        W = ((1-math.exp(-beta))*(Mp+ess))+((math.exp(-beta))*(ts-tr))          ←
        objfnc=W;

    return objfnc
```

We can now define the optimization problem for the PID controller:

```
class PIDProblem(Problem):
    def __init__(self):
        super().__init__(n_var=3,
                         n_obj=1,
                         n_constr=0,
                         xl=0,
                         xu=100,
                         vtype=float)

    def _evaluate(self, X, out, *args, **kwargs):
        f = np.zeros((X.shape[0], 1))
        for i, params in enumerate(X):
            Kp, Ki, Kd = params
            T, t, y =transfer_function(Kp,Ki,Kd)
            error = 1 - y
            f[i]=objective_function(t, np.abs(error), Kp,Ki,Kd, 5)
        out["F"] = f
```

Three decision variables, representing the PID controller's Kp, Ki, and Kd gains

Number of objective functions

No constraints

Lower and upper bounds for the decision variables

Evaluate the objective function.

Next, we can set up and solve the PID tuning problem using GA. The previously defined PIDProblem class is used to model the optimization problem. The GA solver is configured with a population size of 50. Initial solutions are sampled using Float RandomSampling, and the crossover operation employs a two-point crossover with a probability of 0.8. Additionally, polynomial mutation is applied with a probability of 0.3, and the algorithm runs for 60 generations:

```
problem = PIDProblem()

algorithm = GA(
    pop_size=50,
    sampling=FloatRandomSampling(),
    crossover=PointCrossover(prob=0.8, n_points=2),
    mutation = PolynomialMutation(prob=0.3, repair=RoundingRepair()),
    eliminate_duplicates=True
)

res = minimize(problem, algorithm, ('n_gen', 60), seed=1, verbose=True)
```

Let's now print the results:

```
best_params = res.X
print("Optimal PID controller parameters:")
print("Kp =", best_params[0])
print("Ki =", best_params[1])
print("Kd =", best_params[2])
```

And we'll visualize the time response:

```
Kp = best_params[0]
Ki = best_params[1]
Kd = best_params[2]
```

```
T, t, y =transfer_function(Kp,Ki,Kd)

plt.plot(t,y)
plt.title("Step Response")
plt.xlabel("Time (s)")
plt.grid()
```

Figure 8.20 depicts the step response of the system, demonstrating how its outputs change over time when the inputs swiftly transition from 0 to 1.

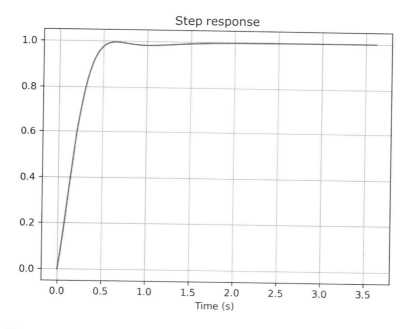

Figure 8.20   Step response

To show the step response characteristics (rise time, settling time, peak, and others), you can use the following function:

```
control.step_info(T)
```

This results in the following output:

```
{'RiseTime': 0.353,
 'SettlingTime': 0.52,
 'SettlingMin': 0.92,
 'SettlingMax': 1.0,
 'Overshoot': 0,
 'Undershoot': 0,
 'Peak': 0.99,
 'PeakTime': 3.62,
 'SteadyStateValue': 1.0}
```

You can experiment with adjusting the algorithm's parameters (such as population size, crossover method and probability, mutation method and probability, number of generations, etc.) and altering the performance metric to observe the effects on the system's performance.

8.8 *Political districting problem*

I introduced political districting in section 2.1.5—it can be defined as the process of grouping n subregions within a territory into m electoral districts while adhering to certain constraints. Suppose we need to merge n neighborhoods in the City of Toronto into m electoral districts while ensuring a sufficient level of population equality. Figure 8.21 shows a sample dataset that contains population and median household income for 16 neighborhoods in East Toronto.

Figure 8.21   The 16 neighborhoods in East Toronto with their population and median household income

In addressing the political districting problem, a viable solution must ensure that there is a satisfactory degree of population equilibrium (i.e., a fair and balanced distribution) in every electoral district. For example, we can evaluate a district's population balance by calculating the deviation from an ideal population size within an upper bound (pop_{UB}) and lower bound (pop_{LB}) as follows:

$$pop_{UB} = \text{ceil}\left(\left(pop_{av} + pop_{margin}\right) \times \frac{n}{m} \right)$$

$$pop_{LB} = \text{floor}\left(\left(pop_{av} - pop_{margin}\right) \times \frac{n}{m} \right)$$

where pop_{av} represents the target population size that can be considered the average of all the neighborhoods and pop_{margin} indicates the acceptable degree of deviation from the ideal population size. n is the number of the neighborhoods, and m is the number of districts.

A district will be regarded as overpopulated if its total population exceeds the upper bound, and conversely, a district will be deemed underpopulated if its total population falls below the lower bound. A district whose population falls within the upper and lower bounds will be regarded as having an appropriate population size. The objective function is to minimize the total number of overpopulated and underpopulated districts. The search process will persist until the objective function's minimum value is obtained, ideally zero. This indicates that no districts are either overpopulated or underpopulated.

The next listing shows how to find the political districts using GA. We'll start by reading the data from a local folder or using a URL.

Listing 8.6   Solving a political districting problem using GA

```
import geopandas as gpd
import pandas as pd
import folium

data_url="https://raw.githubusercontent.com/Optimization-Algorithms-Book/
Code-Listings/main/Appendix%20B/data/PoliticalDistricting/"

toronto = gpd.read_file(data_url+"toronto.geojson")
neighborhoods = pd.read_csv(data_url+"Toronto_Neighborhoods.csv")

range_limit = 16
toronto_sample = toronto.tail(range_limit)
values = neighborhoods.tail(range_limit)
values = values.join(toronto_sample["cartodb_id"])
```

Read the neighborhood information (e.g., names, populations, and median household incomes).

Read the Toronto region administration boundaries.

URL for the data folder

Pick 16 neighborhoods as a subset to represent neighborhoods in East Toronto.

After reading the dataset, we'll do the following data preprocessing to get the population of each neighborhood, and the adjacency relationship among every possible pair of neighborhoods, in a Boolean matrix.

```
import numpy as np

def get_population(lst, table):
    return table["population"].iloc[lst].to_numpy()

eval = get_population(range(range_limit), values)

def get_neighboors(database):
    result = []
    for i in range(database['name'].size):
        tmp = np.zeros(database['name'].size)
        geo1 = database.iloc[i]
        for j in range(database['name'].size):
            if i != j:
```

Get the population of each neighborhood.

Prepare the population dataset.

Represent the adjacency relationship among every possible pair of neighborhoods.

```
                    geo2 = database.iloc[j]
                    if geo1["geometry"].intersects(geo2["geometry"]):
                        tmp[j] = 1
            result.append(tmp)
        return np.stack(result)

neighbor = get_neighboors(toronto_sample)
```

We'll now define the political districting class with a single objective function, three constraints, a given number of districts, a given population margin, and an adjacency matrix between the neighborhoods. `PoliticalDistricting` is a custom problem class that extends the `Problem` class from pymoo. The `Problem` class implements a method that evaluates a set of solutions instead of a single solution at a time, like in the case of the `ElementwiseProblem` class. In the `PoliticalDistricting` class, the following parameters are defined:

- `num_dist`—The number of districts to divide the region into
- `neighbor`—A matrix representing the neighborhood relationships between locations in the region
- `populations`—The population of each neighborhood
- `margin`—The acceptable degree of deviation from the ideal population size
- `average`—The average population
- `n_var`—The number of decision variables, which is equal to the number of neighborhoods
- `n_obj=1`—The number of objectives, which is 1 for this problem
- `n_eq_constr=3`—The number of equality constraints, which is 3 for this problem
- `xl=0`—The lower bound for the decision variables, which is 0 for this problem
- `xu=num_dist-1`—The upper bound for the decision variables, which is `num_dist-1` for this problem
- `vtype=int`—The type of decision variables, which is integer for this problem

The following code shows how to define a `PoliticalDistricting` class with different parameters, such as the number of districts, neighbor information, populations, and margin:

```
from pymoo.core.problem import Problem

class PoliticalDistricting(Problem):
    def __init__(self,
                 num_dist,              Define a constructor
                 neighbor,              with specific parameters.
                 populations,
                 margin
                 ):                                     Hold the population data.

        self.populations = populations         Store the mean population
        self.average = np.mean(populations)    of all districts.
```

```
        super().__init__(n_var=len(self.populations), n_obj=1, n_eq_constr=3,
➤ xl=0, xu=num_dist-1, vtype=int) ◄─────────────────┐
                                                     │ Call the constructor of
                                                     │ the parent class with
        self.n_var = len(self.populations)           │ specific parameters.
        self.n_dist = num_dist
        self.margin = margin            ┌── Evaluate the solution
        self.neighbor = neighbor        │   against the objective
        self.func = self._evaluate ◄────┘   function and constraints.
```

As a continuation and as part of the `problem` class, we'll extract the neighborhoods that belong to a specific district using the following function:

```
def _gather(self, x, district):
    return np.where(x==district, 1, 0)
```

We'll then calculate the upper and lower bounds based on the given population values and margin as follows:

```
def _get_bounds(self):
    ub = np.ceil(self.average + self.margin) *
➤ (len(self.populations)/self.n_dist)
    lb = np.ceil(self.average - self.margin) *
➤ (len(self.populations)/self.n_dist)
    return ub, lb
```

The following function is used to decide whether an electoral district is overpopulated or underpopulated:

```
def _get_result(self, gathered, ub, lb):
    product = gathered * self.populations
    summed_product = np.sum(product, axis=1)
    return np.where((summed_product > ub), 1, 0) + np.where((summed_product <
➤ lb), 1, 0)
```

As all the constraints are equality constraints, the following function returns true if the constraint is satisfied:

```
def _get_constraint(self, constraint):
    constraint = np.stack(constraint)
    return np.any(constraint==0, axis=0)
```

To make sure that there is no isolated neighborhood far from other neighbors within a district, unless the district only has one neighborhood, the following function is used:

```
def _get_neighbor(self, gathered):
    singleton = np.sum(gathered, axis=1)
    singleton = np.where(singleton==1, True, False)
    tmp_neighbor = np.dot(gathered, self.neighbor)
    tmp_neighbor = np.where(tmp_neighbor > 0, 1, 0)
    product = gathered * tmp_neighbor
    return np.all(np.equal(product, gathered), axis=1) + singleton
```

The following function determines the best approximation to make an electoral district a contiguous block:

```
def cap_district(self, gathered):
    result = np.zeros(gathered.shape[0])
    for i in range(len(gathered)):
        nonzeros = np.nonzero(gathered[i])[0]
        if nonzeros.size != 0:
            mx = np.max(nonzeros)
            mn = np.min(nonzeros)
            result[i] = self.neighbor[mx][mn] or (mx == mn)
    return result
```

The last function in the `problem` class is used to evaluate the solution against the objective function, including checking the constraints:

```
def _evaluate(self, x, out, *args, **kwargs):
    x=np.round(x).astype(int) # Ensure X is binary
    pop_count = []
    constraint1 = []
    constraint2 = []
    constraint3 = []
    for i in range(self.n_dist):
        gathered = self._gather(x, i)
        ub, lb = self._get_bounds()
        result = self._get_result(gathered, ub, lb)
        pop_count.append(result)
        constraint1.append(np.sum(gathered, axis=1))
        constraint2.append((self._get_neighbor(gathered)))
        constraint3.append(self.cap_district(gathered))

    holder = np.sum(np.stack(pop_count), axis=0)
    out["F"] = np.expand_dims(holder, axis=1)
    out["H"] = [self._get_constraint(constraint1),
                self._get_constraint(constraint2),
                self._get_constraint(constraint3)]
```

Constraint 1: make sure that there is no empty district,

Constraint 2: make sure there is no lone neighborhood within a district, unless the district only has one neighborhood.

Constraint 3: ensure the electoral district is a contiguous block by achieving the best possible approximation.

```
def create_districting_problem(number_of_districts, neighborlist, population_
 list, margin, seed=1):
    np.random.seed(seed)
    problem = PoliticalDistricting(number_of_districts, neighborlist,
 population_list, margin)
    return problem
```

We can now define the GA solver and apply it to solve the problem as follows:

```
from pymoo.algorithms.soo.nonconvex.ga import GA
from pymoo.operators.sampling.rnd import FloatRandomSampling
from pymoo.operators.crossover.pntx import PointCrossover
from pymoo.operators.mutation.pm import PolynomialMutation
from pymoo.operators.repair.rounding import RoundingRepair
from pymoo.termination import get_termination
from pymoo.optimize import minimize

num_districts = 3
margin=6000
```

```
problem = create_districting_problem(num_districts, neighbor, eval, margin,
seed=1)

algorithm = GA(
    pop_size=2000,
    sampling=FloatRandomSampling(),
    crossover=PointCrossover(prob=0.8, n_points=2),
    mutation = PolynomialMutation(prob=0.3, repair=RoundingRepair()),
    eliminate_duplicates=True
)

termination = get_termination("n_gen", 100)

res = minimize(problem,
               algorithm,
               termination,
               seed=1,
               save_history=True,
               verbose=True)
```

The resultant political districts are listed here and visualized in figure 8.22:

```
Political District- 1 :  ['Woburn', 'Highland Creek', 'Malvern']
Political District- 2 :  ['Bendale', 'Scarborough Village', 'Guildwood',
'Morningside', 'West Hill', 'Centennial Scarborough', 'Agincourt South-
Malvern West']
Political District- 3 :  ['Rouge', 'Hillcrest Village', 'Steeles',
"L'Amoreaux", 'Milliken', 'Agincourt North']
```

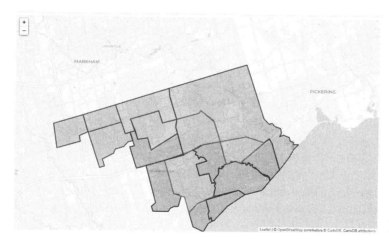

**Figure 8.22
The three political
districts that combine
the 16 neighborhoods**

The problem is treated as a single objective optimization problem where the objective is to minimize the total number of overpopulated and underpopulated districts. The dataset contains the median household income of each neighborhood, so you can replace the objective function to focus on the heterogeneity of the median household income. You can also treat the problem as a multi-objective optimization problem by considering both criteria.

This chapter marks the end of the third part of the book, which focused on genetic algorithms and their applications in solving complex optimization problems. The fourth part of the book will delve into the fascinating realm of swarm intelligence algorithms.

Summary

- The Hamming cliff problem, which results from the inherent nature of binary representation, negatively affects binary-coded GAs by disrupting the search space's smoothness, causing poor convergence and leading to inefficient exploration and exploitation. To address this problem, alternative representations like Gray code or real-valued encoding can be used, as they offer better locality and smoother search spaces, minimizing the disruptive effects of small changes on decoded values.

- Real-valued GA is well suited for optimization problems involving continuous variables or real-valued parameters. It offers benefits such as better representation precision, faster convergence, diverse crossover and mutation operations, and reduced complexity, making it an attractive choice for many continuous optimization problems.

- Permutation-based GA is a class of genetic algorithms specifically designed to handle combinatorial optimization problems where the solutions can be represented as ordered sequences, or permutations, of elements.

- Multi-objective optimization problems can be tackled using either a preference-based multi-objective optimization method or a Pareto optimization approach. In the preference-based method, the multiple objectives are combined into a single or overall objective function by using a weighting scheme. The Pareto optimization approach focuses on identifying multiple trade-off optimal solutions known as Pareto-optimal solutions. These solutions can be further refined using higher-level information or decision-making processes.

- Crossover is primarily exploitative, as it combines the genetic material of two parent individuals to produce offspring, promoting the exchange of beneficial traits between solutions. However, depending on the implementation, crossover can also have some explorative properties, as it can produce offspring with new combinations of genes, leading to the discovery of new solutions.

- Mutation can act as an explorative or exploitative operator depending on influencing factors such as the mutation rate and the mutation step size.

- In general, the crossover rate should be relatively high, as it promotes the exchange of genetic information between parent chromosomes. On the other hand, mutation is typically applied with a low probability, as its main purpose is to introduce random variations into the population.

Part 4

Swarm intelligence algorithms

As we advance in our exploration of optimization algorithms, this part will immerse you in the world of collective intelligence. Here, you'll discover the power of swarm intelligence algorithms, including particle swarm optimization, ant colony optimization, and artificial bee colony. Through the two chapters in this part, you'll witness how nature-inspired swarming behaviors can be harnessed to find optimal solutions.

In chapter 9, you'll learn about swarm intelligence and dive deep into particle swarm optimization (PSO). You'll gain an understanding of how swarms of particles collectively explore solution spaces to find optimal answers. You'll explore continuous PSO algorithms, delve into binary PSO for discrete problems, and understand permutation-based PSO for combinatorial optimization. You'll discover how to adapt PSO to strike a balance between exploration and exploitation and see how it can efficiently solve both continuous and discrete optimization problems.

Chapter 10 will broaden your horizons as you explore other swarm intelligence (SI) algorithms. You'll get familiar with the principles of ant colony optimization (ACO) metaheuristics and understand different variants of ACO that cater to various problem types. Additionally, you'll delve into the world of artificial bee colony (ABC) algorithms and grasp the adaptation aspects that make SI algorithms so versatile. You'll witness how these SI algorithms can be applied to address a wide range of continuous and discrete optimization problems.

Particle swarm
optimization

This chapter covers

- Introducing swarm intelligence
- Understanding the continuous particle swarm optimization algorithm
- Understanding binary particle swarm optimization
- Understanding permutation-based particle swarm optimization
- Adapting particle swarm optimization for a better trade-off between exploration and exploitation
- Solving continuous and discrete problems using particle swarm optimization

In the treasure-hunting mission I introduced in chapter 2, suppose you want to collaborate and share information with your friends instead of doing the treasure-hunting alone. However, you do not want to follow a competitive approach in which you only keep better-performing hunters and recruit new hunters to replace poorer-performing ones, like in the genetic algorithm (GA) explained in the previous chapters. You want to adopt a more cooperative approach and keep all the hunters, without replacing any, but you want to give more weight to the better-performing hunters and try to emulate their success. This scenario uses *swarm intelligence* and corresponds to population-based optimization algorithms such as *particle swarm optimization* (PSO), *ant colony optimization* (ACO), and *artificial bee colony* (ABC) algorithms, which will be explained in this fourth part of the book.

In this chapter, we'll focus on different variants of PSO algorithms and apply them to solve continuous and discrete optimization problems. These variants include continuous PSO, binary PSO, permutation-based PSO, and adaptive PSO. Function optimization, the traveling salesman problem, neural network training, trilateration, coffee shop planning, and the doctor scheduling problem are discussed in this chapter and its supplementary exercises included in appendix C. The next chapter will cover the ACO and ABC algorithms.

9.1   *Introducing swarm intelligence*

Life on this planet is full of astonishing examples of collective behavior. Individual species depend upon one another for sustenance, often forming surprising alliances to achieve a common goal: the continuance of the species. The majority of living things also display amazing altruism in order to protect and provide the best care for their offspring, comparable to any form of sacrifice shown by human beings. They can cooperatively perform complex tasks such as foraging for food, dividing up labor, constructing nests, brood sorting, protecting, herding, schooling, and flocking, to name just a few. These complex collective behaviors emerge from individual interactions between spatially distributed and simple entities without a centralized controller or coordinator and without a script or access to global information. Various cooperation patterns, communication mechanisms, and adaptation strategies are employed to enable such complex collective behaviors.

> ### Swarm intelligence
> Swarm intelligence is a subfield of artificial intelligence that explores how large groups of relatively simple and spatially distributed agents can interact with each other and with their environment in a decentralized and self-organized manner to collectively achieve complex goals.

Several efficient population-based algorithms have been designed to exploit the power of collective intelligence by mimicking the collective behaviors observed in nature to solve complex optimization problems. Table 9.1 provides a non-exhaustive list of swarm intelligence algorithms and their sources of inspiration from unicellular and multicellular living organisms.

Table 9.1   Examples of swarm intelligence algorithms and their sources of inspiration

Organisms	Class	Source of inspiration	Algorithms
Unicellular organisms	Bacteria	Bacterial swarm foraging	Bacterial foraging optimization algorithm (BFO)
			Bacterial swarming algorithm (BSA)
Multicellular organisms	Bird/fish	Bird flocking and fish schooling	Particle swarm optimization (PSO)
	Ant	Ant foraging behaviors	Ant colony optimization (ACO)
	Bees	Foraging behavior of honeybees	Artificial bee colony (ABC)
	Bats	Echolocation behavior of bats	Bat algorithm (BA)
	Fireflies	Flashing behavior of fireflies	Firefly algorithm (FA)
	Butterflies	Foraging behavior of butterflies	Butterfly optimization algorithm (BOA)
	Dragonflies	Static and dynamic swarming behaviors of dragonflies	Dragonfly algorithm (DA)
	Spiders	Cooperative behavior of the social spiders	Social spider optimization (SSO)
	Krill	Herding behavior of krill	Krill herd (KH)
	Frogs	Frog cooperative search for food	Shuffled frog leaping algorithm (SFLA)
	Fish	Gregarious behavior of fish	Fish school search (FSS)
	Dolphins	Dolphins' behavior in detecting, chasing after, and preying on swarms of sardines	Dolphin partner optimization (DPO)
			Dolphin swarm optimization algorithm (DSOA)
	Cats	Resting and tracing behaviors of cats	Cat swarm optimization (CSO)
	Monkeys	Search for food	Monkey search algorithm (MSA)
	Lions	Solitary and cooperative behaviors of lions	Lion optimization algorithm (LOA)
	Cuckoos	Reproduction strategy of cuckoos	Cuckoo search (CS)
			Cuckoo optimization algorithm (COA)
	Wolves	Leadership hierarchy and hunting mechanism of gray wolves	Wolf search algorithm (WSA)
			Grey wolf optimizer (GWO)

For example, bacteria, which are single-celled organisms, possess underlying social intelligence allowing them to cooperate to solve challenges. Bacteria develop intricate communication capabilities like chemotactic signaling to cooperatively self-organize into highly structured colonies with elevated environmental adaptability. Bacterial chemotaxis is the process by which bacterial cells migrate through concentration gradients of chemical attractants and repellents. The E. coli bacterium uses this bacterial chemotaxis during the foraging process. This collective behavior provides the basis for optimization algorithms such as the bacterial foraging optimization algorithm (BFO) and bacterial swarming algorithm (BSA).

Ethology, the study of animal behavior, is the main source of inspiration for swarm intelligence algorithms such as particle swarm optimization (PSO), ant colony optimization (ACO), artificial bee colony (ABC), bat algorithm (BA), firefly algorithm (FA), and social spider optimization (SSO). For example, honeybees are highly cooperative social insects that cooperatively construct hives in which about 30,000 bees can live and work together. They differentiate their work: some make wax, some make honey, some make bee-bread, some shape and mold combs, and some bring water to the cells and mingle it with the honey. Young bees engage in out-of-door work while the elder bees do the indoor work. During the foraging process, rather than expending energy searching in all directions, honeybee colonies use individual foragers to reduce the cost/ benefit ratio. Additionally, colonies concentrate their foraging efforts on the most lucrative patches and disregard those of lesser quality. It has been observed that when a colony's food resources are scarce, foragers recruit more nestmates to food sources they have found, and changes in their dance patterns upon returning to the hive facilitate this increased recruitment.

The fundamental components of swarm intelligence algorithms typically involve numerous decentralized processing agents that operate without central supervision. These agents communicate with neighboring agents and adapt their behavior based on received information. Furthermore, the majority of the research carried out on swarm intelligence algorithms is primarily based on experimental observations of collective behavior exhibited by living organisms. These observations are translated into models, which are then tested through simulations in order to derive the metaheuristics that form the basis of swarm intelligence algorithms, as illustrated in figure 9.1. This experimental approach enables researchers to gain a deeper understanding of the complex interactions between individual agents and how they give rise to collective behavior. By simulating these interactions and testing various scenarios, researchers can refine the algorithms and improve their effectiveness. As an example of such experimental research, you can watch the "The Waggle Dance of the Honeybee" video of the experiment conducted by Georgia Tech College of Computing to understand how honeybees communicate the location of new food sources (www.youtube.com/ watch?v=bFDGPgXtK-U).

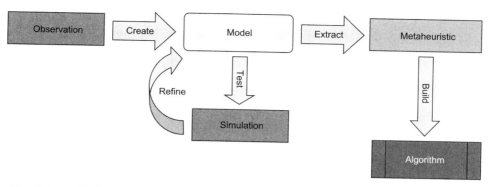

Figure 9.1 Derivation process for swarm intelligence algorithms

Algorithm 9.1 shows the common steps in a swarm intelligence algorithm. The algorithm starts by initializing the algorithm parameters, such as the number of individuals in the swarm, the maximum number of iterations, and the termination criteria. A swarm of initial candidate solutions is then sampled (the different sampling methods were explained in section 7.1). The algorithm then iterates over all the individuals in the swarm, performing the following operations: finding the best so far, finding the best neighbor, and updating the individual.

Algorithm 9.1   Swarm intelligence algorithm

```
Initialize parameters
Initialize swarm
While (stopping criteria not met) loop over all individuals
     Find best so far
     Find best neighbor
     Update individual
```

The individual and the neighbor are evaluated using the defined objective/fitness function. The neighborhood structure and update mechanism depend on the algorithm being used. This loop over all the individuals is repeated until the termination criterion is met, which could be a maximum number of iterations or reaching a satisfactory fitness level. At this point, the algorithm stops and returns the best solution found during the optimization process. In the following sections, we'll dive deep into the PSO algorithm.

9.2   Continuous PSO

Particle swarm optimization (PSO) is a population-based stochastic optimization technique developed by Russell Eberhart and James Kennedy in 1995. Since then, PSO has gained popularity and has been applied to various real-world applications in different domains. This algorithm is inspired by the conduct of social organisms such as birds, fish, ants, termites, wasps, and bees. PSO emulates the actions of these creatures, with each member of the swarm being referred to as a *particle*, akin to a bird in a flock, a fish in a school, or a bee in a colony. Eberhart and Kennedy opted to use the term "particle" to refer to an individual or candidate solution in the context of optimization, as they believed it was more suitable for describing the particle's velocity and acceleration.

Bird flocking

Bird flocking is a behavior controlled by three simple rules, as illustrated in the following figure:

- *Separation*—Prevent getting too close to nearby birds to avoid overcrowding.
- *Alignment*—Adjust the heading to correspond to the average direction of neighboring birds.
- *Coherence*—Move toward the average position of neighboring birds.

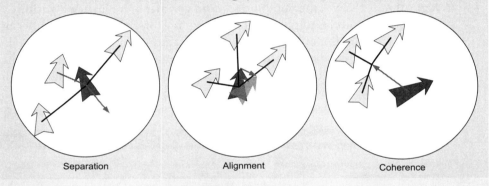

| Separation | Alignment | Coherence |

Bird flocking rules: separation, alignment, and coherence

When birds—spatially distributed agents interacting with each other and with their environment in a decentralized and self-organized manner without access to global information—apply these three simple rules, the outcome is the emergent behavior of bird flocking.

The particles (candidate solutions) move, or fly, through the feasible search space by following the current best particles. Thus, PSO is guided by a straightforward principle: emulate the success of neighboring individuals. Each particle in the swarm operates in a decentralized manner by utilizing both its own intelligence and the collective intelligence of the group. Therefore, if one particle uncovers a favorable route to food, the remaining members of the swarm can immediately adopt the same path.

The PSO algorithm

"This [PSO] algorithm belongs ideologically to that philosophical school that allows wisdom to emerge rather than trying to impose it, that emulates nature rather than trying to control it, and that seeks to make things simpler rather than more complex." J. Kennedy and R. Eberhart, inventors of PSO [1].

Figure 9.2 shows the PSO flowchart. We start by initializing the algorithm parameters and creating an initial swarm of particles. These particles represent the candidate solutions. Each particle in the search space holds the current position x^i and current velocity v^i. The fitness of each particle is then evaluated based on the fitness/objective function to be optimized. The best position each particle has achieved so far is known as the personal best or *pbest*. The best position achieved by the particles in its neighborhood is known as *nbest*. If the neighborhood is restricted to a few particles, the best is called the local best, *lbest*. If the neighborhood is the whole swarm, the best achieved by the whole swarm is called the global best, *gbest*. We'll discuss neighborhood structures in PSO further in section 9.2.3.

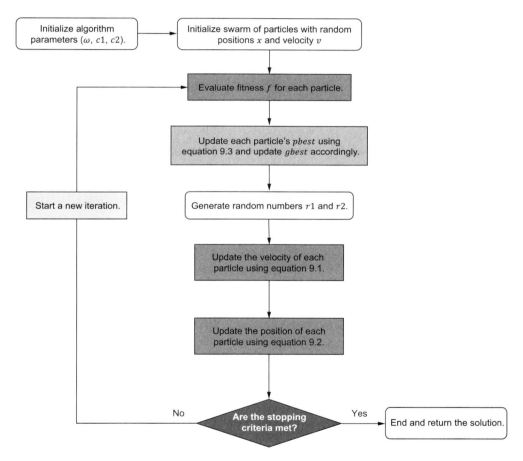

Figure 9.2   The PSO algorithm

After evaluating the fitness of each particle, PSO updates each particle's personal best position if the current fitness is superior, identifies the global best position based on the best fitness in the entire swarm, and adjusts particle velocities and positions using a combination of personal and global information. These steps guide the swarm toward optimal or near-optimal solutions by balancing individual and collective learning, promoting exploration and exploitation in the search space. The process iterates until termination criteria are met.

9.2.1   *Motion equations*

The velocity (v) and position (x) of each particle are updated using the following equations:

$$v_{k+1}^{id} = \omega \times v_k^{id} + c1r1_k^d \left(pbest_k^{id} - x_k^{id} \right) + c2r2_k^d \left(gbest_k^d - x_k^{id} \right)$$ **9.1**

$$x_{k+1}^{id} = x_k^{id} + v_{k+1}^{id}$$ **9.2**

where

- k is the iteration number.
- i and d are the particle number and the dimension. For example, dimension = 1 in the case of a univariate optimization problem with a single decision variable, dimension = 2 in the case of a bivariate problem, etc.
- ω is the inertia weight.
- $c1$, $c2$ are the acceleration coefficients.
- $r1$, $r2$ are random numbers between 0 and 1 and are generated in each iteration for each dimension, and not for each particle.
- *pbest* is the best position achieved by the particle.
- *gbest* is the best position achieved by the whole swarm. *gbest* should be replaced by *nbest or lbest* if you are dividing the swarm into multiple neighborhoods.

As you can see in these two equations, we start by updating the velocity $v_{(k+1)}^{id}$. The position is then updated to $x_{(k+1)}^{id}$ by taking the current position x_k^{id} and adding to it the new displacement $v_{(k+1)}^{id} \times timestamp$ where $timestamp = 1$, which represents a single iteration.

To understand these motion update equations, let's visualize these equations using vectors in the 2D Cartesian coordinate system, as shown in figure 9.3. As you can see, the velocity update equation consists of three primary components, each contributing to the movement of particles in the search space:

- *Inertia component*—The first part of the velocity update equation represents the influence of a particle's inertia, taking into account that a particle (like a fish in a school or a bird in a flock) cannot abruptly change its direction. As you will see later, this inertia component is crucial, as it allows the algorithm to be more adaptive and helps maintain a balance between exploration and exploitation.

- *Cognitive component*—The second part of the equation, referred to as the cognitive component, represents the particle's attraction toward its personal best position, or individual proximity (*i*-proximity). This component reflects the degree of trust a particle places in its own past experiences, without considering the experiences of its neighbors or the swarm as a whole. The cognitive component encourages particles to explore the areas around their personal best positions, allowing them to fine-tune their search in promising regions.

- *Social component*—The third part of the velocity update equation is the social component, which represents the particle's attraction to the swarm's collective knowledge or group proximity (*g*-proximity). This component takes into account the experiences of neighboring particles and the swarm as a whole, guiding the particles toward the global best position found so far. The social component fosters collaboration among particles, helping them converge toward an optimal solution more effectively.

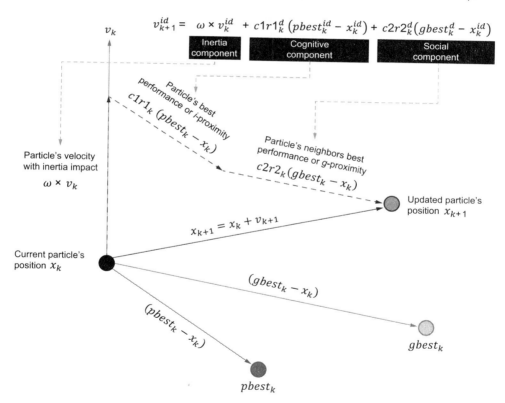

Figure 9.3 **Visualizing the motion equation for a particle in the swarm**

To better understand the meaning of each component, imagine a group of friends visiting a large amusement park for the first time. Their goal is to visit the most thrilling rides in the park as efficiently as possible. The friends can be thought of as particles in the PSO algorithm, with each person's enjoyment of the rides serving as the objective function to optimize. Each person has a preferred way of exploring the available rides, like walking through certain parts of the park or trying specific rides like roller coasters or water slides. This is similar to the inertia component in PSO, where particles maintain their current velocity and direction, ensuring they don't change their exploration pattern too abruptly.

Each friend relies on their own personal experiences to find the most thrilling rides. For instance, one friend might have had a great time on a roller coaster earlier in the day. They're more likely to return to their favorite one or want to find more similar rides, knowing it was a good choice. They trust their judgment and focus on exploring the areas around the roller coaster, seeking out rides that they think they'll enjoy based on their personal experience. This is the cognitive component, where particles in PSO are attracted to their personal best positions, following their past experiences and individual preferences.

The friends then collaborate to find the most thrilling ride based on their shared experiences. Imagine one of the friends has just ridden the most exciting roller coaster and can't wait to tell the others about it. As they share their excitement, the group collectively becomes more attracted to that ride, influencing their individual choices. This is the social component, where particles in PSO are influenced by the global best position or the collective knowledge of the swarm.

The following subsections dive into more detail about the different PSO parameters.

9.2.2   *Fitness update*

After moving, each particle updates its own personal best using the following equation, assuming a minimization problem:

$$pbest_{k+1}^{id} = \begin{cases} x_{k+1}^{id} \ if \ f(x_{k+1}^{id}) \le f(pbest_k^{id}) \\ pbest_k^{id} \qquad otherwise \end{cases}$$

$$9.3$$

After that, each neighborhood updates its best as follows:

$$nbest_{k+1}^{id} = \underset{nbest_{k+1}^{id} \in N}{\arg\min} \ f\left(pbest_{k+1}^{id}\right)$$

$$9.4$$

The neighborhood best (*nbest*) is the same as the global best (*gbest*) if the neighborhood is the whole swarm.

PSO has two main variants based on how particles' positions and velocities are updated—synchronous and asynchronous PSO:

- *Synchronous PSO (S-PSO)*—All particles in the swarm update their positions and velocities simultaneously in a global manner. The local and global best are then updated. This synchronous approach ensures that all particles have access to the same global best position when updating their velocities and positions, promoting global exploration.

- *Asynchronous PSO (A-PSO)*—Particles are updated based on the current state of the swarm. This asynchronous approach allows the particles to update their positions and velocities based on the most recent information available.

Figure 9.4 shows the difference between S-PSO and A-PSO. As you'll notice, in A-PSO, the neighborhood best update is moved into the particle's update loop. This allows particles to evaluate their fitness and update their positions and velocities independently and asynchronously.

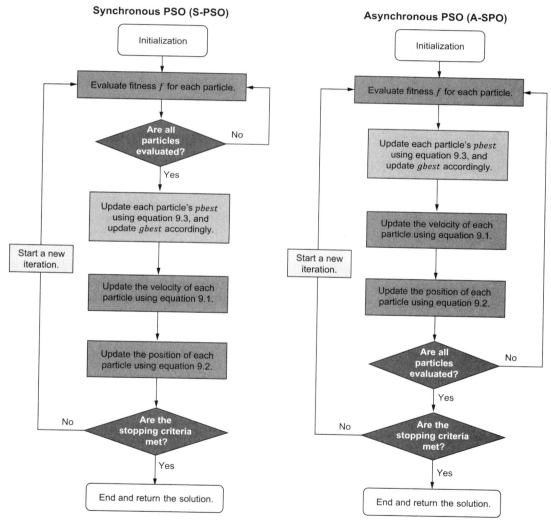

Figure 9.4 **Synchronous and asynchronous PSO**

Although both synchronous and asynchronous PSO strategies can be employed to handle optimization problems, the asynchronous version is generally more effective, as it allows particles to take advantage of the most recent neighbor information.

9.2.3   *Initialization*

PSO initialization includes initializing the particle position, velocity, and personal best, and initializing the algorithm's parameters:

- *Particle position initialization*—Particle positions represent candidate solutions to the problem, and they can be sampled using different sampling methods, as explained in section 7.1. For example, the initial positions of the particles can be randomly assigned within the defined feasible search space.
- *Particle velocity initialization*—The velocities of the particles can be set to zero or small values initially. Initializing them with small velocities ensures that the particles' updates are gradual, preventing them from moving too far away from their starting positions. In contrast, large initial velocities may lead to significant updates, which can potentially cause divergence and hinder the convergence of the algorithm.
- *Personal best position initialization*—The personal best position of each particle, which represents the best solution found by the particle so far, should be initialized to its initial position. This allows the particles to begin their search with their starting points as a reference and to update their personal bests as they discover better solutions.

As shown in equation 9.1, PSO has three primary parameters that play a critical role in controlling the search algorithm's behavior: the inertia weight (ω) and the acceleration coefficients ($c1$, $c2$). These parameters influence the balance between exploration and exploitation within the optimization process:

- *Inertia weight*—Large values of ω encourage exploration, while small values promote exploitation, allowing the cognitive and social components to exert greater control. A widely adopted value for ω is 0.792.
- *Acceleration coefficients*—Setting $c1$ to 0 reduces the PSO algorithm to a *social-only* or *selfless PSO* model. In this case, particles are solely attracted to the group best and ignore their personal bests. This leads to an emphasis on global exploration based on the swarm's collective knowledge. Setting $c2$ to 0 results in a *cognition-only model*, where particles act as independent hill climbers, relying only on their personal bests. In this scenario, the particles do not consider the experiences of other swarm members, focusing on local exploitation based on their individual experiences. In many applications, $c1$ and $c2$ are set to 1.49. Although there is no theoretical justification for this specific value, it has been empirically found to work well in various optimization problems. Generally, the sum of $c1$ and $c2$ should be less than or equal to 4 to maintain the algorithm's stability and convergence properties.

Other parameters to consider include swarm size and neighborhood size. There is no one-size-fits-all solution, as the optimal values depend on the specific problem being solved. However, some best practices and guidelines can help inform your choices:

- *Swarm size*—A large swarm size can promote global exploration and prevent premature convergence, but at the cost of increased computational effort. A small swarm size can lead to faster convergence and reduced computational effort but may increase the risk of premature convergence. For many problems, a swarm size between 20 and 100 particles has been found to yield good results. It is advisable to conduct experiments with different swarm sizes to determine the best trade-off between exploration, exploitation, and computational complexity for the problem at hand.
- *Neighborhood size*—A large neighborhood size can encourage global exploration and information sharing among particles but may reduce the ability to exploit local optima. A small neighborhood size can promote local exploitation and convergence speed but may limit global exploration. You can use different neighborhood structures, as you'll see in the next subsection.

Generally speaking, selecting the best algorithm parameters requires experimentation and fine-tuning based on the specific problem you are trying to solve. It is often beneficial to perform a sensitivity analysis or use a parameter-tuning technique to find the optimal parameter values for your problem. We'll look at this in more detail in section 9.5.

9.2.4 Neighborhoods

In the PSO algorithm, particles within a specific vicinity engage in mutual communication by sharing details about each other's success within that local region. Subsequently, all particles gravitate toward a position that is considered to be an improvement based on a key performance indicator. The efficacy of the PSO algorithm is heavily reliant on the social network structure it employs. Choosing an appropriate neighborhood topology plays a crucial role in ensuring the algorithm's convergence and in preventing it from becoming trapped in local minima.

Some of the prevalent neighborhood topologies utilized in PSO include the star social structure, the ring topology, the Von Neumann model, and the wheel topology:

- *The star social structure, also known as the global best (gbest) PSO*—This is a neighborhood topology where all particles are connected, as shown in figure 9.5a. This structure allows access to global information within the swarm, with the result that each particle is drawn toward the optimal solution discovered by the entire swarm. The *gbest* PSO has been demonstrated to converge more rapidly than other network structures. However, it is more prone to becoming ensnared in local minima without fully exploring the search space. This topology excels when applied to unimodal problems, as it allows for efficient and effective optimization in such cases.

- *Ring topology, also known as the local best (lbest) PSO*—Following this topology, a particle interacts exclusively with its immediately adjacent neighbors (figure 9.5b). Each particle endeavors to emulate its most successful neighbor by gravitating toward the optimal solution discovered within the local vicinity. Although convergence occurs at a slower pace than with the star structure, the ring topology explores a more extensive portion of the search space. This topology is recommended for multimodal problems.
- *Von Neumann model*—In this topology, particles are arranged in a grid-like structure or square topology where each particle is connected with four other particles (the neighbors above, below, and to the right and left), as shown in figure 9.5c.
- *Wheel topology*—In this topology, the particles are isolated from each other, and one particle is randomly selected as the focal point or hub for all information flow, as illustrated in figure 9.5d.

The choice of neighborhood topology depends on the problem's characteristics and the desired balance between exploration and exploitation. Experiment with different topologies to find the best fit for your problem.

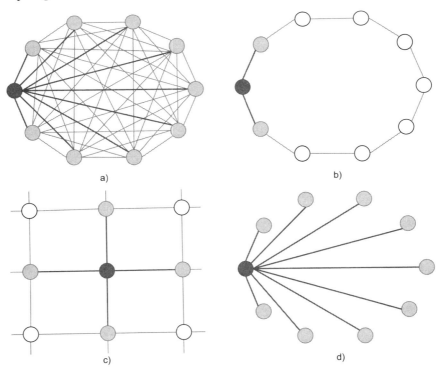

a)   b)

c)   d)

Figure 9.5   PSO neighborhood topologies: a) the star social structure, b) the ring topology, c) the Von Neumann model, and d) the wheel topology

Let's now look at how to solve a continuous optimization problem using PSO. The Michalewicz function is a nonconvex mathematical function commonly used as a test problem for optimization algorithms. This function is given by the following formula:

$$f(x) = -\sum_{j=1}^{d} \sin\left(x_j\right)\left[\sin\left(\frac{jx_j^2}{\pi}\right)\right]^{2m}$$

9.5

where d is the dimension of the problem and m is a constant (usually $m = 10$). This function has d local minima. For $d = 2$, the minimum value is -1.8013 at $(2.20, 1.57)$.

Let's start by defining the Michalewicz function as shown in listing 9.1. This function can accept size-1 arrays with single or multiple rows. If the input position is a size-1 array with a single row, we reshape it to a 2D array with a single row using the `reshape()` function. A *size-1 array*, also known as a *singleton array*, is an array data structure that contains only one element. This reshaping enables uniform handling of both single-row size-1 arrays and arrays with multiple rows. This is evident in the implementation of the PSO solver, where the function addresses solving one solution at a time. Additionally, the function seamlessly manages arrays with multiple rows, a scenario encountered when simultaneously evaluating multiple solutions. This aspect will be further elaborated upon later in the context of pymoo and PySwarms solvers.

Listing 9.1 Solving the Michalewicz function using PSO

```
import numpy as np
import math
import matplotlib.pyplot as plt

def michalewicz_function(position):
    m = 10
    position = np.array(position)
    if len(position.shape) == 1:  #A
        position = position.reshape(1, -1)
    n = position.shape[1]
    j = np.arange(1, n + 1)
    s = np.sin(position) * np.power(np.sin((j * np.square(position)) /
    np.pi), 2 * m)
    return -np.sum(s, axis=1)
```

Reshape to a 2D array with a single row if the position is a size-1 array.

The Michalewicz formula

Let's now create a PSO solver from scratch. As a continuation of listing 9.1, we'll start by defining a particle class with position, velocity, and personal best value as follows:

```
class Particle:
    def __init__(self, position, velocity, pbest_position, pbest_value):
        self.position = position
        self.velocity = velocity
        self.pbest_position = pbest_position
        self.pbest_value = pbest_value
```

The fitness function to be minimized is the Michalewicz function in this example:

```
def fitness_function(position):
    return michalewicz_function(position)
```

We can now define the velocity update function following equation 9.1. The function takes three arguments—particle, which is an object representing the current particle; gbest_position, which is the global best position found by the swarm so far; and options, which is a dictionary containing the algorithm parameters (specifically, the inertia weight w and the cognitive and social acceleration coefficients c1 and c2):

```
def update_velocity(particle, gbest_position, options):
    w = options['w']
    c1 = options['c1']
    c2 = options['c2']
    inertia = w * particle.velocity
    cognitive = c1 * np.random.rand() * (particle.pbest_position -
➥ particle.position)
    social = c2 * np.random.rand() * (gbest_position - particle.position)
    new_velocity = inertia + cognitive + social
    return new_velocity
```

The function computes the three components of the new velocity: the inertia component, the cognitive component, and the social component, as per equation 9.1. It returns the updated velocity as the sum of the three components.

We can now define the PSO solver function. This function takes four parameters as inputs—swarm_size, which is the size of the particle swarm; iterations, which is the maximum number of iterations to run the algorithm for; bounds, which is a list of tuples defining the lower and upper bounds of the search space for each dimension of the input vector; and options, which is a dictionary containing the algorithm parameters (such as the inertia weight and cognitive and social acceleration coefficients):

```
def pso(swarm_size, iterations, bounds, options):
    swarm = []
    for _ in range(swarm_size):
        position = np.array([np.random.uniform(low=low, high=high) for low,
➥ high in bounds])
        velocity = np.array([np.random.uniform(low=-abs(high-low),
➥ high=abs(high-low)) for low, high in bounds])
        pbest_position = position
        pbest_value = fitness_function(position)
        particle = Particle(position, velocity, pbest_position, pbest_value)
        swarm.append(particle)

    gbest_position = swarm[np.argmin([particle.pbest_value for particle in
➥ swarm])].pbest_position
    gbest_value = np.min([particle.pbest_value for particle in swarm])

    for _ in range(iterations):
        for _, particle in enumerate(swarm):
```

Initialize a random swarm.

Initialize the global best.

Update the velocity and position. — options)

```
                          particle.velocity = update_velocity(particle, gbest_position,

                          particle.position += particle.velocity

                          particle.position = np.clip(particle.position, [low for low, high
    → in bounds], [high for low, high in bounds]) ←
```
Apply the bounds.

Update the personal best (pbest).
```
current_value = fitness_function(particle.position)
if current_value < particle.pbest_value:
    particle.pbest_position = particle.position
    particle.pbest_value = current_value
```

Update the global best (gbest).
```
if current_value < gbest_value:
    gbest_position = particle.position
    gbest_value = current_value
```
Update the position.

```
                          particle.position += particle.velocity ←
```
Return the global best position and corresponding value.
```
              return gbest_position, gbest_value ←
```

The function first initializes the particle swarm by randomly generating the initial positions and velocities for each particle within the bounds defined by bounds. It then evaluates the fitness function for each particle and updates its personal best position and value accordingly. The function then enters a loop, where it updates the velocity and position of each particle using the update_velocity function, which takes the global best position found so far as input. The function also applies bounds to the particle position and updates its personal best position and value. The function then updates the global best position and value based on the star topology. Other topologies, such as ring, Von Neumann, and wheel, can be found in the complete code of listing 9.1, available in the book's GitHub repository. Finally, the function returns the global best position and value found by the algorithm.

We can now use this PSO solver to minimize the Michalewicz function after we set up the problem and algorithm parameters as follows:

```
swarm_size = 50
iterations = 1000
options = {'w': 0.9, 'c1': 0.5, 'c2': 0.3}
```
PSO parameters

Use the implemented PSO solver to solve the problem.
```
dimension = 2
bounds = [(0, math.pi)] * dimension
```
Dimension and domain of the Michalewicz function for each variable
```
best_position, best_value = pso(swarm_size, iterations, bounds, options)
```

You can print the optimal solution and minimum value of the function after running PSO:

```
print(f"Optimal solution: {np.round(best_position,3)}")
print(f"Minimum value: {np.round(best_value,4)}")
print()
```

The output would be as follows:

```
Optimal solution: [2.183 1.57]
Minimum value: [-1.8013]
```

Compared to genetic algorithms, there are fewer Python libraries available for PSO. Pymoo provides a PSO implementation for continuous problems. As a continuation of listing 9.1, pymoo PSO can be used to solve the same problem as follows:

```
from pymoo.algorithms.soo.nonconvex.pso import PSO
from pymoo.core.problem import Problem
from pymoo.optimize import minimize                    Define the problem.

class MichalewiczFunction(Problem):                     The 2D Michalewicz
    def __init__(self):                                 function
        super().__init__(n_var=2,
                         n_obj=1,
                         n_constr=0,
                         xl=0,
Set the lower and                xu=math.pi,
   upper bounds.                 vtype=float)           Evaluate the
                                                        objective function.
    def _evaluate(self, x, out, *args, **kwargs):
        out["F"] = michalewicz_function(x)              Create a problem instance.

problem = MichalewiczFunction()

algorithm = PSO(w=0.9, c1=2.0, c2=2.0)
                                                        Define the solver with
res = minimize(problem,                                 the parameters.
               algorithm,
               seed=1,
               verbose=False)       Apply PSO to solve the problem.

print(f"Optimal solution: {np.round(res.X,3)}")         Print the optimal solution and minimum
print(f"Minimum value: {np.round(res.F,4)}")            value of the function after running PSO.
```

This code produces the following output:

```
Optimal solution: [2.203 1.571]
Minimum value: [-1.8013]
```

PySwarms is another open source optimization library for Python that implements different variants of PSO. PySwarms can be used as follows to handle the problem:

```
!pip install pyswarms
import pyswarms as ps           Import the PSO solver from pyswarms.
                                                                    Create bounds for
dimension = 2          Dimension of the Michalewicz function        the search space.
bounds = (np.zeros(dimension), np.pi * np.ones(dimension))

options = {'w': 0.9, 'c1': 0.5, 'c2': 0.3}        Set up the optimizer.

optimizer = ps.single.GlobalBestPSO(n_particles=100, dimensions=dimension,
  options=options, bounds=bounds)          Create an instance of the optimizer.
```

Optimize the Michalewicz function.

```
cost, pos = optimizer.optimize(michalewicz_function, iters=1000)

print(f"Optimal solution: {np.round(pos,3)}")
print(f"Minimum value: {np.round(cost,4)}")
```

Print the optimal solution and minimum value of the function after running PSO.

This code produces the following output:

```
Optimal solution: [2.203 1.571]
Minimum value: -1.8013
```

The pyswarms.single package implements various techniques in continuous single-objective optimization. From this module, we used the global-best PSO (*gbest* PSO) algorithm in the previous code. You can experiment by replacing this solver with local-best.

Figure 9.6 shows the 3D landscape and 2D contours of the Michalewicz function, the optimal solution, and the solutions obtained by PSO, PSO Pymoo, and PSO PySwarms.

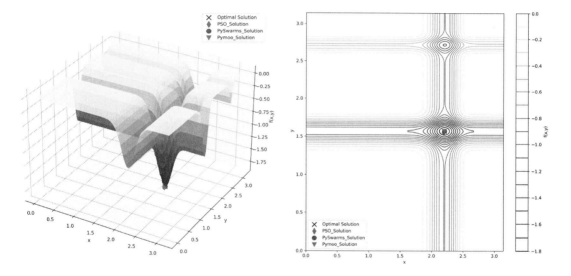

Figure 9.6   3D and 2D plots of the Michalewicz function. The three solutions are all very close to the optimal solution.

The three versions of PSO provide comparable results. However, PSO PySwarms and PSO pymoo are more stable, as they provide more consistent results each time you run the code. The PySwarms library is more comprehensive than pymoo for PSO, as it provides implementations of different variants and topologies of PSO, including discrete PSO, which will be explained in the next two sections.

9.3   Binary PSO

PSO was originally developed for problems that involve continuous-valued variables. However, many real-world problems are discrete or combinatorial in nature, such as TSP, task allocation, scheduling, assignment problems, and feature selection, among others. These types of problems involve searching through a finite set of possible solutions, rather than searching through a continuous space. To handle these discrete problems, PSO variants have been developed, such as binary PSO and permutation-based PSO.

In *binary PSO* (BPSO), each particle represents a position in the binary space, where each element is either 0 or 1. The binary sequence is updated bit by bit based on its current value, the fitness-based value of that particular bit within the particle, and the best value of the same bit observed so far among its neighboring particles. This approach enables the search to be conducted in a binary space rather than a continuous space, which is well suited for problems where the variables are binary.

In BPSO, the velocity is defined in terms of the probability of the bit changing. To restrict the values of the velocity elements to the range of [0,1], the sigmoid function is used:

$$sig\left(v_k^{id}\right) = \frac{1}{1 + e^{-v_k^{id}}}$$

9.6

The position update equation then becomes

$$x_k^{id} = \begin{cases} 1 \text{ if } sig\left(v_k^{id}\right) > r \\ 0 \text{ otherwise} \end{cases}$$

9.7

where r is a randomly generated number in [0, 1]. Figure 9.7 shows the sigmoid function and the probability of the updated position to be 1. For example, if $v = 0.3$, this means that the probability that the updated position will be 1 is 30%, and the probability that it will be 0 is 70%.

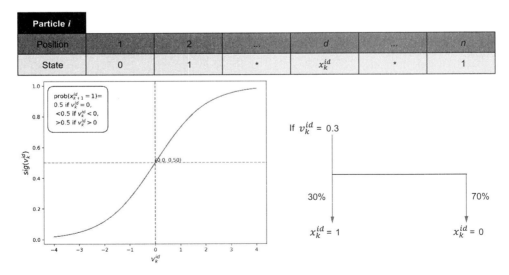

Particle *i*						
Position	1	2	...	d	...	n
State	0	1	*	x_k^{id}	*	1

Figure 9.7   Position and velocity notations in binary PSO (BPSO). Each particle represents a position in the binary space. Velocity is defined in terms of the probability of the bit changing.

As you'll notice, the velocity components will remain as real-valued numbers using the original equation, but these values are then passed through the sigmoid function before updating the position vector. The following equations are the velocity update equations in BPSO:

$$v_{k+1}^{id} = v_k^{id} + \phi_1 \left(pbest_k^{id} - x_k^{id} \right) + \phi_2 \left(gbest_k^{d} + x_k^{id} \right)$$

9.8

$$sig \left(v_{k+1}^{id} \right) = \frac{1}{1 + e^{-v_{k+1}^{id}}}$$

9.9

The positions are updated according to the following equation:

$$x_{k+1}^{id} = \begin{cases} 1 \text{ if } sig \left(v_{k+1}^{id} \right) > r \\ 0 \text{ otherwise} \end{cases}$$

9.10

where

- ϕ_1 and ϕ_2 represent different random numbers drawn from uniform distributions. Sometimes these parameters are chosen from a uniform distribution 0–2, such that the sum of their two limits is 4.0.
- v_{k+1}^{id} is the probability that an individual i will choose 1 for the bit at the dth site in the bit string.
- x_k^{id} is the current state of string i at bit d.
- v_k^{id} is a measure of the string's current probability to choose 1.
- $pbest_k^{id}$ is the best state found so far for bit d of individual i (i.e., a 1 or a 0).
- $gbest_k^{d}$ is 1 or 0 depending on what the value of bit d is in the best neighbor to date.

BPSO example

To illustrate how BPSO works, suppose we have a population of five binary particles, where each particle consists of 6 bits. Let's assume the particles are represented by the following binary strings: 101101, 110001, 011110, 100010, and 001011. We want to update particle 4 (represented by the binary string 100010) at bit 3 (which has a current value of 0). The current propensity (velocity) of this bit to be 1 is assumed to be 0.23. Additionally, we assume that the best value of this particle found so far is 101110, while the best value found by the entire population is 101111. Let's also assume that $\Phi_1 = 1.5$ and $\Phi_2 = 1.9$. Using equations 9.8 and 9.9, we can get the updated velocity of bit 3 in particle 4 as follows:

Particle 4: 100010, $v_k^{43} = 0.23$, $x_k^{43} = 0$, $pbest_k^{43} = 1$, $gbest_k^3 = 1$, $\Phi_1 = 1.5$, $\Phi_2 = 1.9$

$v_{k+1}^{43} = 0.23 + 1.5(1-0) + 1.9(1-0) = 3.63$

$sig(v_{k+1}^{43}) = sig(3.63) = 1/(1 + e^{-3.63}) = 0.974$

(continued)

Generate a random number $r^{43} = 0.6$, and update the position using equation 9.10 as follows:

$$x_{k+1}^{43} = 1 \text{ as } sig(v_{k+1}^{43}) > r^{43}$$

Updated particle 4: 100110

For more information about BPSO, see Kennedy and Eberhart's article "A discrete binary version of the particle swarm algorithm" [2].

9.4   *Permutation-based PSO*

Numerous efforts have been undertaken to employ PSO in solving permutation problems. The challenge of adapting PSO to tackle these problems arises from the fact that the notions of velocity and direction are not inherently applicable to permutation problems. To overcome this obstacle, arithmetic operations like addition and multiplication need to be redefined.

In M. Clerc's 2004 article, "Discrete particle swarm optimization, illustrated by the traveling salesman problem" [3], PSO was applied to solve the TSP. The position of a particle was the solution to a problem (the permutation of cities). The velocity of a particle was defined as the set of swaps to be performed on a particle. As you have seen, the right side of equation 9.1 contains three arithmetic operations: multiplication, subtraction, and addition. These operations are redefined for the new search space as follows:

- *Multiplication*—The velocity vector constrains a number of swaps between cities. Multiplying this vector by a constant c, results in another velocity vector with a different length, depending on the value of the constant. If $c = 0$, the length of the velocity vector (i.e., the included number of swaps) is set to 0. This means that no swap will be performed. If $c < 1$, the velocity is truncated. If $c > 1$, the velocity is augmented as illustrated in figure 9.8. Augmentation means adding a swap taken from the top of the current velocity vector to the end of the new velocity vector.

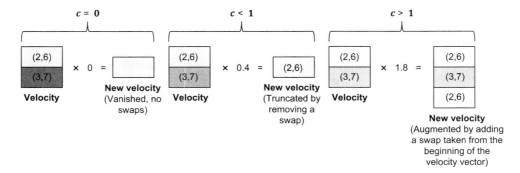

Figure 9.8   Redefined multiplication for permutation-based PSO

- *Subtraction*—Subtracting two positions should produce a velocity. This operation produces the sequence of swaps that could transform one position to the other. For example, let's consider an 8-city TSP. A candidate solution for this TSP is represented by a permutation such as [2, 4, 6, 1, 5, 3, 8, 7]. Figure 9.9 shows how a new velocity vector is produced by subtracting two positions.

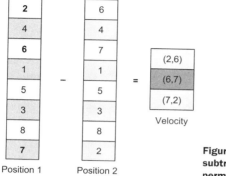

Figure 9.9   Redefined subtraction operation for permutation-based PSO

- *Addition*—The operation is performed by applying the sequence of swaps defined by the velocity to the position vector. Figure 9.10 shows how a new position (i.e., a new candidate solution) is generated by adding the velocity swap vector to the current position.

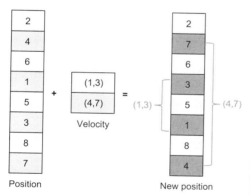

Figure 9.10   Redefined addition operation for permutation-based PSO

These redefined arithmetic operations allow us to update the velocity and position of PSO particles.

9.5   *Adaptive PSO*

The inertia, cognitive, and social components are the primary PSO parameters that can be used to achieve an equilibrium between exploration and exploitation during the optimization process. These three factors significantly influence the behavior of the algorithm, as discussed in the following subsections.

9.5.1   *Inertia weight*

The inertia parameter represents the tendency of a particle to maintain its current trajectory. By adjusting the inertia value, the algorithm can balance its focus on searching the solution space broadly (exploration) or homing in on the best solutions found thus far (exploitation). Large values of ω promote exploration, and small values promote exploitation, as illustrated in figure 9.11. Excessively small values may hinder the swarm's exploration capabilities. As the value of ω decreases, the influence of the cognitive and social components on position updates becomes more dominant.

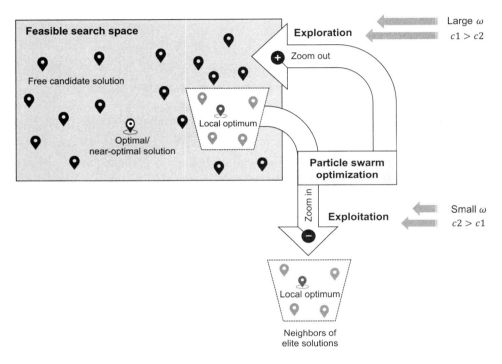

Figure 9.11   Effect of PSO parameters on the search behavior. Large inertia promotes exploration, and small values promote exploitation. $c1 > c2$ results in excessive wandering of individuals through the search space. In contrast, $c2 > c1$ may lead particles to rush prematurely toward a local optimum.

When $\omega > 1$, particle velocities tend to escalate over time, accelerating toward the maximum velocity (provided that velocity clamping is utilized), ultimately causing the swarm to diverge. In this scenario, particles struggle to alter their direction to return to promising regions. On the other hand, when $\omega < 1$, particles may gradually decelerate until their velocities approach 0, depending on the acceleration coefficients' values.

Velocity clamping can be considered by setting a maximum (and minimum) limit for the velocity. If the calculated velocity for a particle exceeds this limit, it is set to the maximum (or minimum) value. This prevents particles from wandering too far off in the problem space or getting stuck in a specific region in the search space.

The following methods can be used to update the inertia weight:

- *Random selection (RS)*—This involves selecting a different inertia weight in each iteration. The weight can be chosen from a distribution with a mean and standard deviation of your choice, but it's important to ensure that the swarm still converges despite the randomness. The following formula can be used:

$$\omega_t = 0.5 + \frac{rand(.)}{2}$$

9.11

  where $rand(.)$ is a uniformly distributed random number within the range $[0,1]$. Therefore, the mean value of the inertia weight is 0.75.

- *Linear time varying (LTV)*—This involves gradually decreasing the value of ω from a starting high value of ω_{max} to a final low value of ω_{min} following this equation:

$$\omega_t = (\omega_{max} - \omega_{min}) \times \frac{(t_{max} - t)}{t_{max}} + \omega_{min}$$

9.12

  where t_{max} is the number of iterations, t is the current iteration, and ω_t is the value of the inertia weight in the tth iteration. Typically, the convention is to set ω_{max} and ω_{min} to 0.9 and 0.4 respectively.

- *Nonlinear time varying (NLTV)*—This approach also involves decreasing the inertia weight from an initial high value, but this decrement can be nonlinear, as shown in the following equation:

$$\omega_{t+1} = (\omega_t - \omega_{min}) \times \frac{(t_{max} - t)}{t_{max} + \omega_{min}} + \omega_{min}$$

9.13

  where $\omega_{t=0} = 0.9$ is the initial choice of ω. By allowing more time to fall off toward the lower end of the dynamic range, NLTV can enhance local search or exploitation.

Figure 9.12 shows these three update methods.

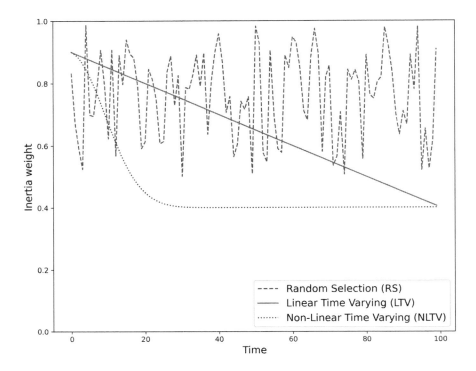

Figure 9.12   Different inertia weight update methods

As you can see, in random selection, a different inertia weight is randomly selected in each iteration. The mean value of the inertia weight is 0.75. LTV linearly decreases the inertia weight. In NLTV, the inertia weight decrement is more gradual than in LTV. In summary, the inertia weight plays a crucial role in the convergence speed and solution quality of the PSO algorithm. A high inertia weight promotes exploration, while a low inertia weight encourages exploitation.

9.5.2   *Cognitive and social components*

The cognitive component $c1$ is a parameter associated with a particle's individual learning capability, where the particle is influenced by its own experiences. The social component $c2$ is a parameter linked to the collective learning capability of all particles within the swarm. It represents the degree to which a particle is influenced by the best solutions found by its neighbors. If $c1 > c2$, the algorithm will show exploratory behavior, and if $c2 > c1$, the algorithm will tend to exploit the local search space, as illustrated in figure 9.11. Setting $c1 = 0$ reduces the velocity model to a social-only model or selfless model (the particles are all attracted to *nbest*). On the other hand, setting $c2 = 0$ reduces it to a cognition-only model (particles are independent, as in the case of the hill climbing algorithm).

Typically, $c1$ and $c2$ are kept constant in PSO. Empirically, the sum of $c1$ and $c2$ should be less than or equal to 4, and any significant deviations from this may result in divergent behavior. In adaptive PSO, it is advisable to gradually decrease the value of $c1$ over time and concurrently increase the value of $c2$ using linear formulas [4], as follows:

$$c1_t = \left(\frac{(c1_{max} - c1_{min}) \times (t_{max} - t)}{t_{max}} \right) + c1_{min}$$

9.14

$$c2_t = c2_{max} - \left(\frac{(c2_{max} - c2_{min}) \times (t_{max} - t)}{t_{max}} \right)$$

9.15

where t is the iteration index, $c1_{max}$ and $c2_{max}$ are the maximum cognitive and social parameters respectively, $c1_{min}$ and $c2_{min}$ are the minimum cognitive and social parameters respectively, and t_{max} is the maximum iteration.

Figure 9.13 shows the linearly changing $c1$ and $c2$. As you can see, we start with $c1 > c2$ to favor exploration. As the search progresses, $c2$ starts to be higher than $c1$ in order to favor exploitation.

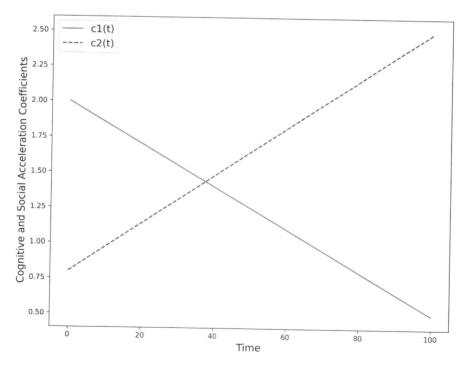

Figure 9.13   Cognitive and social acceleration coefficient updates. c1>c2 results in more exploration, while c2>c1 may lead to more exploitation.

Let's now see how we can use PSO to handle continuous and discrete optimization problems.

9.6   *Solving the traveling salesman problem*

In the previous chapter, you saw how to solve the TSP for 20 major cities in the United States, starting from New York City, using a genetic algorithm. Let's now solve the same problem using PSO, as shown in the next listing. We'll start by defining the latitude and longitude for the twenty US cities and computing the inter-city distances between them.

Listing 9.2   Solving TSP using PSO

```
import numpy as np
import pandas as pd
from collections import defaultdict
from haversine import haversine
import networkx as nx
import matplotlib.pyplot as plt
import pyswarms as ps

cities = {
    'New York City': (40.72, -74.00),
    'Philadelphia': (39.95, -75.17),
    'Baltimore': (39.28, -76.62),
    'Charlotte': (35.23, -80.85),
    'Memphis': (35.12, -89.97),
    'Jacksonville': (30.32, -81.70),
    'Houston': (29.77, -95.38),
    'Austin': (30.27, -97.77),
    'San Antonio': (29.53, -98.47),
    'Fort Worth': (32.75, -97.33),
    'Dallas': (32.78, -96.80),
    'San Diego': (32.78, -117.15),
    'Los Angeles': (34.05, -118.25),
    'San Jose': (37.30, -121.87),
    'San Francisco': (37.78, -122.42),
    'Indianapolis': (39.78, -86.15),
    'Phoenix': (33.45, -112.07),
    'Columbus': (39.98, -82.98),
    'Chicago': (41.88, -87.63),
    'Detroit': (42.33, -83.05)
}
```

Define the latitude and longitude for twenty major US cities.

```
distance_matrix = defaultdict(dict)
for ka, va in cities.items():
    for kb, vb in cities.items():
        distance_matrix[ka][kb] = 0.0 if kb == ka
➥ else haversine((va[0],va[1]), (vb[0], vb[1]))

distances = pd.DataFrame(distance_matrix)
distance=distances.values
city_names=list(distances.columns)
```

Create a haversine distance matrix based on the latitude and longitude coordinates.

Convert the distance dictionary into a dataframe with distances as values and city names as headers.

Next, we can count the number of cities and set up the integer bounds of the decision variables, which represent the order in which the cities are visited. The first function, `tsp_distance`, takes two arguments: `position` and `distance`. `position` is a 1D array that represents the order in which the cities are visited. `distance` is a 2D array that contains the distances between all pairs of cities. The function first defines `tour` as a permutation of the indices that represent the order of visiting the cities. It then calculates the total distance of the tour by summing the distances between adjacent cities as well as the distance between the last city in the tour and the starting city.

The second function, `tsp_cost`, takes two arguments: `x` and `distance`. `x` is a 2D array that contains the decision variables for the TSP problem, with each row representing a different particle in the swarm. `distance` is a 2D array that contains the distances between all pairs of cities. The function calculates the cost of each particle by calling the `tsp_distance` function on each row of `x` and returns a list of the costs:

Define the TSP problem as a permutation optimization problem with integer bounds.

Define the TSP distance function.

```
n_cities = len(city_names)
bounds = (np.zeros(n_cities), np.ones(n_cities)*(n_cities-1))

def tsp_distance(position, distance):
    tour = np.argsort(position)
    total_distance = distance[0, tour[0]]
    for i in range(n_cities-1):
        total_distance += distance[tour[i], tour[i+1]]
    total_distance += distance[tour[-1], 0]
    return total_distance

def tsp_cost(x, distance):
    n_particles = x.shape[0]
    cost=0
    cost = [tsp_distance(x[i], distance) for i in range(n_particles)]
    return cost
```

Convert the permutation to a TSP tour.

Compute the total distance of the tour from New York City as the first city, and add the distance from the last city back to New York City.

Compute and return the cost of each particle in the swarm.

As a continuation of listing 9.2, the following code sets the parameters for the PSO optimizer. `options` is a dictionary that contains the values for the inertia weight (`w`), cognitive (`c1`) and social (`c2`) acceleration coefficients, number of neighbors to consider (`k`), and the p-value for the Minkowski distance (`p`). `n_particles` represents the number of particles used in the optimization, and `dimensions` represents the number of decision variables, which is equal to the number of cities in the TSP problem. The best solution found by the optimizer is converted to a TSP tour by sorting the indices of the solution in ascending order and using them to index the `city_names` list in the same order. This creates a list of city names in the order that they are visited in the best tour. We then print the best route and its length:

Set up the PSO parameters.

```
options = {'w': 0.79, 'c1': 2.05, 'c2': 2.05, 'k': 10, 'p': 2}
optimizer = ps.discrete.BinaryPSO(n_particles=100, dimensions=n_cities,
  options=options)
```

Instantiate the PSO optimizer.

```
cost, solution = optimizer.optimize(tsp_cost, iters=150, verbose=True,
    distance=distance)
```
Solve the problem.

```
tour = np.argsort(solution)
city_names_tour = [city_names[i] for i in tour]
```
Convert the best solution to a TSP tour.

```
Route = " → ".join(city_names_tour)
print("Route:", Route)
print("Route length:", np.round(cost, 3))
```
Print the best route and its length.

Listing 9.2 produces the following output:

```
Route: New York City → Columbus → Indianapolis → Memphis → San Francisco
→ San Jose → Los Angeles → San Diego → Phoenix → Dallas → Fort Worth →
San Antonio → Austin → Houston → Jacksonville → Charlotte → Baltimore →
Philadelphia → Chicago → Detroit
Route length: 12781.892
```

Figure 9.14 shows the obtained route. The complete version of listing 9.2 is available in the book's GitHub repo, and it shows the steps for visualizing the route as a NetworkX graph.

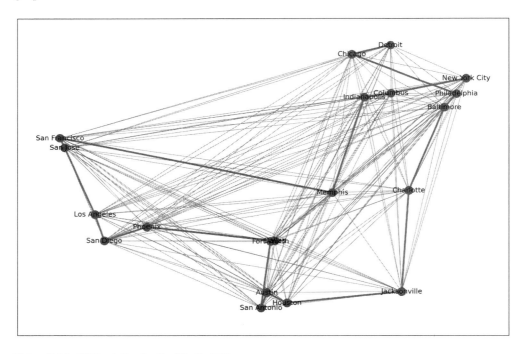

Figure 9.14   PSO solution for the 20-city TSP

Feel free to adjust the code according to your needs by modifying elements such as the problem data, the initial city, or the parameters of the algorithm.

9.7   *Neural network training using PSO*

Machine learning (ML) is a subfield of artificial intelligence (AI) that endows an artificial system or process with the ability to learn from experience and observation without being explicitly programmed. Many ML approaches have been and are still being proposed, and more details about ML will be provided in chapter 11. For now, let's consider neural networks, which are one of the most used and successful statistical ML approaches. The artificial neural network (ANN or NN) approach is inspired by the biological brain and can be considered a highly simplified computational model, as NN is very far from matching a brain's complexity. NN is at the heart of deep learning models that nowadays form the basis of many successful applications that touch everybody's life, such as text, audio, image, and video generation, voice assistants, and recommendation engines, to name just a few.

The human brain

Aristotle (384-322 BC) wrote, "Of all the animals, man has the largest brain in proportion to his size." The human brain is composed of an average of 86 billon interconnected nerve cells or *neurons*. Each biological neuron is connected to several thousand other neurons. It is extremely energy efficient, as it can perform the equivalent of an exaflop (a billion billion mathematical operations per second) with just 20 watts of power.

For simplicity, consider ML as glorified curve fitting, which intends to find a mapping function between independent and dependent variables. For example, suppose a vision-based object recognition model takes as input a digital image taken by the front camera of a vehicle—the output would be recognized objects, such as cars, pedestrians, cyclists, lanes, traffic lights, etc. In fact, ML shares the same ingredients as curve fitting in terms of model, scoring criteria, and search strategy. However, ML approaches, such as NNs, are a way to create functions that no human could write. They tend to create nonlinear, nonmonotonic, nonpolynomial, and even noncontinuous functions that approximate the relationship between independent and dependent variables in a data set.

An NN is a massively parallel adaptive network of simple nonlinear computing elements called neurons that are arranged in input, hidden, and output layers. Each node, or artificial neuron, connects to another and has an associated weight and threshold allowing the node to simulate a neuron firing. Each individual node has its own linear regression model, composed of input data, a bias, a threshold, and an output, as illustrated in figure 9.15. A neuron k can be described with the following equation:

$$z_k = \sum_{i=1}^{n} \omega_{ki} x_i + b$$

9.16

Its output is

$$y_k = \phi \left(z_k - \theta_k \right)$$

9.17

where x_i are the inputs, ω_{ki} are the weights, b is the bias term that defines the ability to fire in the absence of external input to the node, and φ is the activation function. This activation function makes the neuron fire the output when the input z_k reaches a threshold θ_k. There are different forms of activation functions (aka squashing functions) such as sign, step, tanh, arctan, s-shaped sigmoid (aka logistic), softmax, radial basis function, and rectified linear unit (ReLU).

As in the case of curve fitting, a scoring criterion or cost function is used to estimate deviation between the estimated values and the actual values. In this context, training an NN is fundamentally an optimization problem. The goal of training is to find the optimal parameters (weights and biases) that minimize the difference between the network's output and the expected output. This difference is often quantified using a loss or cost function, such as these:

- *Mean squared error (MSE)*—MSE is often used in regression problems. It calculates the square of the difference between the predicted and actual values and then averages these across the dataset. This function heavily penalizes large errors.

- *Cross-entropy loss*—Cross-entropy loss is typically used for binary and multiclass classification problems. It measures the dissimilarity between the predicted probability distribution and the actual distribution. In other words, it compares the model's confidence in its prediction with the actual outcome.

- *Negative log likelihood (NLL)*—NLL is another loss function in multiclass classification. If y is the true label and $p(y)$ is the predicted probability of that label, the negative log likelihood is defined as $-\log(p(y))$. The log function transforms the probabilities, which range between 0 and 1, to a scale that ranges from positive infinity to 0. When the predicted probability for the correct class is high (close to 1), the log value is closer to 0, but as the predicted probability for the correct class decreases, the log value increases toward infinity. Negating the log value thus gives a quantity that is minimized when the predicted probability for the correct class is maximized.

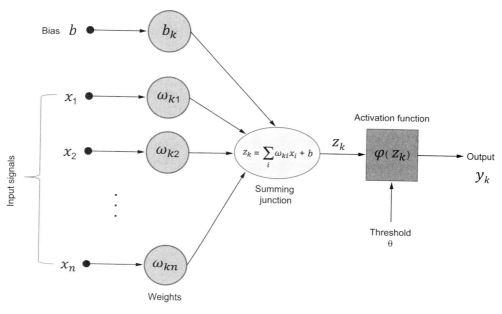

Figure 9.15 Neural network node demonstration

Training an NN involves the following steps:

- *Initialization*—Before training starts, the weights and biases in the network are typically initialized with small random numbers.
- *Feedforward*—In this stage, the input is passed through the network to produce an output. This output is generated by performing computations on the inputs using the initial or current weights, bias, and activation function transformation. The output of one layer becomes the input to the next layer until the final output is produced.
- *Error calculation*—After the feedforward stage, the output is compared with the desired output to calculate the error using a loss function. This function quantifies how far the network's predictions are from the actual values.
- *Backpropagation*—The calculated error is then propagated back through the network, starting from the output layer and moving back toward the input layer. This process computes the gradient or derivative of the loss function with respect to the weights and biases in the network.

- *Weight adjustment*—In this final stage, the weights of the network are updated in an effort to reduce the error. This is typically done using a technique called *gradient descent*. The weights are adjusted in the direction that most decreases the error, as determined by the gradients calculated during backpropagation.

By repeating these steps for many iterations (or epochs), the network gradually learns to produce outputs that are closer to the desired ones, thus "learning" from the input data.

Now that you have a basic understanding of NNs, let's train a simple NN using PSO following a supervised learning approach. During supervised training, the NN learns by initially processing a labeled dataset. By training on a labeled dataset, the network can subsequently predict labels for a new, unlabeled data set during the inferencing stage, after training.

For this example, we will use the Penguins dataset. This is a popular dataset in the data science community, containing information on the size, sex, and species of penguins. The dataset consists of 344 observations collected from three islands in the Palmer Archipelago, Antarctica. It includes the following seven variables:

- `species`—The species of penguin (Adelie, Chinstrap, or Gentoo)
- `island`—The island where the penguin was observed (Biscoe, Dream, or Torgersen)
- `bill_length_mm`—The length of the penguin's bill in millimeters
- `bill_depth_mm`—The depth of the penguin's bill in millimeters
- `flipper_length_mm`—The length of the penguin's flipper in millimeters
- `body_mass_g`—The mass of the penguin's body in grams
- `sex`—The sex of the penguin (male or female)

Our simple NN, described in the PySwarms use cases, has the following characteristics:

- *Input layer size*—4
- *Hidden layer size*—10 (activation function: $\tanh(x)$). The hyperbolic tangent activation function (aka Tanh, tanh, or TanH) maps input values to be between -1 and 1, and it's used to introduce nonlinearity in NNs. Remember that a sigmoid function maps input values to be between 0 and 1. The tanh function is centered at 0, which helps mitigate the vanishing gradient problem, compared to the sigmoid function. However, both tanh and sigmoid activations suffer from the vanishing gradient problem to some degree. Alternatives like rectified linear unit (ReLU) and its variants are often preferred.
- *Output layer size*—3 (activation function: $\text{softmax}(x)$). Softmax is a generalization of the sigmoid function. This function takes as input the *logits* that represent unnormalized outputs of the last layer of the network before they are

transformed into probabilities by applying a softmax function. These logits can be interpreted as a measure of the "evidence" that a certain input belongs to a particular class. The higher the logit value for a particular class, the more likely it is that the input belongs to that class.

The following listing shows the steps for training this simple NN using PSO. We start by importing the libraries we'll need and reading the penguin dataset.

Listing 9.3   Neural network training using PSO

```
import seaborn as sns            ◄──────   Required for loading
import matplotlib.pyplot as plt           the dataset
import numpy as np
import pandas as pd
from sklearn.preprocessing import LabelEncoder   ──┐   Required for target
from sklearn.decomposition import PCA                │   label encoding
import pyswarms as ps ◄──   Required for dimensionality reduction

penguins = sns.load_dataset('penguins')   ◄───   Load the Penguins dataset.
penguins.head() ◄───   Show the dataset rows and columns.
```

This produces the output shown in figure 9.16.

	species	island	bill_length_mm	bill_depth_mm	flipper_length_mm	body_mass_g	sex
0	Adelie	Torgersen	39.1	18.7	181.0	3750.0	Male
1	Adelie	Torgersen	39.5	17.4	186.0	3800.0	Female
2	Adelie	Torgersen	40.3	18.0	195.0	3250.0	Female
3	Adelie	Torgersen	NaN	NaN	NaN	NaN	NaN
4	Adelie	Torgersen	36.7	19.3	193.0	3450.0	Female

Figure 9.16   Penguins dataset

As a continuation of listing 9.3, we can visualize this dataset using the seaborn library as follows:

```
plt.figure(figsize=(8, 6))
sns.scatterplot(data=penguins, x='bill_length_mm', y='body_mass_g',
➥ hue='species', style="species")
plt.title('Bill Length vs. Body Mass by Species')
plt.show()
```

The output is shown in figure 9.17.

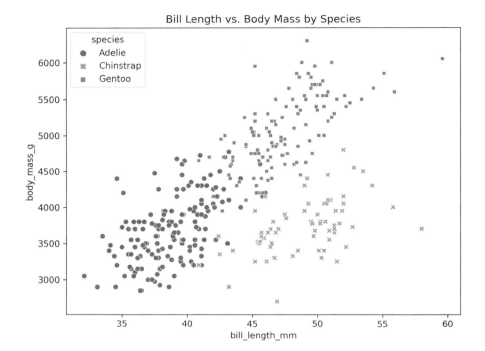

Figure 9.17   Bill length vs. body mass by species in the Penguins dataset

Next, we define a `logits_function` to take in a vector p of parameters for the NN and return the logits (pre-activation values) for the final layer of the network. As illustrated in figure 9.18, this function starts by extracting the weights and biases for the first and second layers of the network from the parameter vector p using indexing and reshaping operations. Then, the function performs forward propagation by computing the pre-activation value z^1 in the first layer as the dot product of the input data X and the first set of weights W^1, plus the bias term b^1. It then applies the tanh activation function to z^1 to obtain the activation value a^1 in the first layer. Finally, the function computes the pre-activation value for the second layer by taking the dot product of a^1 and the second set of weights W^2 and adding the bias term b^2. The resulting values are returned as the logits from the final layer of the network:

```
def logits_function(p):

    W1 = p[0: n_inputs * n_hidden].reshape((n_inputs, n_hidden))
    b1 = p[n_inputs * n_hidden: (n_inputs + 1) * n_hidden].reshape((n_hidden,))
    W2 = p[(n_inputs +1) * n_hidden: -n_classes].reshape((n_hidden, n_classes))
    b2 = p[-n_classes:].reshape((n_classes,))

    z1 = X.dot(W1) + b1
    a1 = np.tanh(z1)
```

Extracting the weights of the first layer

Extracting the weights of the second layer

Extracting the biases of the second layer

Calculate the pre-activation value in the first layer .

```
logits = a1.dot(W2) + b2          Calculate and return the logits.
return logits
```

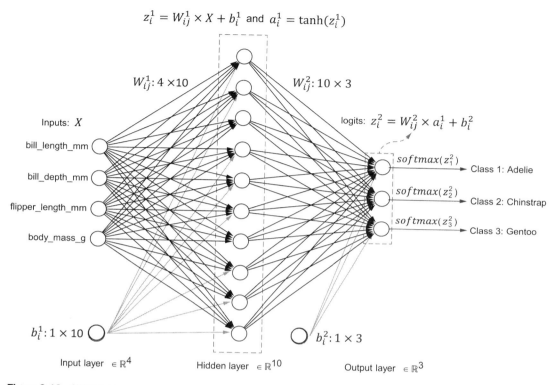

$$z_i^1 = W_{ij}^1 \times X + b_i^1 \text{ and } a_i^1 = \tanh(z_i^1)$$

W_{ij}^1: 4 ×10 W_{ij}^2: 10 × 3

Inputs: X

logits: $z_i^2 = W_{ij}^2 \times a_i^1 + b_i^2$

bill_length_mm

bill_depth_mm

$softmax(z_1^2)$ → Class 1: Adelie

flipper_length_mm

$softmax(z_2^2)$ → Class 2: Chinstrap

body_mass_g

$softmax(z_3^2)$ → Class 3: Gentoo

b_i^1: 1 × 10

b_i^2: 1 × 3

Input layer $\in \mathbb{R}^4$ Hidden layer $\in \mathbb{R}^{10}$ Output layer $\in \mathbb{R}^3$

Figure 9.18 NN layers

Next, we define the `forward_prop` function to perform a forward pass through an NN with two layers. This computes the softmax probabilities and negative log likelihood loss for the output, given a set of parameters `params`. The function first calls the `logits_function` to obtain the logits for the final layer of the network, given the parameters `params`. Then the function applies the softmax function to the logits using the `np.exp` function and normalizes the resulting values by dividing by the sum of the exponentiated logits for each sample, using the `np.sum` function with the `axis=1` argument. This gives a probability distribution over the classes for each sample. The function then computes the negative log likelihood loss by taking the negative log of the probability of the correct class for each sample, which is obtained by indexing the `probs` array using the `y` variable, which contains the true class labels. The `np.sum` function is used to compute the sum of these negative log probabilities across all samples, and the result is divided by the total number of samples to obtain the average loss per sample. Finally, the function returns the computed loss:

```
def forward_prop(params):

    logits = logits_function(params)  ◄──── Obtain the logits for the softmax.

                                              Compute the negative log likelihood.
    exp_scores = np.exp(logits)
    probs = exp_scores / np.sum(exp_scores, axis=1, keepdims=True)

    correct_logprobs = -np.log(probs[range(num_samples), y])  ◄────
    loss = np.sum(correct_logprobs) / num_samples

    return loss
```

Apply softmax to calculate the probability distribution over the classes.

Compute and return the loss.

To perform forward propagation over the whole swarm of particles, we define the following `particle_loss()` function. This function computes the loss for each particle in a PSO swarm, given its position in the search space. It is worth noting that each position represents the NN parameters (w1,b1,w2,b2) with `dimension` calculated as follows:

```
dimension = (n_inputs * n_hidden) + (n_hidden * n_classes) + n_hidden +
     n_classes = 4 * 10 + 10 * 3 + 10 * 3 + 1 * 10 + 1 * 3 = 83.
```

An example of a candidate setting of NN parameters (i.e., a *position* in PSO terminology) is given here:

```
[ 3.65105185e-01 -9.57472869e-02  4.99475198e-01  2.33703047e-01
  5.56295931e-01  6.95323783e-01  8.76045204e-02  5.52892675e-01
  3.33363337e-01  5.60680304e-01  3.24233602e-01  3.40402243e-01
  2.28940991e-01  6.47396295e-01  2.49476898e-01 -2.15041386e-01
  6.61749764e-01  4.50805880e-01  7.31521923e-01  4.55724886e-01
  5.81614992e-01  4.21303249e-01  3.10417945e-01  2.80091464e-01
  3.63352355e-01  7.21593713e-01  4.11009136e-01  3.50489680e-01
  6.82325768e-01  3.60945155e-01  3.34258781e-01  5.53845122e-01
  5.39748679e-01  8.45310205e-01  7.38728229e-01  5.44408893e-01
  4.22464042e-01  4.45099192e-01  4.36914661e-01 -2.40298612e-02
  4.68795601e-01  4.58388074e-01  2.29566792e-01  5.18783606e-01
  1.21226363e-01  2.80730816e-01  4.13249634e-01  1.91229505e-01
  6.30829496e-01 -4.52777424e-01  1.62066215e-01  3.07603861e-01
  1.54565454e-01  5.39974173e-01  4.48241886e-01 -2.81999490e-04
  2.93907050e-01  2.58571312e-01  7.87784363e-01  5.06092352e-01
  1.85010537e-01  8.06641243e-01  8.30985197e-01  4.06314407e-01
  2.20795704e-01  3.25405213e-01  6.02993839e-01  4.21051295e-01
  5.24352428e-01  2.49710316e-01  4.99212007e-01  4.48000964e-01
  4.90888329e-01  3.94908331e-01  6.35997377e-01  5.91192453e-01
  6.16639300e-01  6.85748919e-01  5.40805197e-01 -1.51195135e+00
  3.21751027e-01  3.93555680e-01  5.23679003e-01]
```

The PSO algorithm can then use these loss values to update the positions of the particles and search for the optimal set of parameters for the NN.

```
def particle_loss(x):
    n_particles = x.shape[0]  ◄──── Determine the number of particles.
    j = [forward_prop(x[i]) for i in range(n_particles)]
    return np.array(j)
```

Compute and return the loss for each particle.

The last function we need is `predict`, which uses the NN parameters corresponding to the positions of particles in a PSO swarm to predict the class labels for each sample in the dataset. This function first calls `logits_function` to obtain the logits for the final layer of the network, given the positions `pos` of the particles in the search space. Then the function computes the predicted class labels by taking the `argmax` of the logits across the columns (i.e., along the second axis or `axis=1`), using the `np.argmax` function. This gives the index of the class with the highest probability for each sample. Finally, the function returns the predicted class labels as a numpy array `y_pred`:

Compute and return the predicted class labels.

```
def predict(pos):
    logits = logits_function(pos)     ◀── Obtain logits for the final
    y_pred = np.argmax(logits, axis=1)     layer of the network.
    return y_pred
```

We can now train the NN using different PSOs available in PySwarms. The code starts by setting up several training samples, inputs, and the number of hidden layers and outputs. The dimensions are then computed based on the number of inputs, hidden nodes, and output classes. Three variants of PSO are defined: `globalBest`, `localBest`, and `binaryPSO`. The PSO hyperparameters are set using a dictionary called `options`. These hyperparameters include the inertia weight `w`, the cognitive parameter `c1`, the social parameter `c2`, the number of neighbors to be considered `k`, and the Minkowski distance parameter `p` (`p=1` is the sum-of-absolute values [or the L1 distance], while `p=2` is the Euclidean [or L2] distance):

Get the feature vector.

```
X = penguins[['bill_length_mm', 'bill_depth_mm', 'flipper_length_mm',
➥ 'body_mass_g']].to_numpy()
num_samples = X.shape[0]
n_inputs = X.shape[1]            Set up the number of training samples,
n_hidden = 10                    inputs, hidden layers, and outputs.
n_classes = len(np.unique(y))

dimensions = (n_inputs * n_hidden) + (n_hidden * n_classes) + n_hidden + n_
classes    ◀── Set up the dimensions of the problem.

PSO_varaints = ['globalBest', 'localBest', 'binaryPSO']  ◀── Define the variants of PSO.

options = {'w':0.79, 'c1': 0.9, 'c2': 0.5, 'k': 8, 'p': 2}  ◀──
                                                     Set up the PSO hyperparameters.

for algorithm in PSO_varaints:     ◀── Train the NN using different variants
    if algorithm == 'globalBest':      of PSO, and print the best accuracy.

        optimizer = ps.single.GlobalBestPSO(n_particles=150,
➥ dimensions=dimensions, options=options)
        cost, pos = optimizer.optimize(particle_loss, iters=2000)
        print("#"*30)
        print(f"PSO varaints: {algorithm}")
        print(f"Best average accuracy: {100*round((predict(pos) ==
y).mean(),3)} %")
        print()
```

```
    elif algorithm == 'localBest':
        optimizer = ps.single.LocalBestPSO(n_particles=150,
➥ dimensions=dimensions, options=options)
        cost, pos = optimizer.optimize(particle_loss, iters=2000)
        print("#"*30)
        print(f"PSO varaints: {algorithm}")
        print(f"Best average accuracy: {100*round((predict(pos) ==
y).mean(),3)} %")
        print()
    elif algorithm == 'binaryPSO':
        optimizer = ps.discrete.BinaryPSO(n_particles=150,
➥ dimensions=dimensions, options=options)
        cost, pos = optimizer.optimize(particle_loss, iters=2000)
        print("#"*30)
        print(f"PSO varaints: {algorithm}")
        print(f"Best average accuracy: {100*round((predict(pos) ==
y).mean(),3)} %")
        print()
```

The code then trains an NN, using each variant of PSO in turn, by creating an instance of the PSO optimizer and calling the `optimize` method, passing in the loss function and the number of iterations to run, `iters`. The best loss and particle position found by the optimizer are stored in `cost` and `pos` respectively. The code then prints the variant of PSO used along with the best accuracy that was obtained by using the corresponding particle position to make a prediction and comparing it to the true class label `y`.

Running the complete listing produces the following output:

```
##############################
PSO variant: globalBest
Best average accuracy: 99.1 %
##############################
PSO variant: localBest
Best average accuracy: 69.1 %
##############################
PSO variant: binaryPSO
Best average accuracy: 43.8 %
```

As you can see, `globalBest` PSO is the most efficient PSO variant for training this NN. Binary PSO does not match with the continuous nature of the NN parameters.

You can experiment with the code by changing the problem and algorithm parameters. For example, you could use a reduced feature set such as `bill_length_mm` and `flipper_length_mm` instead of the four features used in this code. You could also change the algorithm parameters and apply velocity clamping. `velocity clamp` is a parameter enabled in PySwarms to set the limits for velocity clamping. It's a tuple of size 2 where the first entry is the minimum velocity and the second entry is the maximum velocity.

In the next chapter, you will be introduced to ant colony optimization (ACO) and artificial bee colony (ABC) as other effective optimization algorithms inspired by swarm intelligence.

Summary

- PSO employs a stochastic approach that utilizes the collective intelligence and movement of a swarm of particles. It is based on the idea of social interaction, which allows for efficient problem-solving.

- The fundamental principle of PSO is to guide the swarm toward the best position in the search space while also remembering each particle's own best-known position, as well as the global best-known position of the swarm.

- PSO is guided by a straightforward principle: emulate the success of neighboring individuals.

- Although PSO was initially designed for solving problems with continuous variables, many real-world problems involve discrete or combinatorial variables. In these problems, the search space is finite, and the algorithm needs to search through a set of discrete solutions. To address these types of problems, different variants of PSO have been developed, such as binary PSO (BPSO) and permutation-based PSO.

- By carefully tuning inertia weight and cognitive and social acceleration coefficients, PSO can effectively balance exploration and exploitation.

Other swarm intelligence
algorithms to explore

This chapter covers

- Getting familiar with ant colony optimization metaheuristics
- Understanding different variants of ant colony optimization
- Understanding artificial bee colony
- Applying these swarm intelligence algorithms to solve continuous and discrete optimization problems

In the previous chapter, we looked at the particle swarm optimization (PSO) algorithm, but ant colony optimization (ACO) and artificial bee colony (ABC) are other widely used swarm intelligence algorithms, drawing inspiration from ants and bees to tackle diverse optimization problems. Let's revisit the treasure hunting mission and assume you still want to follow a cooperative and iterative approach to find the treasure (which is the best solution in the case of an optimization problem). You and your friends are divided into two groups: the ant group and the bee group. Each group has its own unique way of finding the treasure, using ant colony optimization or the artificial bee colony algorithm. You can join either of these two groups.

362

As treasure-hunting ants, you and some of your friends will start at the base camp and explore different paths to find the treasure. As you explore, each of you leaves a trail of special chalk (pheromones) behind. The more promising the path, the more chalk you leave on that path. When your friends find your chalk trail, they can decide to follow it or to explore a new path. Over time, the most promising paths will have the strongest chalk trails, and eventually the whole group will converge on the path that leads to the treasure.

As treasure-hunting bees, you'll use a different approach. You have forager bees and scout bees. Forager bees concentrate on searching nearby areas, while scout bees fly out and randomly explore the island, searching for clues leading to the treasure. When a bee finds a promising clue, it returns to the base camp and performs a "waggle dance" to communicate the location and quality of the clue to the other friends (onlooker bees). This process continues until the group finds the best path to the treasure.

This chapter presents ant colony optimization and artificial bee colony as swarm intelligence algorithms. The open traveling salesman problem, function optimization, routing problem, pump design, and a supply-demand problem are discussed in this chapter and its supplementary exercises in appendix C.

10.1   Nature's tiny problem-solvers

Ants are tiny creatures that can solve complex problems better than some humans. Ants may be small, but when they work together in a colony, they can accomplish some incredible feats. During foraging, they can find the shortest path to a food source, build intricate tunnels, and even take down prey much larger than themselves! During nest construction, some ants cut leaves from plants and trees, others forage for leaves hundreds of meters away from their nest to construct highways to and from their foraging sites, and yet other ants form chains of their own bodies, allowing them to cross wide gaps and pull stiff leaves together to form a nest. In the latter case, the worker ants form a chain along the edge of the leaf and pull the edges together by shortening the chain one ant at a time. Once the leaf edges are in place, weaver ants hold one larva each in their mandibles and gently squeeze the larva to produce silk, which is used to glue the leaf edges together.

Fascinating facts about the mighty ant

- Ants appeared on earth some 100 million years ago, making them one of the oldest groups of insects on the planet.
- Ants have a current total population estimated at 10^{16} individuals. It is estimated that the total weight of ants is in the same order of magnitude as the total weight of human beings.
- Ants are incredibly strong for their size. Some species can carry objects that are 50 times their body weight! To put that in perspective, this is like a human carrying a car!
- About 2% of all insects are social. There are around 12,000 different types of ants, and most ants are social insects.

(continued)

- Ants are considered the densest population in the world. They live in colonies of 30 to millions of individuals. Some colonies like Formica Yesensis have approximately 1,080,000 queens and 306,000,000 workers and live in 45,000 nests connected to each other over an area of 2.7 square kilometers.

- Ants use pheromones as their primary medium of stigmergic communication. However, ants also use other forms of communication, including visual, auditory, and tactile communication. For example, some species of ants use sound to communicate with each other. These sounds can range from simple clicks and pops to more complex signals that convey information about food sources, nest locations, and other important information. Some species of ants produce sounds in the audible range of humans (20Hz to 20kHz). For example, leafcutter ants are known to produce a clicking sound when they communicate with each other. The frequency of these clicks can range from 1 to 10 kilohertz. Other species of ants produce sounds that are beyond the range of human hearing. For example, some species of army ants produce ultrasonic sounds that can be used to locate prey or communicate with each other. If you're interested, take a look at the "What Sound Does an Ant Make?" video on YouTube (http://mng.bz/aEKo).

An ant is a simple stimulus-response creature that is incapable of achieving complex tasks alone. However, as a colony, ants show an amazing capability to perform complex tasks without any planning, a central controller, centralized supervision, or direct communication. Ants employ an indirect communication mechanism known as stigmergic communication. *Stigmergy* is a concept introduced by the French biologist Pierre-Paul Grassé in 1959 as an indirect method of communication among social insects involving environmental modifications. These environmental modifications serve as external or shared memory between the insects.

Ants use pheromones as their primary medium of stigmergic communication. As they travel to and from a food source, they deposit pheromones along their path. Other ants can detect these pheromones, which influences their decision-making when choosing a path. This allows ants to work together as a cohesive unit and accomplish complex tasks such as finding the shortest path from the nest to a food source and vice versa. The absence of direct communication or a central controller makes the actions of ants seem almost as if they are coordinated by some form of collective intelligence. In essence, the phenomenon of stigmergic communication allows social insects like ants to use their collective knowledge and behavior to achieve tasks beyond their individual abilities.

Ant colony optimization (ACO) is inspired by the foraging behavior of ants. As they forage for food, ants initially explore randomly around the nest area. Once an ant discovers a food source, it carries some of the food back to the nest while laying a pheromone trail along its path. Other ants then follow the pheromone trail to the food source, as illustrated in figure 10.1. As more and more ants follow the pheromone trail to the food source, the intensity of the pheromone trail increases, making it more attractive to other ants. In contrast, because pheromone trails are not fixed and will gradually evaporate over time, the pheromone trail on the longer path will evaporate. Eventually, a single pheromone trail becomes dominant, and most of the ants follow this trail to and from the food source. In this way, ants can find the shortest path between the nest and the food source through a process of collective or swarm intelligence.

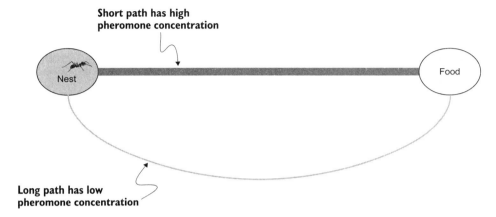

Figure 10.1   Ant foregoing process. A foraging ant deposits a pheromone trail along the path it takes on its way back to the nest. Other ants will likely follow the path with a stronger pheromone trail to reach the discovered food source.

As I explained in the previous chapter, the majority of the research carried out on swarm intelligence algorithms was initially based on experimental observations. To understand the collective behavior of ants during food foraging and to derive heuristics for the ACO algorithm, two famous experiments were conducted: the binary bridge experiment and the bridges with non-equal lengths experiment.

The binary bridge experiment was designed to observe the behavior of ants when presented with two equal-length bridges connecting their nest to a food source (figure 10.2a). The experiment aimed to investigate how ants determine the best path to use and how they adapt their behavior over time. Initially, the ants chose one of the two bridges randomly. As the ants traveled back and forth between the nest and the food source, they deposited pheromones along the path they took. As time progressed, more ants followed the path with the higher concentration of pheromones, which made the path even more attractive to other ants. Eventually, one of the two bridges became dominant, and most of the ants used it to travel between the nest and the food source. The ants' decision-making process was based on the principle of positive feedback, where the ants reinforced the path with the highest pheromone concentration, making it even more attractive to other ants.

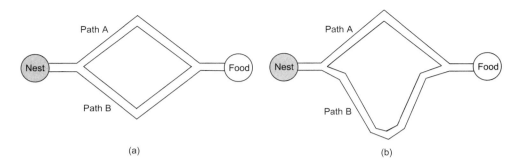

Path A   Path A

Nest   Food   Nest   Food

Path B   Path B

(a)   (b)

Figure 10.2   a) Binary bridge experiment; b) bridges with non-equal lengths experiment

The bridges with non-equal lengths experiment (figure 10.2b) is an extension of the binary bridge experiment with one branch of the bridge being longer than the other. The goal of this experiment was to observe how ants adapted their behavior when presented with two paths of different lengths. The experiment showed that ants tended to select the shorter path over the longer one. This was because ants traveling on the shorter path returned to the nest earlier than those on the longer path. As a result, the pheromone trail on the shorter path was reinforced sooner than that on the longer path, making it more attractive to other ants. This reinforcement behavior is called *autocatalytic behavior.*

The role of pheromones in the collective behavior of ants can be summarized in the following key points:

- The pheromone trail acts as a collective memory for the ants to communicate through by sensing and recording their foraging experience.
- The pheromone trail evaporates over time, introducing changes in the environment that can influence the ants' behavior.
- The concentration of pheromones on the trail represents a feedback signal that influences the ants' decision-making process.

Let's now dive deep into ACO metaheuristics.

10.2   *ACO metaheuristics*

Ant colony optimization (ACO) mimics the behavior of real ant colonies by having a group of "artificial ants" search for the best solution to a problem. These artificial ants leave "pheromone trails" to communicate with each other, just like real ants do, and eventually converge on the best solution.

To simulate the behavior of ants, let's assume we have a nest and a food source connected through two paths with different lengths L_1 and L_2, as in the case of the bridges with non-equal lengths. Let's now assign a computational parameter τ to represent the pheromone deposited by the ants. We'll initially assign equal values of pheromones to each path: $\tau_1 = \tau_2$ as shown in figure 10.3. We then start by placing m ants at the nest. Let's assume that these artificial ants exactly mimic the real ants and take decisions based on the pheromone concentration, but without any knowledge of the lengths of the paths. For each ant k, this ant traverses path 1 with probability

$$p_1 = \frac{\tau_1}{\tau_1 + \tau_2}$$

10.1

This ant thus traverses path 2 with a probability $p_2 = 1 - p_1$.

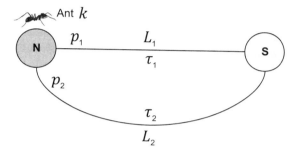

Figure 10.3   ACO simulation

As $\tau_1 = \tau_2$, the ant k will randomly pick one of the two paths, as both have same probability to of being traversed. After traversing the selected paths, pheromone concentration on each path needs to be updated. This pheromone update includes two phases: evaporation and deposit. During the evaporation phase, the pheromone concentration τ is decremented as follows:

$$\tau(t + 1) = (1 - \rho) \times \tau(t), \rho \in (0, 1)$$

10.2

where ρ specifies the rate of evaporation. Figure 10.4 shows the effect of the pheromone evaporation rate during the foraging process based on a NetLogo simulation. NetLogo is a multi-agent programmable modeling environment used to simulate natural and social phenomena. It allows users to create, experiment with, and analyze simulations of complex systems, such as ecosystems, economies, and social networks. The foraging behavior of ants is shown in NetLogo's Ants model (https://ccl.northwestern.edu/netlogo/models/Ants).

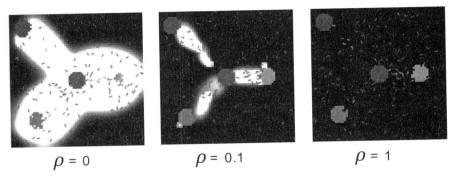

$\rho = 0$ $\rho = 0.1$ $\rho = 1$

Figure 10.4   Effect of evaporation rate during the food foraging process. In the simulation, the ants initiate their search for food from the central nest, which is surrounded by three food sources shown as blobs. The pheromone trails are shown in white. Upon discovering a food item, an ant transports it back to the nest, leaving behind a chemical trail. This trail is then followed by other ants that pick up the scent, directing them toward the food source. As more ants continue to retrieve food, they strengthen the chemical trail.

As you can see, if the evaporation rate is set to 0, the pheromone trail will never evaporate, and the ants will follow the same path repeatedly. This will cause the ants to become trapped in a local optimum, and they will not be able to explore other paths or find a better solution. On the other hand, if the evaporation rate is set to 1, the pheromone trail will evaporate at the maximum rate, which means the ants will not be able to follow any trail, and they will be forced to explore the environment randomly. This can result in slow convergence to the optimal solution.

During the deposit phase, each ant leaves more pheromones on its traversed path. Figure 10.5 shows the different methods used for pheromone updates:

- *Online step-by-step pheromone update*—Each ant deposits a certain amount of pheromones on the path it has traversed. This will increase the probability of another ant choosing the same edge:

$$\tau(t+1) = \tau(t) + \Delta\tau \qquad \textbf{10.3}$$

There are different approaches for choosing the value of $\Delta\tau$. Following the *ant density model*, the ant adds a constant amount Q to each traversed edge. This means that the final pheromone added to the edge will be proportional to the number of ants choosing it. The higher the density of the traffic on the edge, the more desirable that edge becomes as a component of the final solution. This method does not take the quality of the solution (i.e., the edge length) into account. In the *ant quantity model*, the amount of pheromones deposited is proportional to the quality of the solution obtained by the ant. For example, an ant traversing between node i and j will deposit a quantity Q/d_{ij}, where d_{ij} is the distance between i and j. In this case, only local information, d_{ij}, is used to update pheromone concentrations. Lower cost edges are made more desirable.

■ *Online delayed pheromone update (or ant cycle model)*–Once the ant constructs the solution, it retraces its steps and updates the pheromones trails on the edges it has traversed based on the quality of the solution. The amount of pheromones deposited is determined by the quality of the solution obtained by the ant as follows:

$$\Delta\tau_{ij}^{k}(t) = \frac{Q}{L^{k}(t)}$$

10.4

where Q is a constant and L^{k} is the length of the path constructed by ant k. For each edge (i,j) of the corresponding path, and after all the ants have completed their tours, the total amount of pheromones deposited will be

$$\tau_{ij}(t+1) = \tau_{ij}(t) + \sum_{k=1}^{m}\Delta\tau_{ij}^{k}(t)$$

10.5

where m is the number of ants.

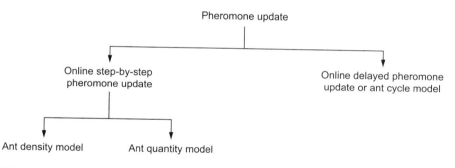

Figure 10.5 **Pheromone update methods**

In summary, with online step-by-step pheromone update, the ant updates the pheromone trail τ_{ij} on the edge (i,j) when moving from node i to node j. In online delayed pheromone update, once a path is constructed, the ant can retrace the same path backward and update the pheromone trails on the traversed edges. Which method you choose depends on the specific problem being solved. Any combination of online step-by-step pheromone updates and online delayed pheromone updates is also possible.

10.3 ACO variants

ACO has been used to solve a wide range of optimization problems, such as vehicle routing problems, scheduling problems, and optimal assignment problems. Over the years, several variants of the algorithm have been developed, as shown in figure 10.6.

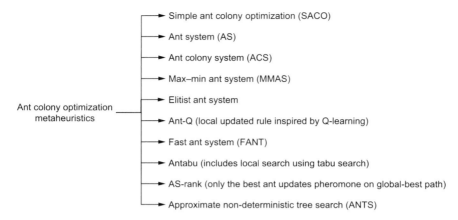

Figure 10.6   Examples of ACO variants

These variants have different strengths and weaknesses, and the choice of variant depends on the specific problem being solved. In the following subsections, we will discuss some of these variants.

10.3.1   *Simple ACO*

Simple ACO (SACO) is an algorithmic implementation of the double bridge experiment. Consider the problem of finding the shortest path between two nodes on a graph, as shown in figure 10.7.

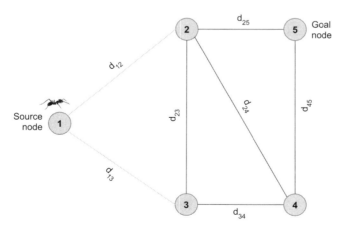

Figure 10.7   Shortest path problem

Let's solve this problem using SACO. On each edge, we'll assign a small random value to indicate the initial pheromone concentration, $\tau_{ij}(0)$. Then we'll place a number of ants, $k = 1,\ldots,m$ on the source node.

For each iteration of SACO, each ant will incrementally construct a path (solution) to the destination node. Initially, an ant will randomly select which edge to follow next. Later, each ant will execute a decision policy to determine the next edge of the path. At each node i, the ant has a choice to move to any of the j nodes connected to it, based on the following transition probability:

$$p_{ij}^k(t) = \begin{cases} \dfrac{[\tau_{ij}(t)]^\alpha \cdot [\eta_{ij}(t)]^\beta}{\sum_{l \in N_i^k} [\tau_{il}(t)]^\alpha \cdot [\eta_{il}(t)]^\beta} & \text{if } j \in N_i^k \\ 0 & \text{if } j \notin N_i^k \end{cases}$$

10.6

where

- N_i^k is the set of feasible nodes connected to node i, with respect to ant k.
- τ_{ij} is the amount of pheromones deposited for transition from state i to j.
- η_{ij} is a heuristic value that represents the desirability of state transition ij (a priori knowledge, typically $1/d_{ij}$, where d is the distance).
- $\alpha \geq 0$ is a parameter that controls the influence of τ_{ij}. α is used to amplify the influence of the pheromone. Large values of α give excessive importance to the pheromone, especially the initial random pheromones, which may lead to rapid convergence to suboptimal paths.
- $\beta \leq 1$ is a parameter that controls the influence of the desirability of the edge η_{ij}.

In the shortest path problem, assume that we use five ants, an initial pheromone value of 0.5, and $\alpha = \beta = 1$. The first ant $(k = 1)$, placed at the source node, has two neighboring nodes {2,3}, as shown in figure 10.8.

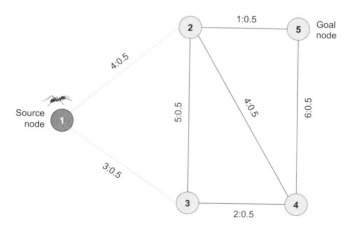

Figure 10.8   The first ant is at source node 1 with neighbors 2 and 3. There are two numbers on each edge separated by a colon. The first number represents the length of the edge, and the second represents the current pheromone concentration on the edge.

Considering the inverse of the edge length as edge desirability, this ant needs to choose between nodes 2 and 3 by applying the transition probability as follows:

$$p_{12}^1 = \frac{\tau_{12}^\alpha \eta_{12}^\beta}{\sum_{l \in N_1^1} \tau_{1l}^\alpha \eta_{1l}^\beta} = \frac{\tau_{12}^\alpha / d_{12}^\beta}{\sum_{l \in N_1^1} \tau_{1l}^\alpha / d_{1l}^\beta}$$
$$= \frac{0.5/4}{0.5/4 + 0.5/3} = 0.43$$

10.7

$$p_{13}^1 = \frac{\tau_{13}^\alpha \eta_{13}^\beta}{\sum_{l \in N_1^1} \tau_{1l}^\alpha \eta_{1l}^\beta} = \frac{\tau_{13}^\alpha / d_{13}^\beta}{\sum_{l \in N_1^1} \tau_{1l}^\alpha / d_{1l}^\beta}$$
$$= \frac{0.5/3}{0.5/4 + 0.5/3} = 0.57$$

10.8

where p_{12}^1 is the probability of node 2 being selected by ant 1 at node 1, and p_{13}^{1} is the probability of node 3 being selected. We then generate a random number r between 0 and 1. If $p_{13}^1 \geq r$, we select node 3; otherwise, we select 2. As node 3 has the highest probability of being selected, it will most likely be selected.

Moving forward, the first ant is now at node 3 and needs to decide between the adjacent nodes 2 and 4 following the same transition probability, which results in $p_{32}^1 = 0.29$ and $p_{34}^1 = 0.71$. Let's assume that node 4 is selected. The ant is now at node 4 and needs to decide between the adjacent nodes 2 and 5 following the same transition probability, which results in $p_{42}^1 = 0.6$ and $p_{45}^1 = 0.4$. Let's assume that node 5 is selected, based on the generated random number. Figure 10.9 shows the path completed by the first ant in the first iteration with length $L^1(t = 1) = 3 + 2 + 6 = 11$. Each ant will generate its own path following the same steps.

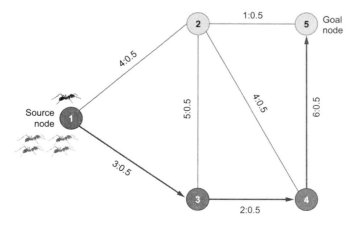

Figure 10.9   The path constructed by the first ant. Each of the other four ants will similarly construct a path.

Before starting a new iteration, the pheromones need to be updated. Following equation 10.2 and assuming that the evaporation rate ρ is 0.7, the new pheromone value will be

$$\tau(t+1) = (1-\rho) \times \tau(t) = (1-0.7) \times 0.5 = 0.15 \qquad \textbf{10.9}$$

Pheromones are also deposited. If the first ant $k = 1$ is selected to deposit pheromones based on the costs of the paths found by each ant, it enforces the edges {1,3}, {3,4}, and {4,5} with the value $Q/L^1 = 1/11$ following the online delayed pheromone update model. Figure 10.10 shows the updated pheromone values on each edge.

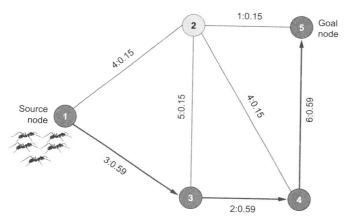

Figure 10.10 **Updated pheromone concentrations**

In this simple example, over three iterations, the ants find the shortest path $1 \rightarrow 3 \rightarrow 4 \rightarrow 5$. In the following sections, we'll discuss the ant system (AS) algorithm, ant colony system (ACS) algorithm, and max–min ant system (MMAS) algorithm as ACO variants proposed to deal with SACO limitations.

10.3.2 *Ant system*

The ant system (AS) algorithm improves on SACO by adding a memory capability via a tabu list. This list, or ant memory, identifies the already-visited nodes. The transition probability used in AS is the same as in equation 10.6. As an ant visits a new node, that node is added to the ant's tabu list for a predefined number of iterations. And as in SACO, after an ant completes a path, the pheromone on each edge is updated. The ant density, ant quantity, and ant cycle models can be used to update the pheromones. As previously explained, in the ant density and ant quantity models, ants deposit pheromones while building, whereas in the ant cycle model, ants deposit pheromones after they have built a complete path.

10.3.3 *Ant colony system*

The ant colony system (ACS) algorithm is an extension of the AS algorithm with a modified transition rule that utilizes an elitist strategy. This strategy, known as the *pseudo-random proportional action rule*, is designed to improve the efficiency and effectiveness of the algorithm. The pseudo-random proportional action rule used in ACS is based on the idea that the best solutions found by the ants should be given more weight in the decision-making process. In ACS, a random number r is generated, and the parameter $r_o \in [0,1]$ is predefined. An ant k, located at node i, selects the next node j to move to using the following decision rule with a double function:

- If $r \le r_o$, the ant selects node j

$$j = \arg\max_{l \in N_i^k} \tau_{il}(t) \cdot [\eta_{il}(t)]^\beta$$

10.10

- Else, a node is probabilistically selected (using a roulette wheel method, for example, which you learned about in chapter 7) according to the following transition probability:

$$p_{ij}^k(t) = \begin{cases} \dfrac{\tau_{ij}(t) \cdot [\eta_{ij}(t)]^\beta}{\sum_{l \in N_i^k} \tau_{il}(t) \cdot [\eta_{il}(t)]^\beta} & \text{if } j \in N_i^k \\ 0 & \text{if } j \notin N_i^k \end{cases}$$

Notice that compared to the transition probability of SACO (equation 10.6), the parameter that controls the influence of the pheromone concentration is $\alpha = 1$ in ACS. The parameter r_0 is used to balance the exploration–exploitation trade-off. When $r \le r_0$, the decision rule exploits the knowledge available about the problem by favoring the best edge, and when $r > r_0$, the algorithm explores. Properly tuning r_0 allows us to strike a balance between exploration and exploitation.

In the previous shortest path example, assume that the ant is at node 4 and needs to choose node 2 or 5 following the ACS decision rule (figure 10.11). Let's assume that we have the values $r_o = 0.5$, $\beta = 1$, and $\eta_{ij} = 1 / d_{ij}$. Let's now generate a random number r.

If $r \le r_o$, the ant will select node

$$j = \arg\max_{l \in N_i^k} \tau_{il}(t) \cdot [\eta_{il}(t)]^\beta$$

$$= \arg\max_{l \in N_i^k} \left\{ 0.5 \times \frac{1}{4},\ 0.5 \times \frac{1}{3} \right\}$$

$$= \arg\max\{0.125,\ 0.1666\} \Rightarrow node\,5$$

10.11

If $r > r_o$, the ant will select a node with maximum transition probability: $p^1_{45} = 0.6$ and $p^1_{42} = 0.4$ as calculated before in section 10.3.1 with $\alpha = 1$. Using the roulette wheel method, node 2 or node 5 may be selected.

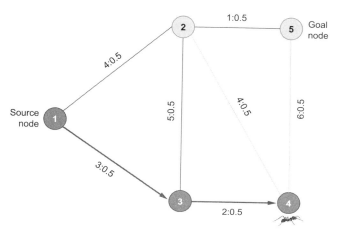

Figure 10.11 **The ant at node 4 selects the next node (2 or 5) following the ACS elitist strategy.**

Unlike in AS, the pheromone reinforcement process in ACS is exclusively performed by the ant with the global-best solution, which corresponds to the best path found so far. However, relying solely on the global-best solution to dictate pheromone deposition may cause the search to converge too rapidly around the global-best solution to date, hindering exploration of other potentially better solutions. The max–min ant system (MMAS) algorithm was developed to address this issue.

10.3.4 *Max–min ant system*

ACS can experience premature stagnation, which occurs when all ants follow the same path and little exploration is done. This issue is especially prevalent in complex problems, where the search space is large and the optimal solution is difficult to find. To overcome this problem, the max–min ant system (MMAS) was proposed.

MMAS employs the iteration-best path instead of the global-best path for pheromone updates. Pheromone trails are only updated using the online delayed pheromone update model, where the edges that were traversed by the best ant in the current iteration receive additional pheromones. Since the best paths can vary significantly between iterations, this approach promotes a higher degree of exploration throughout the search space compared to ACS. Hybrid strategies can also be implemented, in which the iteration-best path is primarily utilized to encourage exploration, while the global-best path is incorporated periodically.

In MMAS, the pheromone concentrations are constrained within an upper bound (τ_{max}) and lower bound (τ_{min}), ensuring that the search remains focused yet flexible. The pheromone trails are initialized to their maximum value τ_{max}, and if the algorithm reaches a stagnation point, all pheromone concentrations are reset to the maximum value. Following this reset, the iteration-best path is exclusively used for a limited number of iterations. The values for τ_{min} and τ_{max} are typically determined through experimentation, although they could also be computed analytically if the optimal solution is known.

10.3.5 *Solving open TSP with ACO*

Let's now implement the ACO algorithm to solve open TSP, considering the 20 major US cities. Our objective is to find the shortest route that a salesperson can follow to visit each of these 20 cities once, starting from New York City and without returning to the home city.

We'll start by defining a `cities` dictionary that contains the names of the 20 US cities and their latitude and longitude coordinates. We'll then use a nested loop to calculate the distance between each pair of cities using the `haversine` distance formula, storing the results in the `distance_matrix` dictionary. The `haversine` distance is used because it takes into account the earth's curvature, providing accurate distance measurements between two points on the earth's surface (see the "Haversine distance" sidebar in section 4.3.3 for more details). The `cost_function` is defined to calculate the total distance of a path. It takes a list of city indices (`path`) and a distance matrix (`distances`) as input arguments. The function then iterates through the path, summing the distance between each consecutive pair of cities. The total path distance is then returned. This code is shown in the next listing.

> **Listing 10.1   Solving shortest path problem using ACO**

```
import numpy as np
import pandas as pd
from collections import defaultdict
from haversine import haversine
import networkx as nx
import matplotlib.pyplot as plt
import random
from tqdm import tqdm

cities = {
    'New York City': (40.72, -74.00),
    'Philadelphia': (39.95, -75.17),
    'Baltimore': (39.28, -76.62),
    'Charlotte': (35.23, -80.85),
    'Memphis': (35.12, -89.97),
    'Jacksonville': (30.32, -81.70),
    'Houston': (29.77, -95.38),
    'Austin': (30.27, -97.77),
    'San Antonio': (29.53, -98.47),
    'Fort Worth': (32.75, -97.33),
    'Dallas': (32.78, -96.80),
    'San Diego': (32.78, -117.15),
    'Los Angeles': (34.05, -118.25),
```

```
                'San Jose': (37.30, -121.87),
                'San Francisco': (37.78, -122.42),
                'Indianapolis': (39.78, -86.15),
                'Phoenix': (33.45, -112.07),
                'Columbus': (39.98, -82.98),
                'Chicago': (41.88, -87.63),
                'Detroit': (42.33, -83.05)
        }
```

Define latitude and longitude for 20 major US cities.

Create a haversine distance matrix based on latitude and longitude coordinates.

```
distance_matrix = defaultdict(dict)
for ka, va in cities.items():
    for kb, vb in cities.items():
        distance_matrix[ka][kb] = 0.0 if kb == ka else haversine((va[0],
➥ va[1]), (vb[0], vb[1]))

distances = pd.DataFrame(distance_matrix)
city_names=list(distances.columns)
city_indices = {city: idx for idx, city in enumerate(city_names)}
city_count = len(city_names)

def cost_function(path):
    distance = 0
    for i in range(len(path) - 1):
        city1, city2 = city_names[path[i]], city_names[path[i + 1]]
        distance += haversine(cities[city1], cities[city2])
    return distance
```

Inter-city values

City names

Define the cost function that represents the path length.

As a continuation of listing 10.1, the next code snippet presents a function called ant_tour that takes two arguments: pheromones, representing the pheromone levels between cities, and distances, representing the distances between cities. It initializes a paths array to store paths for each ant, and it iterates over each ant in the specified range of ants. For each ant, it initializes a path starting from New York City. It enters a while loop that continues until all cities are visited. Within the while loop, it selects the current city as the last city in the path. It then calculates the probabilities for choosing the next city based on the pheromone levels and the inverse of the distances between the current city and unvisited cities. The probabilities are calculated using equation 10.6. The next city is chosen using the random.choices function, based on the normalized probabilities. The chosen next city is removed from the list of unvisited cities, and it is appended to the path:

```
def ant_tour(pheromones):
    paths = np.empty((ants, city_count), dtype=int)
    for ant in range(ants):
        path = [city_indices['New York City']]
        unvisited_cities = set(range(city_count))
        unvisited_cities.remove(path[0])
        while unvisited_cities:
            current_city = path[-1]
```

Initialize an array to store paths for each ant.

Initialize a set of unvisited cities.

Start each ant's path from New York City.

Remove New York City from unvisited cities.

Continue building the path until all cities are visited.

```
        probabilities = []
```
Calculate the probabilities for moving to each unvisited city.
```
        for city in unvisited_cities:
            tau = pheromones[current_city, city]
            eta = (1 / distances[current_city, city])
            probabilities.append((tau** alpha)*(eta ** beta))
```
Choose the next city based on probabilities.
```
        probabilities /= sum(probabilities)
```
Normalize the probabilities.
```
        next_city = np.random.choice(list(unvisited_cities),
    p=probabilities)
        unvisited_cities.remove(next_city)
        unvisited_cities.remove(next_city)
```
Remove the chosen city from the set of unvisited cities.

Add the chosen city to the path.
```
        path.append(next_city)
```
Store the completed path for the current ant.
```
        paths[ant] = path

    return paths
```

Once all the cities have been visited, the path for the current ant is stored in the `paths` array. After all the ants have completed their paths, the function returns the `paths` array containing the optimal tours found by each ant.

The following `update_pheromones` function is used to update the pheromone levels based on the distances and paths of the ants:

```
def update_pheromones(paths, pheromones):
    delta_pheromones = np.zeros_like(pheromones)
```
Initialize a matrix to store the changes in pheromone levels.

Get the indices of the cities in the current path.
```
    for i in range(ants):
        for j in range(city_count - 1):
            city1_idx, city2_idx = paths[i, j], paths[i, j + 1]
            delta_pheromones[city1_idx, city2_idx] += Q / cost_
    function(paths[i])
```
Update pheromones based on the paths taken by the ants.

```
    return (1 - evaporation_rate) * pheromones + delta_pheromones
```
Update the pheromone level between the current and next city.

Evaporate existing pheromones, add the changes in pheromones, and return the updated pheromones.

This function takes two arguments: `paths`, representing the paths taken by ants, and `pheromones`, representing the current pheromone levels on edges between cities. It initializes a matrix `delta_pheromones` to store the changes in pheromone levels. This matrix has the same shape as the `pheromones` matrix. It iterates over each ant in the specified range of ants. Within the loop, it iterates over each city in the ant's path (except the last city). For each pair of consecutive cities, it updates the `delta_pheromones` matrix by adding a value based on the inverse of the cost of the ant's path. After the inner loop, it calculates the updated pheromones by combining the existing pheromones, considering evaporation, and adding the changes stored in `delta_pheromones`. Finally, it returns the matrix of updated pheromones.

As a continuation, the following code snippet shows the `run_ACO` function, which takes the following inputs:

- distances—A 2D array (matrix) that stores the distances between cities
- ants—The number of ants to use in the algorithm
- iterations—The number of iterations
- alpha—A parameter that controls the influence of the pheromone trail on the ant's decision
- beta—A parameter that controls the influence of the distance to the next city on the ant's decision
- evaporation_rate—The rate at which pheromones evaporate from the paths
- Q—A constant used in the calculation of the amount of pheromones deposited by the ants

This function returns the best_path and best_distance, representing the optimal solution found by the ACO algorithm:

```
def run_ACO(distances, ants, iterations, alpha, beta, evaporation_rate, Q):
    pheromones = np.ones((city_count, city_count))   ◄── Initialize the
    best_path = None                                     pheromones array.
    best_distance = float('inf')

    for _ in tqdm(range(iterations), desc="Running ACO", unit="iteration"):
        paths =ant_tour(pheromones, distances)   ◄── Generate paths for each ant.

        distances_paths = np.array([cost_function(path) for path in paths])
        min_idx = distances_paths.argmin()
        min_distance = distances_paths[min_idx]
                                              Find the index of the path
        if min_distance < best_distance:   ◄── with the minimum distance.
            best_distance = min_distance
            best_path = paths[min_idx]        Return the best path and distance
                                                  found during the iterations.
        pheromones = update_pheromones(paths, pheromones)

    return best_path, best_distance   ◄──
```

Calculate the total distance for each path.

Update the pheromones.

Let's now apply ACO to solve the shortest path problem using the following parameters:

```
ants = 30
iterations = 100
alpha = 1              Set ACO parameters.
beta = 0.9
evaporation_rate = 0.5
Q = 100
                                          Run ACO with the defined parameters.
best_path, best_distance = run_ACO(distances.values, ants, iterations, alpha,
beta,
➥ evaporation_rate, Q)   ◄──
```

Given the randomness included in the algorithm, your solution may vary. The following path is what was generated when I ran the solver:

```
Route: New York City → Philadelphia → Baltimore → Detroit → Chicago →
Indianapolis → Columbus → Charlotte → Jacksonville → Memphis → Fort Worth →
Dallas → Houston → Austin → San Antonio → Phoenix → San Diego → Los Angeles →
San Jose → San Francisco
Route length: 7937.115
```

The preceding path is shown in figure 10.12. The complete version of listing 10.1 is available in the book's GitHub repo, which also contains the code to generate this visualization.

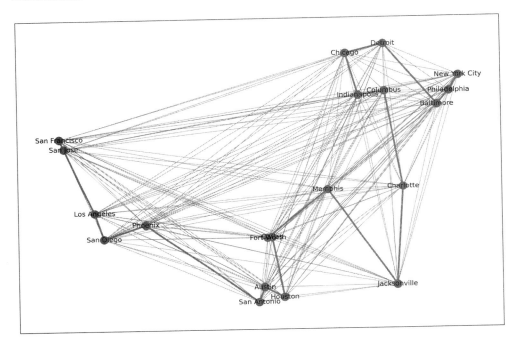

Figure 10.12   Shortest path obtained by ACO

Unlike genetic algorithms and particle swarm optimization algorithms, there are no well-developed and comprehensive Python packages for ACO metaheuristics. The ACOpy project (https://acopy.readthedocs.io/en/latest/index.html) provides an implementation of ACO and can be installed using pip as follows: `pip install acopy`. As a continuation of listing 10.1, let's use ACOpy to solve the shortest path problem.

We'll start by importing the `acopy` and `networkx` libraries. A graph, `G`, is created where the nodes represent cities and the edges represent the distances between them. The `distance_matrix` contains the distances between each pair of cities. The loops iterate over all pairs of cities, adding an edge between each pair of cities to the graph, with the weight of the edge being the distance between the cities. Self-loop edges (edges that connect a node to itself) are then removed from the graph:

```
import acopy
import networkx as nx

G=nx.Graph()

for ka, va in cities.items():
    for kb, vb in cities.items():
        G.add_weighted_edges_from({(ka,kb, distance_matrix[ka][kb])})
G.remove_edges_from(nx.selfloop_edges(G))
```

The parameters for the ACO algorithm are then defined: `evaporation_rate`, `iterations`, and `Q`, as explained previously. An ACO solver is created with the specified `evaporation_rate` and `Q`. The `acopy.Colony` object is initialized with `alpha` and `beta` parameters. The algorithm then iterates for the specified number of iterations. In each iteration, the solver's `solve` method is used to find a tour whose path is a list of edges. For each edge in the path, the code determines the city that hasn't been added to the `path_indices` list yet and adds it. Finally, the path of the tour is updated to be the `path_indices` list, which is a list of city names instead of edges:

```
evaporation_rate = 0.5                      ⌐ ACO parameters
iterations = 100
Q = 100

solver = acopy.Solver(rho=evaporation_rate, q=Q)  ◄─── Set up the ACO solver.

colony = acopy.Colony(alpha=1, beta=0.9)  ◄──── Set up the ACO colony with
                                                 alpha and beta parameters.
for n_iter in range(iterations):     ◄── Run the ACO algorithm.
    tour = solver.solve(G, colony, limit=4)
    path_indices = ['New York City']   ◄──── Start with city 0 (New York City).
    for edge in tour.path:
        next_city = edge[0] if edge[1] == path_indices[-1] else edge[1]
        if next_city not in path_indices:        ◄── Add the other node from the
            path_indices.append(next_city)            edge that is not already in
                                                      the path.
    tour.path=path_indices  ◄──── Return the ordered list of city names included in the path.
```

Let's now print the obtained path and its length as follows:

```
best_path = tour.path
best_distance = tour.cost
Route = " → ".join(best_path)
print("Route:", Route)
print("Route length:", np.round(best_distance, 3))
```

The `best_path` variable is set to the `path` property of the `tour` object obtained by the acopy solver. This path is a list of cities that represents the shortest route found. The `best_distance` variable is set to the `cost` property of the `tour` object, which is the total distance (or cost) of the best path. The `Route` variable is a string that joins all the cities in `best_path` with an arrow (→) in between, representing the sequence of cities to visit in the optimal tour. Finally, the `print` statements display the best route and its total distance. A path like the following will be generated after running the solver:

```
Route: New York City → Columbus → Detroit → Philadelphia → Baltimore →
Charlotte → Jacksonville → Memphis → Houston → Dallas → Fort Worth → Austin →
San Antonio → Phoenix → San Diego → Los Angeles → San Jose → San Francisco →
Chicago → Indianapolis
Route length: 11058.541
```

The obtained path is shown in figure 10.13. The complete version of listing 10.1 available in the book's GitHub repo contains the code to generate this visualization.

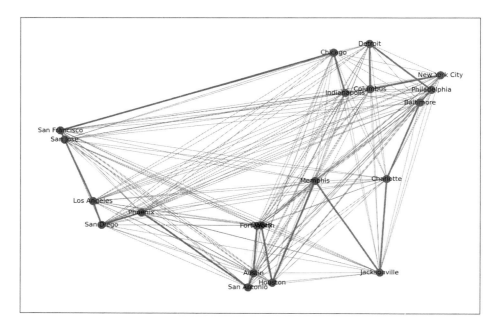

Figure 10.13   Shortest path obtained by ACOpy

It's worth mentioning that ACO, like many other stochastic optimization algorithms, contains elements of randomness. The randomness in ACO comes from two main sources:

- *Initial conditions*—At the start of the algorithm, the ants are usually placed at random positions unless the start position is predefined, such as in the case of TSP where ants start from a predetermined home city. This means that in scenarios where random positions are used, each ant starts exploring from a different city, leading to diverse paths.
- *Path selection*—As the ants move from city to city, they probabilistically choose which city to visit next. This choice is influenced by the amount of pheromones on the path to a city and the distance to the city. Even if two ants are in the same city and have the same information, they might still choose different cities to visit next due to this probabilistic choice.

This inherent randomness means that each run of the ACO algorithm can produce different results. However, over multiple runs, ACO should consistently find near-optimal solutions, even if they are not always the exact same solution.

In the following section, we will delve into another fascinating algorithm that is a product of swarm intelligence. This algorithm again takes its inspiration from the natural world, specifically the food-seeking behavior of honeybees. You'll soon understand how this bee-inspired algorithm operates and how it can be applied in a computational context.

10.4   *From hive to optimization*

Honeybees are remarkable social insects known for their extraordinary cooperation. They build hives capable of accommodating approximately 30,000 bees, all working together harmoniously. Each bee has a designated task, such as producing wax, creating honey, making bee-bread, forming combs, or bringing water to the cells and mixing it with honey. Young bees typically handle tasks outside the hive, while elder bees focus on indoor duties.

Honeybee colonies operate as goal-oriented decision-making systems, with their functions directed by the decentralized control and actions of individual bees. The cooperation between honeybees during the foraging process leads to advantageous behaviors that optimize the hive's overall fitness. By using individual foragers, honeybee colonies aim to minimize the cost/benefit ratio, rather than expending energy searching in all directions indiscriminately. They concentrate their foraging efforts on the most rewarding patches, while disregarding those of lesser quality.

Observations have shown that when colony food resources are scarce, foragers exhibit increased recruitment behaviors, characterized by changes in their dance patterns upon returning to the hive. This enhanced recruitment serves to mobilize more nestmates to exploit available food sources. In addition to foraging, honeybees also cooperate in various other tasks, such as hive construction, hive thermoregulation, and colony defense, showcasing their exceptional teamwork skills.

Discover the fascinating world of honeybees

- Honeybees are the most well-known and important insects that produce food consumed by humans.
- Honeybee colonies consist of a single queen, hundreds of male drones, and 20,000 to 80,000 female worker bees.
- A single worker bee may visit 50 to 1,000 flowers per day. Bees from the same hive can visit up to 225,000 flowers in one day. Honeybees can fly at speeds of 21 to 28 km/h (13–17 mph) and can have a foraging area up to 70 km^2 (27 mi^2).
- Honeybees can maintain a constant temperature of about 33°C (91°F) in their hive, regardless of the outside temperature.
- Honeybees choose the hexagonal shape for their honeycomb cells to hold the queen bee's eggs and store the pollen and honey the worker bees bring to the hive.

(continued)

- The hexagonal structure has several advantages, such as efficient use of space (creating the maximum number of cells that can be built in a given area), structural strength (it's strong and stable), material efficiency (it uses less beeswax), and optimal angle (a slight tilt, ~13 degrees from horizontal, to prevent honey from spilling out of the cells while still allowing bees to move around easily).
- Honeybees communicate with each other through complex dance moves called "waggle dances," explained in "The Waggle Dance of the Honeybee," a video from Georgia Tech College of Computing (http://mng.bz/gvxx).

The artificial bee colony (ABC) algorithm is a swarm intelligence algorithm based on the foraging behavior of honeybees. Specifically, it is inspired by the way honeybees search for food sources and communicate their findings to optimize the gathering of resources. Let's first look at how honeybees forage for food. Figure 10.14 illustrates the steps of their foraging behavior.

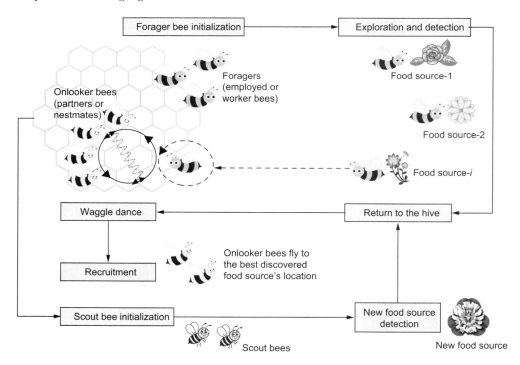

Figure 10.14   Foraging behavior of honeybees

The foraging behavior can be summarized in the following steps:

1   *Initialization*—Forager bees (employed bees) and scout bees begin their foraging for food sources. Forager bees usually gather resources from known sources around the hive to meet the colony's immediate needs. Scout bees locate new food sources to ensure the colony's long-term survival, especially if the food sources around the hive start to deplete. Scout bees only represent a small percentage of colony members, but they save the colony many wasted miles of flight trying to locate abundant new food sources. It is worth noting that forager bees and scout bees are both worker bees (female bees). A worker bee can switch roles from being a forager to a scout, depending on the colony's needs and food source availability. In summary, forager bees concentrate on exploiting the available resources while scout bees focus on exploring to discover new resources.

2   *Exploration*—Forager bees leave the hive and start searching for food sources, such as flowers with nectar and pollen, in the surrounding area. Scout bees explore areas farther away to discover new food sources.

3   *Detection*—When a suitable food source is found, the worker bee lands on the flower and begins to collect nectar in her honey stomach or gathers pollen on her hind legs.

4   *Memorization*—The bee takes note of the food source's location, including its distance and direction from the hive, as well as the flower type and quality.

5   *Return to the hive*—Once the worker bee has collected enough resources or her honey stomach is full, she flies back to the hive. Upon reaching the hive, the forager bee transfers the nectar to a house bee, who then processes and stores it as honey. Pollen is similarly offloaded to other bees for storage and later use as food.

6   *Communication*—The worker bee performs a waggle dance on the hive's dance floor to share the location information with her nestmates (aka *onlooker bees*). The dance communicates the direction, distance, and quality of the food source.

7   *Recruitment*—Onlooker bees observe the waggle dance and decode the information about the food source's location. These bees then fly out to collect the resources.

8   *Repeat*—The worker bee continues to visit the same food source until it is depleted or another bee recruits her to a more promising source. In either case, she repeats the foraging process to ensure the colony's needs are met.

Now let's look at the ABC algorithm in more detail.

10.5   Exploring the artificial bee colony algorithm

The artificial bee colony (ABC) algorithm, proposed by Dervis Karaboga in 2005 [1], simulates the roles of three types of bees: employed bees (foragers), onlooker bees, and scout bees. Algorithm 10.1 shows the steps of the ABC algorithm.

Algorithm 10.1   Artificial bee colony algorithm

```
Initialization Phase: population of candidate solutions (food sources) are
initialized
REPEAT
   Forager Bee Phase: Each forager bee goes to a food source in her memory
and determines a closest source, then evaluates its nectar amount and dances
in the hive
   Onlooker Bee Phase: Each onlooker bee watches the dance of forager bees
and chooses one of their sources depending on the dances, and then goes to
that source. After choosing a neighbor around that, she evaluates its nectar
amount.
   Scout Bee Phase: Abandoned food sources are determined and are replaced
with the new food sources discovered by scout bees.
   Memorize the best food source (solution) achieved so far.
UNTIL (termination criteria are met)
```

As you can see, the ABC algorithm simulates the honeybee foraging behaviors to explore and exploit the search space, balancing global exploration (diversity) and local exploitation (convergence) to efficiently solve optimization problems. In the ABC algorithm, the three types of bees have the following complementary roles:

- *Employed bees (foragers)*—These bees exploit the current food sources, meaning they search around their current position (searching the neighborhood) to find better solutions. These bees perform a local search (intensification), which refines the current best solutions.

- *Onlooker bees*—These bees also contribute to exploitation. They probabilistically choose food sources depending on the fitness of the solutions found by the employed bees. They are more likely to choose better solutions (food sources with more nectar) for further exploitation.

- *Scout bees*—These bees perform the exploration. If a food source is exhausted (if the solution cannot be improved after a certain number of iterations), the employed bee associated with that food source becomes a scout bee. Scout bees perform a global search (diversification) by abandoning the exhausted food source and randomly searching for new food sources in the problem space. This process prevents the algorithm from getting stuck in local optima by exploring new regions of the search space.

In the ABC algorithm, communication between the bees is simulated by sharing the fitness values of solutions among employed and onlooker bees, guiding them toward better solutions. The ABC algorithm adopts a fitness-proportionate selection process inspired by how bees choose food sources based on their quality. In the algorithm, employed bees and onlooker bees select solutions with a probability proportional to their fitness, promoting better solutions to be explored more frequently.

To understand how we can use ABC to solve optimization problems, let's consider minimizing the Rosenbrock function using ABC. The Rosenbrock function, also referred to as the *valley* or *banana function,* is a popular test problem for gradient-based optimization algorithms. This function has n dimensions and takes the following general form:

$$f(x) = \sum_{i=1}^{n-1} \left(100 \times \left(x_{i+1} - x_i^2 \right)^2 + (x_i - 1)^2 \right)$$

10.12

The function is usually evaluated on the hypercube $x_i \in [-5, 10]$ for all $i = 1,...,n$, but the domain may be restricted to $x_i \in [-2.048, 2.048]$ for all $i = 1,...,n$. This function has a global minimum at $f(x^*) = 0.0$ located at $(1,...,1)$.

Let's consider the 2D Rosenbrock function that takes the following form:

$$f(x, y) = 100 \times \left(y - x^2 \right)^2 + (1 + x)^2$$

10.13

Figure 10.15 shows the 2D surface of Rosenbrock function.

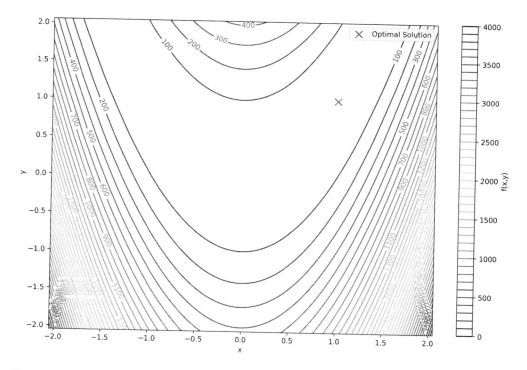

Figure 10.15   **The 2D surface plot of the Rosenbrock function. The dot indicates the global minimum of this function.**

Let's look at how we can minimize this function using ABC:

- *Initialization phase*—Let's assume that we have a swarm of $N = 6$ bees. Each bee tries to find a candidate solution, and each solution i in the population consists of a position vector $X_{mi} = \{x_{mi}, y_{mi}\}$ where $X_{mi} \in [-2.048, 2.048]$ and $m = 1,...,N$. X_{mi} represents a potential solution to the optimization problem. The position of the employed bees is randomly determined within the boundaries. These initial solutions can be generated using the following formula:

$$x_{mi} = l_i + rand(0,\ 1) \times (u_i - l_i)$$ **10.14**

where l_i and u_i are the lower and upper bounds of the decision variables. Let's assume the initial positions (represented as (x, y)) shown in table 10.1.

Table 10.1   Initial food sources

Candidate solution X_m	Objective function $f_m(X_m)$
$X_1 = (-1.04, 0.11)$	98.56
$X_2 = (-1.61, -1.98)$	2097.22
$X_3 = (1.82, 1.22)$	438.49
$X_4 = (-1.64, 1.92)$	66.20
$X_5 = (0.77, 0.04)$	30.62
$X_6 = (-0.66, 1.59)$	136.02

- *Employed bee phase*—In the employed bee phase, each bee generates a new solution in the neighborhood of its current solution using the following formula:

$$v_{mi} = x_{mi} + \phi_{mi} \times (x_{mi} - x_{ki})$$ **10.15**

where v_{mj} is the new solution, x_{mi} is the current solution, ϕ_{mi} is a random number between -1 and 1, and x_{ki} is a randomly chosen solution different from the current solution. Let's assume that all ϕ_{mi} are -0.9 for simplicity, and for each bee, we choose the solution of bee 1 to calculate the new solutions. The best bee, in the initial population (table 10.1), bee 5, can also be used. We then calculate the new fitness values shown in table 10.2.

Table 10.2   New food sources

Candidate solution X_m	Objective function $f_m(X_m)$
$X_1 = (-1.04, 0.11)$	98.56
$X_2 = (-1.10, -0.10)$	174.02
$X_3 = (-0.75, 0.22)$	15.15
$X_4 = (-1.10, 0.29)$	88.87
$X_5 = (-0.86, 0.10)$	43.76
$X_6 = (-1.00, 0.26)$	59.66

- *Onlooker bee phase*—The onlooker bees observe the dance of the employed bees and choose a food source depending on the nectar amount (the *fitness value*). If the new solution has a better fitness value, it is remembered as a global variable, and the position is updated. Otherwise, the old position is retained. The probability value p_m, with which X_m is chosen by an onlooker bee, can be calculated by using the following formula:

$$p_m = \frac{fit_m(X_m)}{\sum_{m=1}^{N} fit_m(X_m)}$$

10.16

where $fit_m(X_m)$ is the fitness value of the solution, which can be calculated using the following expression:

$$fit_m(X_m) = \begin{cases} \frac{1}{1+f_m(X_m)} & \text{if } f_m(X_m) \geq 0 \\ 1 + \text{abs}(f_m(X_m)) & \text{otherwise} \end{cases}$$

10.17

where $f_m(X_m)$ is the objective function of solution X_m. Table 10.3 shows the solution fitness calculations.

Table 10.3 Solution fitness calculations

Candidate solution X_m	Objective function $f_m(X_m)$	Fitness $fit_m(X_m)$	Probability of selection p_m
$X_1 = (-1.04, 0.11)$	98.56	0.010	0.08
$X_2 = (-1.10, -0.10)$	174.02	0.006	0.04
$X_3 = (-0.75, 0.22)$	15.15	0.062	0.49
$X_4 = (-1.10, 0.29)$	88.87	0.011	0.09
$X_5 = (-0.86, 0.10)$	43.76	0.022	0.18
$X_6 = (-1.00, 0.26)$	59.66	0.016	0.13

In this example, the food source discovered by bee 3 is most likely to be chosen. After a food source X_m for an onlooker bee is probabilistically chosen, a neighborhood source v_m is determined by using equation 10.15, and its fitness value is computed.

- *Scout bee phase*—If a position cannot be improved further through a predetermined number of cycles or trials (called the *limit*), that position is abandoned and the bee becomes a scout, searching for a new random position, which can be generated by equation 10.14.

Let's now see how we can implement ABC in Python to solve this problem. In the next listing, we start by importing the libraries we'll use and defining the `rosenbrock_function`. This function takes as an argument a candidate solution (x, y) to the Rosenbrock function and returns its value.

> **Listing 10.2   Solving Rosenbrock function optimization using ABC**

```
import numpy as np
import random
import matplotlib.pyplot as plt

def rosenbrock_function(cand_soln):
    return (1 - cand_soln[0]) ** 2 + 100 * (cand_soln[1] - cand_soln[0] ** 2)
** 2
```

As a continuation of listing 10.2, we'll create a `Bee` that contains the following attributes:

- `position`—The position of the bee in the search space (solution)
- `fitness`—The fitness of the bee's current position (the value of the Rosenbrock function at the current position)
- `counter`—A counter to track the number of unsuccessful trials (iterations without improvement in the bee's fitness):

```
class Bee:
    def __init__(self, position, fitness):
        self.position = position
        self.fitness = fitness
        self.counter = 0
```

Now we need a function to generate a `Bee` with a random position and calculate its fitness using the Rosenbrock function:

```
def generate_bee(dimensions):
    position = np.array([random.uniform(-5, 5) for _ in range(dimensions)])
    fitness = rosenbrock_function(position)
    return Bee(position, fitness)
```

The following function will update the position of a given bee using the position of a partner bee. If the new position has a better fitness value, the bee's position, fitness, and counter are updated. Otherwise, the counter is incremented:

```
def update_position(bee, partner, dimensions):
    index = random.randrange(dimensions)      ◀── Determine which element of the
    phi = random.uniform(-1, 1)                    bee's position will be updated.
    new_position = bee.position.copy()
    new_position[index] += phi * (bee.position[index] - partner.
position[index])
    new_position = np.clip(new_position, -5, 5)  ◀── Clip to ensure it stays
    new_fitness = rosenbrock_function(new_position)   within a specified range.
    if new_fitness < bee.fitness:
        bee.position = new_position
        bee.fitness = new_fitness
        bee.counter = 0
    else:
        bee.counter += 1
```

Next, we'll define an `abc_algorithm` function to implement the ABC algorithm with the following input parameters:

- `dimensions`—The number of dimensions of the problem, which is 2 for the Rosenbrock function
- `num_bees`—The total number of bees in the colony
- `max_iter`—The maximum number of iterations the algorithm should run
- `max_trials`—The maximum number of unsuccessful cycles or trials (iterations without improvement) allowed before a bee becomes a scout bee:

```
def abc_algorithm(dimensions, num_bees, max_iter, max_trials):

    bees = [generate_bee(dimensions) for _ in range(num_bees)]    ◄──
    best_bee = min(bees, key=lambda bee: bee.fitness)    ◄──

    for _ in range(max_iter):        Find the bee with the best fitness value.
        for i in range(num_bees // 2):        Generate an initial population of bees.
            employed_bee = bees[i]
            partner_bee = random.choice(bees)
            update_position(employed_bee, partner_bee, dimensions)

        total_fitness = sum(1 / (1 + bee.fitness) if bee.fitness >= 0 else 1
        + abs(bee.fitness) for bee in bees)
        probabilities = [(1 / (1 + bee.fitness)) / total_fitness if bee.
        fitness >= 0 else (1 + abs(bee.fitness)) / total_fitness for bee in bees]

        for i in range(num_bees // 2, num_bees):    ◄──
            onlooker_bee = random.choices(bees, weights=probabilities)[0]
            partner_bee = min(bees[:num_bees // 2], key=lambda bee: bee.
    fitness)

            update_position(onlooker_bee, partner_bee, dimensions)

        for bee in bees:        Calculate the selection probability according equations 16 and 17.
            if bee.counter > max_trials:    ◄──
                new_bee = generate_bee(dimensions)        Check if each bee's counter
                bee.position = new_bee.position        exceeds max_trials.
                bee.fitness = new_bee.fitness
                bee.counter = 0

        best_iter_bee = min(bees, key=lambda bee: bee.fitness)
        if best_iter_bee.fitness < best_bee.fitness:
            best_bee = best_iter_bee

    return best_bee    ◄──    Return best_bee, which represents the optimal solution.
```

Perform the employed bees phase.

Perform the onlooker bees phase.

Perform the scout bees phase.

Update best_bee with the new best bee.

Now we can set up the parameters of the ABC algorithm and apply it to solve the problem:

Define the problem dimensions.

```
dimensions = 2    ◄──
num_bees = 50        Set the maximum number of iterations used as a stopping criterion.
max_iter = 1000    ◄──
max_trials = 100    ◄──
```

Set the number of bees.

Set the maximum number of unsuccessful trials (iterations without improvement) allowed before a bee becomes a scout bee.

```
best_bee = abc_algorithm(dimensions, num_bees, max_iter, max_trials)
print(f"Best solution: {best_bee.position}")
print(f"Best fitness: {best_bee.fitness}")
```

Print the position of best_bee, which represents the solution and its fitness, which is the value of the Rosenbrock function at the best solution.

Run the ABC algorithm with the parameters specified and store the best bee (the one with the minimum fitness value) in the best_bee variable.

This code will produce output like the following:

```
Best solution: [0.99766117 0.99542949]
Best fitness: 6.50385257086524e-06
```

In contrast to genetic algorithms and particle swarm optimization algorithms, the availability of well-established and comprehensive Python packages specifically designed for the ABC algorithm is relatively limited. However, there is a Python library called MEALPY that offers implementations of population-based metaheuristic algorithms, including ABC. You can install MEALPY using `pip install mealpy`.

As a continuation of listing 10.2, the following code snippet demonstrates using the `OriginalABC` class from the MEALPY library to minimize the Rosenbrock function:

```
from mealpy.swarm_based.ABC import OriginalABC
```
Import the solver from MEALPY library.

```
problem_dict = {
    "fit_func": rosenbrock_function,
    "lb": [-5, -5],
    "ub": [5, 5],
    "minmax": "min",
}
```
Define the problem using dictionary.
Set the number of epochs (iterations).
Set the population size.
Create an instance of the algorithm class.

```
epoch = 200
pop_size = 50
n_limits = 15
```
Set the limit on the number of unsuccessful trials before a scout bee is triggered.

```
model = OriginalABC(epoch, pop_size, n_limits)
```
Run the algorithm.

```
best_position_mealpy, best_fitness_mealpy = model.solve(problem_dict)
```

```
print(f"Best solution: {best_position_mealpy}")
print(f"Best fitness: {best_fitness_mealpy}")
```
Print the results.

We start by importing the `OriginalABC` class from the `mealpy.swarm_based.ABC` module, which is the implementation of the ABC algorithm provided by the MEALPY library. We then define the problem dictionary, which contains the cost function (`fit_func`), lower bound (`lb`), upper bound (`ub`), and whether this is a minimization or maximization problem (`minmax`). The number of epochs (iterations), population size, and the limit on the number of unsuccessful trials before a scout bee is triggered are set. We then create an instance of the `OriginalABC` class, initialized with the specified parameters. The `solve()` method is called on the `model` object, passing the `problem_dict` as an argument. It performs the ABC algorithm optimization process on the defined problem and returns the best solution and fitness value.

Running this code will produce a solution like the following:

```
Best solution: [1.07313697 1.04914444]
Cost at best solution: 0.0009197449137428784
```

Figure 10.16 shows the solution obtained by the ABC solver, ABC MEALPLY, and the ACO solver implemented as part of the complete listing 10.2.

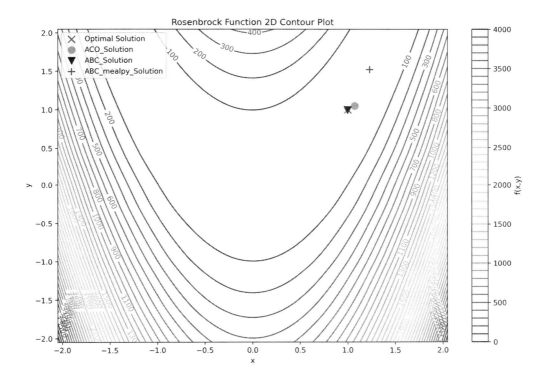

Figure 10.16   The Rosenbrock function contour and solutions using the ABC and ACO algorithms

As you can see, the ABC, ABC MEALPY, and ACO solutions are all close to the optimal solution of this function. With parameter tuning, an optimal solution can be reached by these algorithms. You can use the code in listing 10.2 to experiment with different algorithm parameter settings and different problem dimensions.

This chapter concludes the fourth part of this book. In this part, we've delved deep into the fascinating world of swarm intelligence, exploring how simple entities, like birds in particle swarm optimization (PSO), ants in ant colony optimization (ACO), and bees in the artificial bee colony (ABC) algorithm, can collectively perform complex tasks. These nature-inspired algorithms elegantly balance exploration and exploitation to find optimal or near-optimal solutions to complex optimization problems.

As we move forward, we'll transition to the domain of machine learning. In the last part of this book, we'll look at machine learning methods specifically tailored for search and optimization. We'll explore cutting-edge techniques, such as graph neural networks, attention mechanisms, self-organizing maps, and reinforcement learning, and investigate their applications in search and optimization.

Summary

- Ant colony optimization (ACO) is a population-based algorithm inspired by the foraging behavior of ants. Simple ACO (SACO), ant system (AS), ant colony system (ACS), and max–min ant system (MMAS) are examples of ACO metaheuristics algorithms.

- During foraging, ants discover good solutions, which influence the decisions of other ants. Over time, the pheromone trails intensify along the paths of better solutions, attracting more ants to explore those paths. This is called autocatalytic behavior.

- Pheromone updates include two phases: evaporation and deposit. During the evaporation phase, the pheromone concentration is decreased. Ants can deposit pheromones during the construction of a solution, using the online step-by-step pheromone update method, or after the solution has been built, by revisiting all the states visited during the construction process, using the online delayed pheromone update method. In some cases, both methods can be used together.

- Ant system (AS) improves on simple ACO by adding a memory capability in the form of a tabu list.

- The ant colony system (ACS) algorithm is an extension of the AS algorithm with a modified transition rule that utilizes an elitist strategy.

- The max–min ant system (MMAS) addresses the limitations of AS and ACS by using the iteration-best path for pheromone updates, encouraging exploration and constraining pheromone values between minimum and maximum values. This approach reduces the risk of premature stagnation and improves performance by balancing exploration and exploitation.

- The artificial bee colony (ABC) algorithm is a population-based search algorithm inspired by the foraging behavior of honeybees. The ABC algorithm manages the balance between exploration and exploitation through its three types of bees (employed bees, onlooker bees, and scout bees), each of which perform different complementary roles.

- The inherent randomness in stochastic optimization algorithms due to initial conditions and the probabilistic decision-making process is not necessarily a bad thing. It can help the algorithm avoid getting stuck in local optima—solutions that are the best in their immediate vicinity but are not the best overall. By occasionally taking less promising paths, the algorithm can explore more of the solution space and has a better chance of finding the global optimum—the best possible solution.

Part 5

Machine learning-based methods

In this final part of the book, comprising two chapters, you'll delve into the dynamic world of machine learning techniques and how they can be harnessed to solve complex optimization problems.

In chapter 11, you'll learn how to use the power of artificial intelligence, machine learning, and deep learning to tackle optimization problems. We'll start with a refresher on these foundational concepts, ensuring you have a strong grounding. You'll then delve into the exciting field of graph machine learning, graph embedding, graph convolutional networks, and attention mechanisms, which are invaluable in solving optimization problems with graph-structured data. Additionally, you'll explore self-organizing maps, uncovering their role in optimization tasks. By the end of this chapter, you'll be well-equipped to apply supervised and unsupervised machine learning techniques to handle optimization problems.

Chapter 12 delves into the fascinating realm of reinforcement learning (RL). You'll grasp the fundamental principles underlying RL, understand the concept of a Markov decision process, and delve into the actor-critic architecture and proximal policy optimization algorithms. You'll also become acquainted with multi-armed bandits and contextual bandits and learn how these techniques can be applied to solve optimization problems, where decisions lead to optimal outcomes.

In this part, you'll bridge the gap between machine learning and optimization, gaining insights into how machine learning can be harnessed to find optimal solutions efficiently. This is where the synergy between machine learning and optimization unlocks a new horizon and a shift toward data-driven and intelligent problem-solving.

Supervised and unsupervised learning

This chapter covers

- Reviewing the basics of artificial intelligence, machine learning, and deep learning
- Understanding graph machine learning, graph embedding, and graph convolutional networks
- Understanding attention mechanisms
- Understanding self-organizing maps
- Solving optimization problems using supervised and unsupervised machine learning

Artificial intelligence (AI) is one of the fastest growing fields of technology, driven by advancements in computing power, access to vast amounts of data, breakthroughs in algorithms, and increased investment from both public and private sectors. AI aims to create intelligent systems or machines that can exhibit intelligent behavior, often by mimicking or drawing inspiration from biological intelligence. These systems can be designed to function autonomously or with some human guidance, and ideally, they can adapt to environments with diverse structures, observability levels, and dynamics. AI augments our intelligence by empowering us to analyze vast amounts of multidimensional, multimodal data and identify hidden patterns that would be difficult for humans to recognize. AI also supports our learning and decision-making by providing relevant insights and potential courses of action. AI encompasses various subfields, such as situation awareness (comprising perception, comprehension, and projection), knowledge representation, cognitive reasoning, machine learning, data analytics (covering descriptive, diagnostic, predictive, and prescriptive analytics), problem solving (involving constraint satisfaction and problem-solving using search and optimization), as well as digital and physical automation (such as conversational AI and robotics).

In this last part of the book, we will explore the convergence of two branches of AI: machine learning and optimization. Our focus will be on showcasing the practical applications of machine learning in tackling optimization problems. This chapter provides an overview of machine learning fundamentals as essential background knowledge, and then it delves into applications of supervised and unsupervised machine learning in handling optimization problems. Reinforcement learning will be covered in the next chapter.

11.1 A day in the life of AI-empowered daily routines

AI, and machine learning in particular, forms the foundation of many successful disruptive industries and has successfully delivered many commercial products that touch everybody's life every day. Starting at home, voice assistants eagerly await your commands, effortlessly controlling smart appliances and adjusting the smart thermostat to ensure comfort and convenience. Smart meters intelligently manage energy consumption, optimizing efficiency and reducing costs.

On the route to school or work, navigation apps with location intelligence guide the way, considering real-time traffic updates to provide the fastest and most efficient route. Shared mobility services offer flexible transportation options on demand, while advanced driver assistance systems enhance safety and convenience if you decide to drive. In the not-too-distant future, we will enjoy safe and entertaining self-driving vehicles as a third living space, after our homes and workplaces, with consumer-centric products and services.

Once at school or at the workplace, AI becomes an invaluable tool for personalization and to boost productivity. Personalized learning platforms cater to individual needs, adapting teaching methods and content to maximize understanding and retention. Summarization and grammar-checking algorithms aid in crafting flawless documents, while translation tools bridge language barriers effortlessly. Excel AI formula generators streamline complex calculations, saving time and effort. Human-like text generation enables natural and coherent writing, while audio, image, and video generation from text unlock creative possibilities. Optimization algorithms ensure optimal resource allocation and scheduling, maximizing efficiency in various scenarios, and handle different design, planning, and control problems.

During shopping, AI enhances the experience in numerous ways. Voice search enables hands-free exploration, while searching by images allows for effortless discovery of desired items. Semantic search understands context and intent, providing more accurate results. Recommendation engines offer personalized suggestions based on individual preferences and online shopping behavior, while last-mile or door-to-door delivery services ensure timely, transparent, and convenient package arrival.

In the realm of health, AI revolutionizes personalized healthcare, assisting with diagnosis, treatment planning, and rehabilitation. Lab automation speeds up testing processes, improving accuracy and efficiency. AI-driven drug discovery and delivery enable the development of innovative treatments and targeted therapies, transforming lives.

During leisure time, AI contributes to physical and mental well-being. Fitness planning apps tailor workout routines to individual goals and capabilities, providing personalized guidance and motivation. Trip planning tools recommend exciting destinations and itineraries, ensuring memorable experiences. AI-powered meditation apps offer customized relaxation experiences, soothing the mind and promoting mindfulness.

Machine learning, a prominent subfield of artificial intelligence, has played a pivotal role in bringing AI from the confines of high-tech research labs to the convenience of our daily lives.

11.2 Demystifying machine learning

The goal of learning is to create an internal model or abstraction of the external world. More comprehensively, Stanislas Dehaene, in *How We Learn* [1], introduced seven key definitions of learning that lie at the heart of present-day machine learning algorithms:

- Learning is adjusting the parameters of a mental model.
- Learning is exploring a combinatorial explosion.
- Learning is minimizing errors.
- Learning is exploring the space of possibilities.
- Learning is optimizing a reward function.
- Learning is restricting search space.
- Learning is projecting a priori hypotheses.

Machine learning (ML) is a subfield of AI that endows an artificial system or process with the ability to learn from experience and observation without being explicitly programmed. Thomas Mitchell, in *Machine Learning*, defines ML as follows: "A computer program is said to learn from experience E with respect to some class of tasks T and performance measure P, if its performance at tasks in T, as measured by P, improves with experience E" [2]. In his book *The Master Algorithm*, Pedro Domingos summarizes the ML schools of thought into five main schools [3], illustrated in figure 11.1:

- Bayesians with probabilistic inference as the master algorithm
- Symbolists with rules and trees as the main core algorithm within this paradigm
- Connectionists who use neural networks with backpropagation as a master algorithm
- Evolutionaries who rely on the evolutionary computing paradigm
- Analogizers who use mathematical techniques like support vector machines with different kernels

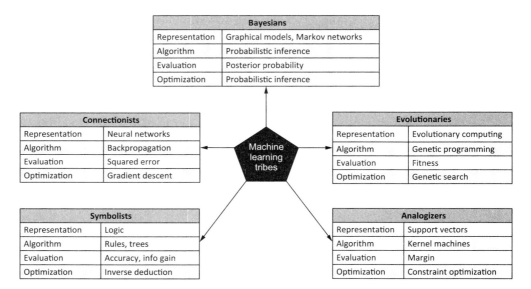

Figure 11.1   Different ML schools of thought according to Domingos' *The Master Algorithm*

Nowadays, connectionist learning approaches have attracted most of the attention, thanks to their perception and learning capabilities in several challenging domains. These statistical ML algorithms follow a bottom-up inductive reasoning paradigm (i.e., inferring general rules from a set of examples) to discover patterns from vast amounts of data.

The unreasonable effectiveness of data

Simple models and a lot of data trump more elaborate models based on less data [4]. This means that having a large amount of data to train simple models is often more effective than using complex models with only a small amount of data. For example, in self-driving vehicles, a simple model that has been trained on millions of hours of driving data can often be more effective in recognizing and reacting to diverse road situations than a more complex model trained on a smaller dataset. This is because the massive amount of data helps the simple model learn a wide range of patterns and scenarios, including adversarial and edge cases it might encounter, making it more adaptable and reliable in real-world driving conditions.

These connectionist learning or statistical ML approaches are based on the experimental findings that even very complex problems in artificial intelligence may be solved by simple statistical models trained on massive datasets [4]. Statistical ML is currently the most famous form of AI. The rapid advancement of this form of ML can be attributed primarily to the widespread availability of big data and open source tools, enhanced computational power such as AI accelerators, and substantial research and development funding from both public and private sectors.

Generally speaking, ML algorithms can be categorized into supervised, unsupervised, hybrid learning, and reinforcement learning algorithms, as illustrated in figure 11.2.

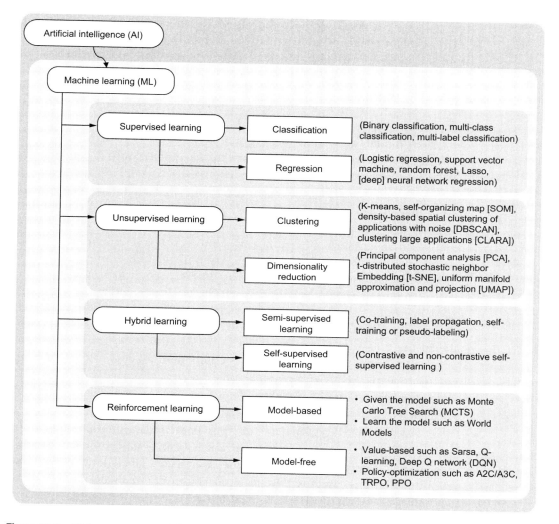

Figure 11.2 ML taxonomy as a subfield of AI

- *Supervised learning*—This approach uses inductive inference to approximate mapping functions between data and known labels or classes. This mapping is learned using already labeled training data. *Classification* (predicting discrete or categorical values) and *regression* (predicting continuous values) are common tasks in supervised learning. For example, classification seeks a scoring function $f: X \times C \rightarrow R$, where X represents the training data space and C represents the label or class space. This mapping can be learned using N training examples of the form $\{(x_{11}, x_{21}, \ldots, x_{m1}, c_1), (x_{12}, x_{22}, \ldots, x_{m2}, c_2), \ldots, (x_{1N}, x_{2N}, \ldots, x_{mN}, c_N)\}$, where x_i is the feature vector of the i-th example, m is number of features, and c_i is the corresponding class. The predicted class is the class that gives the highest score of f, i.e., $c(x) = \text{argmax}_c f(x,c)$. In the context of self-driving vehicles, supervised learning might be used to train a model to recognize traffic signs. The input data would be images of various traffic signs, and the correct output (the labels) would be the type of each sign. The trained model could then identify traffic signs correctly when driving. Feedforward neural networks (FNNs) or multilayer perceptrons (MLPs), convolutional neural networks (CNNs), recurrent neural networks (RNNs), long short-term memory (LSTM) networks, and sequence-to-sequence (Seq2Seq) models are examples of common neural network architectures that are typically trained using supervised learning. Examples of solving combinatorial problems using supervised ML are provided in sections 11.6, 11.7, and 11.9.

- *Unsupervised learning*—This approach deals with unlabeled data through techniques like *clustering* and *dimensionality reduction*. In clustering, for example, n objects (each could be a vector of d features) are given, and the task is to group them based on certain similarity measures into c groups (clusters) in such a way that all objects in a single group have a "natural" relation to one another, and objects not in the same group are somehow different. For instance, unsupervised learning might be used in self-driving vehicles to cluster similar driving scenarios or environments. Using unsupervised learning, the car might learn to identify different types of intersections or roundabouts, even if no one has explicitly labeled the data with these categories. Autoencoders, k-means, density-based spatial clustering (DBSCAN), principal component analysis (PCA), and self-organizing maps (SOMs) are examples of unsupervised learning methods. SOM is explained in section 11.4. An example of a combinatorial problem using SOM is provided in section 11.8.

- *Hybrid learning*—This approach includes *semi-supervised learning and self-supervised learning* techniques. Semi-supervised learning is a mix of supervised and unsupervised learning where only a fraction of the input data is labeled with corresponding outputs. In this case, the training process uses the small amount of labeled data available and pseudo-labels the rest of the dataset—for example, training a self-driving vehicle's perception system with a limited set of labeled driving scenarios, then using a vast collection of unlabeled driving data to improve its ability to recognize and respond to various road conditions and obstacles. Self-supervised learning is an ML process where a model learns meaningful representations of the input data by using the inherent structure or relationships within the data itself. This is achieved by creating supervised learning tasks from the unlabeled data. For instance, a self-supervised model might be trained to predict the next word in a sentence based on the previous words or to reconstruct an image from a scrambled version. These learned representations can then be used for various downstream tasks, such as image classification or object detection. In the context of self-driving vehicles, a perception system can be trained to identify essential features in unlabeled driving scenes, such as lane markings, pedestrians, and other vehicles. Then, the learned features are utilized as pseudo-labels to classify new driving scenes in a supervised manner, enabling the vehicle to make decisions based on its understanding of the road environment.

- *Reinforcement learning (RL)*—This approach learns from interactions through a feedback loop or by trial and error. A learning agent learns to make decisions by taking actions in an environment to maximize some notion of cumulative reward. For self-driving vehicles, reinforcement learning could be used in the decision-making process. For instance, the car might learn over time the best way to merge into traffic on a busy highway. It would receive positive rewards for successful merges and negative rewards for dangerous maneuvers or failed attempts. Over time, through trial and error and the desire to maximize the reward, the car would learn an optimal policy for merging into traffic. More details about RL are provided in the next chapter.

Deep learning (DL) is a subfield of ML concerned with learning underlying features in data using neural networks with many layers (hence "deep") enabling artificial systems to build complex concepts out of simpler concepts. DL enables learning discriminative features or representations and learning at different levels of abstraction. To achieve this, the network uses hierarchical feature learning and employs a handful of convolutional layers. DL revolutionizes the field of ML by reducing the need for extensive data preprocessing. DL models can automatically extract highly discriminative features from raw data, eliminating the need for hand-crafted feature engineering. This end-to-end learning process significantly reduces the reliance on human experts, as the model learns to extract meaningful representations and patterns directly from the input data.

Unlike traditional ML algorithms, DL models have the ability to directly consume and process various forms of structured and unstructured data, such as text, audio, images, video, and even graphs. Graph-structured data is particularly important in the field of combinatorial optimization due to its ability to capture and represent the relationships and constraints between elements in optimization problems. Geometric DL is a subfield of ML that combines graph theory with DL.

The following two sections address graph machine learning and self-organizing maps in more detail. They are essential background knowledge to the use cases described later in this chapter.

11.3 Machine learning with graphs

As explained in section 3.1, a graph is a nonlinear data structure composed of entities known as *vertices* (or nodes) and the relationships between them, known as *edges* (or *arcs* or *links*). Data coming from different domains can be nicely captured using a graph. Social media networks, for instance, employ graphs to depict connections between users and to analyze social interactions, which in turn drive content propagation and recommendations. Navigation applications use graphs to represent physical locations and the paths between them, enabling route calculations, real-time traffic updates, and estimated time of arrival (ETA) predictions. Recommender systems rely on graphs to model user–item interactions and preferences, thereby offering personalized recommendations. Search engines use web graphs, where web pages are nodes and hyperlinks are edges, to crawl and index the internet and facilitate efficient information retrieval. Knowledge graphs offer a structured representation of factual information, relationships, and entities, and they're used in diverse fields from digital assistants to enterprise data integration. Question-answering engines use graphs to understand and decompose complex questions and search for relevant answers in structured datasets. In the realm of chemistry, molecular structures can be viewed as graphs, where atoms are nodes and bonds are edges, supporting tasks like discovering compounds and predicting properties.

Graph-structured data is vital due to its power to model complex relationships and dependencies between entities in an intuitive, self-descriptive, intrinsically explainable, and natural way. Unlike traditional tabular data, graphs allow for the representation of networked relationships and complex interconnectedness between entities of interest, making them an excellent tool for modeling numerous real-world systems. Tabular data can be converted into graph-structured data—the specific definitions of nodes and edges would depend on what relationships you're interested in examining within the data. For example, in the context of a FIFA dataset, we can define nodes and edges based on the information available in this dataset:

- *Nodes*—Nodes represent entities of interest and could be the players, the clubs they play for, or their nationalities. Each of these entities could be a separate node in the graph. For example, Lionel Messi, Inter Miami, and Argentina could all be individual nodes in the graph.
- *Edges*—Edges represent the relationships between the nodes. For instance, an edge could connect a player to the club they play for, indicating that the player is part of that club. Another edge could connect a player to their nationality, showing that the player belongs to that country. So, for example, Lionel Messi could be connected to Inter Miami with an edge indicating that Messi plays for Inter Miami, and another edge could connect Lionel Messi to Argentina, indicating his nationality.

The next listing shows how to convert tabular data for 10 selected soccer players into a graph using NetworkX.

Listing 11.1   Converting tabular data to a graph

```
import pandas as pd
import networkx as nx
import matplotlib.pyplot as plt
```

```
data={'Player':['L. Messi','R. Lewandowski','C. Ronaldo','Neymar Jr','K.
➥ Mbappé','E.Haaland','H. Kane','Luka Modrić','L. Goretzka','M. Salah'],
➥     'Age':[36,34,38,22,24,35,29,37,28,31],
➥     'Nationality':['Argentina','Poland','Portugal','Brazil','France','Norway',
➥     'England','Croatia','Germany','Egypt'],
➥     'Club':['Inter Miami','Barcelona','Al-Nassr','Al-Hilal ','PSG','Manchester
➥     City','Tottenham Hotspur','Real Madrid','Bayern Munich','Liverpool'],
➥     'League':['Major League Soccer ','Spain Primera Division','Saudi Arabia
➥ League','Saudi Arabia League','French Ligue 1','English Premier
➥ League','English Premier League','Spain Primera Division','German 1.
➥ Bundesliga','English Premier League']}
df=pd.DataFrame.from_dict(data)
```

As a continuation of listing 11.1, we can create a NetworkX graph whose nodes represent the player name, club, and nationality and whose edges represent the semantic relationships between these nodes.

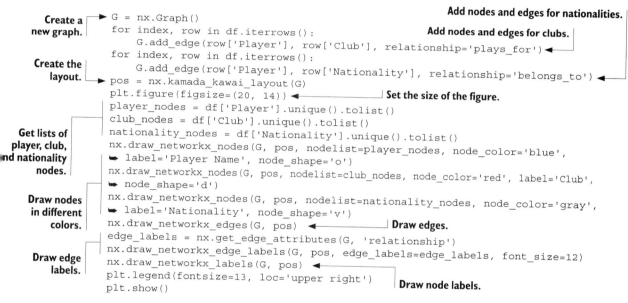

Figure 11.3 shows the data for the 10 selected soccer players in a graph. This graph shows the entities of interest (player, club, and nationality) and their relationships. For example, L. Messi is a player who plays for Inter Miami and is from Argentina.

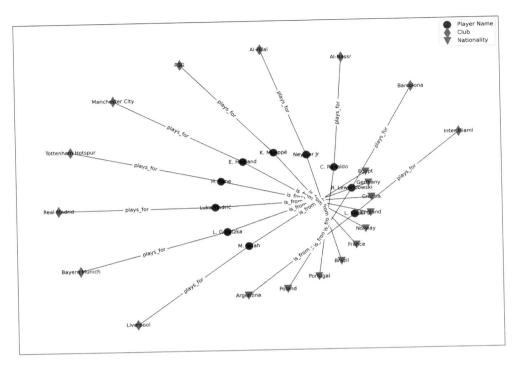

Figure 11.3   Graph-structured data for 10 selected soccer players

Graph data fundamentally differs from Euclidean data, as the concept of distance is not simply a matter of straight-line (Euclidean) distance between two points. In the case of a graph, what matters is the structure of the nodes and edges—whether two nodes are connected by an edge and how they are connected to other nodes in the graph. Table 11.1 summarizes the differences between Euclidean and non-Euclidean graph data.

Table 11.1   Euclidean data versus non-Euclidean graph data

Aspects	Euclidean data	Non-Euclidean graph data
Common data types	Numerical, text, audio, images, videos	Road networks, social networks, web pages, and molecular structures
Dimensionality	Can be 1D (e.g., numbers, text), 2D (e.g., images, heatmaps), or higher-dimensional (e.g., RGB-D images or depth maps, 3D point cloud data)	Large dimensionality (e.g., a Pinterest graph has 3 billion nodes and 18 billion edges)
Structure	Fixed structure (e.g., in the case of an image, the structure is embedded via pixel proximity)	Arbitrary structure (every node can have a different neural structure because the network neighborhood around it is different, as the model adapts to the data)

Table 11.1   Euclidean data versus non-Euclidean graph data (*continued*)

Aspects	Euclidean data	Non-Euclidean graph data
Spatial locality	Yes (i.e., data points that are close together in the input space are also likely to be close together in the output space).	No, "closeness" is determined by the graph structure, not spatial arrangement (i.e., two nodes that are "close" to each other might not necessarily have similar properties or features, such as in the case of a traffic light node and a crosswalk node).
Shift-invariance	Yes (i.e., data-inherent meaning is preserved when shifted; for instance, the concept of a cat in a picture does not change if the cat is in the top left corner or the bottom right corner of the image).	No (in a graph, there's no inherent meaning to the "position" of a node that can be "shifted").
Ordinality or hierarchy	Yes	No, graph data has "permutation invariance"—the specific ordering or labeling of nodes doesn't usually affect the underlying relationships and properties of the graph.
Shortest path between two points	A straight line	Is not necessarily a straight line
Examples of ML models	Convolutional neural networks (CNNs), long short-term memory (LSTM), and recurrent neural networks (RNNs)	Graph neural networks (GNNs), graph convolutional networks (GCNs), temporal graph networks (TGNs), spatial-temporal graph neural networks (STGNNs)

Geometric deep learning (GDL) is an umbrella term for emerging techniques seeking to extend (structured) deep neural models to handle non-Euclidean data with underlying geometric structures, such as graphs (networks of connected entities), point clouds (collections of 3D data points), molecules (chemical structures), and manifolds (curved, high-dimensional surfaces). Graph machine learning (GML) is a subfield of ML that focuses on developing algorithms and models capable of learning from graph-structured data. Graph embedding or representation learning is the first step in performing ML tasks such as node classification (predicting a category for each node), link prediction (forecasting connections between nodes), and community detection (identifying groups of interconnected nodes). The next subsection describes different graph embedding techniques.

11.3.1   Graph embedding

Graph embedding is a task that aims to learn a mapping from a discrete high-dimensional graph domain to a low-dimensional continuous domain. Through the process of graph embedding, graph nodes, edges, and their features are transformed into continuous vectors while preserving the structural information of the graph. For example, as shown in figure 11.4, an encoder, $ENC(v)$, maps node v from the input graph space G to a low-dimensional vector h_v in the embedding or latent space H based on the node's position in the graph, its local neighborhood structure, or its features, or some combination of the three.

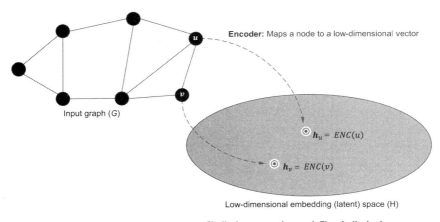

Figure 11.4   Graph embedding

This encoder needs to be optimized to minimize the difference between the similarity of a pair of nodes in the graph and their similarity in the embedding space. Nodes that are connected or nearby in the graph should be close in the embedded space. Conversely, nodes that are not connected or are far apart in the graph should be far apart in the embedded space. In a more generalized encoder/decoder architecture, a decoder is added to extract user-specified information from the low-dimensional embedding [5]. By jointly optimizing the encoder and decoder, the system learns to compress information about the graph structure into the low-dimensional embedding space.

There are various methods for graph embedding which can be broadly classified into transductive (shallow) embedding and inductive embedding:

- *Transductive embedding*—In the transductive learning paradigm, the model learns embeddings only for the nodes present in the graph during the training phase. The learned embeddings are specific to these nodes, and the model cannot generate embeddings for new nodes that weren't present during training. These methods are difficult to scale and are suitable for static graphs. Examples of transductive methods for graph embedding include random walk (e.g., node2vec and DeepWalk) and matrix factorization (e.g., graph factorization and HOPE).

- *Inductive embedding*—Inductive learning methods can generalize to unseen nodes or entire graphs that were not present during training. They do this by learning a function that generates the embedding of a node based on its features and the structure of its local neighborhood, which can be applied to any node, regardless of whether it was present during training or not. These methods are suitable for evolving graphs. Examples of inductive methods for graph embedding are graph neural networks (GNN) and graph convolutional networks (GCNs).

Appendix A contains examples of some of these methods. For more information, see Broadwater and Stillman's *Graph Neural Networks in Action* [6]. We'll focus on GCN, as it is the most relevant approach to the combinatorial optimization application presented in this chapter.

Transductive versus inductive learning

Transductive learning aims to learn from a specific set of data to a specific set of predictions without generalizing to new data. *Inductive learning* aims to learn general rules from observed training cases. These general rules can then be applied to new, unseen data.

The *convolution operation* forms the basis of representation learning in many structured data scenarios, enabling the automatic learning of meaningful features from raw data, thereby obviating the need for manual feature engineering. Convolution is a mathematical operation that takes two functions (input data and a kernel, filter, or feature detector) and measures their overlap or merges the two sets of information to produce a feature map. One critical aspect of convolution is its ability to respect and utilize the known structural relationships among data points, such as the positional associations among pixels, the temporal order of time points, or the edges linking nodes in a network. In traditional ML, convolutional neural networks (CNNs) employ the convolution operator as a key tool for identifying spatial patterns within images. This is made possible by the inherent grid-like structure of image data, which allows the model to slide filters over the image, exploit the spatial regularities, and extract features in a manner akin to pattern recognition.

However, in the realm of graph machine learning (GML), the situation changes considerably. The data in this context is non-Euclidean, as explained previously in table 11.1, meaning that it isn't arranged on a regular grid like pixels are in an image or points are on a 3D surface. Instead, it's represented in the form of a network or graph, which can capture complex relationships. Moreover, this data exhibits order invariance, implying that the output does not change with the rearrangement of nodes.

Unlike CNNs, which operate on a regular grid, GCNs are designed to work with data that's structured as a graph, which can represent a wide variety of irregular and complex structures. Each node is connected to its neighbors without any predefined pattern, and the convolution operation is applied to a node and its direct neighbors in the graph.

How does Google DeepMind predict the estimated time of arrival?

Have you ever wondered how Google Maps predicts the estimated time of arrival (ETA) when you're planning your trip? Google DeepMind uses a GML approach to do so. The traditional ML approach would be to break the route down into a number of road segments, predict the time to traverse each road segment using a feedforward neural network, and sum them up to get the ETA. However, the underlying assumption of feedforward NN is that the road segments are independent of each other. In reality, road segment traffic easily influences the ETA of neighboring road segments, so the samples are not independent.

(continued)

For instance, consider the situation where congestion on a minor road influences the traffic flow on a main road. When the model encompasses multiple junctions, it naturally develops the capacity to predict slowdowns at intersections, delays due to converging traffic, and the total time taken in stop-and-go traffic conditions. A better approach is to use GML to take the influence of the neighboring road segments into consideration.

In this case, the road network will first be converted into a graph where each road segment is represented as a node. If two road segments are connected to each other, their corresponding nodes will be connected by an edge in the graph. Graph embedding is then generated by GNN to map the node features and graph structures from a high-dimensional discrete graph space to a low-dimensional continuous latent space. Information is propagated and aggregated across the graph through a technique called *message passing*, where, at the end, the embedding vector for each node contains and encodes its own information as well as the network information from all its neighboring nodes, according to the degree of neighborhood. Adjacent nodes pass messages to each other. In the first pass, each node knows about its neighbor. In the second pass, every node knows about its neighbor's neighbors, and this information is encoded into the embedding, and so on. This allows us to represent the influence of the traffic in each of the neighboring road segments.

The accuracy of real time ETAs was improved by up to 50% in places like Berlin, Jakarta, São Paulo, Sydney, Tokyo, and Washington DC using this approach [7].

As illustrated in figure 11.5, given an input graph, which includes node features x_v and an adjacency matrix A, a GCN transforms the features of each node into a latent or embedding space H, while preserving the graph structure denoted by the adjacency matrix A. These latent vectors provide a rich representation of each node, making it possible to perform node classification independently.

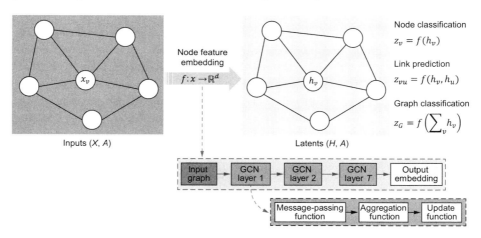

Figure 11.5   Graph embedding and node, link, and graph classification

Moreover, GCNs are also capable of predicting characteristics related to edges, such as whether a link exists between two nodes. Once node embeddings are generated, the likelihood of an edge between two nodes v and u can be predicted based on their embeddings h_v, h_u. A common approach is to compute a similarity measure (e.g., a dot product) between the embeddings of two nodes. This similarity can then be passed through a sigmoid function to predict the probability of an edge. The errors (loss) on predictions will be backpropagated and update the weights in neural networks.

Finally, GCNs enable classification at the level of the entire graph. This can be achieved by aggregating all the latent or embedding vectors (H) for all the nodes. The aggregation function used must be permutation invariant, meaning the output should remain the same regardless of the order of the nodes. Common examples of such functions are summation or averaging or maximizing. Once you've aggregated the latent vectors into a single representation, you can feed this representation into a module (e.g., a neural network layer) to predict an output for the whole graph. In essence, GCNs allow node-level, edge-level, and graph-level predictions.

To better understand how GCN works, let's consider a graph with five nodes, as shown in figure 11.6. For each node in the graph, the first step is to find the neighboring nodes. Let's assume we want to examine how the embedding for node 5 is generated. As you can see in the original graph (upper-left corner of figure 11.6), nodes 2 and 4 are neighbors of node 5. The second step is message-passing, which is the process of nodes sending, receiving, and aggregating messages from their neighbors to iteratively update their features. This allows GCNs to learn a representation for each node that captures both its own features and its context within the graph. The learned representations can then be used for downstream tasks like node classification, link prediction, or graph classification.

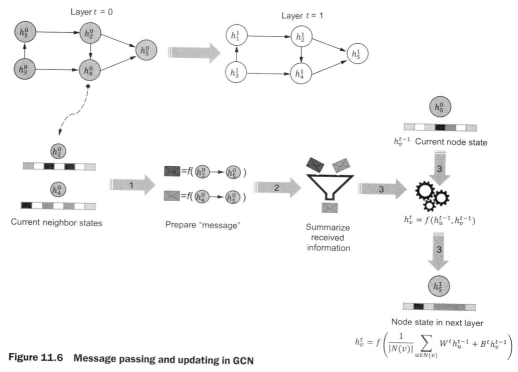

Figure 11.6   Message passing and updating in GCN

The embedding of node v after t layers of neighborhood aggregation considering $N(v)$ neighboring nodes is based on the formula shown in figure 11.7. The initial 0th layer embeddings h_v^0 are equal to node features x_v.

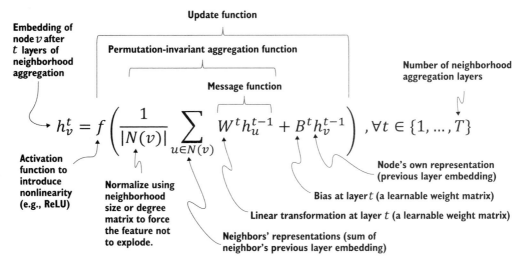

Figure 11.7   Embedding function in GCN

This formula is applied recursively to get another, better vector h at each time step, where h is the vector representation of the nodes in the latent space. The weight matrix is learned through training on given data. At the beginning, each node in the graph is aware only of its own initial features. In the first layer of the GCN, each node communicates with its immediate neighbors, aggregating its own features and receiving features from those neighbors. As we move to the second layer, each node again communicates with its neighbors. However, because the neighbors have already incorporated information from their own neighbors in the first layer, the original node now indirectly accesses information from two hops away in the graph—its neighbors' neighbors. As this process repeats through more layers in the GCN, information is propagated and aggregated across the graph. At the end, the embedding vector for each node contains and encodes its own information as well as the network information from all its neighboring nodes according to the degree of neighborhood, or its *k-hop* neighborhood, to create context embedding. The *k-hop neighborhood*, or neighborhood of radius *k*, of a node is a set of neighboring nodes at a distance less than or equal to *k*.

Listing 11.2 shows how to generate node embedding for the Cora dataset using GCN. The Cora dataset consists of 2,708 scientific publications classified into one of seven classes. The citation network consists of 5,429 links. Each publication in the dataset is described by a 0/1-valued word vector indicating the absence/presence of the corresponding word in the dictionary. The dictionary consists of 1,433 unique words.

PyG (PyTorch Geometric) is used and can be installed as follows:

```
$conda install pytorch torchvision -c pytorch
$conda install torch_scatter
$conda install torch_sparse
$conda install torch_cluster
$conda install torch-spline-conv
$conda install torch_geometric
```

More information about PyG CUDA installation is available in the PyG documentation (https://pytorch-geometric.readthedocs.io/en/latest/notes/installation.html).

We'll start by importing the libraries we'll use.

Listing 11.2   Node embedding using GCN

```
import numpy as np
from sklearn.preprocessing import StandardScaler
from sklearn.decomposition import PCA
from sklearn.pipeline import Pipeline
import torch
import torch.nn.functional as F
from torch_geometric.datasets import Planetoid
from torch_geometric.nn import GCNConv
from torch_geometric.utils import to_networkx
```

PyG provides several datasets that can be loaded directly, such as KarateClub, Cora, Amazon, Reddit, etc. The Cora dataset is part of the Planetoid dataset and can be loaded as follows:

```
dataset = Planetoid(root='/tmp/Cora', name='Cora')
```

As you can see in the following code, the GCN model is defined with two `GCNConv` layers (`GCNConv`) and a `torch.nn.Dropout` layer. `GCNConv` is a graph convolution layer, and `torch.nn.Dropout` is a dropout layer, which randomly zeroes some of the elements of the input tensor with probability 0.5 during training as a simple way to prevent overfitting.

The `forward` function defines the forward pass of the model. It takes a data object as input, representing the graph, and the features of the nodes and the adjacency list of the graph are extracted from the input data. The node features (`x`) are passed through the first GCN layer `conv1`, a `relu` activation function, a dropout layer, and finally the second GCN layer `conv2`. The adjacency list, `edge_index`, is required for the convolution operation in the GCN layers. The output of the network is then returned:

```
class GCN(torch.nn.Module):
    def __init__(self):
        super(GCN, self).__init__()
        self.conv1 = GCNConv(dataset.num_node_features, 16)
        self.conv2 = GCNConv(16, dataset.num_classes)
        self.dropout = torch.nn.Dropout(0.5)
```

```
def forward(self, data):
    x, edge_index = data.x, data.edge_index

    x = self.conv1(x, edge_index)
    x = F.relu(x)
    x = F.dropout(x, training=self.training)
    x = self.conv2(x, edge_index)

    return x
```

As a continuation of listing 11.2, the following code snippet trains the GCN model on a single graph and extracts the node embedding from the trained model. The `model` is trained for 200 epochs. Its gradients are first zeroed, then the forward pass is computed, and the negative log-likelihood loss is calculated on the training nodes (those marked by `data.train_mask`). The backward pass is then computed to get the gradients, and the optimizer performs a step to update the model parameters. The model is set to evaluation mode and is run on the graph again to obtain the final node embeddings:

Create an instance of the GCN model, and move it to the chosen device.

If CUDA is available, the code uses the GPU; otherwise, it will use the CPU.

```
device = torch.device('cuda' if torch.cuda.is_available() else 'cpu')
model = GCN().to(device)
data = dataset[0].to(device)
```

Load the first graph in the dataset, and move it to the device.

```
optimizer = torch.optim.Adam(model.parameters(), lr=0.01, weight_decay=5e-4)
```

Use the Adam optimizer with a learning rate of 0.01 and weight decay (a form of regularization) of 0.0005.

Train the model for 200 epochs.

```
model.train()
for epoch in range(200):
    optimizer.zero_grad()
    out = model(data)
    loss = F.nll_loss(out[data.train_mask], data.y[data.train_mask])
    loss.backward()
    optimizer.step()
```

Set evaluation mode.

Obtain the final node embeddings.

```
model.eval()
embeddings_pyg = model(data).detach().cpu().numpy()
```

The `.detach()` function is used to detach the output from the computational graph and returns a new tensor that doesn't require a gradient. The embeddings are then moved from the GPU (if they were on the GPU) to the CPU. This is done to make the data accessible for further processing, such as converting it to a NumPy array. The generated embedding has a size of (2708, 7), where the number of nodes is 2,708 and the number of classes or subjects is 7. Dimensionality reduction using principle component analysis (PCA) is applied to visualize the embedding in 2D as shown in figure 11.8.

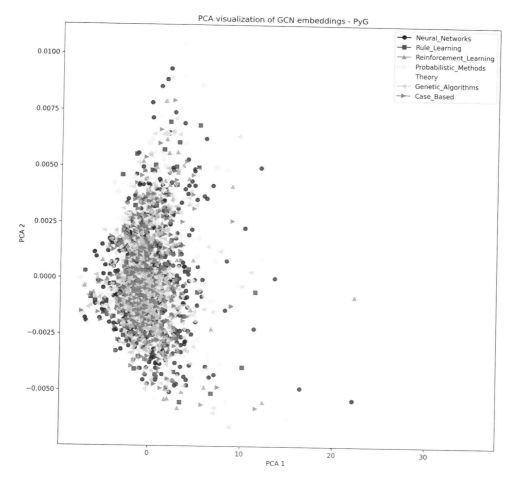

Figure 11.8   Node embedding using GCN in PyG

As you can see, the node embedding makes the nodes belonging to the same classes cluster together. This means increased discrimination power of the features, which results in more accurate predictions.

The complete version of listing 11.2 available in the book's GitHub repo also shows how to generate node embedding using the GCN available in StellarGraph. Stellar-Graph is a Python library for ML on graphs and networks.

11.3.2 Attention mechanisms

As you saw in figure 11.7, the embedding function in GCN consists of message passing, aggregation, and update functions. The message passing function mainly integrates messages from the node's neighbors based on a learnable weight matrix W. This weight matrix does not reflect the degree of importance of neighboring nodes. The convolution operation applies the same learned weights to all neighbors of a node as a linear transformation, without explicitly accounting for their importance or relevance. This might not be ideal because some segments may need more attention than others.

The concept of "attention" in DL essentially permits the model to selectively concentrate on specific segments of the input data as it produces the output sequence. This mechanism ensures that context is maintained and propagated from the initial stages to the end. It also allows the model to dynamically allocate its resources by focusing on the most important parts of the input at each time step. In a broad sense, attention in DL can be visualized as a vector consisting of importance or relevance scores. These scores help quantify the relationship or association between a node in a graph and all other nodes in the graph.

Attention is all you need

The groundbreaking paper "Attention Is All You Need" [8] proposes a new Transformer model for processing sequential data like text. In the world of language processing and translation, models usually read an entire sentence or document word by word, in order (like we do when we read a book), and then make predictions based on that. These models have some difficulties understanding long sentences and recalling information from far away in the text. In the case of long sequences, there is a high probability that the initial context will be lost by the end of the sequence. This is called the *forgetting problem.*

The authors of the paper propose a different way of handling this task. Instead of reading everything in order, their model focuses on different parts of the input at different times, almost like it's jumping around the text. This is what they refer to as "attention." The attention mechanism allows the model to dynamically prioritize which parts of the input are most relevant for each word it's trying to predict, making it more effective at understanding context and reducing confusion arising from long sentences or complex phrases. For more details, see "The Annotated Transformer" [9].

Figure 11.9b shows a graph attention network (GAT), where a weighting factor or attention coefficient α is added to the embedding equation to reflect the importance of the neighboring nodes. GAT uses a weighted adjacency matrix instead of non-weighted adjacency matrix used in case of GCN (figure 11.9a). An attentional mechanism a is used to compute unnormalized coefficients e_{vu} across pairs of nodes v and u based on their features:

$$e_{vu} = a(h_v, h_u) \qquad\qquad \textbf{11.1}$$

An example of this attentional mechanism can be dot-product attention that measures the similarity or alignment between the features of the two nodes, providing a quantitative indication of how much attention node v should give to node u. Other mechanisms may involve learned attention weights, nonlinear transformations, or more complex interactions between node features. Following the graph structure, node v can attend over nodes in its neighborhood only $i \in N_v$.

Attention coefficients are typically normalized using the softmax function so that they are comparable, irrespective of the scale or distribution of raw scores in different neighborhoods or contexts. Note that in figure 11.9b, for simplicity, the attention coefficients α_{vu} are denoted as α_u.

$$\alpha_{vu} = \frac{exp(e_{vu})}{\sum_{i \in N(v)} exp(e_{vi})}$$

11.2

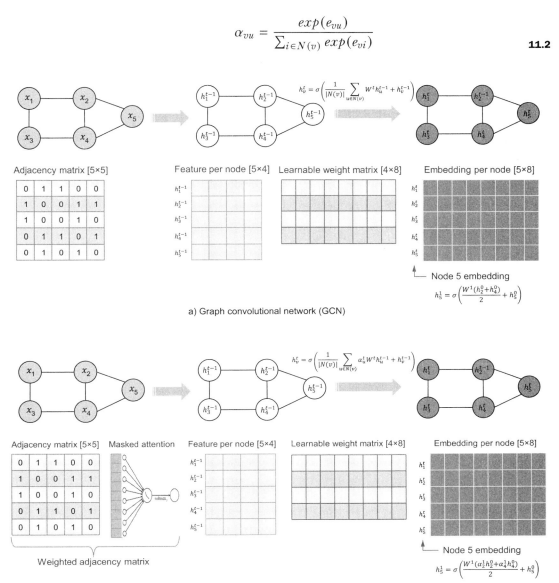

a) Graph convolutional network (GCN)

b) Graph attention network (GAT)

Figure 11.9   Graph convolutional network (GCN) vs. graph attention network (GAT)

Multi-head attention is a key component in GATs and also in the Transformer model discussed in the "Attention Is All You Need" paper. In a multi-head attention mechanism, the model has multiple sets of attention weights. Each set (or "head") can learn to pay attention to different parts of the input. Instead of having just one focus of attention, the model can have multiple focuses, allowing it to capture different types of relationships and patterns in the data. In the context of GATs, a multi-head attention mechanism allows each node in the graph to focus on different neighboring nodes in different ways, as shown in figure 11.10.

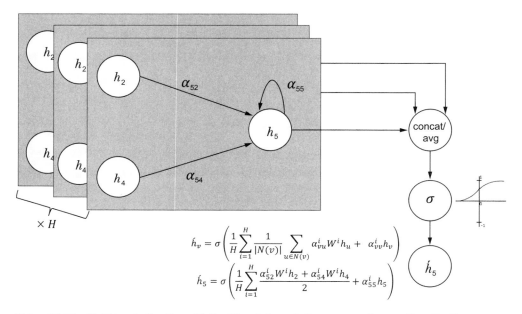

$$\acute{h}_v = \sigma \left(\frac{1}{H} \sum_{i=1}^{H} \frac{1}{|N(v)|} \sum_{u \in N(v)} \alpha_{vu}^i W^i h_u + \alpha_{vv}^i h_v \right)$$

$$\acute{h}_5 = \sigma \left(\frac{1}{H} \sum_{i=1}^{H} \frac{\alpha_{52}^i W^i h_2 + \alpha_{54}^i W^i h_4}{2} + \alpha_{55}^i h_5 \right)$$

Figure 11.10   Multi-head attention with H = 3 heads by node 5. α_{52}, α_{54}, and α_{55} **are the attention coefficients between the nodes. The aggregated features from each head are averaged to obtain the final embedding of the node.**

Once the multiple heads have performed their respective attention operations, their results are typically averaged. This process condenses the diverse perspectives captured by the multiple attention heads into a single output. After the results of the multi-head attention operation are combined, a final nonlinearity is then applied. This step typically involves the use of a softmax function or logistic sigmoid function, especially in classification problems. These functions serve to translate the model's final outputs into probabilities, making the output easier to interpret and more useful for prediction tasks.

11.3.3 *Pointer networks*

Sequential ML involves dealing with data where the order of observations matters, such as time series data, sentences, or permutations. Sequential ML tasks can be classified based on the number of inputs and outputs, as shown in table 11.2. A *sequence-to-sequence* (seq2seq) model takes a sequence of items and outputs another sequence of items. Recurrent neural networks (RNN) and long short-term memory (LSTM) have been established as state-of-the-art approaches in seq2seq modeling.

Table 11.2   Sequential ML

Task	Example
One-to-one	Image classification. We provide a single image as input, and the model outputs the classification or category, like "dog" or "cat," as a single output.
One-to-many	Image captioning. We input a single image into the model, and it generates a sequence of words describing that image.
Many-to-one	Sentiment analysis. We input a sequence of words (like a sentence or a tweet), and the model outputs a single sentiment score (like "positive," "negative," or "neutral").
Many-to-many (type 1)	Sequence input and sequence output, like in the case of named entity recognition (NER). We input a sentence (a sequence of words), and the model outputs the recognized entity, such as a person, organization, location, etc.
Many-to-many (type 2), known as a synchronized sequence model	Synced sequence input and output. The model takes a sequence of inputs but doesn't output anything until the entire sequence has been read. Then it outputs a sequence. An example of this is video classification, where the model takes a sequence of video frames as input and then outputs a sequence of labels for those frames.

In discrete combinatorial optimization problems like the travelling salesman problem, sorting tasks, or the convex hull problem, both the input and output data are sequential. However, traditional seq2seq models struggle to solve these problems effectively. This is primarily because the discrete categories of output elements are not predetermined. Instead, they are contingent on the variable size of the input (for instance, the output dictionary is dependent on the input length). The *pointer network* (Ptr-Net) model [10] addresses this problem by utilizing attention as a mechanism to point to or select a member of the input sequence for the output. This model not only enhances performance over the conventional seq2seq model equipped with input attention, but it also enables us to generalize to output dictionaries of variable sizes.

While traditional attention mechanisms distribute attention over the input sequence to generate an output element, Ptr-Net instead uses attention as a pointer. This pointer is used to select an element from the input sequence to be included in the output sequence. Let's consider the convex hull problem as an example of a discrete combinatorial optimization problem. A convex hull is a geometric shape, specifically a polygon, that fully encompasses a given set of points. It achieves this by optimizing two distinct parameters: it maximizes the area that the shape covers, while simultaneously minimizing the boundary or circumference of the shape, as illustrated in figure 11.11. To understand this concept, it can be useful to imagine stretching a rubber band around the extreme points or vertices of the set. When you release the rubber band, it automatically encompasses the entire set in the smallest perimeter possible, and this is essentially what a convex hull does.

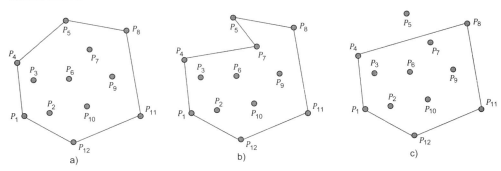

Figure 11.11 The convex hull problem. a) A valid convex hull that encloses all points while maximizing the area and minimizing the circumference. Note that the number of points included in the output sequence of the polygon may be smaller than the number of given points. b) An invalid convex hull, as the circumference is not minimized. c) An invalid convex hull, as not all the points are enclosed.

Convex hulls have a multitude of applications across a variety of disciplines. For example, in the field of image recognition, convex hulls can help determine the shape and boundary of objects within an image. Similarly, in robotics, they can assist in obstacle detection and navigation by defining the "reachable" space around a robot.

The problem of finding or computing a convex hull, given a set of points, has been addressed through various algorithms. For example, the Graham scan algorithm sorts the points according to their angle with the point at the bottom of the hull and then processes them to find the convex hull [11]. The Jarvis march (or the gift wrapping algorithm) starts with the leftmost point and wraps the remaining points like wrapping a gift [12]. The quickhull algorithm finds the convex hull of a point set by recursively dividing the set into subsets, selecting the point farthest from the line between two extreme points, and eliminating points within the formed triangles until the hull's vertices are identified [13].

As shown in figure 11.12, Ptr-Net takes as input a planar set of points $P = \{P_1, P_2, \ldots, P_n\}$ with n elements each, where $P_j = (x_j, y_j)$ are the Cartesian coordinates of the points. The outputs $C_P = \{C_1, C_2, \ldots, C_{m(P)}\}$ are sequences representing the solution associated with the point set P. In this figure, Ptr-Net estimates the output sequence [1 4 2] from the input data points [1 2 3 4]. This output sequence represents the convex hull that includes all the input points with maximum area and minimum circumference. As can be seen, the convex hull is formed by connecting P_1, P_2, and P_4. The third point P_3 is inside this convex hull.

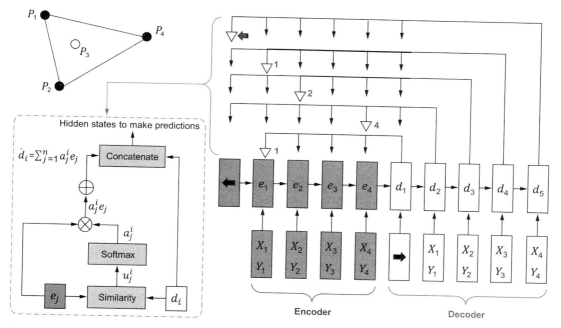

Figure 11.12   Pointer network (Prt-Net) estimating the output sequence [1 4 2] from the input data points [1 2 3 4]

Ptr-Net consists of three main components:

- *Encoder*—The encoder is a recurrent neural network (RNN), often implemented with long short-term memory (LSTM) units or gated recurrent units (GRUs). The encoder's purpose is to process the input sequence, converting each input element into a corresponding hidden state. These hidden states (e_1,..., e_n) encapsulate the context-dependent representation of the elements in the input sequence.

- *Decoder*—Like the encoder, the decoder is also an RNN. It's responsible for generating the output sequence (d_1,..., d_m). For each output step, it takes the previous output and its own hidden state as inputs.

- *Attention mechanism (pointer)*—The attention mechanism in a Ptr-Net operates as a pointer. It computes a distribution over the hidden states output by the encoder, indicating where to "point" in the input sequence for each output step. Essentially, it decides which of the inputs should be the next output. The attention mechanism is a softmax function over the learned attention scores, which gives a probability distribution over the input sequence, signifying the likeliness of each element being pointed at.

The attention vector at each output time i is computed using the following equations:

$$u_j^i = v^T \tanh\left(W_1 e_j + W_2 d_i\right) \quad j \in (1, \ldots, n)$$

11.3

$$a_j^i = softmax\left(u_j^i\right) \quad j \in (1, \ldots, n)$$

11.4

$$d_i' = \sum_{j=1}^{n} a_j^i e_j$$

11.5

where

- u_j is the attention vector or alignment score that represents the similarity between the decoder and encoder hidden states. v, W_1, and W_2 are learnable parameters of the model. If the same hidden dimensionality is used for the encoder and decoder (typically 512), v is a vector, and W_1 and W_2 are square matrices.
- a_j is the attention mask over the input or weights computed by applying the softmax operation to the alignment scores.
- d_i' is the context vector that is fed into the decoder at each time step. In other words, d_i and d_i' are concatenated and used as the hidden states from which the predictions are made. This weighted sum of all the encoder hidden states allows the decoder to flexibly focus the attention on the most relevant parts of the input sequence.

Ptr-Net can process variable-length sequences and solve complex combinatorial problems, especially those involving sorting or ordering tasks, where the output is a permutation of the input, as you will see in section 11.9.

11.4 Self-organizing maps

The *self-organizing map* (SOM), also known as a *self-organizing feature map* (SOFM) or *Kohonen map*, is a type of artificial neural network (ANN) that is trained with unsupervised learning to produce a low-dimensional (typically two-dimensional), discretized representation of the input space of the training samples, called a *map*. SOMs are distinguished from traditional ANNs by the nature of their learning process, known as *competitive learning*. In such algorithms, processing elements or neurons compete for the right to respond to a subset of the input data. The degree to which an output neuron is activated is amplified as the similarity between the neuron's weight vector and the input grows. The similarity between the weight vector and the input, leading to neuron activation, is commonly gauged through the calculation of Euclidean distance. The output unit that demonstrates the highest level of activation, or equivalently the shortest distance, in response to a specific input is deemed the best matching unit (BMU) or the "winning" neuron, as illustrated in figure 11.13. This winner is then drawn incrementally closer to the input data point by adjusting its weight.

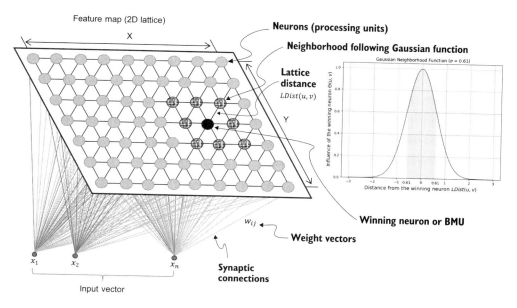

Figure 11.13   Self-organizing map (SOM) with a Gaussian neighborhood function

A key characteristic of SOM is the concept of a *neighborhood function*, which ensures that not only the winning neuron but also its neighbors learn from each new input, creating clusters of similar data. This allows the network to preserve the topological properties of the input space. Equation 11.6 shows an example of a neighborhood function:

$$\theta(u, v) = exp\left(-\frac{LDist(u, v)^2}{2\sigma^2}\right)$$

11.6

where v is the index of the node in the map, u is the index of the winning neuron, $LDist(u,v)$ represents the lattice distance between u and v, and σ is the bandwidth of the Gaussian kernel. In SOMs, σ represents the radius or width of the neighborhood and determines how far the influence of the winning neuron extends to its neighbors during the weight update phase. A large σ means a broader neighborhood is affected. On the other hand, a small σ means that fewer neighboring neurons are influenced. When σ is set to an extremely small value, the neighborhood effectively shrinks to include only the winning neuron itself. This means that only the winning neuron's weights are significantly updated in response to the input, while the weights of the other neurons are barely or not at all affected. This behavior, where only the winning neuron is updated, is referred to as "winner take all" learning.

Algorithm 11.1 shows the steps of SOM, assuming that D_t is a target input data vector, W_v is the current weight vector of node v, $\theta(u,v,s)$ is the neighborhood function that represents the restraint due to the distance from the winning neuron, and α is a learning rate where $\alpha \in (0,1)$.

Algorithm 11.1 Self-organizing map (SOM)

```
Randomly initialize the weights of each neuron
For each step s=1 to iteration limit:
    Randomly pick an input vector from the dataset
        Traverse each node in the map
            Calculate Euclidean distance as a similarity measure
            Determine the node that produces the smallest distance (winning
neuron)
        Adapt the weights of each neuron v according to the following rule
        W_v(s+1)=W_v(s)+ α(s).θ(u,v,s).‖D_t-W_v(s)‖
```

SOMs were initially used as a dimensionality reduction method for data visualization and clustering tasks. For example, the neural phonetic typewriter was one of the early applications of Kohonen's SOM algorithm. It was a system where spoken phonemes (the smallest unit of speech that can distinguish one word from another) were recognized and converted into symbols. When someone spoke into the system, the SOM would classify the input phoneme and type the corresponding symbol. SOMs can be applied to different problems such as feature extraction, adaptive control, and travelling salesman problems (see section 11.8).

SOMs offer a significant advantage in that they preserve the relative distances between points as calculated within the input space. Points that are close in the input space are mapped onto neighboring units within the SOM, making SOMs effective tools for analyzing clusters within high-dimensional data. When using techniques like principal component analysis (PCA) to handle high-dimensional data, data loss may occur when reducing the dimensions to two. If the data contains numerous dimensions and if each dimension carries valuable information, then SOMs can be superior to PCA for dimensionality reduction purposes. Beyond this, SOMs also possess the ability to generalize. Through this process, the network can identify or categorize input data that it has not previously encountered. This new input is associated with a specific unit on the map and is thus mapped accordingly.

The previous sections have offered a fundamental foundation in ML, equipping you with essential background knowledge. The upcoming sections will delve deeply into the practical applications of supervised and unsupervised ML in tackling optimization problems.

11.5   *Machine learning for optimization problems*

The utilization of ML techniques to tackle combinatorial optimization problems represents an emergent and exciting field of study. *Neural combinatorial optimization* refers to the application of ML and neural network models, specifically seq2seq supervised models, unsupervised models, and reinforcement learning, to solve combinatorial optimization problems. Within this context, the application of ML to combinatorial optimization has been comprehensively described by Yoshua Bengio and his co-authors [14]. The authors depict three distinctive methods for harnessing ML for combinatorial optimization (see figure 11.14):

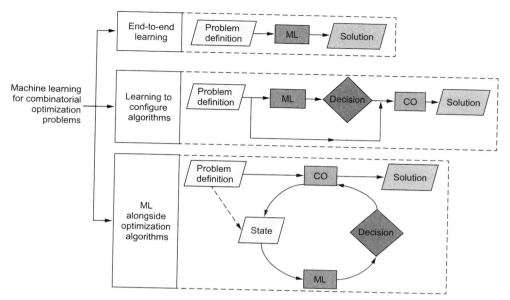

Figure 11.14   **Machine learning (ML) for combinatorial optimization (CO) problems**

- *End-to-end learning*—To use ML to address optimization problems, we need to instruct the ML model to formulate solutions directly from the input instance. An example of this approach is Ptr-Net, which is trained on m points and validated on n points for a Euclidean planar symmetric TSP [10]. Examples of solving combinatorial optimization problems using end-to-end learning are provided in sections 11.6, 11.7, and 11.9.

- *Learning to configure algorithms*—The second method involves applying an ML model to enhance a combinatorial optimization algorithm with pertinent information. In this regard, ML can offer a parameterization of the algorithm. Examples of such parameters comprise, but are not restricted to, learning rate or step size in gradient descent methodologies; initial temperature or cooling schedule in simulated annealing; standard deviation of Gaussian mutation or selective crossover in genetic algorithms; inertia weight or cognitive and social acceleration coefficients in particle swarm optimization (PSO); or rate of evaporation, influence of pheromone deposition, or influence of the desirability of state transition in ant colony optimization (ACO).

- *ML in conjunction with optimization algorithms*—The third method calls for a combinatorial optimization algorithm to repetitively consult the same ML model for decision-making purposes. The ML model accepts as input the current state of the algorithm, which could encompass the problem definition. The fundamental distinction between this approach and the other two lies in the repeated utilization of the same ML model by the combinatorial optimization algorithm to make identical kinds of decisions, approximately as many times as the total number of iterations of the algorithm. An example of this approach is DL-assisted heuristic tree search (DLTS), which consists of a heuristic tree search in which decisions about which branches to explore and how to bound nodes are made by deep neural networks (DNNs) [15].

Another intriguing research paper by Vesselinova et al. delves into some pertinent questions concerning the intersection of ML and combinatorial optimization [16]. Specifically, the paper investigates the following questions:

- Can ML techniques be utilized to automate the process of learning heuristics for combinatorial optimization tasks and, as a result, solve these problems more efficiently?
- What essential ML methods have been employed to tackle these real-world problems?
- How applicable are these methods to practical domains?

This paper offers a thorough survey of various applications of supervised and reinforcement learning strategies in tackling optimization problems. The authors analyze these learning approaches by examining their application to a range of optimization problems:

- The knapsack problem (KP), where the goal is to maximize the total value of items chosen without exceeding the capacity of the knapsack
- The maximal clique (MC) and maximal independent set (MIS) problems, which both involve identifying subsets of a graph with specific properties
- The maximum coverage problem (MCP), which requires selecting a subset of items to maximize coverage
- The maximum cut (MaxCut) and minimum vertex cover (MVC) problems, which involve partitioning a graph in particular ways

In addition, the paper discusses the application of ML approaches to the satisfiability problem (SAT), which is a decision problem involving Boolean logic; the classic TSP, which requires finding the shortest possible route that visits a given set of cities and returns to the origin city; and the vehicular routing problem (VRP), which is a generalized version of TSP where multiple "salesmen" (vehicles) are allowed. More information about benchmark optimization problems is provided in appendix B.

Optimization by prompting (OPRO) is described in Chengrun et al.'s "Large Language Models as Optimizers" article as a simple and effective approach to using large language models (LLMs) as optimizers, where the optimization task is described in natural language [17]. Additional examples showcasing the use of ML in addressing optimization problems can be accessed through the AI for Smart Mobility publication hub (https://medium.com/ai4sm). To stimulate further exploration and draw more researchers into this emerging domain, a competition named Machine Learning for Combinatorial Optimization (ML4CO) was organized as part of the Neural Information Processing Systems (NeurIPS) conference. The competition posed a unique proposition for participants, requiring them to devise ML models or algorithms targeted at resolving three separate challenges. Each of these challenges mirrors a specific control task that commonly emerges in conventional optimization solvers. This competition provides a platform where researchers can explore and test novel ML strategies, contributing to the advancement of the field of combinatorial optimization.

11.6 Solving function optimization using supervised machine learning

Amortized optimization, or *learning to optimize*, is an approach where ML models are used to rapidly predict the solutions to an optimization problem. Amortized optimization methods try to learn the mapping between the decision variable space and the optimal or near-optimal solution space. The learned model can be used to predict the optimal value of an objective function, enabling fast solvers. The computation cost of the optimization process is spread out between learning and inferencing. This is the reason for the name "amortized optimization," as the word "amortization" generally refers to spreading out costs.

B. Amos shows several examples of how to use amortized optimization to solve optimization problems in his tutorial [18]. For example, a supervised ML approach can learn to solve optimization problems over spheres. Here the objective is to find the extreme values of a function defined on the earth or other space that can be approximated with a sphere of the form

$$y^*(x) \in \arg\min_{y \in S^2} f(y, x)$$

11.7

where S^2 is the surface of the unit 2-sphere embedded in real-number space R^3 as $S^2 := \{y \in R^3 \mid \|y\|_2 = 1\}$, and x is some parameterization of the function $f: S^2 \times X \to R$. $\|y\|_2$ refers to the Euclidean norm (also known as the *L2 norm* or *2-norm*) of a vector y. More details about the amortization objective function are available in Amos's "Tutorial on amortized optimization for learning to optimize over continuous domains" [18].

Listing 11.3 shows the steps for applying amortized optimization based on supervised learning to solve the problem of finding the extreme values of a function defined on the earth or other spaces. We'll start by defining two conversion functions, `celestial_to_euclidean()` and `euclidean_to_celestial()`, that convert between celestial coordinates (right ascension, `ra`, and declination, `dec`) and Euclidean coordinates (`x`, `y`, `z`).

The celestial coordinate system

The *astronomical* or *celestial coordinate system* is a reference system used to specify the positions of objects in the sky, such as satellites, stars, planets, galaxies, and other celestial bodies. There are several celestial coordinate systems, with the most common being the equatorial system. In the equatorial system, right ascension (RA) and declination (Dec) are the two numbers used to fix the location of an object in the sky. These coordinates are analogous to the latitude and longitude used in earth's geographic coordinate system.

As shown in the following figure, RA is measured in hours, minutes, and seconds (h:m:s), and it is analogous to longitude in earth's coordinate system. RA is the angular distance of an object measured eastward along the celestial equator from the vernal equinox (the point where the sun crosses the celestial equator during the March equinox). The celestial equator is an imaginary great circle on the celestial sphere, lying in the same plane as earth's equator. Dec is measured in degrees and represents the angular distance of an object north or south of the celestial equator. It is analogous to latitude in earth's coordinate system.

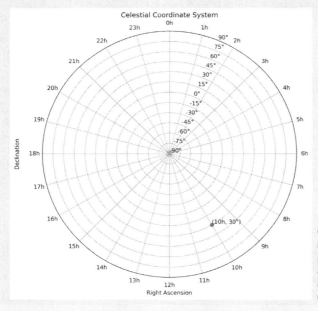

Celestial coordinate system with an example point with a right ascension of 10 hours and a declination of 30 degrees

Positive declination is used for objects above the celestial equator, and negative declination is used for objects below the celestial equator.

The `sphere_dist(x, y)` function calculates the Riemannian distance (the great-circle distance) between two points on the sphere in the Euclidean space. This distance represents the shortest (geodesic) path between two points on the surface of a sphere, measured along the surface rather than through the interior of the sphere. The function asserts that the input vectors are two-dimensional. Then it calculates the dot product of *x* and *y* and returns the arccosine of the result, which corresponds to the angle between *x* and *y*.

> **Listing 11.3** Solving a function optimization problem using supervised learning

```python
import torch
from torch import nn
import numpy as np
from tqdm import tqdm
import matplotlib.pyplot as plt

def celestial_to_euclidean(ra, dec):        ◀──── Convert from celestial coordinates
    x = np.cos(dec)*np.cos(ra)                     to Euclidean coordinates.
    y = np.cos(dec)*np.sin(ra)
    z = np.sin(dec)
    return x, y, z

def euclidean_to_celestial(x, y, z):        ◀──── Convert from Euclidean coordinates
    sindec = z                                     to celestial coordinates.
    cosdec = (x*x + y*y).sqrt()
    sinra = y / cosdec
    cosra = x / cosdec
    ra = torch.atan2(sinra, cosra)
    dec = torch.atan2(sindec, cosdec)
    return ra, dec

def sphere_dist(x,y):                ◀──── Calculate the Riemannian distance
    if x.ndim == 1:                          between two points on the sphere.
        x = x.unsqueeze(0)
    if y.ndim == 1:
        y = y.unsqueeze(0)
    assert x.ndim == y.ndim == 2
    inner = (x*y).sum(-1)
    return torch.arccos(inner)
```

We then define a `c-convex` class as a subclass of `nn.Module`, which makes it a trainable model in PyTorch. Cohen and his co-authors defined *c-convex* in their "Riemannian convex potential maps" article as a synthetic class of optimization problems defined on the sphere [19]. The `c-convex` class models a c-convex function on the sphere with `n_components` components that we can sample data from for training. The `gamma` parameter controls the aggregation of the components of the function, and `seed` is used to initialize the random number generator for reproducibility. It also generates random parameters `ys` (which are unit vectors in the 3D space) and `alphas` (which are scalars between 0 and 0.7) for each component of the c-convex function. The parameters are concatenated into a single `params` vector. The `forward(xyz)` method calculates the value of the c-convex function at the point `xyz`:

```python
class c_convex(nn.Module):    ◀───────────────────
    def __init__(self, n_components=4, gamma=0.5, seed=None):
        super().__init__()
        self.n_components = n_components          Define a c-convex function.
        self.gamma = gamma
```

Sample random parameters.

```
if seed is not None:
    torch.manual_seed(seed)
self.ys = torch.randn(n_components, 3)
self.ys = self.ys / torch.norm(self.ys, 2, dim=-1, keepdim=True)
self.alphas = .7*torch.rand(self.n_components)
self.params = torch.cat((self.ys.view(-1), self.alphas.view(-1)))
```

```
def forward(self, xyz):
    cs = []
    for y, alpha in zip(self.ys, self.alphas):
        ci = 0.5*sphere_dist(y, xyz)**2 + alpha
        cs.append(ci)
    cs = torch.stack(cs)
    if self.gamma == None or self.gamma == 0.:
        z = cs.min(dim=0).values
    else:
        z = -self.gamma*(-cs/self.gamma).logsumexp(dim=0)
    return z
```

Computes the output of the c-convex function given input coordinates xyz on the sphere.

As a continuation of the preceding code, we define an amortized model, which takes a parameter vector as input and outputs a 3D vector representing a point on the sphere. The amortized model uses a neural network to learn a mapping from the parameter space to the 3D space of points on the sphere. The code also initializes a list of c_convex objects with different seeds and sets the number of parameters for the amortized model:

```
seeds = [8,9,2,31,4,20,16,7]
fs = [c_convex(seed=i) for i in seeds]
n_params = len(fs[0].params)
```

Create a list of integers representing different seeds.

Create an fs list that contains different instances of the c_convex class.

Set the number of parameters in the first c_convex object (fs[0]).

The amortized model is represented as nn.Module in the following code. The neural network is defined as a feedforward neural network or a multilayer perceptron that consists of three fully connected (linear) layers with ReLU activation functions:

```
class AmortizedModel(nn.Module):
    def __init__(self, n_params):
        super().__init__()
        self.base = nn.Sequential(

            nn.Linear(n_params, n_hidden),
            nn.ReLU(inplace=True),
            nn.Linear(n_hidden, n_hidden),
            nn.ReLU(inplace=True),
            nn.Linear(n_hidden, 3)
        )

    def forward(self, p):
        squeeze = p.ndim == 1
        if squeeze:
            p = p.unsqueeze(0)
        assert p.ndim == 2
```

Number of parameters in the c-convex function that will be used as input to the neural network

Define the layers of the neural network in sequence.

Define the forward pass of the amortized model, which maps the input p (parameter vector) to a point on the sphere.

```
z = self.base(p)
z = z / z.norm(dim=-1, keepdim=True)
if squeeze:
    z = z.squeeze(0)
return z
```

We can now train the amortized model to learn a mapping from parameter vectors to points on the sphere. It uses a list of c_convex functions (fs) with different random seeds to generate training data. The amortized model is trained using an Adam optimizer, and its progress is visualized using a tqdm progress bar. The resulting output points on the sphere are stored in a tensor xs:

Set the number of hidden units for the AmortizedModel neural network.

Set the random seed to ensure the reproducibility of the training process.

Create an instance of the AmortizedModel.

Create an Adam optimizer to update the parameters with a learning rate of 0.0005.

Store the output points on the sphere for each iteration of training.

```
n_hidden = 128
torch.manual_seed(0)
model = AmortizedModel(n_params=n_params)
opt = torch.optim.Adam(model.parameters(), lr=5e-4)

xs = []
num_iterations = 100

pbar = tqdm(range(num_iterations), desc="Training Progress")
```

Training loop

Store the losses for each c_convex function and the corresponding output points on the sphere (xis).

Iterate over each c_convex function (f) in the list fs.

```
for i in pbar:
    losses = []
    xis = []
    for f in fs:
        pred_opt = model(f.params)
        xis.append(pred_opt)
        losses.append(f(pred_opt))
    with torch.no_grad():
        xis = torch.stack(xis)
        xs.append(xis)
    loss = sum(losses)

    opt.zero_grad()
    loss.backward()
    opt.step()

    pbar.set_postfix({"Loss": loss.item()})

xs = torch.stack(xs, dim=1)
```

After training is complete, all the predicted output points on the sphere are stacked along a new dimension, resulting in a tensor xs with the following shape: number of iterations, number of c_convex functions, 3. Each element in this tensor represents a point on the sphere predicted by the amortized model at different stages of training. It generates a visual representation of the training progress for the amortized model and c_convex functions, as shown in figure 11.15.

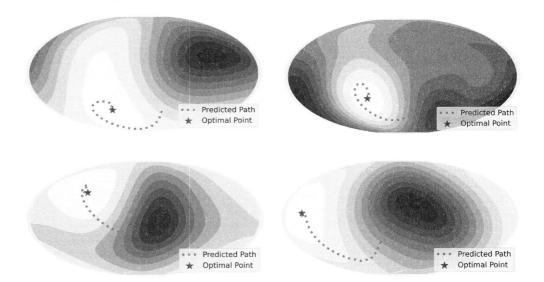

Figure 11.15   Examples of output from the trained amortized model

The complete version of listing 11.3 is available in the book's GitHub repo. It creates a grid of celestial coordinates, evaluates the c_convex functions and the amortized model on this grid, and then plots contour maps of the functions, the predicted paths, and the optimal points on the sphere. The optimal points are the points that give minimum loss, given that supervised learning is used to train the amortized model.

11.7   *Solving TSP using supervised graph machine learning*

Joshi, Laurent, and Bresson, in their "Graph Neural Networks for the Travelling Salesman Problem" article [20], proposed a generic end-to-end pipeline to tackle combinatorial optimization problems such as the traveling salesman problem (TSP), vehicle routing problem (VRP), satisfiability problem (SAT), maximum cut (MaxCut), and maximal independent set (MIS). Figure 11.16 shows the steps of solving TSP using ML.

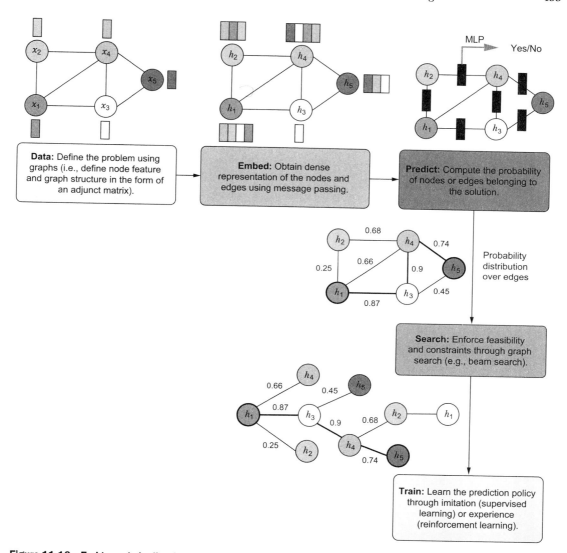

Figure 11.16 End-to-end pipeline for combinatorial optimization problems

Following this approach, we start by defining the graph problem in the form of node features and an adjacency matrix between the nodes. A low-dimensional graph embedding is then generated using GNN or GCN, based on the message-passing approach. The probability of nodes or edges belonging to the solution is predicted using multilayer perceptrons (MLPs). A graph search, such as beam search (see chapter 4), is then applied to search the graph with the probability distribution over the edge to find a feasible candidate solution. Learning by imitation (supervised learning) and learning by exploration (reinforcement learning) are applied. Supervised learning minimizes the loss between optimal solutions (obtained by a well-known solver such as Concorde in the case of TSP) and the model's prediction. The reinforcement learning approach uses a policy gradient to minimize the length of the tour predicted by the model at the end of decoding. Reinforcement learning is discussed in the next chapter.

Training an ML model from scratch and applying it to solve TSP requires a substantial amount of code and data preprocessing. Listing 11.4 shows how you can use the pretrained models to solve different instances of TSP. We start by importing the libraries and modules we'll use. These libraries provide functionality for handling data, performing computations, visualization, and optimization. The Gurobi library is used to eliminate subtours during optimization and to calculate the reduce costs for a set of points (see appendix A). We set the CUDA_DEVICE_ORDER and CUDA_VISIBLE_DEVICES environment variables to control the GPU device visibility.

Listing 11.4   Solving TSP using supervised ML

```
import os
import math
import itertools
import numpy as np
import networkx as nx
from scipy.spatial.distance import pdist, squareform
import seaborn as sns
import matplotlib.pyplot as plt

import torch
from torch.utils.data import DataLoader
from torch.nn import DataParallel

from learning_tsp.problems.tsp.problem_tsp import TSP
from learning_tsp.utils import load_model, move_to

from gurobipy import *

os.environ["CUDA_DEVICE_ORDER"] = "PCI_BUS_ID"
os.environ["CUDA_VISIBLE_DEVICES"] = "0"
```

As a continuation, the following `opts` class contains several class-level attributes that define the following options and configurations:

- `dataset path`—The TSP dataset available in the book's GitHub repo.
- `batch size`—This determines the number of TSP instances (problems) processed simultaneously during training or evaluation. It specifies how many TSP instances are grouped together and processed in parallel.
- `number of samples`—This is the number of samples per TSP size.
- `neighbors`—This is used in the TSP data processing pipeline to specify the proportion (percentage) of nearest neighbors to consider for graph sparsification. It controls the connectivity of the TSP graph by selecting a subset of the nearest neighbors for each node.
- `knn strategy`—This is the strategy used to determine the number of nearest neighbors when performing graph sparsification. In the code, the `'percentage'` value indicates that the number of nearest neighbors is determined by the `neighbors` parameter, which specifies the percentage of neighbors to consider.
- `model`—This is the path for the pretrained ML model. The model used is a pretrained GNN model available in the book's GitHub repo.
- `use_cuda`—This checks if CUDA is available on the system. CUDA is a parallel computing platform and programming model that allows for efficient execution of computations on NVIDIA GPUs. `torch.cuda.is_available()` returns a Boolean value (true or false) indicating whether CUDA is available or not. If CUDA is available, that means a compatible NVIDIA GPU is present on the system and can be utilized for accelerated computations.
- `device`—This is the device to be used for computations:

```
class opts:
    dataset_path = "learning_tsp/data/tsp20-50_concorde.txt"
    batch_size = 16
    num_samples = 1280

    neighbors = 0.20
    knn_strat = 'percentage'

    model =
➥ "learning_tsp/pretrained/tspsl_20-50/sl-ar-var-20pnn-gnn-
max_20200308T172931"

    use_cuda = torch.cuda.is_available()
    device = torch.device("cuda:0" if use_cuda else "cpu")
```

The next step is to create a dataset object using the TSP class with the following parameters:

- `filename`—The path or filename of the dataset to be used, specified by `opts` `.dataset_path`
- `batch_size`—The number of samples to include in each batch, specified by `opts.batch_size`

- `num_samples`—The total number of samples to include in the dataset, specified by `opts.num_samples`
- `neighbors`—The value representing the number of nearest neighbors for graph sparsification, specified by `opts.neighbors`
- `knn_strat`—The strategy for selecting nearest neighbors (`'percentage'` or `None`), specified by `opts.knn_strat`
- `supervised`—A Boolean value indicating whether the dataset is used for supervised learning, set to `True`

The `make_dataset` method creates an instance of the TSP dataset class and initializes it with the provided arguments, returning the `dataset` object:

```
dataset = TSP.make_dataset(
    filename=opts.dataset_path, batch_size=opts.batch_size,
➥ num_samples=opts.num_samples,
➥ neighbors=opts.neighbors, knn_strat=opts.knn_strat, supervised=True
)
```

The following line creates a data loader object that enables convenient iteration over the dataset in batches, which is useful for processing the data during evaluation. The `dataset` object created in the previous line will be used as the source of the data. You can provide other optional arguments to customize the behavior of the data loader, such as `shuffle` (to shuffle the data) and `num_workers` (to specify the number of worker processes for data loading):

```
dataloader = DataLoader(dataset, batch_size=opts.batch_size, shuffle=False,
➥ num_workers=0)
```

We can now load the trained model and assign it to the `model` variable. If the model is wrapped in `torch.nn.DataParallel`, it extracts the underlying module by accessing `model.module`. `DataParallel` is a PyTorch wrapper that allows for parallel execution of models on multiple GPUs. If the model is indeed an instance of `DataParallel`, it extracts the underlying model module by accessing the `module` attribute. This step is necessary to ensure consistent behavior when accessing model attributes and methods. The decode type of the model is then set to `"greedy"`. This means that during inference or evaluation, the model should use a greedy decoding strategy to generate output predictions:

```
model, model_args = load_model(opts.model, extra_logging=True) ◄─────────┐
model.to(opts.device)                                   Load a pretrained model. ┘

if isinstance(model, DataParallel):
    model = model.module          ├─── Extract the underlying module.

model.set_decode_type("greedy") ◄───── Set the decoding type of the model to "greedy".

model.eval() ◄───┐ Set the model's mode to evaluation.
```

The complete version of listing 11.4, including the visualization code, is available in the book's GitHub repo. Figure 11.17 shows the output produced by the pretrained ML model for the TSP50 instance.

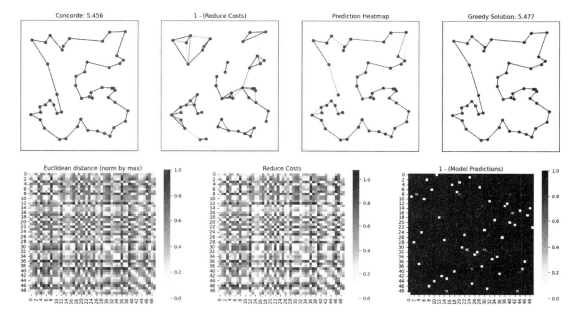

Figure 11.17   The TSP50 solution using a pretrained ML model

The figure shows the following seven plots related to the TSP instance and the model's predictions:

- *Concorde*—The plot in the upper-left corner shows the ground truth solution generated by the Concorde solver, which is an efficient implementation of the branch-and-cut algorithm for solving TSP instances to optimality. It shows the nodes of the TSP problem as circles connected by edges, representing the optimal tour calculated by Concorde. The title of the plot indicates the length (cost) of the tour obtained from Concorde.
- *1 - (Reduce Costs)*—The second plot contains the shortest subtour and shows the reduced costs for the points in these subtours using the Gurobi optimization library. It displays the edges of the TSP as red lines, with the edge color indicating the reduced cost value.
- *Prediction Heatmap*—The third plot presents a heatmap visualization of the model's predictions for the TSP problem. It uses a color scale to represent the prediction probabilities of edges, with higher probabilities shown in darker shades.

- *Greedy Solution*—The fourth plot illustrates the solution generated by the ML model using a greedy decoding strategy. It displays the nodes of the TSP problem connected by edges, representing the tour obtained from the model. The title of the plot shows the length (cost) of the tour calculated by the model.
- *Euclidean Distance (norm by max)*—The lower-left plot is a heatmap visualization of the Euclidean distances between nodes in the TSP problem. It uses a color scale to represent the distances, with lighter shades indicating smaller distances.
- *Reduce Costs*—The lower-middle plot is a heatmap representation of the reduced costs of edges in the TSP problem. It shows the reduced costs as a color scale, with lower values displayed in lighter shades.
- *1 - (Model Predictions)*—The lower-right plot presents a heatmap visualization of the model's predictions for the TSP problem, similar to the third plot. However, in this case, the heatmap displays "1 - (Model Predictions)" by subtracting the model's prediction probabilities from 1. Darker shades represent lower probabilities, indicating stronger confidence in the edge selection.

This example demonstrated how we can employ a pretrained GNN model for solving TSP. Figure 11.17 displays the model's solution alongside the Concorde TSP solver's results for a TSP instance comprising 50 points of interest. More information and complete code, including model training steps, are available in "Learning the Travelling Salesperson Problem Requires Rethinking Generalization" GitHub repo [21].

11.8   *Solving TSP using unsupervised machine learning*

As an example of an unsupervised ML approach, listing 11.5 shows how we can solve TSP using self-organizing maps (SOMs). We start by importing the libraries we'll use. Some helper functions are imported from the som-tsp implementation described in Vicente's blog post [22] to read the TSP instance, get the neighborhood, get the route, select the closest candidate, and calculate the route distance and plot the route. We read the TSP instance from the provided URL and obtain the cities and normalize their coordinates to a range of [0, 1].

Listing 11.5   Solving TSP using unsupervised learning

```
import numpy as np
import matplotlib.pyplot as plt
from matplotlib.animation import FuncAnimation
from IPython.display import HTML
import requests
import os
from tqdm import tqdm                          Define the URL where the
                                               TSP instances are located.
from som_tsp.helper import read_tsp, normalize, get_neighborhood, get_route,
➥ select_closest, route_distance, plot_network, plot_route

url = 'https://raw.githubusercontent.com/Optimization-Algorithms-Book/Code-
➥Listings/256207c4a8badc0977286c48a6e1cfd33237a51d/Appendix%20B/data/TSP/'◄
```

```
tsp='qa194.tsp'
```
TSP instance

```
response = requests.get(url+tsp)
response.raise_for_status()
problem_text = response.text
with open(tsp, 'w') as file:
    file.write(problem_text)
```
Download the file if it does not exist.

```
problem = read_tsp(tsp)
```
Read the TSP problem.

```
cities = problem.copy()
cities[['x', 'y']] = normalize(cities[['x', 'y']])
```
Obtain the normalized set of cities (with coordinates in [0,1]).

We can now set up various parameters and initialize a network of neurons for the SOM:

```
number_of_neurons = cities.shape[0] * 8
```
The population size is 8 times the number of cities.

```
iterations = 12000
```
Set the number of iterations.

```
learning_rate=0.8
```
Set the learning rate.

```
network = np.random.rand(number_of_neurons, 2)
```
Generate an adequate network of neurons.

As a continuation, the following code snippet implements the training loop for SOM. This loop iterates over the specified number of training iterations using tqdm to show a progress bar:

```
route_lengths = []
```
Store the lengths of the TSP routes during the SOM training iterations.

```
paths_x = []
paths_y = []
```
Store the x and y coordinates of the neurons in the network during the training iterations.

```
for i in tqdm(range(iterations)):
```
Training loop

```
    if not i % 100:
        print('\t> Iteration {}/{}'.format(i, iterations), end="\r")
```
Print only if the current iteration index is a multiple of 100.

```
    city = cities.sample(1)[['x', 'y']].values
```
Choose a random city.

```
    winner_idx = select_closest(network, city)
```
Find the index of the neuron (winner) in the SOM network that is closest to the randomly chosen city.

```
    gaussian = get_neighborhood(winner_idx, number_of_neurons // 10,
    network.shape[0])
```
Generate a filter that applies changes to the winner's gaussian.

```
    network += gaussian[:, np.newaxis] * learning_rate * (city - network)
```
Update the network's weights.

```
    paths_x.append(network[:, 0].copy())
    paths_y.append(network[:, 1].copy())
```
Append the current coordinates to the paths.

```
    learning_rate = learning_rate * 0.99997
    number_of_neurons = number_of_neurons * 0.9997
```
Decay the learning rate and the neighborhood radius n at each iteration to gradually reduce the influence of the Gaussian filter over time.

```
    if not i % 1000:
        plot_network(cities, network, name='diagrams/{:05d}.png'.format(i))
```
Check for the plotting interval.

```
if number_of_neurons < 1:  ◀─────┐ Check if any parameter has completely decayed.
    print('Radius has completely decayed, finishing execution',
        ➥ 'at {} iterations'.format(i))
    break
if learning_rate < 0.001:
    print('Learning rate has completely decayed, finishing execution',
        ➥ 'at {} iterations'.format(i))
    break

route = get_route(cities, network)
problem = problem.reindex(route)       ──── Calculate distance, and store
distance = route_distance(problem)          it in the route_lengths list.
route_lengths.append(distance)
```

Indicate that the specified number of training iterations has been completed.
```
else:
    print('Completed {} iterations.'.format(iterations))  ◀───────
```

The following code snippet plots the route length in each iteration.

```
plt.figure(figsize=(8, 6))
plt.plot(range(len(route_lengths)), route_lengths, label='Route Length')
plt.xlabel('Iterations')
plt.ylabel('Route Length')
plt.title('Route Length per Iteration')
plt.grid(True)
plt.show()
```

Figure 11.18 shows the route length per iteration. The final route length is 9,816, and the optimal length for the Qatar TSP instance used, `qa194.tsp`, is 9,352.

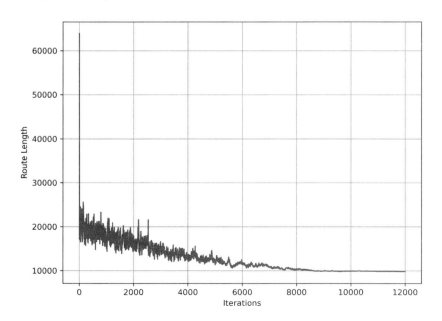

Figure 11.18   Route length per iteration of SOM for the Qatar TSP. The final route length is 9,816, and the optimal solution is 9,352.

The complete version of listing 11.5 is available in the book's GitHub repo, and it contains an implementation based on MiniSom. MiniSom is a minimalistic and Numpy-based implementation of SOM. You can install this library using `!pip install minisom`. However, the route obtained by MiniSom is 11,844.47, which is far from the optimal length of 9,352 for this TSP instance. To improve the result, you can experiment with the provided code and try to tune SOM parameters such as the number of neurons, the sigma, the learning rate, and the number of iterations.

11.9   Finding a convex hull

Ptr-Net can be used to tackle the convex hull problem using a supervised learning approach, as described by Vinyals and his co-authors in their "Pointer networks" article [10]. Ptr-Net has two key components: an encoder and a decoder, as illustrated in figure 11.19.

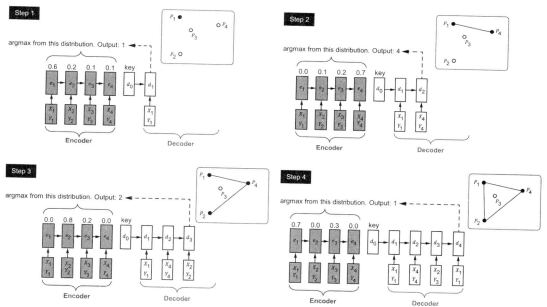

Figure 11.19   Solving the convex hull problem using Ptr-Net. The output in each step is a pointer to the input that maximizes the probability distribution.

The encoder, a recurrent neural network (RNN), converts the raw input sequence. In this case, it coordinates delineating the points for which we want to determine the convex hull into a more manageable representation.

   This encoded vector is then passed on to the decoder. The vector acts as the modulator for a content-based attention mechanism, which is applied over the inputs. The content-based attention mechanism can be likened to a spotlight that highlights different segments of the input data at varying times, focusing on the most pertinent parts of the task at hand.

The output of this attention mechanism is a softmax distribution with a dictionary size equal to the length of the input. This softmax distribution gives probabilities to every point in the input sequence. This setup allows Ptr-Net to probabilistically decide at each step which point should be added next to the convex hull. This is determined based on the current state of the input and the network's internal state. The training process is repeated until the network has made a decision for every point, yielding a complete resolution to the convex hull problem.

Listing 11.6 shows the steps for solving convex hull problem using pointer networks. We start by importing several necessary libraries and modules, such as torch, numpy, and matplotlib. The three helper classes `Data`, `ptr_net`, and `Disp` are imported based on the implementations provided in McGough's "Pointer Networks with Transformers" article [23]. They contain functions for generating training and validation data, defining the pointer network architecture, and visualizing the results. This code generates two datasets for training and validation respectively. These datasets consist of random 2D points, where the number of points in each sample (the convex hull problem's input) varies between `min_samples` and `max_samples`. `Scatter2DDataset` is a custom dataset class used to generate these random 2D point datasets.

Listing 11.6 Solving a convex hull problem using pointer networks

```python
import numpy as np
import torch
from torch.utils.data import DataLoader
import matplotlib.pyplot as plt
from scipy.spatial import ConvexHull

from ptrnets.Data import display_points_with_hull, cyclic_permute,
➥ Scatter2DDataset,Disp_results
from ptrnets.ptr_net import ConvexNet, AverageMeter, masked_accuracy,
➥ calculate_hull_overlap

min_samples = 5
max_samples = 50
n_rows_train = 100000
n_rows_val = 1000

torch.random.manual_seed(231)
train_dataset = Scatter2DDataset(n_rows_train, min_samples, max_samples)
val_dataset = Scatter2DDataset(n_rows_val, min_samples, max_samples)
```

Running this code generates 100,000 training points and 1,000 validation points. We can then set the parameters of the pointer network. These parameters include a TOKENS dictionary containing the following tokens:

- `<eos>`—End-of-sequence token with the index 0
- `c_inputs`—Number of input features for the model
- `c_embed`—Number of embedding dimensions

- c_hidden—Number of hidden units in the model
- n_heads—Number of attention heads in the multi-head self-attention mechanism
- n_layers—Number of layers in the model
- dropout—Dropout probability, which is used for regularization
- use_cuda—A Boolean flag indicating whether to use CUDA (GPU) if available or CPU
- n_workers—Number of worker threads for data loading in DataLoader

The training parameters include n_epochs (number of training epochs), batch_size (batch size used during training), lr (learning rate for the optimizer), and log_interval (interval for logging training progress). The code checks if CUDA (GPU) is available and sets the device variable accordingly:

```
TOKENS = {'<eos>': 0 }
c_inputs = 2 + len(TOKENS)
c_embed = 16
c_hidden = 16
n_heads = 4
n_layers = 3
dropout = 0.0
use_cuda = True
n_workers = 2
n_epochs = 5
batch_size = 16
lr = 1e-3
log_interval = 500
device = torch.device("cuda" if torch.cuda.is_available() and use_cuda else
"cpu")
```

As a continuation, we load the training and validation data with the specified batch_size and num_workers:

```
train_loader = DataLoader(train_dataset, batch_size=batch_size,
➥  num_workers=n_workers)

val_loader = DataLoader(val_dataset, batch_size=batch_size,
➥  num_workers=n_workers)
```

The ConvexNet model is a Ptr-Net model that is implemented as a transformer architecture with an encoder and decoder that use nn.TransformerEncoderLayer and apply multi-head self-attention. The complete code is available in the ptr_net.py class, available in the book's GitHub repo. This model is initialized with the predefined hyperparameters. The AverageMeter class is used for keeping track of the average loss and accuracy during training and validation:

Create a ConvexNet model.   **Use the Adam optimizer for training the model.**

```
model = ConvexNet(c_inputs=c_inputs, c_embed=c_embed, n_heads=n_heads,
➥  n_layers=n_layers, dropout=dropout, c_hidden=c_hidden).to(device)

optimizer = torch.optim.Adam(model.parameters(), lr=lr)
```

```
criterion = torch.nn.NLLLoss(ignore_index=TOKENS['<eos>'])
```
Use negative log-likelihood loss as the loss function.

```
train_loss = AverageMeter()
train_accuracy = AverageMeter()
val_loss = AverageMeter()
val_accuracy = AverageMeter()
```
Keep track of the average loss and accuracy during training and validation.

We can now perform the training and evaluation loop for a model (ConvexNet) using PyTorch. The model is being trained on the train_loader dataset with known labels and evaluated on the val_loader dataset:

Train the model.
```
for epoch in range(n_epochs):
    model.train()
    for bat, (batch_data, batch_labels, batch_lengths) in enumerate(train_
loader):
```
Iterate over batches of training data.
```
        batch_data = batch_data.to(device)
        batch_labels = batch_labels.to(device)
        batch_lengths = batch_lengths.to(device)
```

Set the model's parameters' gradients to zero to avoid accumulation from previous batches.
```
        optimizer.zero_grad()
        log_pointer_scores, pointer_argmaxs = model(batch_data, batch_lengths,
            batch_labels=batch_labels)
```
Calculate the loss.
```
        loss = criterion(log_pointer_scores.view(-1, log_pointer_scores.
    shape[-1]), batch_labels.reshape(-1))
```

```
        assert not np.isnan(loss.item()), 'Model diverged with loss = NaN'
```
A safeguard check to ensure that the loss value during the training process is not a NaN.

```
        loss.backward()
        optimizer.step()
```
Perform a backward pass and optimization step.

Update training loss and accuracy.
```
        train_loss.update(loss.item(), batch_data.size(0))
        mask = batch_labels != TOKENS['<eos>']
        acc = masked_accuracy(pointer_argmaxs, batch_labels, mask).item()
        train_accuracy.update(acc, mask.int().sum().item())
```

```
        if bat % log_interval == 0:
            print(f'Epoch {epoch}: '
                f'Train [{bat * len(batch_data):9d}/{len(train_dataset):9d} '
                f'Loss: {train_loss.avg:.6f}\tAccuracy: {train_accuracy.
avg:3.4%}')
```
Print the training progress.

As a continuation, the trained model (model) is evaluated on a validation dataset (val_dataset) to calculate the validation loss, accuracy, and overlap between the convex hull of the input data and the predicted pointer sequences. We start by setting the model to evaluation mode, where the model's parameters are frozen and the batch normalization or dropout layers behave differently than during training. The code then iterates through the validation dataset using the val_loader, which provides batches of data (batch_data), ground truth labels (batch_labels), and the lengths of each sequence (batch_lengths):

Initialize an empty list to store the overlap values between the
convex hull of the input data and the predicted pointer sequences.

```
model.eval()                                          Set the model to evaluation mode.
hull_overlaps = []
for bat, (batch_data, batch_labels, batch_lengths)
    in enumerate(val_loader):              Iterate through the
  batch_data = batch_data.to(device)       validation dataset.
  batch_labels = batch_labels.to(device)
  batch_lengths = batch_lengths.to(device)       Produce pointer scores
                                                  and argmax predictions.
  log_pointer_scores, pointer_argmaxs = model(batch_data, batch_lengths,
      batch_labels=batch_labels)
  loss = criterion(log_pointer_scores.view(-1, log_pointer_scores.
  shape[-1]),batch_labels.reshape(-1))
```

Calculate the
validation
loss.

Ignore the loss contribution from positions where
the <eos> token is present in batch_labels.

```
  assert not np.isnan(loss.item()), 'Model diverged with loss = NaN'
  val_loss.update(loss.item(), batch_data.size(0))
  mask = batch_labels != TOKENS['<eos>']
  acc = masked_accuracy(pointer_argmaxs, batch_labels, mask).item()
  val_accuracy.update(acc, mask.int().sum().item())
```

Update the
validation loss.

Update the validation accuracy.   **Calculate the masked accuracy.**

```
for data, length, ptr in zip(batch_data.cpu(), batch_lengths.cpu(),
        pointer_argmaxs.cpu()):
    hull_overlaps.append(calculate_hull_overlap(data, length, ptr))

print(f'Epoch {epoch}: Val\tLoss: {val_loss.avg:.6f} '
    f'\tAccuracy: {val_accuracy.avg:3.4%} '
    f'\tOverlap: {np.mean(hull_overlaps):3.4%}')    Print the epoch-wise
train_loss.reset()                                   validation loss, accuracy,
train_accuracy.reset()                               and mean overlap.
val_loss.reset()          Reset the metrics.
val_accuracy.reset()                        Calculate the overlap between the convex hull of the
                                            input data and the predicted pointer sequences.
```

**Iterate through each batch's data,
lengths, and pointer argmax predictions.**

You can display the results of training and validation losses and accuracies using the
`Disp_results` helper function:

```
Disp_results(train_loss, train_accuracy, val_loss, val_accuracy, n_epochs)
```

The preceding line of code will generate output like the following:

```
Best Scores:
train_loss: 0.0897 (ep: 9)
train_accuracy 96.61% (ep: 9)
val_loss: 0.0937 (ep: 7)
val_accuracy: 96.54% (ep: 7)
```

After model training and validation, we can test the model. The following test function will evaluate a trained model (`model`) on a test dataset. The function evaluates the model's accuracy and overlap with the convex hull for different test sample sizes. This test function takes as inputs the model, the number of test samples, and the number of points per sample. The code performs the test for different numbers of points per sample (`i`) by iterating from 5 to 45 in steps of 5. The `AverageMeter` class is used to keep track of average loss and accuracy during testing:

Test function →

Track the loss and accuracy.

Update the overlap between the convex hull and predicted pointer sequences.

```
n_rows_test = 1000  ◄——————  Set the number of test samples to be generated for each test.

def test(model, n_rows_test, n_per_row):
    test_dataset = Scatter2DDataset(n_rows_test, n_per_row, n_per_row)
    test_loader = DataLoader(test_dataset, batch_size=batch_size,
    ➥ num_workers=n_workers)
                                                    Generate the test dataset.
    test_accuracy = AverageMeter()
    hull_overlaps = []
    model.eval()                              Iterate through the batches of test data.

    for _, (batch_data, batch_labels, batch_lengths) in enumerate(test_loader):◄
        batch_data = batch_data.to(device)
        batch_labels = batch_labels.to(device)
        batch_lengths = batch_lengths.to(device)

        _, pointer_argmaxs = model(batch_data, batch_lengths)

        val_loss.update(loss.item(), batch_data.size(0))
        mask = batch_labels != TOKENS['<eos>']
        acc = masked_accuracy(pointer_argmaxs, batch_labels, mask).item()
        test_accuracy.update(acc, mask.int().sum().item())

        for data, length, ptr in zip(batch_data.cpu(), batch_lengths.cpu(),
        ➥ pointer_argmaxs.cpu()):
            hull_overlaps.append(calculate_hull_overlap(data, length, ptr))

    print(f'# Test Samples: {n_per_row:3d}\t '              Print the accuracy
        f'\tAccuracy: {test_accuracy.avg:3.1%} '            and overlap.
        f'\tOverlap: {np.mean(hull_overlaps):3.1%}')

for i in range(5,50,5):                 Iterate and print results for different sample sizes.
    test(model, n_rows_test, i)
```

This code will produce output like the following:

```
# Test Samples:     5      Accuracy: 54.8%      Overlap: 43.7%
# Test Samples:    10      Accuracy: 72.1%      Overlap: 79.1%
# Test Samples:    15      Accuracy: 79.0%      Overlap: 90.1%
# Test Samples:    20      Accuracy: 84.8%      Overlap: 92.7%
# Test Samples:    25      Accuracy: 80.6%      Overlap: 92.3%
# Test Samples:    30      Accuracy: 80.3%      Overlap: 91.6%
# Test Samples:    35      Accuracy: 77.8%      Overlap: 91.9%
# Test Samples:    40      Accuracy: 75.8%      Overlap: 92.1%
# Test Samples:    45      Accuracy: 72.4%      Overlap: 90.4%
```

Let's now test the trained model and see how well this model generalizes to new unseen data. We'll use a dataset with 50 points to test the trained and validated model and calculate the convex hull overlap between the predicted hull and the ground truth hull obtained by SciPy. We pass the batch of input data and its lengths through the model to obtain the predicted scores (`log_pointer_scores`) and the argmax indices (`pointer_argmaxs`) of the pointer network. The ground truth is the convex hull obtained using the `ConvexHull` function from `scipy.spatial`:

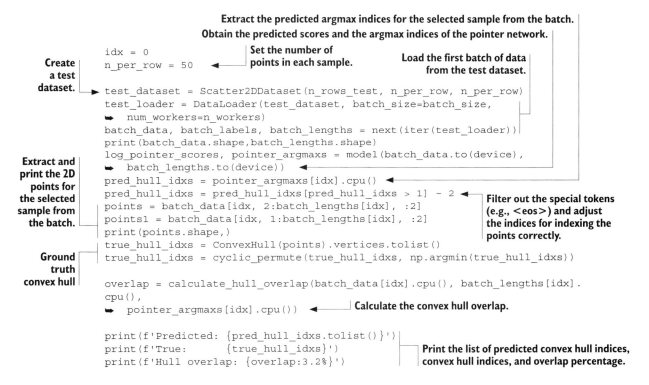

Running the code will produce output like the following. You can run the preceding code snippets multiple times to get a high percentage of hull overlap:

```
torch.Size([16, 51, 3]) torch.Size([16])
torch.Size([49, 2])
Predicted: [0, 3, 5, 31, 45, 47, 48, 40, 10]
True:      [0, 3, 5, 31, 45, 47, 48, 40, 10]
Hull overlap: 100.00%
```

The following code snippet can be used to visualize the convex hull generated by the pointer network (`ConvexNet`) in comparison with the convex hull generated by `scipy.spatial` as a ground truth:

```
plt.rcParams['figure.figsize'] = (10, 6)
plt.subplot(1, 2, 1)
```

Set the default figure size, and create the first subplot.

```
true_hull_idxs = ConvexHull(points).vertices.tolist()
display_points_with_hull(points, true_hull_idxs)
_ = plt.title('SciPy Convex Hull')

plt.subplot(1, 2, 2)
display_points_with_hull(points, pred_hull_idxs)
_ = plt.title('ConvexNet Convex Hull')
```

Display the points and their convex hull in the first subplot.

Create a second subplot.

Display the points and the convex hull generated by ConvexNet.

Compute the convex hull of a set of points (points) using the ConvexHull function from scipy.spatial.

Figure 11.20 shows the convex hulls generated by SciPy and ConvexNet. These convex hulls are identical in some instances (i.e., hull overlap = 100.00%), yet achieving this consistency requires proper training and careful tuning of the ConvexNet parameters.

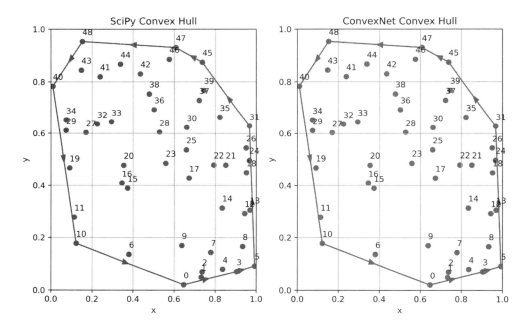

Figure 11.20   **Convex hulls generated by SciPy and Ptr-Net for 50 points**

This chapter has offered a fundamental foundation in ML and discussed the applications of supervised and unsupervised ML in handling optimization problems. The next chapter will focus on reinforcement learning and will delve deeply into its practical applications in tackling optimization problems.

Summary

- Machine learning (ML), a branch of artificial intelligence (AI), grants an artificial system or process the capacity to learn from experiences and observations, rather than through explicit programming.

- Deep learning (DL) is a subset of ML that is focused on the detection of inherent features within data by employing deep neural networks. This allows artificial systems to form intricate concepts from simpler ones.

- Geometric deep learning (GDL) extends (structured) deep neural models to handle non-Euclidean data with underlying geometric structures, such as graphs, point clouds, and manifolds.

- Graph machine learning (GML) is a subfield of ML that focuses on developing algorithms and models capable of learning from graph-structured data.

- Graph embedding represents the process of creating a conversion from the discrete, high-dimensional graph domain to a lower-dimensional continuous domain.

- The attention mechanism allows a model to selectively focus on certain portions of the input data while it is in the process of generating the output sequence.

- The pointer network (Ptr-Net) is a variation of the sequence-to-sequence model with attention designed to deal with variable-sized input data sequences.

- A self-organizing map (SOM), also known as a Kohonen map, is a type of artificial neural network (ANN) used for unsupervised learning. SOMs differ from other types of ANNs, as they apply competitive learning rather than error-correction learning (such as backpropagation with gradient descent).

- Neural combinatorial optimization refers to the application of ML to solve combinatorial optimization problems.

- Harnessing ML for combinatorial optimization can be achieved through three main methods: end-to-end learning where the model directly formulates solutions, using ML to configure and improve optimization algorithms, and integrating ML with optimization algorithms where the model continuously guides the optimization algorithm based on its current state.

Reinforcement learning

12

This chapter covers

- Grasping the fundamental principles underlying reinforcement learning
- Understanding the Markov decision process
- Comprehending the actor-critic architecture and proximal policy optimization
- Getting familiar with noncontextual and contextual multi-armed bandits
- Applying reinforcement learning to solve optimization problems

Reinforcement learning (RL) is a powerful machine learning approach that enables intelligent agents to learn optimal or near-optimal behavior through interacting with their environments. This chapter dives into the key concepts and techniques within RL, shedding light on its underlying principles as essential background knowledge. Following this theoretical exposition, the chapter will proceed to illustrate practical examples of employing RL strategies to tackle optimization problems.

12.1   Demystifying reinforcement learning

Reinforcement learning (RL) is a subfield of machine learning that deals with how an agent can learn to make decisions and take actions in an environment to achieve specific goals following a trial-and-error learning approach. The core idea of RL is that the agent learns by interacting with the environment, receiving feedback in the form of rewards or penalties as a result of its actions. The agent's objective is to maximize the cumulative reward over time.

Reinforcement learning

"Reinforcement learning problems involve learning what to do—how to map situations to actions—so as to maximize a numerical reward signal" (Richard Sutton and Andrew Barto, in their book *Reinforcement Learning* [1]).

Figure 12.1 outlines the common RL algorithms found in the literature. This classification divides RL problems into two main categories: Markov decision process (MDP) problems and multi-armed bandit (MAB) problems. The distinction between the two lies in how the agent's actions interact with and affect the environment.

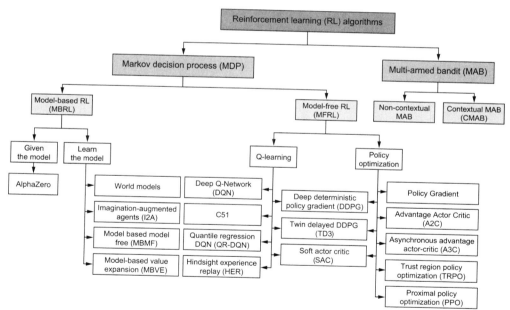

Figure 12.1   Reinforcement learning algorithm taxonomy

In MDP-based problems, the agent's actions influence the environment, and the agent must consider the consequences of its actions over multiple time steps, incorporating the notion of states and transitions. MAB problems, on the other hand, involve scenarios where the agent faces a series of choices (arms) and aims to maximize the cumulative reward over time. Such problems are often used when there is no explicit state representation or long-term planning required. In contextual multi-armed bandit (CMAB) problems, the agent is presented with context or side information that is used to make more informed decisions. The expected reward of an arm (an action) is a function of both the action and the current context. This means the best action can change depending on the provided context. It is worth mentioning that MDPs are a more comprehensive framework that accounts for dynamic decision-making in a broader range of situations.

Before we explore how reinforcement learning can be applied to solve optimization problems, it is essential to understand several relevant reinforcement learning techniques. The following subsections will provide a detailed overview of these methods, and the subsequent sections will demonstrate their use in addressing optimization problems.

12.1.1 *Markov decision process (MDP)*

The purpose of learning is to form an internal model of the external world. This external world, or *environment*, can be abstracted using deterministic or nondeterministic (stochastic) models.

Consider a situation where you're planning to commute from your initial state (e.g., your home) to a designated goal state (e.g., your workplace). A deterministic path-planning algorithm such as A* (discussed in chapter 4) might provide you with multiple options: taking the train, which would take about 1 hour and 48 minutes; driving by car, which could take about 1 hour and 7 minutes; or biking, which could take about 3 hours and 16 minutes (figure 12.2a). These algorithms operate under the assumption that actions and their resulting effects are entirely deterministic.

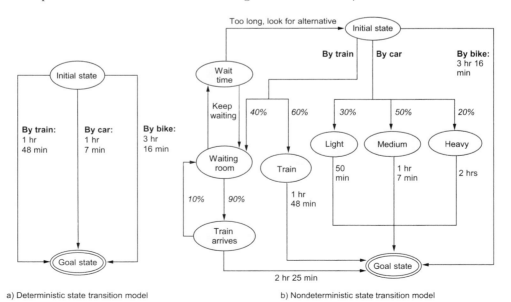

Figure 12.2   Deterministic vs. nondeterministic state transition models

However, if uncertainties come into play during your journey planning, you should resort to stochastic planning algorithms that operate on nondeterministic state transition models to enable planning under uncertainty. In these scenarios, transition probabilities between states become an integral part of your decision-making process.

For instance, let's consider the initial state (your home), as shown in figure 12.2b. If you choose to commute by train, there's a 60% chance that you'll be able to catch the train on time and reach your destination (your workplace) within the expected 1 hour and 48 minutes. However, there's a 40% chance that you could miss the train and need to wait for the next one. If you do end up waiting, there's a 90% chance the train will arrive on time and you'll catch it and arrive at your destination within a total time of 2 hours and 25 minutes. On the other hand, there's a 10% chance the train does not arrive, leading to an extended wait or even having to look for an alternative. On the other hand, if you choose to drive, there's a 30% chance that you'll encounter light traffic and reach your office in just 50 minutes. However, there's also a 50% likelihood of medium traffic delaying your arrival to 1 hour and 7 minutes. In the worst-case scenario, there's a 20% chance that heavy traffic could extend your travel time to 2 hours. If you choose to bike, the estimated travel time of 3 hours and 16 minutes is more predictable and less subject to change.

This scenario describes an environment that is fully observable and where the current state and actions taken completely determine the probability distribution of the next state. This is called a Markov decision process (MDP).

12.1.2 *From MDP to reinforcement learning*

MDP provides a mathematical framework for planning under uncertainty. It is used to describe an environment for reinforcement learning, where an agent learns to make decisions by performing actions and receiving rewards. The learning process involves trial and error, with the agent discovering which actions yield the highest expected cumulative reward over time.

As shown in figure 12.3, the agent interacts with the environment by being in a certain state $s_t \in S$, taking an action $a_t \in A$ at time t based on an observation o and by applying policy π, and then receiving a reward $r_t \in R$ and transitioning to a new state $s_{t+1} \in S$ according to the state transition probability T.

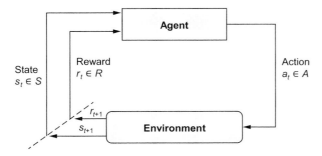

Figure 12.3   An agent learns through interaction with the environment.

The following terms are commonly used in RL:

- *A state,* s—This represents the complete and unfiltered information about the environment at a particular time step. An observation *o* is the partial or limited information that the agent can perceive from the environment at a given time step. When the agent is able to observe the complete state of the environment, we say that the environment is fully observable and can be modeled as an MDP. When the agent can only see part of the environment, we say that the environment is partially observable, and it should be modeled as a *partially observable Markov decision process* (POMDP).
- *An action set,* A—This represents the set of possible or permissible actions that an agent can take in a given environment. These actions can be discrete, like in the case of board games, or continuous, like in the case of robot controls or the lane-keep assist of an assisted or automated driving vehicle.
- *The policy*—This can be seen as the agent's brain. It is the decision-making strategy of the agent or the mapping from states or observations to actions. This policy can be deterministic, usually denoted by μ, or stochastic, denoted by π. A stochastic policy π is mainly the probability of selecting an action $a \in A$ given a certain state $s \in S$. A stochastic policy can also be parameterized and denoted by π_{θ}. This parameterized policy is a computable function that depends on a set of parameters (e.g., the weights and biases of a neural network), which we can adjust to change the behavior via an optimization algorithm.
- *A trajectory, τ (aka episode or rollout)*—This is a sequence of states and actions in the world, $\tau = (s_0, a_0, s_1, a_1, \ldots)$.
- *The expected return*—This refers to the cumulative sum of rewards that an agent can expect to receive over a future time horizon. It is a measure of the overall desirability or value of a particular state-action sequence or policy.

Let's consider a simple Reach the Treasure game where an agent tries to get a treasure and then exits. In this game, there are only four states, as illustrated in figure 12.4. Among them, state 0 represents a fire pit, and state 3 represents the exit—both are terminal states. State 1 contains the treasure, symbolized by a diamond. The game starts with the agent positioned in state 2 and has the options of moving left or right as actions. Upon reaching the treasure, the agent receives a reward of +10. However, falling into the fire pit results in a penalty of –10. Successfully exiting grants a reward of +4.

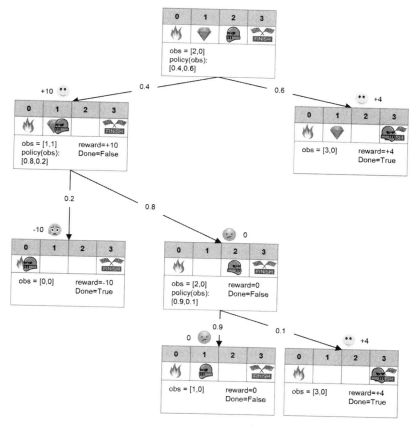

Figure 12.4 Reach the Treasure game

The state *s* provides the complete information about the environment, including the agent's position and the locations of the fire pit, treasure, and exit (state 0 is the fire pit, state 1 is the treasure, state 2 is the current location, and state 3 is the exit). The game's observations are collected and presented as an observation vector, such as obs = [2,0], indicating that the agent is in state 2 and does not perceive the presence of the treasure. This is a partial view of the environment, as the agent does not have access to the complete state information, such as the locations of the fire pit or exit. The policy denotes the probabilities assigned to moving left or right based on the observation. For instance, a policy(obs) of [0.4, 0.6] signifies a 40% chance of moving left and a 60% chance of moving right. In the single trajectory shown in figure 12.4, we can calculate the expected return as follows: expected return (R) = 0.4 * (10) + 0.6 * (4) + 0.4 * 0.2 * (−10) + 0.4 * 0.8 * (0) + 0.4 * 0.8 * 0.9 * (0) + 0.4 * 0.8 * 0.1 * (4) = 5.728.

The goal in RL is to learn an optimal policy that maximizes the expected cumulative discounted reward. Value iteration, policy iteration, and policy gradients are different iterative methods used in reinforcement learning to achieve this goal. The value function in RL defines the expected cumulative reward of the agent starting from a particular state or state-action pair, following a certain policy. There are two types of value functions: the state-value function $V(s)$ and the action-value function $Q(s,a)$. The state-value function $V(s)$ estimates the expected cumulative future rewards an agent may obtain, starting from a particular state s and following a policy π. It quantifies the desirability of a state based on its projected future rewards. The state-value function $V(s)$ is given by the following formula:

$$V^\pi(s) = E_\pi\left[R_t|s_t = s\right] = E_\pi\left[\sum_{k=0}^{\infty} \gamma^k r_{t+k+1}|s_t = s\right]$$ **12.1**

where

- $V^\pi(s)$ is the expected return when starting in s and following π thereafter.
- $E_\pi[]$ denotes the expected value, given that the agent follows policy π.
- t is any time step.
- γ is the discount factor, typically a value between 0 and 1, representing the present value of future rewards relative to immediate rewards. The purpose of discounting is to prioritize immediate rewards more heavily, reflecting the preference for rewards received sooner rather than later. A discount factor close to 0 makes the agent *myopic* (i.e., focused on immediate rewards), while a discount factor close to 1 makes the agent more *farsighted* (i.e., considering future rewards).

The action-value function, $Q(s, a)$, estimates the expected cumulative future rewards an agent can achieve by taking a specific action a from a given state s and following a policy π. It quantifies the "goodness" of taking a specific action in a specific state under a given policy. The action-value function $Q(s, a)$ is given by the following formula:

$$Q^\pi(s, a) = E_\pi\left[R_t|s_t = s, a_t = a\right]$$

$$= E_\pi\left[\sum_{k=0}^{\infty} \gamma^k r_{t+k+1}|s_t = s, a_t = a\right]$$ **12.2**

In *policy iteration methods*, we first compute the value $V^\pi(s)$ of each state following an initial policy, and we use these value estimates to improve the policy. This means that from an initial policy we repeatedly alternate between policy evaluation and policy improvement steps (until convergence).

Policy gradient methods learn a parameterized policy that is used by the agent to choose actions. The goal is to find the values of the policy parameters that maximize the expected cumulative reward over time.

Policy gradient

Policy gradient is a model-free policy-based method that doesn't require explicit value function representation. The core idea is to favor actions that lead to higher returns while discouraging actions that result in lower rewards. This iterative process refines the policy over time, aiming to find a high-performing policy.

Instead of explicitly estimating the value function, policy gradient methods work by computing an estimator of the policy gradient and plugging it in to a stochastic gradient ascent algorithm. Policy gradient loss L^{PG} is one of the most commonly used gradient estimators:

$$L^{PG}(\theta) = \widehat{E}_t \left[\log \pi_\theta(a_t, s_t)\widehat{A}_t \right]$$

12.3

where

- The expectation E_t indicates the empirical average over a finite batch of samples.
- π_θ is a stochastic policy that takes the observed states from the environment as an input and suggests actions to take as an output.
- $\widehat{A}_t$ is an estimate of the advantage function at time step t. This estimate basically tries to assess the relative value of the selected action in the current state. The advantage function represents the advantage of taking a particular action in a given state, compared to the expected value. It is calculated as the difference between the expected rewards from executing the suggested action (which often has the highest Q-value) and the estimated value function of the current state:

$$A(s, a) = Q(s, a) - V(s)$$

12.4

where

- $Q(s, a)$ is the action-value function (also known as the Q-value), which represents the expected cumulative rewards from taking action a in state s following the policy.
- $V(s)$ is the state-value function, which represents the expected cumulative rewards from state s following the policy.

As you can see in equation 12.4, if the advantage function is positive, indicating that the observed return is higher than the expected value, the gradient will be positive. This positive gradient means that the probabilities of the actions taken in that state will be increased in the future to enhance their likelihood. On the other hand, if the advantage function is negative, the gradient will be negative. This negative gradient implies that the probabilities of the selected actions will be decreased if similar states are encountered in the future.

12.1.3 *Model-based vs. model-free RL*

Reinforcement learning is categorized into two main types: model-based RL (MBRL) and model-free RL (MFRL). This classification is based on whether the RL agent possesses a model of the environment or not. The term *model* refers to an internal representation of the environment, encompassing its transition dynamics and reward function. Table 12.1 summarizes the differences between these two categories.

Table 12.1   Model-based RL (MBRL) versus model-free RL (MFRL)

Aspects	Model-based RL (MBRL)	Model-free RL (MFRL)
Environment model	Uses a known model or learns a model of the environment (i.e., transition probabilities)	Skips models and directly learns what action to take when (without necessarily finding out the exact model of the action)
Rewards	Typically known or learned	Unknown or partially known. Model-free RL learns directly from the rewards received during interaction with the environment.
Actions	Selected to maximize the expected cumulative reward using the model	Selected to maximize the expected cumulative rewards based on the history of experiences
Policy	Policy learning is accomplished by learning a model of the environment dynamics.	Policy learning is achieved through trial and error, directly optimizing the policy based on observed experiences.
Design and tuning	MBRL can have a higher initial design and tuning effort due to model complexity. However, advancements are simplifying this process.	Requires less initial effort. However, MFRL hyperparameter tuning can also be challenging, especially for complex tasks.
Examples	AlphaZero, world models, and imagination-augmented agents (I2A)	Q-learning, advantage actor-critic (A2C), asynchronous advantage actor-critic (A3C), and proximal policy optimization (PPO)

Based on how RL algorithms learn and update their policies from collected experiences, RL algorithms can also be classified as off-policy and on-policy RL. Off-policy methods learn from experiences generated by a policy different from the one being updated, while on-policy methods learn from experiences generated by the current policy being updated. Both on-policy and off-policy methods are often considered *model-free* because they directly learn policies or value functions from experiences without explicitly constructing a model of the environment's dynamics, distinguishing them from model-based approaches. Table 12.2 summarizes the differences between off-policy and on-policy model-free RL methods.

Table 12.2   Off-policy versus on-policy RL methods

Aspects	Off-policy RL methods	On-policy RL methods
Learning approach	Learn from experiences generated by a different policy than the one being updated	Learn from experiences generated by the current policy being updated
Sample efficiency	Typically more sample-efficient due to reusing past experiences (recorded data)	Typically less sample-efficient, as the batch of experiences is discarded after each policy update (past experiences are not explicitly stored)
Policy evaluation	Can learn the value function and policy separately, enabling different algorithms (e.g., Q-learning, DDPG, TD3)	Policy evaluation and improvement are typically intertwined in on-policy algorithms (e.g., REINFORCE, A2C, PPO).
Pros	More sample-efficient, can learn from diverse experiences, enables reuse of past data, useful if large amounts of prior data are available	Simpler and more straightforward, avoids off-policy correction, can converge to better local optima, suitable for scenarios with limited data or online learning
Cons	Requires careful off-policy correction, less suitable for online learning or tasks with limited data	Less sample-efficient, discards past experiences, limited exploration diversity, may converge to suboptimal policies

The following two subsections provide more details about A2C and PPO as examples of the on-policy methods used in this chapter.

12.1.4   *Actor-critic methods*

Figure 12.5 shows the advantage actor-critic (A2C) architecture as an example of actor-critic methods. As the name suggests, this architecture consists of two models: the *actor* and the *critic*. The actor is responsible for learning and updating the policy. It takes the current state as input and outputs the probability distribution over the actions that represent the policy. The critic, on the other hand, focuses on evaluating the action suggested by the actor. It takes the state and action as input and estimates the advantage of taking that action in that particular state. The advantage represents how much better (or worse) the action is compared to the average action in that state based on expected future rewards. This feedback from the critic helps the actor learn and update the policy to favor actions with higher advantages.

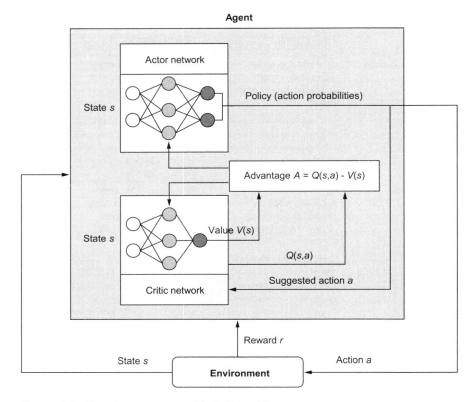

Figure 12.5   The advantage actor-critic (A2C) architecture

A2C is a synchronous, model-free algorithm that aims to learn both the policy (the actor) and the value function (the critic) simultaneously. It learns an optimal policy by iteratively improving the actor and critic networks. By estimating advantages, the algorithm can provide feedback on the quality of the actions taken by the actor. The critic network helps estimate the value function, providing a baseline for the advantages calculation. This combination allows the algorithm to update the policy in a more stable and efficient manner.

12.1.5 *Proximal policy optimization*

The proximal policy optimization (PPO) algorithm is an on-policy model-free RL designed by OpenAI [2], and it has been successfully used in many applications such as video gaming and robot control. PPO is based on the actor-critic architecture.

In RL, the agent generates its own training data through interactions with the environment. Unlike supervised machine learning, which relies on static datasets, RL's training data is dynamically dependent on the current policy. This dynamic nature leads to constantly changing data distributions, introducing potential instability during training. In the policy gradient method explained previously, if you continuously apply gradient ascent on a single batch of collected experiences, it can lead to updates that push the parameters of the network too far from the range where the data was collected. Consequently, the advantage function, which provides an estimate of the true advantage, becomes inaccurate, and the policy can be severely disrupted. To address this problem, two primary variants of PPO have been proposed: PPO-penalty and PPO-clip.

PPO-PENALTY

In *PPO-penalty*, a constraint is incorporated in the objective function to ensure that the policy update does not deviate too much from the old policy. This idea is the basis of trust region policy optimization (TRPO). By enforcing a trust region constraint, TRPO restricts the policy update to a manageable region and prevents large policy shifts. PPO-penalty is primarily inspired by TRPO and uses the following unconstrained objective function, which can be optimized using stochastic gradient ascent:

$$\underset{\theta}{\text{maximize}} \; \widehat{E}_t \left[\frac{\pi_\theta(a_t|s_t)}{\pi_{\theta_{old}}(a_t|s_t)} \widehat{A}_t - \beta . KL \left[\pi_{\theta_{old}}(.|s_t), \pi_\theta(.|s_t) \right] \right] \qquad \text{12.5}$$

where θ_{old} is the vector of policy parameters before the update, β is a fixed penalty coefficient, and the Kullback–Leibler divergence (KL) represents the divergence between the updated and old policies. This constraint is integrated into the objective function to avoid the risk of moving too far from the old policy.

Kullback–Leibler divergence

Kullback–Leibler (KL) divergence, also known as *relative entropy*, is a metric that quantifies the dissimilarity between two probability distributions. KL divergence between two probability distributions P and Q is defined as $KL(P \| Q) = \int P(x) \cdot \log(P(x) / Q(x)) \, dx$, where $P(x)$ and $Q(x)$ represent the probability density functions (PDFs) of the two distributions. The integral is taken over the entire support of the random variable x (i.e., the range of values of the random variable where the PDF is nonzero). The following figure shows the KL divergence between two Gaussian distributions with different means and variances.

(continued)

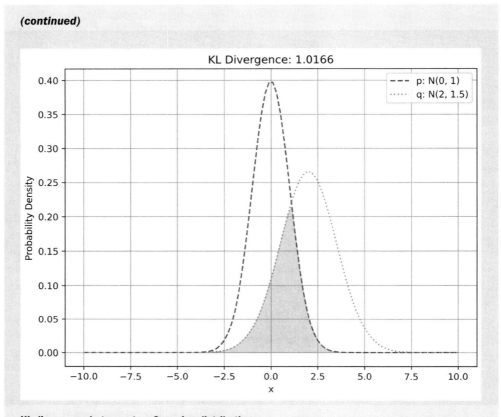

KL divergence between two Gaussian distributions

The KL divergence is equal to zero if, and only if, P and Q are identical distributions.

PPO-CLIP

In *PPO-clip*, a ratio $r(\theta)$ is defined as a probability ratio between the updated policy and the old version of the policy. Given a sequence of sample actions and states, this $r(\theta)$ value will be larger than 1 if the action is more likely now than it was in the old version of the policy, and it will be somewhere between 0 and 1 if it is less likely now than it was before the last gradient step.

The central objective function to be maximized in PPO-clip takes the following form:

$$L^{CLIP}(\theta) = \widehat{E}_t \left[\min \left(r_t(\theta) \, \widehat{A}_t, \, clip \left(r_t(\theta), 1 - \epsilon, 1 + \epsilon \right) \widehat{A}_t \right) \right]$$

and

$$r_t(\theta) = \frac{\pi_\theta(a_t | s_t)}{\pi_{\theta_{old}}(a_t | s_t)}$$

12.6

where L^{CLIP} is the clipped surrogate objective, which is an *expectation operator* computed over batches of trajectories, and epsilon ϵ is a hyperparameter (e.g., $\epsilon = 0.2$). As you can see in equation 12.6, the expectation operator is taken over the minimum of two terms. The first term represents the default objective used in normal policy gradients. It encourages the policy to favor actions that result in a high positive advantage compared to a baseline. The second term is a clipped or truncated version of the normal policy gradients. It applies a clipping operation to ensure that the update remains within a specified range, specifically between $1 - \epsilon$ and $1 + \epsilon$.

The clipped surrogate objective in PPO has different regions that define how the objective function behaves based on the advantage estimate $\hat{A}_t$ and the ratio of probabilities, as illustrated in figure 12.6.

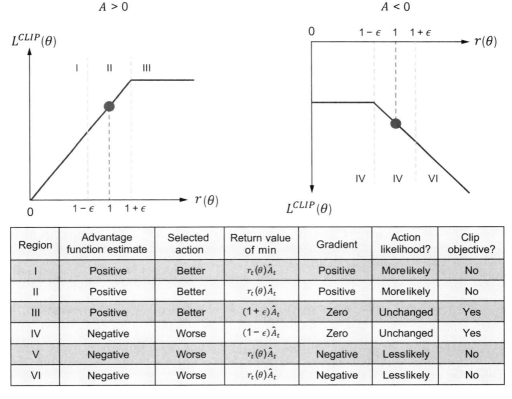

Region	Advantage function estimate	Selected action	Return value of min	Gradient	Action likelihood?	Clip objective?
I	Positive	Better	$r_t(\theta)\hat{A}_t$	Positive	More likely	No
II	Positive	Better	$r_t(\theta)\hat{A}_t$	Positive	More likely	No
III	Positive	Better	$(1+\epsilon)\hat{A}_t$	Zero	Unchanged	Yes
IV	Negative	Worse	$(1-\epsilon)\hat{A}_t$	Zero	Unchanged	Yes
V	Negative	Worse	$r_t(\theta)\hat{A}_t$	Negative	Less likely	No
VI	Negative	Worse	$r_t(\theta)\hat{A}_t$	Negative	Less likely	No

Figure 12.6 Clipped surrogate objective in PPO

On the left side of figure 12.6, where the advantage function is positive, the objective function represents cases where the selected action has a better-than-expected effect on the outcome. It's important to observe how the objective function flattens out when the ratio (r) becomes too high. This occurs when the action is more likely under the current policy compared to the old policy. The clipping operation limits the update to a range where the new policy does not deviate significantly from the old policy, preventing excessively large policy updates that may disrupt training stability.

On the right side of figure 12.6, where the advantage function is negative, it represents situations where the action has an estimated negative effect on the outcome. The objective function flattens out when the ratio (r) approaches zero. This corresponds to actions that are much less likely under the current policy compared to the old policy. This flattening effect prevents overdoing updates that could otherwise reduce the probabilities of these actions to zero.

12.1.6 Multi-armed bandit (MAB)

The *multi-armed bandit* (MAB) is a class of reinforcement learning problems with a single state. In MAB, an agent is faced with a set of actions or "arms" to choose from, and each action has an associated reward distribution. The agent's goal is to maximize the total reward accumulated over a series of actions. The agent does not modify its environment through its actions, does not consider state transitions, and always stays in the same single state. It focuses on selecting the most rewarding action at each time step without considering the impact on the environment's state.

> **Slot machine (one-armed bandit)**
>
> A *slot machine* (aka a fruit machine, pokies, or one-armed bandit) is a popular gambling device typically found in casinos. It is a mechanical or electronic gaming machine that features multiple spinning reels with various symbols on them. Players insert coins or tokens into the machine and then pull a lever (hence the term "one-armed bandit") or press a button to initiate the spinning of the reels. The objective of playing a slot machine is to align the symbols on the spinning reels in a winning combination. The term "bandit" originates from the analogy to a slot machine, where the agent pulls an arm (like pulling the lever on a slot machine) to receive varying rewards. This highlights how people perceive slot machines, especially older mechanical ones, as resembling a thief or bandit taking the player's money.

The MAB agent faces the exploration versus exploitation dilemma. To learn the best actions, it must explore various options (exploration). However, it also needs to quickly converge and swiftly focus on the most promising action (exploitation) based on its current beliefs. In supervised and unsupervised machine learning, the primary goal is to fit a prediction model (in supervised learning) or to discover patterns within the given data (in unsupervised learning), without an explicit notion of exploration, as seen in reinforcement learning, where the agent interacts with an environment to learn optimal behavior through trial and error. MAB problems provide valuable insights into learning from limited feedback and balancing exploration against discovering high-reward actions. In MAB, the agent's objective is to exploit the actions that have historically yielded high rewards while exploring to gather information about potentially more rewarding actions.

To understand MAB, imagine you're in a casino, and in front of you is a row of slot machines (one-armed bandits). Each slot machine represents an "arm" of the MAB. Let's assume that you are presented with three slot machines, as shown in figure 12.7. Every time you decide to play a slot machine, your situation (or state) is the same: "Which slot machine should I play next?" The environment doesn't change or provide you with different conditions; you're perpetually making decisions in this singular state. There's no context such as "If the casino is crowded, then play machine A" or "If it's raining outside, then play machine B." It's always just "Which machine should I play?" Your action is choosing a slot machine to play—you insert a coin and pull the lever. You are allowed to pull the levers of these machines for a total of 90 times, and each slot machine has its own payoff distribution, characterized by its mean and standard deviation. However, at the beginning, you are unaware of the specific details of these distributions. After pulling the lever, the machine might give you a payout (a positive reward) or nothing (a reward of zero). Over time, you're trying to discern if one machine gives a higher payout more frequently than the others.

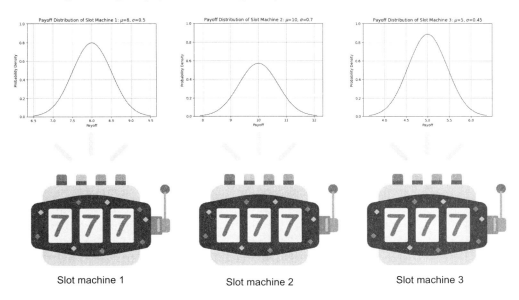

Figure 12.7 Three slot machines as a noncontextual multi-armed bandit (MAB) problem. The payoff distribution's mean and standard deviations of these three machines are (8,0.5), (10, 0.7), and (5, 0.45), respectively.

The objective in this MAB problem is to maximize the total payoff or cumulative reward obtained over the 90 trials by choosing the most rewarding slot machine. In other words, you're trying to learn the payoff distributions of the machines. The term *payoff distribution* refers to the probability distributions of rewards (or payoffs) that each machine (or arm) provides. Since you don't have prior knowledge about these payoff distributions, you need to explore the slot machines by trying different options to gather information about their performance. The challenge is to strike a balance between exploration and exploitation. Exploration involves trying different machines to learn their payoff distributions, while exploitation involves choosing the machine that is believed to yield the highest rewards based on the available information.

You can apply various bandit algorithms or strategies to determine the best approach for selecting the slot machines and maximizing your cumulative reward over the 90 trials. Examples of these strategies include, but are not limited to, explore-only, exploit-only greedy, epsilon-greedy (ε-greedy), and upper confidence bound (UCB):

- *Explore-only strategy*—In this strategy, the agent randomly selects a slot machine to play at each trial without considering the past results. In MAB, "regret" is a common measure, calculated as the difference between the maximum possible reward and the reward obtained from each selected machine. For example, if we apply the explore-only strategy in the 90 trials, and considering the mean of the payoff distribution of each slot machine, we will get a total average return of $30 \times 8 + 30 \times 10 + 30 \times 5 = 690$. The maximum possible reward can be obtained if you use machine 2 during the 90 trials. The maximum reward in this case will be $90 \times 10 = 900$. This means that regret $\rho = 900 - 690 = 210$.

- *Exploit-only greedy strategy*—In this case, the agent tries each machine once and then selects the slot machine that has the highest estimated mean reward. For example, assume that in the first trial, the agent gets payoffs of 7, 6, and 3 from machines 1, 2, and 3 respectively. The agent will then focus on using machine 1, thinking that it is the most rewarding. This can lead the agent to get stuck due to a lack of exploration.

- *ε-greedy strategy*—Here, the agent tries to strike a balance between exploration and exploitation by randomly selecting a slot machine with a certain probability (epsilon). This is the exploration part, where the agent occasionally tries out all three machines to gather more information about them. With a probability of $1 - \varepsilon$, the agent chooses the machine that has the highest estimated reward based on past experiences. This is the exploitation part, where the agent opts for the action that appears to be the best based on data the agent has gathered so far. For example, for the 90 trials and if $\varepsilon = 10\%$, the agent will randomly select a slot machine about 9 times (10% of 90). The other 81 trials (90% of 90) would see the agent choosing the slot machine that has, based on the trials up to that point, yielded the highest average reward.

- *Upper confidence bound (UCB) strategy*—In this strategy, the agent selects a machine based on a trade-off between its estimated mean reward and the uncertainty or confidence in that estimate. It prioritizes exploring machines with high potential rewards but high uncertainty in their estimates to reduce uncertainty and maximize rewards over time. In UCB, the arm (the action A_t) is chosen at time step t using the following formula:

$$A_t = \arg\max_a \left[Q_t(a) + c\sqrt{\frac{\log t}{N_t(a)}} \right]$$

12.7

where $Q_t(a)$ is the estimated value of action a at trial t. $Q_t(a)$ = sum of rewards/ $N_t(a)$. $N_t(a)$ is the number of trials where action a has been selected, prior to trial t. The first term on the right side of equation 12.7 represents the exploitation part. If you always pulled the arm with the highest $Q_t(a)$, you would always be exploiting the current knowledge without exploring other arms. The second term is the exploration part. As the number of trials t increases, the exploration term generally increases, but it's reduced by how often action a has already been selected. The multiplier c scales the influence of this exploration term.

Each strategy employs a different approach to balance exploration and exploitation, leading to different levels of regret. This regret level quantifies the cumulative loss an agent incurs due to not always choosing the optimal action. Intuitively, it measures the difference between the reward an agent could have achieved by always pulling the best arm (i.e., by selecting the optimal action) and the reward the agent actually received by following a certain strategy.

Let's look at Python implementations of the four MAB strategies. We'll start by setting the numbers of arms (actions), the payoff distributions of each slot machine, and the number of trials. We'll also define a `sample_payoff` to sample a payoff from a slot machine and calculate the maximum possible reward.

Listing 12.1 MAB strategies

```
import numpy as np

K = 3                          Set the number of
                               slot machines (arms).
payoff_params = [
    {"mean": 8, "std_dev": 0.5},      Specify payoff distribution.
    {"mean": 10, "std_dev": 0.7},      Set the number of trials.
    {"mean": 5, "std_dev": 0.45}
]                                               Calculate the maximum
num_trials = 90                                 possible reward.

                                        Function to sample a payoff
                                        from a slot machine
def sample_payoff(slot_machine):
    return np.random.normal(payoff_params[slot_machine]["mean"],
        payoff_params[slot_machine]["std_dev"])

max_reward = max([payoff_params[i]["mean"] for i in range(K)])
```

As a continuation of listing 12.1, we'll define a function named `explore_only()` that implements the explore-only strategy. In this function, `total_regret` is initialized, and we iterate over the specified number of trials. A slot machine is randomly selected by generating a random integer between 0 and $K-1$ (inclusive), where K represents the number of slot machines. We then sample the payoff from the selected slot machine by calling the `sample_payoff()` function, which returns a reward value based on the payoff distribution of the selected machine. The regret is calculated by subtracting the reward obtained from the maximum possible reward (`max_reward`). Here, we consider the maximum value of the mean values as the points of maximum probability in the payoff distributions of the three machines. The average regret is returned as output:

```
def explore_only():
    total_regret = 0
    for _ in range(num_trials):
        selected_machine = np.random.randint(K)
        reward = sample_payoff(selected_machine)
        regret = max_reward - reward
        total_regret += regret
    average_regret = total_regret / num_trials
    return average_regret
```

- Sample the payoff from the selected slot machine.
- Calculate the regret.
- Randomly select a slot machine.
- Calculate the total regret.
- Calculate the average regret.

The second strategy is defined in the `exploit_only_greedy()` function. This function selects the slot machine with the highest mean payoff by finding the index of the maximum mean payoff from the list of payoff means (`payoff_params[i]["mean"]`) for each machine (`i`). The `np.argmax()` function returns the index of the maximum mean payoff, representing the machine that is believed to provide the highest expected reward:

```
def exploit_only_greedy():
    total_regret = 0
    for _ in range(num_trials):
        selected_machine = np.argmax([payoff_params[i]["mean"] for i in
        range(K)])
        reward = sample_payoff(selected_machine)
        regret = max_reward - reward
        total_regret += regret
    average_regret = total_regret / num_trials
    return average_regret
```

- Sample the payoff from the selected slot machine.
- Calculate the regret.
- Select the slot machine with the highest mean payoff for exploitation.
- Calculate the total regret.
- Calculate the average regret.

The following `epsilon_greedy(epsilon)` function implements the epsilon-greedy strategy. This function checks if a randomly generated number between 0 and 1 is less than the epsilon value. If it is, the algorithm performs exploration by randomly selecting a slot machine for exploration. If this condition is not satisfied, the algorithm performs exploitation by selecting the slot machine with the highest mean payoff:

```
def epsilon_greedy(epsilon):
    total_regret = 0
    for _ in range(num_trials):
        if np.random.random() < epsilon:
            selected_machine = np.random.randint(K)
        else:
            selected_machine = np.argmax([payoff_params[i]["mean"]
            for i in range(K)])
        reward = sample_payoff(selected_machine)
        regret = max_reward - reward
        total_regret += regret
    average_regret = total_regret / num_trials
    return average_regret
```

- Randomly select a slot machine for exploration.
- Select the slot machine with the highest mean payoff for exploitation.
- Sample the payoff from the selected slot machine.

The following `ucb(c)` function implements the upper confidence bound (UCB) strategy. This function starts by initializing an array to keep track of the number of plays for each slot machine. The function also initializes an array to accumulate the sum of rewards obtained from each slot machine and initializes a variable to accumulate the total regret. The code includes a loop that plays each slot machine once to gather initial rewards and update the counts and sum of rewards:

```python
def ucb(c):
    num_plays = np.zeros(K)          # Initialize an array to keep track of the
                                     # number of plays for each slot machine.
    sum_rewards = np.zeros(K)        # Initialize an array to accumulate the sum of
                                     # rewards obtained from each slot machine.
    total_regret = 0                 # Initialize the total regret of each slot machine.

    for i in range(K):               # Play each slot machine once to initialize.
        reward = sample_payoff(i)
        num_plays[i] += 1
        sum_rewards[i] += reward

    for t in range(K, num_trials):   # Continue playing with the UCB strategy.
        ucb_values = sum_rewards / num_plays + c * np.sqrt(np.log(t) / num_plays)   # Calculate the UCB values.
        selected_machine = np.argmax(ucb_values)
        reward = sample_payoff(selected_machine)
        num_plays[selected_machine] += 1
        sum_rewards[selected_machine] += reward
        optimal_reward = max_reward
        regret = optimal_reward - reward
        total_regret += regret

    average_regret = total_regret / num_trials
    return average_regret
```

The following code snippet is used to run the strategies, calculate average regrets, and print the results:

```python
avg_regret_explore = explore_only()
avg_regret_exploit = exploit_only_greedy()
avg_regret_epsilon_greedy = epsilon_greedy(0.1)   # Set the epsilon value for the epsilon-greedy strategy, and run the strategy.
avg_regret_ucb = ucb(2)                           # Set the value of the exploration parameter c for the UCB strategy, and run the strategy.
```

```python
print(f"Average Regret - Explore only Strategy: {round(avg_regret_explore,4)}")
print(f"Average Regret - Exploit only Greedy Strategy: {round(avg_regret_exploit,4)}")
print(f"Average Regret - Epsilon-greedy Strategy: {round(avg_regret_epsilon_greedy,4)}")
print(f"Average Regret - UCB Strategy: {round(avg_regret_ucb,4)}")
```
Print the results.

Given the random sampling included in the code, your results will vary, but running the code will produce results something like these:

```
Average Regret - Explore only Strategy: 2.246
Average Regret - Exploit only Greedy Strategy: 0.048
Average Regret - Epsilon-greedy Strategy: 0.3466
Average Regret - UCB Strategy: 0.0378
```

MAB algorithms and concepts find applications in various real-world scenarios where decision-making under uncertainty and exploration–exploitation trade-offs are involved. Examples of real-world applications of MABs include, but are not limited to, resource allocation (dynamically allocating resources to different options to maximize performance), online advertising (dynamically allocating ad impressions to different options and learning which ads yield the highest click-through rate, which is the probability that a user clicks on an ad), design of experiments and clinical trials (optimizing the allocation of patients to different treatment options), content recommendation (personalizing content recommendations for users), and website optimization (optimizing different design options).

As you saw in figure 12.1, MABs can be classified into noncontextual and contextual MABs. In contrast to the previously explained noncontextual MABs, a contextual multi-armed bandit (CMAB) uses the contextual information contained in the environment. In CMAB, the learner repeatedly observes a context, selects an action, and receives feedback in the form of a reward or loss specific to the chosen action. CMAB algorithms use supplementary information, known as *side information* or *context*, to make informed decisions in real-world scenarios. For example, in a truck selection problem, the shared context is the type of delivery route (city or interstate). Section 12.5 shows how to use CMAB to solve this problem as an example of combinatorial actions.

Contextual multi-armed bandit applications

Contextual multi-armed bandits (CMABs) have found applications in areas like personalized recommendations and online advertising, where the context can be information about a user. For example, Amazon shows how to develop and deploy a CMAB workflow on SageMaker using a built-in Vowpal Wabbit (VW) container to train and deploy contextual bandit models (http://mng.bz/y8rE). These CMABs can be used to personalize content for a user, such as content layout, ads, search, product recommendations, etc. Moreover, a scalable algorithmic decision-making platform called WayLift was developed based on CMAB using VW for optimizing marketing decisions (http://mng.bz/MZom).

12.2 *Optimization with reinforcement learning*

RL can be used for combinatorial optimization problems by framing the problem as a Markov decision process (MDP) and applying RL algorithms to find an optimal policy that leads to the best possible solution. In reinforcement learning, an agent learns to make sequential decisions in an environment to maximize a notion of cumulative reward. This process involves finding an optimal policy that maps states to actions in order to maximize the expected long-term reward.

The convergence of reinforcement learning and optimization has recently become an active area of research, drawing significant attention from the academic and industrial communities. Researchers are actively exploring ways to apply the strengths of RL to tackle complex optimization problems efficiently and effectively. For example, the generic end-to-end pipeline presented in section 11.7 can be used to tackle combinatorial optimization problems such as TSP, the vehicle routing problem (VRP), the satisfiability problem (SAT), maximum cut (MaxCut), maximal independent set (MIS), etc. This pipeline includes training the model with supervised or reinforcement learning. Listing 11.4 showed how to solve TSP with an ML model pretrained using a supervised or reinforcement learning approach, as described by Joshi, Laurent, and Bresson [3].

An end-to-end framework for solving the VRP using reinforcement learning is presented in a paper by Nazari et al. [4]. The capacitated vehicle routing problem (CVRP) was also handled by reinforcement learning in a paper by Delarue, Anderson, and Tjandraatmadja [5]. Another framework called RLOR is described in a paper by Wan, Li, and Wang[6] as a flexible framework of deep reinforcement learning for routing problems such as CVRP and TSP. A distributed model-free RL algorithm called DeepPool is described in a paper by Alabbasi, Ghosh, and Aggarwal [7] as learning optimal dispatch policies for ride-sharing applications by interacting with the environment. DeepFreight is another model-free RL algorithm for the freight delivery problem described in a paper by Jiayu et al. [8]. It decomposes the problem into two closely collaborative components: truck-dispatch and package-matching. The key objectives of the freight delivery system are to maximize the number of served requests within a certain time limit and to minimize the total fuel consumption of the fleet during this process. MOVI is another model-free approach for a large-scale taxi dispatch problem, described by Oda and Joe-Wong [9]. RL is also used to optimize traffic signal control (TSC) as a way to mitigate congestion. In a paper by Ruan et al. [10] (of which I was a co-author), a model of a real-world intersection with real traffic data collected in Hangzhou, China, is simulated with different RL-based traffic signal controllers. We also proposed a multi-agent reinforcement learning model to provide both macroscopic and microscopic control in mixed traffic scenarios [11]. The experimental results show that the proposed approach demonstrates superior performance compared with other baselines in terms of several metrics, such as throughput, average speed, and safety.

A framework for learning optimization algorithms, known as "Learning to Optimize," is described by Li and Malik [12]. The problem was formulated as an RL problem, in which any optimization algorithm can be represented as a policy. Guided policy search is used, and autonomous optimizers are trained for different classes of convex and nonconvex objective functions. These autonomous optimizers converge faster or reach better optima than hand-engineered optimizers. This is somewhat similar to the amortized optimization concept described in section 11.6, but using reinforcement learning.

RL-based dispatching is described by Toll et al. for a four-elevator system in a 10-floor building [13]. The elevator dispatching problem is a combinatorial optimization problem that involves efficiently dispatching multiple elevators in a multi-floor building to serve incoming requests from passengers. As explained in section 1.4.2, the number of possible states in this case is 10^4 (elevator positions) $\times 2^{40}$ (elevator buttons) $\times 2^{18}$ (hall call buttons) = 2.88 x 10^{21} different states.

Stable-Baselines3 (SB3) provides reliable implementations of reinforcement learning algorithms in PyTorch for several OpenAI Gym-compatible and custom RL environments. To install Stable Baselines3 with pip, execute `pip install stable-baselines3`. Examples of RL algorithm implementations in SB3 include advantage actor-critic (A2C), soft actor-critic (SAC), deep deterministic policy gradient (DDPG), deep Q network (DQN), hindsight experience replay (HER), twin delayed DDPG (TD3), and proximal policy optimization (PPO). Environments and projects available in SB3 include the following:

- *mobile-env*—A Gymnasium environment for autonomous coordination in wireless mobile networks. It allows the simulation of various scenarios involving moving users in a cellular network with multiple base stations. This environment is used in section 12.4.

- *gym-electric-motor*—An OpenAI Gym environment for the simulation and control of electric drivetrains. This environment is used in exercise 6 for this chapter (see appendix C).

- *highway-env*—An environment for decision-making in autonomous driving in different scenarios, such as highway, merge, roundabout, parking, intersection, and racetrack.

- *Generalized state dependent exploration (gSDE) for deep reinforcement learning in robotics*—An exploration method to train RL agents directly on real robots.

- *RL Reach*—A platform for running reproducible RL experiments for customizable robotic reaching tasks.

- *RL Baselines3 Zoo*—A framework to train, evaluate RL agents, tune hyperparameters, plot results, and record videos.

- *Furuta Pendulum Robot*—A project to build and train a rotary inverted pendulum, also known as a Furuta pendulum.

- *UAV_Navigation_DRL_AirSim*—A platform for training UAV navigation policies in complex unknown environments.

- *tactile-gym*—RL environments focused on using a simulated tactile sensor as the primary source of observations.

- *SUMO-RL*—An interface to instantiate RL environments with Simulation of Urban MObility (SUMO) for traffic signal control.

- *PyBullet Gym*—Environments for single and multi-agent reinforcement learning of quadcopter control.

The following sections provide examples of how you can use RL methods to handle control problems with combinatorial actions.

12.3 *Balancing CartPole using A2C and PPO*

Let's consider a classic control task where the goal is to balance a pole on top of a cart by moving the cart left or right, as shown in figure 12.8. This task can be considered an optimization problem where the objective is to maximize the cumulative reward by finding an optimal policy that balances the pole on the cart for as long as possible. The agent needs to learn how to make decisions (take actions) that maximize the reward signal. The agent explores different actions in different states and learns which actions lead to higher rewards over time. By iteratively updating its policy based on observed rewards, the agent aims to optimize its decision-making process and find the best actions for each state.

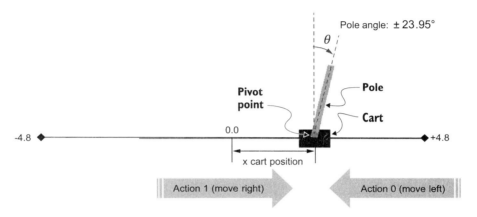

Figure 12.8   CartPole balancing problem

The state of this environment is described by four variables:

- Cart position (continuous)—This represents the position of the cart along the *x*-axis. The value ranges from −4.8 to 4.8.
- Cart velocity (continuous)—This represents the velocity of the cart along the *x*-axis. The value ranges from −inf to inf.
- Pole angle (continuous)—This represents the angle of the pole from the vertical position. The value ranges from −0.418 to 0.418 radians or −23.95° to 23.95° degrees.
- Pole angular velocity (continuous)—This represents the angular velocity of the pole. The value ranges from −inf to inf.

The action space in the CartPole environment is discrete and consists of two possible actions:

- Action 0—Move the cart to the left.
- Action 1—Move the cart to the right.

The agent receives a reward of +1 for every time step when the pole remains upright. The episode ends if one of the following conditions is met:

- The pole angle is more than ±12 degrees from the vertical.
- The cart position is more than ±2.4 units from the center.
- The episode reaches a maximum time step limit (typically 200 steps).

In the CartPole environment, the objective is to balance the pole on the cart for as long as possible, maximizing the cumulative reward. Let's look at the code for learning the optimal policy to balance the CartPole using the advantage actor-critic (A2C) algorithm discussed in section 12.1.4.

As shown in listing 12.2, we start by importing the necessary libraries:

- `gym` is the OpenAI Gym library, used for working with reinforcement learning environments.
- `torch` is the PyTorch library used for building and training neural networks.
- `torch.nn` is a module providing the tools for defining neural networks.
- `torch.nn.functional` contains various activation and loss functions.
- `torch.optim` contains optimization algorithms for training neural networks.
- `tqdm` provides a progress bar for tracking the training progress.
- `seaborn` is used for visualization.

Listing 12.2   Balancing CartPole using the A2C algorithm

```
import gym
import numpy as np
import torch
import torch.nn as nn
import torch.nn.functional as F
import torch.optim as optim
import matplotlib.pyplot as plt
from tqdm import tqdm
import pandas as pd
import seaborn as sns
```

Next, we create the actor and critic networks using PyTorch. The `Actor` class is a subclass of `nn.Module` in PyTorch, representing the policy network, and the `__init__` method defines the architecture of the actor network. Three fully connected layers (`fc1`, `fc2`, `fc3`) are used. The `forward` method performs a forward pass through the network, applying activation functions (ReLU) and returning the action probabilities using the softmax function:

```
class Actor(nn.Module):

    def __init__(self, state_dim,  action_dim):
        super(Actor, self).__init__()
        self.fc1 = nn.Linear(state_dim, 64)
```

```
        self.fc2 = nn.Linear(64, 32)
        self.fc3 = nn.Linear(32, action_dim)

    def forward(self, state):
        x1 = F.relu(self.fc1(state))
        x2 = F.relu(self.fc2(x1))
        action_probs = F.softmax(self.fc3(x2), dim=-1)
        return action_probs
```

The `Critic` class is also a subclass of `nn.Module`, representing the value network. The `__init__` method defines the architecture of the critic network, similar to the actor network. The forward method performs a forward pass through the network, applying activation functions (ReLU) and returning the predicted value:

```
class Critic(nn.Module):

    def __init__(self, state_dim):
        super(Critic, self).__init__()
        self.fc1 = nn.Linear(state_dim, 64)
        self.fc2 = nn.Linear(64, 32)
        self.fc3 = nn.Linear(32, 1)

    def forward(self, state):
        x1 = F.relu(self.fc1(state))
        x2 = F.relu(self.fc2(x1))
        value = self.fc3(x2)
        return value
```

As a continuation, the following code snippet is used to create an instance of the CartPole environment using the OpenAI Gym library and to retrieve important information about the environment:

Create the CartPole environment.

Set the random seed to help make the environment's behavior reproducible.

```
env = gym.make("CartPole-v1")
env.seed(0)
state_dim = env.observation_space.shape[0]
n_actions = env.action_space.n
```

Retrieve the dimensionality of the observation space.

Retrieve the number of actions in the action space.

`state_dim` represents the state space or the observation space and in this example has a value of 4 (the four states being cart position, cart velocity, pole angle, and pole angular velocity). `n_actions` represents the dimensionality of the action space or the number of actions, which in this example is 2 (push left and push right). We can now initialize the actor and critic models as well as the Adam optimizer for the actor and critic models using learning rate `lr=1e-3`. The discount factor, gamma, determines the importance of future rewards compared to immediate rewards in reinforcement learning algorithms:

Create an instance of the Actor class.

Create an instance of the Critic class.

Initialize the Adam optimizer for the actor model.

```
actor = Actor(state_dim, n_actions)
critic = Critic(state_dim)
adam_actor = torch.optim.Adam(actor.parameters(), lr=1e-3)
```

```
adam_critic = torch.optim.Adam(critic.parameters(), lr=1e-3)
gamma = 0.99
```

Set the discount rate.

Initialize the Adam optimizer for the critic model.

After this initialization, we can start the training process, where an agent interacts with the environment for a specified number of episodes. During the training, the agent computes the advantage function, updates the actor and critic models, and keeps track of the training statistics. The following code snippet is used to initialize the training process:

Set the total number of episodes to run.

Create an empty list to store the total rewards obtained in each episode.

```
num_episodes=500
episode_rewards = []
stats={'actor loss':[], 'critic loss':[], 'return':[]}
pbar = tqdm(total=num_episodes, ncols=80, bar_format='{l_bar}{bar}| {n_fmt}/
{total_fmt}')
```

Initialize the tqdm progress bar.

Create a dictionary to store the training statistics, including the actor loss, critic loss, and total return for each episode.

The training loop iterates over the specified number of episodes. In each episode, the environment is reset to its initial state, and the random seeds are initialized to ensure that the sequence of random numbers generated by the environment remains consistent across different runs of the code:

```
for episode in range(num_episodes):
    done = False
    total_reward = 0
    state = env.reset()
    env.seed(0)
```

The agent then interacts with the environment by taking actions based on its policy, accumulating rewards, and updating its parameters to improve its performance in balancing the pole on the cart until the episode is complete. The actor network is used to determine action probabilities given the current state, and a categorical distribution is created using these probabilities. An action is then stochastically sampled from this distribution and executed in the environment. The resulting next state, reward, done flag, and additional information are received from the environment, completing one step of the agent-environment interaction loop:

Obtain action probabilities given the current state.

Create a categorical distribution.

```
while not done:
    probs = actor(torch.from_numpy(state).float())
    dist = torch.distributions.Categorical(probs=probs)
    action = dist.sample()
    next_state, reward, done, info = env.step(action.detach().data.numpy())
```

Sample an action from the categorical distribution.

Pass the action to the environment.

The advantage function is then computed using the rewards, next state value, and current state value.

```
advantage = reward + (1-
   done)*gamma*critic(torch.from_numpy(next_state).float()) -
      critic(torch.from_numpy(state).float())
```
Compute the advantage function.

```
total_reward += reward
state = next_state
```
Update the total reward.

Move to the next state.

This advantage function is used to update the critic model. The critic loss is calculated as the mean squared error of the advantage. The critic parameters are updated using the Adam optimizer:

```
critic_loss = advantage.pow(2).mean()
adam_critic.zero_grad()
critic_loss.backward()
adam_critic.step()
```

The actor loss is calculated as the negative log probability of the chosen action multiplied by the advantage. The actor parameters are updated using the Adam optimizer:

```
actor_loss = -dist.log_prob(action)*advantage.detach()

adam_actor.zero_grad()
actor_loss.backward()
adam_actor.step()
```

The total reward for the episode is then appended to the `episode_rewards` list:

```
episode_rewards.append(total_reward)
```

The actor loss, critic loss, and total reward for the episode are added to the `stats` dictionary. The statistics are printed for each episode:

```
stats['actor loss'].append(actor_loss)
stats['critic loss'].append(critic_loss)
stats['return'].append(total_reward)
print('Actor loss= ', round(stats['actor loss'][episode].item(), 4), 'Critic
   loss= ', round(stats['critic loss'][episode].item(), 4), 'Return= ',
   stats['return'][episode])
```
Print the tracking statistics.

```
pbar.set_description(f"Episode {episode + 1}")
pbar.set_postfix({"Reward": episode_rewards})
pbar.update(1)
```
Update the tqdm progress bar.

Close the tqdm progress bar.

```
pbar.close()
```

Let's now visualize the learning process by plotting the episode rewards obtained during each training episode using a scatter plot with a trend line:

Set the size of the figure to be displayed.

```
data = pd.DataFrame({"Episode": range(1, num_episodes + 1), "Reward":
   episode_rewards})
```
Create a DataFrame for episode rewards.

```
plt.figure(figsize=(12,6))
sns.set(style="whitegrid")
```
Set the style of the seaborn plots to have a white grid background.

```
sns.regplot(data=data, x="Episode", y="Reward", scatter_kws={"alpha": 0.5})
plt.xlabel("Episode")                                     Create the scatter plot with a trend line.
plt.ylabel("Reward")
plt.title("Episode Rewards with Trend Line")
plt.show()
```

When you run this code, you'll get a scatter plot and trend line something like the one in figure 12.9.

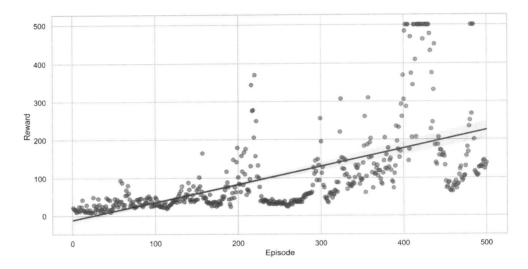

Figure 12.9   Episode rewards with a trend line

As you can see, there are fluctuations in the rewards during the learning process, as depicted by the scatter plot showing increasing and decreasing rewards in different episodes. However, the overall trend or pattern in the rewards over the episodes is improving. Fluctuations in the rewards during the learning process are expected and considered normal behavior in reinforcement learning. Initially, the agent may explore different actions, which can lead to both successful and unsuccessful episodes, resulting in varying rewards. As the training progresses, the agent refines its policy and tends to exploit more promising actions, leading to more consistent rewards.

Stable Baselines3 (SB3) provides more abstract and reliable implementations of different reinforcement learning algorithms based on PyTorch. As a continuation of listing 12.2, the following code snippet shows the steps for handling the CartPole environment using the A2C implementation in SB3. The A2C agent uses `MlpPolicy` as a specific type of policy network, which in turn uses a multilayer perceptron (MLP) architecture. The created agent will interact with the environment for a total of 10,000 timesteps to learn the optimal policy:

Import the gym module.

```
import gymnasium as gym
from stable_baselines3 import A2C
from stable_baselines3.common.evaluation import evaluate_policy
```

Import the A2C model.

To evaluate the performance of the trained model

Create the CartPole-v1 environment.

```
env = gym.make("CartPole-v1", render_mode="rgb_array")

model = A2C("MlpPolicy", env, verbose=1)
```

Create an A2C model with the MlpPolicy (multilayer perceptron) and the environment.

```
model.learn(total_timesteps=10000, progress_bar=True)
```

Start the learning process for the model.

```
mean_reward, std_reward = evaluate_policy(model, model.get_env(),
➥      n_eval_episodes=10)
vec_env = model.get_env()
obs = vec_env.reset()
for i in range(1000):
    action, _states = model.predict(obs, deterministic=True)
    obs, rewards, dones, info = vec_env.step(action)
    vec_env.render("human")
```

Test and evaluate the trained model.

Render the environment in a way that a human can visualize it.

This code snippet sets up the environment, trains an A2C model, evaluates its performance for 1,000 steps, and then visualizes the model's actions in the environment.

We can use PPO instead of A2C to balance the CartPole. The next listing is quite similar to the previous one, but it uses PPO instead of A2C.

Listing 12.3 Balancing CartPole using the PPO algorithm

```
import gymnasium as gym
from stable_baselines3 import PPO
from stable_baselines3.common.evaluation import evaluate_policy

env = gym.make("CartPole-v1", render_mode="rgb_array")

model = PPO("MlpPolicy", env, verbose=1)

model.learn(total_timesteps=10000, progress_bar=True)
```

Import the PPO model from SB3.

Create an instance of the CartPole-v1 environment.

Initialize a PPO model with the MlpPolicy to handle agent's networks.

Start the learning process for 10,000 timesteps.

During the training, the code renders logger output in the following format:

```
-----------------------------------------
| rollout/            |            |
|    ep_len_mean      | 61.8       |
|    ep_rew_mean      | 61.8       |
| time/               |            |
|    fps              | 362        |
|    iterations       | 5          |
|    time_elapsed     | 28         |
|    total_timesteps  | 10240      |
| train/              |            |
|    approx_kl        | 0.0064375857 |
|    clip_fraction    | 0.051      |
|    clip_range       | 0.2        |
```

```
|   entropy_loss         | -0.61    |
|   explained_variance   | 0.245    |
|   learning_rate        | 0.0003   |
|   loss                 | 26.1     |
|   n_updates            | 40       |
|   policy_gradient_loss | -0.0141  |
|   value_loss           | 65.2     |
------------------------------------------
```

The logger output presents the following information:

- rollout/
  - ep_len_mean—The mean episode length during rollouts
  - ep_rew_mean—The mean episodic training reward during rollouts
- time/
  - fps—The number of frames per seconds achieved during training, indicating the computational efficiency of the algorithm
  - iterations—the number of completed training iterations
  - time_elapsed—The time elapsed in seconds since the beginning of training
  - total_timesteps—The total number of timesteps (steps in the environments) the agent has experienced during training
- train/
  - approx_kl—The approximate Kullback-Leibler (KL) divergence between the old and new policy distributions, measuring the extent of policy changes during training
  - clip_fraction—The mean fraction of surrogate loss that was clipped (above the clip_range threshold) for PPO.
  - clip_range—The current value of the clipping factor for the surrogate loss of PPO
  - entropy_loss—The mean value of the entropy loss (negative of the average policy entropy)
  - explained_variance—The fraction of the return variance explained by the value function
  - learning_rate—The current learning rate value
  - loss—The current total loss value
  - n_updates—The number of gradient updates applied so far
  - policy_gradient_loss—The current value of the policy gradient loss
  - value_loss—The current value for the value function loss for on-policy algorithms

We usually keep an eye on the reward and loss values. As a continuation, the following code snippet shows how to evaluate the policy and render the environment state:

Retrieve the vectorized environment associated with the model.

```
mean_reward, std_reward = evaluate_policy(model, model.get_env(),
    n_eval_episodes=10)
vec_env = model.get_env()
obs = vec_env.reset()
for i in range(1000):
    action, _states = model.predict(obs, deterministic=True)
    obs, rewards, dones, info = vec_env.step(action)
    vec_env.render("human")
```

Evaluate the policy of the trained model.

Reset the environment to its initial state and get the initial observation.

Test the trained agent.

As shown in the preceding code, after training the model, we evaluate the policy of the trained model over 10 episodes and return the mean and standard deviation of the rewards. We then allow the agent to interact with the environment for 1,000 steps and render the environment. The output will be an animated version of figure 12.8 showing the behavior of the CartPole learning the balancing policy.

12.4 Autonomous coordination in mobile networks using PPO

Schneider et al. described the mobile-env environment as an open platform for reinforcement learning in wireless mobile networks [14]. This environment enables the representation of users moving within a designated area and potentially connecting to one or multiple base stations. It supports both multi-agent and centralized reinforcement learning policies.

In the mobile-env environment, we have a mobile network formed by a number of base stations or cells (BSs) and user equipment (UE), as illustrated in figure 12.10. Our objective is to decide what connections should be established among the UEs and BSs in order to maximize the quality of experience (QoE) globally. For individual UEs, a higher QoE is achieved by establishing connections with as many BSs as possible, resulting in higher data rates. However, since BSs distribute resources among connected UEs (e.g., scheduling physical resource blocks), UEs end up competing for limited resources, leading to conflicting goals.

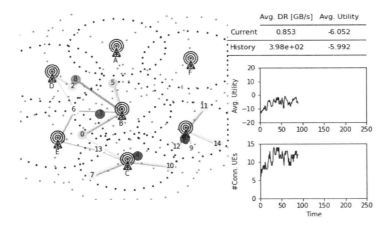

Figure 12.10 The mobile-env environment with a number of base stations and user equipment

To achieve maximum QoE globally, the policy must consider two crucial factors:

- The data rate (DR in GB/s) of each connection is determined by the channel's quality (e.g., the signal-to-noise ratio) between the UE and BS.
- The QoE of individual UEs does not necessarily increase linearly with higher data rates.

Let's create a mobile network environment and train a PPO agent to learn the coordination policy. We'll start in listing 12.4 by importing `gymnasium`, which is a maintained fork of OpenAI's Gym library. `mobile_env` is imported to create an environment related to mobile networks. `IPython.display` enables the use of interactive display features within IPython or Jupyter Notebook environments. We'll create a small instance of `mobile_env` that contains three base stations and five users.

Listing 12.4   Mobile network coordination using PPO

```
import gymnasium
import matplotlib.pyplot as plt
import mobile_env                                    Print the number of users and
from IPython import display                          the number of base stations.

from stable_baselines3 import PPO                    Create an instance of the environment.
from stable_baselines3.ppo import MlpPolicy

env = gymnasium.make("mobile-small-central-v0", render_mode="rgb_array")
print(f"\nSmall environment with {env.NUM_USERS} users and {env.NUM_STATIONS}
    cells.")
```

Next, we'll create an instance of the PPO agent using the multilayer perceptron (MLP) policy (`MlpPolicy`) with the mobile environment (`env`) as the environment. The training progress will be logged to the `results_sb` directory for TensorBoard visualization. You can install and set up `tensorboard logdir` as follows:

```
pip install tensorboard
tensorboard --logdir .
```

The agent is trained for a total of 30,000 time steps:

```
model = PPO(MlpPolicy, env, tensorboard_log='results_sb', verbose=1)
model.learn(total_timesteps=30000, progress_bar=True)
```

The following code snippet can be used to render the environment state after training. During the episode, the trained model is used to predict the action to be taken based on the current observation. The action is then executed in the environment, and the environment responds with the next observation (`obs`), the reward received (`reward`), a Boolean flag indicating whether the episode is terminated (`terminated`), a flag indicating whether the episode was terminated due to the episode time limit (`truncated`), and environment information (`info`):

```
obs, info = env.reset()        Reset the environment, returning the initial
                               observation and environment information.
```

```
done = False
```
Flag to track if the episode is complete.

```
while not done:
    action, _ = model.predict(obs)
    obs, reward, terminated, truncated, info = env.step(action)
    done = terminated or truncated
```
Predict the action to be taken based on the current observation.

Update the flag.

Execute the action and get the environment response.

```
    plt.imshow(env.render())
    display.display(plt.gcf())
    display.clear_output(wait=True)
```
Render the environment state.

The output is an updated version of figure 12.10 showing three stations, five users, and the dynamically changing connections between them. The average data rate and average utility of the established connections are also rendered.

Instead of having a single RL agent centrally control cell selection for all users, an alternative approach is to adopt a multi-agent RL. In this setup, multiple RL agents work in parallel, with each agent being responsible for the cell selection of a specific user. For instance, in the mobile-small-ma-v0 environment, we will use five RL agents, each catering to the cell selection needs of a single user. This approach allows for more distributed and decentralized control, enhancing the scalability and efficiency of the system. We'll use Ray and Ray RLlib in this example. Ray is an open source unified framework for scaling AI and Python applications like machine learning. Ray RLlib is an open source library for RL, offering support for production-level, highly distributed RL workloads while maintaining unified and simple APIs for a large variety of industry applications. To install RLlib with pip, execute `pip install -U "ray[rllib]"`.

As a continuation of listing 12.4, we can import the Ray libraries to learn the optimal coordination policy following a multi-agent approach:

```
import ray
from ray.tune.registry import register_env
import ray.air
from ray.rllib.algorithms.ppo import PPOConfig
from ray.rllib.policy.policy import PolicySpec
from ray.tune.stopper import MaximumIterationStopper
from ray.rllib.algorithms.algorithm import Algorithm
from mobile_env.wrappers.multi_agent import RLlibMAWrapper
```

The following function will create and return a wrapped environment suitable for RLlib's multi-agent setup. Here we create a small instance of `mobile_env`:

```
def register(config):
    env = gymnasium.make("mobile-small-ma-v0")
    return RLlibMAWrapper(env)
```

We'll now initialize Ray using the following function.

```
ray.init(
    num_cpus=2,
    include_dashboard=False,
    ignore_reinit_error=True,
    log_to_driver=False,
)
```
Specify the number of CPUs.

Ignore the forwarding logs.

Disable the Ray web-based dashboard.

Ignore the reinitialization error if Ray is already initialized.

We can now configure an RLlib training setup to use the proximal policy optimization (PPO) algorithm on `mobile-env`'s small scenario in a multi-agent environment:

```
config = (
    PPOConfig()
    .environment(env="mobile-small-ma-v0")          ◄──── Set the environment.
    .multi_agent(
        policies={"shared_policy": PolicySpec()},
        policy_mapping_fn=lambda agent_id, episode, worker, **kwargs:
        ➥ "shared_policy",
    )
                                              Specify that each worker
                                              should use one CPU core.          Indicate that there should
                                                                                be one worker dedicated
    .resources(num_cpus_per_worker=1)   ◄────                                   to performing rollouts.
    .rollouts(num_rollout_workers=1)    ◄──────────────────────────────
)
```

Configure all agents to share the same policy. (points to `)` after multi_agent block)

The following code snippet configures and initiates a training session using the RLlib framework. It sets up a tuner (trainer) for the PPO algorithm and executes the training:

```
tuner = ray.tune.Tuner(                    Specify where the training results and
    "PPO",                                 checkpoints (saved model states) will be stored.     Define the
                                                                                                stopping
    run_config=ray.air.RunConfig(                                                               condition for
        storage_path="./results_rllib",    ◄───────────────────────────────                    the training.
        stop=MaximumIterationStopper(max_iter=10),   ◄─────────────────────
        checkpoint_config=ray.air.CheckpointConfig(checkpoint_at_end=True),
    ),
    param_space=config,        ◄─────────── Specify the training parameters.
)

result_grid = tuner.fit()    ◄──────────── Start the training process.
```

Specify PPO. (points to "PPO")
Configure how checkpoints are saved. (points to checkpoint_config)

After training, we can load the best trained agent from the results:

Extract the best training result from the result_grid based on the metric of average episode reward.

```
best_result = result_grid.get_best_result(metric="episode_reward_mean",
➥ mode="max")
ppo = Algorithm.from_checkpoint(best_result.checkpoint) ◄
```

Load the agent from the best checkpoint (model state) obtained in the training.

Lastly, we can evaluate a trained model on a given environment and render the results:

Reset the environment to its initial state and fetch the initial observation and additional info.

```
env = gymnasium.make("mobile-small-ma-v0", render_mode="rgb_array")
obs, info = env.reset()   ◄
done = False
                                   Initiate a loop to run one episode with the trained model.
while not done:   ◄
    action = {}   ◄                Initialize an empty dictionary to hold actions
                                   for each agent in the multi-agent environment.
    for agent_id, agent_obs in obs.items():
        action[agent_id] = ppo.compute_single_action(agent_obs,
            ➥ policy_id="shared_policy")
```

Initialize the environment. (points to `env = gymnasium.make`)
Iterate through each agent's observations. (points to `for agent_id` loop)

```
obs, reward, terminated, truncated, info = env.step(action)
done = terminated or truncated
```

**Determine if the episode has
ended. An episode ends if it is
terminated or if truncated is True.**

```
plt.imshow(env.render())
display.display(plt.gcf())
display.clear_output(wait=True)
```

**Visualize
the current
state of the
environment.**

**Return the new observations, rewards, termination
flags, truncation flags, and additional information.**

Running this code produces an animated rendering of the environment shown in figure 12.11.

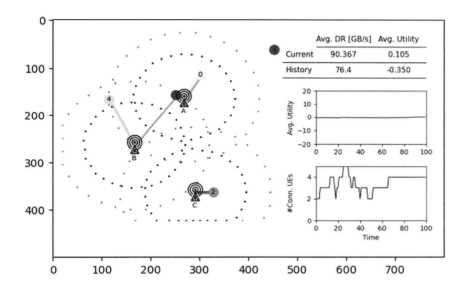

Figure 12.11   Coordination of the mobile environment using a multi-agent PPO

This rendering shows the established connection with the five user units and three base stations and the obtained average data rates and utilities. For more information about the decentralized multi-agent version of the PPO-based coordinator, see Schneider et al.'s article "mobile-env: An open platform for reinforcement learning in wireless mobile networks" and the associated GitHub repo [14].

12.5 Solving the truck selection problem using contextual bandits

Let's consider a scenario where a delivery service provider is planning to assign trucks for different delivery routes, as illustrated in figure 12.12. The goal is to maximize the efficiency of the fleet according to the type of delivery route. The delivery routes are categorized as city deliveries or interstate deliveries, and the company has to select the optimal type of truck according to the following decision variables: size, engine type, and tire type. The available options for each decision variable are as follows:

- Size—Small, medium, or large
- Engine type—Petrol, diesel, or electric
- Tire type—All-season, snow, or off-road

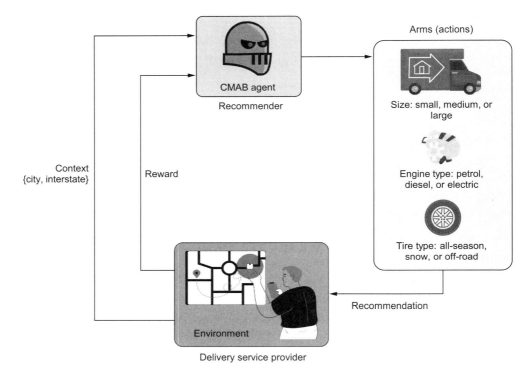

Figure 12.12   A CMAB-based recommender system to select delivery truck size, engine type, and tire type based on a specified context

The reward is based on how suitable the truck selection is for a given delivery route. The reward function receives as arguments the delivery route type and the selected actions for each variable. In order to reflect real-world conditions and add complexity to the problem, we add noise to the reward value, representing uncertainties in weather, road conditions, and so on. The objective is to select the best combination from the available choices in such a way as to maximize the total reward. This means choosing the most suitable truck size, engine type, and tire type for each type of delivery route.

A contextual multi-armed bandit (CMAB) can be used to handle this problem. Vowpal Wabbit (VW), an open source ML library developed originally at Yahoo and currently at Microsoft, supports a wide range of machine-learning algorithms, including CMAB. You can install VW using `pip install vowpalwabbit`.

We'll use CMAB to find the optimal values of the decision variables that maximize the reward based on the given context. The next listing starts by importing the necessary libraries and defining variables for the contextual bandit problem.

Listing 12.5 Contextual bandit for delivery truck selection

```
import vowpalwabbit
import torch
import matplotlib.pyplot as plt
import pandas as pd
import random
import numpy as np
from tqdm import tqdm

shared_contexts = ['city', 'interstate']    ◄──── Set the shared context.

size_types = ['small', 'medium', 'large']
engine_types = ['petrol', 'diesel', 'electric']
tire_types = ['all_season', 'snow', 'performance', 'all_terrain']
```

Set the action options or the arms.

We then define the following reward function that takes as inputs the shared context and indices representing the chosen size, engine, and tire options. It returns the reward value as an output:

```
def reward_function(shared_context, size_index, engine_index, tire_index):
    size_value = [0.8, 1.0, 0.9]    ◄──────
    engine_value = [0.7, 0.9, 1.0]    ◄──────
    tire_value = [0.9, 0.8, 1.0, 0.95]    ◄──────

    reward = (
        size_value[size_index]
        * engine_value[engine_index]
        * tire_value[tire_index]
    )    ◄──── Initial reward is based on the selected options.

    noise_scale = 0.05
    noise_value = np.random.normal(loc=0, scale=noise_scale)
    reward += noise_value

    return reward    ◄──── Return the reward.
```

Higher value indicates better fuel efficiency.

Higher value indicates better performance.

Higher value indicates better comfort.

Add noise to the reward representing uncertainties in weather, road conditions, and so on.

As a continuation, the following `generate_combinations` function generates combinations of actions and examples for the contextual bandit problem. This function takes four inputs: the shared context and three lists representing size, engine, and tire options for the actions. The function returns the list of examples and the list of descriptions once all combinations have been processed. Nested loops are used to iterate over each combination of size, engine, and tire options. The `enumerate` function is used to simultaneously retrieve the index (`i`, `j`, `k`) and the corresponding options (size, engine, tire):

```
def generate_combinations(shared_context, size_types, engine_types, tire_
types):
    examples = [f"shared |User {shared_context}"]
    descriptions = []
    for i, size in enumerate(size_types):
        for j, engine in enumerate(engine_types):
            for k, tire in enumerate(tire_types):
                examples.append(f"|Action truck_size={size} engine={engine}
                    ➥ tire={tire}")
                descriptions.append((i, j, k))
    return examples, descriptions
```

We now need to sample from a probability mass function (PMF) representing truck actions. The `sample_truck_pmf` function samples an index from a given PMF and returns the index along with its probability. The indices are used to retrieve the corresponding size, engine, and tire indices from the indices list:

```
def sample_truck_pmf(pmf):                        │ Convert the pmf to a Torch tensor.
    pmf_tensor = torch.tensor(pmf)  ◄───────────┘
    index = torch.multinomial(pmf_tensor, 1).item()  ◄──────┘ Perform a multinomial sampling.
    chosen_prob = pmf[index]  ◄────────────┘ Capture the probability of the selected action.

    return index, chosen_prob  ◄────────────┐ Return the sampled index and
                                            │ its corresponding probability.
```

Now we need to create a VW workspace for training the contextual bandit model:

```
cb_vw = vowpalwabbit.Workspace(
    "--cb_explore_adf --epsilon 0.2 --interactions AA AU AAU -l 0.05
--power_t 0",
    quiet=True,
)
```

The workspace is defined using the following parameters:

- `--cb_explore_adf`—This parameter specifies the exploration algorithm for contextual bandit learning using the action-dependent features (ADF). In many real-world applications, there may be features associated with each action (or arm), and these are the *action-dependent features*. This enables the model to explore different actions based on the observed context.

- `--epsilon 0.2`—This parameter sets the exploration rate or epsilon value to 0.2. It determines the probability of the model exploring a random action instead of selecting the action with the highest predicted reward. A higher epsilon value encourages more exploration.

- `--interactions AA AU AAU`—This parameter creates feature interactions between namespaces in VW. These interactions help the model capture more complex relationships between features.

- `-l 0.05`—This parameter sets the learning rate to 0.05. It determines the rate at which the model's internal parameters are updated during the learning process.

A higher learning rate makes the model converge faster, but if you adjust the learning rate too high, you risk over-fitting and end up worse on average.

- `--power_t 0`—This argument sets the power value to 0. It affects the learning rate decay over time. A power value of 0 indicates a constant learning rate.
- `quiet=True`—This argument sets the `quiet` mode to `True`, suppressing the display of unnecessary information or progress updates during the training process. It helps keep the output concise and clean.

The following code snippet is used to train the CMAB model:

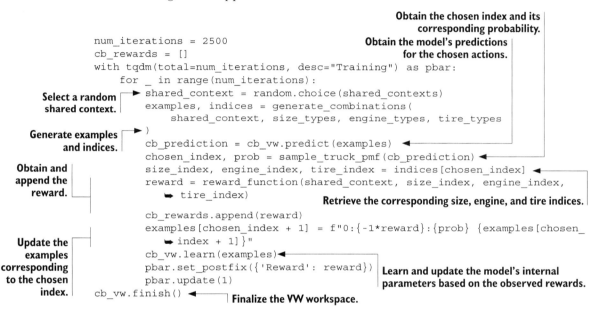

```
num_iterations = 2500
cb_rewards = []
with tqdm(total=num_iterations, desc="Training") as pbar:
    for _ in range(num_iterations):
        shared_context = random.choice(shared_contexts)
        examples, indices = generate_combinations(
            shared_context, size_types, engine_types, tire_types
        )
        cb_prediction = cb_vw.predict(examples)
        chosen_index, prob = sample_truck_pmf(cb_prediction)
        size_index, engine_index, tire_index = indices[chosen_index]
        reward = reward_function(shared_context, size_index, engine_index,
            ➥ tire_index)
        cb_rewards.append(reward)
        examples[chosen_index + 1] = f"0:{-1*reward}:{prob} {examples[chosen_
            ➥ index + 1]}"
        cb_vw.learn(examples)
        pbar.set_postfix({'Reward': reward})
        pbar.update(1)
cb_vw.finish()
```

Callouts: Obtain the chosen index and its corresponding probability. Obtain the model's predictions for the chosen actions. Select a random shared context. Generate examples and indices. Obtain and append the reward. Retrieve the corresponding size, engine, and tire indices. Update the examples corresponding to the chosen index. Learn and update the model's internal parameters based on the observed rewards. Finalize the VW workspace.

After training, we can use the following function to test the trained CMAB model. This code evaluates the trained model by generating examples, making predictions, sampling actions, and calculating the expected reward based on a given shared context:

```
def test_model(shared_context, size_types, engine_types, tire_types):
    examples, indices = generate_combinations(shared_context, size_types,
        ➥ engine_types, tire_types)
    cb_prediction = cb_vw.predict(examples)
    chosen_index, prob = sample_truck_pmf(cb_prediction)
    chosen_action = examples[chosen_index]
    size_index, engine_index, tire_index = indices[chosen_index]
    expected_reward = reward_function(shared_context, size_index,
        ➥ engine_index, tire_index)
    print("Chosen Action:", chosen_action)
    print("Expected Reward:", expected_reward)


test_shared_context = 'city'
test_model(test_shared_context, size_types, engine_types, tire_types)
```

The code will produce output something like the following:

```
Chosen Action: Action truck_size=medium engine=electric tire=snow
Expected Reward: 1.012
```

This output represents the chosen action based on the given shared context during testing. In this case, the chosen action specifies a truck with a medium size, an electric engine, and a snow tire. The obtained reward is 1.012. Note that the maximum reward with noise ≈ 1.0 + 0.15 = 1.15. Given that the maximum values from `size_value`, `engine_value`, and `tire_value` are 1, and considering that the noise is a random value with a standard deviation of 0.05, a value of +3 standard deviations ($3 \times 0.05 = 0.15$) would cover about 99.7% of cases in a normal distribution.

12.6 *Journey's end: A final reflection*

In this book, we have embarked on a comprehensive journey through a diverse landscape of search and optimization algorithms. We first explored deterministic search algorithms that tirelessly traverse problem spaces, seeking optimal solutions through both blind and informed methods. Then we climbed the peaks and valleys of trajectory-based algorithms, witnessing the power of simulated annealing and the ingenious designs of tabu search for escaping local optima. Continuing on our path, we ventured into the realm of evolutionary computing algorithms, witnessing the power of genetic algorithms and their variants in solving complex continuous and discrete optimization problems. Along the way, we embarked on a fascinating journey with swarm intelligence algorithms, starting with particle swarm optimization and offering a glimpse into other algorithms such as the ant colony optimization and artificial bee colony algorithms. Finally, we embraced the realm of machine learning–based methods, where supervised, unsupervised, and reinforcement learning algorithms are used to handle combinatorial optimization problems. Each algorithm covered in this book carries its own set of strengths and weaknesses. Remember, the choice of technique is determined by the task at hand, the characteristics of the problem, and the available resources.

I hope that the knowledge you've gained from this book empowers you to solve real-world problems and embrace the boundless potential of search and optimization in different domains. The fascinating world of search and optimization algorithms continues to expand and evolve. It is up to us to harness this knowledge, to further our capabilities, to solve the problems of today, and to shape the future.

Summary

- Reinforcement learning (RL) can be formulated as an optimization problem wherein the agent aims to learn and/or refine its policy to maximize the expected cumulative reward within a specific environment.
- Reinforcement learning problems can be classified into two main categories: Markov decision processes (MDPs) and multi-armed bandit (MAB) problems. MDP problems involve environments where the agent's actions impact the

environment and its future states. MAB problems focus on maximizing cumulative rewards from a set of independent choices (often referred to as "arms") that can be made repeatedly over time. MABs don't consider the impact of choices on future options, unlike MDPs.

- In MDP-based problems, reinforcement learning uses MDP as a foundational mathematical framework to model decision-making problems under uncertainty. MDP is used to describe an environment for RL where an agent learns to make decisions by performing actions in an environment to achieve a goal.

- RL is classified into model-based and model-free RL, based on the presence or absence of a model of the environment. The model refers to an internal representation or understanding of how the environment behaves—specifically, the transition dynamics and reward function.

- Based on how RL algorithms learn and update their policy from collected experiences, RL algorithms can be classified into off-policy and on-policy RL.

- Advantage actor-critic (A2C) and proximal policy optimization (PPO) are model-free on-policy RL methods.

- By using a clipped objective function, PPO strikes a balance between encouraging exploration and maintaining stability during policy updates. The clipping operation restricts the update to a bounded range, preventing large policy changes that could be detrimental to performance. This mechanism ensures that the policy update remains within a reasonable and controlled distance from the previous policy, promoting smoother and more stable learning.

- Unlike MDPs, Multi-armed bandits (MABs) don't consider the impact of choices on future states, and the agent does not need to worry about transitioning between states because there is only one state. Explore-only, exploit-only greedy, ε-greedy, and upper confidence bound (UCB) are examples of MAB strategies for determining the best approach for selecting the actions to maximize the cumulative reward over the time.

- Contextual multi-armed bandits (CMABs) are an extension of MAB where the decision-making is influenced by additional contextual information about each choice or environment.

- Reinforcement learning can be applied to solve various combinatorial optimization problems, including the traveling salesman problem, traffic signal control, elevator dispatching, optimal dispatch policies for ride-sharing, the freight delivery problem, personalized recommendations, CartPole balancing, coordinating autonomous vehicles in mobile networks, and truck selection.

references

CHAPTER 1

[1] Herbert A. Simon, "The structure of ill structured problems," *Artificial Intelligence* 4, no. 3–4 (1973), 181–201.

CHAPTER 2

[1] M. Held and R.M. Karp, "A dynamic programming approach to sequencing problems," *Journal of the Society for Industrial and Applied Mathematics* 10, no. 1 (1962), 196–210.

[2] M.T. Goodrich and R. Tamassia, *Algorithm Design and Applications* (Wiley, 2015), 513–514.

[3] N. Damavandi and S. Safavi-Naeini, "A hybrid evolutionary programming method for circuit optimization," *IEEE Transactions on Circuits and Systems I: Regular Papers*, 52, no. 5 (2005), 902–910.

[4] P. Jensen and B. Jonathan, *Operations research models and methods* (John Wiley & Sons, 2002).

[5] A. Khamis and M. Ashraf, "A differential evolution-based approach to design all-terrain ground vehicle wheels," *2017 IEEE International Conference on Autonomous Robot Systems and Competitions (ICARSC)*, (IEEE, 2017).

[6] K. Veselić, "Finite catenary and the method of Lagrange," *SIAM Review* 37, no. 2 (1995), 224–229.

[7] J. Kalcsics and Roger Z. Ríos-Mercado, "Districting problems," in Gilbert Laporte, Stefan Nickel, and Francisco Saldanha da Gama (eds.), *Location Science* (Springer, 2019), 705–743.

[8] S.M. Almufti, "Historical survey on metaheuristics algorithms," *International Journal of Scientific World*, 7, no. 1 (2019), 1.

CHAPTER 4

[1] M. Leighton, R. Wheeler, and C. Holte, "Faster optimal and suboptimal hierarchical search," *Proceedings of the Fourth Annual Symposium on Combinatorial Search* (Barcelona, 2011).

[2] P. Sanders and D. Schultes, "Highway hierarchies hasten exact shortest path queries," *Algorithms: ESA 2005* (Springer, 2005), 568–579.

[3] R. Geisberger et al., "Contraction hierarchies: Faster and simpler hierarchical routing in road networks," *Experimental Algorithms: WEA 2008* (Springer, 2008), 319–333.

CHAPTER 5

[1] S. Kirkpatrick, C. Gelatt, and M. Vecchi, "Optimization by Simulated Annealing," *Science* 220, no. 4598 (13 May 1983), 671–680.

[2] Y. Xiang et al., "Generalized simulated annealing algorithm and its application to the Thomson model," *Physics Letters A* 233, no. 3 (1997), 216–220.

[3] L. Ingber, "Adaptive simulated annealing (ASA): Lessons learned," arXiv cs/0001018 (2000).

[4] X. Geng, Z. Chen, W. Yang, D. Shi, and K. Zhao, "Solving the traveling salesman problem based on an adaptive simulated annealing algorithm with greedy search," *Applied Soft Computing* 11, no. 4 (June 2011), 3680-3689.

[5] B. Felgenhauer and F. Jarvis, "Enumerating possible Sudoku grids" (2005).

[6] E. Russell and F. Jarvis, "Mathematics of Sudoku II," *Mathematical Spectrum* 39, no. 2 (2006), 54–58.

CHAPTER 6

[1] F. Glover, "Tabu search and adaptive memory programming—advances, applications and challenges," in *Interfaces in Computer Science and Operations Research*, ed., R. Barr, R. Helgason and J. Kennington (Springer, 1997), 1–75.

[2] F. Glover, M. Laguna, and R. Marti, "Principles of tabu search," in , T.F. Gonzalez, ed., *Handbook of approximation algorithms and metaheuristics* (Chapman & Hall, 2007), chapter 23.

[3] M. Gendreau, "An introduction to tabu search," in Fred Glover, Gary A. Kochenberger, *Handbook of Metaheuristics* (Springer US, 2003).

[4] R. Battiti and G. Tecchiolli, "Training neural nets with the reactive tabu search," *IEEE transactions on neural networks* 6, no. 5 (1995), 1185–1200.

CHAPTER 7

[1] El-Ghazali Talbi, *Metaheuristics: From Design to Implementation* (John Wiley & Sons, 2009).

[2] Julian Blank and Kalyanmoy Deb, "Pymoo: Multi-objective optimization in Python," *IEEE Access* 8 (2020), 89497–89509.

CHAPTER 8

[1] K. Deb and R.B. Agrawal, "Simulated binary crossover for continuous search space," *Complex Systems* 9, no. 2 (1995), 115–148.

[2] K. Deb, K. Sindhya, and T. Okabe, "Self-adaptive simulated binary crossover for real-parameter optimization," in *Proceedings of the 9th annual conference on genetic and evolutionary computation* (July 2007), 1187–1194.

[3] K. Deb, "Multi-objective optimization using evolutionary algorithms: an introduction," in L. Wang, A.H. Ng, K. Deb (eds.), *Multi-objective evolutionary optimisation for product design and manufacturing* (Springer, 2011).

[4] E. Zitzler, "Evolutionary algorithms for multiobjective optimization: Methods and applications," Tik-Schriftenreihe 30 (Swiss Federal Institute of Technology Zurich, 1999).

[5] A.P. Wierzbicki, "The use of reference objectives in multiobjective optimization," in *Multiple criteria decision making theory and application: Proceedings of the third conference* (Springer 1980), 468–486.

[6] Z. Gaing, "A particle swarm optimization approach for optimum design of PID controller in AVR system," *IEEE transactions on energy conversion* 19, no. 2 (2004): 384–391.

CHAPTER 9

[1] J. Kennedy and R. Eberhart, "Particle swarm optimization," in *Proceedings of IEEE International conference on neural networks (ICNN'95)* 4 (1995), 1942–1948.

[2] J. Kennedy and R. Eberhart, "A discrete binary version of the particle swarm algorithm," in *1997 IEEE international conference on systems, man, and cybernetics: Computational cybernetics and simulation* vol. 5 (1997), pp. 4104–4108.

[3] M. Clerc, "Discrete particle swarm optimization, illustrated by the traveling salesman problem," in G. Onwubolu and B. Babu (eds.), *New optimization techniques in engineering: Studies in fuzziness and soft computing*, vol. 141 (Springer, 2004), 219–239.

[4] A. Ratnaweera, S.K. Halgamuge, and H.C. Watson, "Self-organizing hierarchical particle swarm optimizer with time-varying acceleration coefficients," *IEEE Transactions on Evolutionary Computation* 8, no. 3 (2004), 240–255.

CHAPTER 10

[1] Dervis Karaboga, "An idea based on honey bee swarm for numerical optimization," *Technical report TR06*, vol. 200 (Erciyes University, 2005), 1–10.

CHAPTER 11

[1] S. Dehaene, *How we learn: Why brains learn better than any machine... for now* (Penguin, 2021).

[2] T.M. Mitchell, *Machine learning* (McGraw-Hill, 1997).

[3] P. Domingos, *The master algorithm: How the quest for the ultimate learning machine will remake our world* (Basic Books, 2015).

[4] A. Halevy, P. Norvig, and F. Pereira, "The unreasonable effectiveness of data," *IEEE Intelligent Systems* 24, no. 2 (2009), 8–12.

[5] W. Hamilton, R. Ying, and J. Leskovec, "Representation learning on graphs: Methods and applications," arXiv preprint arXiv:1709.05584 (2017).

[6] K. Broadwater and N. Stillman, *Graph Neural Networks in Action* (Manning, 2023).

[7] Oliver Lange and Luis Perez, "Traffic prediction with advanced Graph Neural Networks," *Google DeepMind* blog, www.deepmind.com/blog/traffic-prediction-with-advanced-graph-neural-networks.

[8] A. Vaswani et al., "Attention is all you need," *Advances in neural information processing systems*, 30 (2017).

[9] "The Annotated Transformer," *Harvard NLP*, https://nlp.seas.harvard.edu/2018/04/03/attention.html.

[10] O. Vinyals, M. Fortunato, and N Jaitly, "Pointer networks," arXiv preprint arXiv:1506.03134 (2015).

[11] L. Graham, "An efficient algorithm for determining the convex hull of a finite planar set," *Information Processing Letters* 1 (1972), 132–133.

[12] A. Jarvis, "On the identification of the convex hull of a finite set of points in the plane," *Information Processing Letters* 2 (1973), 18–21.

[13] C. Barber, D.P. Dobkin, and H. Huhdanpaa, "The quickhull algorithm for convex hulls," ACM *Transactions on Mathematical Software* 22, no. 4 (1996), 469–483.

[14] Y. Bengio, A. Lodi, and A. Prouvost, "Machine learning for combinatorial optimization: A methodological tour d'horizon," *European Journal of Operational Research* 290, no. 2 (2021), 405–421.

[15] A. Hottung, S. Tanaka, and K. Tierney, "Deep learning assisted heuristic tree search for the container pre-marshalling problem," *Computers & Operations Research* 113 (2020).

[16] N. Vesselinova et al., "Learning combinatorial optimization on graphs: A survey with applications to networking," *IEEE Access* 8 (2020), 120,388–120,416.

[17] Chengrun Yang et al., "Large Language Models as Optimizers," arXiv preprint arXiv:2309.03409 (2023).

[18] B. Amos, "Tutorial on amortized optimization for learning to optimize over continuous domains," arXiv: 2202.00665 (2022).

[19] S. Cohen, B. Amos, and Y. Lipman, "Riemannian convex potential maps," *Proceedings of the 38th International Conference on Machine Learning, Proceedings of Machine Learning Research* (2021), 2028–2038.

[20] Chaitanya K. Joshi, Thomas Laurent, and Xavier Bresson, "Graph Neural Networks for the Travelling Salesman Problem," from the "Boosting Combinatorial Optimization using Machine Learning" session at the INFORMS annual meeting 2019.

[21] Chaitanya K. Joshi, Quentin Cappart, Louis-Martin Rousseau, Thomas Laurent, code for "Learning the Travelling Salesperson Problem Requires Rethinking Generalization," *27th International Conference on Principles and Practice of Constraint Programming* (CP 2021), GitHub repo, https://github.com/chaitjo/learning-tsp.

[22] Diego Vicente, "Using Self-Organizing Maps to solve the Traveling Salesman Problem," *Diego Vicente* blog post, https://diego.codes/post/som-tsp/.

[23] M. McGough, "Pointer Networks with Transformers," *Towards Data Science* (2021), https://towardsdatascience.com/pointer-networks-with-transformers-1a01d83f7543.

CHAPTER 12

[1] R. Sutton and A. Barto, *Reinforcement Learning: An introduction*, second edition (MIT Press, 2018).

[2] J. Schulman et al., "Proximal policy optimization algorithms," arXiv preprint (2017), arXiv:1707.06347.

[3] C. Joshi, T. Laurent, and X. Bresson, "Graph Neural Networks for the Travelling Salesman Problem," in Boosting Combinatorial Optimization using Machine Learning, NFORMS Annual Meeting 2019.

[4] M. Nazari, et al., "Reinforcement learning for solving the vehicle routing problem," arXiv preprint (2018), arXiv:1802.04240.

[5] A. Delarue, R. Anderson, and C. Tjandraatmadja, "Reinforcement learning with combinatorial actions: An application to vehicle routing," arXiv preprint (2020), arXiv:2010.12001.

[6] C. Wan, Y. Li, and J. Wang, "RLOR: A flexible framework of deep reinforcement learning for operation research," arXiv preprint (2023), arXiv:2303.13117.

[7] A. Alabbasi, A. Ghosh, and V. Aggarwal, "DeepPool: Distributed model-free algorithm for ride-sharing using deep reinforcement learning," *IEEE Transactions on Intelligent Transportation Systems* 20, no. 12 (2019), 4714–4727.

[8] C. Jiayu et al., "DeepFreight: A model-free deep-reinforcement-learning-based algorithm for multi-transfer freight delivery," in *Proceedings of the International Conference on Automated Planning and Scheduling* 31 (2021), 510–518.

[9] T. Oda and C. Joe-Wong, "MOVI: A model-free approach to dynamic fleet management," in *IEEE INFOCOM 2018: IEEE Conference on Computer Communications* (2018), 2708–2716.

[10] J. Ruan et al., "Deep reinforcement learning-based traffic signal control," in *2023 IEEE International Conference on Smart Mobility* (2023), 21–26.

[11] K. Lin et al., "Cooperative variable speed limit control using multi-agent reinforcement learning and evolution strategy for improved throughput in mixed traffic," in *2023 IEEE International Conference on Smart Mobility* (2023), 27–32.

[12] K. Li and J. Malik, "Learning to optimize," arXiv preprint (2016), arXiv:1606.01885.

[13] S. Toll et al., "Efficient Elevator Algorithm," *Chancellor's Honors Program Projects*, University of Tennessee (2020).

[14] S. Schneider et al., "mobile-env: An open platform for reinforcement learning in wireless mobile networks," in NOMS 2022–2022 IEEE/IFIP Network Operations and Management Symposium, 2022. GitHub repo: https://github.com/stefanbschneider/mobile-env/tree/main.

index

A new online reading experience

liveBook, our online reading platform, adds a new dimension to your Manning books, with features that make reading, learning, and sharing easier than ever. A liveBook version of your book is included FREE with every Manning book.

This next generation book platform is more than an online reader. It's packed with unique features to upgrade and enhance your learning experience.

- Add your own notes and bookmarks
- One-click code copy
- Learn from other readers in the discussion forum
- Audio recordings and interactive exercises
- Read all your purchased Manning content in any browser, anytime, anywhere

As an added bonus, you can search every Manning book and video in liveBook—even ones you don't yet own. Open any liveBook, and you'll be able to browse the content and read anything you like.*

Find out more at www.manning.com/livebook-program.

*Open reading is limited to 10 minutes per book daily